"Rich with real-life anecdotes…a ground-breaking book… highly informative reading and well recommended for the parents, relatives, friends, and teachers of [TCKs] as well as the children themselves who, through these pages, will discover they share a common heritage with countless other kids from similar multicultural life experiences."

—The Midwest Book Review

"Essential reading…. It should be available in every school library and brought to the attention of teachers, administrators, board members, and parents…. Pollock and Van Reken must be recognized for their pioneering contribution to an emerging field of great significance."

—The European Council of International Schools Magazine

"Like so many books that break new ground, *Third Culture Kids* provides insights for the rest of us from a new perspective on life…those who have lived an international and intercultural life provide clues about internal events that we are likely to experience now and in the future in an increasingly multicultural world."

—George Simons, George Simons International

Third
Culture
Kids

Third Culture Kids

The Experience of Growing Up Among Worlds

David C. Pollock
and Ruth E. Van Reken

This edition first published by Nicholas Brealey Publishing in association
with Intercultural Press in 2001.

Reprinted 2001

Intercultural Press, Inc.   *nbi*   Nicholas Brealey Publishing
PO Box 700   36 John Street
Yarmouth, Maine 04096 USA   London WC1N 2AT, UK
001-207-846-5168   44-207-430-0224
Fax: 001-207-846-5181   Fax: 44-207-404-8311
www.interculturalpress.com   www.nbrealey-books.com

First published as The Third Culture Kid Experience by Intercultural
Press in 1999

Design and production by Patty J. Topel

ISBN 1-85788-295-4

Printed in Finland

04   03   02   01   00   5   6   7   8   9

**The Library of Congress has
previously catalogued this edition as follows:**

Pollock, David C.
    Third culture kids: growing up among worlds/David C. Pollock and Ruth E.
Van Reken.
        p.   cm.
    Includes bibliographical references
    ISBN 1-877864-72-2
    1. Social interaction in children—Foreign countries.   2. Social skills in chil-
dren—Foreign   countires.   3. Children—Travel—Foreign
countries.   4. Children—Foreign countries—Attitudes.   5. Intercultural communication—Foreign countries.   6. Parents-Employment—Foreign countries.
I. Van Reken, Ruth E., 1945–   II. Title.
HQ784.S56P65   1999
303.3'2—dc21   99–10851
                                                                        CIP

Substantial discounts on bulk quantities are available. For details, discount
information, or to request a free catalogue, please contact the publishers at
the addresses given above.

For Betty Lou and David, our lifelong partners and unfailing supporters throughout our journeys. And to our children, who have taught us so much—TCKs "for true."

Table of Contents

Section Two—Maximizing the Benefits

Appendices

Foreword

It is an honor to have been asked to write the foreword to this perceptively written and valuable book in which Dave Pollock and Ruth Van Reken demonstrate their combined wisdom and their ongoing commitment to the TCK community. They do so with depth and sensitivity. Each has had a profound impact on my own personal and professional development and that of scores of others who live and work in the global corridor.

My association with Dave Pollock began at a SIETAR International conference (International Society for Intercultural Education, Training and Research) in 1984. At that time, Fanchon Silberstein and I gave the very first presentation on *global nomads*, a term I had coined as synonymous with *TCK*, and Dave was in the audience. Two years later he became a founding board member of Global Nomads International (GNI), serving as a source of insight and vision for that body. He is an esteemed colleague, mentor, and forever a friend. I am privileged to have worked with him and continue to enjoy the lively exchange of ideas and possibilities that have marked our collaboration over the years. Our interaction continues to inform my life and my work.

Dave Pollock works tirelessly on behalf of and with the TCK community. His presentations and consultations with TCKs and their families have literally changed lives. For this book he has distilled decades of direct experience with TCKs of all ages and numerous nationalities. The result is a highly distilled body of knowledge that is both anthropological and psychological in nature. Through this knowledge he gives voice to what so many of us have felt soul deep but often cannot articulate. As a result, the outcome of his work runs deeper than an "aha" experience. As lightening thrusts the power of electricity into the earth, so it is when this defining moment occurs in a group he is guiding—the impact of emotional grounding is palpable for those present. Clearly, for many who have grown up globally, having their past validated and placed in the clear context of a shared heritage brings with it a stunning sense of safe homecoming.

On a lighter side, watching spouses during Dave's presentations is a wonder in itself. They sit, wide-eyed and incredulous, listening intently as their beloved's peculiarities are described in detail by a total stranger. As Dave has said, this underlines the critical need for premarital counseling of TCKs and their intendeds. Indeed, too many assume that common nationality means shared culture; they thus unwittingly enter into what is, in actuality, an intercultural marriage.

My first memory of Ruth Van Reken reaches back to 1987 at the International Conference on Missionary Kids (ICMK) in Quito, Ecuador. It was at the Hotel Colon that I stayed up all night in an alcove off the lobby reading her first book, *Letters I Never Wrote* (now *Letters Never Sent*). I had sought refuge there so I could weep with abandon without waking my roommate of the moment. Suffice it to say, I, too, experienced the sense of catharsis commented on by those who have read her powerful personal story.

It was there, also, that Ruth displayed her remarkable ability to relate to others with great simplicity and authenticity. In one lengthy, private conversation during the conference, the two of us discussed being TCKs, the cultures of our respective sponsors—God and the corporation—and the stereotypes each expatriate subgroup smugly held of the other. We got quite the chuckle out of it, but we also decided that it was time to move beyond such judgments. The notion needed to be put forth that we were all grazing in the same pasture separated by—and seeing only—the fences marking boundaries dictated by our sponsorship. Now, as members of the global nomad/TCK community, it was time to look for the gate between our pastures, to understand the power of our shared heritage, and to draw on it for our benefit and for those who come after us. It was Ruth who articulated this vision to our action group the following day, in effect swinging that gate wide open and shepherding us through it.

Her actions there were testimony to her consistent willingness to risk emotionally. She is able to be with TCKs in a way that affirms their worth, draws them to awareness of common strengths as well as pain, and encourages their personal healing in the context of their own community. It is her gift to gently lead others beyond the superficial to the place of greatest vulnerability and growth, where one heart touches another. The Quito conference marked the beginning of what has been for me a valuable and enduring friendship.

What Ruth has done in crafting this book as a writer and a contributor, honing and refining it—yet staying intellectually fresh and emotionally present through its many iterations—demands our utmost respect. It is we readers who benefit most from her persistence and commitment.

Together these two extraordinary people have given us a well-organized, highly readable text that will prove to be a classic in the intercultural field.

For those of us who share the global nomad/TCK heritage, having this experience named, being able to say "I am a TCK," "I am a global nomad," is a powerful gift to our community. In the words of Nori Hsu in the *Global Nomad Quarterly*:

> Suddenly it came out, blurting like a geyser from the
> ground, I am a global nomad. Nothing has felt the
> same since. I now have a culture. After three decades
> of learning other peoples' cultures and still being an
> outsider, I look to the future.... The recognition has

> been life-changing. For me, it is as if three quarters of
> my life has emerged from shadow into full color.

The authors give us a deep understanding of the wide range of hues in the palette of TCK experience. They enable us to add depth, dimension, and definition to the personal portraits of our own lives over time.

Most of us are, I believe, in a lifelong process of integrating our globally nomadic upbringing into our present and our future. We strive, to paraphrase Dr. Kathleen Finn Jordan, to make the pieces of our complex puzzle fit. Just when we feel we have put the mobility/relationship piece securely in place, it is jostled by a pending marriage, another move, a teenager's departure for college, or the prospect of where in the world (literally) to retire. That same old feeling wells up, only this time it's in a different context, buried in a deeper place.

Whatever our life stage may be, then, this book resonates on several levels. It affirms our experience and releases us from self-imposed and external judgments about our TCK-based reactions and behaviors. It offers the renewal born of insight and action. With considerable care, Dave and Ruth have cleared the path, marked it, and given us the tools for self-discovery. By the end of this book, T. S. Eliot's words, elegantly expressed and certainly applicable to the globally nomadic, could be our own:

> We shall not cease from exploration.
> And the end of all our exploring
> Will be to arrive where we started
> And to know the place for the first time.

Owing to the knowledge, skills, and global awareness born, as Paul Seaman has said, of ordinary lives lived in extraordinary circumstances, we TCKs have great potential to effect change. We have the capacity, as Margaret Pusch has said, to view the world whole. So please—let the authors hear from you. Tell them what makes this book work for you, what it sparks in you. Share it with your school, university administrators, or coworkers. Use it as a reference for writing an article for your alumni association. Encourage and support these institutions in acknowledging, valuing, and guiding the TCKs in their midst.

If you haven't already done so, consider the impact of the TCK/ global nomad experience on your life and how you can use it beneficially—within your family as well as locally and globally. After all, after awareness is raised about the characteristics and dynamics of being a TCK, then what? Not surprisingly, the authors take us to that next step—integration. The sections of the book that deal with exploring cycles of mobility, uncovering hidden losses and addressing them and reframing grief, for example, are brilliant. Enlightening suggestions are provided on how TCKs, family, friends, and counselors can engage in dialogue that clears emotional logjams and permits the lifestream to flow freely.

With this book, the authors add a new level of understanding, articulation, and visibility to an emerging interdisciplinary social science field—one with a focus on the children of the globally nomadic community. Undoubtedly it will prompt greater intellectual discourse and synergy.

With that in mind, I would add one cautionary note regarding the definition of *TCK*. The original intent of the term, used by Dr. Ruth Hill Useem in her research in the 1960s, referred to children whose parents' *work* took them abroad to live. The authors have included the children of what they term temporary refugees—those whose parents take them abroad to avoid civil strife, for example. They have also included those who have entered another culture (the Native American community) without leaving their country. In addition, Ruth Van Reken mentions that Dr. Useem herself now refers to TCKs simply as children who accompany their parents into another culture. These, then, broaden the definition of *TCK* to include the children of refugees, immigrants, and those whose experience is domestic, not global. As a result the term risks being diluted beyond use for both researchers and TCKs themselves. If researchers are to be able to exchange research data without contamination, they need clarity on who it is they have been researching. We can only assure this when we maintain the integrity and continuity of past terminology.

Further, in respecting original intent, we also securely establish the starting point for understanding the layering of other related experiences in a global nomad's life.

What are the implications, for example, for a family forced to flee its homeland—or risk death—only to find itself moving again as a result of a parent's career choice? The older children experience both the refugee layer of the journey—complete, perhaps, with all the trauma and violence often associated with such flight—and the TCK layer. Younger offspring, on the other hand, may directly experience only the TCK layer when a parent's job with the World Bank, for example, takes the family to several other elsewheres. These layers of family history, experienced both directly and indirectly, call different issues into play that influence the family dynamic. Clear terminology helps us to articulate the nuances.

As consultant Barbara Schaetti has commented, "We need to disentangle the layers so they can be more clearly understood, while at the same time *respecting their intersection within an integrated identity.*" From there we can explore how the dynamics of each affects the internationally mobile child and the adult she or he becomes.

Because each of us makes use of language in a different way, a healthy and vigorous debate on terminology, such as on the definitions of *TCK* and *global nomad*, has been going on for years—in groups, on listserves, in workshops, at conferences. This is as it should be. It is a dialogue and it, indeed, stimulates inquiry and encourages growth. We invite your participation in this ongoing discussion.

The authors have included two powerful pieces by Sophia Morton and Paul Seaman, both excellent writers. They are not to be missed. Those of you who are not TCKs, prepare to be moved by their stark honesty. Those of you who are TCKs will know well the place in the heart where they take you. Look for them in Appendix B.

Finally, in reflecting on this book, the *mola* as metaphor keeps pushing itself forward. Molas are embroidery pieces crafted in a style unique to the Kuna Indians of Panama. The symbolism inherent in their construction speaks to who I am as a global nomad. I offer it to you in closing.

Pieces of bright-colored fabric, as many as five to eight, are layered upon one another and attached temporarily at each corner. The seamstress cuts down to different layers, folds the edges under in the desired shape to reveal the color beneath, and stitches the folds in place. As she continues to cut, fold, and stitch, a multihued pattern slowly emerges, finally coming together in a richly vibrant image of a fish or a lobster, for instance. The end result is a piece that has a solid hue on one side and emerges brilliantly into full color on the other. Each has the stamp of the creator's individuality but is borne of a distinct cultural heritage.

So it is with our lives as global nomads, as TCKs. During childhood and beyond, all our experiences of mind, heart, body, and spirit—cultural, emotional, physical, geographical—all of the moves, the relationships, the places, the losses, the discoveries, the wonder of the world—are layered one upon another through time. Ultimately, to revel in the beauty of our personal mola-like tapestry means cutting, sometimes deeply, through these layers to reveal the richness and color beneath. This can be painful. It is the legacy of transition and change, and it is also the precursor to growth.

Sometimes the cut feels more like a tear, a violation committed with dull, badly nicked scissors. The stitches on ragged edges are crude. We feel powerless. Restitching takes longer and leaves deep scars on our souls.

Some of the transitions are surprisingly easy. The cut is cleaner. The stitches are neater. We heal faster and settle into the new layer of culture more comfortably. This is so for any number of reasons—good preparation, family interaction, and community support; better continuity (old friends in a new place); familiar routines in a new setting; or the stimulation of the new culture and country. Our mola takes on its own character, its own vibrancy and expression with each successive experience.

Some of us, upon returning home, turn our tapestry over, hide the brilliance of its colors and its uniqueness, deny our heritage or reveal it to few. Perhaps this is done to blend in and gain acceptance, perhaps to deny the impact of loss—what's past is past—perhaps because, frankly, it just seems easier. In that denial, we choose to present ourselves—to ourselves as well as others—as being of one hue.

Dave and Ruth encourage you in this book, as do I, to turn your "life mola" over, to reclaim and proclaim your TCK heritage fiercely. Your mola, unique and complex in its layering of events, emotions, and experiences, in what is folded back and what remains covered, in what is well stitched and what may need mending, is who you are. Hide it and you have little to show for a childhood like no other in its challenges and invaluable gifts. Display its richness, add to it, share it—and you may well change your life and your world, as have many TCKs before you.

—Norma M. McCaig
Founder, Global Nomads International (GNI)
President, Global Nomad Resources

Acknowledgments

Without Lois Stück's original encouragement, transcriptions of seminar tapes, suggestions, and expert help throughout the initial creative process of this book, it would have remained only a dream. Without Professor Barbara Cambridge's guidance in the writing process or Professor Jon Eller's most helpful ideas about organization, the manuscript would never have gotten back to Lois or our publishers. Anthropologist Ken Barger; friends Lori Beuerman, Christine Dowdeswell, Janet Fischer, Stephanie Hock, Barb Knuckles, Ann Kroeker, Erica Lipasti, Paul Pedersen, Paul Seaman, Alan Shea, Francisco West, and Elisabeth Wood; wife Betty Lou Pollock; mother Betty Frame; and daughter Stephanie Van Reken Eriksen have all given most helpful suggestions while reading various drafts of the manuscript. Helen Fail's insights into international schooling have been invaluable. The list could go on and on.

Above all, without each TCK and ATCK who has shared his or her story with us through the years, without the honest dialogue we have witnessed among so many, there would have been no story to tell. In particular, we thank the Global Nomad chapter at Valparaiso University for the time they gave to engage in dialogue specifically designed to address issues we are raising in this book. And a huge thanks to "Erika" not only for letting us use her story, but also for helping in the early stages of writing it.

And many thanks to David Hoopes for having the vision that this is a topic whose time has come—to say nothing of his masterfully helping two people join their different thoughts and writing styles into one text. He did not have an easy job. Thanks also to Toby Frank for her further suggestions and Judy Carl-Hendrick for substantial help in the final editorial process. Without each of them this book couldn't have been written in the readable form we trust it now is. And thanks to Patty Topel for readying this manuscript for publication. We've decided it not only takes a village to raise a child but also to birth a book.

Last, but certainly not least, we thank God not only for life but for the richness of our lives. We have experienced much joy in our journeys as we have studied this topic and lived it as well.

Introduction

David C. Pollock

Third culture kids (TCKs) are not new, and they are not few They have been a part of the earth's population from the earliest migrations. They are normal people with the usual struggles and pleasures of life. But because they have grown up with different experiences from those who have lived primarily in one culture, TCKs are sometimes seen as slightly strange by the people around them.

I have had the joy of working with TCKs since the mid-1970s. In 1986, when David Hoopes, editor-in-chief of Intercultural Press, first asked me to write about TCKs, I struggled with two concerns that still haunt me. First of all, there is much about the highly mobile, transcultural young person that we still don't know or that should be established through research. Second, since we are dealing with people, we are writing about process and progress, not a fixed entity. In the past two decades alone, dramatic changes related to the care of children and adults have occurred in the global nomad community, and undoubtedly new theories and practices will continue to evolve.

We must begin somewhere, however. After more than twenty years of virtually daily interaction with TCKs and their families, we have seen a set of patterns of behavior or reactions to life emerge that stem from the cross-cultural and high-mobility aspects of their upbringing. As I have shared these observations with TCKs, their parents, teachers, and caregivers throughout the world, I have observed a common type of response. Giggles start among the students in one corner of the room. In another, a parent pokes her child in the ribs. Teachers look at each other (and their students) with knowing glances. They all recognize the story. And as I've made this presentation to people in many different kinds of organizations and on every continent except Antarctica, a multitude of TCKs have validated that this is, indeed, their story.

Sometimes the third culture experience is unfairly blamed for problems it didn't generate. At other times it is viewed as a pathology for which therapy is needed and from which one must recover. It is my conviction that being a TCK is not a disease, something from which to recover. It is also not simply okay—it is more than okay. It is a life healthily enriched by this very TCK experience and blessed with significant opportunities for further enrichment.

Since the variety of experience is wide, let's acknowledge that breadth by recognizing that for some, growing up as a TCK has been very difficult, for others much easier. Someone whose experience has been close to ideal isn't in denial for seeing it as so. Someone whose experience has been difficult or painful isn't a wimp, a whiner, or a spoiled child for acknowledging it as such. And those who have known both are also within the normal range of human experience.

My appeal to you as the reader—whether a TCK of any age, a parent, a caregiver for TCKs, or an administrator of agencies with cross-cultural personnel—is that you read carefully and empathetically, act to make a positive difference in the lives of our TCK and adult TCK populations, and provide leadership and support to smooth the way and amplify the advantages for our future TCKs.

I hope the eyes of many will be opened by this book and that it will spark honest thought, sensitive discussion, and productive research into this topic. I pray too that the result will be positive action to help make the TCK experience a strong foundation on which TCKs can build a satisfying and productive adulthood.

A Beginning Word

Ruth E. Van Reken

Sometimes there is a specific moment in a specific day that creeps up so unannounced, it is hardly recognized for its significance, but ever afterward it marks the point when everything changed. Life is never quite the same again. I, and countless others who have grown up in countries and cultures outside that of our parents, have known such a moment. It is that first instant we learn we have a name—that we are third culture kids (TCKs) or adult third culture kids (ATCKs).

My moment came in 1984. It was a typically hot, muggy day in Monrovia, Liberia, where I lived with my husband, David, and our three daughters. I sat on the bed in David's study, sorting through the mail that had just arrived. Mail for me, as for anyone living overseas, was a precious commodity—one to be savored. It looked like a good day.

I organized the letters into piles according to the priority by which I would read them, including a letter from Mom. Ever since my years in boarding school, Mom hasn't missed a week of writing a letter to me when I'm away from her. Faithful as clockwork, never missing a beat. I should have known her letter would be here. It was Monday and the planes came from the States on Friday nights. Mom's letter went on the "slightly later" pile. If there were any earthshaking news, we would have gotten a radio message. Her letter could wait until I finished the rarer one from my school friend.

I read my friend's letter. Nice to get the news, to catch up on what's happening, but nothing particularly unusual. Now for Mom's letter.

"Open carefully, Ruth. Don't tear the stamps." The voice of my philatelist father echoed in my ear even six years after his death. Our mail had always come from so many different countries, each stamp had the potential to be a collector's treasure.

Along with Mom's letter came another two sheets of paper. I casually opened the extra papers to find a two-page article by David C. Pollock called "Ministering to the TCK (Third Culture Kid)." Presumably, Mom had sent it since we were working in what was then called a "Third World Country" and it must have something to do with that. While laying it aside, I wondered if she realized I worked with adults far more than with children. Still, it was nice she'd thought of me.

As I read Mom's letter, I almost forgot about the enclosure. After gathering the other letters and now empty envelopes, I stood up and the article fell to the floor. I bent over to retrieve it, thinking, I might as well read it now as later.

The article began, "He spent sixteen of his first eighteen years in a country where his parents were foreigners. He attended the community schools and spoke the language of the host country better than his parents.... When his parents traveled to the United States for furlough, they spoke of 'going home,' but when furlough was over and they returned to where they were foreigners, he went home."

I couldn't believe it. *This man is writing about me!*

As I continued to read, I was amazed at seeing expressed so many feelings I had experienced but never heard another person put into words. Somehow I had always thought to myself it was my fault for being so "out of it" when I returned to the States from Nigeria for eighth grade. Or when I felt so stupid for not knowing how to swim in high school. But here was someone actually naming some of these kinds of feelings—like always being a square peg in a round hole. Was I truly not the only one in the world to have gone through this? What *was* this third culture kid idea about anyway?

A crack had occurred in my armor that was to grow and later open the way to a whole new world. I didn't know it that day, but this was the moment my life took a new direction and changed forever.

Since then, I have talked to countless other adult TCKs and heard of the moment when they, too, first learned they had a name. That moment is a time to celebrate the many gifts of our backgrounds. It is also a time to begin to understand some of the particular challenges that a highly mobile international childhood can bring. Perhaps, above all else, we've found out we are "normal," whatever that means. Some of our experiences may have been different from those of others we know, but our humanity is the same.

Strangely enough, it took a little longer before I realized that my own father was also a TCK—an American born and raised in Iran. Then I realized I had aunts and uncles and cousins who were all TCKs and that my three daughters were TCKs—Americans reared for nine years in Liberia. Even my husband spent two of his preschool years in China. (And now my first two grandchildren are TCKs in Ghana.)

Since that time, I have discovered a world filled with TCKs from many backgrounds with whom I share a common bond. I hope each one who reads this will have as much joy in discovering his or her connection with this interesting world as I did.

Section One
The Third
Culture Kid
Experience

Part I
Understanding
the World of TCKs

1

Where Is Home? Erika's Story

As the Boeing 747 sped down the runway, Erika sat
inside with seat belt secure, her chin propped against a
clenched fist, staring out the window until the final
sights of her beloved Singapore disappeared from
view.

*How can it hurt this much to leave a country that isn't
even mine?* Erika closed her eyes and settled back in
the seat, too numb to cry the tears that begged to be
shed. *Will I ever come back?*

For nearly half of her twenty-three years, she had
thought of Singapore as home. Now she knew it
wasn't—and America hadn't felt like home since she
was eight years old.

Isn't there anywhere in the world I belong? she
wondered.

Countless people of virtually every nationality and from a great variety of backgrounds identify with Erika's feeling of not belonging
anywhere in the world. Like her, they may be Americans who grew
up in Singapore. But they may also be Japanese children growing
up in Australia, British kids raised in China, Turkish youth reared in
Germany, African children living in Canada, or the child of a Norwegian father and a Thai mother growing up in Argentina. All of

them have one thing in common: like Erika, they are spending, or have spent, at least part of their childhood in countries and cultures other than their own. They are third culture kids (TCKs) or, by now, adult TCKs (ATCKs).

Children are TCKs for many reasons. Some have parents with careers in international business, the diplomatic corps, the military, or religious missions. Others have parents who studied abroad. Still other families live for a period of time outside their home culture because of civil unrest and war.

TCKs are raised in a neither/nor world. It is neither fully the world of their parents' culture (or cultures) nor fully the world of the other culture (or cultures) in which they were raised. This neither/nor world is not merely an amalgamation of the various cultures they have known. For reasons we will explore, in the process of living first in one dominant culture and then moving to another one (and maybe even two or three more and often back and forth between them all), TCKs develop their own life patterns different from those who are basically born and bred in one place. Most TCKs learn to live comfortably in this world, whether they stop to define it or not.

TCKs are not a new phenomenon. They've been around since the beginning of time, but, until now, they have been largely invisible. This has been changing, however, for at least three reasons.

1. *Their number has increased.* In the last half of the twentieth century, the number of people involved in international careers of all types has grown dramatically. In her book *The Absentee American*, Carolyn D. Smith says,

   Since 1946, therefore, when it was unusual for
   Americans to live overseas unless they were missionaries or diplomats, it has become commonplace for
   American military and civilian employees and business-
   people to be stationed abroad, if only for a year. The
   1990 Census counted 922,000 federal workers and
   their families living overseas, and the total number of

Americans living abroad either permanently or
temporarily is estimated at 3 million.[1]

That's a lot of people! But Smith is only talking about Americans. Add to this the burgeoning number of citizens from every other country working and living outside their home cultures and we can only imagine the total worldwide.

Not only do more people have international careers, but now it's easier than ever before for these people to take their children when they move to a new country. Traveling between home and a host country rarely takes more than one day compared to the three weeks to three months it used to take on an ocean liner. International schools exist everywhere; advanced medical care is an airlift away (and soon may be even more accessible via the Internet!). It is now normal for children to accompany their parents overseas rather than to stay home.

2. *Their public voice has grown louder.* As these growing numbers of TCKs become adults, they are becoming more vocal. Through their alumni associations or organizations such as Global Nomads International,[2] they have formed visible, identifiable groups. Through writing or speaking out, their voices are beginning to be heard. As these TCKs and adult TCKs share their stories, they encourage others to do the same.

3. *Their significance has increased.* The TCK experience is a microcosm of what is fast becoming normal throughout the world. Few communities anywhere will remain culturally homogeneous in this age of easy international travel and instant global communication. Growing up among cultural differences is already, or soon will be, the rule rather than the exception—even for those who never physically leave their home country. Sociologist Ted Ward claims that TCKs of the late twentieth century are "the prototype [citizens] of the twenty-first century."[3] Experts are trying to predict the outcome of this cultural juggling. Looking at the TCK world can help us prepare for the

long-term consequences of this new pattern of global cultural mixing.

The benefits of the TCK lifestyle are enormous. Many TCKs and ATCKs are maximizing the potential of these benefits in their lives. Unfortunately, others are not. For some the challenges of the TCK experience have been overwhelming, seemingly canceling out the many benefits—a sad waste for both the TCKs and the world around them. It is our hope that a better understanding of some of these benefits and challenges will help TCKs and ATCKs every-where use the gifts of their heritage well. To this end, throughout this book we examine this paradoxical world of the TCK experience from a variety of perspectives.

We begin by returning to Erika for a better look at one young woman's true story. Only the names and places have been changed.

Erika didn't notice that the captain had turned off the "Fasten your seat belt" sign until a flight attendant interrupted her reverie.

"Would you like something to drink?" he asked.

How many Cokes and roasted peanuts have I eaten on airplanes? she wondered. Far too many to count. But today her grief outweighed any thought of food or drink. She shook her head, and the attendant moved on.

Erika closed her eyes again. Unbidden memories flashed through her mind. She remembered being eight years old, when her family still lived in upstate New York, Erika's birthplace. One day her father entered the playroom as she and her younger sister, Sally, performed a puppet show for their assembled audience of stuffed animals.

"Wanna watch, Dad?" Erika asked hopefully.

"In a few minutes, sweetie. First, I have something special to tell you."

Puppets forgotten, Sally and Erika ran to their dad, trying to guess what it could be. "Are we gonna have a new baby?" Sally began jumping up and down in excited anticipation.

"Did you buy me a new bike?" Erika inquired.

Erika's dad shook his head and sat in the nearby rocking chair, gathering one daughter on each knee. "How would you like to take a long airplane ride?" he asked.

"Wow!"

"Sure."

"I love airplanes."

"Where, Daddy?"

He explained that his company had asked him to move from the United States to Ecuador to start a new branch office. The family would be moving as soon as school ended that June.

A flurry of activity began—shopping, packing, and saying good-bye to relatives and friends. It all seemed so exciting until the day Erika asked, "Mom, how is Spotty going to get there?"

"Honey, it's not easy to take a dog. Grandma's going to take care of him 'til we get home again."

"Mom, we can't leave Spotty! He's part of our family!"

No amount of pleading worked. Spotty was sent to his new home, and finally, with a mixture of eagerness for the adventures ahead and sadness for the people and things they were leaving, Erika and her family flew off to their new world.

Wanting to stop this flood of memories, Erika opened her eyes, trying to focus on her fellow passengers. The diversion didn't work. As soon as she had adjusted her cramped legs and resettled in a more comfortable position, the flashbacks continued. It was almost as if every few seconds a button clicked inside her brain to advance her mental slide show. Pictures of Ecuador replaced those of New York. She had been so scared the first time her family flew into Quito. How would the airplane weave its way between the mountain ranges and find a flat place to land? Yet she remembered how, in time, those same Andes mountains gave her a deep sense of security each morning when she woke to see their towering peaks looming over the city, keeping watch as they had for centuries past.

But what did these memories matter now? She put on her headset, hoping that music would divert her thoughts. Unfortunately, the second channel she switched to carried the haunting music of the hollow-reed flute pipes that always evoked a twinge of melancholy whenever she heard it. The sound brought instant memories of going to fiestas with her Ecuadorian friends and dancing with them while the pipers played. Certainly, listening to this music wouldn't help her now. She took the earphones off, letting them dangle around her neck.

By now the images of the in-flight movie were on the screen in front of her, but Erika never saw them. Her own internal picture show continued with its competing images—the scene changing from towering mountains to the towering skyscrapers of Singapore. After two years in Ecuador, her father had been transferred once more, and for the thirteen years since then—including the four years she attended university in Wisconsin—Erika had considered Singapore her home. Now she knew Singapore would never truly be home. But the question continued to haunt her: where was home?

Still refusing to dwell on that topic, her mind searched for a new cassette of slides to look at. Pictures of countless scenes from other places she had visited with her family through the years appeared— the Kathmandu Valley in Nepal at the beginning of the rainy season, the monkey-cup plants in the Malaysian rain forest, the Karen tribal people in the hills of northern Thailand, winter on the South Island of New Zealand, the water-derrick wells of the Hortobagy in Hungary. One after another the frames appeared in her mind's eye. Even to herself, it seemed incredible how much she had done, seen, and experienced in her first twenty-three years of life. The richness and depth of the world she knew was beyond measure—but what good did that do her today?

Finally, the other pictures ended and Erika was left with the visions of life in Singapore that kept returning, insisting on a paramount spot in the show. Now instead of places, however, she saw people—her amazing collection of friends from the International School in Singapore: Ravi, Fatu, Sam, Kim Su, Trevor, Hilary, Mustapha, Dolores, Joe. One after another they came to her memory. How many races, nationalities, styles of dress, cultures, and religions did these friends represent? With diversity as their hallmark, who could say what was "normal"?

Erika never stopped to wonder that others might be surprised to know that the diversity among her friends reflected the norm rather than the exception of her life. Instead, she reminisced on how she had hated parting from them each summer, when her family returned to the States for vacation. (It was never America or the United States—simply "the States.") Somehow, she always felt much more like a fish out of water with her Stateside peers than she did in Singapore.

For the first time since the airplane had lifted off, a wry smile came to Erika's face. She remembered how strange she had felt the first time her American cousins had asked her to go "cruising." She presumed they meant some type of boat ride—like when she and her friends in Singapore rented a junk and sailed to a small island for a day of sunbathing, swimming, and picnicking. She was eager to go.

To her amazement, cruising for her cousins had nothing to do with boats and water. Instead, it meant endless driving about town with no apparent purpose. Eventually, they parked at a shopping mall and simply stood around. As far as Erika could see, it seemed their purpose was to block aisles rather than purchase any goods. What was the point?

For Erika "going home" meant something entirely different than it did for her parents. When her parents spoke of "going home," they meant returning to the States each summer. For her, "going home" meant returning to Singapore at the end of summer. But where was home now? The nagging question returned.

The temperature dropped inside the airplane as the short night descended. Erika stood up to grab a blanket and pillow from the overhead compartment, hoping for the comfort of sleep. But would sleep ever come on this journey? Not yet. Another set of pictures pushed their way into the muddle of her mind—now with scenes of the time she left Singapore to attend university in the States.

"Don't worry, darling. You'll be fine. I'm sure you'll get a wonderful roommate. You've always made friends so easily. I know you'll have no trouble at all," her parents had reassured her as she faced that transition.

But somehow it hadn't been that easy. Fellow students would ask, "Where are you from?" At first, Erika automatically answered, "Singapore." The universal reply was, "Really? You don't look like it," with the expectation of some explanation of how she was from Singapore.

Soon, Erika decided she would be from New York—where her grandparents lived. She hoped that would simplify these complicated introductions.

Eventually, as she adapted outwardly, picking up the current lingo and attire, others accepted her as one of them. By the end of her freshman year, however, she felt angry, confused, and depressed. How could anyone care so much about who won last week's football game and so little about the political unrest and violence in Bosnia or Rwanda? Didn't they know people actually died in wars? They couldn't understand her world; she couldn't understand theirs.

As time went on, Erika found a way to cope. Once she realized most of her peers simply couldn't relate to what her life had been, she no longer discussed it. Her relatives were happy to tell everyone she was "doing fine."

Just before graduating from university, however, she lost the last internal vestige of home. Her dad was transferred back to the States and her family settled in Dayton, Ohio. For school vacations, she no longer returned to Singapore. Erika closed that chapter of her life. The pain of longing for the past was just too much.

As she stared at the rhythmic, almost hypnotic, flashing red lights on the jet's wings, Erika continued her reflections. *That chapter on Singapore didn't stay closed for very long. When did I reopen it? Why did I reopen it?*

After graduation, she had decided to get a master's degree in history. Thinking about that now while flying somewhere over the Pacific Ocean, she wondered why she had chosen that particular field. *Was I subconsciously trying to escape to a world that paralleled my own—a world that was once exciting but is now gone forever?*

Who could know? All Erika knew was that her restlessness increased in graduate school, and she finally dropped out. At that point, Erika decided only a return to Singapore would stop this chronic unsettledness, this sense of always looking for something that might be just around the corner but never was. But also, she couldn't define what she wanted. Was it to belong somewhere? Anywhere?

Although her family no longer lived in Singapore, she still had many Singaporean friends who had often invited her to stay with them. Why not live her own life overseas? Surely it would be far better to live in a place where she belonged than to wander forever in this inner limbo.

Erika called a travel agent, who knew her well because of all her trips during university days, and booked a flight to Singapore. The next step was to call one of her former classmates still living in Singapore. "Dolores, I want to come home. Can you help me find a job? I'm coming as soon as I get my visa, and I'll need a way to support myself once I'm back."

"That's wonderful! I'm sure we can find some kind of job for you," came the reply. "You can stay with me until you get everything lined up." Erika was ecstatic! It felt so familiar, so normal to be planning a trip overseas again. She couldn't wait to return to the world in which she so obviously belonged.

When she arrived in Singapore, her dream seemed to have come true. What airport in the world could compare to the beauty of Changi? Graceful banners hung on the walls, welcoming weary travelers in their own languages. Brilliantly colored flowers cascaded down the sides of the built-in garden beds throughout the terminal. Trees grew beside waterfalls that tumbled over rocks to a pond below. The piped-in sounds of chirping birds completed her sense of entering a garden in paradise. How could anyone not love this place?

As she walked out of the terminal, she took a deep breath. How wonderfully familiar were the smells: tropical flowers and leaded petrol fumes—what a paradox! Living, life-giving plants, and dead, polluting fuel—intermingled. Was it possible her whole life was a paradox? A life full of rich experiences in totally diverse cultures and places, each experience filled with a special vibrancy that made her want to dance and celebrate the joy of life. And yet, a life in which she always felt a bit like an observer, playing the part for the current scene, but forever watching to see how she was doing.

Erika quickly brushed these thoughts aside. Those times of being an outsider were gone now because she knew where she belonged—in Singapore. How wonderful finally to be home!

As the days progressed, however, life seemed less familiar. She discovered that many things she had taken for granted as a child in the expatriate business community of Singapore were no longer hers to enjoy as a young, single, foreign woman living with a Singaporean family. No maid, no expensive restaurants, no car, fewer friends. Instead, she had to wash her clothes by hand, grab cheap rice dishes from street vendors, and get around the city by walking blocks in the hot sun to take a crowded bus.

While growing up, her family might not have been classified as wealthy, but there had always been enough money for them to be comfortable and not worry about paying the bills, taking little side trips or splurging on a particularly nice outfit. Now she had to consider seriously such mundane questions as how much lunch cost and how she could pay for her barest living expenses.

Finding a job was harder than she had guessed it would be. Jobs that paid enough for her to rent a reasonably modest apartment and buy food and clothes had to be contracted with international companies before entering the country. Now she realized that was what her father had done. To make matters worse, she learned that available jobs were next to impossible for a noncitizen to get. Because the government wanted to save jobs for Singaporeans, it rarely issued a work permit for local jobs to a foreigner. The jobs for local hires that she could find would not pay enough for her to live safely, let alone well. Because a young white woman was so visible in a cheap rent district with high crime rates, Erika feared she would present a far too easy target for someone bent on robbery or assault.

Here, in the world she had always thought of as home, Erika realized she was seen as a foreigner—an outsider. There was no such thing as an international passport.

The sad day came when she finally had to admit that she didn't fit in this country either. Sitting in her friend's tiny apartment in a world she had thought was home, despair swept over her. She was lost. The promises of big dreams seemed foolish and childish. She belonged nowhere. With a muffled sob she picked up the telephone and dialed her parents' number.

"Mom, I can't make it here, but I don't know what to do. I don't fit in Dayton, but I don't fit here either. Somehow I seem to have grown up between two totally different worlds, and now I've found out I don't belong to either one."

With infinite sorrow this time, she made one last airline reservation, and now she was here, forty thousand feet in the air, going—home?

Erika's story is only one of thousands we have heard from TCKs all over the world. The particulars of each tale are different, yet in a sense so many are the same. They are the stories of lives filled with rich diversity but mixed with an underlying question of where TCKs fit among all that diversity. What are some of the reasons for this common thread among TCKs? Who, indeed, are these TCKs and what are some of the benefits and challenges inherent in the experience they have had? These are the questions we will address in the chapters which follow.

Endnotes

[1] Carolyn D. Smith, *The Absentee American* (1991; reprint, Putnam Valley, NY: Aletheia Publications, 1994), 2.

[2] An organization formed by Norma McCaig in 1986 for TCKs of every background and nationality.

[3] Ted Ward, "The MKs' Advantage: Three Cultural Contexts," in *Understanding and Nurturing the Missionary Family,* edited by Pam Echerd and Alice Arathoon (Pasadena, CA: William Carey Library, 1989), 57.

2

Who Are "Third Culture Kids"?

Who or what exactly is a third culture kid? Here's the definition we like best:

> A Third Culture Kid (TCK) is a person who has spent a
> significant part of his or her developmental years
> outside the parents' culture. The TCK builds relation-
> ships to all of the cultures, while not having full
> ownership in any. Although elements from each
> culture are assimilated into the TCK's life experience,
> the sense of belonging is in relationship to others of
> similar background.[1]

Let's look at this definition in detail.

"A Third Culture Kid (TCK)..."

Some of the most vigorous discussions about TCKs start with a debate over the term itself. Over and over people ask, "How can you
possibly say people with such incredibly diverse cultural backgrounds
and experience can make up a 'culture,' when the word *culture*, by
definition, means a group of people who have something in common?"

This is one of the strange paradoxes about TCKs. Looking at
the differences among them—of race, nationality, sponsoring orga-

nizations, and places where they are growing (or have grown) up—you would think TCKs could have little in common. But if you attend a conference sponsored by Global Nomads International and watch the animated, nonstop conversation of the participants throughout the weekend, you will not question the powerful connection between them. What is this almost magical bond? Why have they been called third *culture* kids?

The Third Culture as Originally Defined

A common misconception about third culture kids is that they have been raised in what is often called the "Third World." While this might be true for some, the Third World has no specific relationship to the concept of the third culture. Two social scientists, Drs. John and Ruth Hill Useem, coined the term *third culture* in the 1950s, when they went to India for a year to study Americans who lived and worked there as foreign service officers, missionaries, technical aid workers, businessmen, educators, and media representatives.[2] While in India, the Useems also met expatriates from other countries and soon discovered that "each of these subcultures [communities of expatriates] generated by colonial administrators, missionaries, businessmen, and military personnel—had its own peculiarities, slightly different origins, distinctive styles and stratification systems, but all were closely interlocked."[3] They realized the expatriates had formed a lifestyle that was different from either their home or their host culture, but it was one they shared in that setting.

To best describe this expatriate world, the Useems defined the home culture from which the adults came as the first culture. They called the host culture where the family lived (in that case, India) the second culture. They then identified the shared lifestyle of the expatriate community as an *interstitial culture,* or "culture between cultures," and named it the third culture. The Useems called the children who had grown up in that interstitial culture *third culture kids.*

The Third Culture as Currently Defined

The Useems did their research when most Western expatriates lived in specific communal systems such as military bases, missionary compounds, and business enclaves. Identifying a visible, local expatriate community was relatively easy.

However, the world has changed since then. Today, many expatriates no longer live in defined communities. The Japanese families who live in Kokomo, Indiana, and work for Delco-Remy don't live in a Delco-Remy compound. Their children usually attend local schools instead of going off to boarding schools as TCKs often used to do. Because there are frequently no well-marked expatriate enclaves anymore, some argue that the terms *third culture* or *third culture kid* are now misnomers. How can there be a culture if people don't live together?

When we asked Dr. Useem what she thought about this, she said, "Because I am a sociologist/anthropologist I think no concept is ever locked up permanently.... Concepts change as we get to know more; other times concepts change because what happens in the world is changing."[4]

In her recent report on a survey of adult TCKs, Dr. Useem herself defined the third culture as a generic term to discuss the *lifestyle* "created, shared, and learned" by those who are from one culture and are in the process of relating to another one. In that same article, she defines TCKs simply as "children who accompany their parents into another society."[5]

These larger definitions are justifiable because if culture in its broadest sense is a way of life shared with others, there's no question that, in spite of their differences, TCKs of all stripes and persuasions in countless countries share remarkably important life experiences through the very process of living in and among different cultures—whether or not they grew up in a specific local expatriate community. Further, the kinds of experiences they share tend to affect the deeper rather than the more superficial parts of their personal or cultural being.

Like a double rainbow, two realities arch over the TCK experience that shape the formation of a TCK's life:

1. *Being raised in a genuinely cross-cultural world.* Instead of simply watching, studying, or analyzing other cultures, TCKs actually live in different cultural worlds as they travel back and forth between their home and host cultures. Some TCKs who have gone through multiple moves or whose parents are in an intercultural marriage have interacted closely with four or more cultures.

2. *Being raised in a highly mobile world.* Mobility is normal for the third culture experience. Either the TCKs themselves or those around them are constantly coming or going. The people in their lives are always changing, and the backdrop of physical surroundings may often fluctuate as well.

Members of this broad third culture community usually have other characteristics in common, including:

1. *Distinct differences.* Many TCKs are raised where being physically different from those around them is a major aspect of their identity. Even when external appearances are similar to either their host or home culture, TCKs often have a substantially different perspective on the world from their peers.

2. *Expected repatriation.* Unlike immigrants, third culture families usually expect at some point to return permanently to live in their home country.

3. *Privileged lifestyle.* Historically, employees of international businesses and members of missions, the military, and the diplomatic corps have been part of an elitist community—one with special privileges bestowed on its members by either the sponsoring organization or the host culture or both. Often, there are systems of logistical support or "perks": those in the military can use the commissary or PX; embassy or missionary compounds may employ home repair or domestic service person-

nel; diplomatic families may have chauffeurs to drive the children to school or around town. Even without the perks, there are entitlements such as worldwide travel to and from their post—all at the expense of the sponsoring agency.

4. *System identity.* Members of specific third culture communities may be more directly conscious than peers at home of representing something greater than themselves—be it their government, their company, or God. Jobs can hinge on how well the adults' behavior, or that of their children, positively reflects the values and standards of the sponsoring agency.

The first two characteristics of living in a cross-cultural and highly mobile world are true for virtually every third culture person. The degree to which TCKs may differ from their host culture, expect to repatriate, enjoy a privileged lifestyle, or identify with the organizational system varies a bit more depending on where and why their families are living outside the home culture.

A Sample Slice of the "Neither/Nor" Third Culture

ATCKs Rob and Heather are citizens of different countries who grew up on opposite sides of the globe. The only thing they share is the fact they were both raised outside their parents' home cultures. After hearing a lecture at a Global Nomads International conference about both the original and broader meaning of the term *third culture,* they talked together during a break.

> Rob spoke first. "I felt pretty skeptical before coming to this conference, but maybe there is something to this third culture bit. It never occurred to me that the military lifestyle I grew up in had a culture that was different from my home or host cultures. I just thought of myself as an American in Japan."
>
> "Why?" Heather asked.
>
> "I was nine when my family moved from Oregon to the 'American Bubble' in Japan—that's what everyone called our Army base. It seemed completely American.

Through the commissary or PX we could get Cheerios for breakfast, Nikes to run in, and even Pringles for snacks. The movies in our base theater were the same ones being shown in the States. Man, we even had tennis courts and a swimming pool just like I did at my YMCA in Portland!"

Heather looked at Rob with amazement. "I can't believe it!" she said. "I'm at least twenty years older than you, I've never been to Japan, my dad worked for the British government in Nigeria, but I can relate to what you're saying!"

"How come?" asked Rob.

"Well, I really don't know. I guess I never thought about it before. Maybe because we lived in a 'British Bubble'? We just didn't call it that. Although we didn't have a PX or commissary, we did have Kingsway stores in every major city. They imported all those wonderful British things like Marmite, Weetabix, and Jacob's Cream Crackers. We also had a swimming pool and tennis courts at the local British club. It all seemed very British and very normal."

Rob responded, "Yeah, well, I don't know about you, but for me, even with so many American trappings, life in Japan still wasn't like living in Portland. When I left the base and took the train to town, I suddenly felt isolated because I couldn't understand the people chattering around me or read most of the signs."

"I know what you mean," Heather responded. "With all our British stuff around, it still wasn't like living in England. I had a Nigerian nanny who taught me how to speak Hausa and how to *chiniki*, or bargain, for things as I grew up. I wouldn't have done that in England. But I probably got more into the local culture than you did, since we moved to Nigeria when I was two."

"Well, I got into the local culture too," Rob said, a bit defensively. "I mean, after a few months I found Japanese friends who taught me how to eat sushi, use chopsticks, bathe in an *ofuro*, and sleep on a futon. But my life wasn't like theirs any more than it was like life back in Portland. For one thing, I went to the local international school, where I studied in English instead of Japanese."

"I understand that, too!" Heather exclaimed. "My life wasn't the same as my Nigerian friends' lives either—even if I could speak their language. I had a driver who took me back and forth from school each day, while most of my friends had to walk long distances in the heat of the day to attend their schools."

"So did your life overseas seem strange?" Rob and Heather looked up in surprise to see that someone had joined them.

Both shook their heads at the same time in response to the stranger's question.

"Nope, not to me," said Rob.

"Me either," interjected Heather.

The newcomer persisted. "But how could you feel normal when you lived so differently from people in either your own countries or Japan or Nigeria? Seems to me that would make you feel somewhat odd."

Rob thought for a quick moment. "Well, I suppose it's because all the other American kids I knew were growing up in that same neither/nor world the speaker talked about today. All my Army and international friends had moved as often as I had. We were used to saying good-bye to old friends and hello to new ones. No big deal. That's life. Nothing unusual, since we were all doing it. I don't know—it just seemed like a normal way to live, didn't it, Heather?"

"Exactly. I lived the same way all my other British

and expatriate friends did. They had house help. So did
we. They flew from one continent to another regularly. So did I. When we went out to play, all of us
wore the same kind of pith helmets so we wouldn't
get sunstroke. To me, it's just how life was."

While both Rob and Heather happened to grow up in an easily identifiable expatriate community, third culture families who live in less
defined communities still find ways to keep some expression of their
home culture. In Indiana the Japanese community has organized
special swimming classes at the local YMCA for their TCKs because they want to maintain their traditionally more disciplined approach to training children. They also conduct Saturday classes, when
all academic subjects are taught in Japanese, so their TCKs maintain both written and verbal language skills.

But all this talk about the third culture should not distract us
from understanding the most crucial part of the TCK definition, the
fact that a TCK:

"...is a person..."

Why are these words critical to all further discussion on third culture kids? Because we must never forget that above all else, a TCK
is simply a person. Sometimes TCKs spend so much time feeling
different from people in the dominant culture around them that they
(or those who notice these differences) begin to feel TCKs are, in
fact, intrinsically different—some sort of special breed of being.
While their experiences may be different from other people's, TCKs
have the same need as non-TCKs for building relationships in which
they love and are loved, ones in which they know others and are
known by them. They need a sense of purpose and meaning in their
lives and have the same capacities to think, learn, create, and make
choices as others do. The characteristics, benefits, and challenges
that we describe later arise from the interactions of the various aspects of mobility and the cross-cultural nature of this upbringing,
not from some fundamental difference in them as persons.

"...who has spent a significant part..."

Time by itself doesn't determine how deep an impact the third culture experience has on the development of a particular child. Other variables such as the child's age, personality, and participation in the local culture have an important effect. For example, living overseas between the ages of one and four will affect a child differently than if that same experience occurs between the ages of eleven and fourteen.

While we can't say precisely how long a child must live outside the home culture to develop the classic TCK characteristics, we can say it is more than a two-week or even a two-month vacation to see the sights. Some people are identifiable TCKs or ATCKs after spending as little as one year outside their parents' culture. Of course, other factors such as the parents' attitudes and behavior or policies of the sponsoring agency add to how significant the period spent as a TCK is or was in shaping a child's life.

"...of his or her developmental years..."

Although the length of time needed for someone to become a true TCK can't be precisely defined, the time *when* it happens can. It must occur during the developmental years—from birth to eighteen years of age. We recognize that a cross-cultural experience affects adults as well as children. The difference for a TCK, however, is that this cross-cultural experience occurs during the years when that child's sense of identity, relationships with others, and view of the world are being formed in the most basic ways. While parents may change careers and become former international businesspeople, former missionaries, former military personnel, or former foreign service officers, no one is ever a former third culture kid. TCKs simply move on to being adult third culture kids because their lives grow out of the roots planted in and watered by the third culture experience.

"...outside the parents' culture."

The home culture is defined in terms of the parents' culture. Most often, TCKs grow up outside the parents' home country as well as culture, and the stories throughout our book predominantly feature this more typical TCK experience. It's important to recognize, however, that TCKs can be children who never leave their parents' country but are still raised in a different culture. Jennifer is one.

> Both of Jennifer's parents grew up in upper-middle-class suburbs of Toronto. When Jennifer was nine, they became teachers for five years on a First Nation (Native American) reservation near Vancouver. Jennifer went to school, played, ate, and visited with her First Nation playmates almost exclusively during those years—yet her lifestyle was not the same as theirs. For example, there were celebratory rituals in the First Nation culture that Jennifer's family never practiced. Her parents had rules for curfew and study hours that many friends didn't have, but Jennifer accepted these differences between her and her friends.
>
> When she was fourteen, Jennifer's parents returned to Toronto. They wanted her to have a more "normal" high school experience. Unfortunately, it wasn't as normal as they had hoped. For one thing, Jennifer's new classmates seemed to judge one another far more critically by what styles of clothes they did and didn't wear than she had ever experienced before. Far worse, however, it seemed to her that this emphasis on apparent trivia stemmed from a lack of concern for what she considered the *real* issues of life. When newspapers reported the ongoing conflict of land issues between the First Nation people and the Canadian government, she read the accounts with keen interest. She personally knew friends whose futures were directly affected by these political

decisions. But when she tried to discuss such things
with fellow classmates or their parents, the response
was almost dismissive. "I don't know what those
people are complaining about. Look at all we've
already done for them." The more she tried to explain
why this topic needed attention, the more they labeled
her as radical, and the more she labeled them as
uncaring. Jennifer sobbed herself to sleep many nights,
wishing for the comfortable familiarity of the world
and friends she'd known before.

Although she had never left Canada, Jennifer had become a TCK—
someone raised in that world between worlds—within her own country. Military children who have never moved outside their countries
may also share many TCK characteristics. The military subculture
(see Mary Edwards Wertsch, *Military Brats)* is quite different from
that of the civilian population around it. When military parents return to civilian life, their children often experience many of the same
feelings that internationally mobile TCKs describe when they return to their passport countries.

Raised on Navy bases in California and Washington,
DC, Bernadette was fourteen when her father retired
from the Navy and her family settled in the
midwestern town of Terre Haute, Indiana. Bernadette
later described the experience as one of total alienation from her peers, whose life experience was
completely foreign to her.

"…The TCK builds relationships to all of the cultures, while not having full ownership in any."

This brings us back to Erika.

As she flew back to the United States, Erika wondered
how it could be that life felt like such a rich dance in
and through so many cultures while at the same time

that same richness made it seem impossible to stop
the dance. To land in Singapore would mean she could
celebrate the hustle and bustle of that wonderful city
she loved so much, but then she would miss the
mountains of Ecuador and the joy of touching and
seeing the beautiful weavings in the Otavolo Indian
markets. To end the dance in Ecuador meant she
would never again see the magnificent colors of fall in
upstate New York or taste her grandmother's special
Sunday pot roast. But to stop in New York or Dayton,
where her parents now lived, meant she would miss
not only Singapore and Ecuador but also all the other
places she had been and seen. Erika wished for just
one moment she could bring together the many
worlds she had known and embrace them all at the
same time, but she knew it could never happen.

This is at the heart of the issues of rootlessness and restlessness
discussed later. This lack of full ownership is what gives that sense
of belonging "everywhere and nowhere" at the same time.

"...Although elements from each culture are assimilated into the TCK's life experience,..."

Obviously, there are specific ways each home and host culture shape
each TCK (Rob loves peanut butter and jelly, Heather prefers
Marmite; Rob eats his Cheerios and speaks Japanese, while Heather
eats Weetabix and speaks Hausa). But it's not only food and language that shape them. Cultural rules do as well.

- After living in London where his dad served as ambassador for
  six years, Musa had trouble with how people dealt with time
  when he returned to Guinea. Instead of relaxing as others from
  his home culture could when meetings did not begin and end as
  scheduled, he felt the same frustration many expatriates experienced. Musa had exchanged the more relational worldview of
  his home culture for a time-oriented worldview during his time
  abroad.

- At his summer job in Canada, Gordon's boss thought he was dishonest and lazy because Gordon never looked anyone in the eye. But where Gordon had grown up in Africa, children always kept their eyes to the ground when talking with adults.

Certainly cultural practices are incorporated from the unique aspects of both host and home cultures, but the third culture is more than the sum total of the parts of home and host culture. If it were only that, each TCK would remain alone in his or her experience.

"...the sense of belonging is in relationship to others of similar background."

Erika returned to Dayton, Ohio, after her long, final flight back from Singapore. She began teaching high school French and Spanish during the day; tutoring international businesspeople in English filled her evenings. Once more she tried to accept the reality that her past was gone. Life must go on, and she couldn't expect anyone else to understand her when she didn't understand herself.

Then a remarkable thing occurred. Erika met Judy.

One evening she went to see a play and got there a few minutes early. After settling in her seat, she opened her program to see what to expect.

Before she could finish scanning the first page, a middle-aged woman with curly, graying hair squeezed past her, sitting in the next seat.

Why couldn't she have a ticket for the row in front? That's wide open. Erika rolled her eyes to the ceiling. *All I wanted was a little space tonight.*

Then it got worse. This woman was one of those friendly types.

"Hi, there. I'm Judy. What's your name?"

Oh, brother, lady. I'm not into this kind of chitchat. "I'm Erika. It's nice to meet you." *There, that's over with.* And she turned her eyes back to study the program again.

"Well, I'm glad to meet you too."

Why won't she let me alone?

The lady went on. "I come for the plays every month but I haven't seen you before. Are you new here? Where are you from?"

C'mon, lady. Erika was becoming more internally agitated by the moment. *This is the theater, not a witness stand. Besides, you don't really want to know anyway.* "I live here in Dayton," Erika replied, with cool politeness. *That ought to end it.*

But Judy continued. "Have you always lived here?"

Why does she care? Erika was definitely losing composure at this point. "No, I've only lived here for two years." *Now shut up, lady.*

"Oh, really? Where did you come from before that?"

With a sigh, Erika half turned to look at this pesky woman and said, "I've lived in lots of different places." *So there.*

"Hey, that's great. So have I! Where have you lived?"

For the first time, Erika looked Judy in the eye. She couldn't believe it. This lady genuinely wanted to know. Erika hesitated. "I lived in Ecuador and Singapore."

"How long?"

"Oh, about ten years between the two places, if you're talking about actually living and going to school there full-time."

"You're kidding! I grew up in Venezuela. I'd love to talk to you about it. It's not always easy to find someone here in Dayton who understands what it's like to grow up in another country."

Just then the curtain went up for the play, so they stopped talking. Afterward, they went for coffee and Erika found herself amazed. Here they were, two

women from two totally different backgrounds—
Judy's parents had been in the foreign service while
Erika's were in business; Judy had lived in Venezuela
and Erika had lived in Ecuador and Singapore. Judy was
forty-seven, married, the mother of four grown
children, while Erika was twenty-five, single, with no
children. Yet they were soon talking and laughing
together like long-lost friends.

"I remember when the CEO's wife first came to
our house for dinner," Erika said with a chuckle. "She
had just arrived in Singapore and kept talking about
how awful everything was. My sister and I made up all
sorts of stories about how big the roaches were and
how poisonous the spiders were just to scare her."

Judy laughed. "I know how you felt. I hated it when
new people arrived and complained about everything.
I always felt so protective for what seemed like my
personal Venezuela."

"Well, I guess it was kind of mean," Erika said, "but
we didn't like her barging into our world without
trying to understand the parts we loved so much. We
thought she was arrogant and narrow-minded and
didn't deserve to be there—and she probably thought
we were the same!"

They laughed together and continued talking for
three hours. Erika couldn't believe it. For the first time
in years she could speak the language of her soul
without needing a translator. A space inside that had
almost dried up suddenly began filling and then
overflowing with the joy of being understood in a way
that needed no explanation.

TCKs around the world instinctively feel this connection when they
meet each other. But why? How can someone from Australia who
grew up in Brazil understand that inner experience of someone from
Switzerland who grew up in Hong Kong?

A video of TCKs meeting at Cornell University clearly demonstrates this bond.[6] Among the TCK panelists are

- Kelvin—born in Hong Kong, raised in Nigeria and England;

- Marianne, a Danish citizen who grew up in the United States;

- Kamal, an Indian who lived in Japan as a child;

- a young Turkish man who spent his childhood in Germany, England, and the United States;

- one American who grew up in the Philippines; and

- another American reared in France.

Although each person in the video has differing points of identification with his or her host culture (e.g., the Turkish man feels he is extremely punctual as a result of living in Germany for many years), throughout the discussion it's obvious that their commonalities of feelings and experiences far outweigh their differences. It is equally obvious that they are delighted to finally find a forum where simply naming how they have felt in various circumstances brings instant understanding. No further explanation is needed to elicit a sympathetic laugh or tear from their peers.

But the question remains: what is it about growing up in multiple cultures and with high mobility that creates such instant recognition of each other's experiences and feelings?

Endnotes

[1] "The TCK Profile" seminar material, Interaction, Inc., 1989, 1.

[2] Ruth Hill Useem, "Third Culture Kids: Focus of Major Study," *Newslinks*, Newspaper of the International School Services 12, 3 (January 1993): 1.

[3] Ruth Hill Useem, "Third Cultural Factors in Educational Change," in *Cultural Challenges to Education: The Influence of Cultural Factors in School Learning,* edited by Cole S. Brembeck and Walker H. Hill (Lexington, MA: Lexington Books, 1973), 122.

[4] Personal letter to David C. Pollock, February 1994.

[5] Useem, "Third Culture Kids," 1.

[6] *Global Nomads: Cultural Bridges for the Future*, coproduced by Alice Wu and Lewis Clark in conjunction with Cornell University.

3

Why a Cross-Cultural Childhood Matters

I am
a confusion of cultures.
Uniquely me.
I think this is good
because I can
understand
the traveller, sojourner, foreigner,
the homesickness
that comes.
I think this is also bad
because I cannot
be understood
by the person who has sown and grown in one place.
They know not
the real meaning of homesickness
that hits me
now and then.
Sometimes I despair of
understanding them.
I am

> an island
> and
> a United Nations.
> Who can recognise either in me
> but God?[1]
>
> —"Uniquely Me" by Alex Graham James

Who Am I?

This poem by Alex, an Australian TCK who grew up in India, captures the paradoxical nature of the TCK experience—the sense of
being profoundly connected yet simultaneously disconnected with
people and places around the world. The question, however, is this:
what makes Alex, like Erika and most TCKs, feel this way?

Before we can answer that question, we need to take a closer
look at the world in which they grow up, a world filled with cross-
cultural transitions and high mobility. These two related but distinct
forces play a large role in shaping a TCK's life.

We recognize, of course, that TCKs aren't the only ones who
experience cross-cultural differences or high mobility. In large met-
ropolitan centers around the world, children may live their entire
lives in one place with neighbors from a great variety of ethnic or
racial backgrounds and become aware of cultural differences at an
early age. Children may also experience high mobility within their
own country for various reasons. Without doubt, these factors will
shape a non-TCK's life as well. After Dave Pollock presented "The
TCK Profile" in Washington, DC, one non-TCK said, "I'm an American who has never lived outside the States, but my dad climbed the
corporate ladder while I grew up. We moved every two years or so,
whenever he got his next promotion. I have all the challenges of the
mobility issues without the benefits of the cross-cultural experience."
We also realize that many adults experience both cross-cultural transitions and high mobility as they embark on international careers;
their lives, too, are inevitably changed in the process.

So what makes the TCK experience different from that of these children or adults? Children who grow up amid people from many cultures in one locality usually learn to be comfortable with the diversity. It's a relatively stable diversity. The child isn't being chronically uprooted, and the unwritten rules for how the groups coexist and relate to one another are clearly defined and practiced. The difference for TCKs is that they not only deal with cultural differences in a particular location, but the entire cultural world they live in can change overnight with a single airplane ride. Relationships are subject to equally dramatic changes as they or others around them constantly come and go. When non-TCK children move within the same culture, they miss old friends and need to go through grief at losing familiar people and places, but they don't have to relearn basic cultural rules and practices when they unpack in the next city. The language remains the same, the currency still works, and they already know who the president is.

When people first go to another culture as adults, they experience culture shock and need a period of adjustment, but their value system, sense of identity, and the establishment of core relationships with family and friends have already developed in the home culture. They clearly see themselves as Americans, Australians, Kenyans, or Indonesians who happen to be living in another place or culture. Their basic sense of who they are and where they belong is intact. Unlike adults with similar experiences, however, for TCKs the moving back and forth from one culture to another happens before they have completed the critical developmental task of forming a sense of their own personal or cultural identity. A British child taking toddling steps on foreign soil or speaking his or her first words in Chinese with an amah (nanny) has no idea of what it means to be human yet, let alone "British." He or she simply responds to what is happening in the moment.

To have any meaningful discussion about TCKs, it is essential to remember that it is an *interplay* of these factors—living in both a culturally changing *and* highly mobile world during the *formative* years—rather than any single factor alone that leads to the evolution of both the benefits and challenges we describe as well as the personal characteristics. To better understand how the interplay of these factors works, we need to look at each one separately and in more depth to determine how a TCK's experience differs from that of the child who grows up among diverse cultures in one place or with high mobility alone. We will begin in this chapter by taking a look at the cross-cultural nature of the TCK's childhood. Then, in chapter 4, we will move on to high mobility.

The Significance of Culture

One of the major developmental tasks that help us form our sense of identity and belonging is to successfully learn the basic cultural rules of our society while we are children, to internalize those principles and practices as we move through adolescence, and then use them as the basis for how we live and act as adults. In order to look at this normal process and then why it is so significant for TCKs, we need to first answer these questions: What is culture? How do we learn it? Why is it important?

When we first think of the word *culture*, the obvious things such as how to dress and act like those around us come to mind. But learning culture is more than learning to conform to external patterns of behavior. Culture is also a system of shared assumptions, beliefs, and values.[2] It is the framework from which we interpret and make sense of life and the world around us. As cultural anthropologist Paul G. Hiebert emphasizes, culture is learned rather than instinctive behavior—something caught from, as well as taught by, the surrounding environment and passed on from one generation to the next.[3] Author and cross-cultural trainer and consultant L. Robert Kohls suggests we look at culture as a kind of iceberg, with one part clearly visible above the surface of the water and another, much larger part hidden below. The part above the water can be identified as the *surface culture* and includes behavior, words, customs, and traditions. Underneath the water where no one can see is the *deep culture,* and it consists of beliefs, values, assumptions, and thought processes. Here is a representation of Dr. Kohls' culture iceberg.

behavior
words
customs
traditions

beliefs
values
assumptions
thought processes

No group can be cohesive without its members sharing a basic consensus in the deeper dimensions of culture. Merely mimicking behavior—such as clothing styles or food preferences—will not hold a group together.[4]

Perhaps one of the best illustrations of the traditional role of culture is seen in *Fiddler on the Roof,* a musical about a farmer named Tevye and his Russian Jewish village of Anatevka. For years Tevye's culture has remained basically the same. Everyone knows where he or she fits in relationship to one another and to God. There have been no major outside influences. The way things have always been is the way things still are, with the milkman, matchmaker, farmer, and all others clearly aware of their assigned roles in the village. Roles assigned by whom? By *tradition,* which is another word for how cultural beliefs are worked out in practice. Tevye says,

> Because of our traditions, we've kept our balance for
> many, many years. Here in Anatevka we have tradi-
> tions for everything—how to eat, how to sleep, how
> to wear clothes. For instance, we always keep our
> heads covered and always wear a little prayer shawl.
> This shows our constant devotion to God. You may
> ask, how did this tradition start? I'll tell you—I don't

> know! But it's a tradition. Because of our traditions,
> everyone knows who he is and what God expects him
> to do.... Without our traditions, our lives would be as
> shaky as—as a fiddler on the roof![5]

Tevye then laments that tradition is breaking down. During the story, as the old ways rapidly change, he loses his former sense of balance. His grip on life is slipping, his comfortable world shattered. Mentally and emotionally, Tevye can't keep up, and he begins to feel disoriented and alienated, even from his own children.

Why is *cultural balance*—that almost unconscious knowledge of how things are and work in a particular community— important? Because when we are in cultural balance, we are like a concert pianist who, after practicing for years to master the basics, now no longer thinks about how to find the right piano keys or when to pedal or how to do scales or trills. Those functions have become almost automatic responses to notations in the score of music, and this freedom allows the pianist to use these basic skills to create and express richer, fuller music.

Cultural balance gives us that same kind of freedom. Once we have stayed in a culture long enough to internalize its behaviors and the assumptions behind them, we have an almost intuitive sense of what is right, humorous, appropriate, or offensive in any particular situation. Instead of spending excessive time worrying if we are dressed appropriately for a business appointment, we can concentrate on coming up with a new business plan. Being "in the know" gives us a sense of stability, deep security, and belonging. Like Tevye, we may not understand *why* cultural rules work as they do, but we know *how* our culture works.

Conversely, when we are having to learn and relearn the basic rules by which the world around us is operating, our energies are spent in surviving rather than thriving. It's as if we are still figuring out the fingering for the scales on the piano while others around us are playing a Rachmaninoff concerto. Being out of cultural balance leaves us struggling to understand what is happening rather than fully participating in the event.

A World of Changing Cultures

Through the years, many TCKs have told us they wonder what is wrong with them, because they never seem to "get it." No matter what situation they are in, they often make what looks like a dumb remark or mistake. Others wonder at their apparent stupidity, while they are left with the shame that somehow they can never quite fit in socially as others do.

Perhaps ironically, the struggle many TCKs face in trying to find a sense of cultural balance and identity is not because they learn culture differently from the way others do. In fact, the real challenge comes *because* they learn culture as everyone does—by "catching it" from their environment rather than by reading a book or getting a master's degree in cultural anthropology. What TCKs and those who know them seem to forget is that their life experiences have been different from someone who grows up in a basically stable, traditional, monocultural community such as Tevye's. As TCKs move with their parents from place to place, the cultural values and practices of the communities they live in often change radically. What was acceptable behavior and thinking in one place is now seen as crude or ridiculous in the next. Which culture are they supposed to catch? Do they belong to all of them, none of them, or some of each of them? Where in the world (literally) do they fit?

Another factor for TCKs in finding cultural balance is that cultural norms are as unconsciously taught as they are caught. Parents, community, school, and peers are all part of the cultural teaching process, whether the members of those groups think about it or not. When everyone in a community such as Tevye's holds the same basic values and customs, each group unthinkingly reinforces the next group's instructions. For TCKs, however, not only do the overall cultural rules often change overnight, but equally often the individual members of these four basic groups in any given place may hold markedly different world- and lifeviews from one another. Let's take a look at how the normal process of learning cultural balance may be complicated by each of these groups in a TCK's life.

Parents

Parents communicate both the "above water" and "below water" cultural norms in various ways. They do it by example, dressing differently for a business meeting than for a tennis match, or speaking respectfully of others. They do it by correction: "Don't chew with your mouth open." "If you don't stop hitting your brother, you'll have to take a time-out." Or they do it by praise: "What a good boy you are to share your toys with your sister!"

Wherever TCKs are being raised, their families' cultural practices and values are usually rooted in the parents' home culture or cultures and may be markedly different from the practices of the surrounding culture. This includes something as simple as the style of clothing. Girls from the Middle East may continue wearing a head covering no matter which country they live in. Dutch children wear Western dress in the forests of Brazil. Of course, it's far more than that as well. Telling the truth at all costs may be a prime value at home, while shading the truth to avoid shaming another person is the paramount value in the host culture.

Increasing numbers of TCKs are also being born to parents who are in an intercultural marriage or relationship. In 1960 one-quarter of American children living overseas had parents from two cultures, according to Ruth Hill Useem.[6] In 1995 Helen Fail found that 42 percent of her ATCK survey respondents had grown up in bicultural families.[7] One young man, for example, was born in the Philippines to a German father married to a Cambodian mother, and they speak French as their common family language. That's a lot of cultures for a young child to learn, and it complicates this most elemental step of learning cultural rules and practices from parents.

Community

In a community like Tevye's, other adults reinforce what the parents teach at home because the rules are uniform. The same characteristics—such as honesty, hard work, and respect for adults—bring approval (or, in their absence, disapproval) from the community as well as from parents. No one stops to question by whose standards some cultural behaviors and customs are defined as proper and others as improper, but everyone knows what they are.

TCKs interface with different local communities, each having different cultural expectations, from the moment they begin their odyssey in the third culture experience. Unless they are isolated in a military, embassy, mission, or company compound and never go into the surrounding community, the host culture certainly affects them. They learn to drop in on friends without calling ahead. They call adults by their first names. When TCKs return to their home culture, they usually have to switch to a different set of cultural customs and practices. Now an unexpected visit becomes an intrusion. Addressing a playmate's mother or father by her or his first name is rude enough to be a punishable offense. Woe to the TCK who forgets where he or she is.

Besides the home and host cultures, in many situations TCKs are also conditioned by the overall expatriate community as well as the subcommunity—missionary, business, military, diplomatic corps—in which they grow up. Each of these groups also has its own subculture and clear expectations of behavior. In *Military Brats,* Mary Edwards Wertsch writes,

> Certainly by the time a military child is five years old, the values and rules of military life have been thoroughly internalized, the military identity forged, and the child has already assumed an active stage presence as an understudy of the Fortress theater company.[8]

Whatever the rules are in any TCK's given subculture—be they matters of correct dress, correct faith, or correct political views—TCKs know that to be an accepted member of that group, they must conform to those standards.

School

Although culture isn't taught from a book, no educational system develops in a cultural vacuum. A curriculum, along with how it is taught, is a direct reflection of the cultural values and beliefs of the society. Those who believe in the curriculum do so because they feel the values and practices it emphasizes are correct. As long as the community is in basic cultural agreement, the school will reinforce its views and practices because teachers and administrators (who also come from that community) will make choices for what is taught that are consistent with what parents and others in the community believe and teach.

For many TCKs, however, what and how things are taught at school may be vastly different as they shift from school to school while moving from one place to another. In addition, in an international community the individual teachers themselves often come from many different cultures. This can add significant confusion to the TCK's cultural development. Joe's story is an excellent example.

> My siblings and I found ourselves the only Americans in an Anglo-Argentine culture and we went to British schools. But the Argentines also thought their education was pretty good, so Peron mandated an Argentine curriculum for every private school and, with what time was left over, the school could do what it wanted. We went to school from 8:00 to 4:00 with four hours in Spanish in the morning and four hours of an English public school in the afternoon.
>
> Meanwhile, our parents fought desperately to keep some semblance of Americanism at home. They lost the battle of the "crossed 7s." They lost the spelling battle. Worse, when they were told that in a given year there would be a focus on North American history, geography, and literature, they discovered, to their dismay, North America meant Canada.[9]

It isn't only Americans going to British-oriented schools who struggle. Some of the most difficult situations are those of children who are from non-English-speaking countries who go to American-oriented schools. One Norwegian girl who attended such a school writes:

Norway became my well-kept secret. I was a fiercely patriotic little girl, and every May 17 I would insist on celebrating Norway's independence day. My American classmates had their Thanksgiving and Halloween parties. I was never invited, except for once, when I left the party in tears because I didn't understand the English in the video they were watching. Little did it help that we had a teacher from Texas who taught us U.S. history that year. When I put Florida on the wrong side of the map she scolded me for it. That memory is still very vivid in my mind. I was forced to hear about the wonders of America, and no one cared to hear about Norway. No one seemed to care that English wasn't my first language, and the school wouldn't give us time to learn Norwegian during school hours—we had to study Norwegian during our vacations. I used to think that was really unfair.[10]

If school is a place for learning the values as well as the behavior of culture, what happens when children attend a school with completely different customs, values, or religious orientation from that of their parents? This often occurs for globally nomadic families when the choices for schools that teach the academic curriculum of their home country may be limited to schools based on a belief system which does not match their own.

TCKs who go to boarding school experience another distinct subculture twenty-four hours a day rather than only during school. Without question, different rules are needed to organize scores of children in a dormitory environment rather than two or three in a home. Some TCKs talk of being raised by their peers more than by adults in such a setting. Some consider this the most positive thing about boarding school; others say it was the most difficult. Either way, it is a different experience from going to a day school and returning to parents each night.

Peers

When children play together, they instinctively parrot the cultural rules they have been taught: "You're cheating!" "Don't be a sissy!" As children grow, shaming one another this way enforces the norms of the community.

Most TCKs attend school and play with peers from many cultures—each culture valuing different things. Some friends practically live and die for soccer and cricket; others love American football and baseball. Some children are raised to believe that academic success is the highest priority; others value peer relationships over high grades. How does a child decide which is really most important?

While virtually all children learn culture from their parents, community, school, and peers, TCKs often have two additional sources of cultural input: caregivers and sponsoring agencies.

Caregivers

Some TCKs are left with a caregiver for perhaps as long as all day, five days a week, while both parents work. These caregivers are often members of the host culture and may speak only their national language. A German child being cared for by a Scottish nanny will likely hear no German during the time they spend together. Methods of child care in various cultures can be radically different. Instead of being pushed in a pram, Russian children raised in Niger will be carried on their African nanny's back until they can walk. Shaming may be the main method of training a child in the host culture rather than the positive reinforcement typical of the home culture.

Caregivers inevitably reflect their culture's attitude toward children and life. The story goes that when Pearl Buck was a child in China, someone asked how she compared her mother to her Chinese amah. It is said that Buck replied, "If I need to hear a story read, I go to my mother. If I fall down and need comforting, I go to my *amah*." One culture valued teaching and learning while the other placed a greater value on nurture, and as a child, Buck instinctively knew the difference.

Sponsoring Agencies

Many TCKs' parents belong to sponsoring agencies that have special behavioral or philosophical expectations of not only their employees but of the employees' families as well. This may result in situations that people in the home culture could never imagine. Two examples follow.

- A child's indiscretions (such as spraying graffiti on the wall of a public building) in a foreign service community might be written up and put in a parent's file, forever influencing future promotions, while that same behavior wouldn't cause a ripple in a parent's career if it happened in a suburban community in the home country.

- In the military, if a parent doesn't come in for a teacher-parent conference, the teacher can speak with the parent's officer-in-charge and the officer will require the parent to come in. If a military child does something as serious as getting drunk in school or setting off a firecracker, for example, he or she might be sent back to the home country, the parent won't be promoted that year, and the incident goes on the parent's permanent record.

In addition to such specific expectations for families in certain organizational subcultures, we have historically often neglected to look at how the root or home culture of the sponsoring agency itself may affect TCKs, particularly those who come from a different culture. The increasing internationalization of organizations throughout the world will soon force us to do so. When the policies and operational processes of an agency are rooted in a nationality or culture other than an employee's home culture, it means that without very careful planning, the decisions made by the executives of that organization which deeply affect the employee and his or her family may no longer coincide with the TCK's parental culture. Look at Ilpo's story to see what a major effect this one factor alone can have on a TCK's life. This relates to schooling options provided for him.

Ruth Van Reken met Ilpo, a Finnish TCK who had grown up in Taiwan, while he was finishing his medical residency program at the University of Chicago. He had completed all his post-secondary school education in the United States, including medical school. She asked why he had chosen to come to the United States rather than returning to school in Finland.

"Well, it sort of just happened," Ilpo replied. "My folks taught in a seminary in Taiwan, but the other missionaries were from America and Norway. Even though the curriculum for our little mission school was supposedly an international one, we had an American teacher, so all our classes were in English." Ilpo went on to explain how at age twelve he had gone to the American boarding school in Taichung and he lived in a small dorm run by the Finnish mission. Although he spoke Finnish in the dorm, his classes and interactions with fellow students took place in English. It was about this time that Ilpo faced his first cultural crisis. If he had been in Finland, after ninth grade he would have competed with all other Finnish students in a special test to decide who could continue their academic schooling and who would go to a trade or vocational school. When the time came for Ilpo to take that exam, he encountered a major problem. His education had been in English and the exam was in Finnish. Although he spoke Finnish fluently with his family, his written language skills in that language and his knowledge of the curriculum content from which the tests came were deficient. Ilpo knew he wanted to be a doctor, but if he went back and competed with students who had been studying in Finnish schools, the chances of his scoring high enough to attend university were slim. Ultimately, he felt his only option was to attend university in the States within the educational system he knew. But that also meant he had to stay in the United States for medical training because in Finland, medical training begins during university, not after it.

When Ruth asked Ilpo where he expected to live after his training, he said it would be very difficult to go back to Finland. Not only was its system different, but he didn't know medical vocabulary in Finnish. Even if he learned that, fellow physicians would look down on him because he had trained somewhere else. Ruth asked how he felt about that and Ilpo said, "That's what I'm coming to grips with now. I didn't realize before how nearly impossible it would be ever to return to Finland. It's a choice that slipped out of my hands. I feel like my world slipped away."

TCKs in Relationship to Surrounding Dominant Culture

There is another aspect of cross-cultural living that has a significant influence on a TCK's life—the changing nature of how he or she fundamentally relates to the surrounding dominant culture, be it the home or host culture. Sometimes people presume we only mean a TCK's relationship to the host culture when we talk of his or her relationship to the "dominant culture," but they forget that one of a TCK's most stressful times may be trying to sort out the relationship to the home culture itself. So let us be clear—the patterns of how a TCK relates to the surrounding culture that we are about to describe are possible in both host and/or home cultures.

We said earlier that no group can hold together for long if they share only the visible or surface parts of culture such as dress, language, behavior, and traditions. That is true. Traditionally, however, people have used their surface culture (e.g., tribal scarifications, heraldry, or the chador) to identify themselves as people who also share a common deep culture; in other words, they have similar beliefs, assumptions, and values. In some places, various tribes and nation-alities may have coexisted side by side, but everyone readily knew by appearance who was and was not part of his or her group and, thus, who did or didn't share a common outlook in the deeper culture values as well.

Things are not so simple anymore. Across the world, external patterns of behavior are changing. TV, videos, and the Internet expose people all over the world to similar styles and fashions. Traditional garb is replaced by business suits (or blue jeans). Increased contact through trade, communication, and travel also causes the influences of music, food, and language to spread from one place to another with dizzying speed. We are careening toward the global village Marshall McLuhan and Bruce R. Powers predicted, where the campfire in the middle is a TV set telling us what we should all buy and how we should all look.[11]

But the deeper levels of culture that Kohls mentions are far slower to change than the surface ones. This creates a major problem. Why? As long as we look different from another person, or have some way to quickly and easily identify that we are different, we don't expect the other to behave or believe as we do. But when a person looks and acts much like us on the outside, we assume sameness on the inside and fully expect that other person to respond in a situation as we would. The truth is, the *appearance* that we are the same hides the fact that in those deeper places of culture—the ones from which we make our life decisions—we may be as different as ever. This actually increases cultural stress. We are far more offended if people who look like us don't behave as we assumed they would than if we never have any expectations of similarity in the first place.

How does this characteristic of cultural interaction affect the TCK experience? And how does that relate to our discussion of cultural differences?

Despite the fact that our world is becoming more of a global village, whatever country TCKs live or travel in, there is still a predominant national or local culture. The language and currency used for trade, the view of the elderly, whether tasks or relationships are most valued, and the racial or ethnic makeup of the majority of the population are examples of what might be part of the prevailing, overall cultural milieu. Wherever a TCK lives, he or she may or may not resemble the physical appearance of the majority of the members of that culture. In addition, the pervading cultural beliefs and assumptions may or may not be the same ones from which the TCK operates. In other words, wherever they live, at both the superficial and deeper levels of culture, TCKs either appear similar to and/or think like members of the surrounding dominant culture or they appear different and/or think differently from members of that culture. This means that there are four possible ways they relate to the surrounding culture, be it the home or host culture. For our purposes, we have called these relational patterns *foreigner, adopted, hidden immigrant,* and *mirror.*

Foreigner Look different Think different	Hidden Immigrant Look alike Think different
Adopted Look different Think alike	Mirror Look alike Think alike

1. *Foreigner—look different, think different.* This is the traditional model for TCKs in the host culture. They differ from those around them in both appearance and worldview. They know and others know they are foreigners. In a few cases (e.g., international adoption), this category may apply to TCKs in their official home culture as well.

2. *Adopted—look different, think alike.* Some TCKs appear physically different from members of the surrounding culture, but they have lived there so long and immersed themselves in the

culture so deeply that their behavior and worldview are the same as members of that culture. While TCKs may feel very comfortable relating to the surrounding culture, others may treat them as foreigners.

3. *Hidden immigrant—look alike, think different.* When TCKs return to their home culture, or when they grow up in countries where they physically resemble the majority of the citizens of that country, they appear like those around them, but internally these TCKs view life through a lens that is as different from the dominant culture as any obvious foreigner. People around them, however, presume they are the same as themselves inside, since they appear the same outside.

4. *Mirror—look alike, think alike.* Some TCKs not only physically resemble the members of their host culture, but they have lived there so long that they have adopted the deeper levels of that culture as well. No one would realize they aren't citizens unless they show their passports. TCKs who return to their home culture after spending only a year or two away or who were away only at a very young age may also fit in this category. Although they have lived abroad, their deeper levels of culture have remained rooted solidly in the home culture and they identify with it completely.

Of course, non-TCK children and adults may fall into one or another of these boxes at any given time, but the difference for TCKs is that throughout childhood they are constantly changing which box they're in depending on where they happen to be. They may be obvious foreigners one day and hidden immigrants the next. To complicate the matter further, many TCKs do not make a simple move from one culture to another but are in a repetitive cycle of traveling back and forth between at least home and host cultures throughout childhood. But why does that matter? Because as they move in and out of various cultures TCKs not only have to learn new cultural rules, but more fundamentally, they must understand who they *are* in relationship to the surrounding culture.

Defining this relationship is relatively simple when they are in the foreigner or mirror categories. In both cases, they are who they seem to be. Those in the foreigner box look around and realize that the people around them are different from themselves. People in the community look back at the TCKs and realize they are different as well. Neither TCK nor the member of that culture expects the other person to necessarily think or act like he or she does; they automatically know they are not the same—and they're not. Of course, TCKs in the mirror box look at the community and the community looks back and both expect the other to share similar fundamental principles for life as they do—and they are right again. In both the foreigner and mirror categories the expectations of who others are in the deeper levels as well as superficial levels of culture matches reality—for both TCKs and those in the community.

When TCKs are in the adopted or hidden immigrant categories, however, the expectations no longer hold true. What they and those around them presume is not what they get. Sometimes adopted TCKs feel frustrated when community members overexplain simple things they already know or speak to them slowly, presuming they can't understand the local language. Community members don't realize that in spite of physical differences these TCKs are remarkably like them inside. On the other hand, community members look at the hidden immigrant TCKs, presuming they can do every common task others around know how to do. A Cameroonian TCK who is raised in London and then returns to Cameroon at fourteen, however, probably has no idea how to husk a coconut just off the palm tree like other Cameroonian children can. Members of the community wonder how one of its own could be so ignorant. That same TCK may also be shocked, however, that friends at home don't yet know how to surf the Internet. Based on similar appearances, both TCKs and those in the community are expecting the others to be like themselves in every basic way. This time their expectations are wrong, but neither side forgives the other as they would a true immigrant or obvious foreigner for unexpected behavior or even ignorance. Relating as a hidden immigrant in any culture may be one of the greatest cultural challenges that many TCKs face.

It's not hard to see how growing up cross-culturally can affect a child's attempts to understand who he or she is in relation to the world around, but how does the highly mobile nature of a TCK's childhood also influence the very development of who they are? This will be the subject of chapter 4.

Endnotes

1 Alex Graham James, "Uniquely Me," in *Scamps, Scholars, and Saints*, edited by Jill Dyer and Roger Dyer (Kingswood, SA, Australia: MK Merimna, 1991), 234.

2 Paul G. Heibert, *Cultural Anthropology*, 2d ed. (Grand Rapids, MI: Baker Book House, 1983), 28–29.

3 Ibid., 25.

4 L. Robert Kohls (unpublished manuscript). Used by permission.

5 Book by Joseph Stein, music by Jerry Bock, lyrics by Sheldon Harnick, based on Sholom Aleichem's stories, *Fiddler on the Roof*, 4th Limelight Edition (New York: Crown Publishers, 1994), 2, 9.

6 Useem, "Third Cultural Factors," 126.

7 Helen Fail, "Some of the Outcomes of International Schooling" (master's thesis, Brookes University, Oxford, England, 1995), 76.

8 Mary Edwards Wertsch, *Military Brats* (1991; reprint, Putnam Valley, NY: Aletheia Publications, 1996), 6.

9 Joseph McDonald, MK e-mail communication, October 1995. Used by permission.

10 Personal correspondence from TCK to David C. Pollock, November 1995. Used by permission.

11 Marshall McLuhan and Bruce R. Powers, *The Global Village: Transformations in World Life and Media in the 21st Century* (New York: Oxford University Press, 1989).

4

Why High Mobility Matters

I had adored the nomadic life. I had loved gallivanting
from Japan to Taiwan to America to Holland and
onward. In many ways, I had adapted well. I had
learned to love new smells and vistas and the mysteries inherent to new cultures.... I had conquered the
language of internationalists, both the polite exchange
of conversation in formal settings and the easy intimacy
of globetrotters. I was used to country-hopping. To
move every couple of years was in my blood. In spite
of the fact that foreign service life is one long continuous meal of loss—loss of friends and beloved places—I
loved it. The warp of my life was the fact of moving
on.[1]

—Sara Mansfield Taber

We have looked at the cross-cultural nature of the TCK experience
in some detail. We also want to clarify how we define the term *high
mobility* and why it is the second major factor in the life of most
TCKs.

People often ask how we can say that high mobility is one of the
two nearly universal characteristics for TCKs when mobility patterns vary so widely among them. Some move to a different country
every two or three years with parents who are in the military or

diplomatic corps. It's obvious that their lives are highly mobile. Others stay in one country from birth to university, and mobility wouldn't appear to be an issue for them.

All TCKs, however, deal with mobility issues at one level or another. Children of parents in business like Erika or those with parents in the foreign service usually take home leave each summer. Missionaries' children may only go on furlough every four years, but they usually stay away from the host country for a longer period of time, sometimes up to a year. Each leave means good-bye to friends in the host country, hello to relatives and friends at home; then good-bye to those people a short time later, and hello again to the host country friends—if those friends are still there. TCKs who attend boarding school have other major patterns of mobility. Whether they go home once or twice a year or spend three months at school followed by one month at home, each coming and going involves more greetings and farewells—and more adjustments. Paul Seaman describes this pattern of mobility well.

> Like nomads we moved with the seasons. Four times a year we packed up and moved to, or back to, another temporary home. As with the seasons, each move offered something to look forward to while something had to be given up.... We learned early that "home" was an ambiguous concept, and, wherever we lived, some essential part of our lives was always someplace else. So we were always of two minds. We learned to be happy and sad at the same time. We learned to be independent and [accept] that things were out of our control.... We had the security and the consolation that whenever we left one place we were returning to another, already familiar one.[2]

Besides a TCK's personal mobility, every third culture community is filled with people who continually come and go. Short-term volunteers arrive to assist in a project for several weeks and then they are gone. A favorite teacher accepts another position a continent away. Best friends leave because their parents transfer to a new post.

Older siblings depart for boarding school or university at home. The totality of all these comings and goings—of others as well as the TCKs themselves—is what we mean when we use the term *high mobility* throughout this book, and any time there is mobility, everyone involved goes through some type of transition experience as well. To understand better why high mobility is the second major factor in a TCK's developmental process, we need to look at the normal process of transition.

The Transition Experience

In a certain sense, life for everyone, TCK or not, is a series of transitions—a "passage from one state, stage, subject, or place to another."[3] Each transition changes something in our lives. Some transitions are normal and progressive—we expect them, as in the transition from infancy to childhood or from middle age to old age. Sometimes these life transitions include physical moves from one place to another, such as when a young person goes off to university in another state. In most cases, we know these transitions are coming and have time to prepare for them.

Other transitions, however, are sudden and disruptive—such as the unexpected loss of a job, a serious injury, or the untimely death of a loved one. Life after these transitions is drastically different from what it was before. The abruptness of the change disorients us and we wonder, "What am I ever going to do?"

TCKs also experience expected and unexpected transitions. There are two important reasons, however, why this topic deserves special focus in a discussion on TCKs. First, because of the high mobility inherent in their lifestyle, TCKs go through major transitions far more frequently than those born and raised in one basic area. Psychologist Frances J. White says, "Because of the nature of their work, [third culture families] are particularly vulnerable to separations. They experience not only the...usual share of situational separations faced by the world at large but also a number of partings idiosyncratic to their profession."[4]

Second, TCKs not only go through the transition process more often than most people, but when it involves their personal movement from one location to another, TCKs usually change cultures as well as places. This increases the degree of impact from that experience as the issues related to what is commonly referred to as *culture shock* are piled on top of the normal stress of any transition.

Although there are many types of transitions, for our purposes we will concentrate on describing transition within the context of physical mobility. In any particular transition, of course, we may be a member in the sending or receiving community, but our discussion will primarily focus on how the process takes place from the perspective of the one who is leaving. Basically, each transition experience goes through these five predictable stages:

1. Involvement

2. Leaving

3. Transition

4. Entering

5. Reinvolvement

Involvement Stage

We barely recognize this first stage of transition because life seems too normal to be a "stage." We feel settled and comfortable, knowing where we belong and how we fit in. Under ideal circumstances, we recognize we are an *intimate* part of our community and are careful to follow its customs and abide by its traditions so that we can maintain our position as a valued member. We feel a responsibility to be involved in the issues that concern and interest our community, and we're focused on the present and our immediate relationships rather than thinking primarily about the past or worrying over the future.

Involvement is a comfortable stage for those around us as well. People hear our name and instantly picture our face and form. They know our reputation, history, talents, tastes, interests, and our place in the political and social network.

Leaving Stage

One day life begins to change. We learn we will be leaving, and deep inside we begin to prepare. At first we may not realize what's going on—especially if our departure date is more than six months away. With shorter warning, however, the mostly unconscious leaving process starts immediately. We begin loosening emotional ties, backing away from the relationships and responsibilities we have had. We call friends less frequently. We don't start new projects at work. During the last year before graduation from high school or university, this leaning away is called "senioritis."

While it may be normal—and perhaps necessary—to begin to detach at some level during this stage, it is often confusing as well to both our friends and ourselves. This detachment can produce anger and frustration in relationships that have been close or in the way we handle our job responsibilities.

> During one transition seminar, Dave Pollock talked about this loosening of ties as part of the leaving stage. Soon he noticed a general buzz in the room. One gentleman sat off to the side, blushing rather profusely as others began to laugh. When Dave stopped to ask what was happening, the blushing gentleman said, "Well, I guess I better confess. I'm the manager here, and just yesterday those working under me asked to meet with me. They complained about my recent job performance and told me I don't seem to care; I take far too much time off; I'm unavailable when they need me, and so on. As you've been talking, I just realized what's been happening. Last month, my CEO told me I would be transferred to a new assignment, so mentally I've already checked out."
>
> "That's pretty normal," Dave said rather sympathetically.

> "I know," he replied. "The only problem is I'm not
> due to leave for two more years. Maybe I'd better
> check back in again!"

We may not upset an entire office staff as this man did, but unless we consciously choose to maintain and enjoy relationships and roles as long as possible, at some point all of us will back away in one form or another. It's part of the state of denial that comes during the leaving stage as we unconsciously try to make the leaving as painless as we can. Other forms of self-protective denials surface as well.

Denial of feelings of sadness or grief. Instead of acknowledging sadness, we begin to think, "I don't really like these people very much anyway. Susie takes way too much of my time with all her problems. I'll be glad when I'm out of here and she can't call me every day." We can also deny our sadness at leaving by focusing only on what is anticipated. We talk about the wonderful things to do, eat, and see in the next location and seemingly make a mental leap over the process of getting there.

> One Canadian ATCK began to weep at this point in a
> transition seminar. Later he said, "Dave, I feel terrible.
> I grew up in a remote tribe in Papua New Guinea.
> When I left to return home for university, I could only
> think about how much I'd enjoy having Big Macs, TV,
> and electricity. I looked forward to new friends. When
> my PNG friends came to say good-bye, they started to
> cry, but I just walked away. Now all I can think about is
> them standing there as my little plane took off. They
> thought I didn't care. I want to go back and hug them
> one last time. What should I do?"

Of course, there was nothing wrong with this TCK developing a positive view of the coming move, but when he didn't acknowledge the losses involved in the leaving, he had no way to deal with them. Denying our feelings may get us through an otherwise painful moment, but the grief doesn't go away, and we simply hold on to it into the next stage of transition.

Denial of feelings of rejection. As friends plan for future events (e.g., next year's annual company picnic or the school play), we suddenly realize they are talking around us. No one asks what we would like to do or what we think about the plans. We have become invisible. Of course, we understand. Why should they include us? We'll be gone. In spite of what we know, however, we can still feel intense rejection and resentment. If we deny those feelings and push them aside as ridiculous and immature behavior (obviously we *shouldn't* feel like this), then that underlying sense of rejection and resentment easily produces a seething anger, which results in almost unbelievable conflicts—especially with those who have been close friends and colleagues. Failing to acknowledge that we are beginning to feel like outsiders (and that it hurts) only increases the chances that we will act inappropriately during this stage.

We may not consciously realize it, but as we're loosening our ties to the community, it's loosening its ties to us. Not only do people forget to ask our opinion about future events, they begin giving our jobs to others. They choose someone else for committees and announce the name of the teacher replacing us next year. The same types of denials we use are being used by them. Suddenly our flaws as friends or coworkers seem glaringly obvious, and they secretly wonder why they've maintained this relationship for so long in the first place.

Denial of "unfinished business." The closer we come to separation, the less likely we are to reconcile conflicts with others. We talk ourselves out of mending the relationship, unrealistically hoping that time and distance will heal it—or at least produce amnesia. Once more, the unfortunate reality is that we arrive at our next destination with this unfinished business clinging to us and influencing new relationships. Bitterness in one area of our lives almost always seeps out in another.

Denial of expectations. To prevent disappointment or fear, we may deny anything we secretly hope for. "It doesn't matter what kind of house I get; I can live anywhere." We deny we would like people to give us a nice farewell. We presume that if we have no expectations, we can't be disappointed. In reality, however, we all have expectations for every event in our lives. When they are too high, we're disappointed. When they're too low, we create fear, anxiety, or dread for ourselves.

One thing, however, helps save the day for everyone. This is the time when communities also give us special attention. There are ceremonies of recognition—a watch presented for years of faithful service or a plaque given to say thanks for being part of a team. Graduation ceremonies remind us this school will never be the same without our shining presence. This special attention and recognition help us forget for a moment that even though we are promising never to forget each other, already there is a distance developing between us and those we will soon leave behind.

Transition Stage

At the heart of the transition process is the transition stage itself. It begins the moment we leave one place and ends when we not only arrive at our destination but make the decision, consciously or unconsciously, to settle in and become part of it. It's a stage marked by one word—*chaos!* Schedules change, new people have new expectations, and living involves new responsibilities, but we haven't yet learned how everything is supposed to work. Norma M. McCaig, founder of Global Nomads, says the transition stage is a time when families moving overseas become at least temporarily dysfunctional. This dysfunctionality doesn't last (we hope), but it can be painfully discomfiting at the time.

First, we and all family members making the move with us lose our normal moorings and support systems at this point. Suddenly we aren't relinquishing roles and relationships—they're gone! We've lost the comfort they gave but haven't formed new ones yet. We're not sure where we fit in or what we're expected to do.

Second, this sense of chaos makes us more self-centered than normal. We worry about our health, finances, relationships, and personal safety to a far greater degree than usual. Problems that aren't generally a big deal are exaggerated. Headaches become brain tumors and sneezes become pneumonia. The loss of a favorite pen causes despair. We know we'll never find it again because the usual places we would look for it are gone.

Third, parents who are focusing on their own survival often forget to take time to read their children stories, stop to pick them up, or sit on the floor with them for a few minutes as they did in the past. Children wonder what's happening. The insecurity of each family member contributes to everyone's chaos. Family conflicts seem to occur for the smallest reason and over issues that never mattered before.

The enormous change between how the old and new communities take care of the everyday aspects of life—banking, buying food, cooking—can create intense stress. To make matters worse, we may be scolded for doing something in the new place that was routine in the old one.

> TCK Hanna grew up in an area of chronic drought. The local adage for flushing the toilet was "If it's brown, flush it down. If it's yellow, let it mellow." Breaking that rule meant serious censure from her parents or anyone else around.
>
> Unfortunately, Hanna's grandma in the States had never heard this wonderful rule. At age thirteen, Hanna visited her grandma. Imagine Hanna's chagrin and embarrassment when Grandma pulled her aside and scolded her for not flushing the toilet.

A severe loss of self-esteem sets in during this transition stage. Even if we physically look like adults, emotionally we feel like children again. Not only are we getting scolded for things about which we "should have known better," but, particularly in cross-cultural moves, it seems we have to learn life over practically from scratch. As teenagers and adults, probably nothing strikes at our sense of self-esteem with greater force than learning language and culture, for these are the tasks of children. Suddenly, no matter how many decibels we raise our voices, people don't understand what we're trying to say. We discover gestures we have used all our lives—like pointing someone out in a crowd using our index finger—have completely opposite meanings now (in some cultures, it's a curse). Our cultural and linguistic mistakes not only embarrass us but make us feel anxious and ashamed of being so stupid.

Initially, the community may welcome us warmly—even overwhelmingly. But in every culture the newcomer is still exactly that—and newcomers by definition don't yet fit in. Our basic position in the new community is one of *statuslessness*. We carry knowledge from past experiences—often including special knowledge of people, places, and processes—but none of that knowledge has use in this new place. No one knows about our history, abilities, talents, normal responses, accomplishments, or areas of expertise. Sometimes it seems they don't care. Soon we question whether our achievements in the previous setting were as significant as we thought.

People may now see us as boring or arrogant because we talk about things, places, and people they have never heard mentioned before. We feel the same way toward them because they talk about local people and events about which *we* know nothing.

Even with an initial warm welcome, we may discover it's not as easy as we thought it would be to make close friends. Circles of relationships among our new acquaintances are already well defined, and most people aren't looking to fill a vacant spot in such a circle. It's easy to become resentful and begin to withdraw. Fine, we say inside, if they don't need me, I don't need them.

Sadly, this type of withdrawal results in more feelings of isolation and alienation, for it continues to cut us off from any hope of making new friends. This increasing sense of loneliness can lead to more anger—which makes us want to withdraw even more.

The transition stage is a tough time because we often feel keenly disappointed. The difference between what we expected and what we're experiencing can trigger a sense of panic. All connection and continuity with the past seem gone, and the present isn't what we had hoped it would be. How can we relate the different parts of our lives into a cohesive whole? Is the orderliness of the past gone forever? We look longingly to the future—hoping that somehow, sometime, life will return to normal.

Entering Stage

> Standing on the edge of the Quad at Houghton College, TCK Ramona quietly said to no one in particular, "I think I'll go to my dorm and unpack my suitcase…and my mind."
>
> Ramona had graduated from an international school more than a year before. For fifteen months she'd been traveling and visiting relatives while working at short-term jobs. Without her own place to nest, Ramona could never finish the transition stage. Finally, with her arrival at school and the decision to settle in, she began the entering stage of the overall transition process.

During this stage life is no longer totally chaotic. We have made the decision that it is time to become part of this new community: we just have to figure out how to do it. Although we very much want to move toward people in this new place, however, we still feel rather vulnerable and a bit tentative. What if we make a serious social faux pas? Will others accept us? Will they take advantage of us? We often deal with these fears through an exaggeration of our normal personality traits as we begin to interact with others in our new location. People who are usually shy, introverted, or quiet may become more so. Normally gregarious or outgoing individuals may become loud, overbearing, and aggressive. Then, of course, we're mad at ourselves for acting so "stupid" and worry even more that people won't like us.

This stage is also when we feel a lot of ambivalence. We start to learn the new job, feel successful on a given day, and think, "I'm glad I'm here. This is going to be all right." Next day, someone asks us a question we can't answer, and we wish we were back where we knew most of the answers. Our emotions can fluctuate widely between the excitement of the new discoveries we're making and the homesickness that weighs us down. When we say *boot* and *bonnet* instead of *trunk* and *hood* (or vice versa), everyone laughs and tells us we're so funny. We laugh with them, but inside there is that feeling that nobody thought this was strange in our last place. There we were "normal," not different. On the other hand, tomorrow we catch ourselves just before we say the wrong word and use the local term instead. When it passes without a flicker from those around us (in spite of how strange it sounds to our ears!), we realize we are actually beginning to learn how life works here.

Entering is the stage, more than any other, where we need a good mentor. While we'll discuss that in detail later, suffice it to say that the day finally comes when we actually recognize someone from our new community in the grocery store and can call that person by name. We drive to the other side of town, down quiet, unmarked streets, without anyone telling us where to turn—and we find the house we are looking for! Someone calls with a procedural question at work and this time we *do* know the answer. Hope begins to grow that we will, in fact, one day have a sense of belonging to this community.

Of course, we must not forget that this entry stage is a bit uncomfortable for members of our new community as well, although they may have been eagerly anticipating our arrival. Before we came, everyone's roles were clear. Relationships—whether positive or negative—were established. Life functioned without explanation. We show up, and life changes for them too. Now *everything* seems to need an explanation. They also have to adjust their social order at least slightly to help us find our way in. In the end, however, people in the community begin to remember our names, include us in the events going on, realize we are here to stay rather than simply visiting, and start to make room for us in their world.

Reinvolvement Stage

And then the day finally comes. The light at the end of the proverbial tunnel is that in any transition, cross-cultural or not, a final, recognized stage of reinvolvement is possible. Although there have been moments of wondering if it will ever happen, given enough time and a genuine willingness to adapt, we will once again become part of the permanent community. We may not be native to that community, but we can ultimately belong.

We have learned the new ways and know our position in this community. Other members of the group see us as one of them, or at least they know where we fit in. We have a sense of intimacy, a feeling that our presence matters to this group. We feel secure. Time again feels present and permanent as we focus on the here and now rather than hoping for the future or constantly reminiscing about the past.

This is the normal process of transition. Knowing about the various stages doesn't keep them from happening, but it does help us to not be surprised by what happens at each stage, to recognize we are normal, and to be in a position to make the choices that allow us to gain from the new experiences we encounter while dealing productively with the inevitable losses of any transition experience.

****

Just as TCKs learn culture in the same ways others do, so they are quite as capable as anyone else of navigating their way through these stages of transition and being enriched by them. As with the cultural overlay, however, we need to be aware of some extra stresses TCKs may encounter during the transition process because of their particular lifestyle. Some globally nomadic families make international moves every two years or so, and their TCKs may chronically move from the leaving to entering to leaving stages without knowing the physical or emotional comfort and stability of involvement, let alone reinvolvement. When a tree is transplanted too often, its roots can never grow deep. So it is with these young people. Some TCKs refuse to get involved in a new place because they fear that liking this new place would mean betraying the friends and places they have known and loved before. Others don't settle in as a protection against being hurt again in a future move they know will inevitably come. If they refuse to make close friends, it won't matter when they have to say good-bye next time.

All of this raises the question, "How can any child survive so much cultural confusion and chronic change?" Perhaps one of the strangest things about TCKs is that for most of them this type of lifestyle itself becomes normal. Even the mobility becomes part of the routine. What Pico Iyer describes as the international culture[5] is, in fact, their world and, like Rob and Heather, our American and British ATCKs, they have found a comfortable place and sense of identity and security in it.

What we have also discovered, however, in doing seminars around the world is that because theirs is an intangible world, not tied to one visible place, most TCKs have lived their experience without the words to define it. Our presentations are often not so much about giving new information as much as they are about putting words to matters TCKs and their families already know without realizing they know it. They just never had words to describe their total life experiences before. With the hope that this book will do the same for many more, we proceed to look at the specific benefits and challenges as well as other characteristics we have observed through the years and call "The TCK Profile."

Endnotes

1   Sara Mansfield Taber, *Of Many Lands: Journal of a Traveling Childhood* (Washington, DC: Foreign Service Youth Foundation, 1997), 1.

2   Paul Seaman, *Paper Airplanes in the Himalayas: The Unfinished Path Home* (Notre Dame, IN: Cross Cultural Publications, 1997), 7–8.

3   *Merriam-Webster's Collegiate Dictionary,* 10th ed., *s.v.* "transition."

4   Frances J. White, "Some Reflections on the Separation Phenomenon Idiosyncratic to the Experience of Missionaries and Their Children," *Journal of Psychology and Theology* 11, no. 3 (Fall 1983): 181–88.

5   Pico Iyer, "The Empire Writes Back," *Time,* 8 February 1992, 48.

Part II
The TCK Profile

5

Benefits and Challenges

Besides the drawbacks of family separation and the very real adjustment on the permanent return to the [home country], a child growing up abroad has great advantages. He [or she] learns, through no conscious act of learning, that thoughts can be transmitted in many languages, that skin color Is unimportant...that certain things are sacred or taboo to some people while to others they're meaningless, that the ordinary word of one area is a swearword in another.

We have lived in Tulsa for five years...I am struck again and again by the fact that so much of the sociology, feeling for history, geography, questions [about] others that our friends' children try to understand through textbooks, my sisters and I acquired just by living.[1]

—Rachel Miller Schaetti

Introduction: The TCK Profile

In Part I we focused primarily on defining third culture kids and describing their world. Now we want to look in depth at the specific benefits and challenges of this experience. Then we will examine the character traits this lifestyle fosters along with how it affects interpersonal relationships and developmental patterns. Because this is a group profile, not every characteristic will fit every person. But the "Aha!" moment of recognition, which we have seen among countless TCKs and ATCKs, tells us these characteristics are valid as an overall representation of their world.

The often paradoxical benefits and challenges of this profile are sometimes described as being like opposite sides of the same coin, but in reality they are more like the contrasting colored strands of thread woven together into a tapestry. As each strand crosses with a contrasting or complementary color, a picture begins to emerge, but no strand alone tells the full story. For example, the high mobility of a TCK's life often results in special relationships with people throughout the world, but it also creates sadness at the chronic loss of these relationships. That very pain, however, provides opportunity to develop a greater empathy for others. A TCK's expansive worldview, which enriches history classes and gives perspective to the nightly news, also makes the horror of the slaughter of Hutus and Tutsis in refugee camps a painful reality. That same awareness can be what motivates a TCK's concern for solving those kinds of tragic problems. And so it goes.

Some of the characteristics as well as the benefits and challenges are primarily a result of the cross-cultural nature of the third culture experience. Others are more directly shaped by the high mobility of the lifestyle. Most of the profile, however, is this weaving together of these two dominant realities. We begin by discussing some of the most common general benefits and challenges we have seen among TCKs, but before we do, let us make clear that when we use the word *challenge*, we purposefully do not infer the word *liability*. A challenge is something people have the choice to face, deal with, and grow from. A liability can only be something which pulls someone down. Some may say we concentrate too much on the challenges, but if that criticism is valid, it is for a reason. We have seen the benefits of this experience enrich countless TCKs' lives, whether or not they stop to consciously define or use them. Many have also found unconscious ways to deal with the challenges and make them a productive aspect of their lives in one way or another. We have also seen, however, that for some TCKs (and those around them) the unrecognized challenges have caused years of frustration as they struggle to deal with matters that have no name, no definition. It is our hope that in not only naming these challenges but also offering suggestions on how to deal with them productively, many more TCKs will be able to maximize the great gifts that can come from their lives and not be trapped by the challenges. We begin.

Expanded Worldview versus Confused Loyalties

Benefit: Expanded Worldview

An obvious benefit of the TCK experience is that while growing up in a multiplicity of countries and cultures, TCKs not only observe firsthand the many geographical differences around the world but they also learn how people view life from different philosophical and political perspectives. Some people think of Saddam Hussein as a hero; others believe he's a villain. Western culture is time and task oriented; in Eastern cultures, interpersonal relationships are of greater importance. The TCK's awareness that there can be more than one way to look at the same thing starts early in life. Once we listened to some rather remarkable stories during a meeting in Malaysia with younger TCKs—ages five to twelve.

> "You know, last year we had to hide on the floor for four days because of typhoons."
>
> "We couldn't go out of our compound in Bangladesh for a week when everybody in town started fighting."
>
> "On our vacation last month we got to ride on the backs of elephants and go look for tigers."
>
> "Well, so did we!" countered another seven-year-old from across the room. "We saw six tigers. How many did you see?"

> And so it went.
>
> Eventually New Year's Day came up as part of a
> story. We asked what we thought was a simple
> question. "When is New Year's Day?" Instead of the
> simple "January 1" that we expected, many different
> dates were given—each young TCK trying to defend
> how and when it was celebrated in his or her host
> country. We knew that if we had asked most groups of
> five- to twelve-year-olds in the United States about
> New Year's Day, this discussion wouldn't be occurring.
> Most of them probably had no idea that "New Year's
> Day" could mean anything but January 1.

This may seem like a small detail, but already these children are
learning how big and interesting the world they live in is and how
much there will be to discover about it all through life.

Challenge: Confused Loyalties

Although their expanded worldview is a benefit, it can also leave
TCKs with a sense of confusion about such complex things as politics, patriotism, and values. Should they support the policies of their
home country when those policies are detrimental to their host country? Or should they support the host country, even if it means oppos-
ing policies of their own government?

Joe, the American TCK raised in Argentina and educated in a
British school, writes about divided loyalties:

> When I came to the U.S., there was the matter of
> pledging allegiance to the American flag. I had saluted
> the Union Jack, the Argentine flag, and now I was
> supposed to swear loyalty to a country which, in 1955,
> didn't even have decent pizza or coffee. Worse,
> Americans, many of them, were still McCarthyites at
> heart, and feared anything tainted with foreignisms.
>
> The unfortunate side effects of a multicultural
> upbringing are substantial, of course. Whose side are
> you on? I had a dickens of a time with my loyalties
> during the Islas Malvinas war (no, make that the

Falkland Islands war). After all, as an eleven-year-old I
had sworn undying fealty to Juan Domingo Peron and
his promise that he would free the Malvinas from
British enslavement. After the army booted him out of
Argentina, I figured I was off the hook. But could I
really be sure? On the other hand, I whistled "Rule
Britannia" at least three times a week and really felt
proud to know that a massive British force was headed
to the Falklands and that British sovereignty would be
asserted, unequivocally. I was dismayed by the profound indifference to this war exhibited by Americans.[2]

Confused loyalties can make TCKs seem unpatriotic and arrogant
to their fellow citizens. If Joe is a good American, how could he
ever pledge allegiance to Argentina and Britain—or be angry with
his own country for not getting involved in someone else's war? If
British TCKs who grew up in India try to explain negative remnants
of the colonial era to fellow classmates in England, they can seem
like traitors.

In *Homesick: My Own Story,* Jean Fritz writes of her experiences as an American TCK in China during the 1920s. She attended
a British school in China but defiantly refused to sing "God Save
the King" because it wasn't *her* national anthem. She was an American, although she had never spent a day in the United States in her
life. Throughout the growing turmoil that led to the revolution in
1927, Jean dreamed of her grandmother's farm and garden in Pennsylvania, fantasizing over and over about what it would be like to
live and go to school in America. Finally, after an endless boat ride
and many struggles, Jean arrived at that long-awaited first day in an
American school. Here's what happened.

"The class will come to order," she [Miss Crofts, the
teacher] said. "I will call the roll." When she came to
my name, Miss Crofts looked up from her book. "Jean
Guttery is new to our school," she said. "She has come
all the way from China, where she lived beside the
Yangs-Ta-Zee River. Isn't that right, Jean?"

"It's pronounced *Yang-see*," I corrected. "There are just two syllables."

Miss Crofts looked at me coldly. "In America," she said, "we say *Yangs-Ta-Zee*."

I was working myself up, madder by the minute, when I heard Andrew Carr, the boy behind me, shifting his feet on the floor. I guess he must have hunched across his desk, because all at once I heard him whisper over my shoulder:

"Chink, Chink, Chinaman
Sitting on a fence,
Trying to make a dollar
Out of fifteen cents."

I forgot all about where I was. I jumped to my feet, whirled around, and spoke out loud as if there were no Miss Crofts, as if I'd never been in a classroom before, as if I knew nothing about classroom behavior. "You don't call them Chinamen or Chinks," I cried. "You call them *Chinese*. Even in America you call them *Chinese*."

"Well, you don't need to get exercised, Jean," she [Miss Crofts] said. "We all know that you are American."

"But that's not the *point!*" Before I could explain that it was an insult to call Chinese people *Chinamen*, Miss Crofts had tapped her desk with a ruler.

"That will be enough," she said. "All eyes front."[3]

Which country had Jean's greatest loyalty and devotion—the United States or China? Did she know? All her life she had thought of herself as American—now here she was defending the Chinese. Certainly Miss Crofts and Jean's classmates couldn't understand why she would want to defend a people and a country halfway around the world from them—particularly at the expense of getting along with people from her own country.

More difficult than the questions of political or patriotic loyalties, however, are the value dissonances that occur in the cross-cultural experience. As we said earlier, TCKs often live among cultures with strongly conflicting value systems. One culture says female circumcision is wrong. Another one says female circumcision is the most significant moment in a girl's life; it is when she knows she has become an accepted member of her tribe. One culture says abortion is wrong. Another says it is all right for specific reasons up to certain points in the pregnancy. Still other cultures practice abortion based on the gender of the baby: males are wanted; females are not.

In each situation, which value is right? Which is wrong? Is there a right and wrong? If so, who or what defines them? Conflicting values cannot be operational at the same time, in the same place. How do TCKs decide from all they see around them what their own values will and won't be?

This expanded worldview and its resulting confusion of loyalties and values can be a problem for those who return to cultures that remain relatively homogeneous. In a study of Turkish TCKs, Steve Eisinger discovered that "the statistics regarding public opinion…indicate that this expanded worldview may not be necessarily viewed as a positive characteristic."[4] The new ideas that the TCKs bring back, and their refusal to follow unthinkingly the cultural patterns of preceding generations, can make them unwelcome citizens in their own countries.

Three-Dimensional View of the World versus Painful View of Reality

Benefit: Three-Dimensional View of the World

As TCKs live in various cultures, they not only learn about cultural differences but they also experience the world in a tangible way that is impossible to do through reading books, seeing movies, or watching nightly newscasts alone. Because they have lived in so many places, smelled so many smells, heard so many strange sounds, and been in so many strange situations, throughout their lives when they read a story in the newspaper or watch it on the TV screen, the flat, odorless images there transform into an internal 3-D panoramic picture show. It's almost as if they were there in person, smelling the smells, tasting the tastes, perspiring with the heat. They may not be present at the event, but they have a clear awareness of what is going on and what it is like for those who are there.

> Each summer Dave Pollock leads transition seminars for TCKs. During one of these, he asked the attendees, "What comes to your mind if I say the word *riot*?" The answers came back, "Paris," "Korea," "Iran," "Ecuador."
>
> Next question. "Any details?"
>
> More answers: "Broken windows," "Water cannons," "Burned buses," "Tear gas, mobs," "Burning tires."
>
> Burning tires. Who would think about burning tires except somebody who had smelled that stench?
>
> "Tacks."

Anyone might think of guns in a riot, but why tacks? Because this TCK had seen tacks spread on the streets of Ecuador to flatten tires, so people couldn't travel during a riot. Makes sense, but probably only someone who had seen it would name it.

Having a 3-D view of the world is a useful skill not only for reading stories but for writing them. For TCKs who like to write, their culturally rich and highly mobile childhoods give them a true breadth of hands-on experiences in many places to add life to their work. In a feature article for *Time* called "The Empire Writes Back," Pico Iyer gives an account of an entirely new genre of award-winning authors, all of whom have cross-cultural backgrounds.

> Authors from Britain's former colonies have begun to capture the very heart of English literature, transforming the canon with bright colors and strange cadences and foreign eyes. They are revolutionizing the language from within. Hot spices are entering English, and tropical birds…magical creations from the makers of a new World Fiction.[5]

Iyer goes on to describe the great diversity of each writer's background and then states,

> But the new transcultural writers are something different. For one, they are the products not so much of colonial division as of the *international culture* that has grown up since the war, and they are addressing an audience as mixed up and eclectic and uprooted as themselves.[6]

Without ever using, or perhaps knowing, the term *third culture kids*, Iyer has conveyed vividly the richness of their experience.

Challenge: Painful View of Reality

With this three-dimensional view of the world, however, comes the painful reality that behind the stories in the news are real flesh-and-blood people—not merely flat faces on a TV screen. When an airplane crashes in India, TCKs find it appalling that U.S. newscasters only say how many Americans died—as if the other lives lost didn't matter. As they watch a Serbian woman weep for her child who has been killed in war, TCKs know her loss is as painful as their own would be if they were in that situation. Many of them know that when bombs drop on Iraq, people scream with fear and horror there just as they do when a bomb explodes in Oklahoma City. Many TCKs have seen war or faced the pain of evacuation and its disruption of their world, school, and friendships. Others have parents living and working in dangerous areas of the world, while they themselves are back in the home country.

> During the Gulf War, Courtney's American parents lived in Saudi Arabia, while she lived with relatives and attended secondary school in the States. Unfortunately, her parents' home in Saudi happened to be in a target area for SCUD missiles. Naturally, she felt anxiety and fear for her family. While other friends waited to hear the headlines on the evening news, Courtney checked the news throughout the school day so she could keep up with events in Saudi.

Although her worry for her folks was intense, one of
the hardest things about the experience came when
she realized that none of her American friends could
relate to what she felt. To Courtney, the desert images
on the television were home; to most of her friends,
the war was far away and incomprehensible. She found
herself resenting her classmates for their seeming lack
of interest in not only her family, but all the Saudis,
Iraqis, and Kuwaitis who were suffering as well.

Cross-Cultural Enrichment versus Ignorance of the Home Culture

Benefit: Cross-Cultural Enrichment

TCKs usually have a sense of ownership and interest in cultures
other than just that of their passport country. During university they
run to the radio whenever they hear their host country named. They
have learned to enjoy many aspects of the host culture others might
not appreciate so highly. While the smell of the Southeast Asian
fruit, *durian*, would precipitate a gag reflex in most of us, TCKs
who grew up in Malaysia inhale the scent with glee, for it is the
smell of home. TCKs from India use chapatis (a flat bread) to pick
up the hottest curry sauce. Still other TCKs sit cross-legged on the
floor whenever they have a choice between that and a lounge chair.
TCKs consider these aspects of their lifestyle part of the wealth of
their heritage.

Perhaps more important than what they have learned to enjoy
from the more surface layers of other cultures, however, is the fact
that most TCKs have also gained valuable lessons from the deeper
levels as well. They have lived in other places long enough to learn
to appreciate the reasons and understanding behind some of the behavioral differences rather than simply being frustrated by them as
visitors tend to be. For example, while a tourist might feel irritated
that the stores close for two hours in the middle of the day just when

he or she wants to go shopping, most TCKs can understand that this custom not only helps people survive better if the climate is extremely hot, but it's a time when families greet the children as they return from school and spend time together as a family. Many TCKs learn to value relationships above convenience as they live in such places, and it is a gift they carry with them wherever they may later go.

Challenge: Ignorance of the Home Culture

The irony of collecting cross-cultural practices and skills, however, is that TCKs may know all sorts of fascinating things about other countries but little about their own.

> Tamara attended school in England for the first time when she was ten. Until then she had attended a small American-oriented school in Africa. In early November, she asked her mother, "Mom, who is this Guy Fawkes everybody's talking about?"
>
> Tamara's mom, Elizabeth, a born and bred Englishwoman, tried to hide her shock at her daughter's ignorance. Tamara seemed so knowledgeable about countless global matters—how could she not know a simple fact about a major figure in British history? And particularly one whose wicked deed of trying to blow up the Parliament was decried each year as people throughout the country burned him in effigy? Elizabeth hadn't realized that while Tamara had seen the world, she had missed learning about this common tradition in her own country.

TCKs are often sadly ignorant of national, local, and even family history. How many rides to various relatives' homes are filled with parents coaching TCKs about who is related to whom? Many kids simply haven't been around the normal chatter that keeps family members connected.

Although this may be changing in the Internet age, TCKs have also often missed the rise to renown of the currently famous—movie stars, politicians, musicians, and other public figures. Household names in one country mean nothing in another.

> In 1958, TCK Jordan returned to the States at age thirteen and heard friends discussing Elvis. Imagine the look on their faces when he innocently asked, "Who's Elvis?"

When people switch cultures, humor is another unknown. Jokes are often based on a surprise, an indirect reference to something current, or a play on words with a double meaning specific to that culture or language. Few things make anyone, including TCKs, feel more left out than seeing everyone else laughing at something they can't understand as funny. Or conversely, they try to tell a joke that was hilarious in their boarding school, but none of their new friends laughs. Adelle writes,

> Early in my dating relationship with my [now] husband, something happened and he hummed the theme to the TV show, "The Twilight Zone." I guess I didn't react properly so he said, "You don't know what that is, do you?" I replied, "I know it's supposed to be funny, but I don't know why."[7]

Probably most TCKs have some story about getting caught in an embarrassing situation because they didn't know some everyday rule of their passport culture that is different in their host culture. One TCK couldn't pay her bill because she had forgotten to mentally add the tax to the amount listed on the menu. Another was shamed by his visiting relatives because he came into the room and sat down before making sure that all the oldest guests had found their places. Not knowing cultural rules can also be dangerous.

> In the village in Mali where Sophie had grown up, passing anyone—male or female—on the street and not saying hello created instant social disfavor. In New York the rules were different, as she learned in a police seminar on rape prevention during her first semester at university. "Never look a stranger in the eye," the

policeman said. "After attacking someone, a man often accuses the woman of having invited him with her look." And Sophie had been smiling at strange men all over the city!

All the above benefits and challenges are a mere beginning of the TCK Profile. We continue our discussion by looking at common personal strengths and struggles many TCKs seem to share.

Endnotes

1   Rachel Miller Schaetti, comments from a questionnaire for Jack
    O. Claypoole, George Williams College, 1957. Used by permis-
    sion of the Schaetti family.

2   Joseph McDonald, e-mail message on MK Net, October 1995.
    Used with permission.

3   Jean Fritz, *Homesick: My Own Story* (Santa Barbara, CA: Cor-
    nerstone Books, 1987), 148–50.

4   Steve Eisinger, "The Validity of the 'Third Culture Kid' Defini-
    tion for Returned Turkish Migrant Children" (report submitted
    upon the partial completion of research done in the country of
    Turkey, 31 August 1994), 16.

5   Pico Iyer, "The Empire Writes Back," *Time,* 8 February 1992.

6   Ibid., 48. Italics ours.

7   Adelle Horst Ward, personal e-mail to Ruth E. Van Reken, No-
    vember 1995. Used by permission.

Personal Characteristics

The benefits of this upbringing need to be under-
scored: In an era when global vision is an imperative,
when skills in intercultural communication, linguistic
ability, mediation, diplomacy, and the management of
diversity are critical, global nomads are better
equipped in these areas by the age of eighteen than are
many adults.... These intercultural and linguistic skills
are the markings of the cultural chameleon—the
young participant-observer who takes note of verbal
and nonverbal cues and readjusts accordingly, taking
on enough of the coloration of the social surroundings
to gain acceptance while maintaining some vestige of
identity as a different animal, an "other."[1]

—Norma M. McCaig
Founder, Global Nomads International

Norma M. McCaig, one of the true pioneers in raising global awareness of the issues facing TCKs, is a business ATCK herself and now
works with international companies preparing employees and their
families for overseas assignments. In this chapter and the next we
will discuss many of the characteristics and skills (their benefits and
their corresponding challenges) of the TCK that she mentions, beginning with the cultural chameleon McCaig describes above.

Cultural Chameleon: Adaptability versus Lack of True Cultural Balance

Benefit: Adaptability

TCKs usually develop some degree of cultural adaptability as a primary tool for surviving the frequent change of cultures. Over and over TCKs use the term *chameleon* to describe how, after spending a little time observing what is going on, they can easily switch language, style of relating, appearance, and cultural practices to take on the characteristics needed to blend better into the current scene. Soon their behavior is almost indistinguishable from longtime members of this group and they feel protected from the scorn or rejection of others (and their own ensuing sense of shame) that often comes with being different from others.

Cultural adaptability may begin as a survival tool, but it also has immensely practical benefits. TCKs usually learn to adjust with relative calm to life where meetings may start the exact minute for which they have been scheduled or two hours later, depending on which country they're in. Partly because of the frequency with which they travel and move, TCKs learn to think on their feet and can often "roll with the punches," even in unusual circumstances.

> Nona and her ATCK friend, Joy, waited in vain for a bus to carry them from Arusha to Nairobi. They finally found a taxi driver who would take them to the Tanzanian/Kenyan border and promised to find them a ride the rest of the way. At the border, however, the driver disappeared. Night was approaching, when travel would no longer be safe.
>
> As Nona watched in amazement, Joy walked across the border to find another taxi. She soon came back to the Tanzanian side, got Nona and the bags, and returned to a waiting driver who took them to Nairobi. Later, Nona complimented Joy, "If it was me by myself, I'd still be sitting at the border, waiting for that first driver to come back."

> Joy replied, "Well, there are times when all I can
> think is that this is going to make a great story in three
> months, but right now it's the pits. But I always know
> there's a way out if I can just think of all the options.
> I've been in these kinds of situations too many times to
> just wait."

Challenge: Lack of True Cultural Balance

Becoming a cultural chameleon, however, brings special challenges as well. For one thing, although in the short term the ability to "change colors" helps them fit in with their peers day-by-day, TCK chameleons may never develop true cultural balance anywhere. While appearing to be one of the crowd, inside they are still the cautious observer—always checking to see how they are doing. In addition, others may notice how the TCK's behavior changes in various circumstances and begin to wonder if they can trust anything the TCK does or says. It looks to them as if he or she has no real convictions about much of anything.

Some TCKs who flip-flop back and forth between various behavioral patterns have trouble figuring out their own value system from the multicultural mix they have been exposed to. It can be very difficult for them to decide if there are, after all, some absolutes in life they can hold on to and live by no matter which culture they are in. In the end, TCKs may adopt so many personas as cultural chameleons that they don't know who they really are.

> Ginny returned to Minnesota for university after many
> years in New Zealand and Thailand. She looked with
> disdain on the majority of her fellow students, who
> seemed to be clones of one another, and decided she
> would be anything but like them. She struck up an
> acquaintance with another student, Jessica, who was a
> member of the prevailing counterculture. Whatever
> Jessica did, Ginny did. Both wore clothing that was
> outlandish enough to be an obvious statement that
> they weren't going to be swayed by any current fads.

Only years later did Ginny realize that she too had
been a chameleon—copying Jessica—and had no idea
of what she herself liked or wanted to be. She had
rejected one group to prove she wasn't like them, but
she had never considered the possibility that among
their styles of dress or behavior there might be some
attributes she did, in fact, like. Since she had totally
aligned herself with Jessica, Ginny never stopped to
think that some of Jessica's choices might not work for
her. Was it all right for her to like jazz when Jessica
didn't? What types of clothes did she, Ginny, really
want to wear? It was some time before she was able
to sort out and identify what her own gifts, talents, and
preferences were in contrast to those she had borrowed from Jessica.

Hidden Immigrants: Blending In versus Defining the Differences

While virtually all TCKs make cultural adaptations to survive wherever they live, traditionally, most TCKs—such as the children of
early colonialists—were physically distinct from members of the
host culture and still easily recognizable as *foreigners* when living
there. Even today, the child of the Norwegian ambassador in China
would never be mistaken for a citizen of the host culture. As mentioned earlier, when TCKs are obvious foreigners, they are often
excused—both by others and by themselves—if their behavior
doesn't exactly match the local cultural norms or practices. No one
expects them to be the same based on their appearance alone. Only
when these TCKs, who are true foreigners in their host culture, reenter their home culture do they face the prospect of being the hidden immigrants we described in chapter 3.

A frequently overlooked factor, however, is that in our increasingly internationalizing world, many TCKs are becoming hidden
immigrants in the host culture as well. British children in Canada
appear the same as most of their classmates; a Ugandan diplomat's

child may look just like the African Americans in his classroom in Washington, DC. So, why is this an important issue? For one thing, being a hidden immigrant gives those TCKs who desire it the choice to not only be *cultural* chameleons, but *physical* chameleons as well. Often people around them have no idea they are actually foreigners, and the TCK may like this type of relative anonymity. A second reason for noticing this new development in the TCKs' world, however, is that those TCKs who prefer *not* to totally adapt to the surrounding scene have to find some way other than their skin color or facial features to proclaim they are different from others. This may explain what otherwise might seem like rather bizarre behavior. Take a look at three TCKs who were hidden immigrants in their host cultures.

Benefit: Blending In

The first is Paul, an international business TCK who was born in Alaska and then lived in California and Illinois until he was nine. At that time his family moved to Australia, where his father worked for an oil company. Paul tells us his story.

> My first year of school in Australia was horrible. I learned that Americans weren't very popular because of a nuclear base they'd set up near Sydney. People protested against the "ugly Americans" all the time. I felt other students assigned me guilt by association just because I was a U.S. citizen. Looking back, I realize the only kids who were good to me didn't fit in either.
>
> By the end of the first year, I'd developed an Australian accent and learned to dress and act like my Australian counterparts. Then I changed schools so I could start over and no one knew I was American. I was a chameleon.

As a hidden immigrant, Paul made a choice an obviously foreign TCK could never make. Until he chose to reveal his true identity, no one had to know that he was not Australian. Theoretically, some might argue that he made a poor choice, but from Paul's perspective as a child, blending in to this degree gave him the opportunity to not only be accepted by others but also to more fully participate in school and social events while he remained in Australia.

Challenge: Defining the Differences

While Paul chose to hide his identity, Nicola and Krista are TCKs who reacted in an opposite way. Because they looked like those around them, they felt they would lose their true identity if they didn't find some way to shout, "But I'm *not* like you." This is how each of them proclaimed their differences.

> Nicola, a British TCK, was born in Malaysia while her dad served with the Royal Air Force. He retired from the service when Nicola was four years old. The family moved to Scotland, where Nicola's dad took a job flying airplanes off the coast of Scotland for a major oil company.
>
> At first, Nicola tried to hide her English roots, even adopting a thick Scottish brogue. In spite of that, by secondary school she realized something inside her would never fit in with these classmates who had never left this small town. She looked like them, but when she didn't act like them, they teased her unmercifully for every small transgression. It seemed the more she tried to be like them, the more she was having to deny who she really was inside.
>
> Finally, Nicola decided to openly—rather defiantly, in fact—espouse her English identity. She changed her accent to a proper British one and talked of England as home. She informed her classmates that she couldn't wait to leave Scotland to attend university in England. When Nicola arrived in Southampton on her way to university, she literally kissed the ground when she alighted from the train.
>
> Krista is an American business TCK raised in England from age six to sixteen. She attended a British

school for six months before attending the local
American school. We were surprised to hear her tell
of how fiercely anti-British she and her fellow classmates in the American school became. In spite of the
prevailing culture, they steadfastly refused to speak
"British." They decried Britain for not having Ameri-
can-style shopping malls and bought all their clothes at
American stores like The Gap and The Limited during
their summer leave in the States. And why did everyone insist on queuing so carefully anyway? It looked so
prim and silly. She couldn't wait to return to the U.S.
permanently, where everything would be "normal."

The difficulty for Nicola and Krista, however, is that in trying to
proclaim what they consider their true identity, they ultimately form
an "anti-identity"—be that in clothes, speech, or behavior. Unfortunately, this also tends to cut them off from the many benefits they
could be experiencing in friendships and cultural exchange with those
around them from the local community. In addition, as TCKs scream
to others, "I'm not like you," people around soon avoid them and
they are left with a deep loneliness—although it might take them a
long time to admit such a thing.

Prejudice: Less versus More

Benefit: Less Prejudice

The opportunity to know people from diverse backgrounds as
friends—not merely as acquaintances—and within the context of
their own cultural milieu is another gift TCKs receive. They have
been members of groups that include a striking collection of culturally and ethnically diverse people, and most have the ability to truly
enjoy such diversity and to believe that people of all backgrounds
can be full and equal participants in any given situation. Sometimes
their unconscious, underlying assumptions that people of all backgrounds are still just that—people—can surprise others, and the TCKs

in turn are surprised that such acceptance isn't necessarily "normal" for everyone else.

> One white ATCK living in suburban U.S.A. had an African American repairman arrive to fix a leaky faucet. As the repairman prepared to leave, he said, "I can tell you've been around black people a lot, haven't you?" Since the ATCK had grown up in Africa, she had to agree, but asked, "Why do you say that?" He replied, "Because you're comfortable with me being here. A lot of white people aren't." And she was surprised, because she hadn't been thinking about racial relationships at all. To her, they had simply been talking about fixing faucets and paying the bill.

TCKs who use their experiences well learn there is always a reason behind anyone's behavior—no matter how mystifying it appears—and may be more patient than others might be in a particular situation.

> When ATCK Anne-Marie returned to Mali as a United Nations worker, she heard other expatriates complaining that the Malians who worked in the local government hospital never planned ahead. The medicine, oxygen, or other vital commodities were always completely gone before anyone reported that it was time to reorder. This had caused endless frustration for the UN workers.
>
> While listening to the usual grumbling during morning tea one day soon after she arrived, Anne-Marie interrupted the flow of complaints. "I understand your annoyance," she said, "but did it ever occur to you what it's like to be so poor you can only worry about each particular day's needs? If you haven't got enough money for today, you certainly aren't worrying about storing up for tomorrow."

Of all the gifts we hear TCKs say they have received from their backgrounds, the richness and breadth of diversity among those they truly count as friends is one they consistently mention as among the greatest.

Challenge: More Prejudice

Unfortunately, however, there are a few TCKs who appear to become *more* prejudiced rather than less. Perhaps it is because historically many TCKs' parents are part of what others consider a special, elite group (such as diplomats or high-ranking military personnel) in the host country and their positions often bring special deference. Their standard of living is usually well above the mean for that particular country, and their lifestyle may include servants, drivers, and other special privileges such as extensive travel.

> The movie *Empire of the Sun* gives a clear picture of what this privileged lifestyle has been for some TCKs. The story opens with the scene of a young British lad being driven home from school in the back seat of a chauffeured limousine while he stares uncaringly out the windows at starving Chinese children on the streets. As he enters his home, the young man begins to order the Chinese servants around as if they were his slaves.
>
> One day all is changed. When the British boy tries to tell the maid what to do, she runs up and slaps him. The revolution has come, and years of suppressed bitterness at his treatment of her erupt. It takes World War II and several years of incarceration in a concentration camp before this TCK finally understands that the world is not completely under his control.

While this may seem like an exaggeration, when adults from any expatriate community constantly speak poorly of the host culture residents in their presence, TCKs can pick up the same disdain and thereby waste one of the richest parts of their heritage.

Decisiveness: The Importance of Now versus the Delusion of Choice

Benefit: The Importance of Now

Because their lifestyle is transitory, many TCKs have a sense of urgency that life is to be lived *now*. They may not stop to deliberate long on any particular decision because the chance to climb Mt. Kilimanjaro will be gone if new orders to move come through. Do it now. Seize the day! Sushi is on the menu at the shop around the corner today. Better try it while you can. Some may fault them for impulsiveness, but TCKs do get a lot of living done while others are still deciding what they do or don't want to do.

Challenge: The Delusion of Choice

Ironically, for the same reason that some TCKs seize every opportunity, other TCKs seem to have difficulty in making or feeling excited about plans at all. So often in the past, their desires and intentions to do such things as act in a school play, run for class office, or be captain of the soccer team were denied when Dad or Mom came home one day and said, "Well, I just received orders today; we are shipping out to Portsmouth in two weeks." No matter how much the TCKs thought they had a choice to do things they wanted to do at school or in the neighborhood, it turned out they had no choice at all. They weren't going to be there for the next school year or the next soccer season after all. Off they went, their dreams vanishing. In Portsmouth, or wherever their next post was, the TCKs asked themselves, "Why even make plans for what I want to do? I'll just have to leave again."

These preempted plans can lead to what some mental health professionals call a "delusion of choice." In other words, a choice to act is offered ("Would you like to run for class president next year?"), but circumstances or the intervention of others arbitrarily eliminates that choice ("Pack your bags, we're leaving tomorrow"). In reality, the person has no choice at all. The achievement of a goal, the development of a relationship, or the completion of a project can all be cut short by some unexpected event or the decision of a personnel director.

For some TCKs, decision making has an almost superstitious dimension. "If I allow myself to make a decision and start taking the necessary steps to see it through, something will happen to stop what I want." For others, this delusion of choice is wrapped in a theological dimension. "If God finds out what I really want, he'll take it away from me." Rather than be disappointed, they refuse to acknowledge to themselves, let alone to others or to God, what they would like to do.

Other TCKs and ATCKs have difficulty in making a choice that involves a significant time commitment because they know a new and more desirable possibility may always appear. Signing a contract to teach in Middleville might be a wise economic move, but what if a job opportunity opens in Surabaya next week? It's hard to choose one thing before knowing all the choices. Experience has taught that life not only offers multiple options, but those options can appear suddenly and need to be acted on quickly or they are gone—yet the very fact that one choice might preclude another keeps some TCKs and ATCKs from making any choice at all.

Chronically waiting until the last minute to plan rather than risk disappointment or having to change plans can be particularly frustrating for spouses or children waiting for decisions to be made that will affect the entire family. Adult TCKs may also miss significant school, job, or career opportunities. It becomes such a habit to wait, they never follow through on leads or fill out necessary forms by the deadline.

Of course, many TCKs have parents who have given them significant opportunities for meaningful choices—even within what appeared to be "no choice" situations—and they have developed the ability to look for possible options and ramifications of those possible choices in any circumstances and make solid decisions based on those facts.

Relation to Authority:
Appreciative versus Mistrustful

Benefit: Appreciative of Authority

For some TCKs, living within the friendly confines of a strong organizational system is a strong and happy fact of their lives. Relationships with adults in their community are basically positive and nurturing. There may be almost a cocoon atmosphere on their military base or at their embassy, business, or mission compound. The struggles of others in the world can be shut out, at least for some period of time, and perks such as generators, special stores, and paid vacations are all part of a wonderful package deal. As adults, they look back on their TCK childhoods and those who supervised their lives with nothing but great fondness.

Challenge: Mistrustful of Authority

Other ATCKs and TCKs feel quite different. For all the reasons (and maybe more) mentioned under "The Delusion of Choice," they begin to mistrust the authority figures in their lives, easily blaming virtually all of their problems in life on parents or organizational administrators who made autocratic decisions about where and when they would move with little regard for their needs or the needs of their family. One of them told us:

> My parents finally got divorced when Mom said she
> wouldn't make one more move. The company had
> moved my dad to a new position every two years.
> Each time, we went to a different place, even a
> different country—sometimes in the middle of the
> school year, sometimes not. My mom could see how it
> was affecting us children as well as herself. We would
> finally start to find our own places within the new
> group, when it was time to move again. Mom asked
> Dad to talk to the managers of his company and
> request they leave us in one place while we went

> through high school at least. They said they couldn't do
> it; they were amalgamating their headquarters and the
> office in our town was being phased out. Dad didn't
> want to find a new job, and Mom wouldn't move, so
> they got divorced. I've always been angry about both
> my dad's decision and the company's.

In the end, some TCKs who have had their life unhappily affected because of decisions made by others tell us they will starve before risking the possibility that the direction of their lives will be so profoundly changed once more by the decision of someone in authority over them.

Arrogance: Real versus Perceived

Sometimes the very richness of their background creates a new problem for TCKs. Once, after a seminar, a woman came up to Dave Pollock and said, "There's one issue you failed to talk about tonight and it's the very thing that almost ruined my life. It was my arrogance."

Unfortunately, arrogance isn't an uncommon word when people describe TCKs or ATCKs. It seems the very awareness which helps TCKs view a situation from multiple perspectives can also make TCKs impatient or arrogant with others who only see things from their own perspective—particularly people from their home culture. This may happen for several reasons.

1. A cross-cultural lifestyle is so normal that TCKs themselves don't always understand how much it has shaped their view of the world. They easily forget it's their life experiences that have been different from others', not their brain cells, and they may consider themselves much more cosmopolitan and just plain smarter than others.

2. This impatience or judgmentalism can sometimes serve as a point of identity with other TCKs. It becomes one of the markers of "us" versus "them." It's often easy for a get-together of

TCKs to quickly degenerate into bashing the stupidity of non-TCKs. The irony is that the TCKs are then doing unto others what they don't like having done unto themselves—equating ignorance with stupidity.

Sometimes TCKs and ATCKs appear arrogant because they have chosen a permanent identity as being "different" from others.

> Todd, an ATCK, was angry. His parents could do no right. His sponsoring organization had stupid policies, and his American peers ranked among the dumbest souls who had ever been born. Todd castigated everyone and everything. Mark, his good friend, finally got tired of the tirades and pointed out the pride and arrogance coming out in his words.
>
> "You know, Todd," Mark said, "it's your experiences that have been different—not your humanity. I think if you try, you might discover you are not as different from the rest of the world as you seem to feel. You know, you're a normal person."
>
> At that, Todd fairly jumped out of his chair. "The last thing I want to be is 'normal.' That idea is nauseating to me."

This "I'm different from you" type of identity is often a defense mechanism to protect against unconscious feelings of insecurity or inferiority. But a "different from" identity has a certain arrogance attached to it. TCKs who put other people down often do so as a way to set themselves apart or boost their sense of self-worth. "I don't care if you don't accept me, because you could never understand me anyway." TCKs chalk up any rejection they feel or interpersonal problems they have to being different rather than taking a look to see if they themselves might have added to this particular problem.

At other times, however, what is labeled as arrogance in TCKs is simply an attempt to share their normal life experiences. People who don't understand their background may feel the TCKs are bragging or name-dropping when they speak of places they have been or people they have met. Non-TCK friends don't realize TCKs have no other stories to tell.

And sometimes there may be a mix of both real and perceived arrogance. The conviction or passion with which TCKs speak because of what they have seen and/or experienced makes them seem dogmatic and overly sure of their opinions. Is that arrogance? It's hard to know.

While these are some of the general personal characteristics we have repeatedly seen among TCKs, there are others McCaig also referred to that can develop into true life skills. We look at them in chapter 7.

Endnote

[1] Norma M. McCaig, "Understanding Global Nomads," *Strangers at Home* (New York: Aletheia Press, 1996), 101.

7

Practical Skills

> One day I poured out my bitter complaints to a senior
> missionary. I could not understand why the mission
> imported thirty Canadian and U.S. young people to do
> famine work, when not one of the more than fifteen
> resident MKs [missionary kids]—experienced in
> language and culture—had been asked to help. He told
> me to quit complaining and sign on. I did.[1]
>
> —Andrew Atkins

The feelings Andrew expresses reflect the fact that growing up as a
TCK not only increases an inner awareness of our culturally diverse
world, but the experience also helps in the development of useful
personal skills for interacting with and in it. Some of these skills are
acquired so naturally they aren't recognized, acknowledged, or effectively used—either by ATCKs or others—as the special gifts they
are. At the same time, some of these skills also have a flip side,
where a skill becomes a liability, as we will see in the discussion of
social and linguistic skills below.

Cross-Cultural Skills

As TCKs have the opportunity not only to observe a great variety of
cultural practices but also to learn what some of the underlying as-

sumptions are behind them, they often develop strong cross-cultural skills. More significant than the ease with which they can change from chopsticks to forks for eating or from bowing to shaking hands while greeting is their ability to be sensitive to the more hidden aspects or deeper levels of culture and to work successfully in these areas. For ATCKs who go into international or intercultural careers, this ability to be a bridge between different groups of people can be useful in helping their company or organization speak with a more human voice in the local community and be more sensitive to the dynamics of potentially stressful situations in the work environment.

> ATCK Jamal became a prime negotiator for his company during tense negotiations between executives from the home office in the United States and members of the host country who oversaw daily operations in the company's branch overseas. He told us: "Everyone gets mad at me because I can see both sides in the discussions." But ultimately he played a key role in bringing resolution when he pointed out to both sides that much of the impasse related to different cultural styles of negotiation rather than a difference in what each side wanted. The executives from the home office presumed frank, confrontational discussions were most useful, while host culture members believed that saving face was more important. To them, confrontation meant openly shaming another person—a cardinal offense in that particular culture. Once Jamal helped them understand their different outlooks, both sides were able to step back and consider each other's views more objectively and work to a mutually satisfactory conclusion.

Because of their experience in very different cultures and places around the world, ATCKs often find themselves particularly qualified when it comes to jobs or situations such as teaching or mentoring. For those who choose teaching as a career, the fact that most TCKs have themselves attended schools with a wide variety of cultural learning and teaching styles helps them understand and be sensitive to their students' struggles with language, spelling, and conceptual differences. They have every potential of being particularly effective in cross-cultural educational processes—even if it is only with one child in their classroom who has recently immigrated to the area from another country or culture. ATCKs, of all people, should be willing to allow for some differences in writing as well as thinking and learning styles.

ATCKs may also be particularly effective teachers because they have many firsthand stories to augment the facts recorded in geography or social studies textbooks. They may be able to bring life to the textbook's chapter on how the Netherlands reclaimed its land from the sea because they have walked on those dikes. Maybe they have seen the cells in the Philippines where American and Filipino POWs were held during World War II. Whatever countries they have lived or traveled in, they can, one hopes, bring their students fresh ways of looking at the world.

Children who grow up playing and going to school with children of other races and cultures naturally learn that friendship and respect have nothing to do with skin color or cultural differences. Those who have moved often and been the new kid on the block several times over also realize how painful it can be if no one reaches out to a newcomer or, conversely, how wonderful it is when someone does.

Because of their own experience, TCKs and ATCKs can be effective mentors for new students coming to their school or community from different countries or cultures or even from different parts of their own country. They already know some of the hazards of this process and can effectively help others settle in more quickly—and less traumatically—than might happen otherwise.

Sometimes TCKs can be connectors or mediators between groups that are stereotypically prejudiced against one another.

> Francisco is a black Panamanian TCK. At age six, he
> moved to the States while his stepfather pursued a

military career. Initially, Francisco lived in the predominantly white culture in the community surrounding the
army base. Here he learned firsthand the shock of
being the target of racist slurs and attacks. Later, his
parents moved and he went to a more racially diverse
high school where he became a chameleon who
apparently fit perfectly into the African American
community. Eventually most of his friends saw him as
Francisco and forgot, if they ever knew, that his roots
were not the same as theirs.

One day, however, a heated discussion erupted
among his black friends about why "foreigners"
shouldn't be allowed into the country. Finally, Francisco
spoke up and said, "You know, guys, what you're
saying about them, you're saying about me. I'm not a
citizen either. But foreigners have flesh and blood like
me—and like you." Then Francisco pointed out how
this kind of group stereotyping was why he and they as
black people had known prejudice. Francisco reminded them that he—their personal friend, a foreigner—was living proof that people of all backgrounds, races, colors, and nationalities were just
that—people, not statistics or embodiments of other
people's stereotypes.

Observational Skills

TCKs may well develop certain skills because of the basic human
instinct for survival. Sometimes through rather painful means, they
have learned that particularly in cross-cultural situations it pays to
be a careful observer of what's going on around them and then try to
understand the reasons for what they are seeing.

One TCK received the "nerd for life" award when, on
his first day of school "at home," he carried his books
in a brand-new briefcase—just like his dad's. The
briefcase served a most utilitarian purpose—keeping

books together in an easily transportable manner. But in this new school, a backpack slung over one shoulder (and one shoulder only) served the same purpose in a far more socially acceptable manner.

Through such experiences, TCKs learn firsthand that in any culture these unwritten rules govern everyone's acceptance or rejection in a new setting. In addition, they have seen how behavior unnoticed in one place may cause deep offense in another. Something as seemingly insignificant as raising a middle finger or pointing at another person has distinctly different meanings depending on the culture. Mistakes in conscious and unconscious social rules—whether eating style, greetings, or methods of carrying schoolbooks—often send an unwanted message to people in the new culture. Observing carefully and learning to ask "How does life work here?" before barging ahead are other skills TCKs can use to help themselves or others relate more effectively in different cultures.

Mariella, a German ATCK who had grown up in India, took a job working for an NGO hospital in Ghana. It wasn't long before she heard complaints from the expatriate staff that the patients often threw their prescriptions away immediately after exiting the doctor's office. That seemed odd to her as well, so Mariella began investigating.

She soon noticed that when the new doctor from Germany dispensed these prescriptions, he always sat sideways at the desk. The patients were on the doctor's left side as he wrote notes on their charts using his right hand. Whenever the doctor finished writing the prescription, he would pick it up with his free left hand and give it to the patient.

This process probably would not have caused a second thought in Germany, but Mariella knew from her childhood in India that there the left hand is considered unclean by many because it is the one used for dirty tasks. Giving someone anything with that hand is both an insult and a statement that the object being offered is worthless. She wondered if that might be the case in Ghana as well and asked her new Ghanaian friends if the way a person handed something to another person made a difference in their culture. When their replies confirmed her suspicion that using the left hand in Ghana had the same connotation as she remembered from her childhood in India, Mariella understood why the patients didn't fill the prescriptions! She suggested the doctor turn his desk around so all the patients sat at his right and that way he would naturally give out the prescriptions in a culturally appropriate manner. He followed her advice and the problem disappeared.

Social Skills

In certain ways, learning to live with the chronic change which often characterizes their lifestyle gives many TCKs a great sense of inner confidence and strong feelings of self-reliance. While not always liking change—sometimes even hating it—TCKs do expect to cope with new situations. They generally approach upheavals with some degree of confidence because past experience has taught them that given enough time, they will make more friends and learn the new culture's ways. This sense that they'll be able to manage new situations—even when they can't always count on others to be physically present to help in a crisis—often gives them the security to take risks others might not take. A Belgian ATCK, Helga, planned to go alone on a five-week trip to Australia and New Zealand. Some friends were shocked.

"Do you know anyone there?" they asked.

"Not yet," she replied.

"Well, how can you just go? Aren't you scared? How will you find your way? What kind of food will you eat?"

Actually, she hadn't thought of it. She'd just pre-

sumed one way or another it would all work out. As a
teenager and university student, she'd often traveled
halfway around the world alone to see her parents
each school vacation. Customs and language barriers
were no longer intimidating. Lost luggage could be
dealt with. She had a great time.

But there is a flip side to this type of confidence as well. While
TCKs develop feelings of confidence in many areas of life, there are
other times or situations in which they may be so fearful of making
mistakes they are almost paralyzed. Paul, an American TCK who
grew up in Australia, moved once more as a teenager. Here's what
he said about that move.

I changed worlds once more at age fourteen when my
dad's company moved him from Australia to Indonesia.
But the consequence of switching worlds at that age is
you can't participate in the social scene. Everyone else
seems to know the rules except you. You stand at the
edge, and you shut up and listen, mostly to learn, but
you can't participate. You only sort of participate—not
as an initiator, but as a weak supporter in whatever
goes on—hoping that whatever you do is right and flies
okay. You're always double-checking and making sure.

Just as true chameleons move slowly while constantly checking
which color they should be to blend into each new environment, so
TCKs can appear to be socially slow while trying to figure out the
operative rules in their new situations. To avoid looking foolish or
stupid, they retreat from these situations in such ways as overem-
phasizing academics, belittling the new culture, or withdrawing in
extreme shyness. Even those who have been extremely social in one
setting may refuse to join group activities in the next place because
they have no idea how to do what everyone else already can. Maybe
they have returned home to Sweden from a tropical climate, never
having learned to ice skate, toboggan, or ski. They would rather not
participate at all than let anyone know of their incompetence.

Insecurity in a new environment can make TCKs withdraw even

in areas where they have knowledge or talent. It's one thing to join the choir in a relatively small international school overseas. It's quite another to volunteer when you are suddenly in a school of three thousand students. Who knows what might be expected? Who knows how many others are better than you? And so the TCK holds back to wait and watch, even when it might be possible to be involved.

While TCKs are trying to figure out the new rules and if or where they might jump in, people around them wonder why they are holding back. If the TCKs do jump into the fray, it's easy for them to make dumb mistakes and be quickly labeled as social misfits. This can lead to another problem. Because TCKs often don't feel a sense of belonging, they, as did both Paul and Ginny, can quickly identify with others who don't fit in. Unfortunately, this is often the group that is in trouble with the school administration or one in which scholastic achievement is disdained. Later, if the TCKs want to change and make friends with those more interested in academic success, it may be difficult because they have already been labeled as part of the other group.

Linguistic Skills

Acquiring fluency in more than one language is potentially one of the most useful life skills a cross-cultural upbringing can give TCKs. Children who learn two or more languages early in life, and use these languages on a day-to-day basis, develop a facility and ease with language unlike those who learn a second language for the first time as teenagers or adults.

Bilingualism and multilingualism have advantages in addition to the obvious one of communicating with different groups of people. For instance, Dr. Jeannine Heny, an English professor, believes learning different languages early in life can sharpen thinking skills in general and can actually help children achieve academically above their grade level.[2] Learning the grammar of one language can strengthen grammatical understanding in the next one.

Strong linguistic skills also have practical advantages as the TCK becomes an adult. Some careers are available only to people fluent in two or more languages. One American ATCK works for a large international company as a Japanese/English translator. She learned Japanese while growing up and attending local schools in a small town in Japan. Another American ATCK works as an international broadcaster using the Hausa he learned as a child in Nigeria.

Even if a career isn't directly involved with language, opportunities to take jobs in certain countries may require language acquisition. There's no doubt that a job applicant who can already speak the country's language will see his or her resume land a lot closer to the top of the pile than those who will have to spend a year in language school along the way. And if the language required doesn't happen to be the one the ATCK already knows, the fact that he or she can obviously learn more than one language improves job opportunities as well.

When we first learn a new language as an adult, the thinking process of our mother language often superimposes itself on the second language and makes learning the new language more difficult. It also inhibits us from fully understanding the thinking patterns of those who use that language. When children learn languages, they instinctively pick up the differing nuances of how people in that culture think and relate to one another. Adults often translate word for word and never understand that the same word can have a different meaning in another language. Ironically, however, learning the nuances for certain words in their adopted language can sometimes keep TCKs from fully understanding the nuances of the translation of that same word in their own mother tongue. This happened to JoAnna.

> For years, ATCK JoAnna's American friends told her she was the most guilt-ridden person they'd ever met. No matter what happened—if a glass fell out of someone's hand, a friend lost her notebook, or someone bit his lip—JoAnna always said "Sorry."
> The instantaneous answer always came back.

"What are you sorry for? You didn't do anything."

JoAnna's equally instantaneous reply was also always the same. "I know I didn't do anything. I'm just sorry."

It was a point of significant frustration for both JoAnna and her friends for years. She couldn't get out of the habit of saying sorry and her friends couldn't get over being irritated by it. None of them understood the impasse.

In her forties, JoAnna went to live in Kenya for a year. During a hike in the woods with Pamela, another American, Pamela said, "I'll be glad when I get back to America where everyone doesn't say sorry all the time."

JoAnna wondered why that was a problem.

"It drives me crazy," Pamela said. "No matter what happens, everyone rushes around and says *Pole, pole sana* (which means 'Sorry, very sorry'). But most of the time there's nothing to apologize for."

For the first time, JoAnna understood her lifelong problem with the word *sorry*. For Pamela, an American, *sorry* was only an apology. She had never realized in this African context that people were expressing sympathy and empathy rather than apologizing when they used that word. For JoAnna, in the African language she had learned as a child and in the two she had learned as an adult, sorry was used as both an apology and as an expression of sympathy. It had never occurred to her it was only an apology word in American English. No wonder she and her American friends had misunderstood each other. They weren't speaking the same language!

Although the linguistic gifts for TCKs are primarily positive ones, there are a few pitfalls to be aware of. These include being limited in any one language, becoming a "creative speller," and losing fluency and depth in the child's native language. As we saw earlier with Ilpo, no matter how bright the child is, the specialized terminology needed for studying medicine (or fixing cars, discussing computers, studying science, etc.) may be missing if someone is working in many languages. Ultimately, he or she may never have time to learn the more specialized meanings and usage of each. JoAnna's story above demonstrates how idiomatic expressions or nonliteral meanings of common words can also cause confusion in such situations.

Interestingly enough, it's not simply those who work or study in entirely different languages that may find themselves linguistically challenged. Perhaps for the very reason it seems so minor, TCKs who speak and write English find it very difficult to keep American and English spelling straight. Is it *color* or *colour? Behavior* or *behaviour? Pediatrician* or *paediatrician?* Even worse, how do you remember if it's *criticise* or *criticize* when criticism is spelled the same everywhere? While this may seem a minor irritation, it can become a major issue when, for example, a British student transfers to a school in the United States (or an American-based school in another country), where teachers may not be sensitive to this issue.

These differences in spelling provide a special challenge to schools everywhere that have a mix of nationalities among their students. Many solve the problem by keeping both an English and American dictionary available to check on the variations that come in on assigned papers. With a sense of humor, an understanding teacher, or a spell checker appropriate for the current country, most TCKs weather this particular challenge successfully.

The most serious problem related to learning multiple languages at an early age is that some people never become proficient in their supposed mother tongue—the language of their family roots and personal history. Among TCKs, this occurs most often among those who come from non-English-speaking countries but attend international schools overseas where classes are predominantly taught in English. When that is a boarding school with little home (and thus language) contact for months at a time, language can become a major issue when the TCK returns to his or her parents, with the supposed mother tongue becoming almost a foreign language. Families whose members lack fluency in a common language by which they can express emotions and profound ideas lose one critical tool for developing close, intimate relationships.

> Kwabena is a Ghanaian TCK who faced the problem of never gaining fluency in his parents' languages. His father was from the Ga tribe, his mother from the Anum tribe. Kwabena was born in predominantly English-speaking Liberia, where his father worked for several years. Eventually, the family moved to Mali, where French was the official language. The family could only make occasional visits back to the parents' villages in Ghana, where his grandparents spoke only the local languages. By the time Kwabena reached his teens, he sadly realized he could never talk to his grandparents and ask for the family stories all children love to hear, because he couldn't speak enough of any of their languages and they couldn't speak the English, French, or Malian languages he knew.

Most TCKs we know, however, would count the benefits of having facility in two or more languages another of their greatest practical blessings. What is more, it's just plain fun to watch a group of ATCKs at an international school reunion suddenly break into the greetings or farewells of the language they all learned in some faraway land during their youth. At that moment, language becomes one more marker of all they have shared in the world that now may seem invisible to them.

Endnotes

[1] Andrew Atkins, "Behavioral Strings to Which MKs Dance," *Evangelical Missions Quarterly* (July 1989): 239–43.

[2] Jeannine Heny, "Learning and Using a Second Language," in *Language: Introductory Readings,* 5th ed., edited by Virginia Clark, Paul A. Eschholz, and Alfred F. Rosa (New York: St Martin's Press, 1994), 186.

8

Rootlessness and Restlessness

> Being a TCK has given me a view of the world as my
> home and a confidence in facing new situations and
> people, particularly of other countries and cultures.
> However, it has its negative side [because] Americans
> and foreigners have a problem relating to me, for I am
> not a typical American! The hardest question still to
> answer is where I am from. What is my place of origin?[1]
> —Response to ATCK Survey

While this writer obviously enjoyed the type of confidence a TCK childhood can foster, he or she also brings up two very common characteristics TCKs often share—a deep sense of rootlessness and restlessness. These are such key aspects of the TCK Profile that they deserve a chapter of their own.

Rootlessness

There are several questions many TCKs have learned to dread. Among them are these two: "Where are you from?" and "Where is home?"

Where Are You From?

Why should anyone dread such a simple question? Consider Erika again.

Like most other TCKs, when someone asks Erika that question, her internal computer starts the search mode. *What does this person mean by "from"? Is he asking my nationality? Or maybe it's "Where were you born?" Does he mean "Where are you living now?" or "Where did you come from today?" Or does he mean "Where do your parents live now?" or "Where did you grow up?" Actually, does he even understand what a complicated question he asked me, or care? Is he simply asking a polite "Let's make conversation about something while we stand here with shrimp on our plates" question, or is he really interested?*

Erika decides what to answer by how she perceives the person who asked or what she does and doesn't feel like talking about. If the new acquaintance seems more polite than interested or if Erika doesn't want a lengthy conversation, she gives the "safe" answer. During college she simply said, "Wisconsin." Now she replies, "Dayton." It's the "where I'm living now" answer.

If Erika does want to extend the conversation slightly or test out the questioner's true interest, she throws out the next higher-level answer: "New York"—still a fairly safe answer. It's where she visited during each home leave and where her family roots are.

If the person responds with more than a polite "Oh" and asks another question such as, "Then when did you leave New York?" Erika might elevate her reply to a still higher level, "Well, I'm not really from New York, but my parents are." Now the gauntlet is thrown down. If the potential new friend picks up on this and asks, "Well, where are *you* from then?" the conversation begins and Erika's fascinating life history begins to unfold. Of course, if the newcomer doesn't follow up that clue and lets the comment go, Erika knows for sure she or he wasn't really interested

anyway and moves the conversation on to other
topics—or simply drops it altogether.

On days when Erika feels like talking more or wants
to make herself stand out from among the crowd,
however, she answers the question "Where are you
from?" quite differently. "What time in my life are you
referring to?" she asks. At this point the other person
has virtually no choice but to ask Erika where she has
lived during her life and then hear all the very interesting details Erika has to tell!

Where Is Home?

While this question at first seems to be the same as "Where are you
from?" it is not. In some cases, TCKs have a great sense of "at-
homeness" in their host culture. As long as Erika's parents remained
in Singapore, "Where's your home?" was an easier question to answer than "Where are you from?" She simply said, "Singapore."
Both her emotional and physical sense of home were the same.

Other TCKs who have lived in one city or house during each
leave or furlough may have a strong sense of that place being home.
In January 1987 the U.S. ambassador to Ecuador spoke at a conference about TCKs in Quito and said, "I think every expatriate family
should buy a home before going abroad so their children will have
the same base for every home assignment. My kids feel very strongly
that Virginia is home even though they've lived outside the States
over half their lives." This is undoubtedly an excellent idea, and one
to be seriously considered when at all possible.

When, for various reasons, buying a house in the home country
isn't a viable option, some TCKs still develop a strong sense of
"home" in other ways. Often those whose parents move every two
years rarely consider geography as the determining factor in what
they consider home. Instead, home is defined by relationships.

When Dave Pollock asked Ben, a TCK from the
diplomatic community, "Where's your home?" Ben
replied, "Egypt." Dave was somewhat surprised as he

had not previously heard Ben talk about Egypt, so
Dave asked how long he had lived there.

"Well," Ben replied, "actually, I haven't been to
Egypt yet, but that's where my parents are posted
now. They moved there from Mozambique right after I
left for university, so when I go home for Christmas
vacation, that's where I'll go."

For some TCKS, however, "Where is home?" is the hardest question of all. *Home* connotes an emotional place—somewhere you truly belong. There simply is no real answer to that question for many TCKs. They may have moved so many times, lived in so many different residences, and attended so many different schools that they never had time to become attached to any. Their parents may be divorced and living in two different countries. Some TCKs have spent years in boarding schools and no longer feel a close attachment to their parents. In fact, they may feel more emotionally at home at boarding school than when thinking of their parents' home. Paul Seaman writes,

"Home" might refer to the school dormitory or to the
house where we stayed during the summer, to our
family's home where our parents worked, or, more
broadly, to the country of our citizenship. And while
we might have some sense of belonging to all of these
places, we felt fully at home in none of them. Boarding
life seemed to have the most consistency, but there we
were separated from our siblings and shared one
"parent" with other kids. As it grew colder, we could
look forward to going home for the holidays. We were
always eager to be reunited with our families, but after
three months of separation from our friends, we were
just as eager to go back. Every time we got on the
train, we experienced both abandonment and communion.[2]

No matter how home is defined, the day comes for many TCKs when they realize it is irretrievably gone. For whatever reasons, they, like Erika, can never "go home." Now when someone asks Erika where her home is, she simply says, "Everywhere and nowhere." She has no other answer.

Restlessness—The Migratory Instinct

In the end, many TCKs develop a *migratory instinct* that controls their lives. Along with their chronic rootlessness is a feeling of restlessness: "Here, where I am today, is temporary. But as soon as I finish my schooling, get a job, or purchase a home, I'll settle down." Somehow the settling down never quite happens. The present is never enough—something always seems lacking. An unrealistic attachment to the past, or a persistent expectation that the next place will finally be home, can lead to this inner restlessness that keeps the TCK always moving.

> Inika had waited for what seemed like forever to return to her host country, Guatemala. She finally found a job which offered her the prospect of staying there for many years, possibly even until she retired. Two weeks after arriving, however, Inika felt a wave of panic. For the first time in her life, there was no defined end point. Now she had to be involved with the good and bad of whatever happened in this community. She wondered why she felt like this so soon after reaching her goal. Then she realized that throughout her life no matter where she had lived, any time things got messy (relationships with a neighbor, zoning fights in the town, conflicts at church), internally she had leapfrogged over them. There was always an end point ahead when she knew she would be gone—the end of school, the end of home leave, or something. Suddenly, that safety net had disappeared. For the first time in her life Inika either had to engage completely in the world around her or start forming another plan to leave.

Obviously, it is good to be ready to move when a career choice mandates it, but to move simply from restlessness alone can have disastrous effects on an ATCK's academic life, career, and family.

Without question there are legitimate reasons to change colleges or universities. Sometimes TCKs who live a continent away must enroll in university without having the opportunity to visit beforehand. After arriving, they discover that that school doesn't offer the particular courses or majors they want. Perhaps they change their interest in a career they want to pursue and this school doesn't offer concentrated studies in that field. In such situations, there is no choice but to change. Some TCKs, however, switch schools just because of their inner migratory instinct. Their roommates aren't quite right; the professors are boring; the weather in this place is too hot or too cold. They keep moving on, chronically hoping to find the ideal college or university experience. Unfortunately, frequent transfers can limit what TCKs learn and inhibit the development of their social relationships.

Once through with school (or after dropping out), a TCK who has moved often and regularly may feel it's time to move even when it's not. Some ATCKs can't stay at one job long enough to build any sort of career. Just as they are anticipating a position of new responsibility and growth, that old rolling-stone instinct kicks in. They submit their letters of resignation, and off they go—again always thinking the next place will be "it."

> Sylvia raced through life. In the ten years following her
> university graduation, she acquired two master's
> degrees, had seven career changes, and lived in four
> countries. One day it struck her that while she had a
> vast amount of broad knowledge and experience, her
> career was going nowhere. And she wasn't sure she
> still wanted, or knew how, to settle down.

Some feel almost an obligation to be far from their parents, siblings, or even their own children. When it is possible to live closer, these adult TCKs choose not to. They have spent so much time separated from family that they don't know how to live in physical proximity, or don't want to. Others, like Bernie, have learned to deal with interpersonal conflict—including family conflict—by separating from the situation. He said, "I loved growing up with high mobility. Every time there was a problem, all I had to do was wait and either the people causing the problem left or I left. I have handled all of my life's conflicts the same way." Peggy is another example of how this restlessness works.

> Peggy, a foreign service ATCK, attended twelve schools in sixteen years all around the globe. Now, every two years, an internal clock goes off that says, "This assignment is up. Time to move." She has either changed jobs, houses, cities, and—twice—husbands in response to that message.
>
> Unfortunately, her migratory instinct has affected Peggy's children. Although she has noticed their insecurities developing as she perpetually uproots them, Peggy appears powerless to settle down. The overt reason for change always seems clear, "I don't like the neighborhood we're in," or "My boss simply doesn't understand me," or "I have a nasty landlord." It never occurs to her that she is replaying a very old tape that says, "No place can ever become permanent. Don't get too attached" or "If you have a problem, just leave." Nor does she realize it might be possible to replace the old tape with a new one that plays a message that could serve her better.

Some TCKs have an opposite response to their highly mobile background. They have moved so many times, in so many ways, and to so many places, they swear they will find a place to call their own, put up the white picket fence, and never, ever move again. Lorna, a non-TCK married to an ATCK, told us,

> When I met Dwight, I think I fell in love with his passport as much as I did with him. I was intrigued with all the places he had been and everything he had

seen. I envisioned a life of worldwide travel and living in all sorts of exotic places. Unfortunately, I assumed wrong. When my father surprised us with an old farmhouse for our wedding present, Dwight was thrilled. That was the first time he shared with me how he had always dreamed of finding a place to call his own and settle down. This was it. So I'm still reading my travel magazines and dreaming.

Now we take a further look at how the TCKs' experience, including this rootlessness and restlessness, shapes the patterns of their relationships.

Endnotes

[1] From Ruth E. Van Reken, unpublished original research on ATCKs, 1986.

[2] Seaman, *Paper Airplanes in the Himalayas*, 8.

9

Relational Patterns

Multiple separations tended to cause me to develop deeper relationships quicker. Also, when I was with family or friends, we tended to talk about things that matter spiritually, emotionally, and so on. I still become impatient with [what I see as] superficiality.[1]
—Response to ATCK Survey

Because TCKs often cope with high mobility by defining their sense of rootedness in terms of relationships rather than geography, many TCKs will go to greater lengths than some people might consider normal to nurture relational ties with others—be they family members, friends with whom the TCKs have shared boarding school years, or other important members of their third culture community. Unfortunately, that same mobility can result in relationships being a source of great conflict and pain as well. The cycle of frequent goodbyes inherent in a highly mobile lifestyle not only creates strains on specific relationships—such as parents and children, when it's time for the kids to fly an ocean away for school—but it can also lead to patterns of protecting themselves against the further pain of goodbyes that affect relationships throughout their lives. Here, within the context of relationships, is another example of both the gifts and challenges of the TCK experience. Through relational patterns we can see even more why the TCK life can be a rich source of meeting our basic human need for relationships for many, while making it very difficult for others.

Large Numbers of Relationships

TCKs usually develop a wide range of relationships as they or people around them habitually come and go. New friends enter their lives, while old friends become another entry in their burgeoning address books.

"I could travel to almost any country in the world and stay with a friend," Tom bragged after one transition seminar. This may sound like an exaggeration, but for many adult TCKs it's the truth. With friends from their childhood now in countless places, TCKs build a rich international network that is useful for all sorts of things—from finding cheap room and board while traveling to setting up business connections later in life.

The problem with having this many relationships, however, is that eventually they simply can't all be maintained. Renee learned this the hard way.

> ATCK Renee's personal address list grew to over eight hundred names. No matter how hard she tried to keep up with her correspondence, she couldn't. The stack of letters to answer always exceeded the time available—especially since many of those missives came from friends whom she thought deserved long letters in reply. Eventually, Renee had to resort to a yearly Christmas form letter, but it still took a month of constant work, as she always added personal notes before mailing them off. One year Renee was simply short of time. Presuming her friends would understand, and hoping they would rather have some news than none at all, she mailed the letters with no personal notes.
>
> Four months later she attended a wedding and met an African friend from her five years in Malawi. When

Renee rushed to greet him warmly, his response was exceedingly cool.

"Seems like you've forgotten us," he said.

Renee was dumbfounded. "How can you say that?"

"Well, you haven't called for months, and when you sent out your Christmas letter there wasn't even a personal note on it. My wife and I have been wondering what we've done to offend you."

Renee finally had to accept the sad reality that she wasn't going to be able to keep up with every wonderful person she had ever met.

Deep and Valued Relationships

Relationships everywhere move through various levels of communication as people get to know each other. While this happens in different ways in various cultures, here is one common pattern for how relationships are established.

1. *Superficial level:* This involves conversation generally referred to as "small talk"—How are you? Where are you from? The weather or today's headlines.

2. *"Still safe" level:* This is an exchange of no-risk facts. Where did you go on vacation last year? What sights did you see?

3. *Judgmental level:* Here, we begin to risk a few statements about our opinions on politics, religion, or other matters about which our new friend might disagree with us.

4. *Emotional level:* We begin sharing how we feel about life, ourselves, and others (e.g., that we're sad, happy, worried, or depressed).

5. *Disclosure level:* We reveal our most private thoughts and feelings to another person, confessing secret dreams as well as painful failures. This stage involves an honesty and vulnerability that lead to true intimacy. Most of us only have a few people in our lives with whom we share at this level. Some people have no one to share such a place.

One common complaint from at least Canadian and U.S. American TCKs is that they feel people in their home cultures are "shallow." Conversations with peers seem boring, and the TCKs long for the good old days with their international friends. Why is this such a common complaint? It has to do with these levels of relationships. People in different cultures not only enter but move through the various levels at different paces. Some cultures jump past the small talk quickly and treat strangers like long-lost cousins, inviting them to stay the night, eat what they want, and come as often as they wish. In other cultures nobody bothers to go next door to say hello to the family that just moved in from who knows where.

For various reasons, TCKs seem prone to passing quickly through levels one and two and moving immediately into topics that fall into level three. In other words, while others are still at the polite stages, TCKs are offering opinions on and asking what others think about such topics as how the president's term is going, what the government should do on its immigration policy, or whether the United Nations should intervene in some new world crisis. When others either don't seem to care about such things, or don't want to express their opinions, TCKs deem them shallow—and who knows what these others think of the TCKs?

Why do TCKs often jump into these at least supposedly deeper levels of communication faster than others? There are a number of reasons. One of these is cultural habit. On an Internet list serve for TCKs, this matter of relational levels became a hot topic of discussion. An interesting response came from a Dutch ATCK, Ard A. Louis, who grew up in Gabon and now lives in New York.

> At least among educated Europeans it's very common to discuss politics or other potentially divisive topics upon a first encounter. In fact, sometimes we look for something to argue about on purpose. Part of being "educated" is being able to talk about art, philosophy, politics, and so on.... and argue your points if need be.
>
> This is very different with Americans, who seem always to look for points of common interest. For

example, how often when you meet someone do they
ask where you're from and then try to find some point
of commonality like "I've been there" or "Do you
know so and so?"

Another very common topic of discussion is pop
culture, especially movies/TV shows most people have
seen. (Pop culture is the great unifying factor in the
U.S.—and being well versed in its history helps
tremendously in fitting in.) Thus, a very common first
impression of Europeans arriving in the U.S. is that
Americans are superficial because they seem to have
no opinions about even their own political situation, let
alone what's happening in the rest of the world.[2]

Ard's point is that the methods and styles of relating to one another
differ from culture to culture according to cultural habit. When we
discuss entering relationships at a "deeper level," perhaps this is
only in comparison to particular cultures, as in the case above—
U.S. culture. In reality, discussing politics in some cultures may be
no closer to true intimacy than talking about the weather in other
cultures. This, of course, calls into question the universality of how
the levels themselves are defined.

Another ATCK recounted how this mix-up of culturally appropriate relationship levels and styles caught her unaware:

I'd never met this Israeli businessman before that
evening, but during supper I asked him how the
political situation in Israel was doing.... Another
American eating with us almost spit out his food and
instantly changed the subject of conversation. When
we finished that new topic and I went back to my
original question, the American had the same reaction.
Afterwards he told me how horribly rude I'd been to
ask such a question of someone I barely knew. Frankly,
I was stunned. Here was a guy with lots of information
about key world issues and this American thought I
shouldn't talk about it. So I asked him why. He told me
in his family you were never allowed to talk about

> religion or politics because that always caused trouble.
> Until I heard about these different levels of communi-
> cation and personal relationships, I couldn't understand
> why I shouldn't start with political questions.[3]

There are three other reasons TCKs may jump more quickly than others into what we are calling deeper levels of relationship.

1. *Practice:* Many TCKs know how to get into relationships fairly quickly simply because they have had to start so many. They have learned to observe the dynamics of a situation, ask questions that can help open a door, hopefully be sensitive to cultural cues of what is or is not appropriate for this group, and respond appropriately when others approach them.

2. *Content:* The store of knowledge and experience they have acquired feeds into many different topics, so they often think they have something relevant to say. Because of their parents' careers, TCKs often grow up in homes where discussions on a current political crisis, starving children, religious views, or solutions to the economic woes of the country are standard fare. To express opinions on these topics is normal, and people around seem interested because the TCK's firsthand insights may help others understand the complexity of issues in the newspaper or on television that are happening a world away.

3. *Sense of urgency:* TCKs may also jump into deeper levels of communication quickly because there is little time to develop a particular relationship. They understand that if something doesn't happen now, perhaps it never will. TCKs routinely meet people of incredible diversity who can teach them so much about their part of the world. Why waste time in small talk? In one sense, almost everyone can be an instant friend. Because they have connected at a relatively deep level, many of these quick relationships do become long-term friendships—or at least part of that bulging address book for occasional telephone calls and yearly letters.

In *Military Brats*, Mary Edwards Wertsch talks about the "forced extroversion" the military lifestyle fosters because time is too short to wait to make friends. She says one technique she used to break in to new groups was the "confessional impulse." In quickly spilling family secrets (a level 4 or 5 disclosure), she sent a message that she wanted to invest in a new friendship. Often her confession was met by a mutual confession from the new friend. Wertsch also says that military kids might be more willing to be open than their civilian counterparts because they probably won't be around to deal with any negative consequences from these confessions.[4]

Non-TCKs, who are used to staying at the first or second level of relationship for relatively long periods, may misread TCKs who jump in at a deeper level. This type of confusion happened at a camp where Dave Pollock served as a seminar leader.

> Several days after camp started, a group of tearful, non-TCK young women sought Dave out. They felt completely confused by actions of the TCK males. A young man would engage one of these young women in, to them, deep and meaningful conversation, and she would think he was interested in her. But the next day he would do the same with someone else. After three days the young women were confused, angry with each other, and angry at the young men.
>
> When Dave spoke to the guys, they were shocked that these girls thought they had even considered anything more than a friendship for this week at camp. The TCK young men said they had no romantic presuppositions whatsoever. They just wanted to get to know these young women, find out what they thought about life, the world, their faith, and other assorted interesting topics. It seemed like a perfect chance to understand more about Americans. But the seriousness of the conversation communicated a level of warmth and relationship that meant something quite different to the young women.

TCKs usually place a high value on their relationships—especially those from their TCK world. Often the style and intensity of friendship within the international third culture are quite different from the types of friendship they have in their home country. Most expatriate families live far from relatives and tend to reach out to one another as surrogate families in times of need. When there is a coup, for example, it's the friends in this international community who band together in the fear, the wondering, the packing, and the leaving. Without doubt, a great deal of bonding that lasts a lifetime takes place at such times.

Relationships—both with friends and family at home as well as with friends from their third culture world—are also valued because they give the TCKs a sense of connectedness. These relationships offer the one place where TCKs can say, "Do you remember when...?" and someone actually does!

> A TCK's wedding is usually quite a sight. When Robin married Kevin, her high school sweetheart from boarding school, you would have thought you were in Africa rather than in New York. Papier-mâché palm trees framing a painted mural of a tropical beach decorated the reception hall. Kevin and his grooms-men all wore flowing robes from Sierra Leone. Robin's dad wore a country-cloth chief's robe as he walked her down the aisle. Friends came from far and near, filling the pews with equally colorful attire. The wedding had turned into a minireunion. Watching these TCKs chatter unceasingly throughout the reception was like watching long-lost family members reunite. There was no question about how they viewed their relationships from the past.

Effects of Cycles of Multiple Losses on Relationships

While many TCKs jump into relationships with both feet, others approach any new relationship with caution. In a 1986 survey of three hundred ATCKs, 40 percent of the respondents said they struggled with a fear of intimacy because of the fear of loss.[5] Too many close friends have moved away. Frequent, painful good-byes make some TCKs unwilling to risk emotional involvement again.

Often these TCKs are labeled as quiet or shy. They never take available opportunities to be deeply engaged in their schools or communities. Even TCKs who are regarded as gregarious, open, and friendly because of their skill at jumping into the second and third levels of communication often refuse to move on to the fourth and fifth levels of true intimacy. They manage to erect walls, usually without realizing it, to keep out anyone trying to come closer.

> When Karen became engaged to Jack, she couldn't believe that someone would actually be with her for the rest of her life, so she prepared for what seemed the inevitable loss by presuming Jack would have a fatal car wreck before their marriage. When that didn't happen, she feared it would happen on their honeymoon. After safely returning from their honeymoon, Karen worried whenever Jack was a few minutes late coming home from work. On their first anniversary, he was over two hours late due to an electrical failure in the mass transportation system. By the time he got home, she had started crying with an "I knew it would happen" despair, had begun to plan his funeral, and was wondering how long you had to be married before you didn't need to return the wedding gifts.
>
> Although Jack is living to this day, for a long time after the wedding, Karen couldn't understand why she always seemed to fuss over insignificant details—like whose turn it was to take out the garbage—just when she and Jack felt especially close. She finally realized that deep inside such closeness terrified her because she still feared losing it. Fussing was her way to keep up a wall of safety. Karen had been losing people she loved dearly since first separating from her parents at

> age six, when she left for boarding school, and it took a
> long time for her to let her guard down and dare to
> believe Jack would be staying.

As we saw in our discussion on the stages of transition, people try to protect themselves from the pain of losing a precious, or at least valued, relationship in various ways. TCKs are no different. Some try to limit their vulnerability to impending grief by refusing to acknowledge they care for anyone or anything. In the end, however, they know a pain of loneliness far greater than the one they are running from. The independence they have been so proud of turns into a profound isolation, which keeps them prisoner until the day they become willing to once more feel the pain of loss in order to know the joy of closeness.

A second common response for people trying to avoid the pain of losing a relationship is called the "quick release." When friends are about to leave, or when TCKs think they themselves might be leaving, their response is frequently to let go too soon. Friends quit calling each other and don't visit, play together, or go out for lunch. Each wonders what he or she did to upset the other one. A "quick release" also happens at points where some kind of temporary separation is about to occur. Many ATCKs talk of how easily they have an argument with a spouse the night before one of them is leaving for a short business trip the next day, in an unconscious attempt to let go.

Some ATCKs who have commonly used anger themselves (or had it used by those they were separating from) as a shield against future pain may see any type of anger as a precursor to separation and emotionally detach at the first sign of it.

> Garth and his new bride had their first argument. He
> told us later, "I knew right then she was going to leave
> me." Inside, he went stone-cold toward her. Let her
> leave. I don't care. I don't know why I married her
> anyway, he thought. When he finally realized his wife
> had no intention of leaving, he began to think through

his reaction and what had happened. He remembered
frequent arguments with his parents just before he left
for boarding school, probably each of them unconsciously trying to make the leaving easier. Garth began
to realize that because of that previous pattern, he
made automatic assumptions that any conflict meant
the impending loss of a relationship.

Refusing to feel the pain is a third common response of TCKs to the
multiple losses due to the high mobility of their lives. Even when
TCKs feel intensely about leaving a friend or relative, some refuse
to acknowledge the hurt to others or to themselves. They say they
don't like messy good-byes and, in fact, refuse to say them. Becky
and Mary Ann were two ATCKs caught in this pattern.

Becky and Mary Ann met at a Global Nomads International conference. For both of them, this was the first
time they had consciously reflected on how their pasts
as TCKs had affected them. Each had basked in the joy
of discovering another person who understood her
deep, inner, secret places. They had laughed together,
cried together, and talked incessantly. Suddenly the
conference was over, and that inevitable moment of
saying good-bye had come.

Becky and Mary Ann stood by the elevator as Mary
Ann prepared to leave for the airport. Chances were
great they would never see each other again; they
lived an ocean apart. As they looked at one another,
each knew she had let the other into a space usually
kept off-limits. What did they do now?

After a brief, uncomfortable stare, both broke into
wry smiles of understanding.

"So what do we say?" Becky asked first.

"I guess there's not much to say but the usual," and
Mary Ann paused, bent her right arm up so the palm of
her hand faced Becky. Like a windshield wiper making
one sweep across the windscreen, Mary Ann moved

> her forearm from left to right while saying, *"Byyeee."*
>
> "I guess you're right, Mary Ann. So *Byyeee*," and Becky mirrored the perfunctory farewell wave Mary Ann had just made.
>
> Then they laughed. For some, this might have seemed an incredibly cold way to say good-bye after they had shared their lives so intensely. For them, however, it was a moment of recognition, of understanding how each had learned to avoid painful farewells. They simply didn't acknowledge them! But in another way, it also represented the sum of all they had shared that needed no verbal explanation.

Unfortunately, however, not all who exercise the protective mechanism of emotional flattening realize it as poignantly as Mary Ann and Becky did at the moment of farewell. Even more unfortunately, this flat emotional response can be transferred from avoiding the pain of farewells to all areas of life. Sometimes what is praised as confidence and independence among TCKs may actually be a form of detachment. In his book *Your Inner Child of the Past,* psychiatrist Hugh Missildine cites the work of John Bowlby and says that whenever there is a prolonged loss of relationship between parent and child, for *whatever* reason, children go through grief, despair, and finally, detachment in trying to cope with that loss.[6] Certainly, many TCKs have known profound separation from their parents at an early age. But in addition to that, some have separated so repeatedly from friends and other relatives, they simply refuse to let themselves care about or need anyone again. The sad thing is, when pain is shut down, so is the capacity to feel or express joy.

This response can be devastating in a marriage. The ATCK's partner feels rejected because there are too few external demonstrations of love from the ATCK. Conversely, no matter how many romantic gestures are offered to the ATCK, nothing seems to spark a warm response.

It can be equally painful for the child of such an ATCK. Some ATCK parents seem genuinely unable to delight openly in the pure joy of having a child, of watching that child grow, of playing games together, or of reading stories at bedtime. Not only do the children miss the warmth and approval they long for, but the ATCK parent also loses out on one of the richest relationships possible in life.

On the other hand, however, we have seen how TCKs who learn to deal in healthy ways with the cycle of relationships they face become richer for it. They do, in fact, have a wealth of experiences to share and rich diversity among those they have met, and they have every possibility for making truly deep friendships that last across the years and miles. As TCKS become skilled at going through the process of transition in healthy ways, they can learn to enjoy each relationship they have, whether it be a long- or short-term friendship. Because all people lose relationships at one time or another, they can share the transitional skills they've learned for themselves to help others cope during their life transitions as well.

Endnotes

1 From Ruth E. Van Reken, unpublished original research on ATCKs, 1986.

2 Ard A. Louis, e-mail letter on MK-Issues, August 1996, used by permission.

3 E-mail letter from MK-Issues, August 1996, used with permission of author.

4 Wertsch, *Military Brats,* 263–65.

5 Van Reken, original research.

6 Hugh Missildine, *Your Inner Child of the Past* (New York: Simon and Schuster, 1963), 245–46.

10

Developmental Issues

Sometimes I think the cement of my being was taken from one cultural mould before it cured and forced into other moulds, one after the other, retaining bits of the form of each but producing a finished sculpture that fit into none. At other times I think of myself like the fish we caught [while we were] snorkelling off Wewak. My basic shape camouflages itself in the colours of whatever surroundings I find myself in. I am adept at playing the appropriate roles. But do I have a colour of my own apart from those I appropriate? If I cease to play any role would I be transparent? To mix metaphors, if I peeled away the layers of the roles I adopt would I find nothing at the centre? Am I after all an onion—nothing but the sum of my layers?[1]

—Sophia Morton

In her powerful essay, "Let Us Possess One World," Sophia is reflecting on the basic question we have been talking about that TCKs (and all others) must ultimately answer, Who am I? What does it mean to be human, and what does it mean to be *this* human—me?

Developing Personal Identity

In 1984 Sharon Willmer, an ATCK and therapist for TCKs, spoke at a conference about TCK issues and said that one of the greatest challenges she faced among her clients was that few of them had any idea what it meant to be a person. In particular, they had little sense of their own personal identity. During her talk, Sharon explained how every person—regardless of race, nationality, background, economic status, educational experience or lack thereof—has been created with specific, legitimate needs.[2] These include the need for strong relationships; a sense of belonging, of being nurtured and cared for, of internal unity, of significance; and a feeling of knowing ourselves and being known by others. Every human also has the need to express in one way or another the emotional, creative, intellectual, volitional, and spiritual aspects of his or her being. These needs are what define us as human, and to deny any of them is to deny something precious and important about ourselves as human beings. Furthermore, it is the specific mix and manner in which we meet or express these universal needs that lead to our sense of unique, personal identity.

So why is that such a particular problem for TCKs? Obviously, this is an important issue for non-TCKs as well. At first glance, it may seem that finding a sense of identity is difficult for TCKs simply because of all the cultural or national confusion we've talked about: "Am I an Austrian or a Brazilian?" "Do I fit better in a village setting or a city?" they ask themselves. But having a strong sense of who we are is more than just knowing our nationality or culture, though that is part of it. It's a matter of answering these questions: What is a person? Who am I as *this* person? What are my gifts, my strengths, my weaknesses? Where do I fit or belong? We seek answers to these questions in any culture.

How does that relate to TCKs any differently than non-TCKs? Throughout the preceding chapters and as we complete our look at the TCK Profile in the next chapter, it is becoming clear that the

TCK lifestyle itself affects how TCKs meet these fundamental needs that help them develop a strong sense of personal identity. In the formation of a sense of personhood and identity, the TCK experience has the same paradoxical potential, as we have been discussing, to be either a source of rich blessing or a place of real struggle. Often it is both. Many ATCKs tell us they have felt very nurtured and cared for—by biological parents, dorm parents, other expatriates, their friends among the host nationals, and friends and relatives at home. An Indian TCK raised in the United States said she felt more nurtured than most of her American peers because all the gatherings at the local Indian community center included the children as well as adults, while few American parents included their children in the same way for their social activities. Other TCKs, however, use the word *abandonment* when they reflect on their childhood. For whatever reason, the sense that parents were too busy for them, or were physically or emotionally absent, has left a chronic feeling of emptiness. Nothing and no one else seems to be able to fill this need.

For now, however, we want to look at the first two personal needs we mentioned above—a need for strong relationships and a sense of belonging—and see how the TCK experience presents special challenges as well as opportunities for fulfilling those needs.

Each of us has a strong need to be in relationship with other human beings. "No man is an island" is more than a trite phrase by some ancient poet. Babies who are left alone without human touch will die, no matter how often they are fed. Solitary confinement is considered the worst punishment next to death for a convicted criminal. In relationships we can share and begin to discover many aspects of ourselves. It is also where we receive the love and support we need as the foundation for living a life that is rich and meaningful. But for those things to happen, we must have lasting relationships in our lives, ones in which we don't need to constantly re-explain ourselves and our history. When a person moves continually, however, it's not easy to establish the ongoing relationships that fill this basic human need.

A sense of belonging is the second need we must all have filled to live fully. That can mean belonging to a family, a group of people, a culture, and/or a nation. Certainly it is an extension of our need for relationships, but it's also feeling secure in knowing how a place and people work and how and where we fit into the larger picture. This sense of belonging gives us the freedom we need to continue developing rather than having to repeat the basics constantly. Without that security, it seems we almost go in circles, continually repeating the same lessons of life rather than moving on to new ones.

Now that we know more about the need for relationship and belonging, we can focus a bit more closely on particular developmental issues TCKs may face while they are continuing to sort out their personal identity—a pattern of uneven maturity and delayed adolescence.

Uneven Maturity

People often tell TCKs, "I can't believe you're only fourteen (or whatever). You seem much older." Equally often (and probably behind their backs), these same people marvel at the TCKs' lack of sophistication or social skills. TCKs feel this discrepancy too and soon begin to wonder which person they really are: the competent, capable, mature self or the bungling, insecure, immature self? That's part of the problem in trying to figure out who they are: in many ways they're both.

Early Maturity

It's not only others who see TCKs as "more mature." They often feel more comfortable with older students than with fellow classmates when they begin college or university back in their home countries, probably for several reasons. Among them:

1. *Broad base of knowledge.* TCKs often have an "advanced-for-their-years" knowledge of geography, global events, and poli-

tics in other countries and are interested in topics not usually discussed by younger people in their home cultures. Many have learned unusual practical skills at a very young age as well—such as how to set up solar energy panels to keep computers going for translation work in the Amazon jungle.

2. *Relationship to adults.* TCKs generally feel quite comfortable with adults because they have had lots of experience with them. Generations usually mix much more in third culture communities than often takes place in the home country. Why? Because, at least traditionally, international expatriate communities are often small and quite communal—that is, most of the kids attend the same school; parents appear at the same international or organizational functions; many may go to the only international church in town; and people bump into each other in the one or two grocery stores that carry foods imported from their particular homeland. Since the children may already be friends from school, families visit as families rather than as adults only. In certain situations, some spend more time with adults than other children and almost come across as "mini-adults."

3. *Communication skills.* Children who speak two or more languages fluently also seem like mini-adults. How could they have learned to speak like this so soon in life? Multilingual TCKs generally feel at ease using their languages to communicate with quite diverse groups. In fact, TCKs often serve as translators for their parents—again, a task usually reserved for adults. All this continues to increase their exposure to, participation in, and comfort with a world of culturally diverse adults as well as other children and gives them an unusual air of maturity.

4. *Early autonomy.* In certain ways, many TCKs have an earlier sense of autonomy than peers at home. By their early teenage years, they literally know how to get around in this world and enjoy functioning in quite diverse ways and places. This may be a result of traveling alone to boarding school or having the

opportunity as young children to explore their surroundings freely by trikes, bikes, and hikes. A reliable, safe public transportation system in some countries adds to that sense of autonomy. Many TCKs in Japan take the train to school for two hours each way, every day in early elementary grades. When Paul lived in Australia, he took a ferry and bus by himself to school every day at age eleven, while his friends back in the States were going to the corner of their street and waiting for the school bus to pick them up.

Delayed Adolescence

Ironically, while there are many ways TCKs seem advanced for their years, there are also many ways they seem to lag far behind. In a survey of nearly seven hundred ATCKs, Dr. Ruth Hill Useem and Ann Baker Cottrell observed that it wasn't unusual for TCKs to go through a delayed adolescence, often between the ages of twenty-two and twenty-four, and sometimes even later.[3] TCKs who have never heard the expression "delayed adolescence" have still sensed that they are definitely out of sync with their peers but can't figure out why.

The first question then is—What does *delayed adolescence* mean? The second is—Why is it a characteristic of many TCKs?

Every person must go through certain stages of life successfully in order to function as an independent adult. At least in Western culture, it is during the teenage years that several of these critical developmental steps take place. Each of these tasks relates to a core need of human beings, and going through this process properly is one of the major ways we form a clear picture of who we are—that is, our identity. Below are some of these critical developmental tasks.

1. *Establishing a personal sense of identity.* This is what we talked about earlier in this chapter: the need to figure out—Who am I? What makes me *me*? Where do I fit in my family and group?

2. *Establishing and maintaining strong relationships.* Young children may be bonded to their immediate families, but the teenage years are when relationships with the larger world of peers become critical.

3. *Developing competence in decision making.* Competent decision making is based on the assumption that the world is predictable and that we have some measure of control. In an ideal situation, adolescents learn to make decisions under the protection of the family and then move on to making their own choices.

4. *Achieving independence.* When we have the stability of knowing what the rules of family and culture are and have learned to make competent decisions, we can begin moving toward the independence of adulthood. We realize that not only can we make choices for ourselves, but we are also now accountable for the consequences of our decisions. We—not someone else— become responsible for whether or not we accomplish our goals.

For TCKs, this developmental process may be delayed for a number of reasons. The first one relates back to why cross-cultural transitions and high mobility *during developmental years* are so significant. If establishing a personal sense of identity is a major task of adolescence, how do we do it? One critical way is by taking the cultural rules learned during our childhood and testing them out during adolescence. Often this involves the type of direct challenges teenagers' parents around the world know only too well: Why do I have to be in by midnight? Who says I can't wear my hair like this? After the testing is a period of integrating the cultural practices and values we decide (often unconsciously) to keep. We then use these to make decisions about how we will live as autonomous adults rather than continuing to live as children guided by external, parental rules alone.

When the cultural rules are always changing, however, what happens to this process? This is, again, why the issues of cultural balance and mobility—and the age or ages when they occur—become very important. Often, at the very time TCKs should be testing and internalizing the customs and values of whatever culture they've grown up in, that whole world, its familiar culture, and their relationship to it can change overnight with one plane ride. While peers in their new (and old) community are internalizing the rules of culture and beginning to move out with budding confidence, TCKs are still trying to figure out what the rules are. They aren't free to explore their personal gifts and talents because they're still preoccupied with what is or isn't appropriate behavior. Children who have to learn to juggle many sets of cultural rules at the same time have a different developmental experience from children growing up in one basically permanent, dominant culture that they regard as their own.

Some TCKs experience delayed development because of an extended compliance to cultural rules. In certain situations, TCKs are not as free as peers at home might be to test cultural rules during their teenage years. For instance, some TCKs need to comply with the status quo in a given situation for their own safety and acceptance. Instead of freedom to hang out with friends in shopping malls or on the street corners, many TCKs find themselves restricted, perhaps for safety reasons, to the military base or missionary compound. If they don't want to be kidnapped or robbed, they must obey regulations that might not be necessary in the home country. Also, some TCKs belong to organizations with fairly rigid rules of what its members (and their families) may and may not do. An embassy kid doing drugs or a missionary daughter who gets pregnant can result in a quick repatriation for the family. In such cases not only might the parents lose their jobs, but the TCKs might also lose what they consider to be home. This adds pressure to follow community standards longer than they might otherwise. When TCKs aren't as free as their friends in the home country might be to make some of the decisions about where they will go and what they will do, they must often wait to begin the normal adolescent process of testing parental and societal rules until a later period in life than usual—often to the shock of their parents.

As we saw with "The Delusion of Choice," the fact that life is often unpredictable makes it hard for many TCKs to make decisions. It's hard to make a competent decision if the basis used to decide something is always changing. Also as mentioned before, a TCK's lifestyle in many third culture communities is frequently dictated by the sponsoring agency. If the U.S. Navy assigns a parent for a six-month deployment, it doesn't matter what the TCK does or doesn't decide about it—that parent will be going. For these reasons and probably more, some TCKs don't learn to take responsibility for the direction of their lives. They are more prone to just "letting it happen."

TCKs who are separated from their parents during adolescence may not have the normal opportunity of challenging and testing parental values and choices as others do. Those who were separated from their parents in early years find themselves wanting to cling to parental nurturing to make up for early losses. They don't want to move into adulthood yet. Still others who have spent years away from home may idealize their parents in almost fantasy form. To challenge anything about their parents would call that dream into question. In situations such as these above, we've seen many TCKs delay the normal adolescent process of differentiating their identity from that of their parents until their late twenties, or even into their thirties.

Incompatible educational and social factors also contribute to at least the appearance of delayed adolescence. The Danish TCK who graduates from an American-based international school may return to Denmark and discover that she must do two more years at the secondary level before moving on to university. Suddenly she is grouped with those younger than herself and treated as their peer. This is especially traumatic if she's become accustomed to being seen as older than her years.

The social slowness discussed earlier can contribute to delayed adolescence by severely impeding the normal developmental task of establishing and maintaining strong relationships—particularly with peers and members of the opposite sex. Judith Gjoen, a Dutch

ATCK who grew up in Indonesia and is now a clinical counselor in Norway, wrote about the difficulties Europeans face on their return home after attending a predominantly international school.

> Dating is very American. Scandinavian ways of interrelating between the sexes are much more informal. There is much more flexibility in the sex roles. All boys learn to knit, all girls learn carpentry. Furthermore, a young person's identity is not so strongly connected to "dating status." From a Scandinavian perspective, the American way can be slightly overdone and hysterical. You are not prepared for the European way of being together [males and females] when you are socialized into an American system.[4]

The development of other social skills may also be delayed by not knowing the unwritten rules in the TCK's age group back home or in the new culture. How loud do you play music? How long do you talk on the phone? When do you engage in chitchat and when in deeper conversations? How do you behave with a friend of the opposite sex? When the rules around them have changed, TCKs sometimes retreat into isolation from others rather than try to cope.

Sometimes the very maturity noted earlier coupled with the sometimes more hidden delayed adolescence may lead to unforeseen problems. The initial attraction of a young TCK to older, more mature people may result in the choosing of an older marriage partner. Unfortunately, while the "early maturity" of the TCK may make such a match seem like a good idea, the deeper delay in development may scuttle the relationship later on. Sometimes the TCK isn't as ready for the responsibility or partnership of marriage as he or she appeared to be because the issues of personal identity, good decision making, and ability to build strong relationships haven't been resolved. Other times, as in any marriage, when the younger partner goes on to develop a deeper, truer maturity, the older spouse doesn't always continue to grow at the same rate. This can leave the younger partner disappointed, disillusioned, or dissatisfied.

Uneven maturity offers almost paradoxical benefits and challenges, as do all other TCK characteristics. The very reasons for some of the delays in adolescence are rooted in the greatest benefits of the third culture experience. Once they are aware of and understand the process, however, TCKs and/or their parents can guard against a certain smugness or sense of elitism they sometimes exhibit about how "mature" they are, while at the same time not panicking about areas where they still need to catch up. Given time, the maturity process will sort itself out into a more even flow as they, like others, move on through adolescence—delayed or not—into adulthood.

Delayed Adolescent Rebellion

A delayed adolescence is painful enough for the TCK who keeps wondering why he or she can't be like others, but even more painful—not only for TCKs but for their families as well—is a delayed adolescent rebellion, a time when the normal testing of rules either starts unexpectedly late or becomes exaggerated in an all-out, open defiance of nearly every possible convention the family and/or community holds dear and extends far beyond the adolescent years. Obviously, this type of rebellion also occurs in families that don't live abroad, but we want to look at some specific reasons for a delayed rebellion in some TCKs and then at why it often continues later than the normal teenage years.

1. *Extension of delayed adolescence.* In any journey to adulthood, there are always those who, in the process of testing the rules of their upbringing, decide they will avoid adults' expectations, no matter what. For whatever reasons, they assume an "anti-identity." This process of rebellion is often an offshoot of normal adolescent testing of cultural norms. When the time for that normal process is delayed for all the reasons mentioned above, the rebellion that often comes during that time will also be delayed.

2. *End of the need for compliance.* Sometimes it seems that young people who have been forced to comply with a fairly rigorous system throughout their teenage years decide to try everything they couldn't do before, once they are finally free from those external restraints. Rather than the usual process of testing rules a few at a time while still under a parent's watchful eye, they go off to university and seemingly "go off the deep end."

This form of rebellion may actually be a positive—though slightly misguided—move toward independence. In these situations, parents and others may need to understand the reason for the behavior and be patient in the process, while also pointing out (when possible) that some of this behavior may be counterproductive to the goal of independence they seek.

3. *Loneliness.* Sometimes the rebellion is a plea for help. We have met many TCKs who have tried to express to their parents that they need a home base; that they feel desperately lonely when vacation time comes and everyone else goes home and they stay in the dorm because their parents are still overseas and relatives in the home country seem like strangers; or that they are struggling in school and want to quit. But the parents never seem to hear. Instead, they send e-mail messages with platitudes like "Cheer up," "It will get better," or "Trust God"; or they explain once more why they need to stay in the job they're in.

Eventually, some TCKs finally scream, through their behavior, the message they have not been able to communicate verbally: "I need you to come *home*—to be near me." When they get arrested for drugs, or get pregnant, or try to commit suicide, they know their parents will come—at least for a short period. Unfortunately, the parents who didn't hear the earlier verbal or nonverbal messages often don't understand, even at this point of major rebellion, the deep loneliness and longing their child is experiencing. They judge the rebellion without understanding the reason, and a deeper wedge than ever is driven between parent and child.

At that point, the TCK's behavior may become more extreme than before, and whatever form the rebellion takes—drugs, alcohol, workaholism, some esoteric cause—becomes a way in itself to numb the pain of longing for some type of security and home base. The sad thing is that until the loneliness and longing are addressed, the TCK will stay walled off, often in very destructive behavior, fulfilling the worst prophecies made about him or her.

4. *Anger.* One of the common manifestations of unresolved grief, anger, may erupt in this time of rebellion and intensify it. The anger may be directed at parents, the system they've grown up in, their home country, God, or other targets. Unfortunately, once again people don't always stop to find out what's behind the explosion. The judgment and rejection of the TCK's experience increases the pain and leads to further anger and rebellion.

There is another situation that may be the cause of anger. TCKs who have spent many years physically apart from their parents may, as we said, unrealistically idealize them. As young adults, these TCKs begin to discover their own imperfections, realize their parents aren't perfect either, and not only become angry at the loss of their fantasy but also begin to blame their parents for the lack of perfection in *themselves*. "If I'd just lived a normal life or had better parents, I wouldn't be struggling the way I am now." While anger against parents for imperfections in ourselves is probably a normal part of the developmental process for everyone, TCK or not, when parents remain overseas, working through it can be difficult for all concerned.

The bottom line is that no matter what the reason for the anger, it's often turned against the parents and may be expressed in an almost punitive rebellion—the TCKs want to hurt those whom they feel hurt them.

A major problem with delayed adolescent rebellion, however, is that rebellion in the mid to late twenties may have a destructive effect far beyond that of teenage rebellion.

> Pierre was a diplomat's son from Switzerland, who grew up in four different South American countries. During his early twenties, when friends asked how he had liked his nomadic lifestyle, he always replied, "Oh, I loved it! It never bothered me to pack up and move. We always knew there was something very exciting ahead. I've lived in nine different countries."
>
> After marriage and three children, however, the story changed. Certain job situations didn't work out. He became tired of trying to find ways to support his wife and children. In the end, he became totally disenchanted with family life and the attendant responsibilities and simply walked away from every-thing he'd apparently valued before. "I've spent my life," he replied to those who questioned him, "doing what everyone else wanted me to do and I'm tired of it. Now I'm finally going to do whatever I want to do."

We stress that this type of rebellion is neither desirable nor neces-sary. The TCK as well as parents, family, and friends are all wounded in this process. Being aware of some of the reasons delayed rebel-lion occurs may sometimes prevent it, or it may help the family deal with delayed adolescence in its early stages, so they aren't held pris-oners to destructive behavior. Perhaps the best preventive measure parents and other adults can take against this type of rebellion is to make sure, even in situations where their TCKs are raised in a strong organizational (or family) system, that there are opportunities for the children to make real choices in matters that don't compromise their safety or the agency's effectiveness. Most important, TCKs and ATCKs who read these lines and recognize themselves need to know they have the choice to take responsibility for their own ac-tions and find help for their behavior rather than continuing to blame others for how awful their lives have been or become. (See chapter 18 for further help in this area.)

Identity in a "System"

TCKs who grow up in the subculture of the parents' sponsoring organization have a few extra factors to deal with in this process of establishing a sense of identity. Although in reality these issues are extensions of what we have already talked about, it's important to understand how growing up in what is often a fairly structured community can be one more factor in a TCK's developmental process.

There can be many strong benefits to living in a carefully defined system. In many situations, the whole system of the sponsoring organization serves to some extent as both family and community. It provides materially as a good parent might, with air travel paid for, housing provided, and perhaps special stores made available. In many cases, as mentioned earlier, it also provides specific guidance or regulations for behavior.

An organizational system is one of the places where the need for belonging can truly be fulfilled because there are clear demarcations of who does and doesn't belong. Some TCKs have a deeper sense of belonging to that community than they will ever have with any other group and feel secure within the well-ordered structure of their particular system.

Other TCKs, however, feel stifled by the organizational system in which they grew up. They may be straining at the bit to get out of what they see as the rigid policies of the system. They realize that they have had almost no choice in countless matters that have deeply affected their lives—such as when and where their parents moved, where they could go to school, how to behave in certain common circumstances, or how they could express their inner passions. They see their organization as an uncaring nemesis and they feel intense rage at a system that requires conformity to rules and regulations regardless of individual preferences. Some blame the system for ruining their lives.

Certainly anyone who grows up in a clearly defined system is very much aware of how the group expects its members to behave. Failure to conform brings great shame on the TCK or the whole family. In many cases, the rules of these systems are a higher priority than the rules of the family, superseding decisions parents would normally make for their own children—such as when and where the children go to school.

What might make the difference in how or why an organizational system seems so positive for one person and restrictive for another?

At the risk of oversimplifying, and recognizing that there are many differences in how each agency may be run, we have identified four basic ways TCKs relate to the system in which they grew up—from the perspective of their own personal makeup, gifts, and personality. Understanding this picture can help us answer the above question.

1. *A TCK who fits the system.* Feeling comfortable is relatively easy for those whose personality and interests fit pretty well within the structure or rules of the system under which they have grown up. It might be an easygoing military kid who never seems to question authority, a pragmatic missionary kid who doesn't see the point of the fancy accessories in a Lexus, or a diplomat's kid who is an extrovert and thrives on meeting new people. They can go along with how life works in this system, and it doesn't conflict with how they think, what they like to do, what they want to be, or, most important, who they are by their very nature. There is room in this system to express who they are. It's a pretty good match.

2. *A TCK who doesn't fit the system but attempts to conform.* Other children don't match the system as well. Secretly, they prefer rap, while others around are denouncing it as junk. They long for color and beautiful decor but live in a plain, brown, adobe-type home within a system that feels it isn't spiritual to focus on worldly beauty. They find crowds of new people frightening, but they paste on a smile and act cordial to the dignitaries at never-ending receptions. They have learned not to reveal their feelings or desires because they learned early on that it was

wrong to feel or think that way. Instead of being able to explore the mystery of their own personality and set of gifts, they feel ashamed of this secret longing and try harder and harder to be what they perceive the system says they should be.

The major problem for members of this second group is that their sense of identity comes almost totally from an external system rather than from who they are deep within. If this type of conformity doesn't change at some point, people in this group may become more and more rigid over the years in adhering to the system that now defines them. They fear that if they let any part of it go, they will lose themselves because they don't know who they are without this structure to hold them together.

3. *A person who doesn't completely fit the system but doesn't realize (or at least doesn't seem to mind) it.* People in this group go ahead and listen to rap—not to be rebellious but because they like it. It doesn't occur to them—or worry them—that others might disapprove. If told that others might disapprove, they would likely respond, "That's O.K. If they do, I'll use my earphones." They stay in their rooms and read—not because they're rejecting the social scene, but because they love to read. They make decisions that don't quite match those of everyone else—not for the sake of being different but simply because they prefer the way they've chosen. They don't feel compelled to be exactly like everyone else but are happy to join with others when they do share an interest. Perhaps they have the inner security to be independent because many of their foundational needs for relationship and belonging have been well met in early years within their family. Maybe it just happens to be one of the attributes of their personality. Either way, they are discovering and operating from who they are inside rather than letting their environment define them.

4. *A person who doesn't fit the system, knows it, and spends his or her life proving it.* People in this fourth group like to think of themselves as members of the group just discussed, but they're

not. For whatever reasons, they learned early on that at least parts of them didn't fit the system. Perhaps they cried their first night at boarding school and were told to be brave—but they couldn't stop crying. Maybe they honestly wanted to know why things should be done one way rather than another but were given the unsatisfactory reply, "Because I said so." Still, the burning question inside wouldn't go away. Unfortunately, as they keep bumping into something that doesn't fit them inside, some TCKs finally decide—consciously or unconsciously—to throw out everything the system stands for. They'll be anything *but* that system.

The irony is that these outwardly rebellious TCKs actually get their identity from the very system they're rejecting. People who are determined to prove who they are *not* rarely go on to discover who they *are*.

It's important to remember that it's not wrong to be part of a strong organizational system. An organization is an efficient and necessary way of forming a community into functional groups, usually for the purpose of accomplishing a common goal. We can relate to it; be part of it; and even have some of our core needs of belonging met by it. But it's not, by itself, who we are.

Once that's understood, TCKs and ATCKs can take a better look at their group and determine which parts of the system do or don't fit with who they are, keeping in mind that they don't have to reject or retain an entire system.

By the time we sort through these many challenges, it's easy to wonder once again how any TCK can survive. Dirk, a German TCK who grew up in Taiwan and went to university in the United States, has learned to live with the challenge of many cultures and places by living fully in whichever one he is currently in while not denying the others are also part of his life. He uses a computer metaphor to describe this phenomenon.

> I just build windows. When I'm in America, I activate
> the American window. When I'm in Germany, I
> activate the German window and the American
> window goes on the back burner—and so do the
> people in it.

In summary, when thinking about TCKs' identity and development issues, don't forget the interweaving of challenges with great benefits. TCKs find in their experience numerous opportunities for fulfilling their basic human needs in the most profound ways of all, and they often emerge with a very secure self-identity. We have seen that TCKs who dare to wrestle through the hard questions of life can develop a deep and solid sense of purpose and values that go deeper than those who are not forced to sort through such questions to the same degree. In addition, the exposure to philosophical, political, and social matters which are almost part and parcel of the TCK experience means there is every potential for substantive intellectual development. By its diversity alone, a TCK's world creates questions to ponder. This is one aspect of personhood that has every potential of being filled to overflowing for TCKs. Of all the TCKs we have met or worked with, very few would ever exchange the richness of their lives to avoid the inevitable challenges they have faced along the way.

Endnotes

[1] Sophia Morton, "Let Us Possess One World," see Appendix B.

[2] Sharon Willmer, "Personhood, Forgiveness, and Comfort," in *Compendium of the ICMK: New Directions in Mission: Implications for MKs*, edited by Beth Tetzel and Patricia Mortenson (West Brattleboro, VT: ICMK): 103–18.

[3] Ruth Hill Useem and Ann Baker Cottrell, "TCKs Experience Prolonged Adolescence," *Newslinks* 13, no. 1 (September 1993): 1.

[4] Judith Gjoen, personal letter to David C. Pollock, November 1995.

11

Unresolved Grief

There was no funeral.
No flowers.
No ceremony.
No one had died.
No weeping or wailing,
Just in my heart.
I can't...
But I did anyway,
and nobody knew I couldn't.
I don't want to...
But nobody else said they didn't.
So I put down my panic
and picked up my luggage
and got on the plane.
There was no funeral.[1]

—"Mock Funeral"
by Alex Graham James

Next to sorting out their sense of personal identity, unresolved grief ranks as the second greatest challenge TCKs face. "But what do TCKs have to grieve about?" people often ask. "They've had such exciting lives."

Yes, many have. For that very reason, some TCKs refuse to accept the idea that unresolved grief could possibly be an issue for them. They agree they've had wonderful, interesting lives. Who else has seen the world, traveled to all sorts of fascinating places where few others have been, speaks exotic languages, and enjoys different foods the way they have? What is there to grieve for?

While there is no single reason unresolved grief is a major—and often unrecognized—factor for countless TCKs, many of them experience this grief *because* of the very richness of their lives. We only grieve when we lose people or things we love or that matter greatly to us, and most TCKs have much they love in their childhoods. Much of what they love—and then lose—however, are intangible parts of their world (e.g., the sights, sounds, and smell of market day or the call of a particular bird each morning). Other losses, such as never seeing a best friend again, are more tangible and certainly happen to non-TCKs as well, but as we have seen, for most TCKs the collection of significant losses and separations before the end of adolescence is often more than most people experience in a lifetime. Still, while we may agree that all losses (whether recognized or not and no matter how small or how big) set in motion a grief reaction, the question remains: why do a significant number of TCKs struggle with *unresolved* grief? Some of the reasons we suggest in this chapter—followed by ways TCKs express unresolved grief—may seem obvious now that we better understand the totality of their experience. However, because this unresolved grief is such a major and potentially crippling issue for TCKs if not dealt with, we want to collect the many possible causes of it—both tangible and intangible— that have been touched on throughout our discussion of the TCK Profile and bring them all into direct focus. With a clearer definition of the problem, we hope to prepare the reader for the discussion in the ensuing chapters on how to make the most of the TCK experience.

Reasons for Unresolved Grief

Fear of Denying the Good

It seems some TCKs believe that acknowledging any pain in their past will negate the many joys they have known. To admit how sad it was to leave Grandma in the home country feels like a denial of how glad they were to return to their friends in the host country. To say it was hard to leave the village they grew up in might mean they don't appreciate all the effort relatives in the home country have gone to in preparing for their return. Until these TCKs can acknowledge that proper mourning for the inevitable losses in their lives is an affirmation of the richness of the past rather than a negation of the present, they will continue to deny any grief they have felt.

Hidden Losses

Many intangible losses are tucked in amid the many benefits of a TCK's life, creating a special problem for dealing with the grief related to each loss. Because these losses are hidden, they are most often unnoticed. Because they are unrecognized, the TCK's grief for them is also unrecognized—and thus unresolved. We call them the "hidden losses."

Many of these hidden losses are also recurring ones. The exact loss may not repeat itself, but the same *types* of losses happen again and again, and the unresolved grief accumulates. What are some of these hidden losses?

Loss of their world. With one plane ride a TCK's whole world can die. Every place that's been important, every tree they've climbed, every pet they've had, and virtually every close friend they've made are gone with the closing of the airplane door. TCKs don't lose one thing at a time; they lose everything, but there's no funeral. In fact, there's no time or space to grieve, because tomorrow they'll be in Bangkok to see the sights, then fly to four other exciting places before getting to Grandma's house and seeing the relatives who are eagerly awaiting their return. How could they be sad? As they continue to move from one world to another, this type of loss occurs over and over.

Loss of status. With that plane ride also comes a loss of status. Whether in their home or host country, many TCKs have settled in enough to establish a place of significance for themselves. They know where they belong in the current scene and are recognized for who they are and what they can contribute. All at once, not only their world but their place in it is gone. As they travel back and forth between home and host country, this loss is also repeated.

Loss of lifestyle. Whether it's biking down rutty paths to the open-air market, taking a ferry to school, buying favorite goodies at the commissary or PX, or having dependable access to electricity and water—that too can change overnight. Suddenly, there's too much traffic for bike riding, stuffy buses carry everyone to school, local stores don't have what you want, or electricity and water supplies can go off for three days at a time. All the patterns of daily living are gone and with it the sense of security and competency that are so vital to us all. Indeed, these are major losses.

Loss of possessions. This loss doesn't refer to possessions of monetary value but to the loss of things that connect TCKs to their past and, again, their security. Because of weight limits on airplanes, favorite toys are sold. Tree houses remain nested in the foliage waiting for the next attaché's family. Evacuations during political crises mean nothing can be taken along. And so it goes.

> At one conference, TCKs were asked to name some of their hidden losses. All sorts of answers popped up:
>
> "My country" (meaning the host country).
>
> "Separation from my siblings because of boarding school."
>
> "My dog."
>
> "My history."
>
> "My tree."
>
> "My place in the community."

"Our dishes."

Dishes? Why that?

"We'd lived in Venezuela the whole eighteen years since I'd been born. I felt so sad as I watched my parents sell our furniture. But when we got back to England and my mom unpacked, I suddenly realized she hadn't even brought our dishes. I said, 'Mum, how could you do that? Why didn't you bring them?' She replied, 'They were cracked, and it's easier to buy new ones here.' She didn't understand those were the dishes we'd used whenever my friends came over, for our family meals, for everything. They were not replaceable because they held our family history."

The lack of opportunity to take most personal possessions from one place to another is one of the differences in international mobility compared with mobility within a particular country. If someone moves from Amsterdam to Rotterdam, usually a mover comes, loads up the furniture and dishes along with everything else, and drives the truck to the new home. Although the house and city may be different, at least familiar pictures can go up on the wall, the favorite recliner can be placed in the living room, and some sense of connectedness to the past remains.

In international and intercontinental moves, shipping the entire household is often impossible. Shipping costs a lot more than the furniture is worth. Instructions come from the organization or business (or parents) to keep only those possessions that can fit into a suitcase. Many things are too big or bulky to pack. It seems simpler to start over again at the next place with new things.

Loss of relationships. Not only do many people constantly come and go in the TCKs' world, but among these chronically disrupted relationships are the core relationships of life—the ones between parent and child, siblings, grandparents, aunts, uncles, cousins, and close friends. Dad or Mom may go to sea for six months. Grandparents and other extended family members aren't merely a town or state away, they're an ocean away. Education choices such as boarding school or staying in the home country for high school can create major patterns of separation for families when the children are still young. Many TCKs who return to their home countries for secondary school grow up as strangers to their brothers and sisters, who remain in the host country with their parents during those same years.

> Until Ruth Van Reken was thirty-nine and started writing the journal that turned into *Letters Never Sent* (the story of her own TCK journey), she had no idea that the day her parents and siblings left her in the States and returned to Nigeria for four years was the day her family, as she had always known it, died. Never again did all six children live with two parents as a family unit for any extended period of time. As she wrote, Ruth allowed herself to experience for the first time the grief of that moment twenty-six years before—a grief almost as deep as if she had just had a phone call that her family had been killed in a car wreck.

> In another case, Courtney stayed with grandparents in the States for high school, while her folks were in Saudi Arabia. She says, "I didn't feel nearly so much that I was always going somewhere as that I was always being left. I felt abandoned."

Loss of role model. In the same way we "catch" culture almost instinctively from those around us, we also learn what to expect at upcoming stages of life by observing and interacting with people already in those stages.

In a gathering of older ATCKs, we again asked the question, "What are your hidden losses?" One gentleman answered, "Role models." He had only recently realized that during his twelve years in a boarding school from ages six to eighteen, he had not had a model for a father who was involved in his family's life. Although a successful businessman, he had been married and divorced four times and remained estranged from his adult children.

From our role models, we decide what and who we want to be like when we are adults. We also believe that another potential factor in some TCKs' delayed adolescent response is that while living overseas as teenagers, they aren't around peers from their home culture in the age group just ahead of them—the university or beginning career age group—and so they are deprived of role models for young adulthood.

Loss of system identity. As mentioned before, many TCKs grow up within the friendly (a few might say unfriendly) confines of a strong sponsoring organizational structure, which becomes part of their identity. They have instant recognition as a member of this group. Then at age twenty-one the commissary card is cut up, the support for education stops, invitations to organizational functions cease, and they are on their own as "adults." TCKs understand this mentally and probably maintain personal friends within the original system, but their sense of loss that they are no longer part of that system is real. In fact, some have told us it feels like they were disowned by their own families

Loss of the past that wasn't. Some TCKs feel deep grief over what they see as the irretrievable losses of their childhood. They remember the graduation ceremony parents couldn't attend because they were a continent away and know the chance will never come again. They wish they could have gone to school where they could have studied in their native language. Some regret that they had to return to their home country when their parents did; they wanted to stay in the host country.

> Chris, a Finnish TCK, returned to Helsinki after a childhood in Namibia. While living there, separation from extended family seemed normal. All the other TCKs she knew had done the same. But that hadn't been the experience of her Finnish relatives. One evening, just after Christmas, Chris listened to her cousins reminisce about their childhood in Finland. They talked of family Christmas traditions, summer

vacations at the family cottage on the lake, birthday celebrations and weddings when the family gathered. Suddenly, Chris felt overwhelmed by what she had missed growing up. Later, in a gathering of TCKs from various countries, Chris spoke of how living overseas had robbed her of knowing the closeness of her extended family back home.

Loss of the past that was. While some TCKs grieve for experiences they missed, other TCKs grieve for the past no longer available to them. People who live as adults in the same country where they grew up can usually go back and revisit their old house, school, playground, and church. In spite of inevitable changes, they can still reminisce "on site," but a highly mobile TCK often lacks this opportunity.

****

In any of the types of hidden losses we've just mentioned, the main issue again is not the grief, per se. The problem is that in these types of losses, no one actually died or was divorced, nothing was physically stolen. Contrary to obvious losses, there are no markers, no rites of passage recognizing them as they occur—no recognized way to mourn. Yet, each hidden loss relates to the major human needs of belonging, of feeling we are significant to others, and of being understood. The majority of TCKs are adults before they acknowledge and come to terms with the depth of their grief over any or all of these areas of hidden loss.

Hidden losses aren't the only reason for unresolved grief, however. Even when losses are recognized, other factors may prevent a healthy resolution of grief.

Lack of Permission to Grieve

ATCK Harry wrote the alumni magazine of his school in response to earlier letters in which various ATCKs had talked about painful issues from their childhood. "Stop fussing," he wrote. "Don't you think any kid in

the Harlem ghetto would trade places with you in a
second?"

Sometimes TCKs receive a very direct message that lets them know
it's not okay to express their fears or grief. Many are asked to be
"brave soldiers," perhaps particularly in the military and missionary
context. Colonialists' offspring were encouraged to "keep a stiff upper
lip." In *Military Brats,* Mary Wertsch writes of a girl who came
down the stairs one morning and asked her mom, "What would happen if Dad got shot in Vietnam?" The mother's instant reply was
"Don't—you—*ever*—say—that!"[2]

Also, when parents are doing such noble things—saving the
country from war or representing the government on delicate nego-
tiations or preaching salvation to a lost world—how can a child admit grief or fear? The child would feel too much shame for being
selfish, wrong, or not spiritual or patriotic enough if she or he acknowledged how much it hurt to leave or be left. In such situations,
TCKs may easily learn that negative feelings of almost any kind,
including grief, aren't allowed. They begin to wear a mask to cover
those feelings but conform to the expectations and socially approved
behavior of the community.

TCKs who grow up in a missionary community may face an
added burden. Some mission people see an admission of painful
feelings as weakness or, worse, a lack of faith. TCKs who want to
keep their faith often feel they can't acknowledge any pain they have
experienced. Conversely, other TCKs from such communities take
the opposite tack; they believe that in order to deal with their grief,
they must deny the faith they've been taught. They, too, have forgotten the paradoxical nature of the TCK experience.

Lack of Time to Process

Unresolved grief can also be the result of insufficient time to process the losses. Any person who experiences loss needs a period of
time to face the pain, mourn and accept the loss, come to closure,
and move on. In the era when most international travelers went over-

seas by ship, the trip could take weeks, providing a built-in transition period that allowed time for the grieving process. In today's world of jet travel, however, there is literally no transition, no time or space to deal properly with the inevitable grief of losing what has been left behind.

Lack of Comfort

The presence or lack of comfort is another huge factor in whether grief is resolved. In 1984 Sharon Willmer first identified this as a key issue when she wrote Dave Pollock, "If someone were to ask me, 'From your experience as a therapist and friend of [TCKs], what do you see as the [TCKs'] greatest need?' I would reply, beyond the shadow of a doubt...that they need to be comforted and helped to understand what it means to be a person."[3] We've already looked at the issues relating to personal identity, but to understand why we need comfort and why it's often missing for TCKs, we must first look at what comfort is and isn't and how it differs from encouragement.

Merriam-Webster's Collegiate Dictionary defines *comfort* as "consolation in time of trouble or worry."[4] Comfort doesn't change the situation itself, nor can it take away the pain, but it relays the message that someone cares and understands. Comfort validates grief and gives permission for the grieving process to take place. For example, when a person walks up to a widow standing by her husband's casket and puts an arm around her shoulder, that gesture, with or without words, is comforting. It can't bring the husband back to life or stop the tears or the pain, but it lets the widow know her grief is accepted and understood. She's not alone in her sorrow.

Unfortunately, in their very efforts to help another person "feel better," people often confuse comfort with encouragement and end up giving neither. Encouragement is a person's attempt to change the griever's perspective. It may be a reminder to look at the bright side of a situation instead of the loss or to think about a past success and presume this present situation will turn out just as successfully.

Obviously there's a time for both comfort and encouragement, but what happens if the two are confused? When the grieving widow is told that it's a good thing her husband at least had a substantial life insurance policy, how does she feel? Neither comforted nor encouraged! When encouragement is given before comfort, the subtle or not so subtle message is "Buck up, you *shouldn't* feel so low." It becomes a shame message rather than encouragement.

Perhaps because a TCK's losses are often far less visible than the widow's, it's this mix-up between comfort and encouragement that can sometimes keep TCKs from being comforted. There are several ways people may unknowingly try to encourage rather than comfort TCKs and thus do neither.

Discounting grief. As TCKs and their families prepare to board the plane, Mom and Dad admonish them not to cry, and say, "Don't worry. You'll make new friends quickly once we get there." In not acknowledging the pain involved in the good-bye, they communicate the hidden message that their son or daughter *shouldn't* be so sad. What's the big deal about saying good-bye to these friends when they can be so easily replaced? Somehow, though, the TCKs still feel sad and end up thinking something must be wrong with *them*. After a while there is nothing to do but bury the pain.

Comparing grief to a higher good. When TCKs express sadness at an approaching move or loss, adults may try to cheer them up with the reminder that the reasons behind this lifestyle—and thus the losses involved—are of such importance (defending or representing the country, saving the world, earning enough money to pay for the child's later educational bills) that the TCKs *shouldn't* complain about a few hardships along the way. Unfortunately, this is not comforting. Often, TCKs already understand—and often agree with—the reason why their parents have a particular career and lifestyle. Most TCKs aren't asking their parents to change. All they're trying to say is that, in spite of what they *know*, it still hurts to leave friends and a place they love dearly. When that opportunity to express sadness is denied, some TCKs begin to develop a sense of shame regarding their feelings.

Denying grief. It's not only TCKs who may deny their grief. Adults around them often do the same. To comfort another person, to say "I understand," is to admit there's a reason for grieving. Adults who busily mask their own sense of loss by denial can't afford to admit they understand the sad TCK. If they did, their own internal protective structures might tumble down and leave them quite un-protected. One therapist asked us if anyone had ever done a study on how parents react when they know they must send those kids away to school at age six. Bowlby[5] and others have written about how early separations between parents and children affect a child's abil-ity to later attach to those parents or others, but we know of no offi-cial study regarding how parents cope in such situations. We have heard, however, from ATCKs who speak of how their parents stopped hugging them in their early years so they wouldn't "miss it" when they left for school at age six.

Again, the losses TCKs encounter—recognized or unrecog-nized—and the grief that follows aren't, in themselves, the biggest problems. They are natural and when we can grieve openly for what we have lost, it's "good grief"—a productive way to deal with the pain. The problem is *unresolved* grief, and because it isn't dealt with directly, it emerges in other forms—forms that are destructive and that can last a lifetime. That's "bad grief."

Expressions of Unresolved Grief

Unresolved grief will always express itself somehow. Often it will be in ways that appear completely unrelated to feelings of grief. The following are some typical reactions to unresolved grief.

Denial

Some TCKs refuse to admit to themselves the amount of sadness they have felt. "It didn't bother me to leave my parents for boarding school when I was six. I was so excited to go that once I got on the train, I didn't even think about them anymore." While this may be their conscious recollection of events, they forget that if a six-year-old *doesn't* miss Mommy and Daddy when he or she leaves for months at a time, something must be fundamentally wrong with that relationship—or they have already disconnected. Grief is normal when separating from those we love.

Others admit these separations were painful but claim to have gotten over them. Yet, as we've already seen, they continue to live lives that wall out close relationships to others—including spouses and children.

Anger

The most common responses triggered by unresolved grief are defensiveness and a quick, flashing anger at seemingly small circumstances. These types of responses can have devastating consequences in every context: marriage, work, social relationships, and parenting. For some, the anger is sublimated and eventually finds expression when TCKs take up a "righteous cause." They can defend the need for justice, environmental matters, civil rights, political reform, or religious practices with adamancy and vigor because no one can argue with their sense of outrage on such matters. Those who try will, of course, be seen as fools. This is not to say TCKs and others shouldn't be involved with such issues, but there is often a level of intensity which seems to go beyond the cause itself.

In any of these situations, people complain about how difficult the angry TCK is to live, work, or deal with, but few try to understand the pain behind the anger. Somewhere along the way, the TCK decided the pain was simply too much to bear and replaced grieving with anger as anesthesia for the pain. Unfortunately, anger ultimately increases the pain as the TCK's world becomes more isolated and lonely; no one wants to be near such an angry person.

Depression

Depression is another manifestation of unresolved grief. When there's no opportunity to acknowledge their feelings externally, people often turn those feelings inward. When too much grief gets bottled up for too long, depression can set in. Of course, depression (as well as denial, anger, and withdrawal) is a normal stage of any grieving process and must be respected as such. The problem, however, is getting stuck in this stage, because they have never been able to name the grief and mourn the loss.

Withdrawal

Grief can also be expressed through withdrawal. For parents, a child's withdrawal can be painful. How many parents have been deeply hurt by only sporadic letters from their child? by phone calls that are erratic and monosyllabic at best? by only superficial conversation during infrequent reunions? They don't realize withdrawal is a way to protect from pain. This withdrawal may also be a conscious or unconscious way to strike out at parents and hurt them for "dragging me away from the place I love"—be it home or host country.

We've heard story after story from parents of TCKs whose adult children were in the midst of a life crisis but told their parents, "Don't come. You can't do anything." Parents are often confused, not knowing what to do. They fail to recognize that their children might well deny their need for support rather than risk being disappointed once more that no one will be physically or emotionally present in their times of crisis.

Rebellion

If the normal anger felt in any grief situation isn't dealt with, it can easily take the form of extreme rebellion. For some, rebellion takes an inward, silent form; for others, it's blatant and loud. Either way, rebellion becomes the nearly impenetrable shield behind which the pain is deeply hidden. Each time a new circumstance comes that threatens to break through the fragile protection and expose the pain, it's like something inside the TCK metaphorically grabs a trowel and plaster to reinforce the shield. Until he or she is willing to let the protection be gently removed so the wound can be exposed to light and air, however, healing cannot begin.

Vicarious Grief

Transferring the focus from personal grief to that of others is another way to express unresolved grief. A TCK might sit at an airport weeping as he or she watches total strangers say good-bye. Some TCKs go into professions where this vicarious grief finds a more active, long-term expression.

> As a child, ATCK Joan spent twelve years in boarding schools. On a conscious level, she remembered the fun of game nights, the senior banquet, and the lifelong friends she had made. She denied any particular sadness from these years of family separation, outside of the initial tears of farewell in first and second grades.
>
> After university, however, Joan found herself working in a day-care center. She explained her choice of career by saying, "I just want to help kids whose parents must work not to feel lonely. I like to sit and hug them all day so they know they're wanted and loved. Kids need to be nurtured,"
>
> Joan realized after several years that she was excessively involved with every child under her care, trying to protect each one from emotional pain. Her anger sparked against parents who forgot to bring their child's favorite teddy bear. She fought with other workers if they sharply reprimanded a child.
>
> Finally, Joan began to recognize that her deep involvement with these children reflected more than a normal concern for them. It stemmed from the extreme loneliness she had felt when separated from her own parents during her years at boarding school, which began when she was six. Instead of directly dealing with the loss of day-to-day parenting she had experienced, Joan had unconsciously tried to deal with her own grief by making sure no child under her care would feel that same pain.

Even ATCKs who don't express their grief through a profession often become the "rescuers" of the community. For whatever reasons, they are the unofficial dorm counselors, the ones who befriend lonely people, who may take in the homeless. All of these can, in fact, be noble and positive gestures, but if their activities substitute for working out their own grief, eventually their behavior will become counterproductive. They may be so involved in rescuing others that they never rescue themselves.

Delayed Grief

TCKs may go through life without showing or consciously feeling any particular sadness and suddenly find to their great surprise that a seemingly small incident triggers a huge reaction.

> For ATCK Dan, it was the first day his son, Tommy, went off to kindergarten. Dan should have been happy that Tommy was starting this new phase of life. School was only one block away, so Dan walked Tommy right to the door, said good-bye, turned around to walk away—and found himself unable to see the sidewalk for the tears that filled his eyes. Once back home, his body sagged against the door as he sobbed uncontrollably. His wife couldn't imagine what had happened. "Is everything all right? Is Tommy O.K.?" Dan could only shake his head as his body continued to shudder with pain.
>
> Dan was experiencing delayed grief. As he left his son at school, he suddenly had a flashback of his own departure for first grade. But the picture was different from how his son was beginning school. For Dan, the new picture put him inside a small, one-engine plane with four other schoolkids as it took off from a grassy airstrip. He could still see his parents standing on the edge of the forest waving to him. The memory of what he had felt while returning their farewell wave hit like an engulfing tide as he turned away from Tommy that morning.

Often the people most surprised by the delayed grief are those feeling it. What amazes so many ATCKs is that the grief from losses they have never consciously defined seems to hit them hardest between the ages of twenty-five and forty. Often the first glimmerings of their unrecognized grief begin when they have their own children. Sometimes that's when they first ask themselves, "If my parents loved me as much as I love this baby, how could they have ever let me go away?" Or they must face the fact they aren't the perfect parents they were expecting to be. Even without children, many begin to realize there's a good chance that the rootlessness, withdrawal from close relationships, or whatever they're experiencing isn't going to change no matter how much they change their circumstances. At that point, it's easy for ATCKs to think that if they had lived a "normal" life, they wouldn't have problems. They begin to blame others; then family and friends are shocked that this ATCK who "never had any problems" seems suddenly to be conjuring up all sorts of fantastic painful experiences. Finally, most ATCKs begin to face the fact that some answers for their reactions to life reside inside themselves rather than in outside events and situations. This is the time many finally examine some of this unresolved grief, work through it, and move on in productive, adult ways from having gone through the grieving process.

****

Now that we have looked in detail at the TCK experience itself, we will move on to specific, constructive ways we all—TCK, ATCK, parents, relatives, friends, and sponsors alike—can be involved in maximizing the great potential benefits of this third culture life and dealing with the challenges in healthy ways so that the drawbacks, too, become part of the TCK's strength and gifts.

Endnotes

1   Unpublished poem by ATCK Alex Graham James, used with permission.

2   Wertsch, *Military Brats*, 44.

3   Sharon Willmer (personal letter to David C. Pollock, 1984).

4   *Merriam-Webster's Collegiate Dictionary,* 10th ed., *s.v.* "comfort."

5   John Bowlby, cited in Terry M. Levy and Michael Orlans, "Intensive Short-term Therapy with Attachment-Disordered Children," in *Innovations in Clinical Practice: A Source Book,* Vol. 14, edited by L. VandeCreek, S. Knapp, and T. L. Jackson (Sarasota, FL: Professional Resource Press, 1995).

Section Two
Maximizing the
Benefits

12

Building a Strong Foundation

Wise cross-cultural parenting doesn't just happen. Moving to a new culture far from familiar support systems causes new stress for everyone, and parents often need to learn new parenting skills and practices. Below are some questions parents should consider before committing their family to such a major move.

1. *What are family needs that require attention regardless of location?* A child's age and level in school can be especially important factors to consider. For example, the last two years of secondary school aren't usually a good time to uproot teenagers. Not only will they miss graduating with their friends, but they probably won't be able to plan for what they want to do after they graduate. If they decide to further their education they won't have the opportunity to visit different universities and evaluate which would be the best one to attend the following year. Does any child have a learning or physical disability or a chronic medical condition that requires special care? If so, parents must make sure those needs can be met in the new location. Will home schooling or tutoring be sufficient if special education programs aren't available in the regular school? Will medical facilities be adequate?

2. *What are the policies of the sending agency?* Does the agency look carefully at family and educational needs when moving its personnel? Parents need to read the stated policies, but more important, perhaps, they need to talk with others who work for the organization and have already faced similar situations. This will give a much clearer picture of the reality of these policies.

3. *How will existing family patterns and relationships be affected by the move?* In the home culture, parents generally have a support system of extended family, friends, and people from school and church to help raise their kids. A cross-cultural move radically disrupts that support system.

> A Nigerian man told of the surprise he'd felt when he and his wife first moved to the States so he could pursue a graduate program. In Nigeria their family had lived in proximity to grandparents, aunts, and uncles, who often functioned as surrogate parents for their children. Finding a baby-sitter was never a problem. In the States, they were on their own. No one offered to take their children when they needed to go to class or to the store. The special nurturing that comes from living in an extended family had disappeared, and the couple had to develop completely new patterns of parenting.

4. *Do both spouses favor the move?* This is a key question. If both spouses aren't fully committed to a cross-cultural move, the experience often ends in disaster. A reluctance on the part of one spouse easily turns to resentment and hostility under the pressure of adjusting to the cross-cultural assignment. That unwilling spouse often uses extremely damaging passive-aggressive methods (e.g., emotional withdrawal, drug or alcohol addiction, generalized hostility, or destructive levels of personal criticism) to sabotage the experience for the entire family. One military spouse refused to hang curtains or pictures in the house and kept all the household possessions in boxes as a daily re-

minder to her husband and children that she was only waiting to leave.

5. *How does the family—and the individuals in it—handle stress?* It's important for parents to realize that not only they but also their children will experience the new stresses of a cross-cultural move. Stress is part of everyone's life, causing all sorts of reactions including depression, anger, and withdrawal. But sometimes specific individuals or families seem to have a particularly hard time handling stressful conditions. If someone in the family, or the family as a whole, becomes seriously depressed or reacts in an extreme way to stress in general, parents would be wise to seek outside counsel before planning a cross-cultural move.

6. *If the family does decide to move, how will it take advantage of the cross-cultural opportunities ahead?* It's a sad waste for families to live in another country and culture and not be enriched by the experience. When families don't think ahead about how they want to explore their new world, they often never do it. Soon after moving, life becomes as filled with daily routines as it was in the home country, and the vast resources for learning—whether it be about the history of this new country or the geographical and cultural differences they see around them— are unthinkingly ignored. During her college years, one TCK chided her mother, "Mom, we lived in the middle of a tropical rain forest, and you never taught me a thing about it." The truth was that Mom had never *thought* a thing about it. She had lived there a long time and considered the trees and plants around them in their host country the same way she had those in their home country—simply as part of their environment to be lived in, not a rain forest to be studied or explored.

7. *What educational options are available in the new setting?* This is a crucial matter to consider before accepting any particular assignment. Will children be required to go to boarding school?

Are parents expected to home school them? If so, how will this affect family dynamics? What are the local school options? Are international schools available? What are some of the pros and cons of each choice? The matter of education is so critical, in fact, we've devoted all of chapter 14 to it.

8. *How will the family prepare to leave?* Once parents have decided to make the move, there's a lot they can do to help their children through the transition process (see chapter 13). Closure is as important to a child as it is to an adult. It's important that parents make specific plans to help their children settle relationships and think about what's ahead. Leaving well has as profound an impact on the ability of children to enter and adjust successfully as it does on adults.

There are always trade-offs and sacrifices in making a cross-cultural move, but parents must never sacrifice their children. When considering such an assignment, parents need to make use not only of their own good sense and faith but also that of others, such as school guidance counselors, successful cross-cultural sojourners, and family and friends who know them well, to make the best decision possible. Cross-cultural living can be a wonderful experience in countless ways, but it is far better when it begins with clear thinking and good planning rather than with naive visions of a romantic adventure.

Foundation Blocks for Healthy TCKs

When parents make the decision to take their family into a cross-cultural situation, they are also deciding that they will be raising TCKs. Fortunately, this isn't a malady they inflict on their children. In fact, in most situations it's a great gift. Nevertheless, as we've noted at length, some TCKs do well, while others don't. What can parents do to help their kids maximize the great benefits of this experience and deal most effectively with the challenges?

Unfortunately, there's no perfect formula for "how to raise TCKs 100 percent successfully." But there are specific principles parents can follow to build a foundation strong enough to support their children while they try out the options and opportunities of a TCK lifestyle. It's great to watch countless TCKs build on such foundations as they use the gifts of their background and grow from the challenges rather than being hurt or overwhelmed by them.

The following four foundation blocks are important to all children, but for TCKs, whose world is in continual flux, they are critical.

Parent-to-Parent Relationship

We realize not all third culture families have two biological parents in the home. Some families are blended through marriage or adoption; other TCKs are raised in single-parent families. When there is a two-parent household, however, the relationship between parents is of vital importance. If a poor parental relationship is added to all the other challenges TCKs face, the consequences can be devastating. There are three critical areas parents must examine.

1. *Commitment to each other. Commitment* is an unfashionable word these days, but any lasting relationship must begin with it. Commitment is what gets us through those days when we wonder if the struggle makes it worth sticking around. Commitment forces us to work out our differences rather than throwing in the towel. It's how we grow. When approaching a change as major and as stressful as a cross-cultural move, it's especially important for both parents to decide if they are sufficiently committed to one another, their relationship, and their family to make the necessary personal sacrifices to achieve their common goals.

2. *Respect and support for one another.* These go hand in hand with commitment. When kids know their parents' relationship is solid, they feel secure. They also need to see that their parents *like* each other. Small signs of affection—pecks on the cheek while passing or holding hands while watching TV—may not seem very important, but for children, these types of actions

assure them that all is well with Mom and Dad. That's one area they don't have to worry about.

3. *Willingness to nurture the relationship.* A new cultural environment can severely hamper a couple's traditional ways of nurturing their relationship. Elegant restaurants aren't available for a lovely anniversary meal. Servants or nannies restrict the opportunities for quiet, private conversations. Visitors pop in unannounced any time of day or night. Couples in cross-cultural settings often have to look hard for new and creative ways to carve out enough uninterrupted time to help their relationship not only survive but thrive.

Parent-to-Child Relationship

Parents are the most important caregivers in any child's life. The relationship between parent and child must be as consciously nurtured as the one between parents. Research indicates that this relationship is the single most significant factor in determining how TCKs (or any kids) ultimately fare.[1] It is here that the most basic human needs for meaningful relationship, for a true sense of belonging, and for a feeling of significance are met in early, foundational years.

But cross-cultural living introduces new challenges to parenting. In this section, we will look at ways third culture parents can specifically help meet those needs.

Children need to be valued. Having a sense that we are valued—that what we think and feel makes a difference to those around us—is part of feeling significant as a human being. But for that to happen, someone must know us well enough to be sensitive to and supportive of our thoughts and feelings. And that's what parents do for children. Parents of TCKs communicate that they value their children in all the usual ways parents normally do—by listening when children talk, by asking good questions, by seeking clarification when a child talks or acts in a way parents don't quite understand, or by giving a quiet hug.

Perhaps one of the special challenges for parents in a third culture experience is that their children are growing up in a different world from the one in which they themselves grew up. Because of this, they may not realize that some cross-cultural situations can become far more stressful to children than they had thought. Some ATCKs have told us of their extreme fear when they tried to do such normal things as go to market, because they were the targets of constant attention and rude remarks simply because they were foreigners. Others have known tremendous stress because of the political climate in the new country. For all these reasons, parents need to listen carefully and not brush off their child's concern or behavior as silly until they understand the reason for it.

> International businessman Byron and his family
> survived a coup, seemingly unscathed in spite of
> machine-gun fire in their front yard one night. Shortly
> after the coup, however, one daughter became
> panicked when the family car developed a flat tire and
> they stopped by the side of the road to fix it. After a
> second flat tire the very next day, this daughter refused
> to take any more car trips with the family.
>
> But why should a simple flat tire cause her so much
> panic? When questioned, she said something about the
> "soldiers"; when she was questioned further, however,
> the cause of her panic finally became apparent: the
> first tire went flat near an army barracks, where
> soldiers walked around with guns prominently dis-
> played. Their daughter had panicked, afraid that if the
> soldiers came after them or started to shoot, there
> would be no way for the family to escape because of
> the flat tire. With soldiers present throughout the city,
> she didn't want to risk being caught in such a situation
> again.

It's particularly important for parents to listen not only to the words their children say but also to what lies behind the words when they're discussing upcoming transitions. Sometimes parents try to protect their children and keep them from worrying by not telling them about an impending move until just before it happens. Of course, kids don't usually have the final say in their parents' career choices, but if they are included early on in discussions and preparations, they will get the all-important message that their needs are respected. They will know they are valued members of the family.

This list of questions from cross-cultural educator Shirley Torstrick helps parents assess how well they have been listening to their child.

> What makes your child really angry?
> Who is your child's best friend?
> What color would your child like his or her room to
>   be?
> Who is your child's hero?
> What embarrasses your child most?
> What is your child's biggest fear?
> What is your child's favorite subject in school?
> What is the subject your child dislikes most?
> What is your child's favorite book?
> What gift from you does your child cherish most?
> What person outside your family has most influenced
>   your child?
> What is your child's favorite music?
> What is your child's biggest complaint about the family?
> Of what accomplishment is your child proudest?
> Does your child feel too big or too small for his or her
>   age?
> If you could buy your child anything in the world, what
>   would be his or her first choice?
> What has the biggest disappointment in your child's life
>   been?
> What does your child most like to do as a family?
> When does your child prefer to do her or his home-
>   work?
> What makes your child sad?
> What does your child want to be as an adult?[2]

It's likely the more of these the parents can answer, the more their kids will feel valued.

Children need to be special. There's no greater gift parents can give children than to let them know beyond any doubt that there is at least one place in this world where they will always belong and are so special that no one else could ever replace them. That place is here in this family.

For many TCKs, however, the need to feel special is an area of particular vulnerability. So many parents are involved in important, high-energy, people-oriented jobs that it's easy for TCKs to feel they are less important than the people their parents work with. This is an issue that often surfaces in ATCKs years after the fact, and it surprises parents who thought their children didn't mind their busy lifestyle. To help prevent the sense of being orphaned or abandoned that we've heard some TCKs express, parents need to make sure that amid all the busyness of their schedules, there are spaces reserved for their family to spend that time together we mentioned above—no matter what other apparently urgent matters arise.

Children need to be protected. Children need to know beyond all doubt that their parents love them enough to protect them from unnecessary hurt or harm and that Mom and Dad will be available to comfort and console them when painful times are unavoidable. All of us—including children—feel especially vulnerable in a new setting, and we require a sense of safety before we can take the risks needed to adjust.

Protecting their children can become more complicated than parents expect, however, when they move to a place with different rules not only for what is acceptable, but also for what is safe. For example, an important parental job in every culture is to provide physical and emotional protection for children while still encouraging a healthy independence. But what does that mean in different places or cultures? Walking alone to the store might be safe in one environment and risky in another. Since cultural rules and practices often change rapidly for third culture families, parents must find a balance between protection and independence. Otherwise, it's easy to move from guiding and maintaining boundaries to smothering. When that happens, children either want to break out of what they see as excessive restraints, or they wind up with a lot of unnecessary fears themselves.

We stress the importance of protection, because some of the deep expressions of pain we have heard come from TCKs who have felt unprotected by parents or other caregivers. Sometimes they felt pushed out on their own too soon into a new school or community, especially when they didn't know the language yet. It has also happened on leave, when the TCKs felt they were put on display against their will for church congregations or relatives.

The worst stories, however, are from those who were left with a caregiver—whether a domestic worker or fellow expat in the host country, a friend or relative in the home country, or a dorm parent at boarding school—and were emotionally, physically, or sexually abused by the very person parents trusted to take care of them. The trauma was intensified, of course, if the parents refused to believe what was happening, sometimes sending their child back to that very situation. The fact that their parents put these abusers in charge made the children assume at some probably unconscious level that the parents themselves sanctioned the abuse. This is one reason it often takes years before the child (now an adult) will tell the parents what really happened. Most parents weren't trying to hurt their kids, but they just didn't think about how vulnerable their children might feel or actually be in such situations, or perhaps they simply didn't listen well enough when the child tried to tell them at the time.

Parents can help children not only feel but also *be* protected. If the kids have to attend school in a new language, parents can arrange for tutoring before landing on the doorstep of the school. TCKs who express resistance at being "little missionaries" or "little ambassadors" shouldn't be forced into that role. Children are persons in their own right, and *not merely extensions of their parents*. They need to be respected as such.

Parents must make sure that anytime they are separated from their children, clear, open lines of communication are established. Children must have access to their parents with no one else able to intercept or divert the messages.

If a young child must live away from home, it's extremely important to teach and frequently reinforce concepts of personal safety and private body zones. Children need to be reminded that their parents will always believe them and protect them—no matter what anyone else might say. And then, if the child *does* report some potential or actual infringement, parents must be prepared to intervene on their child's behalf—even if doing so may put their career at risk.

Children need to be comforted. We talked extensively about comfort in chapter 11. Being comforted communicates that parents care enough to understand and be sensitive to their children's feelings, even if the situation can't be changed. Parents should remember, particularly in any transition experience, that the quietest, most compliant child may be grieving and may need comforting the most.

TCKs' Perception of Parents' Work

Nietzsche once said, "I can endure any *how* if I have a *why*." The resilience of human beings is often related to whether or not they have a reason to be resilient; hence, the third foundation block is how TCKs view their parents' work. TCKs will be able to tolerate the most difficult adjustment challenges if the reasons are good enough.

For many, seeing their parents' work as significant and life-changing is a great asset of the TCK experience. They feel pride that their parents are involved in a career that can make at least a small difference in the world. They feel a sense of ownership in that work—and thus a sense of significance themselves—because their family has traveled the globe together to do the job. The challenges of their upbringing are insignificant compared with the sense of what is being accomplished.

Other TCKs, however, express great bitterness toward parents who are involved in these types of international careers. What makes the difference? Certainly the parents' attitude toward the job, the host country and culture, and the sincerity of the political or religious beliefs that have motivated them to go abroad in the first place are critical factors. Parents who feel and act positively toward their situation and the host country people with whom they are working communicate that attitude to their children.

On the other hand, the parent who shows disrespect for the people or culture of the host country can make the young TCK observer wonder why the family is there at all. When the going gets tough, the question can quickly change from "Why are we here?" to "Why don't we go home?"

Once that question is raised, TCKs often begin acting out. International business kids may conclude that money isn't a good enough motivation for living abroad; they end up breaking local laws, hoping their parents will be expelled. Foreign service kids may become so disillusioned with what they perceive as the hypocrisy of governmental politics that they start covering the embassy walls with graffiti. Missionary kids who see a major discrepancy between what their parents preach and what they practice at home can feel that spreading such an apparently ineffective faith isn't worth the cost. They blatantly smoke, drink, use drugs, or get pregnant, hoping the mission will send the family home. Military kids who see their government's presence in a particular conflict as a matter of economic advantage rather than principle may join an antiwar demonstration.

A particular irony sometimes results when parents who have done a good job of convincing their children how important their overseas assignment is decide to return home. How could they think of leaving, the TCK wonders, if it's as important as they said it was? They question whether the parents ever really valued the work they were doing, casting a retrospective doubt on their whole experience. In such cases, as always, parents need to have an open discussion of the upcoming move and make sure their children understand the true reasons for it—even if the children have difficulty listening.

Positive Spiritual Core

The fourth foundation block is the child's awareness that there is a stable spiritual core in their parents' lives and in the life of the family as a whole.

In a world where moral values and practices can be radically different from one place to another, this block is the key to true stability throughout life. When TCKs have a core personal faith and a stable set of values, they will be equipped to remain on a steady course no matter which culture or cultures they live in.

Endnotes

1   Leslie Andrews, "The Measurement of Adult MKs' Well-Being," *Evangelical Missions Quarterly* (October 1995): 418–26.

2   Shirley Torstrick, (seminar handout, used with permission).

13

Dealing with Transition

It's vital that highly mobile families learn to deal well with the entire process of transition. Earlier we discussed the common characteristics of the five stages in any transition experience: involvement, leaving, transition, entering, and reinvolvement. Here, then, are some concrete ways to not only survive but also grow while moving through each stage.

From Involvement through Leaving

The time has finally come. After carefully thinking through the pros and cons, the decision is made: the family will be moving to a new place and, for many TCKs, a new world. With that decision, each member of the family moves from the comfortable stage of involvement they have hopefully been in to the leaving stage. Whether this move is between countries or even to new locations in the same country, leaving is a critical stage for everyone to navigate well.

Since denials—our own or those of friends around us—and moments of special recognition such as graduation or farewell ceremonies don't change the ultimate reality of our leave-taking, it's essential that we face and deal with the normal grief inherent in leaving a place and people we love. Doing this rather than running away from it will allow a healthy transition process to continue. We also need to look ahead realistically and optimistically. How can we do both—face our approaching losses squarely while still looking forward with hope? The best way is by making sure we go through proper closure during this leaving stage. Without that, the rest of the transition process can be very bumpy indeed, and settling on the other side will be much more difficult. Leaving right is a key to entering right.

Building a "RAFT"

The easiest way to remember what's needed for healthy closure is to imagine building a raft. By lashing four basic "logs" together, we will be able to keep the raft afloat and get safely to the other side.

Reconciliation
Affirmation
Farewells
Think Destination

Reconciliation. Any time we face a move from one place to another, it's easy to deal with tensions in relationships by ignoring them. We think, "In two weeks I'll be gone and never see that friend again anyway. Why bother trying to work out this misunderstanding?"

Unfortunately, when we refuse to resolve interpersonal conflicts, two things can happen. First, we are so focused on how good it will be to get away from this problem that we not only skip over the reconciliation needed for good closure but also ignore the total process of closure and don't move on to building the rest of the RAFT. Second, the difficulties don't go away when we move. Instead, as we leave, we carry with us our mental baggage of unresolved problems. This is a poor choice for three reasons: bitterness is never healthy for anyone; the old discontentment can interfere with starting new relationships; and if we ever move back to this same place and have to face these people again, it will be much harder to resolve the issues then.

Reconciliation includes both the need to forgive and to be forgiven. How that happens may vary among cultures. In one culture, it might mean going directly to the person with whom we have a conflict and addressing the issues. In another culture, it may mean using an intermediary. Obviously, true reconciliation depends on the cooperation and response of the other party as well, but we at least need to do all we can to reconcile any broken relationships before leaving.

Affirmation. Relationships are built and maintained through affirmation—the acknowledgment that each person in the relationship matters. Again, styles or customs of affirmation vary from culture to culture, but in every culture we must let others know we respect and appreciate them. Here are four ways to do so:

1. Take the time to tell coworkers you have enjoyed working with them.

2. Tell friends how important their friendship has been, perhaps leaving them some memento of a special time you have shared.

3. Send a note with a small gift to your neighbors to let them know what you've learned about kindness, faith, love, or perseverance through your interactions with them.

4. Reassure parents, siblings, and close friends of your love and respect and that you don't leave them lightly. A bouquet of flowers might be ordered for delivery the day after you leave.

Affirming others helps us as well as those we affirm. It not only solidifies our relationships for future contact, but in expressing what they have meant to us, we are also reminded of what we have gained from living in this place. Part of good closure is acknowledging our blessings—both to rejoice in them and to properly mourn their passing.

Farewells. Saying good-bye to people, places, pets, and possessions in culturally appropriate ways is important if we don't want to have deep regrets later. We need to schedule time for these farewells during the last few weeks and days.

> One woman forgot to take into account that everyone
> comes to the departing friend's house on the last day
> to bid a final farewell. In order not to offend the
> countless people who streamed in all day long, she
> visited with each one in turn. By the end of the day,
> her bags still weren't packed and she missed her flight!

Here are some suggestions for saying good-bye in four key areas, all of which just happen to begin with *p:* people, places, pets, possessions.

Farewells to significant people in our lives are crucial. Parents should take special care to help their children say good-bye to people with whom they have had meaningful relationships in the past as well as the present. Helping kids say good-bye may include writing a note or baking cookies together for that special person—anything that acknowledges the importance of that relationship and says "Thank you for being a special person in my life. I will miss you."

Everyone has places that evoke an emotional response. It may be a spot tied to a special moment in our lives (our engagement, for instance) or where we go when we are upset or where certain events always occur. These are the places we come back to visit, either alone or to show our children years later. Part of healthy closure includes visiting such sites to reminisce and say farewell. This is particularly important for TCKs who may be losing their whole world with next week's plane ride. Many TCKs we have talked to mourn for the favorite tree they used to climb years after they have left the land of their childhood.

People say good-bye to places in different ways. Some plant a tree that will grow long after they are gone, symbolizing a living, ongoing connection to this part of their lives. Others leave a hidden secret message or "treasure" to look for in case they should return. No matter how it is done, openly acknowledging this time as a true good-bye is important, as is recognizing that this stage in life and all that these places represent to us are passing.

Pets aren't equally important in every culture, but they can be significant when it comes to good-byes. TCKs need to know how their pets will be cared for, who will love them. If the pet must be put to sleep, everyone who cares for that pet, particularly children, should say good-bye. Some TCKs tell us how devastated they were after parents promised their pet would be happy in a new home, only to find out months or years later that the dog was euthanized or the chicken given to someone for food.

One problem (some might say blessing!) international sojourners face is that they can rarely take all their possessions with them when they move. Parents may delight in the chance to throw out a child's rock collection, never realizing how precious those rocks were to their child. Certainly, we realize part of life is letting go, but parents should talk with their children about what to take and what to leave as they pack. Everyone in the family needs to carry some treasured items to the new location. These become part of the collection of *sacred objects* that help connect one part of a global nomad's life to the next.

But sometimes even treasures must be left behind. When that happens, it's important to part with them consciously. Placing a precious object in the hands of someone else as a gift or taking photographs of it are two ways to say good-bye to an inanimate but important old friend.

The celebratory rituals of farewell commonly associated with certain types of transitions (e.g., graduations, retirement parties, etc.) are another important part of building this RAFT. Taking the time for "rites of passage" gives us markers for remembering meaningful places and people and directly addressing the fact that we are saying farewell. Many international families permanently return to their home country after the oldest child graduates from secondary school abroad. The graduating TCK goes through the rites of passage—the graduation ceremony, the "wailing wall" afterward, where all line up and say good-bye to one another. However, the needs of the younger children for the same types of closure when they leave for home are often overlooked. This can later add greatly to the younger child's sense of "unfinished business," while the older TCK in the same family is off and running once he or she gets to the homeland. Remember, *every* member of the family needs to build the RAFT during any leaving process.

Thinking destination. Even as we are saying the good-byes and processing the sad reality of those good-byes, we need to think realistically about our destination: Where are we going? What are some of the positives and negatives we can expect to find once we get there? Will we have electricity and running water? How will we learn to drive on the other side of the road? Do we need to take a transformer with us to keep our 110-volt appliances from burning out on a 220-volt electrical system?

This is also the time to look at our external (e.g., finances, family support structure) and internal (e.g., ability to deal with stress or change) resources for coping with problems we might find. What resources will we find in the new location and what will we need to take with us? Who can help us adjust to the new culture when we get there? This is the best time to find out from the sponsoring agency who will meet us at the airport, where we will stay until housing is located, and what that housing will be.

If we don't think through some of these issues, our adjustment may be rockier once we arrive at the new destination. If we are expecting too much, we'll be disappointed. If we don't expect enough, we may not use the resources available, thereby making life more complicated than necessary. Of course, we can never have a perfect picture of what life in the new place will be like, but doing our best to prepare beforehand can prevent a lot of problems later on.

After all of this thorough preparation in the leaving stage, it's time to move on into the transition stage itself.

Maintaining Stability through the Transition Stage

When people ask how they can avoid the chaos and confusion of the transition process, we have to say they can't. They can, though, keep in mind that it's normal and will pass if they hang on long enough. Also, there are a few steps we can take to help us maintain some sense of equilibrium and connectedness with the past and to smooth the way for the future stages of entry and reinvolvement.

One way is through sacred objects—those mementos we mentioned earlier that specifically reflect a certain place or moment of our lives. That's why the choice of which possessions to keep and which to give away is so important during the leaving stage. A favorite teddy bear pulled out of the suitcase each night during the travels from one place to another reminds the child that there is one stable thing in his or her life amidst the general chaos. At the same time Mom or Dad may be reading a treasured book they brought along, which reminds them of other times and places where they have read those same inspiring or comforting words. Other sacred objects are worn. Did you ever look around a group of TCKs or their parents and see how many were wearing some article of clothing or jewelry that connected them with their past? It might be a Taureg cross hanging on a gold chain or a V-ring on a finger. Perhaps they're wearing a sari instead of a sweater. Often an ATCK's home is quite a sight to behold—with artifacts gathered from around the world, all proving that "I was there! It's part of my history." Each sacred object serves as a good reminder that the current moment or scene is part of a bigger story of that person's life.

Pictures are another way we connect with special moments and memories in our past. One ambassador asked each staff member to list what he or she would put in the one bag allowed for an emergency evacuation. Photographs headed the list for every person, far above things with much more intrinsic worth. Why? Because each picture reminds us of some relationship, an experience we have had, a place we have visited. Pictures add a value to our lives that money alone can't buy. A small picture album of photographs representing significant highlights of our past life and location gives us a lovely place to visit when we need a few reflective moments in the middle of this sometimes turbulent stage. Pictures can also be helpful for letting people in the new place know something more of our history.

Of course, we recognize that everyone we would like to show these pictures and sacred objects to may not see the same value in them that we do. (And often it's vice versa when they try to show us theirs!) Why don't most people particularly enjoy another person's slide or video show? Because friends who weren't there can't see anything interesting in a skinny cow walking down the middle of a road; it seems rather bizarre to them. And they certainly don't want to hear a twenty-minute story about the man with the shaved head in the back row. For the person who was there, though, that picture or video segment brings back a flood of memories, and every detail is fascinating. That's why globally nomadic people should make a pact to look at each other's slides or home videos. It's how they can affirm their experiences!

Even if we built our RAFT perfectly in the leaving stage, transition is usually the stage where we begin to mourn most acutely the loss of things and people left behind. We feel unbearable emptiness when we realize we can't call our best friend to meet us for a cup of coffee. We miss the comfort of knowing everyone in our factory or office by name. The permanence of the move and the irretrievability of the past stare us in the face and we wonder if we have made a terrible mistake. During the leaving stage we knew these losses were coming, but now they are here. This is a critical moment and one which can affect us for years to come: we must decide what we will do with the grief. Will we deal with it or try to pack it away, out of sight, out of mind? Sometimes the chaos of the moment is so great we simply can't afford to deal fully with the reality of what we are losing, and our only choice to survive seems to be to ignore those feelings. This is a common means of getting through this transition stage, but if we feel we must shut out our feelings for simple survival's sake, we need to make an agreement with ourselves that we will go back and work through these feelings fully as soon as life stabilizes a bit more. And then we need to keep that agreement. Too many people get through transition by packing away these painful feelings of loss and never taking them out consciously at a later stage.

Years later they continue to exhibit the patterns of behavior we have already talked about.

Other people, of course, seem to be able to deal more easily with the losses as they are happening. Whenever we choose to deal with the inevitable losses in our move—during this stage itself or later—there are some specific ways we can help ourselves and those we love come through this normal process in a healthy way. A professor of philosophy, Jim Gould, says that loss always produces grief, conscious or unconscious, and it will come out one way or another, whether the person intends it to or not.[1] Mourning is the conscious acknowledgment of loss, and by finding ways and rituals that will help us recognize and mourn our loss, we will not only survive this painful period but also be ready to move on to the challenges of our new location unencumbered by a heavy burden of grief.

Mourning the Losses

Any healthy mourning process requires permission, people, and process time. The first of these, permission, includes the internal permission we must give ourselves to recognize that it's not immature, unspiritual, or childish to grieve our losses. In fact, it's most appropriate to mourn the loss of a home, friends, pets, or status. We also need other people who will give us this same permission by letting us express our feelings without judging us. Being willing to acknowledge their own grief is one important way parents and other adults let children know it's okay to be sad for what they themselves are about to lose. We hope the days are gone when parents, as well as children, are told—either by a voice inside or from others around—not to cry.

During this time, we not only need permission to mourn, we also need people who can provide support while we do so. A good comforter helps us maintain balance during our grieving process by being available to help with physical needs and to express empathy, both verbally and in other ways. Listening quietly, asking appropriate questions, reminiscing, and allowing us to be silent are ways people can help us to move through the process of grief.

Even with permission and people to help in the process, however, grief is not dispelled in a moment. It takes time to move from shock through pain, anger, and guilt until there is a return to the normal flow of life. How long it takes people to go through each stage varies from person to person. Few people move smoothly through the grief process. Usually we go forward and then backward several times between various stages as we move on toward a final sense of acceptance. Healthy mourning acknowledges that we need time to sort through these many conflicting emotions before we can get on with the rest of life. Rushing this process only transforms normal grief into unresolved grief.

The grieving stage, however, isn't only about looking at our losses. It also includes the need to plan for the future—immediate and long-range. Such planning can be something as simple as deciding to make a long-distance phone call for Grandma's birthday next week to say "Happy Birthday" and to let her know we miss her, or it can be figuring out what subjects we will study in the new school we are about to attend. Planning ahead in such ways is realistic; it also helps us move through the grieving process by reminding us and our children that life does go on in spite of great loss.

The good news is that with a proper foundation during the leaving stage, and by using these few tips to survive the transition, we can move on to making a positive entry and finding our way in this new world.

Entering Right

Physical arrival alone doesn't mean we have begun the entering stage. Sometimes the chaos of the transition stage remains for some days or weeks after our initial arrival. The more we have thought ahead about this time, however, and the more we are consciously aware of what we and our family will need to make a positive entry, the sooner and smoother we can begin to positively move into our new life. It's important that we recognize that we don't have to wait helplessly for the new community to reach out and receive us; there are many ways we can proactively help ourselves in this process. So how, then, can we (and the new community) move from the desire to establish ourselves in our new community to actually accomplishing it?

Choosing and Using Mentors

The key to successfully negotiating the entry stage is to find a *mentor*—someone who answers questions and introduces the new community to us and us to it. These mentors function as "bridges" and can smooth our way in, significantly shorten the time it takes for us to get acclimated to the new surroundings, and help us make the right contacts.

The problem, of course, lies in finding the *right* mentor. After all, the mentor is the person who determines the group of people we will meet, the attitude we will absorb about this new place, and from whom we learn the acceptable behavioral patterns. Ultimately, the mentor not only affects our long-term relationship to this new community but often determines our effectiveness in it as well. If we find the right one, we're in great shape. The wrong mentor, however, can be a disaster. If our mentor is negative about the place, its people, or our organization, we begin to doubt whether we should have come and become afraid to try new things. If this mentor has a bad reputation in the community, others may put us in the same category and avoid us too.

How can we as newcomers know who is or isn't trustworthy? Often people who themselves are on the fringes of the receiving community will be the first to introduce themselves to a newcomer. We, of course, are so happy *someone* has reached out to us that we can easily jump into this new relationship before we understand what the ramifications of such a relationship might be. How can we make a wise decision at this point?

Our suggestion is to be appreciative and warm to all who reach out a helping hand during this entry time, but inwardly you need to be cautious about making a wholehearted commitment to this relationship by asking yourself a few questions: Is this person one who fits into the local community or is he or she definitely marginalized in one way or another? Does this person exhibit the positive, encouraging attitudes we would like to foster in ourselves or make negative remarks and display hostile attitudes about almost everything?

When we take a little time to evaluate a potential mentor, we may discover that this person who greeted us so warmly is, in fact, one of those wonderful people who belong to the heart of any organization and have the great gift of making newcomers feel almost instantly at home. That person could well go on to be the best possible mentor and a great friend. If, however, we find out that this person who is so eager to be our friend is a marginal member of the community, then we must ask the next question: why does she or he want to befriend us?

Some are marginal simply because they, like us, are relative newcomers and are still looking to establish new friendships. While they may not yet be members of the inner circle, they have learned the basics of how life is lived in this place and can be most helpful. In fact, they often have more time to spend orienting newcomers than those whose plates are already full with well-defined roles and relationships. Relationships that start like this often turn into lifelong friendships.

If, however, we find out that the first person who approaches us so invitingly has been intentionally marginalized from the community, we need to be cautious about adopting this person as our mentor. Such people are often in some kind of trouble within the community. Perhaps they rebel against the accepted standards of behavior, break laws, or defy teachers, and they often want to recruit naive newcomers for their own agenda.

Besides using our common sense in situations such as we have just described, how else can we find good mentors? Some groups have active mentoring programs already in place. Other agencies set up "matching families" for those coming to their community. Many international schools have set up a "big brother/big sister" program, with good mentors already identified, to help new students through their first few weeks at school. One potential problem is that an agency may have a mentoring program for the adults in the family, but the children's need for a mentor is forgotten. In such cases, parents can ask advice from other adults already in the community. They usually know who would and wouldn't be a positive mentor for their children.

How else can or does the community deal with this entry stage? In communities with chronically high mobility, we have noticed two interesting, though rather opposite, responses to newcomers. Some have a regular routine to help new members get oriented. There are maps of the town with the key places to shop marked and instruction guides for dealing with the local host culture—all tucked in a basket of goodies. One person is specifically assigned to take the new family around, and the whole system of orientation goes like clockwork because it has happened so many times. Members of other highly mobile communities, however, are so tired of seeing people come and go they basically don't do much at all for the newcomer. Their thought process goes like this: "What's the use? These people will just be gone again," or "Why bother getting to know them? I've only got three months left here myself."

Most of our discussion on this entry stage applies to any kind of move. But there are extra stresses recognized by experts around the world for those trying to enter a completely new culture. Lisa and Leighton Chinn, a couple who work with international students, have outlined four stages of cultural stress that occur during this phase: fun, flight, fight, and fit. It's important to acknowledge them for a moment because they often happen in spite of all we have done right to prepare for our move and can make us feel that none of our other preparations mattered. The process can go something like this.

As we have looked ahead, we have developed a sense of anticipation and excitement for our new assignment. We decide it will be fun to explore the new environment, learn its history, and enrich our lives through meeting new people. The first few days after arrival, we busily engage with all we meet, feel excitement that we can actually answer the greetings in this new language we tried to study before we came, and all seems well. We think, "What fun!" A few more days pass, however, and things aren't quite as exciting. We don't like not knowing how to get to the store on our own because we haven't learned yet how to drive on the "wrong" side of the road, we're tired of not being understood past simple greetings by those around us, and we wish we could go "home"—back to where we knew how to function and where we fit. This is the flight stage.

Soon, however, we get tired of feeling so useless or out of place and begin to get angry. After all, we used to fit. We were competent individuals in our last home, so it can't be our fault that we feel so lost and insecure, so we begin to blame everything and everyone in this new location for our discomfort. If they would only do things "right" (meaning the way we are used to doing them), everything would be fine. Internally, and sometimes externally, we begin to fight with the way things are being done here—perhaps even becoming angry at our mentor who is doing his or her best to teach us these new ways.

Knowing that these reactions might happen doesn't necessarily stop them, but, again, knowledge helps us at least make more appropriate choices. In this case we might choose not to be quite so vocal about all we despise in our new situation.

These are the moments we need to remind ourselves that entry also takes time, to remember that six months from now we can presume that somehow we will have learned to drive here, discovered where the stores are for the things we want to buy, and most likely made new friends by then.

Reinvolvement Stage

The light at the end of the proverbial tunnel is that in any transition, cross-cultural or not, a final, recognized stage of reinvolvement is possible. We settle into our new surroundings, accepting the people and places for who and what they are. This doesn't always mean that we like everything about the situation, but at least we can start to see *why* people do what they do, rather than only *what* it is they do. We've learned the new ways and know our position in this community. Other members of the group see us as one of them, or at least they know where we fit. We have a sense of intimacy, a feeling that our presence matters to this group, and once more we begin to feel secure. Time again feels present and permanent as we focus on the here and now rather than hoping for the future or constantly reminiscing about the past.

In all transitions, we gain as well as lose. Perhaps one more paradox of the TCK experience is that learning to deal in healthy ways with the losses of transition can become a great asset in a TCK's life. When TCKs learn these lessons well, they no longer have to shut down their emotions or shut out relationships. Instead, they can risk the pain of another loss for the sake of the gain that goes with it. Learning to live with this kind of openness affects all areas of life in a positive way and can help TCKs become good listeners to friends dealing with loss for other reasons as well.

Endnote

[1]   Personal conversation with Ruth E. Van Reken, July 1997.

14

Meeting Educational Needs

Dave and Betty Lou Pollock will never forget that warm September morning in Old Bridge, New Jersey, U.S.A., when they sent their oldest child, Danny, to his first day of school. After outfitting him with new clothes, Dave took his five-year-old son's hand and together they walked to the John Glenn Elementary school.

Although Dave and Betty Lou experienced the nostalgic emotions many parents feel when their offspring take that first step away from home, the decision about where and when to send Danny to school hadn't been a difficult one. Schooling patterns for children in Old Bridge followed a predictable cycle that had gone on for generations. Every September each five-year-old in town headed for the neighborhood school to begin his or her academic career.

Years later, however, when Dave and Betty Lou's daughter, Michelle, turned seven, things were different. By then the Pollocks lived in Kenya and suddenly the simple, routine formulas for "how to do school" were gone. No familiar John Glenn Elementary School down the road, nor Timothy Christian School reached

> by carpooling with others. The Pollocks faced many
> choices, as did their colleagues. Would they teach
> Michelle and her three older brothers at home, send
> them to a local national school or to an international
> day school? Would it be necessary to consider a
> boarding school? Dave and Betty Lou discovered that
> the issues of schooling in a cross-cultural world aren't
> nearly as straightforward as at home.

Third culture families face a variety of choices when it comes to deciding how to educate their children, and every option has distinct advantages and disadvantages. How can parents know which one is best for each particular child?

Unfortunately, parents often face this major decision with little or no awareness of the different types of opportunities available for schooling in a cross-cultural setting, let alone the pros and cons accompanying each method. Yet, for many TCKs, their experiences in school dramatically shape how they view their childhood and whether they look back on it with joy or regret. Because making the right choice for schooling is so crucial for TCKs, we want to look at this issue in depth.

As we mentioned earlier, before parents accept any cross-cultural assignment, it's important that they ask the sponsoring organization about its current educational opportunities and policies. These can vary greatly from one group to another: Are families required to send children away to a boarding school? Are parents expected to home school the children? Are all children required to attend the local international school?

Once parents know the answers to these questions, they must decide whether the organization's policies will or won't accommodate their children's educational needs. If a family feels that an agency's policy won't work well for them, they are generally better off to seek another sponsor than try to force the organization to change its policy—or perhaps worse, to compromise the family's needs.

If parents discover an organization gives complete freedom of choice to its employees regarding their children's schooling, there are still important questions to ask: What, in fact, are the available options? What language and curriculum do local national schools use? What language and curriculum does the local international school use? Who will pay for the extra costs of schooling (including vacation travel for secondary school or university students left at home to join the rest of the family), since some options are very expensive?

Under the stress of raising kids in settings markedly different from their own upbringings, parents often go to extremes. On one hand, because they want to make sure their children have the best education possible, some parents become supervigilant and overly critical of both the school personnel and programs. Nothing is done right or as it would have been at home. On the other hand, well-meaning parents may place a child in an educational setting, especially a boarding school, expecting that the school will fully substitute for the parents. Neither works.

Making the Best Choice

Through the years, we have come to realize that there is no perfect schooling formula that guarantees a happy outcome for all TCKs. There are, though, some underlying principles about the educational process that can help parents make the best choices possible.

Some parents fear taking their children into a cross-cultural setting at all because they believe their children will miss out on too many educational opportunities offered in the home country. But the educational process for any child includes more than school; it includes *all* learning, in every dimension of a person's life. Everyone acquires information and masters skills by a variety of formal and informal means.

One great advantage TCKs have is the wealth of learning opportunities available to them from their travels, cross-cultural interactions, and the third culture experience itself. When TCKs move through the *suk* in Sanaa, eat in an Indian friend's home in Bombay, or watch the murky brown river flow through the greenery of the Brazilian or Vietnam jungle, they are learning in the most dynamic way of all—through the five senses. This hands-on education in geography, history, basic anthropology, social studies, and language acquisition is a great benefit of the TCK experience and more than replaces some of the deficits in equipment or facilities that might be present in an overseas school.

Parents must also remember that in terms of preparing their children for life, they themselves are the primary educators. Schools can't substitute for the home in building values, developing healthy attitudes, and motivating children in positive directions.

Dr. Brian Hill, professor of education at Murdoch University in Australia, suggests seven basic outcomes parents in cross-cultural settings should look for from their children's educational experience. The experience should enable them to maintain a stable and positive self-image while learning new things; acquire survival skills appropriate to their own culture; identify and develop their personal creative gifts; gain access to the major fields of human thought and experience; become aware of the dominant worldviews and value orientations influencing their social world; develop the capacity to think critically and choose responsibly; and develop empathy, respect, and a capacity for dialogue with other persons, including those whose primary beliefs differ from their own.[1] Any specific choice for schooling should be measured in terms of how well it will help meet these larger goals of the educational process.

Educational Philosophies Differ among Cultures

Parents must examine the total approach to education in any system of schooling, not merely the academics. Styles of discipline, teaching, and grading can vary widely from one culture to another. These differences can have an enormous impact on children. Those who always make straight As and a few Bs in one system are devastated when they bring home mostly Cs with only one or two Bs when they switch. In Britain, 50 percent is passing, 70s and 80s are considered great, and scores in the 90s are practically unheard-of. In the United States, 50 percent is failure, but As are given to those with 94 percent and higher. An American child going to a British school can panic when she sees these lower marks. She knows if her transcript is filled with 70s and 80s and is sent to universities in the States without interpretation, she may never be admitted.

Corporal punishment is a common practice in certain places, while it would be unthinkable in others. Some school systems stress learning by rote. Others use only problem-based learning, where students must personally seek out the answers to each assignment. In some cultures discussion and other forms of student participation are encouraged, or even required. In others, this type of behavior is considered disrespectful.

Ways of motivating students vary from culture to culture too. In some places, external methods are emphasized. Homework is assigned and graded each day. Every six weeks parents are notified of their child's progress, or lack thereof. Instant rewards and punishments are the major means of encouraging students in these systems. Other school systems rely far more on internal motivation. Students are assumed to be responsible for their own learning, daily homework is neither assigned nor checked, and class attendance is optional. Only the final exam matters.

We have seen this one difference between motivational philosophies cause great consternation for TCKs and their families. When a student who is used to homework assignments every night goes to a school with no daily assignments, he or she often has trouble knowing how to organize the study time necessary to cover the assigned work before the end of the semester. Parents may wonder why their child seems to go out and socialize with little regard for schoolwork, but since no reports come home to tell them otherwise, they presume all is well. Only when the final exam comes and the TCK fails does anyone know something is wrong.

Conversely, a student who is used to working independently may see no reason to do the daily homework assignments; they seem trivial. Perhaps he or she also sees no reason to attend class regularly; studying in the library seems more important. Only when the first reports come home with failing grades does it become clear that things like homework and class attendance matter in this new setting.

In considering a particular school, parents must ask for an explanation of its philosophy of education, its methods of teaching, and its policy toward discipline and then decide if this school is a good match for their child. Even when an educational option seems like a good one from the parents' view or has been great for other children in the same family, some of these differences in the philosophical or psychological approaches to education can cause enough stress for a particular TCK that a change to a school with a different method of teaching is justified.

School Teaches More than Academic Subjects

As we said in an earlier chapter, school is one of the principal means whereby one generation communicates its culture and its values to the next. As long as everyone comes from the same culture, we hardly notice this process and what's taught is accepted as "right."

In international schools the transmission of cultural values and expectations takes place as it does in any other school, because there is no such thing as value-free education. The difference is that teachers and peers who come from many countries and cultures, along with the curriculum itself, may represent value systems that vary markedly from that of the parents of any given TCK. Parents who forget this are often surprised to discover that the cultural values and behaviors of their children's teachers and peers have influenced their children far more or in different ways than expected.

> One Korean father told us how shocked he was during an exchange with his son. The son had attended an American-oriented school in an Asian country. As the

Korean community in that country grew, they started their own school. The Korean parents believed the American school wasn't preparing their children to take the exams necessary for them to continue school in Korea. They also felt their children were forgetting Korean culture.

When the father told his son he would soon be changing schools, the son refused. "No, I'm not. I've attended the American school all my life, my friends are there, and I'm going to graduate from there."

This conversation distressed the father—not because his son refused the improved educational opportunity but because he dared to disobey. "When I was my son's age, I would never have considered resisting my father," he said. "No matter what I felt, I would have obeyed without question."

For good or ill, educating this Korean student in a school based on the American values of independence, free speech, and individualism had deeply affected a family's cultural heritage.*

Schooling Should Not Make It Impossible for the Child to Return to the Home Country

Attending school in what may almost amount to a "third or fourth culture" can make it extremely difficult—or even impossible—for some TCKs to return to the system in their home country. But it isn't only the difference in school systems or curriculum that can pose problems.

Judith Gjoen, a Dutch TCK from Indonesia, was educated in American schools in Malaysia and now lives with her Norwegian husband in Oslo. She is a practicing counselor who has expressed particular

---

* Many international schools are now attempting to address such issues of identity and cultural mixing their students may face. Wise parents might want to ask about such opportunities when considering whether to send a child to one school or another.

> concern about TCKs who return to their passport
> culture wanting to continue their education but lacking
> proficiency or confidence in using their mother tongue.
> A young woman from a Nordic country observed that
> her speaking, reading, and writing ability in her mother
> tongue was fine for home and social use, but her
> school language was English, the language of her high
> school education. She finally had to pursue her
> university education in the United States. This, of
> course, further alienated her from her home country.

Parents, educators, and agency administrators have a responsibility to provide the opportunity for TCKs to learn their native language so that they have the option of returning to their passport country for further formal education and settling down there, if that's what they choose.

However, there's another potential barrier to TCKs acquiring fluency in their own language. Sometimes the TCKs themselves resist. For a child, nothing may seem more important than being like his or her peers. If everyone else around is speaking French (or in the case above, English), why take more time away from socializing or be labeled as different, just to learn another language? School-age children are not able to look ahead to long-term consequences. Most don't think about life after secondary school. Parents and educators need to be sensitive to this possibility and try to help their TCKs see how learning their own language is an expansion of their world rather than a limitation.

Different Schooling Choices Are Available

Having said all of this, one fact remains: school is, in fact, important; it's the place where we learn things that can't be assimilated by pure observation. The only questions are where and when.

To help parents make wise choices, let's look at specific options generally available to third culture families. Although the variety may seem a little confusing at first, these choices give parents the necessary flexibility to help meet the needs of each individual child. The most common methods for formally educating TCKs include the following: home and correspondence schooling, satellite schools, local national schools, local international schools, overseas boarding schools, and preuniversity schooling in home country. Here are some of the specific pros and cons of each choice.

Home and Correspondence Schooling

Pros	Cons
Child lives with parents	Lack of parental teaching skills
Individual instruction	Parent-child stress
Moral and spiritual values of parents taught	Lack of peer contact
Parent- and home-centered	Lack of healthy competition
Child can continue schooling in home country without interruption	
Can use curriculum of choice	

An increasing number of internationally mobile families use various methods of home schooling, particularly for younger TCKs. Some parents create their own curriculum. During home leave, one mother went to the local public grade school in Chicago, found out what textbooks they used, ordered those books directly from the publisher, and made her own lesson plans from them for each of her four school-age children.

Other parents combine materials offered by several home-schooling groups to design their own curriculum. Still others use a syllabus offered by a specific correspondence school, including videos. In some of these cases, the lessons are monitored by the parents but graded by teachers back home.

Some parents have gone a step further and successfully put together a smorgasbord of educational options by combining modified home schooling and correspondence courses with national schools. A few have worked this out under the supervision of school counselors from their home country or from the nearest international school.

For this, or any type of home schooling or correspondence plan, parents must have access to educational tools and resources in order to do a good job. They must also have the testing apparatus necessary to be certain of proper progress and development for their TCK, and they must be sure that the content and sequencing of the curriculum will be compatible with the next step in the education of the child. It's fine to use these options of home schooling or correspondence school as long as steps are taken to ensure the children can maintain the standards that would be required of them in a more structured school setting.

The obvious main benefit of home schooling is that kids remain with their parents, thereby decreasing some of the disadvantages of separation. Another benefit—especially to those with erratic home leave or frequent relocations—is that the children can maintain continuity in school without having to jump from one system to another in the middle of the year.

Home schooling, however, isn't always the best option—even in its most creative form. First, TCKs may be isolated from peers—particularly those raised in remote areas. This may not be a significant problem during early childhood, when parental support is more crucial than peer approval, but it can be serious during the teenage years.

Second, the dynamics in some families simply aren't suited to this type of schooling. Perhaps the parents have neither the natural nor professional skills to properly teach academic subjects. Or one or both parents may be so disorganized that instruction is haphazard or never takes place at all. Some kids habitually refuse to do anything their parents suggest, causing constant friction and confusion in the home.

In those situations, the benefits of home schooling may not be worth the frustrations. That doesn't mean the parents or children have failed. It only means that home schooling wasn't the best option for this particular family.

Satellite Schools

Pros	Cons
Living at home with parents More chance for interaction with peers than home schooling Trained teacher Externally organized curriculum Parents still closely involved	Labor-intensive for sponsoring agency Still may have limited social opportunities Inadequate equipment for certain subjects High teacher attrition

In recent years, satellite schools have been introduced as another option for TCKs. These are usually small groups of students who have clustered together into a slightly more formalized setting than the individual home. Sometimes the sponsoring agency sends out a qualified teacher to conduct the classes, which resemble the old-fashioned one-room schoolhouse. Other satellite schools depend primarily on videotapes or interactive computer programs. While an adult supervises the proceedings, the teaching itself takes place through these electronic tutors. In certain situations, these schools may also use correspondence courses.

Satellite schools usually have a good teacher/student ratio, with each child receiving individual attention. They provide a bit more socialization than a strictly home-school setting, but the TCK is still able to live at home with parents.

Local National Schools

Pros	Cons
Child lives with parents Cross-cultural relationships Language acquisition Good education in many places Relatively low cost Strong exposure to host culture	Religious/philosophical differences from parents Total cultural identification with host culture—loss of own cultural identity Tension or rejection due to nationality Competes with host nationals for available space in school

National schools may be one of the best educational options in some countries, enabling children to become immersed in the culture, learn the language quickly, make friends in the locality, and become truly bicultural. Often national schools cost far less than the international schools. In fact, in the United States, they're free. TCKs can remain home while having strong peer relationships.

However, there are special issues to consider as well. If school is taught in a language different from a child's mother language, the TCK must know enough of the local language *before* entering the school to function comfortably. We know of several sad cases where kids were put in classrooms before learning the local language. Two weeks of absolutely no communication (not even the ability to ask for directions to the toilet) is an eternity to an eight-year-old. Parents must make certain their children have at least elementary language skills before the first day of school.

Parents should also understand the basic philosophical and methodological underpinnings of this local system, as stated earlier in this chapter. Another thing to consider is the degree of animosity to the child's nationality in the host culture. If negative perceptions exist, a TCK might be designated an "outsider" and find the school situation intolerable.

Finally, there's the issue of assimilation. While one benefit of attending local schools is that it helps TCKs become part of the surrounding community faster, will this method of schooling facilitate their entering the culture more quickly and completely than the parents wish? How will acculturation affect their ultimate sense of cultural identity?

> Dave Pollock was confronted with the assimilation issue at a seminar on TCKs at the United Nations, where none of the attendees was from the U.S. To start out he asked them why they had come. After a period of silence one father said, "Most of us are here to find out how to keep our children from becoming too American." The other participants laughed and nodded in agreement.
>
> Dave replied, "Well, I have some bad news and some good news for you. Whether you knew it or not, when you decided to become a globally nomadic family and move to the United States (or any other country), you decided that your children would become third culture kids. That means they will be influenced by the culture they live in and become in some degree bi- or multicultural; it's inevitable. Now the good news: it doesn't have to ruin their lives. In fact, it will add a lot to them. It's okay to be a TCK."

While it isn't necessarily bad for TCKs to identify closely with the local culture, sometimes the cultural immersion is so complete that the TCK chooses to never repatriate. This can be a painful choice for a TCK's parents, because they may feel their child is rejecting them along with their culture. It's unfair, however, for parents to encourage in-depth cross-cultural relationships throughout their child's schooling and then object when that same child wants to marry and settle down permanently in the host country. The possible long-term implications of school and culture need to be thought through at the beginning of the TCK experience, not the end.

Local International Schools

Pros	Cons
Academically high standards	Expensive
Excellent facility and equipment	Potential lack of preparation for school in home country
Enrichment and specialized programs	Economic imbalance among students
Potential continuity with schooling during leave in home country	
Usually home with parents	
Good preparation for reentry if curriculum is based on home country's system	

International schools are another popular option for TCKs. A significant problem arises, however, in trying to identify what the term *international school* actually means. In her master's thesis, "Some of the Outcomes of International Schooling," Helen Fail raises these issues:

> Are there certain characteristics which define an international school, and if so what are they? Is it because children from several nationalities attend? If so, then many schools in Britain could be described as international. Is it determined by the curriculum? If so, then only the schools offering the International Baccalaureate would qualify. There are many schools overseas offering a U.S. or U.K. curriculum or another mixture which would presumably [result in their being] rated as national schools overseas. It may well be that many schools overseas consider themselves and indeed call themselves international yet never consider that while teaching an international curriculum to a group of students from many different nationalities, the teaching faculty is 95 percent British or American and inevitably they perpetuate certain national and cultural values.[2]

As international educators continue working on this matter, undoubtedly the term *international school* will be more precisely defined in the future. For our discussion here, we will include a broad spectrum of schools under the term *international school* and loosely define it as meaning any school that has students from various countries and whose primary curriculum is different from the one used by the national schools of the host country.

So what are particular elements to consider when thinking of sending a child to an international school? First, curriculum. Many international schools are beginning to incorporate broader choices in their subject material, including the International Baccalaureate degree and the International General Certificate of Secondary Education. Languages such as Japanese, Chinese, or Russian may now be included, when before only the more standard French, Latin, Spanish, and English were available. Many schools offer different choices in history courses, including the history of the host country.

Second, cultural framework. While offering more diversity of subject matter, most international schools still primarily operate from one cultural system of grading, style of teaching, basic curriculum, and philosophy of education. Jill and Roger Dyer write about the disadvantage Australian TCKs face when they take placement tests at many supposedly international schools which are, in reality, based on American standards in testing and curriculum content.

> Why are such [placement] tests invalid? Firstly, such aptitude testing is rarely carried out in Australian schools.... There has long been a belief among Australian educators that no scores are conclusive because of the enormous range of variables involved.... Secondly, there is no doubt that the U.S. tests are biased in content. Small children may be asked to complete a sheet by filling in the initial letter of a word represented on the page by a picture. One example of this is of a window with flowing material covering much of the glassed area. The Australian child would automatically write *C* for curtains and be

> marked incorrect, as the required answer is a *D* for
> drapes. Further evidence of testing which requires
> cultural understanding is a general knowledge test for
> primary-school children asking what is eaten with
> turkey at Thanksgiving...the answer required is
> cranberry sauce.[3]

Parents must look at the whole picture of any so-called international school to make sure their child's needs will be met within the variety of subjects offered and the philosophy or cultural base of education practiced there. Probably no two international schools are alike, given the diversity of the cultural and educational backgrounds among those who administer them.

The above issues aside, there are several significant benefits of international schooling. High on the list is that children usually remain at home, allowing the parents to have a more active role in school activities and in monitoring their children's progress. In fact, the very availability of group activities similar to those in schools back in the home country is another advantage. One of the greatest blessings is the diversity of backgrounds among students. When ATCKs look back on their international school experiences, many say they value most what they learned from their relationships with peers from many different nationalities. These global friendships opened the door to knowledge and understanding for a much larger worldview.[4]

Another important benefit offered by international schools is their general understanding of the internationally mobile experience. Many international schools have a 30 percent turnover each year as families are transferred in and out. Students understand what it is like to be "the new kid in school" and typically extend themselves toward the newcomer. Administrators, teachers, and counselors also understand the transition experience; while some may become blasé about what such a normative experience is, the best recognize the mandate they hold as international educators to support students and families in transition. Indeed, when parents have two or more international schools to choose between (not an uncommon situation in European and Asian capitals), they can factor into their decision which school provides ongoing, institutionalized transition programming. The school that offers transition activities to facilitate the adjustment of arrivals and departures and that integrates intercultural skill building and cultural identity explorations into the academic curriculum is probably the school to choose.[5]

The major drawback of international schools is their great expense. If parents are working for an agency that doesn't pay educational costs, the tuition may be prohibitive.

Overseas Boarding Schools

Pros	Cons
Academically good	Isolated from "real life"
Low or moderate expense	Early separation from parents
Usually closer than a school in the home country	Living away from parents
	Separation from host culture
Peer group relationships	Individualized care difficult
Good preparation for reentry if based on home-country curriculum	Different religious/philosophical values from parents

Many overseas boarding schools (meaning boarding schools outside the TCK's home country, though not always in the host country) originally developed in the days when strong formal educational programs of any kind were severely limited in many of the countries where third culture families worked. When missionary parents worked in remote jungles or when government officials moved to faraway lands to administer colonial regimes, few educational options were available for their children. Generally, the two choices these families had were to either home school their children or leave them behind.

In the early years of the twentieth century, however, various mission and colonial agencies founded boarding schools as an attempt to help TCKs remain closer to their parents. The schools catered to students primarily from Britain or the United States, and the curriculum was generally either British- or American-based. Children from other countries had to adjust as best they could.

Much of this has changed and is still changing. Now many of these same boarding schools not only have students from a broad spectrum of the international population, they have students and teachers from the host country as well. Some obvious benefits of these boarding schools are the opportunities students have to make close friends with their peers, to have healthy competition in sports or other areas, and to have trained teachers and a committed staff caring for them. In addition, children are usually closer to parents than they would be if left behind in the home country.

The negatives mainly have to do with the separation from parents and home. In the past, many children left home for boarding school at five or six years of age and were separated from their parents for long periods of time. This had been a common practice in Britain for years, and these schools were held up as proof that children fared well in such settings. Unfortunately, we've met many people who, as adults, have to deal with deep feelings of abandonment stemming from these early patterns of separation.

Another major problem with boarding schools is that it's almost impossible for parents to monitor what is happening on a day-to-day basis. There are many times when parents don't know until long afterwards if their child is having academic or personal problems or difficulties with a staff member. Some TCKs feel they were raised by older students, or even peers in the boarding school, rather than by adults. In the extreme, there is the risk of child abuse. While certainly not the norm, mistreatment occurs often enough to be of legitimate concern to parents.

Our suggestions for parents considering the boarding school option are to take into account the child's age and temperament, the character and reputation of the school, how often they will be able to see the child, and whether their child's communication with them is unhindered (some schools in the past have monitored their students' contact with parents).

As new findings continue to stress the importance of strong bonding with parents during a child's early years, and after listening to so many adults struggle to come to terms with early separations, we believe it's not wise, with so many other options available, to send young children—particularly those as young as five or six—to boarding school unless there are absolutely no other alternatives. It is simply impossible to measure how that kind of separation affects the children, or which ones will struggle with the effects of separation later on and which won't.

While it's good to include children in all discussions regarding their schooling, the decision about boarding school is one area in which this type of inclusion is vital. The feeling of *abandonment* expressed by ATCKs seems most often to come from those who say they were "sent off." When parents include children in the decision-making process, acknowledge the pros and cons of each schooling option, and listen carefully to the children's concerns and preferences, it makes a long-term difference. Children whose opinions are taken into account see that their thoughts and feelings matter; they do, indeed, feel valued.

Preuniversity Schooling in Home Country

Pros	Cons
Education compatible with higher education Reentry adjustment minimized Educational/enrichment opportunities	Extended separation from parents Lack of personalized care Cultural influence without parental guidance Loss of cross-cultural advantage and language acquisition

As we mentioned, leaving children with relatives or at a boarding school in the homeland used to be a common practice for third culture families. In fact, the normal practice for internationally mobile families until the late 1950s and early 1960s involved leaving TCKs in the homeland for secondary school, which often meant four or more years of separation from parents—all without benefit of e-mail, fax, or phone.[6]

Although sending preuniversity TCKs to school in the home country while parents remain overseas is no longer a common practice, it remains an option. Some families feel that nothing else suits their needs. Perhaps the TCK prefers living with relatives at home rather than going to a boarding school overseas, which was why Courtney left Saudi Arabia and returned to the States to live with her grandparents. She felt that if the only other option was to go to a boarding school where her American expatriate peers made up most of the student body, she would rather be with her grandparents. There can be any number of legitimate reasons for this choice.

The major benefit, of course, is that an early start in the school system of the home country makes it easier for TCKs to continue successfully in that system through university. But such a benefit must be weighed against the trauma of leaving their lifelong friends overseas (unless those friends are also moving) before the normally accepted time of secondary school graduation. Also, this question remains: how does changing cultures and facing all the issues of reentry during the height of identity formation in the early teen years affect TCKs compared with those who make the same switch a few years later?

For some TCKs, of course, it may be essential to return home before university. Those who face competitive exams in their midteens may find this the only real option if they wish to pursue certain careers. We've noticed a major difference in schooling patterns among Australian and New Zealand TCKs as compared with Americans. Most Americans can easily return to the States at age seventeen or eighteen and go directly to university, but TCKs from down under generally return to their home countries by the age of fifteen so they can prepare for the exams that determine which courses they will take during university.

The major drawback of schooling in the home country is the great distance from parents. In these days of e-mail and faxes, certainly communication is far easier than it was earlier in this century; nevertheless, an ocean apart is still pretty far to be away.

* *

It's obvious that there are many good choices for educating TCKs, and statistics show that, as a group, they do well academically. A survey of 608 adult missionary kids carried out by the MK CART/ CORE (a research organization composed of ten mission agencies) committee came out with these statistics:

- 30 percent of the respondents graduated from high school with honors
- 27 percent were elected to National Honor Society
- 94 percent went on to university-level studies
- 73 percent graduated from university
- 25 percent graduated from university with honors
- 3 percent were Phi Beta Kappas
- 11 percent were listed in *Who's Who in American Colleges and Universities*[7]

Another survey on ATCKs confirms that a strikingly high percentage of TCKs go on to postsecondary school education. In 1993 a study of 680 ATCKs done by John and Ruth Hill Useem and their colleagues showed that while only 21 percent of the American population as a whole has graduated from a four-year college or university, 81 percent of the ATCKs they surveyed had earned at least a bachelor's degree. Half of them went on to earn master's or doctorate degrees.[8] Undoubtedly, with thoughtful planning and wise choices, the educational process for TCKs has every chance of being a rich one indeed.

Endnotes

1   Brian Hill, "The Educational Needs of the Children of Expatriates," in *International Conference on Missionary Kids: New Directions in Missions: Implications for MKs*, edited by Beth A. Tetzel and Patricia Mortenson (Compendium of the International Conference on Missionary Kids, Manila, November 1984), 340.

2   Helen Fail, "Some of the Outcomes of International Schooling" (master's thesis, Oxford Brookes University, June 1995), 8.

3   Jill Dyer and Roger Dyer, *What Makes Aussie Kids Tick?* (Kingswood, SA, Australia: MK Merimna, 1989), 139–40.

4   Fail, "Some of the Outcomes."

5   Personal correspondence to David C. Pollock by Barbara F. Schaetti, Transition Dynamics, October 1998.

6   From Ruth E. Van Reken (unpublished original research on ATCKs, 1986).

7   Leslie Andrews, "The Measurement of Adult MKs' Well-Being," *Evangelical Missions Quarterly* 31, no. 4 (October 1995): 418–26.

8   John Useem, Ruth Hill Useem, Ann Baker Cottrell, and Kathleen Jordan, "TCKs Four Times More Likely to Earn Bachelor's Degrees," *Newlinks* 12, no. 5 (May 1993): 1.

15

Enjoying the Journey

One of the best aspects of a TCK lifestyle is the fun it can be. In his book *Living Overseas,* Dr. Ted Ward emphasizes the importance of enjoying the adventure—of *living!*[1] Parents of third culture kids don't need to wake up at 3:30 in the morning feeling terribly guilty because they have imposed a horrible experience on their children.

Ironically, the richness of their lives can become so routine that TCKs and their families forget to notice it. People who live at the foothills of the Alps soon take them for granted. Those living in tropical climates beside an ocean beach become so accustomed to waving palms and the roar of the sea that they rarely pause to wonder at the beauty. What's exotic and exciting to others has become ordinary for them.

How *do* third culture families make the most of their experiences in other cultures and places? Here are some practical tips.

Set Aside Special Times for Family and Make Family Traditions

At least once a week parents should close out the rest of the world and plan some family time. This might be a weekly outing, table games together one evening a week, or some other activity the family enjoys. In cultures where visitors stop by with no forewarning, families often have to leave home and find a park, beach, or restaurant to have this kind of uninterrupted time together.

Traditions bind people and groups together because they are visible markers affirming a shared history and celebrating a current unity of thought, purpose, or relationship. Every nation has them, every ethnic group has them, and, one hopes, every family has them. Traditions help families everywhere build their unique sense of identity and give each family member a sense of belonging as well.

Often a family's traditions evolve without special planning. Uncle Fred pulls out his mandolin at every reunion and family members old and young sing along. No one has consciously decided this will be a tradition, but the family gathering wouldn't be the same if Uncle Fred and his mandolin weren't there.

Third culture families have at least as much need for traditions as other families do—maybe more. But because they won't always be around to go to the family reunions and "hear Uncle Fred," they may have to do a little more conscious planning to develop traditions that are transportable and can be replicated in different places. These traditions can be as simple as giving each family member the chance to pick the menu for his or her birthday dinner every year or as complicated as making a piñata stuffed with candy for a particular holiday once a year.

Developing traditions in cross-cultural settings isn't only important, it's fun. New ideas from different places can be incorporated to help each tradition become a marker of family history. In Liberia a hot-dog roast on the beach defined Christmas Eve for some expatriates—not a traditional custom in most snow-covered lands but a nice one to carry back home (even if the hot dogs have to be roasted in a fireplace!) as a distinctive reminder of the family's history.

Build Strong Ties with the Community

TCKs usually grow up far from blood relatives, but there can be substitute "aunts," "uncles," and "grandparents" wherever TCKs live. Sometimes these people will be host country citizens; sometimes they will be from the third culture community itself. Parents can foster such relationships by inviting these special people to join in celebrating the TCK's birthday, allowing their child to go shopping with them—whatever is appropriate for the situation. This "created" extended family gives TCKs the experience of growing up in a close community, even without blood relatives. As ATCKs remember their childhood, some of these relationships rank among their fondest memories.

Build Strong Ties with Relatives

Relatives back home are another important part of a TCK's life, and relationships with them need to be fostered also. A great way to do this is to bring a grandma, grandpa, aunt, uncle, or cousin out to visit. This not only helps TCKs get to know their relatives better, it lets relatives see TCKs in their own environment—the place where they do, in fact, shine. On top of that, TCKs love to return "home" and be able to talk to family members who know what they're talking about. But even if relatives cannot make such a trip, it's important for TCKs to maintain contact with them as much as possible through letters, e-mail, faxes, telephone, and pictures.

Developing closeness with relatives at home is especially important if and when the time comes for TCKs to repatriate while parents continue living overseas.

> During the four years that Lois attended university in the States, she never once received a care package or an invitation to visit during the holidays from any of her numerous aunts and uncles. Lois was a good kid, and her relatives were warm, caring people, but it apparently never crossed their minds that she might need

them. Lois was too shy to ask, and her parents never
thought to alert their brothers and sisters that Lois
would need care from the extended family.

Fortunately Lois knew one family—friends from her
early childhood—who opened their hearts to her.
Now, many years later, Lois's own home is continually
open to other TCKs whose parents are overseas.

Build Strong Ties with Friends

To begin with, TCKs should work at making new friends everywhere they go so that they won't try to escape the challenges of
entering a new culture or dealing with reentry into their home culture by isolating themselves. Friends from the past are also important, because they validate the TCK experience and prove that the
third culture world and experience aren't a dream. It's also important, when possible, for TCKs to attend school reunions and return
to visit the home or homes of their childhood.

Return to the Same "Home" during Each Leave

Whenever practical, third culture families should return to the same
place each time they go on home leave. Children who change countries every two or three years as well as those who stay in one host
country their whole lives all need the sense that there is at least one
physical place to identify as home in their passport country. When
staying in the same physical house isn't possible, families should
try to locate nearby so TCKs can have the same school, church, and
friends. It's also helpful when taking trips to visit friends or relatives in other places to stay long enough to establish at least some
basis for a relationship that can be built upon during the next leave.

While it's good to foster all these relationships in the home country, families shouldn't spend the entire leave visiting people. When
every evening is spent with the adults chatting happily in one room
and the TCKs and children from the host family eyeing each other

warily in another, and when every night is spent in a different bed, this overload of travel can be stressful. Third culture families should also plan for nights in motels, camping trips, or other private times during their travel to reinforce their sense of being a family in this land as well as in the host country.

Tour When Traveling between Countries

As families go back and forth between host and home countries, they need to get off the plane, find a place to stay, and tour the countries in between. Making stops along the way not only expands the TCKs' world; it also creates memories that last a lifetime. Courtney had this to say about her experiences of travel:

> My memory is much bigger than most of my friends' because of all the exciting places my parents took me on our trips between Saudi and America. When we went to England or Germany, for example, knowing I loved art, my mom would take me to the museums while my sister and dad went off on other excursions. I learned so much by absorbing the cultures we encountered—we would take tours and soak up the information the guides told us.

> My parents may not realize that the most profound thing they did for me was to take me to Dachau. I must have been about eleven or twelve. We walked the grounds; we looked at everything; I cried. My parents did not protect me; they exposed me to everything—including the crematoriums, gas chambers, photos. When you read about World War II and the concentration camps, I can't imagine how you can truly understand it without seeing one of the camps. I just stood there, overwhelmed, and thought, how is this possible? It was so big.

> I am filled up when I think of all that I've seen and touched, and how much I want to return and touch it all again.

Explore and Become Involved in the Surroundings

Don't neglect actively learning about the history, geography, and culture of the host country. Families should pretend they are tourists once or twice a year and plan trips just to see the sights. Courtney's parents also helped her to explore their host country—Saudi Arabia. "My parents often took us out into the desert to look at various natural treasures such as sharks' teeth, sand roses, and arrowheads. It was exciting to imagine this place under water millions of years ago." These may seem like simple memories, but they've left Courtney with a deep sense of connection to her past.

As a corollary, a common regret we hear from ATCKs is they never really got involved with the surrounding culture when they were children. Whether it happened because they lived on a military base, went off to boarding school, or played only with expatriate friends, many consider this a loss. As adults they realize they could have learned so much more and wish they had studied the language or taken time to learn how to cook the wonderful local dishes they enjoyed when they went out to dinner.

Acquire "Sacred Objects"

As we have mentioned before, artifacts from countries where they have lived or visited eventually become the TCKs' portable history to cart around the world in future years. It helps connect all the places and experiences of their lives. During her childhood, ATCK Sandra acquired a set of carved ebony elephant bookends, a lamp (whose base included more elephants), feather paintings, and other ebony carvings to hang on the wall. At university and in the sixteen locations where she has lived since her wedding, when the bookends are in place, the paintings and carvings hung on the wall, and the lamp turned on, she's home.

****

In the end, one German TCK, Dirk, summed up best what we are trying to say. When we asked him what he thought of his experience as a TCK, he said, "The thing I like best about my life is living it!"

That's what it's all about—living and enjoying the TCKs' world.

Endnote

[1] Ted Ward, *Living Overseas: A Book of Preparations* (New York: Free Press, 1984).

16

Coming "Home": Reentry

And now we have come full circle. After all these years of careful planning to make the most of their years in a host culture, the time has finally come for the family, or at least the TCKs themselves, to go "home." As we said at the beginning of this book, one of the factors that distinguishes the TCK experience from a true immigrant is the full expectation that after living for a significant period of their developmental years outside their passport culture, there will come the day when TCKs make a permanent return to that country and culture. Oddly enough, for many TCKs this is one of the most difficult transitions they go through no matter how many other moves they have already made. Commonly called *reentry,* for a great number this process more closely resembles an entry. How TCKs do or don't cope with the reentry experience can shape their lives for years to come.

Why is reentry so hard for so many?

Reentry Stresses

Many reasons for reentry stress are simply extensions of the factors we have already talked about, particularly the normal challenges of any cross-cultural transition: the grief of losing a world they have come to love, the discomfort of being out of cultural balance once more, and the struggle to find a sense of belonging in a new place with new people. There are also some very particular and additional stresses TCKs face during this transition to their home culture, however, and they are worth examining carefully.

False Expectations

One of the most basic, but unrecognized, reason for reentry stress has to do with unconscious expectations of both the TCKs and those in their home culture. As you remember, we talked earlier about the TCKs' various relational patterns with their surrounding community and used the following model to identify each one.

Foreigner Look different Think different	**Hidden Immigrant** Look alike Think different
Adopted Look different Think alike	**Mirror** Look alike Think alike

As we mentioned in chapter 3, traditionally most TCKs have been recognized as foreigners while they were living in their host culture. Some have lived there as hidden immigrants, and a few fit into either the adopted or mirror category. When TCKs return to their passport culture, however, almost all are hidden immigrants. Now everything Dr. Kohls talks about in his model of the iceberg and how that relates to cultural expectations and stress starts to make even more sense. People at home take one look at these returning TCKs and expect them to be in the "mirror" box—persons who think and look like themselves. Why wouldn't they? After all, these TCKs are from the same racial, ethnic, and national background as those "at home" are.

TCKs look around them and they, too, often expect to be in the mirror box. For years they've known they were "different" but excused it because they knew they were Asians living in England, Africans living in Germany, or Canadians living in Bolivia. That justification for being different is now gone, and they presume they will finally be the same as others; after all, these are their own people. Wrong. Take another look at Krista and Nicola, our look-alike TCKs who let their host culture peers in England and Scotland know how eager they were to return to their home countries where they knew they would finally fit in and belong.

> When Krista first returned to the States, she felt euphoric at finally being "home." It didn't take long, however, before Krista realized, to her horror, that she couldn't relate to her American classmates either. Somehow she was as different from them as from her English peers.
>
> The same thing happened to Nicola when she returned to England. After literally kissing the tarmac when she disembarked from the plane in London, a strange thing soon happened. Nicola found herself increasingly irritated with her English student peers. Their world seemed so small. Internally, she began resisting becoming like them, and within a year, virtually all of her friends were international students and other TCKs. She wondered why she could never completely fit into the world around her, whether it was Scottish or English. Both Krista and Nicola's disappointment was greater because they had always presumed if they could only make it "home," they would no longer feel so different from others.

Many TCKs have similar experiences to those of Krista and Nicola, where all seems well at the beginning of reentry. Relatives and old friends welcome the TCKs warmly, while the school bends over backward in its efforts to assess how transcripts from some exotic foreign school relate to the local curriculum. Soon, however, unexpected differences begin to pop up. Classmates use slang or idioms that mean nothing to the returning TCKs. Everyone else is driving a car; they only know how to ride a bike. Friends, relatives, and classmates are shocked at the TCKs' ignorance of the most common practices necessary for everyday living. If they were true immigrants, no one would expect them to know all these things, but because they are presumed to be in the mirror box, those in the home country begin to peg them as "strange" or, at least, slightly stupid.

Conversely, TCKs aren't doing much better in their opinions of newfound peers. When they saw themselves as true foreigners in Romania, they never expected their local friends to know where Utah was on the U.S. map. Now they can't believe how dumb their friends in Utah are because they have no idea where Romania is.

Reentry might not be quite so difficult if the unexpected differences were merely in some of these more obvious ways. But deeper levels of cultural dissonance lurk beneath the apparently similar surface. Every time someone takes them to McDonald's for a hamburger, the TCKs mention how many people could eat for a whole week back in their host country for the money this one meal costs. Even worse, they watch how much food people throw out and express their shock and horror. The person who bought their hamburger sees the TCKs as ungrateful at best, condemning at worst. The fact is that while TCKs and their peers at home may indeed look exactly alike, they don't share a common worldview because their life experiences have been totally different.

And so the problems continue to mount. TCKs who have grown up in a culture where the commitment to honesty and respect is accompanied by orderliness and quiet find entry into a confrontational, loud, self-centered home culture quite offensive. Those who have grown up in a boisterous, activity-centered, individualistic culture may find people from their own country docile and self-effacing. Often TCKs begin to realize they don't even like what is considered their home culture. And those in the home culture may soon realize they're not so sure they like the TCKs either. But no one stops to think through how these reactions are related to the cultural expectations they had for one another in the first place. They still presume their insides match as well as their outsides and that something is "wrong" with the other person.

Of course, there are other reasons besides erroneous expectations that make reentry a tough transition. Here are two false fears that also contribute.

False Fears

Sometimes TCKs fear that allowing themselves to repatriate totally will mean being disloyal to their host country. "If I allow myself to like it here, it may mean I really didn't like it there," or "If I adjust and fit in, I may lose my memory of and commitment to return to the place where I grew up." Such fears can make them lose the delight in their present, which is as much a part of their life experience as their past has been. They need to know it's okay to enjoy a chapati, a Big Mac, and a taco quite interchangeably—that to embrace a particular part of any of their worlds doesn't deny the reality and/or goodness of another part.

Other TCKs fear losing their identity. "If I let go of the place and the people where I have always identified most and fit in best to align myself with my home country and culture, will I lose some important part of me?" This makes for "reentry shock," a close relative to the culture shock experienced by those going to live abroad for the first time. Any threat to our identity calls up deep and complex emotions, which lead to the kinds of symptoms that signal culture shock: sleeplessness, anxiety, irritability, homesickness, depression, and others.

Common Reactions to Reentry Stress

Despite many of their contradictory feelings, however, most TCKs' basic desire is to be "home," to be "the same." How do they react when they find they are not? TCKs choose all sorts of ways to cope. Some, like Paul (our American in Australia), try to be perfect external chameleons. To fit in, they refuse to tell anyone of their past life. Where they have lived or grown up becomes a well-guarded secret. A teacher explains the whys and wherefores of the tribal practices of a group in the TCKs' host country, and they never say a word—although they're boiling inside at the misconceptions being taught. Basically these TCKs deny one entire side of their life to try and blend in with their new peers.

Others cope by getting angry. They will do almost anything to prove they aren't like their fellow citizens. One American girl refused to give up her British accent when she returned to Washington, DC, and displayed it when telling people how dumb she thought American foreign policy was.

Why is anger such a common reaction? There are several likely reasons. A cross-cultural lifestyle is so normal for TCKs that they themselves don't always understand how much it has shaped their view of the world. They easily forget that others haven't had the same exposure to different cultures and lifestyles as they have had. Also, the easiest way for anyone to deal with the stress of feeling uncomfortable in a new situation is to put others down. This impatience can be a defense against the feelings of insecurity or inferiority TCKs may have in their home culture. This impatience or judgmentalism sometimes also serves as a means of identifying with other TCKs. It becomes one of the markers of "us" versus "them." Unfortunately, a get-together of TCKs can quickly degenerate into bashing the perceived stupidity of non-TCKs.

At times it seems TCKs can be culturally tolerant anywhere but in their own culture. When people move to a new host culture, they usually keep quiet if they have strongly negative opinions about that culture. At most, they only express them to fellow expatriates. These rules seem to change, however, on reentry. Some TCKs appear to feel quite free to express every negative opinion they can possibly think of about their home culture, no matter who is around. While chronic put-downs may be an unconscious defense for the TCKs' own feelings of insecurity or rejection, such remarks further alienate them from everyone around them. But, like it or not, they are a member of this group by birth and citizenship. In affirming one part of their experience and themselves, they reject another.

Other TCKs, of course, simply withdraw. Some do it in obvious forms. They have a hard time getting out of bed, or they sit in their rooms and watch TV all day rather than joining any activities at school or church. These, too, are culture shock reactions. Withdrawal can have less obvious forms, however. Some students retreat into their studies and earn straight As—but who can fault them for that? Others spend hours practicing their favorite instrument and winning every musical contest they enter. While everyone congratulates them for their achievement, no one realizes this is another form of escape.

For a few TCKs, however, this period of looking for a way to relate to their home cultures can be a dangerous time. After trying various ways of coping, they realize that for all their external adaptation, something inside still doesn't fit, and they believe this something will never change. Psychiatrist Esther Schubert, an ATCK herself who has done research among TCKs, reports that suicide rates go up among TCKs after their first year home.[1] For them, it's the ongoing struggle to fit in that leads to despair rather than simply the initial reentry.

Helping in the Reentry Process

While there are no foolproof ways to ensure a perfect reentry, the basic key to helping TCKs find their way is to first understand what they are going through. Then there are some practical steps to help TCKs get through this process in a healthy rather than a harmful way.

When parents decide to move to another culture, they and others must accept that their children may wind up with a completely different sense of home and rootedness than their own. As we've said before, in spite of feeling so different in their home culture, many TCKs do have a sense of home, or at least cultural balance—either in one particular host culture or in the internationally mobile

community and its characteristic lifestyle. Dirk, the German business TCK who grew up in Taiwan, said,

> I've always thought I felt more connected to Asia than
> to any other place. In fact, I glamorize Asian culture. I
> pick it up like my favorite pie. It's always been such a
> wonderful thing for me. My long-term goal is to go
> right back there.
>
> But I've begun to realize that it isn't only Asia that I
> feel so connected to. I also feel very connected to
> people who have lived in the international community,
> no matter which part of the world they have lived in.
> I've been doing everything I can since I've gotten here
> to get back to Asia, but if I can't go there, I'll have to
> go somewhere in the international community to feel
> truly at home.

Understanding that this type of reaction is normal for those with a
third culture upbringing is one of the most positive ways to work
through reentry. It gives TCKs the needed permission to work through
reentry in much the same way they would approach coming into any
new culture. Some good ways to approach the reentry process include talking with others who have already been through it, attending seminars, and reading the growing number of books available
for third culture families, including *Strangers at Home,*[2] a book of
essays on the reentry experience, and *The Art of Coming Home.*[3]

Instead of presuming it's everyone else's task to understand them,
TCKs need to make an effort to understand the life experiences of
their home peers. Asking thoughtful questions and listening more
actively are great ways to learn more about the variety of backgrounds
and experiences of peers in their own country. It also helps them
realize that their own story is simply one of many and to understand
why others may not see the world exactly as they do.

> One ATCK, Eleanor, worked in a nursing home, where
> most of the nurse's aides had never lived out of the
> state or spent one day at university. The things they
> talked about—boyfriends and babies—seemed

unbearably dull to her. When she tried to liven the conversations up with stories of her past exciting life in Chile, they listened politely but never asked a follow-up question. At first she felt affronted and judged them as shallow souls. But one day it occurred to Eleanor that she knew no more about their lifestyle and interests than they did about hers. She realized she needed to start getting to know them better instead of waiting for them to get to know her.

Since reentry is actually the entering stage of the larger transition experience they are going through at this point, don't forget that this is when TCKs most need a good mentor. Reentry is the key period when they are most vulnerable to being swept up in a group of friends they would never have chosen under normal circumstances, and they can get into drugs, alcohol, and other behavior they previously spurned. One thing that can make it difficult to find a good mentor, however, is that when TCKs return to their home country and are seen by others as "different" or "weird," often the peers who could be positive role models and friends don't reach out to the TCKs because they appear so odd. This means that parents often need to help identify a suitable mentor such as a relative, caring friend, youth leader, or sympathetic school staff member and enlist that person's help in positively introducing their child to this culture and community.

The chosen mentor also needs to understand that part of the mentoring process is helping the TCK learn the basic survival skills for this culture. These should include new technologies (like how to use a cell phone or the Internet) and significant changes in youth culture. Are bell-bottoms in again? What movies, rock groups, or particular shoe styles are popular? Sometimes these things are so common that the mentor may forget to specifically go over them with the TCK. Attending a transition or reentry seminar is often extremely helpful for many high school- and college-age TCKs during reentry. These seminars with other TCKs take up many of the issues discussed in this book and help TCKs realize they are not alone and aren't weird. (See the list of reentry seminars in Resources and Bibliography, pages 319–33.)

Ultimately, one of the ways to help TCKs resettle in their home country on a long-term basis is to provide an opportunity for them to revisit the host country where they feel most deeply rooted. It's easy for that past experience to become so idealized or romanticized in the transition to their home culture that it grows to larger-than-life proportions. Going back can help put it into perspective. Going back does something else as well. It connects the past and present worlds of TCKs and reminds them that their past is not a myth or totally inaccessible. In addition, such a journey reminds them that things never stay the same, and ultimately the past is now a foundation for the future.

With the increasing number of children from many cultures joining the ranks of TCKs, there are new concerns to consider. For citizens of some countries that have strong cultural traditions to which all children carefully adhere and in which the TCK is a new phenomenon, TCKs can be seen as a threat to the stability of the home culture. In one country, some government officials suggested reprogramming for TCKs because their new independent ways of thinking were unacceptable and disturbing for that culture.

We conclude with perhaps the most important matter we can mention regarding a TCK's transition home. It is this simple fact: whether parents return home with their TCK or send him or her on ahead, they must realize that ultimately it is their responsibility to help their child through the reentry phase. It's such a basic fact, it seems almost silly to say, but believe it or not, we've seen TCKs arrive at universities with no clear idea of where they will go during school breaks, for long weekends, or during summer vacations. It seems as if parents have shipped them back home in the rather vague, blissful assumption that everything will work out by itself—perhaps relying on other relatives to take care of their children, even when those relationships have never been nurtured.

It's not enough to presume that relatives at home will automatically pitch in to take care of a "homeless" TCK. We can't state this point strongly enough. Any time parents send their children back home while they themselves remain overseas, parents are still responsible for making sure their children are protected and cared for. It's their absolute responsibility to make sure their children have a designated "home-away-from-home." A strong extended family helps that process greatly, one where both the relatives and the TCKs already feel comfortable and at home with one another. If it's possible for TCKs to attend university near their relatives, this can also help ease them through reentry.

If no extended family is available, close friends can help. But if there is no safe harbor available for their TCK, parents should think seriously about staying home themselves until their child is secure in his or her new life. This may cost the parents of such TCKs a few years of their careers, but failure to do so may cause their children lifelong harm because of mistakes these TCKs make or the abandonment they feel as they try to adjust to a world they have never known.

In the end, while many TCKs look back on their reentry period as one of the more stressful parts of their TCK experience, they still wouldn't have wanted to miss much of what they learned from the process. Often they emerge from reentry with an awareness of how their own culture operates in ways that those who have never left may never see. This awareness can help them decide, perhaps more proactively than they might have otherwise, which values of their own culture they want to keep or let go of. Most also come to appreciate the special gifts they have received from each culture that has been part of their lives, including this one finally known as "home."

Endnotes

1   Esther Schubert, "Keeping Third-Culture Kids Emotionally Healthy: Depression and Suicide among Missionary Kids," in *International Conference on Missionary Kids: New Directions for Missions: Implications for MKs,* edited by Beth A. Tetzel and Patricia Mortenson (Compendium of the International Conference on Missionary Kids, Manila, November 1984).

2   Carolyn D. Smith, ed., *Strangers at Home* (Putnam Valley, NY: Aletheia Publications, 1996).

3   Craig Storti, *The Art of Coming Home* (Yarmouth, ME: Intercultural Press, 1997).

17

How Sponsoring
Organizations Can Help

In addition to personal and parental choices that can help TCKs thrive in their experience, the policies and the programs (or lack thereof) of sponsoring organizations weigh heavily in the equation. Even if parents and TCKs do everything we've suggested to maximize the TCK experience, administrative decisions or policies within the sponsoring agency can still create problems. For example, a company orders its employee to move in the middle of a school year, or an organization only pays for one type of schooling. Administrators of international organizations need to realize that their personnel policies have a profound effect on the employee's family. At home, employers rarely have any influence on the schooling and living choices of their employees, but in cross-cultural situations the ramifications of corporate and organizational decisions filter down through the family of every employee affected by them.

Administrative decisions based solely on the interests of the international organization are shortsighted. Agencies should consider family needs as well as corporate needs when planning to send an employee overseas, for at least two reasons. First, it's for the long-term benefit of the company. Cross-cultural consultant Germaine

W. Shames states that "approximately 30 percent of managers from the United States return home early from an overseas assignment. The reason? Personal and family stress."[1] When agencies help employees meet their family's needs—whether for schooling, travel, or home leave—parents who work for the agencies are far more likely to stay with the company longer and be more productive. Since the cost of sending an employee overseas usually runs two to five times that employee's annual salary,[2] agencies benefit financially if they can keep their seasoned, internationally experienced employees from departing prematurely.

Keeping employees with strong cross-cultural skills also helps an agency's performance in relationship to the host culture. New people trying to learn those skills are bound to make more professional and social gaffes that hinder their effectiveness in a strange culture than someone who has already gone through the process of cross-cultural adaptation. After all, there are lessons about crossing cultures that only time can teach.

Second, sound corporate decisions and policies are for the long-term good of the family. When corporate or organizational decisions are made with families in mind, the family feels protected and cared for, a relationship that any organization should wish to cultivate as part of the organizational or corporate culture. With each family member having space to grow and develop, parents can make decisions only they are qualified to make—decisions that will help their children effectively use their cross-cultural heritage.

How Agencies Can Help Prior to the Overseas Assignment

One of the most important steps an organization can take for its overseas employees is to compile a list of schooling options well before the date of departure and make their policies and practices regarding educational costs and choices clear. Families need to know their educational options prior to accepting an assignment abroad.

A second valuable step is to plan a preassignment orientation. Some international agencies are doing an excellent job of this, offering workshops for both the employee and the employee's spouse and children. Other agencies, however, still think only of the employee and make no preparation for the intercultural adjustments that the family will inevitably face. Such agencies should seek outside help from cross-cultural training consultants and organizations.

Finally, and perhaps even preceding the two strategies above, organizational managers need to gather information on how often and why personnel are transferred to new locations. Since many challenges of the TCK experience are so closely tied to high mobility, administrators must look for ways to minimize the frequency and severity of the transition cycles. For example, why do military and embassy personnel change posts at least every two years? Is it always because of staffing needs, per se, or is it simply tradition? Some say if military or diplomatic personnel stay in one place too long and get attached to people in the host country, they will no longer be able to represent their own government effectively. Has this theory been tested? Similarly, when a business decides to send a person overseas, is it essential that the employee go in the middle of the school year?

Unnecessary, abrupt decisions by administrators can create tremendous stress for an employee's family. Simple matters like examining the options for moving a family during a school vacation or after a child graduates can make all the difference as to whether a family thrives or barely survives in a cross-cultural lifestyle.

How Agencies Can Help During the Third Culture Experience

An agency's responsibility to the family's well-being doesn't end after the final plans for departure are made or good-byes said. To increase a family's chances of success while they are abroad, the agency should have in place a plan that includes the following components.

1. *Have an entry team or a designated employee to welcome new employees on site.* Each agency should have a formal plan for introducing new people to both the host and expatriate communities as quickly as possible. It's important for newcomers to know the people they need to contact locally for business connections as well as for the practical issues of life that long-time residents take for granted. We know of one young couple who went overseas to an area where, after their initial welcome at the airport, they were left on their own to figure out how to get their driver's licenses, find someone to install a phone, and even locate a doctor to call when a family member became sick. It was three months before they met anyone who explained to them where they could buy meat they could actually chew. The problem there was that the home office presumed that families in the overseas branch would take care of properly orienting new arrivals but had no formal plan in place to make sure it was done.

   Sometimes people are assigned to a post where they are the only employees from their particular home country. Those from the local culture may work hard to make the newcomers feel welcome and to introduce them to local customs and stores, but it is also helpful during this time if they can find others from their home culture as well. These people are the ones who know the types of products the newcomers can substitute for things they have been accustomed to using at home. They are also the only ones who might think to explain, for example, that a siren going off in bad weather means a tornado may be approaching. Local residents are so accustomed to this warning system that they don't even think to explain it or realize these new friends have never been around tornadoes before.

2. *Help employees evaluate schooling options using the compiled list put together before departure.* Agencies should never insist on one particular method of schooling for their families. As

we've said, parents must have freedom to consider each child's personality and special needs when making this critical choice.

Agencies must also take into account the additional costs of education for expatriate children. Part of the employee's salary and benefits should include helping with those costs. In the home country, educational expenses for children are rarely discussed when negotiating a job contract, but schooling is often a complex and costly issue for expatriates, especially in certain countries.

3. *Establish a flexible leave policy.* Policies for leave vary from agency to agency. Some insist their employees remain on site for four years, followed by a one-year home leave. Others have a cycle of sending people overseas for eleven months, then home for a month. Between those two ends of the spectrum lie other alternatives. There are pros and cons to each—both for the sponsoring organizations and for the families. Wise administrators are willing to negotiate mutually beneficial leave packages if the standard policy for that organization doesn't work for a particular person or family.

4. *Make provision for children who are attending school in the home country to visit parents during vacations.* Traditionally, many sponsoring organizations have paid for TCKs to return home for vacations if they were away for schooling through secondary school, but once those children returned to their home culture for university, those benefits ended. It's during those postsecondary years, however, that many major life decisions are made, years when parental support and guidance are crucial. Many organizations lose valuable employees whose children are at this critical life juncture; many would rather resign than be separated for several years—particularly if they are in a situation where they can't afford to pay personally for such trips.

We believe there is a fairly simple answer. Paying for children attending postsecondary institutions in the home country to visit their parents for vacations should be a normal benefit for those working for international organizations. That policy change alone would likely prolong the careers of many of their employees, and it would also go a long way toward reducing many of the most challenging aspects of this globally mobile lifestyle.

5. *Support international community efforts to provide ongoing expatriate family services.* Research surveys that assess the factors contributing to the relative success or failure of an overseas assignment now include the degree to which a sponsoring organization provides ongoing assistance abroad.[3] Barbara F. Schaetti, a consultant to the international expatriate community, suggests that the challenge for a company lies in how to provide such assistance in every one of its international locations. She notes that, historically, most have relied upon their network of expatriate spouses. Support has been limited to paying membership dues to international women's clubs and contributing funds to international school parent/teacher association programs. Increasingly, however, companies are taking a more proactive approach. Many are now contracting with International Employee Assistance Programs (IEAPs) to provide expatriates with access to confidential mental-health services on demand. Others are underwriting spouse-managed information centers and providing access to the Internet so that spouses in diverse locations may link together. Still others sponsor such regional events as the European-based Women on the Move conferences.[4]

One of the most exciting developments in the way companies are providing ongoing expatriate family services is their support of community-based transition programs. Schaetti describes this corporate/community partnership as one in which local operating companies provide the funding, while the community, often with the leadership of the international school, provides a "transition resource team." This team is typically composed of ten to fifteen parents, educators, and students and represents the diversity of the community in terms of nationality and international experience. Its purpose is to design and implement ongoing, institutionalized, year-round transition programming customized to the needs of its own community. Although the specific goals will thus vary by community, the common commitment of community-based transition programs is to help expatriates take the lead regarding their own experience.[5]

6. *Help families prepare for repatriation and organizational reentry.* Not only do companies lose valuable employees during the posting abroad, but disappointing statistics indicate that 20 to 25 percent of expatriate families leave the company within one year of repatriation.[6] Repatriating, or returning home, is frequently more difficult than moving abroad in the first place. Many, especially corporate employees, have been out of the loop while they were overseas. Their old job has been filled by someone else, their career is off track, and the company doesn't know what to do with them or how to use the international and cross-cultural skills they have acquired. Also, overseas these employees may have had a good bit of autonomy as decision makers or leaders, but at home their position is subordinate. Plus, they no longer fit into old patterns—not only at work but also at home in their former community.

Unfortunately, agencies and employees who prepared well for the original cross-cultural transition often forget to prepare equally carefully for the transition home. Ideally, before the family leaves the host country, a formal or informal briefing should be provided by people who have experienced this type of transition before. Families should be reminded that it is as important to build the RAFT we discussed earlier during this transition home as it is prior to a transition anywhere else. If the family has been overseas for a long time, agencies should provide a mentor to help the family navigate the various changes that have occurred at home in their absence.

7. *Offer reentry seminars for both parents and TCKs soon after repatriation.* Several organizations sponsor week-long seminars every summer for TCKs who are returning to their home country, and some agencies hold debriefing seminars for the adults. Recently, some groups have begun offering programs for the entire family (see Resources and Bibliography, pages 319–33, for a list of reentry seminars).

How Agencies Can Help Their TCKs in the Long Term

Because so many TCKs grow up with a strong sense that friends from the sponsoring agency or their international school are a part of their extended family, belonging to this group becomes part of their very identity. It may be the one place outside their family where they have a deep sense of belonging. They want and need to stay connected with this support system in some way.

Helping TCKs and ATCKs stay connected with one another and their past is beneficial for those directly involved as well as for the organization. Think of the benefit it would be for a company if these children return with their cross-cultural skills when they are ready for their own careers. Here are some ways administrators can play a vital role in helping TCKs who have grown up in their communities continue to thrive, ways that can also help in the healing process for those ATCKs who still need help dealing with some of these matters of adjustment.

1. *Support an alumni newsletter.* A growing number of agencies and international schools already help their TCKs and ATCKs maintain a sense of connectedness by helping them put out a newsletter. This forum not only distributes information, it also

gives them the opportunity to discuss relevant issues from their past, to offer suggestions for the present, and to stay part of the "family."

2. *Use the experience of TCKs and ATCKs.* It's ironic to see an organization bring in "experts" about a particular subject or country while ignoring the wealth of knowledge and experience of their own ATCKs.

> One ATCK sat through a meeting where a medical facility to be established in Brazil—modeled after one in the States—was being described and discussed. She knew from the beginning that the project would fail, because the philosophical concepts on which it was based were very different from those which shaped Brazilian thinking. When she attempted to raise a few questions, she was disdainfully put down. Three years later, after vast sums of money had been spent on the project, it folded, a complete failure.

Perhaps all prophets are without honor in their own country, but agencies shouldn't overlook the great resources they have in their ATCKs.

3. *Apologize for past organizational mistakes.* Unfortunately, as a direct result of poor administrative decisions from the company or sponsoring agency, some TCKs suffer the consequences. Some policies on relocating families, for example, have caused needless separations. An unfortunate choice of caregiver in a boarding school may have done harm to some children. The errors may not have been willful but they happened nonetheless. Even though those who made the decision may have since left the organization, it helps the employees—and the TCKs who were hurt by those policies—to know that the system itself is taking responsibility and that someone representing that system or organization is willing to apologize for past mistakes and, where needed, offer restitution.

4. *Pay for a TCK's "journey of clarification."* Some agencies already offer a trip back to the host culture during or immediately after university for all of their TCKs who grew up overseas, even if the parents are no longer abroad. As mentioned before, going back to their roots and validating past experiences helps TCKs move on more smoothly to the next stages of life, but when the agency itself is willing to pay for such a trip, the journey becomes even more healing. TCKs receive the important message that they do indeed belong to a community that cares for them—not one that discards them at a certain age with no concern for the impact growing up as a member of that overseas community had on them. It's another way of validating the value of their heritage and inviting them to build on that heritage rather than disowning it.

****

In conclusion, international organizations must face the fact that they bear responsibility not only to their individual employees but also to their families once they begin to transplant their workers cross-culturally and ask them to be global nomads. Too often administrators have blamed failures totally on the person who failed rather than looking at the part their agency or corporate policies and decisions may have played in the matter. We're grateful for the growing awareness among companies and sponsoring organizations of their role in helping cross-cultural families be successful.

Endnotes

[1] Germaine W. Shames, "Transnational Burnout," *Hemispheres*, (February 1995), 39.

[2] Mel Mandell and Lindsey Biel, "Global Repatriation," *Solutions*, (February 1994), 23–26.

[3] Berlitz International and HFS Mobility Services, 1996–1997 International Assignee Research Project, Princeton, NJ.

[4] Personal correspondence to David C. Pollock from Barbara F. Schaetti, Transition Dynamics, October 1998.

[5] Ibid.

[6] Cornelius Grove and Willa Hallowell, "On Trade and Cultures," *Trade and Culture* (September–October 1994), 4–6.

18

It's Never Too Late

In spite of the growing efforts to help current TCKs better understand and use their cross-cultural experiences, most TCKs from previous generations grew up with little assistance in sorting out the full effect of their third culture upbringing. No one understood that help might be needed, let alone what to do if it were.

Even so, many ATCKs have successfully found their way through the morass of conflicting cultures and lifestyles, come to terms with the inherent losses, and developed a positive sense of identity. They have learned to use their heritage in personally and/or professionally productive ways. But what about ATCKs who are still struggling to put it all together?

Unfortunately, we have met many who continue to be so confused or wounded by the challenges of their childhood that they have never been free as adults to celebrate the benefits. Depression, isolation, loneliness, anger, rebellion, and despair have ruled their lives instead of joy. Some ATCKs may outwardly continue to be successful chameleons, but inwardly the questions "Who am I?" "Where am I from?" "Why can't I seem to move on in life?" still rage. They can't figure out why they have always felt different from their peers.

Other ATCKs believe they are just fine, but spouses, children, friends, and coworkers know better. There is a shell around them that no one can penetrate—even in the closest of relationships. Some of them grew up in organizational systems where extended periods of separation from their family seemed so normal at the time that they never considered how these separations might have affected their lives. Others went through periods of war or conflict in their host country with or without their parents being present. TCKs have experienced emotional, mental, physical, and spiritual abuse, or at least trauma, as they have traversed their worlds, but because these worlds vanished with a plane ride, they have never stopped to sort things out. The experiences and their contexts simply disappeared. Often ATCKs are stuck in one of the stages of unresolved grief without realizing it. All they know is that they are trapped in some place or behavior from which they can't break free.

So what can they do now? Is it too late for wounded ATCKs to put the pieces together? When they have been stuck for a long time in a self-destructive lifestyle, is it possible for them to learn to use their past constructively rather than be bound by it? The answer is, simply, yes. It's never too late to deal with unresolved grief, identity issues, or other challenges related to the TCK lifestyle.

But how does healing occur? Obviously, ATCKs and their parents can't go back and relive their transitional experiences, nor can they undo the separations. The years of family life lost are irretrievable. In fact, most ATCKs can't recover any of their hidden losses. They can't reclaim the sights, sounds, or smells that made home "home" as a child. They can't stop the war that displaced them or the abuser who stole their innocence. What they can do is learn to put words to their past, name their experiences, validate the benefits as well as the losses, and ask for help from their families and others.

What ATCKS Can Do

Name Themselves and Their Experience

For many ATCKs, putting a name to their past—"I grew up as a third culture kid"—opens a new perspective on life. Discovering there are legitimate reasons for their life experiences and the resulting feelings not only helps them understand themselves better, it also normalizes the experience. Some, who have spent a lifetime thinking they're alone in their differentness, discover they have lived a normal life after all—at least normal for a TCK.

Somehow the concept of normality is very liberating. It doesn't solve every problem, but it gives permission for a lot of self-discovery and frees ATCKs to make some changes they may not have thought possible. For example, rather than remaining eternal chameleons and continuing to try fitting in everywhere, they can focus on examining who they are, where they do fit, and where they can best use their gifts. If ATCKs can understand, for example, why they chronically withdraw before saying good-bye to others, they can purposefully choose to stay engaged in relationships until the end.

> Since one ATCK discovered withdrawal was her consistent pattern before moving, she now tells her friends a month before the departure date, "I want to let you know what a great friend you've been, because I might not be able to tell you at the end. I also need to tell you that I've hurt a lot of people by acting like I don't care when it comes time to say good-bye. I'm going to try not to do that, but if I start to withdraw, you let me know." And her friends do.

This simple acknowledgment both helps others understand this ATCK's potential behavior and helps her remain emotionally present in relationships both before and after she leaves.

For other ATCKs, discovering they have a name—that they are adult third culture kids—and are members of a group whose membership extends around the world finally gives them a feeling of belonging. Instead of feeling their history is a piece of life's puzzle that will never fit, they now see it as the key piece around which so many others fall into place.

Name Their Behavioral Patterns

Once ATCKs realize their past has undoubtedly influenced their present life and their choices, it's time for them to make an honest assessment. Are there certain lifelong, repetitive behaviors (such as constantly moving or failure to allow intimacy in one relationship after another) that they have always excused as "That's just the way I am"? Is their anger, depression, or other behavior often out of proportion to its context?

After looking at such repetitive cycles of behavior, ATCKs need to ask themselves some questions: Is this behavior related to a confusion of identities? Is it related to one of the expressions of unresolved grief? Is it totally unrelated to anything except a personal or family matter? If it seems to be a personal matter, how might the influences of cross-culturalism and high mobility have added to that stress?

Name Their Fears

Often a major barrier to healing is fear—fear of facing the pain, fear of taking a risk again, fear of rejection. This fear is hidden behind such statements as "I don't see any reason to look back. Life is to be lived in a forward direction." Or "That TCK stuff is bunk. I'm just me, and my life experiences have nothing to do with the way I am. I'd have been the same no matter where or when I grew up."

It is scary to go back, but it can be helpful for ATCKs to realize that no matter how badly a certain situation hurt, they have already survived it and that situation is now past. Facing the pain will hurt for a bit, but it can be grieved and dealt with in the end. Not facing it may well continue to drive the ATCK into far more pain-producing behaviors than they can currently imagine.

Name Their Losses

After deciding that healing is worth the risk of pain, it's important for ATCKs to look back and try to identify some of the losses they haven't been fully aware of before. Journaling is one effective way to do this, answering such questions as these:

> Did you properly say good-bye to a country you loved dearly?
>
> What ever happened to your pets?
>
> Where is your amah now?
>
> Have your relationships with your siblings ever been restored?
>
> What do you need to do to heal parental relationships?
>
> Have you rediscovered your role in a group?

Having named the losses, it's not too late to go back and do the work of grieving that should have been processed as the losses occurred. We have been astounded at the severity of losses some ATCKs have experienced in their childhood: death in the family while the TCKs were away at boarding school, sexual abuse they never told anyone about, war that uprooted them in the middle of the night. So many of these have been covered over with no proper period of mourning or comfort to deal with the losses. Many ATCKs have simply disassociated themselves from the pain, but the grief merely surfaces in all the other forms mentioned earlier.

If ATCKs dare to face the losses in their lives, to acknowledge and grieve for them, they will discover that proper mourning takes away the power of those losses to drive their behavior in ever more destructive ways. When the pain has been severe, good friends who listen well are essential. Therapists with understanding of the TCK experience can be helpful in identifying and dealing with the ATCK's losses from the past if he or she finds it difficult to do alone or with friends.

One word of warning: we have noticed that when ATCKs first acknowledge some of their hidden losses, part of the grief process is a newly found or at least newly expressed anger at various people whom they feel are responsible for those losses. Lots of ATCKs (to say nothing of the people they're angry at) are so upset by this phase that they back off from going further. Don't give up on the process if this begins to happen! The anger phase *can* be a very difficult period of the healing process for everyone involved, but remember it is a normal stage of grief, which can be worked through to a stage of resolution as the ATCKs (and those around them) persist and give the healing process time.

Name Their Wounds

Even retrospectively, it's important for ATCKs to name not only their losses but also the ways in which they have been hurt and how they have hurt others. Why is this important? Everyone has been hurt by other people, and each of us has hurt others. Some of the wounds, whether intentional or not, have been significant, and they must be acknowledged to be dealt with properly.

Once we have identified a wound, we then have to make a critical decision. Will we hold on to our anger forever or will we forgive the ones who have hurt us? Some ATCKs we have met are living lives bound by bitterness. They have turned their pain into a weapon with which they beat not only the offender but themselves and everyone else as well. It seems that the hurt becomes part of their identity. To let it go would be to leave them hollow, empty. The problem is that the anger and bitterness destroy as much as, or more than, the original wound. Many are unwilling to forgive because they feel the offender will "go free." They believe that saying "I forgive you" means "It doesn't really matter what happened."

Forgiveness is not something lightly given, bestowed without looking at what the situation cost the person who was wounded. Without forgiveness, however, the offended person's life continues to be ruled by the offender. It's important to acknowledge the offense, but forgiveness is making a decision to let go of the need and desire for vengeance—even if the offender never has to pay. Forgiveness is the only thing that ultimately frees the wounded one to move on to true healing.

None of us is perfect. Healing also involves looking at how we ourselves have knowingly or unknowingly hurt others and asking their forgiveness. It's amazing to listen to stories of rage against parents, siblings, relatives, friends, and administrators in the sponsoring organizations from ATCKs who seem to have no perception that they are doing similar damage to their own children. Some who complain of emotional abuse or separation from parents one moment are yelling at their own children the next. Some who complain of abandonment in their childhood are workaholics who may not send their children away to boarding school but still never seem to have time for them.

Until and unless we are willing to acknowledge our own sins and failures against others, true healing is stymied, for we will have to continue living in our self-protective modes, shutting out those who would dare approach us and mention our offenses against them. We need to identify specific occurrences where we have wounded others, and when we recognize the offense, we need to be the first ones to go and ask for forgiveness, not waiting for them to approach us. Doing this both heals important relationships in our lives and also frees us from having to defend and protect ourselves. Instead, we can begin to live more openly and with greater joy.

Name Their Choices

Dealing with the past in a healthy way frees us to make choices about the future. We are no longer victims. Each of us must ultimately accept responsibility for our own behavior, regardless of the past. That doesn't mean that we are responsible for all that happened to us. A sexually abused child isn't responsible for the abuse, a child who felt abandoned is not responsible for the parents' choices. But as adults, we *are* responsible for how we deal with our past, how we relate to those around us in the present, and what we choose for the future. ATCKs must ask themselves several questions as they sort through their past in order to get on with their future: Will I forgive? Will I retaliate? Will I succumb to the message that I am worthless? Will I look at what it means to be a person and realize that it's okay to think, to create, to have emotion? Will I dare to find ways to express these parts of myself?

The choices ATCKs make in response to these questions can make all the difference for those who feel bound by the past but are longing to move on to freedom in the future.

We have started this final chapter focusing on what ATCKs can do for themselves because, in the end, how they deal with their history and how they can best use it is ultimately their responsibility. They can heal and find fulfillment in life even if others never understand their background. However, those close to the ATCKs can be immensely helpful if they try to understand the struggle and freely give their support during the time of healing.

How Can Parents Help Their ATCKs?

We have been saying throughout this book that family relationships are key to a TCK's well-being while he or she is growing up. This is also true for ATCKs who are still struggling with the challenges from their TCK experience. Parents can often be partners with their ATCKs during this healing process. If parents can be supportive and understanding rather than defensive or threatened when ATCKs are sorting through the past, they can help open the way to much faster healing for their adult children. Support throughout an ATCK's healing process is the greatest gift a parent can give. Here are some specific ways that parents can help.

Listen and Try to Understand

This may seem simple, but it's not. ATCKs sometimes turn against their parents when they begin verbalizing their feelings about the past. When the accusations rage, parents often try to defend themselves with the facts: "We *didn't* send you away for six months. It was only three." "We never *made* you wear those hand-me-down clothes. You *wanted* to."

The facts aren't the main issue here. The issue is how ATCKs *perceived* the event. For them, the separation *felt* like six months. In other words, they really missed their parents. When they were laughed at for their attire, they felt they had had no choice in what to wear. Like everyone else in the world, the ATCKs' perceptions of reality have been shaped by the emotional impact of their experiences. That emotional reaction is real, and it's far more important at this point for parents to deal with those perceptions of certain events and the feelings behind them than to argue about the facts. Arguing the facts only proves to the ATCK that the parents never understood anyway—and still don't.

Sometimes parents not only argue with the facts ATCKs bring up during this time but also with the feelings ATCKs express. For example, the ATCK tries to express how lonely he or she felt when leaving for boarding school, and the parent replies, "You never minded going off to school. Why, you smiled and waved and always said you had a great time there." Or the ATCK talks of how hard it was to leave the host country and the parent interjects, "How can you say you were heartbroken to leave Port-au-Prince? You always told us it was too hot and you couldn't wait to get back to France." Perhaps nothing will shut down communication faster between parents and their ATCK than such a response, because no one can tell what another person did or did not feel. Outer behavior often masks inner feelings. That's why it is critical that when ATCKs try to tell their parents, even years later, what they were feeling as they grew up, parents need to listen and accept those feelings. This kind of acceptance opens doors for far more fruitful discussion between parents and ATCKs than trying to prove this isn't what the ATCKs felt.

Parents may be stunned when suddenly confronted with feelings their ATCKs have never expressed before—especially when the ATCKs are in their thirties and forties. This won't be easy, but it's important for parents to realize that life has stages and that, often, people can't fully deal with or understand what is happening at a certain time in their lives. They wait until later, when it is safer to examine the full impact of a situation. This applies not only to ATCKs. It happens to adults from all sorts of backgrounds. Children basically have to deal with life's traumas in a survival mode—whether it be someone calling them a bad name, their own physical handicap, parental divorce, a major separation from either or both parents, abuse, or death. Some kids escape into fantasy. Others block out the feelings of pain with denial or rationalization. Compulsions may be another child's attempt to control the pain. It's not the *how* that's significant; it's the fact that children have to survive, and they must use everything at their disposal to do so.

As life proceeds, however, the pain remains until, finally, the day comes when adults decide to face their inner wounds.

Many people have asked Ruth how she remembered so many details of her childhood to include in *Letters Never Sent*. She always explains, "I didn't remember; I reexperienced those moments. But as an adult, I had words to describe the feelings I felt but couldn't explain as a child." After one such discussion, Faye, another ATCK who had been through a similar process of retracing her own childhood, challenged Ruth: "I don't think we reexperience those feelings. I think we allow them to be felt for the first time."

On further reflection, Ruth agreed. She realized that when she was six and the lights went off at bedtime her first night in boarding school, she felt an immense sense of isolation, aloneness, and homesickness that threatened to squeeze her to death. To give in to that much pain would surely have meant annihilation. So, like most kids, she tried everything she knew to dull the pain, to control it somehow. Ruth's solution involved "trying harder." She prayed with great attention to style—carefully kneeling, giving thanks in alphabetical order for everyone and everything she could think of. This so God would stay happy with her and grant the requests that she would sneak onto the end of the prayer to see her family again. She tried to meticulously obey all the rules at school so she wouldn't get in trouble. Keeping track of the details of life took a lot of focus and attention away from the pain.

When she picked up her pen at age thirty-nine and wrote, "I want my mommy and daddy" as part of the letter her six-year-old self would have written if she'd had the words, Ruth felt that same horrible squeezing in her chest that she had known as that six-year-old child. This time, however, she didn't need to put it away or work against it. She had already survived it and could allow herself to feel the anguish all the way to the bottom of her soul in a way she couldn't have when the separation actually happened.

This pattern of midlife clarification of the past seems to be common for many ATCKs, but it's a process that brings great consternation to some parents. It's helpful for parents to accept that their ATCKs may need to deal with their emotions many years after the events themselves. They also need to see that their ATCKs' attempts to share feelings with them—though initially expressed in anger—are because the ATCKs still want and need their parents to understand what they felt during their moments of separation or other experiences of childhood. Consciously or unconsciously, the ATCKs want to be in a closer relationship with their parents or they wouldn't bother trying to communicate these feelings. After all, these are the only parents the ATCK will ever have.

Dialogue and healing can begin if parents will listen and try to understand their adult child's accounting of the past without defending themselves, their sponsoring organization, the facts, or anything else. They also need to remember that just because their ATCK never told them these things before doesn't mean the ATCK didn't feel them.

Comfort and Be Gentle

Offering comfort is a key factor in any grieving process—even when that process is delayed by decades. Remember, comfort is not encouragement. It is being there with understanding and love, not trying to change or fix things.

> One ATCK took courage and finally wrote his parents some of the things he had felt through some of the early separations from them as a child. His mother wrote back, "Thank you for telling us how you felt. As I read your letter, of course I cried. I wish I could give you a big hug right now. I'm sorry we didn't know then what you expressed now or we might have made some different decisions—but we didn't. I love you and trust your story will help others."

Obviously, the first piece of comfort came with the acknowledgment that his mom understood the feelings he had expressed. The second came with the words, "I wish I could give you a big hug." Then his mom expressed her own sorrow with a simple acknowledgment that as parents they had not realized what he was feeling. His mother never denied his feelings, nor did she wallow in self-blame or defensiveness. Instead, she blessed her son. Parental listening, understanding, comfort, and blessing are huge, wonderful steps in the healing process that parents can provide for their children—even when those children are now adults.

Don't Preach

Almost all parents find it difficult not to preach, but this may be especially so for parents of adult missionary kids. These parents have spent their lives dedicated to a religious cause. There is probably no greater anguish parents can feel than when their ATCKs reject the system for which the parents have stood—particularly when it is the faith they have gone halfway around the world to share. Often, the sense of urgency to convince their children to believe in what they themselves believe grows as parents watch their ATCKs fall into increasingly self-destructive behavior: "If they'd just get their lives right with God, they'd be fine."

To that we would respond with a "yes, but" answer. Yes, what the parents desire for their children is valuable, but ATCKs who suffered within a religious system must first sort out their pain in terms of who God actually is compared with the rules and culture of the religious system that seeks to represent God. Until then, preaching, or worse, words of spiritual reprimand, will only fuel the anger.

Is there never a time for third culture parents to talk forthrightly with their ATCKs in response to both the accusations that are being made as well as the destructive behavior parents see? Of course there is. When parents have listened and understood what their adult child is feeling, there *is* an appropriate time to express their own feelings and beliefs. But it must come as a sharing of who they are and their perspectives rather than as a denial of what the ATCK has shared or is feeling.

Forgive

Sometimes parents need to ask their ATCKs for forgiveness. They have made mistakes too and shouldn't run from acknowledging them. If their ATCK has been extremely hurtful and rebellious toward them, parents will also have much to forgive. This can be very difficult, particularly if their child is not yet acknowledging how badly he or she has hurt them. But if parents are able to forgive and ask for forgiveness, it can be a major factor in their adult child's healing process.

Assume You Are Needed

Parents should assume their adult children still need and want them as part of their lives. They may tell parents not to bother coming for a birth, graduation, or wedding, saying "It isn't that big a deal," and these ATCKs probably believe that's how they really feel. But it makes a big difference—even to those who don't think they need their parents any longer—when parents make the effort to remain involved in a caring way in their children's lives as adults. Sometimes those years together as adults finally make up for the separations of the past.

What Friends and Other Relatives Can Do

Sometimes friends and other relatives can help ATCKs take the first major step in the healing process because they stand outside the emotionally reactive space occupied by the ATCKs and their parents. What can they do for the ATCKs they love to help in the healing process?

Listen to the Story and Ask Good Questions

Many ATCKs feel their childhood story is so far removed from their present lives that they have nearly forgotten it themselves. Few people cared to know more than the cursory details when they first returned from their third culture experience, and they quit talking about it long ago. To have someone invite them for lunch, ask to hear about their experiences, and then actually listen may be such a shock to some that they seem to at least temporarily forget everything that has happened to them. But persist. When friends or relatives initiate the conversation and clearly express their interest, the ATCK knows it's bona fide. It may even give them the first chance they've ever had to put words to their experiences.

Questions such as these can also help the process: "How did you feel when you said good-bye to your grandma?" "What was the hardest thing about returning to your home country?" "What did you like best about growing up that way?"

These kinds of questions prove the friend is listening closely enough to hear the behind-the-scenes story and may even challenge ATCKs to consider issues they never stopped to think about before.

Don't Compare Stories

Friends and relatives shouldn't point out how many other people have had it worse. Generally, ATCKs already know they have had a wonderful life compared with many others. That has often been part of their problem in trying to understand their struggles.

Most ATCKs will first relate the positive parts of their story. They won't tell the difficult aspects until they feel safe and comfortable with the listener. Once they do begin to share the darker times, don't try to cheer them up by reminding them of the positives. Both sides of the story are valid.

Comfort If Possible

Sometimes friends are the first ever to comfort an ATCK, and it can be hard initially for the ATCK to accept it. Many feel as if admitting to any pain is the same as disowning their parents, their faith, or the organizational system in which they grew up. Sometimes ATCKs become angry when others try to comfort them, because they refuse to admit they might need it. So, offer comfort—but don't push if your friend isn't ready to receive it.

How Therapists Can Help

We don't presume to tell therapists how to counsel ATCKs, since professional therapy is outside our domain. We hope, however, that we can help therapists understand the problems specific to the TCK experience, such as where TCK grief often comes from, where the early attachments between parents and children might have been broken, and how TCKs' concepts of identity and worldview have been affected by cultural and mobility issues. Our goal is to help therapists understand the basic life patterns of the third culture experience so they will be better prepared to assist their TCK clients. An interesting occurrence when we have given seminars for therapists is that after our presentations, our audience begins to redefine the topic by explaining it back to us—and to each other—from therapeutic models such as attachment theory or post-traumatic stress syndrome with which they are already familiar.

> After attending a conference on TCK issues, one therapist said, "We used to think that if a child was

adopted at birth, that child would have no different
issues to deal with than a child born to the adoptive
couple. Now we know anytime a client comes in who
was adopted, there are certain questions to ask.

It seems to me the TCK issue falls in that category.
Being aware of this experience can help us ask better
questions when we realize our clients are TCKs or
ATCKs.

Recognize Hidden Losses

Therapists who understand the nature of the third culture experience may be the first to help ATCKs identify the hidden losses that
are part of the TCK experience but that the TCKs themselves are
often not aware of. A "Cycles of Mobility" chart (see Chart 1) can
be a useful tool in this process. Many ATCKs do not recognize the
degree to which separation has been an integral part of their lives
and how it has contributed to feelings of loss and grief.

Chart 1 Cycles of Mobility

Instructions: Make a time chart of the separation patterns for the
first eighteen years of the ATCK's life, using different colors to fill
in the spaces for when and where he or she lived, for example:

Blue = time living with parents in home country

Green = time living with parents in host country #1

Purple = time living with parents in host country #2

Yellow = time living with parents in host country #3

Brown = time spent away from parents in boarding school in host
            country

Pink = time spent away from parents in boarding school in home
            country

Orange = time living with anyone other than parents or in boarding
            school

Chart 1
Cycles of Mobility

	1	2	3	4	5	6	7	8	9	10	11	12	13	14	15	16	17	18
January																		
February																		
March																		
April																		
May																		
June																		
July																		
August																		
September																		
October																		
November																		
December																		
Age in years																		

This chart can be modified to fit the specific situation of each ATCK. What's important is for the therapist—and the ATCK—to see the overall patterns of mobility—where the transitions between various cultures occurred, at what ages, and so forth. As the times of transition, separation, and loss become obvious, therapists may discover the roots of some of the issues they see in their ATCK clients. This insight can help them aid their ATCK clients in recognizing the areas that need healing.

Therapists should also help their ATCK clients carefully think through the issues regarding the impact of culture on a TCK's developmental process. Some of the feelings ATCKs struggle with may, in fact, be largely a result of cultural imbalance.

Recognize the Impact of the System

One major factor that many therapists of ATCKs overlook or fail to understand is the powerful influence of the military, mission, business, or other organizational system under which these ATCKs grew up. Often the ATCKs' anger or hurt stems directly from policies that either controlled their lives on a daily basis or took away choice when it came to schooling, moving, and so on. On the flip side, ATCKs who were used to being protected or nurtured in that system (for example, the perks like free medical care or inexpensive housing) may not know how to cope comfortably in a larger, less structured world, where they are expected to depend more on themselves. Therapy is sometimes stymied if issues are dealt with only in the context of family relationships rather than understanding the operative system that often superseded family decisions.

Recognize the Paradox

Often ATCKs are defensive in therapy when asked about the painful parts of their past. They don't want to negate the way of life that is the only one they have known and is a core element of their identity. Missionary kids may have particular trouble acknowledging the pain because they feel that to do so will negate their faith. It is hard for many to know how much of that system they can examine, and potentially give up, without giving up God in the process.

Acknowledging the paradoxical nature of his or her experience may be particularly important in relationship to a client who attended a boarding school. These ATCKs may have so many great memories of the camaraderie experienced there and friendships made and maintained down through the years that they can't imagine there could be any negatives. In addition, for some TCKs who were boarding students for as long as twelve years, their identity is deeply tied to the boarding school experience. To acknowledge anything but the good could threaten their entire sense of self. But young boarding students often feel unprotected; a six-year-old child going to boarding school may actually experience something akin to becoming an orphan. How can ATCKs acknowledge the loneliness they felt without seeing it as a denial of the good they have also known at school? For these, or any ATCKs who grew up in strong systems and feel closely identified to that system, questions about system policies can be such a threat to their core identity that they may refuse to go on with the therapy they need.

That is why those working with ATCKs must never forget to recognize—and help the ATCK recognize—that when we look at the TCK experience from the perspective of the adult TCK, we will see many paradoxes. Therapists must affirm the positive elements as well as identify the stress points to give their ATCK clients the permission they need to look at all sides of their past experiences. It's also helpful to remind them once more that if there hadn't been so much good to lose, there often wouldn't have been so much grief at its passing.

Final Thoughts

We have now reached both an ending and a beginning—the end of sharing what we have already learned from and about TCKs and ATCKs and the beginning of watching the rest of this story unfold. We haven't begun to look fully at the many possible variations in the TCKs' world. Instead of the traditional pattern of having parents among the elite of the community, some TCKs grow up in the homes of migrant workers or domestic servants. Does that shade the picture differently? If so, how? What about TCKs who, for reasons of war or some other unforeseen event, never have the choice of returning to their home country? There is so much more to study and learn not only about TCKs themselves but also about how their experience compares with others who are raised outside their home culture because they have been adopted cross-culturally or their parents are immigrants or refugees.

We're also encouraged to see the end of apathy and the beginning of real awareness that there are some valid issues to deal with in this lifestyle. Sponsoring agencies are developing new strategies for taking better care of their families. Schools throughout the world are making changes in curriculum and approaches to teaching that will make it easier for students of any country to fit back into the school system of their home country. Parents are making careful, thoughtful decisions that take into account their own TCKs' needs. Everywhere, we see ATCKs taking ownership of their past so that they may use it well.

On the other hand, as the world tries to move toward increased globalization, we also see that many of the same challenges TCKs have faced in their multicultural upbringings will be encountered in the larger world arena as well. We hope this book will help all of us begin to consider some of the ramifications of globalization so that we can avoid at least some of the major pitfalls of intercultural living.

But after all is said and done, we say this: it's exciting to be a TCK or an ATCK. It's also exciting to know, love, and work with them. We wish each of you, our readers, much joy in your own journeys as well.

Appendix A
Adult Third Culture
Kid Survey Results

An Historical Overview of Mobility Patterns for TCKs and Their Long-Term Impact on ATCKs

People often ask, "Is it fair to look at adult TCKs and project their experience onto current TCKs when conditions for third culture living are so different [and presumably better] than they were during the first half of the twentieth century?"

That's a valid question, and in our early days of working with TCKs, we wanted to find an answer. Were the long-term effects of both benefits and challenges of the third culture experience valid for current and future TCKs or simply fading products of an earlier day and way of life?

In 1986, the few surveys that had already been done among TCKs mostly reflected the benefits of the experience but seemed to miss any major discussion of the challenges. We soon realized that because boarding schools and universities were the easiest place to access this population, every survey that had been conducted among TCKs picked up mostly missionary kids, and all were teenagers or

in their early twenties. That raised the next question. Did the "positive only" nature reflect that the younger TCKs didn't face the issues of former generations or did it reflect another possibility—that
young people often don't have a full perspective on their life experiences and perhaps haven't yet started to deal with some of the long-
term ramifications of their experience? Certainly we had found a
pattern among the many ATCKs we had talked to. Most had not
begun to deal consciously with issues relating to their TCK experience until their mid to late twenties—or even into their thirties. Armed
with this information, we decided to do a simple survey ourselves.

In 1986 we gathered 800 names of ATCKs from a variety of
sources—personal contacts, referrals by friends, and alumni lists of
various TCK boarding schools. Most of these prospects were adult
missionary kids, so our sample pool in parental occupational orientation closely reflected that of the initial surveys we had seen. All
were postuniversity ATCKs, and the 282 who responded ranged in
age from twenty-two to seventy-five years of age.

The questionnaire focused on two major issues:
1. What were the patterns of separation from family, home, and
   host countries—both in kind and amount—during the first eighteen years of the ATCK's life?

2. How did the respondent think these separations had affected
   him or her?

The results were revealing. We not only learned the ways many
ATCKs felt their lives had been affected by these patterns of separation, but a vivid picture of the changes occurring in the third culture
community emerged as well. The findings painted a clear historical
picture of the TCK world as well as showing changing trends.

When we began noticing some significant differences in certain
statistics among ATCKs of the pre- and post-World War II eras, we
decided we could best compare the past and present world of TCKs
by dividing our respondents into two major categories. Those born
before 1947 we called the "older ATCKs"; those born in 1947 and

later we called the "younger ATCKs." To study the data more precisely, we broke these two larger groups down into subgroups representing all the respondents born within five-year spans. Each of the
following graphs and discussions is based on this framework.

Graph 1
Place of Birth—Home or Host Country

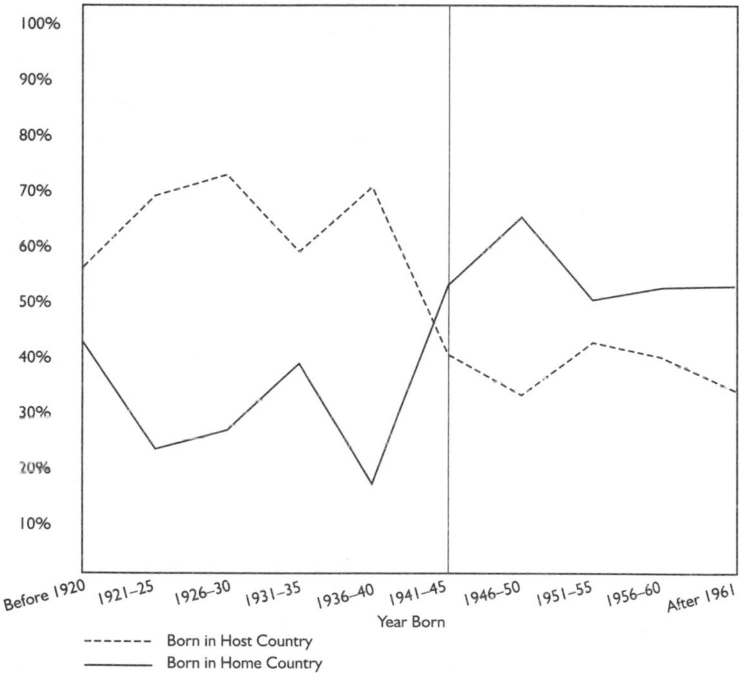

------- Born in Host Country
———— Born in Home Country

Our first clue about the changing patterns in the third culture world
came when we graphed out place of birth. In every five-year group of
the older ATCKs—those born during or before World War II—the
majority were born in the host country. It was exactly the opposite
for every five-year age group of TCKs born after the war. The majority of these younger ATCKs were born in their home countries.

There are undoubtedly several reasons for this marked difference. In the prewar years, most missionaries (the major group from

which our sample came) went overseas for at least four years at a time—some much longer. It could easily take six weeks to three months on an ocean freighter before they arrived at their destination.

In those early days, many mission boards didn't accept people over thirty years of age, feeling that by the time anyone older than that learned the language in a new country, they would be too old for useful, long-term service. Agencies also believed only younger people could better stand up to the health risks involved in overseas living. This meant people went overseas in their early twenties, often before the birth of their children. When babies came later, they were born wherever their parents were—usually in the host country.

In the post-World War II era, children were and are still being born wherever parents are, but patterns for how and when people engage in international careers are vastly different from before. Long, uninterrupted stints in faraway lands are less common now than they used to be. Because people can travel by jet rather than ship, it means they come and go between countries far more easily. Leaves or furloughs are scheduled more frequently. Women who choose to do so can fly home for the delivery of their babies rather than stay in a host culture that may have less adequate facilities. Short-term assignments are also possible because the business or mission started by the lifelong pioneers of earlier days is now well established. It's easy to identify a place where people can plug in to meet a specific need of the moment. For these reasons, and doubtless others, more TCKs are being born in their home country now than formerly.

Graph 2
Those Separated from Parents for a
Significant Period before Age Six

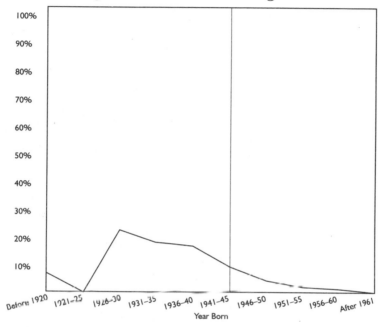

Year Born

The next difference between the older and younger ATCK groups became clear when we looked at how many had been separated from their parents for a significant period of time before the age of six. Many ATCKs born just before and during World War II were in this category. There were two common reasons children were left in the home country at an extremely early age while parents went overseas.

1. Children weren't allowed to travel overseas during the war because of the risks involved. In 1944 this ban on children traveling across the ocean meant Ruth Van Reken's parents faced a major dilemma when they discovered Ruth's mom, Betty, was pregnant while they were preparing to go to Africa for the first

time. They could either go while Betty was pregnant, not go at all, or wait in the States for the baby to be born and then go on to Africa, leaving the baby with caregivers until the war was over. Ruth's folks chose to cross the ocean while her mom was still pregnant. (Sadly, the ship that carried them to Europe was torpedoed and sunk by enemy fire on its return trip to the States; there were obviously good reasons for the ban on travel for children.)

2. Even before the war, many parents chose to leave their young children at home for educational purposes. Others left their children behind because they feared the disease and other perils they might face in an overseas post such as West Africa, which in the colonial era was called "the white man's grave."

Graph 3
Those Who Lost a Family Member to Death before Respondent Was Eighteen

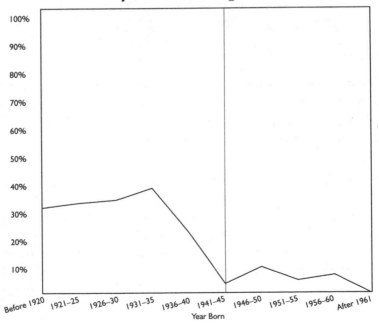

During their first eighteen years of life, the older ATCKs surveyed had suffered a much higher mortality rate in their immediate family than had the younger ATCKs. Before antibiotics and antimalarial drugs became available, death rates were high for expatriates in many tropical countries. When an article came out in the early 1990s in *Christianity Today* discussing the children's graves at a mission station in Nigeria, Ruth realized she'd known every one of those children personally except for two. They'd either been her friends, or she had baby-sat them, or they were the children of her parents' close friends. Death was a sad, but common, occurrence among the expatriate community in those earlier days.

Graph 4
Total Years of Separation from Parents
before Age Eighteen and Longest Single Stretch of Time
without Seeing Parents Even Once in First Eighteen Years

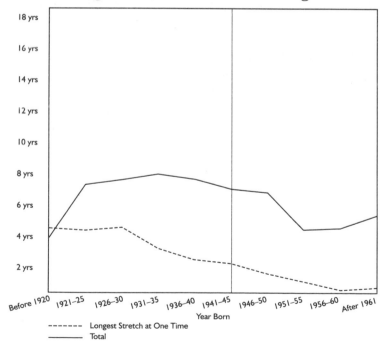

Year Born

------- Longest Stretch at One Time

———— Total

Aside from the TCKs mentioned in Graph 2, who were left at home for fear of war or disease, most separations for TCKs occurred because of schooling. The figures in this graph reflect some interesting possibilities regarding educational patterns. The higher number of total years away for the oldest ATCKs likely reflects not only time away in boarding school overseas but long stretches in their home country as well.

The graph stays relatively steady until we see those born after the war, in the fifties and sixties. Suddenly, the total number of years away drops. The trend toward home schooling and the more varied options offered by satellite schools and by local national and international schools are likely reflected in these statistics.

The greatest difference between the older and younger ATCKs, however, is in the average *longest* period of time TCKs went without seeing their parents at all during those same first eighteen years of life. These figures tell a remarkable story.

In the older group, the average length of time for not seeing parents even once was 3.6 years. The normal pattern for most missionaries in those days was four years overseas and one year back in the home country for furlough. With few American or British secondary schools available overseas, many TCKs stayed in the States, Canada, or England and went to boarding schools or lived with relatives in the home country during their teenage years. Meanwhile, parents returned overseas for the next four-year stint. With slower transportation and the high costs involved for travel, TCKs rarely visited their parents overseas during those four-or-more-year stretches.

The average length of time the younger TCKs went without seeing parents once was only eleven months. Quite a change.

Graph 5
Percent of Those Separated from Parents for Longer
Than One Year at a Time before Age Eighteen

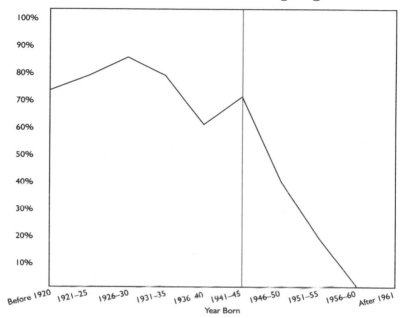

Year Born

A quick look at this graph shows how common these long separations were for older ATCKs. They were accepted as a normal and inevitable part of an international, or at least a missionary, career. The dramatic lowering in this pattern of extended separations for the younger ATCKs (among those born in 1956 and later, not one ATCK during the first eighteen years had gone a full year without seeing parents at least once) clearly reflects several points. Like Graph 4, this decline no doubt reflects the trend toward home schooling and the more varied options offered by satellite schools and by local national and international schools. These figures also reflect the trend for sending children who are in their home country back to see their parents in the host country during the school vacation periods.

Graph 6
Age at Permanent Return to Home Country

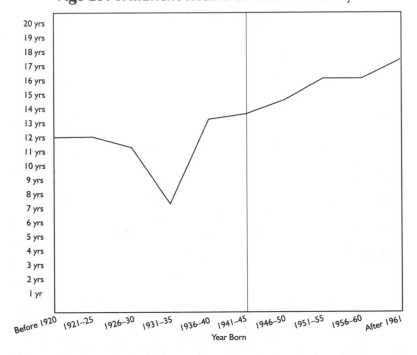

The rising average age when TCKs permanently reentered the home country clearly reflects the increased availability of international schooling options around the world. Instead of returning at age twelve or thirteen for secondary school in the home country as the older ATCKs did, the great majority of younger TCKs stayed in the host country until an average age of almost seventeen. They only returned to the home country for university.

Graph 7
Impact of Multiple Separations on Relationships

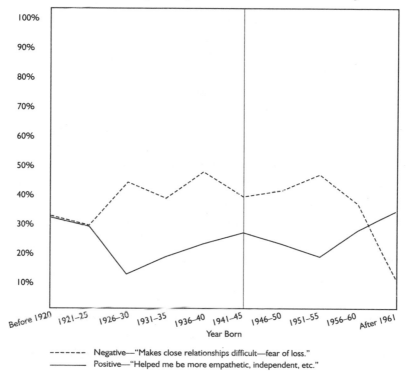

-------- Negative—"Makes close relationships difficult—fear of loss."
————— Positive—"Helped me be more empathetic, independent, etc."

After looking at the notable differences in type, amount, and patterns of separation experienced by the older and younger ATCK groups, we expected to find that the issues TCKs from previous generations faced weren't relevant for today's culturally mobile kids. We presumed there would be a significant difference in how the older and younger groups responded to our question of how the separations had affected them—with the older generation saying they had been hard and the younger group barely noticing them.

The specific question we asked was "How do you feel the cycle of separations affected you?" Here are some of the replies.

"Don't know."

"Hard to communicate and make friends."

"I am sympathetic with those who have to be separated from loved ones."
"Have never made intimate friends."
"Because of internment by Japanese, I was spared
separation. [Apparently this ATCK was in internment
camp with the parents.] My brother, who was separated, was affected."
"Am very interested in people and their needs."

There were three basic types of response: positive, negative,
and both. Positive responses were judged as those that included such
statements as "It made me more independent," although we have no
way to assess if that is a healthy independence or the isolation we
talked about in chapter 6. We judged as negative those remarks which
included *only* challenges with no benefits listed. Here's one example.
"I have become very protective emotionally. I do not easily let others get close emotionally. I find it very hard to communicate in an
intimate relationship for fear of rejection. It has crippled my marriage." A major recurring theme in many of the remarks reflected
the ATCKs' fear of intimacy because of the fear of loss.

The responses we marked as "both" included replies such as
this respondent's: "I struggled with depression for years but now
find my own struggle gives me greater empathy for others." None
of these were listed in the negative responses.

To our surprise, in spite of all the differences in separation patterns between older and younger ATCKs, 47 (40.1%) of the 117
respondents in the older group said the chronic cycles of separation
had a negative impact on them and 62 (39.2%) of the 158 in the
younger group said the same thing. A mere 1 percent difference!

How could this be? With further reflection, and many intervening years to test our hypothesis, our conclusion was, and remains,
that it is the *cycles* of separation and the loss itself that affect TCKs
and ATCKs—not merely the longevity or amount. Though TCKs
may now return from boarding school every three months instead of
being separated from parents for four years, these children still know,

and internally stay prepared for, the fact that they will soon be leaving again. If TCKs see grandparents and relatives back home more often than before, they know it's not a permanent settling down. In fact, some ATCKs who experienced the long periods of separation from parents adjusted to it much as they would to death. Perhaps they experienced less of the *cycle* of separation by staying with the same relatives in one place rather than saying "hello" and "good-bye" to parents every three months—although other types of losses are certainly inherent in such prolonged separations between parents and children. It was this graph which made us begin to look more carefully at the hidden—rather than the obvious—losses we discuss in this book.

Surely there is much more research to do in this whole area. While other surveys have been done in the intervening years on ATCKs as well as TCKs, many questions remained unanswered. Perhaps because this is such a highly paradoxical experience, it is hard to measure the "both/andedness" in any quantitative survey. For those interested, we would suggest that any survey designed for TCKs and ATCKs take into account the inherent paradoxes and leave room for open-ended responses as well as those designed to gather statistical data.

Appendix B
Writings by Adult
Third Culture Kids

Let Us Possess One World

Sophia Morton

Sophia is an Australian TCK who grew up in Papua
New Guinea and now lives in Sydney. This fictional
piece reflects the struggle for intimacy many TCKs
know well.

You stare out the window in hurt defeat. I suppress a sigh and continue to stir my coffee aimlessly, casting my mind back into the depths of high school geography, trying to remember whether flotsam or jetsam is the appropriate name for the froth on top of the coffee. The levels of my mind continually amaze me. While I'm pondering the flotsam-jetsam dilemma, I'm simultaneously recognising the pondering as an attempt to distract myself from the question at hand, which threatens to overwhelm me. It's an old coping strategy. At another level I'm observing you and wondering what you'd think of my ponderings. I am indeed a curious mix.

We have circumnavigated the proverbial bush often and ferociously in the afternoon. It's not that I don't want to push through, but I don't know how. I can't make you understand. Instead of communicating myself to you, I get stuck defining and redefining the terms of reference. I thought we spoke the same language. But it seems that even though our words are the same, their meanings must be different.

Sometimes I think the cement of my being was taken from one cultural mould before it cured and was forced into other moulds, one after the other, retaining bits of the form of each but producing a finished sculpture that fitted into none. At other times I think of myself as the fish we caught snorkeling off Wewak. My basic shape camouflages itself in the colours of whatever surroundings I find myself in. I am adept at playing the appropriate roles. But do I have a colour of my own apart from those I appropriate? If I cease to play any role, would I be transparent? To mix metaphors, if I peeled away the layers of the roles I adopt, would I find nothing at the centre? Am I, after all, an onion—nothing but the sum of my layers?

The slipping sun casts its rays across the table, creating a wall of light and dancing dust particles between us. An intangible but definite barrier. I am halfway through thinking cynically that if communication can't be achieved between individuals, then it must be truly impossible across cultures, before I remember I am communicating across cultures—that is the problem.

You came to me with questions. We had promised each other honesty and openness, but you felt mine could be queried. I gave but I didn't share. There was a depth of intimacy we weren't achieving. You said I was shutting doors in your face. Staring out across the light barrier, I realise I have no answers for you, only a plea for understanding, which you think is an excuse, a justification for my lack of commitment (read: a commitment less than yours).

I tried to explain I was as committed to you as you are to me but that I find it nearly impossible to demonstrate that fact. You said I was splitting hairs. How can I make you understand I'm afraid? You got mad. You wanted to know why I didn't trust you. I said I do trust you. I'm not afraid of you necessarily; I'm just afraid. You said that people are always afraid of something. I agreed there's always a reason for fear but it's not necessarily a fear of something. So you wanted to know what the reason was. Words failed me. I tried. I tried to explain.

How can I make you understand that? Once my world stopped spinning, people, places, things, behaviours, and even a language were ripped from my life and I was thrust naked, except for the skimpy garment of family and the rags of memory, into a cold, new, and unfamiliar world. The more I invest in the world you and I are creating, the more there will be to grieve for when our world stops spinning.

If, I think quickly, *if.*

I am training myself slowly to the belief that worlds don't have to end. It is a measure of my intimacy with and trust in you that I can change the "when" to "if," even as an afterthought.

It is a mark of how much I trust you that I don't play the roles completely with you. I forget to. I lapse into pidgin, point with my chin, pick things up with my toes in your presence. You are amused. I've tried to explain to you that this is who I am. But I'm beginning to realise you have no way of understanding. It is totally outside your experience.

There was the day we went to the cricket match and I borrowed your binoculars. You asked me what was going on in the centre. I had to say I didn't know. I'd been watching a West Indian outfielder chewing gum. You laughed, yet a trifle impatiently. But I scarcely noticed. The sight of brown faces, with the occasional contrastive glimpse of shell-white teeth and dusky pink tongue, chewing casually but continuously, had brought the pungent smell of betel nut vividly to mind. I fully expected their saliva to be saffron when they spit. I was lost in my childhood. It is now that I remember.

Or the day we were shopping at the Queen Victoria Building and I dragged you into the Papua New Guinea shop. I was madly examining bilems and carvings, staring at story boards, transfixed by the chilling evil that fear fetishes always cast over me, and inhaling deeply the odour of the market and the village. I sensed your restless movements beside me and looked up into a bored but inquiring glance. We left. You exhaled suddenly and commented on the smell. For me it was a familiar and pleasant odour.

I was reexamining the world I lost, giving the globe in my mind a flick. In the part of me that belongs to that world, I was pretending the few revolutions caused by the flick were the continuous spinning of a living world, however unsatisfactory, artificial, and transient the indulgence. That globe haunts my present world. The truth is the old world informs the present. I am a composite, a citizen of the two. You couldn't participate in my other world. How can I expect you to accept the fear its loss creates and accommodate it? You have often questioned the veracity of my effort in maintaining contact with friends down south. Simply, I refuse to let another world stop. Spin more slowly, yes; halt, no.

If I could make you understand, I know what you'd say. As you grasped at the fragments of the conversation that made sense to you, I could see you heading down that track. *Willpower*, you'd say. *You simply have to push your fears to one side, take a risk, and open up to me. I won't fail you.*

And if I told you I can't, you'd interpret my insufficient willpower as a lack of real desire to do so. That's not it. I yearn for oneness with you with every fibre of my being. I don't like the still sparse landscape I inhabit. The people I've let into my heart have been like the tropical downpour that ends the dry season and fills up the tank again. I know it would be worthwhile. But fear creates an inertia that I, for all my oft-discussed strength of character, willpower, even stubbornness, cannot simply set aside. It's not you I fear, it's losing you. I'm trying to minimise the loss.

The last Christmas someone gave us two giant teddy bears—three months before we left. I remember sorting through my possessions, trying to decide what to take and what to leave. It was the teddy bears I cried for. I remember Mum trying to comfort me, pointing out all the things I could take and saying that I really hadn't had the teddies for long, they weren't my favourite toys. But that was precisely why I was so upset. I didn't have a chance for them to become well-loved favourites. I was crying not for the past I was leaving, nor even the present, but for the future, the might-have-beens. I think I sensed I could take my history with me but not my future. My world was slowly grinding to a halt. It was going to be arrested at a fixed point. While I would always have it, while I could examine it, while I could mount it on a stand and have it as a globe in my memory to give an occasional spin, I could never give it life, never keep it spinning, never develop it beyond the point at which it stopped.

Your hands come down onto the table. *Long, lean, attractive hands*, I muse absentmindedly.

The coping strategy again. You look searchingly into my face. I hope the desperate need, the pleading are clear in my eyes, but I fear the mask of independence I have long since learnt to wear has been permanently grafted onto my face. I want you to know without me having to tell you. I want you to cross the barriers within, without me having to open them. I want intimacy without vulnerability, I realise in a blinding flash of insight. The ludicrousness of it is nearly overwhelming.

"I have to go," you say wearily. Your knuckles whiten as you push yourself to a standing position. There is a luminosity to this moment. I have been here before.

"Call me?" I hear myself asking.

It is an effort to display even that much need, to make myself that vulnerable. Your smile is whimsical, and a shadow chills your calm blue eyes. Inside me the little girl is weeping for her teddy bears again. *Don't do it*, I think. *If you bring this world to a close, how will I ever find the courage to begin another?*

You stop to kiss me good-bye and your lips are cool against my mouth. For the first time I begin to doubt my logic. Suddenly my fear of investing too heavily in an uncertain future is swamped by the knowledge of losing a present that is just starting to pay dividends on my past investments. The realisation slams into my consciousness. Now is a future that *has* arrived. Tears fill my eyes and overflow down my cheeks. You feel the wetness and pull back in surprise.

"I need you." The words come out in a sob, surprising me more than I think they surprise you. I weep, my eyes drowning in the warm, equatorial waters of grief, guilt, and relief. I am vaguely aware of the group at the next table staring, but adrift in a liberating moment of nakedness I couldn't care less. In my mind I see children playing naked and carefree on the banks of the Sepik and I recognise their wisdom—*naked and unashamed.*

The child in me is weeping too—for the market, for favourite toys, for the lagoon, for school friends and courtesy relatives, for the everyday sights, sounds, and smell. She is weeping for her present.

I am aware also of your indecision. If our world has stopped spinning, I will have myself to blame as much as my history. I hate my own culpable blindness. Amazingly, I feel your hands under my elbows drawing me up into your arms. A line flows up from my memory—*Let us possess one world, each hath one and is one.* And I recognise its truth. Now is reality.

The Long Good-bye: Honoring Unresolved Grief

Paul Asbury Seaman

Paul is the son of United Methodist missionaries and grew up in Pakistan. He is also a former president of Global Nomads, Washington area, and author of *Paper Airplanes in the Himalayas: The Unfinished Path Home* and *Far above the Plain.*

Dealing with the accumulated grief of too many leavings is an essential part of the global nomad legacy. Why then are we so reluctant to talk about it? Hushing up heartache only means that it will take longer to let go and move on.

I moved recently, bringing to an end the longest period of geographic stability in my life. It was a big event. After three and a half years in the same apartment, I packed up and moved...a block down the street. I didn't have to say good-bye to any friends, learn a new currency, or adjust to a new job. The new apartment was comparatively spacious, filled with light, and, most importantly, contained the woman I loved. Like "an outward sign of an inward grace," this transition reflected some very positive developments in my life.

So why, a month later, was I so depressed? Stress counselors emphasize that even good changes are stressful. But I suspect there was another factor: the grief of leaving familiar places is a distinctive part of my identity as a global nomad. Many of us have experienced such transitions multiple times, and because they occurred during our formative years, their impact is deeply embedded. We might deny or may not recognize the effects of accumulated losses, but they will make their influence felt through other voices. Depression, anger, withdrawal, arrogance, exhaustion, and righteousness are some of the voices grief has borrowed in my life.

Grief is a current that goes unarticulated in many people's lives, and even within the very organizations that seek to understand and serve global nomads, grief seems almost like a taboo subject. There is a curious reticence about publicly exploring this key aspect of our experience. Informal discussions of grief as a global nomad issue are often characterized by hyperbole and judgmental generalizations: "Everyone who says that they had a great experience growing up and that they are content now is in denial." Or "Everyone who is grieving is using their global nomad background as a crutch, as a catchall excuse, for all their current problems"; they are "wallowing in a victim mentality" and need to "get a life."

I readily grant that some global nomads had perfectly happy childhoods; others have experienced horrendous disorientation, abandonment, or abuse, the impact of which they will struggle with for the rest of their lives. And, yes, some individuals are obsessed and crippled by grief, allowing themselves to be defined by it. I suspect, however, that the majority of us simply live with ambivalent memories, and whether the dominant feeling is nostalgia, regret, or bitterness, the sense of loss is essentially the same.

Sometimes we cushion our grief under blankets of explanations and pillows of dimming memories. To hear someone articulate a vaguely familiar pain can be quite threatening to these careful arrangements. Even if there is nothing unresolved within ourselves to be disturbed, most of us aren't very good with public expression of vulnerability. It is too intimate and may often be viewed as a sign of weakness or social maladjustment. Dealing with an emotional individual is awkward enough, but a whole group of people displaying their raw feelings can really make us uncomfortable.

Some time after the Second International Conference for Global Nomads in September 1992, one person remarked to me that the event seemed to be "overrun with grieving MKs [missionary kids]." This was not my experience, but supposing grief was an insistent if unofficial theme at the conference, it is worth asking why this was the case—and why among missionary kids more than other global nomads. An emotional atmosphere can seem manipulated, ungenuine, or self-absorbed, but genuine opportunities to face grief directly and honestly will be missed—or can be comfortably avoided—as long as the topic itself remains so highly charged.

A curious phenomenon happens when global nomads are called upon to talk about their past, especially in more formal situations such as a panel discussion or interviews. Invariably, they end their already very positive accounts with "...but it was great. I wouldn't trade it for anything." There is a subtle defensiveness in this kind of summary that begs the question: What is it that they feel needs this reassurance? Or are they reassuring themselves?

The parents of many global nomads were involved in high-profile or morally weighty service professions. They were on a mission, representing the home country, a particular ideology, or even God. Sacrifice—of family or emotional stability, of reliable friends or circumstances—was just part of pursuing the noble cause. We were trained from an early age to believe in the cause; to show our pain, to acknowledge the cost, was disloyal.

But acknowledging grief or anger does not invalidate the positive aspects of an otherwise cherished experience. When I unexpectedly shed a few tears at the loss of my old apartment, it did not mean I regretted the decision to move. Rather, it was honoring all that place had given me, the things that I had learned and experienced during the time I lived there, and acknowledging that a particular period of my life, not just my location, had come to an end.

Give Grief a Chance: Acknowledgment and Closure

Why is grief such a persistent, unresolved issue for many of us? There are at least four reasons:

1. incomplete good-byes or a lack of closure at the time a loss occurs;

2. not recognizing the symptoms, such as anger and depression;

3. guilt or embarrassment about having "negative" feelings, which can lead to denial or repression; or

4. the lack of adequate forums for expressing grief.

David Pollock's presentations of the TCK Profile and transition workshops by Norma McCaig always emphasize the importance of having closure rituals. These can take many forms, from simply having the opportunity to say farewell to your friends to something more elaborate, perhaps with spiritual overtones. This may include saying good-bye privately to familiar buildings, to a favorite spot, or to the landscape itself. The day I left my old apartment I stood in the empty rooms and suddenly felt the pangs of parting. I took a few minutes to cherish the many memories contained in that place. Going back to the places where we were raised to complete our good-byes can be a powerful release and brings an added dimension to what might otherwise be merely a nostalgic trip.

Our backgrounds were often wondrously unusual, sometimes exotic, even glamorous. We do feel privileged. Often there was excitement in the transitions themselves: the anticipation of going "home" or to an interesting new place. In the eager hustle and earnest efforts to embrace a new setting, we often didn't understand how much we were leaving behind. When grief showed up as depression or other forms of stress, we attributed it to culture shock. Years later we are confused by an uncharacteristic sentimentality, triggered by certain movies, even television advertisements, that evoke a sense of community or home. What we think is nostalgia may really be some part of ourselves that is being given permission to grieve. The tears may be as much from relief, from finally letting go, as they are about the grief itself. I remember seeing *Out of Africa* several years ago when it was first released. After the movie ended, I sat in the theater and wept for twenty minutes.

We need to give dignity to our grief and create social structures—personal ones, if not institutional—where we can name the pain of lost friendships, lost places, lost identities. To finally bring closure and healing to lingering grief some people may need to practice "constructive indulgence" for a time.

Western society is famously bad about dealing with grief. Death is the only severe loss for which we have public grieving rituals (and *they* are usually pretty restrained). We have no tradition that offers socially sanctioned support for the many other causes of grief. Severe illnesses or natural disasters may be exceptions, but even in these cases, when the symptoms are gone, the affected individual or family is expected to return to "normal."

From my own struggles with grief and depression I have learned that the process of healing always takes longer than other people think it should and, further, that those who have not experienced a similar loss or identity struggle will never really understand.

How then, once we face our grief, can we know if the way we are dealing with it and the length of time it takes are appropriate? Some questions to ask might be:

- Can we see progress—is the grief evolving, going deeper, beginning to dissipate?

- Is the grief clearly not the primary attribute that defines our identity?

- Does it lead to a sense of solidarity and kinship with others that is healing, empowering, change-inducing?

- Are we moving away from a sense of victimization, or powerlessness, toward a greater sense of control of our life that is still connected with but not overly dependent on others?

Trauma experts emphasize that talking is a critical step in healing. If survivors of an airplane crash or victims of a hurricane simply describe *what happened* in detail, while difficult, it significantly hastens the recovery from shock and helplessness. Like Vietnam veterans, global nomads have been deprived of social validation of their experience. We didn't get a hero's welcome. For the most part society—friends, relatives, school officials, parents' sponsoring agencies—couldn't appreciate the "big deal" about what had happened to us. They did not recognize the trauma of uprooting and cultural dislocation, because many aspects of this were beyond their own experience and, thus, their ability to comprehend.

For friends and family the importance of listening cannot be overstated. For some global nomads, the chance to reminisce with an empathetic group, to laugh together about the hard memories, is enough. Others need to express their grief more directly. Grieving people sometimes talk a lot because they've never really felt heard. This is, of course, a vicious cycle, as impatience sometimes causes others to tune out. But when a grieving person finally feels accepted and understood, the compelling need to talk about his or her woundedness usually dissipates. A pain that has been named and honored by the empathy of others can be let go of. This is one reason that the company of other global nomads can be so exhilarating and healing.

While we cannot recover what we've lost, we can celebrate those aspects of ourselves that we may associate with another time and place. For instance, we cannot become children again, but we can seek to recover a childlike sense of wonder, spontaneity, and vulnerability—or perhaps just a sense of contentment about our place in the world. Ultimately, coming to terms with grief means learning to feel at home within ourselves.

Resources and Bibliography

Resources for TCKs and ATCKs

Australia/New Zealand

Australasian MK Association
23 Bundoran Parade
Box Hill North
Victoria 3129
Australia
Group of primarily adult missionary kids helping one another and new returnees in adjusting to home country.

MK Merimna
PO Box 205
Kingswood, South Australia 5062
Australia
61 08 272-5419
"Committed to caring for cross-cultural kids." Directors Roger and Jill Dyer have been involved in issues relating to helping international schools with curriculum development so non-North American TCKs can fit better into their own culture.

Denmark

DUO-Denmark, Borgmestervej 12,
DK-6070 Christiansfeld, Denmark
Postal Giro 1199-081 88 36
Organization working with returned TCKs through conferences and seminars.

United States

Around the World in a Lifetime (AWAL)
c/o FSYF
PO Box 39185
Washington, DC 20016
Organization for Foreign Service teens. Circulates newsletter and sponsors local meetings for TCKs.

Cultural Connexions
PO Box 90402
Indianapolis, IN 46290-0402
Phone: 317-465-8760
Fax: 317-251-4933
e-mail: RDvanreken@aol.com
Organization of conferences and seminars for internationally mobile families. Special focus on issues related to non-North American families living and raising their TCKs in the United States.

Global Nomads International
PO Box 9584
Washington, DC 20016-9584
Phone: 202-466-2244
e-mail: info@gni.org
Website: globalnomadsassociation.com
Organization founded for those with internationally mobile childhoods of all backgrounds. Sponsors conferences and publishes newsletter with articles pertaining to such a lifestyle.

Global Nomad Resources
Norma M. McCaig, President
PO Box 8066
Reston, VA 20191
Phone/Fax: 703-758-7766
e-mail: gmu.edu
Workshops, presentations, consultations, and publications related to
global nomads and their families.

Interaction, Inc.
PO Box 158
Houghton, NY 14744-0158
716-567-8774
Directed by David C. Pollock. Conducts reentry seminars and TCK
profile seminars throughout the year for international organizations
and individuals throughout the world.

Intercultural Press, Inc.
PO Box 700
374 US Route One
Yarmouth, ME 04096
Phone: 207-846-5168
Fax: 207-846-5181
e-mail: books@interculturalpress.com
Website: www.interculturalpress.com
The premier publisher and distributor of books, videos, simulations,
and other materials on intercultural topics.

Mu Kappa International
PO Box 1388
De Soto, TX 75115
One of the first support groups started by and for TCKs. Primarily
for missionary kids.

Overseas Brats
PO Box 29805
San Antonio, TX 78229
Group designed to help adults raised as dependents of parents in
U.S. military, government, or civilian organizations to connect with
one another.

Third Culture Family Services
Elsie Purnell, Director
2685 Meguiar Drive
Pasadena, CA 91107
Phone: 626-794-9406
Strong emphasis on organizing and facilitating support groups for
ACTKs. Presentations for international organizations on how to
maximize third culture experience for families involved.

Transition Dynamics
Barbara F. (Bobbie) Schaetti, Principal
2448 NW 63rd St.
Seattle, WA 98107
Phone: 206-789-3290
Fax: 206-781-2439
e-mail: bfschaetti@transition-dynamics.com
Website: www.transition-dynamics.com
A consultancy committed to serving the children, women, and men
for whom international mobility and cultural transitions are a part of
daily life.

Practical Books on TCK Issues

Austin, Clyde N., ed. *Cross-cultural Reentry: A Book of Readings.*
1986. Abilene, TX: Abilene Christian University.
> A collection of articles on how to identify and deal
> with problems which occur when reentering the home
> country after a period overseas.

————. *Cross-cultural Reentry: An Annotated Bibliography.* 1983.
Abilene, TX: Abilene Christian University.
> A review of literature on cross-cultural reentry
> issues.

Bell, Linda. *Hidden Immigrants: Legacies of Growing Up Abroad.*
1997. Cross Cultural Publications, PO Box 506, Notre Dame,
IN 46556.
> Linda explores the TCK experience by interviewing
> six men and seven women who were raised as TCKs.
> They share their reactions to things such as culture
> shock and matters of identity, marriage, career, and
> grief along with what helped or hindered them in
> dealing with these matters.

Blohm, Judith M. *Where in the World Are You Going?* 1996. Intercultural Press, PO Box 700, Yarmouth, ME 04096. 800-370-
2665; fax: 207-846-5181.
e-mail: books@interculturalpress.com
Website: www.interculturalpress.com
> An entertaining activity book for children ages five
> to ten to help them prepare for an overseas move
> with their families.

Bowers, Joyce, ed. *Raising Resilient MKs: Resources for Caregivers,
Parents, and Teachers.* 1998. ACSI, PO Box 35097, Colorado Springs, CO 80935.
> A collection of materials from a variety of authors
> all designed to be helpful for caregivers, teachers, and
> parents of TCKs. Many of the articles were originally

presented as seminars at the first three International Conferences on Missionary Kids. Other chapters are from various magazine articles published later on this topic.

Dyer, Jill. *Harold and Stanley Say Goodbye*. 1998. MK Merimna, PO Box 205, Kingswood, SA, Australia 5062.
This delightful story featuring a bear family about to make a cross-cultural transition is designed to help young TCKs understand and talk about their own feelings as they face a similar uprooting. A great tool for parents to use with their children.

Dyer, Jill, and Roger Dyer, eds. *"...and Bees Make Honey."* 1995. MK Merimna, PO Box 205, Kingswood, SA, Australia 5062.
Second anthology of TCK writings—including many from non-North American TCKs. Interesting—and short—readings.

———, eds. *Scamps, Scholars, and Saints*. 1991. MK Merimna, PO Box 205, Kingswood, SA, Australia 5062.
First volume of collected anecdotes, reflections, poems, and drawings by TCKs. Many good insights expressed even by young TCKs.

———. *What Makes Aussie TCKs Tick?* 1989. MK Merimna, PO Box 205, Kingswood, SA, Australia 5062.
A practical resource book primarily written for Australian families living overseas, but also helpful to any non-North American family in dealing with the strong North American influences in schooling and culture present in many expatriate communities.

Eakin, K. B. *The Foreign Service Teenager—At Home in the U.S.: A Few Thoughts for Parents Returning with Teenagers*. 1988. Washington, DC: Overseas Briefing Center/Foreign Service Institute, Department of State.
Written by a veteran diplomat spouse, educator, and officer in the Family Liaison Office of the State

Department, this book deals with specific issues of teenage children whose parents are in the diplomatic corps.

Echerd, Pam, and Alice Arathoon, eds. *Understanding and Nurturing the Missionary Family.* 1989. (Compendium of the International Conference on Missionary Kids, Quito, Ecuador, January 4-8, 1987, vol. 1). William Carey Library, PO Box 41029, Pasadena, CA 91114.

————. *Planning for MK Nurture.* 1987. (Compendium of the International Conference on Missionary Kids, Quito, Ecuador, January, 1989, vol. 2.) William Carey Library, PO Box 41029, Pasadena, CA 91114.

The above two books contain transcripts of the various plenary sessions and seminars from the conference held in January 1987.

Foyle, Marjory. *Missionary Stress.* 1987. EMIS, PO Box 794, Wheaton, IL 60189. (Originally published in Britain as *Honourably Wounded.)*

British psychiatrist Marjory Foyle, herself an experienced missionary, writes of particular stresses faced by the missionary community in its cross-cultural endeavors.

Gordon, Alma. *Don't Pig Out on Junk Food: The MKs Guide to Survival in the U.S.* 1993. EMIS, PO Box 794, Wheaton, IL 60189. 708-653-2158.

A humorous yet practical guide by ATCK Alma Gordon, based on her years of experience as the daughter of an ATCK, as a TCK herself, and in raising her own TCKs in South America.

Hess, J. Daniel. *The Whole World Guide to Culture Learning.* 1994. Intercultural Press, PO Box 700, Yarmouth, ME 04096. 800-370-2665; fax: 207-846-5181.
e-mail: books@interculturalpress.com
Website: www.interculturalpress.com

.A substantive introduction to culture learning, designed especially for students going abroad. Contains a series of guides to help students get the most out of their overseas experience.

Hughes, Katherine L. *The Accidental Diplomat: Dilemmas of the Trailing Spouse.* 1998. Aletheia Publications, 46 Bell Hollow Road, Putnam Valley, NY 10579. 914-526-2873; fax: 914-526-2905.
e-mail: AlethPub@aol.com
Website: http://members.AOL.com/AlethPub

A close-up look at the world of women whose identities are shaped by the professional commitments of their husbands to the Foreign Service. In the context of frequently shifting locales, they are often forced to reinvent their lives every two or three years.

Janssen, Gretchen. *Women on the Move: A Christian Perspective on Cross-Cultural Adaptation.* 1989. Intercultural Press, PO Box 700, Yarmouth, ME 04096. 800-370-2665; fax: 207-846-5181. Out of print.
e-mail: books@interculturalpress.com
Website: www.interculturalpress.com

Kalb, Rosalind, and Penelope Welch. *Moving Your Family Overseas.* 1992. Intercultural Press, PO Box 700, Yarmouth, ME 04096. 800-370-2665; fax: 207-846-5181.
e-mail: books@interculturalpress.com
Website: www.interculturalpress.com

Designed for use by the entire family, this book provides practical information on the steps involved in preparing for and successfully managing an overseas move.

Kohls, L. Robert. *Survival Kit for Overseas Living.* 3d ed. 1996. Intercultural Press, PO Box 700, Yarmouth, ME, 04096. 800-370-2665; fax: 207-846-5181.
e-mail: books@interculturalpress.com
Website: www.interculturalpress.com

Practical information and insights into the process of
cross-cultural adaptation along with suggestions on
how best to go about it.

Marshall, Terry. *The Whole World Guide to Language Learning.*
1990. Intercultural Press, PO Box 700, Yarmouth, ME 04096.
800-370-2665; fax: 207-846-5181.
e-mail: books@interculturalpress.com
Website: www.interculturalpress.com
Practical guide to successful, self-directed language
learning while abroad. The learning program includes
maximum use of and involvement with the local
community.

McCluskey, Karen Curnow, ed. *Notes from a Traveling Childhood:*
Readings for Internationally Mobile Parents and Children.
1994. Foreign Service Youth Foundation, PO Box 39185,
Washington, DC 20016.
A helpful, easily readable handbook filled with short
essays and writings by ATCKs and others on not only
the issues involved for internationally mobile families,
but practical charts on what to do.

Pascoe, Robin. *Culture Shock: Successful Living Abroad.* 1953, 1993.
Graphic Arts, Portland OR. 800-452-3032.
Website: www.gacpc.
Robin takes a critical look at the issues of settlement for the entire family in the light of the role and
relationships of the trailing spouse in maintaining sanity
in the home.

———. *Surviving Overseas: A Wife's Guide to Successful Living*
Abroad. 1953, 1992. Times Books International, Times Centre, 1 New Industrial Road, Singapore.
Robin's sensitivity to the issues she so clearly spells
out regarding the "trailing spouse"—and how to best
deal with them—stems from her own firsthand
experience as a Canadian diplomat's wife who served
in China and Korea.

Piet-Pelon, Nancy J., and Barbara Hornby. *Women's Guide to Overseas Living.* 2d ed. 1992. Intercultural Press, PO Box 700, Yarmouth, ME 04096. 800-370-2665; fax: 207-846-5181.
e-mail: books@interculturalpress.com
Website: www.interculturalpress.com
A perceptive examination of issues critical to women (and their families) who relocate abroad.

Romano, Dugan. *Intercultural Marriage: Promises and Pitfalls.* 2d ed. 1997. Intercultural Press, PO Box 700, Yarmouth, ME 04096. 800-370-2665; fax: 207-846-5181.
e-mail: books@interculturalpress.com
Website: www.interculturalpress.com
A wise look at the various factors and stresses of intercultural marriage from one who has been there.

Schmeil, Gene, and Kathryn Schmeil. *Welcome Home: Who are You? Tales of a Foreign Service Family.* 1998. Aletheia Publications, 46 Bell Hollow Road, Putnam Valley, NY 10579. 914-526-2873; fax: 914-526-2905
e-mail: AlethPub@aol.com
Website: http://members.AOL.com/ AlethPub
From the bizarre and unpredictable to the peaceful and reassuring, the vignettes offer vivid portrayals of the life of a Foreign Service family living and working on three continents.

Shames, Germaine W. *Transcultural Odysseys: The Evolving Global Consciousness.* 1997. Intercultural Press, PO Box 700, Yarmouth, ME 04096. 800-370-2665; fax: 207-846-5181.
e-mail: books@interculturalpress.com
Website: www.interculturalpress.com
Through stories of those who have gone overseas, the author explores how an individual can become a "global" person.

Smith, Carolyn D. *The Absentee American.* 1991; reprint, 1994.
Aletheia Publications, 46 Bell Hollow Road, Putnam Valley,
NY 10579. 914-526-2873.
e-mail: AlethPub@aol.com
Website: www.members.AOL.com/ AlethPub
    A Foreign Service ATCK writes specifically about
    how American ATCKs view their home country and its
    place in the contemporary world. Includes helpful
    statistical data about the American expatriate commu-
    nity as well as stories gathered from over three
    hundred questionnaires to which ATCKs responded.

————, ed. *Strangers at Home.* 1996. Aletheia Publications, 46 Bell
Hollow Road, Putnam Valley, NY 10579. 914-526-2873
e-mail: AlethPub@aol.com
Website: www.members.AOL.com/ AlethPub
    Essays on the reentry experience of TCKs. Includes
    the findings of the ATCK survey done by sociologists
    Ruth Hill Useem and Ann Baker Cottrell along with
    reflections by ATCKs themselves. David Pollock,
    Norma McCaig, and Ruth Van Reken are among the
    authors.

Storti, Craig. *The Art of Coming Home.* 1997. Intercultural Press,
PO Box 700, Yarmouth, ME 04096. 800-370-2665; fax: 207-
846-5181.
e-mail: books@interculturalpress.com
Website: www.interculturalpress.com
    This book addresses in detail the reentry process
    after a cross-cultural sojourn.

————. *The Art of Crossing Cultures.* 1990. Intercultural Press, PO
Box 700, Yarmouth, ME 04096. 800-370-2665; fax: 207-846-
5181.
e-mail: books@interculturalpress.com
Website: www.interculturalpress.com

An essential book for anyone returning to his or her
country after a time abroad. Storti also discusses the
substantial emotional and financial costs of unsuccessful
reentry for the sending organizations as well.

Taber, Sara Mansfield. *Of Many Lands: Journal of a Traveling Child-hood.* 1997. Foreign Service Youth Foundation (Publications), PO Box 39185, Washington, DC 20016. Fax 703-875-7979.

Evocative "snapshots" of the author's life as a TCK
invite response from fellow TCKs or ATCKs as they
reflect on their own experience. Written in journal
form, this workbook can be used both personally and
also as a tool for family members or groups of TCKs or
ATCKs to share their stories.

Tetzel, Beth A., and Patricia Mortenson, eds. *International Conference on Missionary Kids: New Directions in Missions: Implications for MKs.* (Compendium of the International Conference on Missionary Kids, Manila, November 1984.) Missionary Internship, Box 457, Farmington, MI 48024. 313-474-9110.

Based on the plenary sessions and workshops of the
first international conference on TCKs in Manila,
specifically missionary TCKs.

Walters, Doris L. *An Assessment of Reentry Issues for Missionary Children.* New York: Vantage Press, 1991.

Psychologist Walters reports on what she considers
the primary reentry issues facing missionary children
based on her work with them through the Southern
Baptist mission.

Ward, Ted. *Living Overseas: A Book of Preparations.* New York: Free Press, 1984.

This book specifically deals with preparing to make
the move overseas; what to look for, how to deal with
conflicts, and much more useful advice.

Wertsch, Mary Edwards. *Military Brats.* 1991. Reprint, 1996. Aletheia Publications, 46 Bell Hollow Road, Putnam Valley, NY 10579. 914-526-2873.
e-mail: AlethPub@aol.com
Website: www.members.AOL.com/AlethPub
> A groundbreaking book on life in the military. Filled with stories, facts, and philosophizing about this subset of the TCK world. Insightful and helpful.

Williams, K. L. *When Africa Was Home.* New York: Orchard Books, 1991.
> Many beautiful pictures accompany the text of this story about a TCK childhood. It is written for children of all ages.

Biographies, Autobiographies, and Fictionalized Personal Accounts of TCK Experience

Addleton, Jonathan. *Some Far and Distant Place.* Athens and London: University of Georgia Press, 1996.
> A memoir of a TCK childhood spent in Pakistan. Addleton was born in the mountains of northern Pakistan in 1957, the son of missionary parents who had themselves grown up in rural Georgia. The book includes many reflections on the challenges that come with continuously confronting and, on occasion, crossing boundaries of race, class, religion, and ethnicity. It offers an interesting perspective on the various subcultures arising within missionary communities and within overseas boarding schools established by and large to educate the children of expatriates.

Fritz, Jean. *Homesick: My Own Story.* Santa Barbara, CA: Cornerstone Books, 1987.
> A charming, slightly fictionalized story of a childhood spent in China in the prerevolutionary days. It covers not only time in China but also reentry to a

country Fritz had always considered home without
having once been there. TCKs everywhere will
recognize much in this story as their own.

Gilkey, Langdon. *Shantung Compound.* San Francisco: Harper-
Collins, 1975.

This is a story based on Langdon Gilkey's two and a
half years spent in Japanese internment camps with
two thousand other expatriates, including many TCKs.
It is a reflection on people's reaction under stress as
well as an accounting of prison life.

Michell, David J. *A Boy's War.* Republic of Singapore: Overseas
Missionary Fellowship, 1988.

One man's account of his internment in a Japanese
concentration camp along with his fellow students
from the Chefoo School in China. Includes interesting
insights of fellow detainee, Eric Liddell, the runner
featured in *Chariots of Fire*.

Seaman, Paul, ed. *Far above the Plain.* Pasadena, CA: William Carey
Library, 1996.

An anthology of stories written by alumni of Murree
Christian School, a missionary kid boarding school in
Pakistan.

————. *Paper Airplanes in the Himalayas: The Unfinished Path
Home.* Notre Dame, IN: Cross Cultural Publications, 1997.

A well-written account of Seaman's life as a TCK
growing up in Pakistan. Includes a powerful history of
the era and country as well as accounts of his school
days. The description of "the train ride"—that long
trek back and forth from boarding school—will move
any who have made similar journeys.

Van Reken, Ruth E. *Letters Never Sent* (formerly *Letters I Never
Wrote*). 1986. "Letters," PO Box 90084, Indianapolis, IN
46290-0084. 317-251-4933.

This is a thoughtful look at the hitherto unexamined

impact of the many cycles of separation and loss from Ruth Van Reken's missionary kid childhood. Using the format of letters to her parents, Ruth explains—at the age of thirty-nine—the feelings she could never articulate to them when she was a child.

TEXT BOOK

Writing through Literature

THIRD EDITION

Robert Scholes
Brown University

Nancy R. Comley
Queens College, CUNY

Gregory L. Ulmer
University of Florida

Bedford/St. Martin's

BOSTON ♦ NEW YORK

. Conroy

Marketing Manager: Richard Cadman
Art Director: Donna Lee Dennison
Text Design: Sandra Rigney
Copy Editor: Joan Torkildson
Cover Design: Donna Lee Dennison
Composition: the dotted i
Printing and Binding: Haddon Craftsmen, Inc., an R. R. Donnelley & Sons Company

President: Charles H. Christensen
Editorial Director: Joan E. Feinberg
Editor in Chief: Karen S. Henry
Director of Marketing: Karen R. Melton
Director of Editing, Design, and Production: Marcia Cohen
Managing Editor: Erica T. Appel

Library of Congress Control Number: 2001095589

Manufactured in the United States of America.

7 6 5
f e

For information, write: Bedford/St. Martin's, 75 Arlington Street, Boston, MA 02116
(617-399-4000)

ISBN: 0-312-24879-2

Acknowledgments

Margaret Atwood, "you fit into me" from *Power Politics* copyright © 1996 by Margaret Atwood. Reproduced by permission of Stoddart Publishing Company, Ltd., Toronto.

W. H. Auden, "Let us honor . . . ," copyright 1934 and renewed 1962 by W. H. Auden, from *W. H. Auden: Collected Poems* by W. H. Auden, edited by Edward Mendelson. Used by permission of Random House, Inc. and Faber and Faber, Ltd.

Paul Auster, "Tell Me a Story." From *The Invention of Solitude*, by Paul Auster. Reprinted by permission of Carol Mann Agency.

Russell Banks, "*Bambi:* A Boy's Story," from *The Movie That Changed My Life.* Copyright © 1991 by Russell Banks. Reprinted by permission of Ellen Levine Literary Agency, Inc.

Acknowledgments and copyrights are continued at the back of the book on pages 377–380, which constitute an extension of the copyright page.

Preface for Instructors

THE TITLE OF THIS TEXTBOOK is not a joke. It is meant to signify our intention to offer an alternative approach to the traditional course called "Writing about Literature" or "Introduction to Literature." By substituting the concept of *text* for the concept of *literature,* we accomplish a number of things. We allow for the presentation of a wider range of material and a broader spectrum of approaches to literary study. And we close or reduce the gaps that have separated reading from writing, creative from critical work, and literature from ordinary language.

And our subtitle, "Writing through Literature"—what can that mean? It could mean a lot of things, but let us tell you what we mean by it here and now, in the case of this book. Most obviously—and most importantly—we mean something different from "writing *about* literature." It is our belief, based on a lot of years in classrooms all over this country, that we teachers make a mistake when we separate the writing done by students from the texts they write about. What literature has to offer us—teachers and students alike—is pleasure, information, and something else: the most powerful and creative ways to use language—those things that make literature literary.

Our mistake—and we have all made it—is to serve up literary texts on a pedestal, to be admired. Of course they may be admirable. Why else would we care about them? But putting them on a pedestal does them no service, and it leads students to believe that the way writers write has nothing to do with the way students write. This book is an attempt to correct that mistake. We offer those who use this book a chance to escape, however briefly, from the common practices of literary study, and to open the real creative joys of literature to every student who will make the effort to work through this book.

The structure of the book is simple. In Chapter 1, "Texts as Representation," we examine the basis of narrative and dramatic texts, starting with simple forms like the anecdote and the character conflict. In this chapter you'll find, for instance, selections ranging from anecdotes by Walter Benjamin and Brent Staples to Kate Chopin's short story "The Kiss." Then in Chapter 2, "Texts, Thoughts, and Things," we move to the basis of poetic texts (and of all creative uses of language), the metaphorical processes that are pervasive in all our forms of textuality: literary, commercial, and scientific. The point of poetic study is not to find a few hidden meanings but to learn to think as poets think, to become accustomed to metaphor, to be equally able to comprehend and compose metaphors. Selections in this chapter, such as Roger Brown's "What Words Are: Metaphor" and W. S. Merwin's "Separation," help students construct a theory on the uses of metaphor and test that theory against literary examples.

The study of metaphor leads naturally to problems of interpretation and to forms that are based on extended metaphors, like the parable and the allegory. We examine these forms with examples from Jorge Luis Borges and Franz Kafka, among others. It also leads to the cultural study of the ways that common metaphors organize our thinking and feeling—even in scientific modes of thought. The study of interpretation in Chapter 3, "Texts and Other Texts," includes several versions of "Sleeping Beauty" as well as theoretical texts from Umberto Eco and Susan Sontag. This work leads to a major project, discussed in Chapter 4, "Texts and Research: The Mystory." The mystory is not the traditional research paper, which emphasizes all over again the great difference between the literary and the academic text. Instead, it incorporates the writer's own stake in the object of study and the writer's own position. This position should be not outside the literary texts seeking an impossible objectivity, but inside them, going through them, using their language and their strategies in the process of understanding them.

Several decades of literary theory have led us to this position—and to these conclusions:

- We cannot learn about literature from the outside; we must go through it.
- We can gain the theoretical knowledge we need by finding it in the literary works themselves, when the right questions are asked about them.
- The knowledge and power we keep is the knowledge that we have used and continue to use. Everything else falls away and is lost.

- Having learned how to write "through" literature, we return to the conventions of argument with a new understanding of the literariness of all writing.

Believing these things, we have developed a book based on doing things, on writing through literature rather than writing about it, and on learning literary theory by emulating literary practice. The book will work best for those who follow it from the relatively simple procedures and questions of the opening sections to the intricacies of the later sections and the mystory. But it can be used in other ways by creative teachers. We believe in the creativity of teachers and students—both.

NEW TO THIS EDITION

In the Third Edition, we've included more—and more varied—selections, ranging from traditional to experimental literature. Of the 101 readings in the book, 57 are new. Exciting new pieces exemplify and help students learn important composing processes such as revision and the use of metaphor. New works include Paul Auster's "Tell Me a Story," André Breton's "Surrealist Methods," Emily Martin's "The Egg and the Sperm," Umberto Eco's "The Intention of the Text," Susan Griffin, from A Chorus of Stones—and many more.

We also have scores of new assignments to provide more opportunities for working with, rather than simply reading, texts. These assignments—which are now titled in this edition—draw on students' creative imaginations and analytical skills to turn them from passive consumers into active producers of critical and creative texts. New assignments include "Proposing Your Own Theory of Literary Interpretation" and "The Familiar and the Unfamiliar."

To extend the work of Text Book into the ever-more-prevalent electronic realm, we now include unique instruction in, and opportunities to explore, hypertextuality. A new companion Web site at **www.bedfordstmartins .com/textbook** extends the work of a new section on hypertext in Chapter 3 and offers exercises that allow students to work directly and practically with literary hypertexts on the Web. The site features the complete hypertext of Robert Coover's Briar Rose and James Michael Jarrett's "A Jarrett in Your Text," along with discussion suggestions, opportunities to comment, additional research links, and more.

We have also streamlined Text Book to allow students to move more easily from interpreting texts to research-based writing projects. In response to instructor suggestions, the previous edition's chapter on "Fragments and Signatures" has been combined with its chapter on the mystory to make it easier for students to move directly from learning about interpretation to research writing. This new streamlined Chapter 4 provides a new introduction and explanation of the method of the mystory as well as a new archive of literary texts.

Finally, we have updated *Resources for Teaching* Text Book: Writing Through Literature, Third Edition. This resource includes sample syllabi to help instructors plan the course; a discussion of each reading and each assignment to provide classroom-tested suggestions for teaching with the book; and student writing samples based on the assignments in *Text Book* to show what kinds of responses are possible.

ACKNOWLEDGMENTS

We would like to thank the following at Bedford/St. Martin's: Chuck Christensen and Joan Feinberg, John Sullivan, Bernard Onken, Steve Scipione, Karen Melton, Caroline Thompson, Elizabeth Schaaf, and Dennis Conroy.

We would also like to acknowledge the assistance of the following instructors who took the time to give detailed written comments on *Text Book*, and we are very grateful to them: Michelle Baillif, The University of Georgia; Mary Ellen DuPree, University of Nevada; Rosemary Hennessy, The University at Albany, SUNY; Anne Kress, Santa Fe Community College; David McDowell, Anne Arundel Community College; and Brendan Pieters, Santa Fe Community College.

We are also grateful to the following instructors who completed a questionnaire for us: Kenneth Baldwin, University of Maryland, Baltimore County; Robin Dizard, Keene State College; Neil Easterbrook, Texas Christian University; Nona Fienberg, Keene State College; Clayton E. Hudnall, University of Hartford; Lyn Isaacson, Central College; Virginia Nees-Hatlem, University of Maine; Kathleen A. Nesbitt, Spalding University; Joseph Ng, Metro State College; Melissa Sprenkle, University of Tennessee, Knoxville; Peter Staffel, West Liberty State College; Kathleen Swaim, University of Massachusetts, Amherst; Ann Trubek, Oberlin College; and Robin Varnum, American International College.

Table of Contents

2 Texts, Thoughts, and Things   62

4 Texts and Research: The Mystory   240

A Letter to the Student

You may, of course, have read our preface to this edition, or reviewed the table of contents, or even skimmed through a reading selection. Nevertheless, in these few paragraphs we will assume that you have just opened this book for the first time and want to know why you are using this book of all books, and what you may get out of using it. We consider these fair questions and will try to answer them fairly, but first we must warn you that verbal education is a lot like physical education. You build your mind in the same way you build your body: through your own efforts. We can provide the most interesting and useful material for you to work on, based on the most recent information about language and literature, but the benefits to you will depend on your own efforts—"No pain, no gain," as the iron-pumpers say.

Our goal is to help you to a better mastery of your verbal environment. We all live in a world that constantly bombards us with texts. To survive—and above all to do more than just survive: to flourish—we need to deal with all kinds of texts confidently. This book is called *Text Book* because it offers an entrance into the world of textuality: to the higher and more developed forms of reading and writing.

As you enter this book you will find all kinds of texts: some are usually called "literary" and some are not. This mixture is essential to our method. We do *not* want to offer you a collection of "master" works that ask for your passive submission, but a set of texts that you can work and play with, increasing your own understanding of fundamental textual processes and your own ability to use the written word. We hope to help you feel more at home in the house of language, and we are confident that a better command of written language will contribute to a better life. That is saying a lot, we realize, but we want you to know that, though this book is often playful, we are serious about its purpose. It is different from other books, and that has made it harder to write—and more fun. We have worked on it for years, trying to make it as effective and attractive as we could.

Come on in and see for yourself.

Sincerely,

Robert Scholes
Nancy R. Comley
Gregory L. Ulmer

1

Texts as Representation

B Y *REPRESENTATION*, we mean both the act of representing an idea, concept, or action and the expression of that idea, concept, or action. In this chapter, we will be concentrating primarily on narrative and drama as representation, exploring the ways in which people and their actions get into texts. Human events can be recounted (narrative) or enacted (drama), but either way they become *textualized*, taking on a certain formal structure that is found in much the same form in every culture: the structure of stories, which extends from personal anecdotes to literary novels and plays. That this should be the case is interesting in itself, but even more interesting is the way this formal structure returns into our lives, shaping our thoughts and actions. If you have ever found yourself wondering how something that was happening to you would sound in the telling, you know what we mean. If you have ever wondered how some experience in your life would "come out," you were applying a concept from storytelling to the interpretation of your own experience, even as it was happening: because experience does not "come out" — it just goes on and on.

The point of all this is that texts and life exist in a very complex relationship. Our thinking and even our feeling are shaped by texts in ways that we are dimly aware of in our normal day-to-day existence. We all use narrative structures and dramatic devices every day in our thoughts and in our actions — living out stories, playing roles, recounting events, enacting gestures and deeds. To learn more about how narrative and dramatic texts work, then, is to be a little more conscious of our own situations, a little more in control of our own lives.

The reading, discussion, and writing opportunities presented in this chapter are designed to help you strengthen your command of narrative and dramatic processes, building on the awareness you already have—having come this far in life—of narrative and dramatic forms. We will present you with some texts designed to reveal connections between these "literary" forms and ordinary life, and with some opportunities to move back and forth between the forms, developing your awareness and mastery of textual processes.

STORY AND STORYTELLER

Natural Narrative

Mary Louise Pratt

We think of literature as something special, as something above or beyond the way we use language in our daily lives—and so, in certain respects, it is. Literature is language used with special care and precision, or special energy and imagination. But the forms taken by literary works, and even the language used by poets and playwrights, are based on forms and ways of speaking that we all use, all the time. Literature is different from other uses of language, but it is also the same; it overlaps ordinary speech. Most approaches to the study of literature emphasize the differences, concentrating on the unique powers of literature. Without denying that these powers exist, we are taking the opposite tack in this book. We are going to emphasize the continuities, showing how literary forms and uses of language are connected to the ways that we use language on ordinary occasions. The point of doing it this way is to show that the passage from ordinary language to literature can be negotiated by any of us. It is not some impassable abyss that only a genius can leap across. It is a craft, a skill, that will benefit from study, effort, and practice. Our presentation begins with the anecdote, a basic form of storytelling that links the personal narratives we tell one another with the literary narratives produced by professional writers.

A few years ago, Mary Louise Pratt, a literary critic, discovered that the great novels of world literature were similar in their structure to the personal narratives exchanged among people with very little formal education. She based her discovery on studies of inner-city speech by the sociolinguist William Labov. In the following selection we have reprinted a section of the second chapter of her book, A Speech-Act Theory of Literary Discourse, *in which she presents Labov's work and discusses its significance.*

For our purposes, the most important thing to learn from Pratt is the six-part structure of the ordinary personal narrative. You will find versions of this structure—or interesting deviations from it—in every kind of text that presents a story.

Much of Labov's research over the past ten years has been devoted to docu-   1
menting dialect variations in American English and above all to exploring the
ways in which those divisions reflect and reinforce a speaker's place in the
class hierarchy of the larger speech community. He has concentrated especially on those dialects of American English considered by most Americans
to be not only nonstandard but also substandard. In his first book, *The Social Stratification of English in New York City* (1966), Labov showed that
phonological variation in the speech of New Yorkers could not be systematically specified independently of the social pressures acting on the speakers
in the given speech situation. This was an important realization for linguis-
tics since it provided support for building information about social context
into the grammar.

Labov's interest in oral narrative stems mainly from a study of Black En-   2
glish Vernacular (BEV), "that relatively uniform dialect spoken by the majority of black youth in most parts of the United States today, especially in the
inner city areas" (Labov, 1972:xiii). The project, which resulted in the volume
of essays titled *Language in the Inner City* (1972), was originally undertaken
to find out whether dialect differences had anything to do with the consistent
reading problems of inner city black children. It was conducted in Harlem.
As he analyzed the phonological and grammatical differences between BEV
and Standard English, Labov made an important observation:

> The major reading problems did not stem from structural inter-
> ference in any simple sense. . . . The major causes of reading failure
> are political and cultural conflicts in the classroom, and dialect
> differences are important because they are symbols of this conflict.
> We must then understand the way in which the vernacular culture
> uses language and how verbal skills develop in this culture. (Labov,
> 1972:xiv)

BEV speakers had trouble reading not because they lacked verbal skills
(the contrary proved to be the case) but because the verbal skills they
had were of no use in school. All this seems a far cry from aesthetics, and
it is true that Labov's interest in "verbal art" rose from his research quite
indirectly. I quote here Labov's own description of this development. The
passage is long but worthwhile as an introduction to my own discussion
to follow:

> In the course of our studies of vernacular language, we have
> developed a number of devices to overcome the constraints of the
> face-to-face interview and obtain large bodies of tape-recorded ca-
> sual speech. The most effective of these techniques produce *narra-
> tives of personal experience*, in which the speaker becomes deeply in-
> volved in rehearsing or even reliving events of his past. The "Danger
> of Death" question is the prototype and still the most generally used:
> at a certain point in the conversation, the interviewer asks, "Were

you ever in a situation where you were in serious danger of being killed, where you said to yourself—*'This is it'?*" In the section of our interview schedule that deals with fights, we ask "Were you ever in a fight with a guy bigger than you?" When the subject says "Yes" we pause and then ask simply, "What happened?" The narratives that we have obtained by such methods form a large body of data on comparative verbal skills, ranging across age levels, classes and ethnic groups. Because they occur in response to a specific stimulus in the interview situation, they are not free of the interactive effect of the outside observer. The form they take is in fact typical of discourse directed to someone outside of the immediate peer group of the speaker. But because the experience and emotions involved here form an important part of the speaker's biography, he seems to undergo a partial reliving of that experience, and he is no longer free to monitor his own speech as he normally does in face-to-face interviews. (1972:354–55)

Labov was fascinated by the high degree of verbal virtuosity displayed by   3
many of his informants in these narratives and by the high value placed on that virtuosity by the vernacular speech communities. This interest and the fact that, despite cultural differences, the narratives had great structural similarities led him to attempt a structural description of the oral narrative of personal experience as a speech act. The results of his study are found in two papers, "Narrative Analysis: Oral Versions of Personal Experience" (1967), written in collaboration with Joshua Waletzky, and "The Transformation of Experience in Narrative Syntax," in *Language in the Inner City*. (Unless otherwise specified, all subsequent references are to the latter article.) Before presenting Labov's analysis of these narratives, let me offer two contrasting examples, both taken from Labov's data. The first is a story told by a middle-aged white male speaker from Martha's Vineyard:

(1)

I never believed a whole lot in licking. I was never—
with my children, and I never—when it was with my animals,
dogs; I never licked a dog, I never had to. A dog knew
what I meant; when I hollered at a dog, he knew the—what
I meant. I could—I had dogs that could do everything   5
but talk. And by gorry, sir, I never licked 'em.
   I never come nearer bootin' a dog in my life. I
had a dog—he was a wonderful retriever, but as I say he
could do everything but talk. I could waif him that way,
I could waif him on, I could waif him anywhere. If I   10
shot a crippled duck he went after it; he didn't see it
in the water, he'd always turn around look at me, and I'd
waif him over there, if the duck was there, or if it was

on the other side of where we're on, I could waif him
straight ahead, and he'd turn and he'd go. If he didn't   15
see me, he'd turn around, he'd look at me, and I'd keep
a-waifin' him on. And he'd finally catch sight of him,
and the minute he did, you know, he would beeline and
get that duck.

    I was gunnin' one night with that dog—we had to   20
use live decoys in those days—a fellow named Jack Bumpus
was with me; I was over at a place called Deep Bottom,
darker than pitch. And—uh—heard a quackin' off shore.
And I said to Jack, "Keep quiet. There's one comin' in."
And uh—finally Jack said to me, "I think I see 'im." I   25
said, "Give 'im a gun. Give 'im a gun. Try it."

    So he shot, and this duck went for the shore with
his wings a-goin' like that for the shore. Went up on the
shore. Well this dog never lost a crippled duck on shore,
he'd take a track just the same as a hound would take a   30
rabbit track. And I sent him over. I said, "Go ahead."

    So he went over there. And—gone a while and come
back and he didn't have the duck. And that was unusual—
I said, "You git back there and get that duck!" And he
went back there; and he stayed a little while longer,   35
longer than he did the first time, and he come back and
he didn't have the duck.

    And I never come nearer shootin' a dog. By gorry,
I come pretty near. *"You git back there and get that
duck!"* And that dog went back there, and he didn't come   40
back. And he didn't come back. By gorry, we went over
there—I walked over there, and here he was; one of my
tame ducks that I had tethered out there had got the
strap off her leg, and had gone out there, and when
this fellah shot he hadn't hit the duck. The duck   45
came to the shore, he hadn't hit the duck; but the
duck was scared and come for the shore. My dog was
over there, and he had his paw right on top of that
duck, holdin' him down just as tight as could be, and—
by gorry, boy, I patted that dog, I'll tell you if I   50
had ever walloped that dog I'd have felt some bad. He
knew more'n I did; the dog knew more than I did. He
knew that was that tame duck; he wasn't gonna pick him
up in his mouth and bring him, you know. He was just
holdin' him right down on the ground.   55

(Labov, 1967:14–15)

The second is a fight story told by a black adolescent male from Harlem referred to as Larry:

(2)

An' then, three weeks ago I had a fight with this other dude
outside. He got mad 'cause I wouldn't give him a cigarette
Ain't that a bitch? (Oh yeah?)
Yeah, you know, I was sittin' on the corner an' shit, smokin'
my cigarette, you know. I was high, an' shit. He walked over   5
to me:
    "Can I have a cigarette?"
He was a little taller than me, but not that much. I said:
    "I ain't got no more, man."
'Cause, you know, all I had was one left. An' I ain't gon'   10
give up my last cigarette unless I got some more. So I said:
    "I don't have no more, man."
So he, you know, dug on the pack, 'cause the pack was in my
pocket. So he said:
    "Eh, man, I can't get a cigarette, man? I mean—I mean   15
we supposed to be brothers, an' shit."
So I say:
    "Yeah, well, you know, man, all I got is one, you dig it?"
An' I won't give up my las' one to nobody. So you know, the
dude, he looks at me, an' he—I 'on' know—he jus' thought   20
he gon' rough that motherfucker up. He said:
    "I can't get a cigarette."
I said:
    "Tha's what I said, my man."
You know, so he said: 25
    "What you supposed to be *bad* an' shit?"
So I said:
    "Look here, my man, I don't think I'm bad, you understand?
But I mean, you know, if I had it, you could git it. I like
to see you with it, you dig it? But the sad part about it,   30
you get to do without it. That's all, my man."
So the dude, he 'on' to pushin' me, man.
(Oh, he pushed you?)
An' why he do that? *Everytime somebody fuck with me,* why
they do it? I put that cigarette down, an' boy let me tell you. I   35
beat the shit outa that motherfucker. I tried to *kill* 'im—over
one cigarette! I tried to *kill* 'im. Square business! After I got
through stompin' him in the face, man, you know, all of a
sudden I went crazy! I jus' went crazy. An' I jus' wouldn't stop
hittin' the motherfucker. Dig it, I couldn't stop hittin'   40
'im, man, till the teacher pulled me off o' him. An' guess
what? After all that I gave the dude the cigarette, after
all that. Ain't that a bitch?
(How come you gave 'im the cigarette?)
I 'on' know. I jus' gave it to him. An' he smoked it, too!   45

(Labov, 1972:356–58)

Labov's (1972) analysis of these "natural narratives," as they are com-   4
monly called, will seem self-evident to literary critics, and it is for precisely
this reason that I want to outline it here. Labov defines narrative as:

> one method of recapitulating past experience by matching a verbal
> sequence of clauses to the sequence of events which (it is inferred)
> actually occurred. . . . Within this conception of narrative, we can define
> a *minimal narrative,* as a sequence of two clauses which are *tempo-*
> *rally ordered:* that is, a change in their order will result in a change in
> the temporal sequence of the original semantic interpretation. (p. 360)

Narrative clauses are clauses with a simple preterite verb or, in some   5
styles, a verb in the simple present. Here is an adult "danger of death" narrative which consists of four such ordered clauses: (This and all further examples in this chapter are taken from Labov's data.)

(3) Well, this person had a little too much to drink and he attacked
     me and the friend came in and she stopped it.

Narratives like (3), which consist only of narrative clauses, are not very interesting, nor are they very common. A fully developed natural narrative, according to Labov, is made up of the following sections:

1. abstract
2. orientation
3. complicating action
4. evaluation
5. result or resolution
6. coda

"A complete narrative," he concludes, "begins with an orientation, proceeds
to the complicating action, is suspended at the focus of evaluation before the
resolution, concludes with the resolution, and returns the listener to the present time with the coda." I shall summarize briefly Labov's description of the
six sections:

Complicating action and *resolution* are, of course, the core of the narra-   6
tive. The former begins with the first narrative clause in the speech act; the
latter usually ends with the last such clause.

The *abstract* is a short (usually one or two sentence) summary of the   7
story that narrators generally provide before recounting the story proper. The
abstract "encapsulates the point of the story." In narrative (1) above, the single sentence "I never come nearer bootin' a dog in my life" has this function;
in narrative (2), lines 1–2 are the abstract.

The *orientation* serves to "identify in some way the time, place, persons,   8
and their activity or situation" and occurs immediately before the first narrative clause, as a rule. The orientation often includes "an elaborate portrait of
the main character" as in (1), whose narrator describes at length the prowess

of his retriever before going on to the situation orientation (11.20–22). In (2), some information is already available in the abstract, and the orientation section (11.4–5) gives a more detailed picture of the situation. Syntactically, orientations often contain many past progressive verbs "sketching the kind of thing that was going on before the first event of the narrative occurred or during the entire episode."

The *coda*'s general function is to "close off the sequence of complicating 9 actions and indicate that none of the events that followed were important to the narrative." In addition to this mechanical function, "a good coda . . . leaves the listener with a feeling of satisfaction and completeness that matters have been rounded off and accounted for." Labov notes a number of forms codas can take. Sometimes they consist of a single sentence like "And that was that"; sometimes they "bring the narrator and the listener back to the point at which they entered the narrative," as does this coda, which closes out a story in which the teller was saved from drowning:

(4) And you know, that man who picked me out of the water? He's a detective in Union City, and I see him every now and again.

and this coda to a fight story:

(5) Ever since then I haven't seen the guy 'cause I quit. I quit, you know. No more problems.

In narrative (1) above, the narrative proper ends at "just as tight as could be" (1.49) and the coda, starting with a pause and the phrase "by gorry," echoes the abstract ("If I had ever walloped. . . .") and provides an additional explication and recapitulation of the story's climax. In narrative (2), the fight story ends with the teacher's intervention, and the coda, beginning with "Guess what?" (1.41), contains additional information about the ultimate effects of the events, as in (5) above. The narrator of (2), like that of (1), echoes the abstract in the coda, here by repeating the line "Ain't that a bitch?"

Evaluation is considered by Labov to be "perhaps the most important ele- 10 ment in addition to the basic narrative clause." By evaluation, Labov means "the means used by the narrator to indicate the point of the narrative, its raison d'être: why it was told and what the narrator was getting at." He elaborates:

> There are many ways to tell the same story, to make very different points, or to make no point at all. Pointless stories are met (in English) with the withering rejoinder, "So what?" Every good narrator is continually warding off this question; when his narrative is over, it should be unthinkable for a bystander to say, "So what?" Instead, the appropriate remark would be "He did?" or similar means of registering the reportable character of the events of the narrative. (p. 366)

> To identify the evaluative portion of a narrative, it is necessary to know why this narrative—or any narrative—is felt to be tellable;

in other words, why the events of the narrative are reportable. Most of the narratives cited here concern matters that are always reportable: danger of death or of physical injury. These matters occupy a high place on an unspoken permanent agenda. . . . The narrators of most of these stories were under social pressure to show that the events involved were truly dangerous and unusual, or that someone else really broke the normal rules in an outrageous and reportable way. Evaluative devices say to us: this was terrifying, dangerous, weird, wild, crazy; or amusing, hilarious and wonderful; more generally, that it was strange, uncommon, or unusual—that is, worth reporting. (p. 371)

The evaluation of a natural narrative is usually concentrated in one section immediately preceding the resolution. However, as Labov notes, evaluative devices are generally strung throughout the entire narrative, forming what he calls "a secondary structure." Labov's discussion of evaluation is long, and I shall only partially summarize here his preliminary typology of the evaluative devices used by his informants. Again, the examples are Labov's.

A. *Evaluative commentary*

The narrator interrupts the progress of the narrative with a statement reaffirming the tellability of the story or assessing the situation. Such commentary may be

1. *External:* The narrator himself asserts the point of the story as in statements like "it was quite an experience" or "it was the strangest feeling" and so on.
2. *Internal:* The evaluative statements are embedded in the story. The narrator may
   a. present the statement as having occurred to him at the time in the story, e.g., "I just closed my eyes, I said, 'O my God, here it is!'"
   b. present the evaluation as statements addressed by himself to another character. Larry's evaluation, addressed (in rhymed couplets, no less) to his adversary (11.28–31) is an example of this type.
   c. attribute evaluative remarks to a witness or neutral observer in the story as in this example, referring to a knife wound: "And the doctor says, 'Just about this much more' he says, 'and you'd a been dead!'"
   (a) to (c), you will notice, involve progressively deeper embedding of the evaluation in the story. As Labov notes, the more deeply embedded the evaluation, the more effective it is.

B. *Sentence-internal evaluation devices*

1. *Intensifiers:* These are devices superimposed or added onto the basic narrative syntax without affecting the unmarked (simple past) form of the narrative verb phrase. Examples:
   a. gestures.
   b. expressive phonology such as lengthened vowels ("a loooong time").

    c. repetition; there are many examples in (1) and (2).

    d. ritual interjections like "Well, sir," "By gorry," and so on.

2. *Comparators:* These are devices which involve the use of some verb phrase construction other than the simple past of the narrative clause. They include negatives, futures, modals, questions, commands, comparatives, and others.

The category called comparators merits some explanation. Labov observed that complex auxiliary constructions tended to be concentrated in the evaluation sections of natural narratives, and he concluded upon analysis that most, if not all, verb constructions that depart from the simple past tense in natural narrative can be shown to be performing an evaluative role. The comparators do so by referring to hypothetical events that are then compared to the observed events. Comparators, in other words, "draw upon a cognitive background considerably richer than the set of events which were observed." Negatives, for example, talk about what didn't happen but could have; futures allude to what could happen but hasn't yet; modals refer to hypothetical events; questions and commands are attempts to produce future events and function often as disguised threats in narratives, implying future consequences (see, for example, narrative [2] above). Generally speaking "a comparator moves away from the line of narrative events to consider unrealized possibilities and compare them with events that did occur." Labov uses the following evaluation taken from a schoolboy's narrative of a fight with "the baddest girl in the neighborhood" to exemplify the evaluative role played by complex auxiliary structures: 12

(6) So I says to myself, "There's *gonna* be times my mother won't give me money, because we're a poor family and I *can't* take this every time she *don't* give me any money." So I say, "Well, I just *gotta* fight this girl. She *gonna hafta* whup me. I hope she *don't* whup me" (emphasis mine).

The passage contains four negatives, four futures, and three modals, all involving speculation about hypothetical events or situations which are compared to the present state of affairs. In the resolution of the story which follows, the simple narrative syntax is restored: 13

(7) I hit the girl, powww! I put something on it. I win the fight.

Larry's fight narrative above (11.7–12 and elsewhere) is similarly organized. The grammatical comparative of course always performs an evaluative function, as do similes and metaphors. Interestingly, such overt comparisons are found mainly in the syntax of older, more highly skilled narrators like that of (1) (see for example, 11.7, 30, 52).

    One of the most striking aspects of Labov's model, as I suggested earlier, is its self-evidence. I think it is self-evident for two reasons. First, the oral narrative of personal experience is a speech act exceedingly familiar to us all, regardless of what dialect we speak. We all spend enormous amounts of con- 14 versational time exchanging anecdotes, though these may only occasionally involve fights or danger of death. Most speakers of English have a distinctive speech style for this type of narration with special intonation and in many cases special grammatical constructions not used in other contexts.* We are all perfectly aware of the "unspoken agenda" by which we assess an experience's tellability. We know that anecdotes, like novels, are expected to have endings. We now that for an anecdote to be successful, we must introduce it into the conversation in an appropriate way, provide our audience with the necessary background information, keep the point of the story in view at all times, and so on. And as with any speech situation, literary or otherwise, we form firm judgments all the time about how "good" an anecdote was and how well it was brought off by its teller; in fact, we are expected to express this judgment as soon as an anecdote ends. We recognize narrative expertise when we hear it, and when narrative speech acts fail, we can almost always say why: the experience was trivial, the teller long-winded, or we "missed the point." Should anyone be in doubt about any of these points, I would urge him to spend an hour some day listening to real "everyday language," watching for narratives and for people's responses to them.

The second reason Labov's analysis seems so obvious is that his subdivision of the narrative into six main components corresponds very closely indeed to the kind of organization we are traditionally taught to observe in narrative literature. Every high school student knows that novels and plays have an introduction, a gradual rising action, a climax followed by a swift dénouement and resolution with the option of an epilogue at the end. That novels and natural narratives both have a structurally similar "narrative core" is not so surprising, since both are attempts to render experience. . . . 15

FOR DISCUSSION AND WRITING: TELLING AND WRITING ANECDOTES

1. *Complicating action* and *resolution* are two elements of narrative that Pratt does not discuss at length, because she assumes that "every high school student knows that novels and plays have an introduction, a gradual rising action, a climax followed by a swift dénouement and resolution with the option of an epilogue at the end." Is she right? Do you know these things? In any case, it might be a good idea to review your understanding by discussing the complicating action and resolution of the two complete examples Pratt quotes from Labov. Try to summarize

---

*For example, adverbial constructions like "down we fell" or "over it went" are apparently exclusively narrative. In many languages, including North American English, speakers often switch to the present tense for narration or alternate between present and simple past as in "So yesterday he comes into my office and I told him he was fired." Many North American English dialects use irregular first person forms like "I says," "I comes," "I runs" exclusively for narration. Needless to say, these phenomena are much in need of study, but their very existence strongly supports the hypothesis that, independent of any literary considerations, narration must be identified as a speech act in its own right. [More recently, "I go" is the preferred irregular form for narration. *Eds.*]

the *action* of each narrative, ignoring the other elements of the speech act. Can you locate a "rising" action, climax, and dénouement or resolution in both cases?

2. What makes a good anecdote good? Discuss the two examples given by Pratt. How much depends upon the events narrated and how much upon the way the narrator handles such matters as abstract, orientation, evaluation, and coda?

3. Take Pratt's example (3), which presents a whole story in a single sentence, and make something of it. That is, retell it as a full-fledged anecdote, using all six elements and adding descriptive details that will make it interesting. (This can be done as a group project.)

4. In preparation for writing your own anecdote (exercise 5, which follows), your instructor may ask you to tell your anecdote to the class or to a group of students. As you listen to one another's anecdotes, take note of the evaluative commentary used by each speaker. You might want to discuss the writing strategies necessary to substitute for gestures used by the speaker to emphasize a point. Remember, it is not easy to convey a tone of voice in writing.

5. Write an anecdote based on personal experience. Your narrative may concern something that happened to you, or it may concern something that you witnessed but that happened to someone else. You may, like most of Labov's speakers, tell about a situation in which you felt yourself to be in danger, but, as Labov points out, memorable events can be "weird, wild, crazy; or amusing, hilarious and wonderful" as well. After you have written out your anecdote, refer to Pratt's list of six parts of the anecdote to make sure that yours is formally complete.

THE "LITERARY" ANECDOTE

Mary Louise Pratt has helped us to understand that all narratives—from a story told in the street to a great literary novel—share the same formal building blocks. Every story is "literary" to some degree. Still, there are differences of degree possible. Having looked at some anecdotes, thought about the anecdote as a form of narrative, and produced an anecdote of your own, you should be ready to consider the ways in which even the anecdote— that simplest of narrative forms—can be made more literary in the hands of a skilled writer. Many a musician can carry a tune, but the great improvisers—in classical variations on a theme, or in jazz, or any other musical form—will do things that make a simple melody endlessly fascinating.

Here are five examples of writers playing with the anecdote form, using the six features identified by Labov, but rearranging them or omitting some, or playing games with time and space. We ask you, in reading and discussing them, to use the six basic elements as a way of looking at these texts, to help you see what is and is not going on in them. Remember, the point is not to check for all six features and take points away for any that are missing. The point is to see what these professional writers do with the basic form. To see that, of course, you have to start by looking for it.

Anecdote (1)

Ordnance

Walter Benjamin

"Ordnance" refers to gunnery. A metaphor of gunpowder (a "magazine" is a supply of explosive powder) runs through this anecdote. Riga is a city in Latvia. This story takes place in the 1920s. Walter Benjamin, a literary critic and cultural philosopher, died trying to escape the Nazis during World War II.

I had arrived in Riga to visit a woman friend. Her house, the town, the language were unfamiliar to me. Nobody was expecting me, no one knew me. For two hours I walked the streets in solitude. Never again have I seen them so. From every gate a flame darted, each cornerstone sprayed sparks, and every streetcar came toward me like a fire engine. For she might have stepped out of the gateway, around the corner, been sitting in the streetcar. But of the two of us I had to be, at any price, the first to see the other. For had she touched me with the match of her eyes, I should have gone up like a magazine.

Anecdote (2)

Polar Bears

Patricia J. Williams

This is a fragment of a larger essay in which the polar bears return more than once, but it is also readable in itself as an anecdote about the refusal to tell anecdotes, among other things. Patricia J. Williams, an African American, is a professor of law and writer on women's issues and racial questions. Professor Williams prefaces this anecdote with a quotation from Walter Benjamin's essay, "The Storyteller."

"Familiar though his name may be to us, the storyteller in his living immediacy is by no means a present force. He has already become something remote   1 from us and something that is getting even more distant. . . . Less and less frequently do we encounter people with the ability to tell a tale properly. . . . It is as if something that seemed inalienable to us, the securest among our possessions, were taken from us: the ability to exchange experiences" (from *Illuminations*, New York: Schocken, 1969, p. 83).

My mother's cousin Marjorie was a storyteller. From time to time I would   2
press her to tell me the details of her youth, and she would tell me instead stories about a child who wandered into a world of polar bears, who was prayed over by the polar bears, and in the end eaten. The child's life was not in vain because the polar bears had been made holy by its suffering. The child had been a test, a message from god for polar bears. In the polar bear universe, she would tell me, the primary object of creation was polar bears, and the rest of the living world was fashioned to serve polar bears. The clouds took their shape from polar bears, trees were designed to give shelter and shade to polar bears, and humans were ideally designed to provide polar bears with meat.

The truth, the truth, I would laughingly insist as we sat in her apartment   3
eating canned fruit and heavy roasts, mashed potatoes, pickles and vanilla pudding, cocoa, Sprite, or tea. What about roots and all that, I coaxed. But the voracity of her amnesia would disclaim and disclaim and disclaim, and she would go on telling me about the polar bears until our places were full of emptiness and I became large in the space which described her emptiness and I gave in to the emptiness of words.

Anecdote (3)

Tell Me a Story

Paul Auster

The following is a section of "Portrait of an Invisible Man," an essay about Auster's search for the truth about his father. Auster interrogates his own memories, as well as family photographs, newspaper clippings, family members, and even the empty "Auster Family Album" in assembling a narrative about a man "incapable or unwilling to reveal himself."

I remember a day very like today. A drizzling Sunday, lethargy and quiet in   1
the house: the world at half-speed. My father was taking a nap, or had just awoken from one, and somehow I was on the bed with him, the two of us alone in the room. Tell me a story. It must have begun like that. And because he was not doing anything, because he was still drowsing in the languor of the afternoon, he did just what I asked, launching into a story without missing a beat. I remember it all so clearly. It seems as if I have just walked out of that room, with its gray light and tangle of quilts on the bed, as if, simply by closing my eyes, I could walk back into it any time I want.

He told me of his prospecting days in South America. It was a tale of high 2
adventure, fraught with mortal dangers, hair-raising escapes, and improbable
twists of fortune: hacking his way through the jungle with a machete, fighting off
bandits with his bare hands, shooting his donkey when it broke its leg. His language was flowery and convoluted, probably an echo of the books he himself
had read as a boy. But it was precisely this literary style that enchanted me. Not
only was he telling me new things about himself, unveiling to me the world of
his distant past, but he was telling it with new and strange words. This language
was just as important as the story itself. It belonged to it, and in some sense
was indistinguishable from it. Its very strangeness was proof of authenticity.

It did not occur to me to think this might have been a made-up story. For 3
years afterward I went on believing it. Even when I had passed the point when
I should have known better, I still felt there might have been some truth to it.
It gave me something to hold on to about my father, and I was reluctant to let
go. At last I had an explanation for his mysterious evasions, his indifference
to me. He was a romantic figure, a man with a dark and exciting past, and his
present life was only a kind of stopping place, a way of biding his time until
he took off on his next adventure. He was working out his plan, figuring out
how to retrieve the gold that lay buried deep in the heart of the Andes.

Anecdote (4)

Departures

Storm Jameson

*This selection is the conclusion of a chapter from Margaret Storm Jameson's au-
tobiography,* Journey from the North. *In it she begins to tell of a train journey
from Yorkshire (in the north of England) to London made with her husband during World War I. But, in the telling, her mind moves back through memories of
other departures to an anecdote of an earlier departure from Yorkshire, this one
with her mother (the wife of a sea captain). Jameson was the author of many
novels and other books.*

The September day we left for London was cold and cloudily sunny. In the 1
few minutes as the train drew out past the harbour, I felt myself isolated by
a barrier of ice from every living human being, including the husband facing
me. Like a knot of adders uncoiling themselves one departure slid from another
behind my eyes—journeys made feverish by unmanageable longings and
ambitions, night journeys in wartime, the darkened corridors crammed with
young men in clumsy khaki, smoking, falling asleep, journeys with a heavy baby
in one arm. At last I come to the child sitting in a corner of a third-class carriage, waiting, silent, tense with anxiety, for the captain's wife to return from
the ticket office. A bearded gentleman in a frock coat—the stationmaster—

saunters up to the open door and says, smiling, something she makes no attempt to hear. Her mother walks lightly across the platform. "Ah, there you are, Mrs. Jameson. Your little girl was afraid you weren't coming," he said amiably. Nothing less amiable than Mrs. Jameson's coldly blue eyes turned on him, and cold voice.

"Nonsense. My child is never afraid."   2

Not true . . .   3

Anecdote (5)

Blake

Brent Staples

This is an excerpt from "A Brother's Murder," an essay originally published in the New York Times *Magazine in 1986, in which Brent Staples reflects on the murder of his twenty-two-year-old younger brother two years earlier. Both grew up with violence, but Staples notes, "As I fled the past, so Blake embraced it."*

I saw that Blake's romance with the street life and the hustler image had   1
flowered dangerously. One evening that late December, standing in some Roanoke dive among drug dealers and grim, hair-trigger losers, I told him I feared for his life. He had affected the image of the tough he wanted to be. But behind the dark glasses and the swagger, I glimpsed the baby-faced toddler I'd once watched over. I nearly wept. I wanted desperately for him to live. The young think themselves immortal, and a dangerous light shone in his eyes as he spoke laughingly of making fools of the policemen who had raided his apartment looking for drugs. He cried out as I took his right hand. A line of stitches lay between the thumb and index finger. Kickback from a shotgun, he explained, nothing serious. Gunplay had become part of his life.

I lacked the language simply to say: Thousands have lived this for you   2
and died. I fought the urge to lift him bodily and shake him. This place and the way you are living smells of death to me, I said. Take some time away, I said. Let's go downtown tomorrow and buy a plane ticket anywhere, take a bus trip, anything to get away and cool things off. He took my alarm casually. We arranged to meet the following night—an appointment he would not keep. We embraced as though through glass. I drove away.

FOR DISCUSSION AND WRITING: ANALYZING ANECDOTES

1. If we think of Labov's six elements as a basic plan for all anecdotes, consider the ways in which each of these five "literary" anecdotes deviates from the basic plan, either by rearrangement of the basic six elements or

by omission of one element or more. For instance, checking the first anecdote against Labov's list, we might get something like this:

a. Abstract? Missing
b. Orientation? Yes, explanation of reason for visit
c. Complicating action? Yes, wandering the streets
d. Evaluation? Yes, in the last sentence
e. Result or resolution? No—we are never told what happened.
f. Coda? Yes, combined with evaluation, and no, since the resolution is missing. Because the last sentence is not in the simple past tense of narration but in the conditional (*if* she *had* even looked at him, he *would* have exploded), the story cannot be resolved as a story is resolved. Narration requires the past tense.

This simple analysis would then enable us to probe further into the "literary" quality of this anecdote. It establishes suspense but then, instead of providing a result or resolution, it shifts the point of the tale to the evaluation, suggesting that what actually happened is not as important as the state of the author's emotions at the time—feeling like a powder keg ready to explode under the gaze of his friend. By shifting the emphasis from the events to the metaphor of explosive longing, the author has moved the anecdote in the direction of the "literary."

The question to begin with, then, has two parts:

a. Check each anecdote against Labov's six elements of narrative.
b. Consider the effect of any omissions or modifications in the use of these elements.

2. Later on, you may study metaphor more formally. For the moment, however, it will be enough to consider metaphor as a sort of comparison, a way of talking about one thing in terms of another. For instance, as we have noted, Benjamin's anecdote depends upon the metaphor or comparison of his emotional state to an explosive charge needing only a match to set it off. Examine the other anecdotes for their use of comparison or metaphor: the polar bears in anecdote (2), for instance, or the snakes (adders) in anecdote (4). What do the comparisons contribute toward the "literary" quality of those anecdotes?

3. Anecdote (2) begins with a quotation from the author of anecdote (1) about the loss of the ability to "tell a tale properly." Consider all of the anecdotes in relation to what it means to "tell a tale properly"—and do not worry if you cannot reach absolutely firm conclusions about this. Does Benjamin himself tell his tale "properly"?

Benjamin is talking partly about the loss of a tradition of oral storytelling and its replacement by written narratives, which were more "literary" but perhaps less satisfactory as stories. Considering the five anecdotes collected here, do you find any particularly good or bad, strong or weak? Try to explain your judgment—to yourself and others. That is, try not only to justify your opinion but also to explore the reasons why you came to it in the first place. This could be done in the form of an essay

about the anecdote(s), which could also include discussion of the anecdotes considered in Pratt's essay (pp. 2–11).

4. In writing these questions, we have been putting the word "literary" in
   quotation marks to indicate that the category of "literature" is not something fixed and given but is itself a matter of discussion and debate. We
   have suggested that *literary* may mean nothing more than "what is written" as opposed to what is told orally, or it can mean something that is
   inventive, surprising. "Literature" can also refer to texts that seem to refer more widely to common experiences than others. An anecdote is always a singular story, a tale of some one thing that happened to some
   one person (or possibly to a group of people). A literary anecdote might
   be seen as a story about one person who becomes the representative of
   others, as the scared girl and tough mother in anecdote (4) might represent
   the childish fears and maternal toughness of other children and mothers.
   Consider each of these anecdotes from this point of view. That is, to what
   extent can the anecdotes the authors tell be seen as representative of more
   common or general experiences?

THE SHORT STORY

As a form, the short story derives from the tale, as in the folktales passed
down from one storyteller to another. As a literary form, the short story was
fully developed in the nineteenth century by such writers as Nathaniel
Hawthorne and Edgar Allan Poe in the United States and Gustave Flaubert
and Guy de Maupassant in France. But where Hawthorne and Poe frequently based their stories on folktales or, in Poe's case, on mythic or gothic
material, Flaubert and de Maupassant were concerned with matters of
everyday life, and transformed their close observations of people and
events into fiction. Like the anecdote, the short story tells a story of what
happened; but where we assume that the anecdote is telling us of something that really happened to the narrator, we assume that the short story
is fictional. Sometimes, however, the distinction is not so obvious. If we
look at William Carlos Williams's "The Use of Force," which is written as
a first-person narrative, it is easy at first to assume that we are reading
a description of a real event. Indeed, the story is based on a real incident
from Williams's medical practice, but his giving his story a title is the first
sign of his fictionalizing of the event. We want to know what it means.
For where the anecdote is likely to spell out the meaning of events, the
short story is more likely to require the reader to interpret the meaning of
the story. As you read each of the following three stories, consider what
makes each of them fictional. Labov's six elements can be useful here.
Which ones are missing? Which contribute most to the effect of the story?

The Kiss

Kate Chopin

This selection is a short story by the American writer Kate Chopin, who lived in Louisiana a century ago. She was unique for her time, in that she wrote frequently about a powerful female sexuality trapped within an elaborate code of manners.

It was still quite light out of doors, but inside with the curtains drawn and the   1
smouldering fire sending out a dim, uncertain glow, the room was full of deep shadows.

Brantain sat in one of these shadows; it had overtaken him and he did   2
not mind. The obscurity lent him courage to keep his eyes fastened as ardently as he liked upon the girl who sat in the firelight.

She was very handsome, with a certain fine, rich coloring that belongs to   3
the healthy brune type. She was quite composed, as she idly stroked the satiny coat of the cat that lay curled in her lap, and she occasionally sent a slow glance into the shadow where her companion sat. They were talking low, of indifferent things which plainly were not the things that occupied their thoughts. She knew that he loved her—a frank, blustering fellow without guile enough to conceal his feelings, and no desire to do so. For two weeks past he had sought her society eagerly and persistently. She was confidently waiting for him to declare himself and she meant to accept him. The rather insignificant and unattractive Brantain was enormously rich; and she liked and required the entourage which wealth could give her.

During one of the pauses between their talk of the last tea and the next   4
reception the door opened and a young man entered whom Brantain knew quite well. The girl turned her face toward him. A stride or two brought him to her side, and bending over her chair—before she could suspect his intention, for she did not realize that he had not seen her visitor—he pressed an ardent, lingering kiss upon her lips.

Brantain slowly arose; so did the girl arise, but quickly, and the new-   5
comer stood between them, a little amusement and some defiance struggling with the confusion in his face.

"I believe," stammered Brantain, "I see that I have stayed too long. I—I   6
had no idea—that is, I must wish you good-by." He was clutching his hat with both hands, and probably did not perceive that she was extending her hand to him, her presence of mind had not completely deserted her; but she could not have trusted herself to speak.

"Hang me if I saw him sitting there, Nattie! I know it's deuced awkward   7
for you. But I hope you'll forgive me this once—this very first break. Why, what's the matter?"

"Don't touch me; don't come near me," she returned angrily. "What do   8
you mean by entering the house without ringing?"

"I came in with your brother, as I often do," he answered coldly, in self-   9
justification. "We came in the side way. He went upstairs and I came in here
hoping to find you. The explanation is simple enough and ought to satisfy
you that the misadventure was unavoidable. But do say that you forgive me,
Nathalie," he entreated, softening.

"Forgive you! You don't know what you are talking about. Let me pass.   10
It depends upon—a good deal whether I ever forgive you."

At that next reception which she and Brantain had been talking about   11
she approached the young man with a delicious frankness of manner when
she saw him there.

"Will you let me speak to you a moment or two, Mr. Brantain?" she   12
asked with an engaging but perturbed smile. He seemed extremely unhappy;
but when she took his arm and walked away with him, seeking a retired corner, a ray of hope mingled with the almost comical misery of his expression.
She was apparently very outspoken.

"Perhaps I should not have sought this interview, Mr. Brantain; but—   13
but, oh, I have been very uncomfortable, almost miserable since that little
encounter the other afternoon. When I thought how you might have misinterpreted it, and believed things"—hope was plainly gaining the ascendancy
over misery in Brantain's round, guileless face—"of course, I know it is nothing to you, but for my own sake I do want you to understand that Mr. Harvy
is an intimate friend of long standing. Why, we have always been like cousins
—like brother and sister, I may say. He is my brother's most intimate associate and often fancies that he is entitled to the same privileges as the family.
Oh, I know it is absurd, uncalled for, to tell you this; undignified even," she
was almost weeping, "but it makes so much difference to me what you think
of—of me." Her voice had grown very low and agitated. The misery had all
disappeared from Brantain's face.

"Then you do really care what I think, Miss Nathalie? May I call you   14
Miss Nathalie?" They turned into a long, dim corridor that was lined on either side with tall, graceful plants. They walked slowly to the very end of it.
When they turned to retrace their steps Brantain's face was radiant and hers
was triumphant.

Harvy was among the guests at the wedding; and he sought her out in a   15
rare moment when she stood alone.

"Your husband," he said, smiling, "has sent me over to kiss you."   16

A quick blush suffused her face and round polished throat. "I suppose   17
it's natural for a man to feel and act generously on an occasion of this kind.
He tells me he doesn't want his marriage to interrupt wholly that pleasant intimacy which has existed between you and me. I don't know what you've been
telling him," with an insolent smile, "but he has sent me here to kiss you."

She felt like a chess player who, by the clever handling of his pieces, sees   18
the game taking the course intended. Her eyes were bright and tender with a
smile as they glanced up into his; and her lips looked hungry for the kiss
which they invited.

"But, you know," he went on quietly, "I didn't tell him so, it would have   19
been ungrateful, but I can tell you. I've stopped kissing women; it's dangerous."

Well, she had Brantain and his million left. A person can't have every- 20
thing in this world; and it was a little unreasonable of her to expect it.

FOR DISCUSSION AND WRITING: COMPARING "NATURAL" AND "LITERARY" NARRATIVES

1. This is a sophisticated story of a sophisticated world. Begin your study of
   it by comparing its structure to that of "natural" narratives. Does it have
   all six of Labov's analytic elements? Discuss what is omitted, compressed,
   or rearranged in this story.

2. Retell the story as a personal narrative recounted by Mr. Harvy. Imagine
   him in his club, telling this tale to a small circle of intimate friends. You
   will have to develop his character and motivation a bit to do this, but try
   to keep your additions in harmony with the material in Chopin's version
   of this story. Aim for a "complete" narrative, with all six Labovian elements.

3. In a written essay, take up the question of the relationship between "natural" narratives and "literary" narratives, exploring both their similarities
   and their differences. Use Pratt and Chopin as your primary sources, but
   feel free to add material from the anecdotes of Benjamin, Williams, Auster,
   Jameson, or Staples, or from William Carlos Williams if you have studied
   this material. Try to reach some conclusion about which is more important:
   the differences or the similarities between popular and literary storytelling.

The Use of Force

William Carlos Williams

*The following selection is a personal experience recounted by the American poet
William Carlos Williams. Williams was a physician—a general practitioner—
and this is a story drawn from his practice.*

They were new patients to me, all I had was the name, Olson. Please come 1
down as soon as you can, my daughter is very sick.

When I arrived I was met by the mother, a big startled looking woman, 2
very clean and apologetic who merely said, Is this the doctor? and let me in.
In the back, she added. You must excuse us, doctor, we have her in the
kitchen where it is warm. It is very damp here sometimes.

The child was fully dressed and sitting on her father's lap near the 3
kitchen table. He tried to get up, but I motioned for him not to bother, took
off my overcoat and started to look things over. I could see that they were all
very nervous, eyeing me up and down distrustfully. As often, in such cases,
they weren't telling me more than they had to, it was up to me to tell them;
that's why they were spending three dollars on me.

The child was fairly eating me up with her cold, steady eyes, and no ex- 4
pression to her face whatever. She did not move and seemed, inwardly, quiet;
an unusually attractive little thing, and as strong as a heifer in appearance.
But her face was flushed, she was breathing rapidly, and I realized that she
had a high fever. She had magnificent blonde hair, in profusion. One of those
picture children often reproduced in advertising leaflets and the photogravure sections of the Sunday papers.

She's had a fever for three days, began the father and we don't know what 5
it comes from. My wife has given her things, you know, like people do, but it
don't do no good. And there's been a lot of sickness around. So we tho't you'd
better look her over and tell us what is the matter.

As doctors often do I took a trial shot at it as a point of departure. Has 6
she had a sore throat?

Both parents answered me together, No . . . No, she says her throat don't 7
hurt her.

Does your throat hurt you? added the mother to the child. But the little 8
girl's expression didn't change nor did she move her eyes from my face.

Have you looked? 9

I tried to, said the mother, but I couldn't see. 10

As it happens we had been having a number of cases of diphtheria in the 11
school to which this child went during that month and we were all, quite apparently, thinking of that, though no one had as yet spoken of the thing.

Well, I said, suppose we take a look at the throat first. I smiled in my best 12
professional manner and asking for the child's first name I said, come on,
Mathilda, open your mouth and let's take a look at your throat.

Nothing doing. 13

Aw, come on, I coaxed, just open your mouth wide and let me take a 14
look. Look, I said opening both hands wide, I haven't anything in my hands.
Just open up and let me see.

Such a nice man, put in the mother. Look how kind he is to you. Come 15
on, do what he tells you to. He won't hurt you.

At that I ground my teeth in disgust. If only they wouldn't use the word 16
"hurt" I might be able to get somewhere. But I did not allow myself to be
hurried or disturbed but speaking quietly and slowly I approached the child
again.

As I moved my chair a little nearer suddenly with one catlike movement 17
both her hands clawed instinctively for my eyes and she almost reached them
too. In fact she knocked my glasses flying and they fell, though unbroken,
several feet away from me on the kitchen floor.

Both the mother and father almost turned themselves inside out in em- 18
barrassment and apology. You bad girl, said the mother, taking her and shaking her by one arm. Look what you've done. The nice man . . .

For heaven's sake, I broke in. Don't call me a nice man to her. I'm here 19
to look at her throat on the chance that she might have diphtheria and possibly die of it. But that's nothing to her. Look here, I said to the child, we're
going to look at your throat. You're old enough to understand what I'm saying. Will you open it now by yourself or shall we have to open it for you?

Not a move. Even her expression hadn't changed. Her breaths however 20
were coming faster and faster. Then the battle began. I had to do it. I had to
have a throat culture for her own protection. But first I told the parents that
it was entirely up to them. I explained the danger but said that I would not
insist on a throat examination so long as they would take the responsibility.

If you don't do what the doctor says you'll have to go to the hospital, the 21
mother admonished her severely.

Oh yeah? I had to smile to myself. After all, I had already fallen in love 22
with the savage brat, the parents were contemptible to me. In the ensuing
struggle they grew more and more abject, crushed, exhausted while she surely
rose to magnificent heights of insane fury of effort bred of her terror of me.

The father tried his best, and he was a big man but the fact that she was 23
his daughter, his shame at her behavior and his dread of hurting her made
him release her just at the critical times when I had almost achieved success,
till I wanted to kill him. But his dread also that she might have diphtheria
made him tell me to go on, go on though he himself was almost fainting,
while the mother moved back and forth behind us raising and lowering her
hands in an agony of apprehension.

Put her in front of you on your lap, I ordered, and hold both her wrists. 24

But as soon as he did the child let out a scream. Don't, you're hurting 25
me. Let go of my hands. Let them go I tell you. Then she shrieked terrifyingly,
hysterically. Stop it! Stop it! You're killing me!

Do you think she can stand it, doctor! said the mother. 26

You get out, said the husband to his wife. Do you want her to die of 27
diphtheria?

Come on now, hold her, I said. 28

Then I grasped the child's head with my left hand and tried to get the 29
wooden tongue depressor between her teeth. She fought, with clenched teeth,
desperately! But now I also had grown furious—at a child. I tried to hold myself down but I couldn't. I know how to expose a throat for inspection. And I
did my best. When finally I got the wooden spatula behind the last teeth and
just the point of it into the mouth cavity, she opened up for an instant but before I could see anything she came down again and gripping the wooden blade
between her molars she reduced it to splinters before I could get it out again.

Aren't you ashamed, the mother yelled at her. Aren't you ashamed to act 30
like that in front of the doctor?

Get me a smooth-handled spoon of some sort, I told the mother. We're 31
going through with this. The child's mouth was already bleeding. Her tongue
was cut and she was screaming in wild hysterical shrieks. Perhaps I should
have desisted and come back in an hour or more. No doubt it would have
been better. But I have seen at least two children lying dead in bed of neglect
in such cases, and feeling that I must get a diagnosis now or never I went at
it again. But the worst of it was that I too had got beyond reason. I could have
torn the child apart in my own fury and enjoyed it. It was a pleasure to attack
her. My face was burning with it.

The damned little brat must be protected against her own idiocy, one 32
says to one's self at such times. Others must be protected against her. It is a

social necessity. And all these things are true. But a blind fury, a feeling of adult shame, bred of a longing for muscular release are the operatives. One goes on to the end.

In a final unreasoning assault I overpowered the child's neck and jaws. 33 I forced the heavy silver spoon back of her teeth and down her throat till she gagged. And there it was—both tonsils covered with membrane. She had fought valiantly to keep me from knowing her secret. She had been hiding that sore throat for three days at least and lying to her parents in order to escape just such an outcome as this.

Now truly she was furious. She had been on the defensive before but 34 now she attacked. Tried to get off her father's lap and fly at me while tears of defeat blinded her eyes.

FOR DISCUSSION AND WRITING: EVALUATING AND INTERPRETING ANECDOTE AND STORY

1. Later in this book, we will discuss more formally the question of how to produce "interpretations" of literary texts. For the moment we can think of interpretation simply as an extension of what Labov calls evaluation. It is a matter of explaining the significance or meaning of the events narrated. In Williams's story there is actually very little evaluation. You might confirm this by checking the text of the story against the six Labovian features of narrative. The absence of overt evaluation in many literary texts is a way of drawing the reader into the creative process. The reader must supply an appropriate evaluation for the events in order to complete the narrative structure.

   With this in mind, how do you evaluate or interpret the events in this story? What is the story about? What does it mean? You might begin by locating anything in the text that does seem to you to belong to orientation or evaluation. What about the title, for instance? Would you consider that a step toward an interpretation of the story? Try to develop, either in writing or in discussion, a full evaluation or interpretation of the story.

2. At this point, you might begin discussing the similarities and differences between the natural narratives of Labov and Pratt and the literary anecdote or story as exemplified by "The Use of Force." What seem to you to be the important features common to both types of narrative, and what differences do you find notable? Which seem to you the most important— the similarities or the differences?

A Conversation with My Father

Grace Paley

This is a story about storytelling. Grace Paley, the daughter of Russian immigrants, grew up in a New York City community of stories and storytelling. The influence of this oral tradition can be heard in this story, whose narrative flow is broken as the story within the story is revised.

My father is eighty-six years old and in bed. His heart, that bloody motor, is equally old and will not do certain jobs any more. It still floods his head with brainy light. But it won't let his legs carry the weight of this body around the house. Despite my metaphors, this muscle failure is not due to his old heart, he says, but to a potassium shortage. Sitting on one pillow, leaning on three, he offers last-minute advice and makes a request.   1

"I would like you to write a simple story just once more," he says, "the kind de Maupassant wrote, or Chekhov,[1] the kind you used to write. Just recognizable people and then write down what happened to them next."   2

I say, "Yes, why not? That's possible." I want to please him, though I don't remember writing that way. I *would* like to try to tell such a story, if he means the kind that begins: "There was a woman . . ." followed by plot, the absolute line between two points which I've always despised. Not for literary reasons, but because it takes all hope away. Everyone, real or invented, deserves the open destiny of life.   3

Finally I thought of a story that had been happening for a couple of years right across the street. I wrote it down, then read it aloud. "Pa," I said, "how about this? Do you mean something like this?"   4

Once in my time there was a woman and she had a son. They lived nicely, in a small apartment in Manhattan. This boy at about fifteen became a junkie, which is not unusual in our neighborhood. In order to maintain her close friendship with him, she became a junkie too. She said it was part of the youth culture, with which she felt very much at home. After a while, for a number of reasons, the boy gave it all up and left the city and his mother in disgust. Hopeless and alone, she grieved. We all visit her.

"O.K., Pa, that's it," I said, "an unadorned and miserable tale."   5

"But that's not what I mean," my father said. "You misunderstood me on purpose. You know there's a lot more to it. You know that. You left everything out. Turgenev[2] wouldn't do that. Chekhov wouldn't do that. There are in fact Russian writers you never heard of, you don't have an inkling of, as good as anyone, who can write a plain ordinary story, who would not leave out what you have left out. I object not to facts but to people sitting in trees talking senselessly, voices from who knows where. . . ."   6

"Forget that one, Pa, what have I left out now? In this one?"   7

"Her looks, for instance."   8

---

[1][Guy de Maupassant (1850–1893), French short-story writer and novelist. Anton Chekhov (1860–1904), Russian dramatist and short-story writer. *Eds.*]
[2][Ivan Turgenev (1818–1883), Russian novelist, playwright, and short-story writer. *Eds.*]

"Oh. Quite handsome, I think. Yes."   9

"Her hair?"   10

"Dark, with heavy braids, as though she were a girl or a foreigner."   11

"What were her parents like, her stock? That she became such a person.   12
It's interesting, you know."

"From out of town. Professional people. The first to be divorced in their   13
county. How's that? Enough?" I asked.

"With you, it's all a joke," he said. "What about the boy's father? Why   14
didn't you mention him? Who was he? Or was the boy born out of wedlock?"

"Yes," I said. "He was born out of wedlock."   15

"For Godsakes, doesn't anyone in your stories get married? Doesn't any-   16
one have the time to run down to City Hall before they jump into bed?"

"No," I said. "In real life, yes. But in my stories, no."   17

"Why do you answer me like that?"   18

"Oh, Pa, this is a simple story about a smart woman who came to N.Y.C.   19
full of interest love trust excitement very up to date, and about her son, what
a hard time she had in this world. Married or not, it's of small consequence."

"It is of great consequence," he said.   20

"O.K.," I said.   21

"O.K. O.K. yourself," he said, "but listen. I believe you that she's good-   22
looking, but I don't think she was so smart."

"That's true," I said. "Actually that's the trouble with stories. People start 23
out fantastic. You think they're extraordinary, but it turns out as the work
goes along, they're just average with a good education. Sometimes the other
way around, the person's a kind of dumb innocent, but he outwits you and
you can't even think of an ending good enough."

"What do you do then?" he asked. He had been a doctor for a couple of   24
decades and then an artist for a couple of decades and he's still interested in
details, craft, technique.

"Well, you just have to let the story lie around till some agreement can   25
be reached between you and the stubborn hero."

"Aren't you talking silly now?" he asked. "Start again," he said. "It so   26
happens I'm not going out this evening. Tell the story again. See what you
can do this time."

"O.K.," I said. "But it's not a five-minute job." Second attempt: 27

Once, across the street from us, there was a fine handsome woman,
our neighbor. She had a son whom she loved because she'd known
him since birth (in helpless chubby infancy, and in the wrestling, hugging ages, seven to ten, as well as earlier and later). This boy, when
he fell into the fist of adolescence, became a junkie. He was not a
hopeless one. He was in fact hopeful, an ideologue and successful
converter. With his busy brilliance, he wrote persuasive articles for
his high-school newspaper. Seeking a wider audience, using important
connections, he drummed into Lower Manhattan newsstand distri-
bution a periodical called *Oh! Golden Horse!*

In order to keep him from feeling guilty (because guilt is the stony heart of nine tenths of all clinically diagnosed cancers in America today, she said), and because she had always believed in giving bad habits room at home where one could keep an eye on them, she too became a junkie. Her kitchen was famous for a while—a center for intellectual addicts who knew what they were doing. A few felt artistic like Coleridge[3] and others were scientific and revolutionary like Leary.[4] Although she was often high herself, certain good mothering reflexes remained, and she saw to it that there was lots of orange juice around and honey and milk and vitamin pills. However, she never cooked anything but chili, and that no more than once a week. She explained, when we talked to her, seriously, with neighborly concern, that it was her part in the youth culture and she would rather be with the young, it was an honor, than with her own generation.

One week, while nodding through an Antonioni film,[5] this boy was severely jabbed by the elbow of a stern and proselytizing girl, sitting beside him. She offered immediate apricots and nuts for his sugar level, spoke to him sharply, and took him home.

She had heard of him and his work and she herself published, edited, and wrote a competitive journal called *Man Does Live by Bread Alone*. In the organic heat of her continuous presence he could not help but become interested once more in his muscles, his arteries, and nerve connections. In fact he began to love them, treasure them, praise them with funny little songs in *Man Does Live. . . .*

the fingers of my flesh transcend
my transcendental soul
the tightness in my shoulders end
my teeth have made me whole

To the mouth of his head (that glory of will and determination) he brought hard apples, nuts, wheat germ, and soybean oil. He said to his old friends, From now on, I guess I'll keep my wits about me. I'm going on the natch. He said he was about to begin a spiritual deep-breathing journey. How about you too, Mom? He asked kindly.

His conversion was so radiant, splendid, that neighborhood kids his age began to say that he had never been a real addict at all, only a journalist along for the smell of the story. The mother tried several times to give up what had become without her son and his friends a

---

[3][Samuel Taylor Coleridge (1772–1834), English Romantic poet, was an opium addict. *Eds.*]

[4][Timothy Leary (1920–1996), sometime Harvard professor of psychology and early advocate of the use of LSD. *Eds.*]

[5][Michelangelo Antonioni (1912–), Italian film director who favors long takes of what appear to be random events. *Eds.*]

lonely habit. This effort only brought it to supportable levels. The boy and his girl took their electronic mimeograph and moved to the bushy edge of another borough. They were very strict. They said they would not see her again until she had been off drugs for sixty days.

At home alone in the evening, weeping, the mother read and re-read the seven issues of *Oh! Golden Horse!* They seemed to her as truthful as ever. We often crossed the street to visit and console. But if we mentioned any of our children who were at college or in the hospital or dropouts at home, she would cry out, My baby! My baby! and burst into terrible, face-scarring, time-consuming tears. The End.

First my father was silent, then he said, "Number One: You have a nice 28 sense of humor. Number Two: I see you can't tell a plain story. So don't waste time." Then he said sadly, "Number Three: I suppose that means she was alone, she was left like that, his mother. Alone. Probably sick?"

I said, "Yes." 29

"Poor woman. Poor girl, to be born in a time of fools, to live among fools. 30 The end. The end. You were right to put that down. The end."

I didn't want to argue, but I had to say, "Well, it is not necessarily the 31 end, Pa."

"Yes," he said, "what a tragedy. The end of a person." 32

"No, Pa," I begged him. "It doesn't have to be. She's only about forty. She 33 could be a hundred different things in this world as time goes on. A teacher or a social worker. An ex-junkie! Sometimes it's better than having a master's in education."

"Jokes," he said. "As a writer that's your main trouble. You don't want to 34 recognize it. Tragedy! Plain tragedy! Historical tragedy! No hope. The end."

"Oh Pa." I said. "She could change." 35

"In your own life, too, you have to look it in the face." He took a couple 36 of nitroglycerin. "Turn to five," he said, pointing to the dial on the oxygen tank. He inserted the tubes into his nostrils and breathed deep. He closed his eyes and said, "No."

I had promised the family to always let him have the last word when ar- 37 guing, but in this case I had a different responsibility. That woman lives across the street. She's my knowledge and my invention. I'm sorry for her. I'm not going to leave her there in that house crying. (Actually neither would Life, which unlike me has no pity.)

Therefore: She did change. Of course her son never came home again. 38 But right now, she's the receptionist in a storefront community clinic in the East Village. Most of the customers are young people, some old friends. The head doctor has said to her, "If we only had three people in this clinic with your experiences. . . ."

"The doctor said that?" My father took the oxygen tubes out of his nos- 39 trils and said, "Jokes. Jokes again."

"No, Pa, it could really happen that way, it's a funny world nowadays." 40

"No," he said. "Truth first. She will slide back. A person must have char- 41 acter. She does not."

"No, Pa," I said. "That's it. She's got a job. Forget it. She's in that store- 42
front working."

"How long will it be?" he asked. "Tragedy! You too. When will you look 43
it in the face?"

FOR DISCUSSION AND WRITING: WHAT MAKES A "GOOD STORY"?

1. Does this story contain all six of Labov's analytic elements? Which elements predominate? How does this story complicate the concept of resolution both through its structure and through the fact of the father's condition?

2. Both and father and daughter take storytelling seriously, but they seem to disagree on certain points. Describe the father's concept of a "plain ordinary story." How does it seem to differ from his daughter's way of telling a story?

3. Take the anecdote of personal experience that you wrote earlier for the Labov material and read it to a classmate. Work together toward revising one another's anecdotes into stories, keeping in mind the criteria set forth in Paley's story. You may not agree on what makes a "good story," but your discussions should spur you to new ideas for further development. When you have completed your revision, write a paragraph in which you discuss the changes you made and why you made them.

CHARACTER AND CONFRONTATION

In the previous section, the object of study was the basic structure of narrative texts. Beginning with personal, or "natural," narrative, we considered the ways in which Labov's six elements of narrative can be applied to texts of every size and shape. In the present section, we will approach the study of dramatic texts through the ways in which they resemble and differ from narrative, using Labov's six elements as the basis of our comparison.

Trifles

Susan Glaspell

To begin with, let us consider a sample of dramatic literature that is drawn from ordinary life. The following selection is a one-act play by Susan Glaspell, written in 1916 and set in a midwestern farm community in the early years of the twentieth century. The drama centers on the investigation of the murder of a farmer, with his wife as the main suspect. Evidence of a motive is lacking, and

*as the farmhouse is being searched, tension is built through the differences in
how the women read the facts of daily life in the house as compared with the
men's interpretations. As you read the play over a couple of times, notice how
much of the drama is conveyed through silence and the looks that pass between
the two women. We suggest a reading of the play in class to get a better sense
of the dramatic confrontations that occur through speech and those that occur
through the silence of the look.*

CHARACTERS

George Henderson, County Attorney
Henry Peters, Sheriff
Lewis Hale, A Neighboring Farmer
Mrs. Peters
Mrs. Hale

SCENE: *The kitchen in the now abandoned farmhouse of John Wright, a gloomy kitchen,
and left without having been put in order—unwashed pans under the sink, a loaf of
bread outside the breadbox, a dish towel on the table—other signs of incompleted work.
At the rear the outer door opens and the* Sheriff *comes in followed by the* County Attorney *and* Hale. *The* Sheriff *and* Hale *are men in middle life, the* County Attorney *is a
young man; all are much bundled up and go at once to the stove. They are followed by
two women—the* Sheriff's *wife first; she is a slight wiry woman, a thin nervous face.* Mrs.
Hale *is larger and would ordinarily be called more comfortable looking, but she is disturbed now and looks fearfully about as she enters. The women have come in slowly, and
stand close together near the door.*

County Attorney: [Rubbing his hands.] This feels good. Come up to the fire,
    ladies.
Mrs. Peters: [After taking a step forward.] I'm not—cold.
Sheriff: [Unbuttoning his overcoat and stepping away from the stove as if to
    mark the beginning of official business.] Now, Mr. Hale, before we move
    things about, you explain to Mr. Henderson just what you saw when you
    came here yesterday morning.
County Attorney: By the way, has anything been moved? Are things just as
    you left them yesterday?
Sheriff: [Looking about.] It's just the same. When it dropped below zero last
    night I thought I'd better send Frank out this morning to make a fire for
    us—no use getting pneumonia with a big case on, but I told him not to
    touch anything except the stove—and you know Frank.
County Attorney: Somebody should have been left here yesterday.
Sheriff: Oh—yesterday. When I had to send Frank to Morris Center for that
    man who went crazy—I want you to know I had my hands full yester-
    day, I knew you could get back from Omaha by today and as long as I
    went over everything here myself—
County Attorney: Well, Mr. Hale, tell just what happened when you came
    here yesterday morning.

Hale: Harry and I had started to town with a load of potatoes. We came
along the road from my place and as I got here I said, "I'm going to see
if I can't get John Wright to go in with me on a party telephone." I spoke
to Wright about it once before and he put me off, saying folks talked too
much anyway, and all he asked was peace and quiet—I guess you know
about how much he talked himself; but I thought maybe if I went to the
house and talked about it before his wife, though I said to Harry that I
didn't know as what his wife wanted made much difference to John—

County Attorney: Let's talk about that later, Mr. Hale. I do want to talk about
that, but tell now just what happened when you got to the house.

Hale: I didn't hear or see anything; I knocked at the door, and still it was all
quiet inside. I knew they must be up, it was past eight o'clock. So I knocked
again, and I thought I heard somebody say, "Come in." I wasn't sure, I'm
not sure yet, but I opened the door—this door *[Indicating the door by
which the two women are still standing]* and there in that rocker—*[Point-
ing to it.]* sat Mrs. Wright. *[They all look at the rocker.]*

County Attorney: What—was she doing?

Hale: She was rockin' back and forth. She had her apron in her hand and
was kind of—pleating it.

County Attorney: And how did she—look?

Hale: Well, she looked queer.

County Attorney: How do you mean—queer?

Hale: Well, as if she didn't know what she was going to do next. And kind
of done up.

County Attorney: How did she seem to feel about your coming?

Hale: Why, I don't think she minded—one way or other. She didn't pay
much attention. I said, "How do, Mrs. Wright, it's cold, ain't it?" And she
said, "Is it?"—and went on kind of pleating at her apron. Well, I was
surprised; she didn't ask me to come up to the stove, or to set down, but
just sat there, not even looking at me, so I said, "I want to see John." And
then she—laughed. I guess you would call it a laugh. I thought of Harry
and the team outside, so I said a little sharp: "Can't I see John?" "No,"
she says, kind o' dull like. "Ain't he home?" says I. "Yes," says she, "he's
home." "Then why can't I see him?" I asked her, out of patience. "'Cause
he's dead," says she. *"Dead?"* says I. She just nodded her head, not getting a bit excited, but rockin' back and forth. "Why—where is he?" says
I, not knowing what to say. She just pointed upstairs—like that *[Himself
pointing to the room above]*. I got up, with the idea of going up there. I
walked from there to here—then I says, "Why, what did he die of?" "He
died of a rope round his neck," says she, and just went on pleatin' at her
apron. Well, I went out and called Harry. I thought I might—need help.
We went upstairs and there he was lyin'—

County Attorney: I think I'd rather have you go into that upstairs where you
can point it all out. Just go on now with the rest of the story.

Hale: Well, my first thought was to get that rope off. It looked . . . *[Stops, his
face twitches.]* . . . but Harry, he went up to him, and he said, "No, he's
dead all right, and we'd better not touch anything." So we went back

down stairs. She was still sitting that same way. "Has anybody been notified?" I asked. "No," says she, unconcerned. "Who did this, Mrs. Wright?" said Harry. He said it businesslike—and she stopped pleatin' of her apron. "I don't know," she says. "You don't *know?*" says Harry. "No," says she. "Weren't you sleepin' in the bed with him?" says Harry. "Yes," says she, "but I was on the inside." "Somebody slipped a rope round his neck and strangled him and you didn't wake up?" says Harry. "I didn't wake up," she said after him. We must 'a looked as if we didn't see how that could be, for after a minute she said, "I sleep sound." Harry was going to ask her more questions but I said maybe we ought to let her tell her story first to the coroner, or the sheriff, so Harry went fast as he could to Rivers' place, where there's a telephone.

County Attorney: And what did Mrs. Wright do when she knew that you had gone for the coroner?

Hale: She moved from that chair to this one over here *[Pointing to a small chair in the corner.]* and just sat there with her hands held together and looking down. I got a feeling that I ought to make some conversation, so I said I had come in to see if John wanted to put in a telephone, and at that she started to laugh, and then she stopped and looked at me—scared. *[The* County Attorney, *who has had his notebook out, makes a note.]* I dunno, maybe it wasn't scared. I wouldn't like to say it was. Soon Harry got back, and then Dr. Lloyd came, and you, Mr. Peters, and so I guess that's all I know that you don't.

County Attorney: *[Looking around.]* I guess we'll go upstairs first—and then out to the barn and around there. *[To the* Sheriff*]* You're convinced that there was nothing important here—nothing that would point to any motive.

Sheriff: Nothing here but kitchen things.

[The County Attorney, *after again looking around the kitchen, opens the door of a cupboard closet. He gets up on a chair and looks on a shelf. Pulls his hand away, sticky.]*

County Attorney: Here's a nice mess.

[The women draw nearer.]

Mrs. Peters: *[To the other woman.]* Oh, her fruit; it did freeze. *[To the* County Attorney*]* She worried about that when it turned so cold. She said the fire'd go out and her jars would break.

Sheriff: Well, can you beat the women! Held for murder and worryin' about her preserves.

County Attorney: I guess before we're through she may have something more serious than preserves to worry about.

Hale: Well, women are used to worrying over trifles.

[The two women move a little closer together.]

County Attorney: *[With the gallantry of a young politician.]* And yet, for all their worries, what would we do without the ladies? *[The women do not unbend. He goes to the sink, takes a dipperful of water from the pail and, pouring it into a basin, washes his hands. Starts to wipe them on the roller towel, turns it for a cleaner place.]* Dirty towels! *[Kicks his foot against the pans under the sink.]* Not much of a housekeeper, would you say, ladies?

Mrs. Hale: *[Stiffly.]* There's a great deal of work to be done on a farm.

County Attorney: To be sure. And yet *[With a little bow to her]* I know there are some Dickson county farmhouses which do not have such roller towels.

[He gives it a pull to expose its full length again.]

Mrs. Hale: Those towels get dirty awful quick. Men's hands aren't always as clean as they might be.

County Attorney: Ah, loyal to your sex, I see. But you and Mrs. Wright were neighbors. I suppose you were friends, too.

Mrs. Hale: *[Shaking her head.]* I've not seen much of her of late years. I've not been in this house—it's more than a year.

County Attorney: And why was that? You didn't like her?

Mrs. Hale: I liked her all well enough. Farmers' wives have their hands full, Mr. Henderson. And then—

County Attorney: Yes—?

Mrs. Hale: *[Looking about.]* It never seemed a very cheerful place.

County Attorney: No—it's not cheerful. I shouldn't say she had the home-making instinct.

Mrs. Hale: Well, I don't know as Wright had, either.

County Attorney: You mean that they didn't get on very well?

Mrs. Hale: No, I don't mean anything. But I don't think a place'd be any cheerfuller for John Wright's being in it.

County Attorney: I'd like to talk more of that a little later. I want to get the lay of things upstairs now.

[He goes to the left, where three steps lead to a stair door.]

Sheriff: I suppose anything Mrs. Peters does'll be all right. She was to take in some clothes for her, you know, and a few little things. We left in such a hurry yesterday.

County Attorney: Yes, but I would like to see what you take, Mrs. Peters, and keep an eye out for anything that might be of use to us.

Mrs. Peters: Yes, Mr. Henderson.

[The women listen to the men's steps on the stairs, then look about the kitchen.]

Mrs. Hale: I'd hate to have men coming into my kitchen, snooping around and criticising.

[She arranges the pans under sink which the County Attorney had shoved out of place.]

Mrs. Peters: Of course it's no more than their duty.

Mrs. Hale: Duty's all right, but I guess that deputy sheriff that came out to make the fire might have got a little of this on. *[Gives the roller towel a pull.]* Wish I'd thought of that sooner. Seems mean to talk about her for not having things slicked up when she had to come away in such a hurry.

Mrs. Peters: *[Who has gone to a small table in the left rear corner of the room, and lifted one end of a towel that covers a pan.]* She had bread set.

[Stands still.]

Mrs. Hale: *[Eyes fixed on a loaf of bread beside the breadbox, which is on a low shelf at the other side of the room. Moves slowly toward it.]* She was go-ing to put this in there. *[Picks up loaf, then abruptly drops it. In a manner of returning to familiar things.]* It's a shame about her fruit. I wonder if it's all gone. *[Gets up on the chair and looks.]* I think there's some here that's all right, Mrs. Peters. Yes—here; *[Holding it toward the window.]* this is cherries, too. *[Looking again.]* I declare I believe that's the only one. *[Gets down, bottle in her hand. Goes to the sink and wipes it off on the outside.]* She'll feel awful bad after all her hard work in the hot weather. I remember the afternoon I put up my cherries last summer.

[She puts the bottle on the big kitchen table, center of the room. With a sigh, is about to sit down in the rocking-chair. Before she is seated realizes what chair it is; with a slow look at it, steps back. The chair which she has touched rocks back and forth.]

Mrs. Peters: Well, I must get those things from the front room closet. *[She goes to the door at the right, but after looking into the other room, steps back.]* You coming with me, Mrs. Hale? You could help me carry them.

[They go in the other room; reappear, Mrs. Peters *carrying a dress and skirt,* Mrs. Hale *following with a pair of shoes.]*

Mrs. Peters: My, it's cold in there.

[She puts the clothes on the big table, and hurries to the stove.]

Mrs. Hale: *[Examining her skirt.]* Wright was close.[1] I think maybe that's why she kept so much to herself. She didn't even belong to the Ladies Aid. I suppose she felt she couldn't do her part, and then you don't enjoy things when you feel shabby. She used to wear pretty clothes and be lively, when she was Minnie Foster, one of the town girls singing in the choir. But that— oh, that was thirty years ago. This all you was to take in?

Mrs. Peters: She said she wanted an apron. Funny thing to want, for there isn't much to get you dirty in jail, goodness knows. But I suppose just to make her feel more natural. She said they was in the top drawer in this cupboard. Yes, here. And then her little shawl that always hung behind the door. *[Opens stair door and looks.]* Yes, here it is.

[Quickly shuts door leading upstairs.]

Mrs. Hale: *[Abruptly moving toward her.]* Mrs. Peters?

Mrs. Peters: Yes, Mrs. Hale?

Mrs. Hale: Do you think she did it?

Mrs. Peters: *[In a frightened voice.]* Oh, I don't know.

Mrs. Hale: Well, I don't think she did. Asking for an apron and her little shawl. Worrying about her fruit.

Mrs. Peters: *[Starts to speak, glances up, where footsteps are heard in the room above. In a low voice.]* Mr. Peters says it looks bad for her. Mr. Henderson is awful sarcastic in a speech and he'll make fun of her sayin' she didn't wake up.

Mrs. Hale: Well, I guess John Wright didn't wake when they was slipping that rope under his neck.

Mrs. Peters: No, it's strange. It must have been done awful crafty and still. They say it was such a—funny way to kill a man, rigging it all up like that.

Mrs. Hale: That's just what Mr. Hale said. There was a gun in the house. He says that's what he can't understand.

---

[1][close: stingy, miserly; also, secretive, unsociable. *Eds.*]

Mrs. Peters: Mr. Henderson said coming out that what was needed for the case was a motive; something to show anger, or—sudden feeling.

Mrs. Hale: *[Who is standing by the table.]* Well, I don't see any signs of anger around here. *[She puts her hand on the dish towel which lies on the table, stands looking down at table, one half of which is clean, the other half messy.]* It's wiped to here. *[Makes a move as if to finish work, then turns and looks at loaf of bread outside the breadbox. Drops towel. In that voice of coming back to familiar things.]* Wonder how they are finding things upstairs. I hope she had it a little more red-up[2] up there. You know, it seems kind of *sneaking.* Locking her up in town and then coming out here and trying to get her own house to turn against her!

Mrs. Peters: But Mrs. Hale, the law is the law.

Mrs. Hale: I s'pose 'tis. *[Unbuttoning her coat.]* Better loosen up your things, Mrs. Peters. You won't feel them when you go out.

*[*Mrs. Peters *takes off her fur tippet, goes to hang it on hook at back of room, stands looking at the under part of the small corner table.]*

Mrs. Peters: She was piecing a quilt.

[She brings the large sewing basket and they look at the bright pieces.]

Mrs. Hale: It's log cabin pattern. Pretty, isn't it? I wonder if she was goin' to quilt it or just knot it?

[Footsteps have been heard coming down the stairs. The Sheriff *enters followed by* Hale *and the* County Attorney.*]*

Sheriff: They wonder if she was going to quilt it or just knot it!

[The men laugh; the women look abashed.]

County Attorney: *[Rubbing his hands over the stove.]* Frank's fire didn't do much up there, did it? Well, let's go out to the barn and get that cleared up.

[The men go outside.]

Mrs. Hale: *[Resentfully.]* I don't know as there's anything so strange, our takin' up our time with little things while we're waiting for them to get the evidence. *[She sits down at the big table smoothing out a block with decision.]* I don't see as it's anything to laugh about.

Mrs. Peters: *[Apologetically.]* Of course they've got awful important things on their minds.

[Pulls up a chair and joins Mrs. Hale *at the table.]*

Mrs. Hale: *[Examining another block.]* Mrs. Peters, look at this one. Here, this is the one she was working on, and look at the sewing! All the rest of it has been so nice and even. And look at this! It's all over the place! Why, it looks as if she didn't know what she was about!

[After she has said this they look at each other, then start to glance back at the door. After an instant Mrs. Hale *has pulled at a knot and ripped the sewing.]*

Mrs. Peters: Oh, what are you doing, Mrs. Hale?

Mrs. Hale: *[Mildly.]* Just pulling out a stitch or two that's not sewed very good. *[Threading a needle.]* Bad sewing always made me fidgety.

Mrs. Peters: *[Nervously.]* I don't think we ought to touch things.

---

[2][red-up: readied, made up. *Eds.*]

Mrs. Hale: I'll just finish up this end. *[Suddenly stopping and leaning forward.]* Mrs. Peters?

Mrs. Peters: Yes, Mrs. Hale?

Mrs. Hale: What do you suppose she was so nervous about?

Mrs. Peters: Oh—I don't know. I don't know as she was nervous. I sometimes sew awful queer when I'm just tired. *[Mrs. Hale starts to say something, looks at Mrs. Peters, then goes on sewing.]* Well, I must get these things wrapped up. They may be through sooner than we think. *[Putting apron and other things together.]* I wonder where I can find a piece of paper, and string.

Mrs. Hale: In that cupboard, maybe.

Mrs. Peters: *[Looking in cupboard.]* Why, here's a birdcage. *[Holds it up.]* Did she have a bird, Mrs. Hale?

Mrs. Hale: Why, I don't know whether she did or not—I've not been here for so long. There was a man around last year selling canaries cheap, but I don't know as she took one; maybe she did. She used to sing real pretty herself.

Mrs. Peters: *[Glancing around.]* Seems funny to think of a bird here. But she must have had one, or why would she have a cage? I wonder what happened to it.

Mrs. Hale: I s'pose maybe the cat got it.

Mrs. Peters: No, she didn't have a cat. She's got that feeling some people have about cats—being afraid of them. My cat got in her room and she was real upset and asked me to take it out.

Mrs. Hale: My sister Bessie was like that. Queer, ain't it?

Mrs. Peters: *[Examining the cage.]* Why, look at this door. It's broke. One hinge is pulled apart.

Mrs. Hale: *[Looking too.]* Looks as if someone must have been rough with it.

Mrs. Peters: Why, yes.

[She brings the cage forward and puts it on the table.]

Mrs. Hale: I wish if they're going to find any evidence they'd be about it. I don't like this place.

Mrs. Peters: But I'm awful glad you came with me, Mrs. Hale. It would be lonesome for me sitting here alone.

Mrs. Hale: It would, wouldn't it? *[Dropping her sewing.]* But I tell you what I do wish, Mrs. Peters. I wish I had come over sometimes when *she* was here. I—*[Looking around the room.]*—wish I had.

Mrs. Peters: But of course you were awful busy, Mrs. Hale—your house and your children.

Mrs. Hale: I could've come. I stayed away because it weren't cheerful—and that's why I ought to have come. I—I've never liked this place. Maybe because it's down in a hollow and you don't see the road. I dunno what it is but it's a lonesome place and always was. I wish I had come over to see Minnie Foster sometimes. I can see now—

[Shakes her head.]

Mrs. Peters: Well, you mustn't reproach yourself, Mrs. Hale. Somehow we just don't see how it is with other folks until—something comes up.

Mrs. Hale: Not having children makes less work—but it makes a quiet house, and Wright out to work all day, and no company when he did come in. Did you know John Wright, Mrs. Peters?

Mrs. Peters: Not to know him; I've seen him in town. They say he was a good man.

Mrs. Hale: Yes—good; he didn't drink, and kept his word as well as most, I guess, and paid his debts. But he was a hard man, Mrs. Peters. Just to pass the time of day with him—*[Shivers.]* Like a raw wind that gets to the bone. *[Pauses, her eye falling on the cage.]* I should think she would 'a wanted a bird. But what do you suppose went with it?

Mrs. Peters: I don't know, unless it got sick and died.

[She reaches over and swings the broken door, swings it again. Both women watch it.]

Mrs. Hale: You weren't raised round here, were you? [Mrs. Peters *shakes her head.*] You didn't know—her?

Mrs. Peters: Not till they brought her yesterday.

Mrs. Hale: She—come to think of it, she was kind of like a bird herself—real sweet and pretty, but kind of timid and—fluttery. How—she—did—change. *[Silence; then as if struck by a happy thought and relieved to get back to everyday things.]* Tell you what, Mrs. Peters, why don't you take the quilt in with you? It might take up her mind.

Mrs. Peters: Why, I think that's a real nice idea, Mrs. Hale. There couldn't possibly be any objection to it, could there? Now, just what would I take? I wonder if her patches are in here—and her things.

[They look in the sewing basket.]

Mrs. Hale: Here's some red. I expect this has got sewing things in it. *[Brings out a fancy box.]* What a pretty box. Looks like something somebody would give you. Maybe her scissors are in here. *[Opens box. Suddenly puts her hand to her nose.]* Why—[Mrs. Peters *bends nearer, then turns her face away.*] There's something wrapped up in this piece of silk.

Mrs. Peters: Why, this isn't her scissors.

Mrs. Hale: *[Lifting the silk.]* Oh, Mrs. Peters—it's—

[Mrs. Peters bends closer.]

Mrs. Peters: It's the bird.

Mrs. Hale: *[Jumping up.]* But, Mrs. Peters—look at it! Its neck! Look at its neck! It's all—other side *to.*

Mrs. Peters: Somebody—wrung—its—neck.

[Their eyes meet. A look of growing comprehension, of horror. Steps are heard outside. Mrs. Hale slips box under quilt pieces, and sinks into her chair. Enter Sheriff *and* County Attorney. Mrs. Peters *rises.]*

County Attorney: *[As one turning from serious things to little pleasantries.]* Well, ladies, have you decided whether she was going to quilt it or knot it?

Mrs. Peters: We think she was going to—knot it.

County Attorney: Well, that's interesting, I'm sure. *[Seeing the birdcage.]* Has the bird flown?

Mrs. Hale: *[Putting more quilt pieces over the box.]* We think the—cat got it.

County Attorney: *[Preoccupied.]* Is there a cat?

[Mrs. Hale glances in a quick covert way at Mrs. Peters.]

Mrs. Peters: Well, not *now*. They're superstitious, you know. They leave.

County Attorney: *[To Sheriff Peters, continuing an interrupted conversation.]* No sign at all of anyone having come from the outside. Their own rope. Now let's go up again and go over it piece by piece. *[They start upstairs.]* It would have to have been someone who knew just the—

[Mrs. Peters sits down. The two women sit there not looking at one another, but as if peering into something and at the same time holding back. When they talk now it is in the manner of feeling their way over strange ground, as if afraid of what they are saying, but as if they can not help saying it.]

Mrs. Hale: She liked the bird. She was going to bury it in that pretty box.

Mrs. Peters: *[In a whisper.]* When I was a girl—my kitten—there was a boy took a hatchet, and before my eyes—and before I could get there—*[Covers her face an instant.]* If they hadn't held me back I would have—*[Catches herself, looks upstairs where steps are heard, falters weakly.]*—hurt him.

Mrs. Hale: *[With a slow look around her.]* I wonder how it would seem never to have had any children around. *[Pause.]* No, Wright wouldn't like the bird—a thing that sang. She used to sing. He killed that, too.

Mrs. Peters: *[Moving uneasily.]* We don't know who killed the bird.

Mrs. Hale: I knew John Wright.

Mrs. Peters: It was an awful thing was done in this house that night, Mrs. Hale. Killing a man while he slept, slipping a rope around his neck that choked the life out of him.

Mrs. Hale: His neck. Choked the life out of him.

[Her hand goes out and rests on the birdcage.]

Mrs. Peters: *[With rising voice.]* We don't know who killed him. We don't know.

Mrs. Hale: *[Her own feeling not interrupted.]* If there'd been years and years of nothing, then a bird to sing to you, it would be awful—still, after the bird was still.

Mrs. Peters: *[Something within her speaking.]* I know what stillness is. When we homesteaded in Dakota, and my first baby died—after he was two years old, and me with no other then—

Mrs. Hale: *[Moving.]* How soon do you suppose they'll be through, looking for the evidence?

Mrs. Peters: I know what stillness is. *[Pulling herself back.]* The law has got to punish crime, Mrs. Hale.

Mrs. Hale: *[Not as if answering that.]* I wish you'd seen Minnie Foster when she wore a white dress with blue ribbons and stood up there in the choir and sang. *[A look around the room.]* Oh, I *wish* I'd come over here once in a while! That was a crime! That was a crime! Who's going to punish that?

Mrs. Peters: *[Looking upstairs.]* We mustn't—take on.

Mrs. Hale: I might have known she needed help! I know how things can be—for women. I tell you, it's queer, Mrs. Peters. We live close together and we live far apart. We all go through the same things—it's all just a different kind of the same thing. *[Brushes her eyes; noticing the bottle of fruit, reaches out for it.]* If I was you I wouldn't tell her her fruit was gone. Tell her it *ain't.* Tell her it's all right. Take this in to prove it to her. She— she may never know whether it was broke or not.

Mrs. Peters: *[Takes the bottle, looks about for something to wrap it in; takes petticoat from the clothes brought from the other room, very nervously begins winding this around the bottle. In a false voice.]* My, it's a good thing the men couldn't hear us. Wouldn't they just laugh! Getting all stirred up over a little thing like a—dead canary. As if that could have anything to do with—with—wouldn't they *laugh!*

[The men are heard coming down stairs.]

Mrs. Hale: *[Under her breath.]* Maybe they would—maybe they wouldn't.

County Attorney: No, Peters, it's all perfectly clear except a reason for doing it. But you know juries when it comes to women. If there was some definite thing. Something to show—something to make a story about—a thing that would connect up with this strange way of doing it—.

[The women's eyes meet for an instant. Enter Hale *from outer door.]*

Hale: Well, I've got the team around. Pretty cold out there.

County Attorney: I'm going to stay here a while by myself. *[To the* Sheriff.*]* You can send Frank out for me, can't you? I want to go over everything. I'm not satisfied that we can't do better.

Sheriff: Do you want to see what Mrs. Peters is going to take in?

[The County Attorney *goes to the table, picks up the apron, laughs.]*

County Attorney: Oh, I guess they're not very dangerous things the ladies have picked out. *[Moves a few things about, disturbing the quilt pieces which cover the box. Steps back.]* No, Mrs. Peters doesn't need supervising. For that matter, a sheriff's wife is married to the law. Ever think of it that way, Mrs. Peters?

Mrs. Peters: Not—just that way.

Sheriff: *[Chuckling.]* Married to the law. *[Moves toward the other room.]* I just want you to come in here a minute, George. We ought to take a look at these windows.

County Attorney: *[Scoffingly.]* Oh, windows!

Sheriff: We'll be right out, Mr. Hale.

[Hale goes outside. The Sheriff *follows the* County Attorney *into the other room. Then* Mrs. Hale *rises, hands tight together, looking intensely at* Mrs. Peters, *whose eyes make a slow turn, finally meeting* Mrs. Hale's. *A moment* Mrs. Hale *holds her, then her own eyes point the way to where the box is concealed. Suddenly* Mrs. Peters *throws back quilt pieces and tries to put the box in the bag she is wearing. It is too big. She opens box, starts to take bird out, cannot touch it, goes to pieces, stands there helpless. Sound of a knob turning in the other room.* Mrs. Hale *snatches the box and puts it in the pocket of her big coat. Enter* County Attorney *and* Sheriff.]*

County Attorney: *[Facetiously.]* Well, Henry, at least we found out that she was not going to quilt it. She was going to—what is it you call it, ladies?

Mrs. Hale: *[Her hand against her pocket.]* We call it—knot it, Mr. Henderson.

CURTAIN

FOR DISCUSSION AND WRITING: STAGING AND WRITING DRAMA

1. Stage a reading of the play.

2. Plays are meant to be acted. We often forget this little fact when we encounter the texts of plays in books. A printed play is more like a printed story than an acted play is. For one thing, a printed play usually has stage directions. At this point we would like you to consider the full range of differences between narration and enactment as ways of representing events. What seem to you the special strengths and limitations of each form? What do plays have that stories don't—and vice versa? Base your answers on the texts you have already considered in this course. You might also consider the difference between your private reading of Glaspell's text and the public staging or reading of it that you have just witnessed. The point of this inquiry is to refine your understanding of the ways that events are made into texts in these different forms. If you have a preference for one form over the other, try to explain the reasons for your preference.

3. Write your own version of a scene that presents the differences in the way something is perceived by a man and by a woman. Possibilities: a husband and wife arguing over the actions, desires, or attire of their child; a couple trying to decide where to go on their first date; or, dramatize a newspaper account of an actual murder trial in which you include a character confrontation that demonstrates how the homicide might be considered justifiable by one sex more than the other.

4. Using Glaspell's play as a source, write a narrative of the possible outcome of events. Start by considering the questions the reader is left with at the end of the play. For example, what will Mrs. Hale do with that box in her pocket? Will Mrs. Peters, the sheriff's wife, ever tell her husband what passed between her and Mrs. Hale? What do you suppose will happen to Mrs. Wright?

The Kiss (dialogue from the story)

Kate Chopin

This selection should look familiar to you. It consists of all the spoken dialogue from Kate Chopin's little story, "The Kiss." Look this material over before considering the assignment.

Brantain: I believe, I see that I have stayed too long. I—I had no idea— that is, I must wish you good-by.

Harvy: Hang me if I saw him sitting there, Nattie! I know it's deuced awkward for you. But I hope you'll forgive me this once—this very first break. Why, what's the matter?

Nathalie: Don't touch me; don't come near me. What do you mean by entering the house without ringing?

Harvy: I came in with your brother, as I often do. We came in the side way. He went upstairs and I came in here hoping to find you. The explanation is simple enough and ought to satisfy you that the misadventure was unavoidable. But do say you forgive me, Nathalie.

Nathalie: Forgive you! You don't know what you're talking about. Let me pass. It depends upon—a good deal whether I ever forgive you.

Nathalie: Will you let me speak to you a moment or two, Mr. Brantain?

Nathalie: Perhaps I should not have sought this interview, Mr. Brantain; but—but, oh, I have been very uncomfortable, almost miserable since that little encounter the other afternoon. When I thought how you might have misinterpreted it, and believed things—of course, I know it is nothing to you, but for my sake I do want you to understand that Mr. Harvy is an intimate friend of long standing. Why, we have always been like cousins—like brother and sister, I may say. He is my brother's most intimate associate and often fancies that he is entitled to the same privileges as the family. Oh, I know it is absurd, uncalled for, to tell you this; undignified even, but it makes so much difference to me what you think of—of me.

Brantain: Then you really do care what I think, Miss Nathalie? May I call you Miss Nathalie?

Harvy: Your husband has sent me over to kiss you.

Harvy: I suppose it's natural for a man to feel and act generously on an occasion of this kind. He tells me he doesn't want his marriage to interrupt wholly that pleasant intimacy which has existed between you and me. I don't know what you've been telling him, but he has sent me over here to kiss you.

Harvy: But you know, I didn't tell him so, it would have seemed ungrateful, but I can tell you. I've stopped kissing women; it's dangerous.

FOR DISCUSSION AND WRITING: CHANGING DIALOGUE TO DRAMA

Your task is to add everything that is needed to make this into a play that is as complete as the story from which it has been taken. You might begin by considering what is missing from this version that is in the story, using Labov's formula to aid your investigation. Then consider how to compensate for what is lacking. Some of the things you should consider adding are these:

1. Scene divisions and settings
2. Stage directions
3. Additional dialogue (monologue? soliloquy?)
4. Additional characters (a confidante? a commentator?)

You should undertake your revision of the dialogue with a staged production in mind: something that could be performed in class.

Character Contests

Erving Goffman

A personal narrative or a dramatic scene can be thought of as a form imposed upon the chaos of life—and we are often encouraged to think of literature in this way. But in fact, as sociologists have been demonstrating for some time, such forms are already present in life itself. Because life is social, it often has many of the features of a scene played before an audience. No one has developed this view more eloquently than Erving Goffman, a sociologist who has studied the dramatic or literary aspects of ordinary human interaction.

Ordinary interaction is not always ordinary, of course, and Goffman has argued persuasively that the smooth running of society requires a rhythm of crisis and relaxation, a rhythm caused by attempts of individuals to live out the roles or characters that they have adopted in order to function within a social structure. Our characters, says Goffman, are illusions encouraged by society. Our behavior in moments of crisis or confrontation depends upon our feeling that what we do will reveal what we are. Goffman puts it this way:

> And now we can begin to see character for what it is. On the one hand, it refers to what is essential and unchanging about the individual—what is *characteristic* of him. On the other, it refers to attributes that can be generated and destroyed in a few fateful moments.
>
> (*Interaction Ritual*, p. 238)

Because we want to have a good character—to be known as brave or honest or faithful—we try to behave in moments of stress so as to enact our ideas of bravery, honesty, fidelity. For Goffman, one of the most interesting social moments arrives when the characters of two individuals are at stake in a contest. He describes the "character contest"—a form of life that is also a form of art—in Interaction Ritual *as "a special form of moral game":*

These engagements occur, of course, in games and sports where opponents   1
are balanced and marginal effort is required to win. But character contests
are also found under conditions less obviously designed for contesting, sub-
jecting us all to a stream of little losses and gains. Every day in many ways
we can try to score points, and every day in many ways we can be shot down.
(Perhaps a slight residue remains from each of these trials, so that the moment one individual approaches another, his manner and face may betray
the consequences that have been usual for him, and subtly set the interaction off on a course that develops and terminates as it always seems to do for
him.) Bargaining, threatening, promising—whether in commerce, diplomacy,
warfare, card games, or personal relations—allow a contestant to pit his capacity for dissembling intentions and resources against the other's capacity
to rile or cajole the secretive into readability. Whenever individuals ask for or
give excuses, proffer or receive compliments, slight another or are slighted, a

contest of self-control can result. Similarly, the tacit little flirtations occurring between friends and between strangers produce a contest of unavailability—if usually nothing more than this. And when banter occurs or "remarks" are exchanged, someone will have out-poised another. The territories of the self have boundaries that cannot be literally patrolled. Instead, border disputes are sought out and indulged in (often with glee) as a means of establishing where one's boundaries are. And these disputes are character contests.

The character contest is of interest to a social scientist like Goffman because it is a place where individual actions reveal the social codes by which people judge others and themselves. As he says, "When a contest occurs over whose treatment of self and other is to prevail, each individual is engaged in providing evidence to establish a definition of himself at the expense of what can remain for the other." Human behavior has a certain literary quality built in, as individuals play roles (dramatically) in order to define (verbally) themselves. Goffman is especially interested in what happens when human interaction is carried to the point of serious conflict. When one person offends or challenges another and neither will apologize or give in, we have what Goffman calls a "run-in," which is an especially intense form of character contest. Such encounters, it should be emphasized, are not just about who gets to have their way but about character itself: who is seen to have acted with what the social group—and the individuals themselves—consider to be good character. This is the way he elaborates on the possibilities of the run-in:

When the run-in has occurred and the contest begun, the characterological implications of the play can unfold in different ways, and not necessarily with "zero-sum" restrictions.   2

One party can suffer a clear-cut defeat on the basis of properties of character: he proves to have been bluffing all along and is not really prepared to carry out his threatened deed; or he loses his nerve, turns tail and runs, leaving his opponent in the comfortable position of not having to demonstrate how seriously he was prepared to carry through with the contest; or he collapses as an opponent, abases himself and pleads for mercy, destroying his own status as a person of character on the tacit assumption that he will then be unworthy as an opponent and no longer qualify as a target of attack.   3

Both parties can emerge with honor and good character affirmed—an outcome carefully achieved, apparently, in most formal duels of honor, a considerable achievement since injury was also usually avoided.   4

And presumably both parties can lose, just as one party may lose while the other gains little. Thus, that ideal character contest, the "chicken run," may end with both vehicles swerving, neither vehicle swerving, or one swerving so early as to bring great dishonor to its driver but no particular credit to the opponent.   5

Obviously, the characterological outcome of the contest is quite independent of what might be seen as the "manifest" result of the fray. An overmatched player can gamely give everything he has to his hopeless situation and then go down bravely, or proudly, or insolently, or gracefully, or with an ironic smile   6 on his lips.[1] A criminal suspect can keep his cool in the face of elaborate techniques employed by teams of police interrogators, and later receive a guilty sentence from the judge without flinching. Further, a well-matched player can grimly suffer while his opponent stoops to dishonorable but decisive techniques, in which case a duel is lost but character is won. Similarly, an individual who pits himself against a weak opponent may acquire the character of a bully through the very act of winning the match. And a bully who ties is lost indeed, as this news story from Fresno, California illustrates:

> A barmaid and a bandit played a game of "chicken" with loaded pistols early yesterday and although no shots were fired, the barmaid won.
>
> The action took place at The Bit, a proletarian beer and wine oasis on the southern fringe of town, where lovely Joan O'Higgins was on duty behind the bar.
>
> Suddenly a towering bandit walked into the establishment, ordered a beer, flashed a small pistol and commanded Miss O'Higgins to clean out the cash register.
>
> The barmaid placed $11 on the bar, an amount that failed to satisfy the bandit, whose height was estimated at six feet five.
>
> "Give me the rest," he demanded.
>
> Barmaid O'Higgins reached into a drawer for the main money bag and the .22 caliber pistol beneath it.
>
> She pointed the gun at the man and asked:
>
> "Now, what do you want to do?"
>
> The bandit, realizing that he had met his match in The Bit, blinked at the sight of the gun and left, leaving his beer and the $11 behind.[2]

FOR DISCUSSION AND WRITING: ANALYZING AND WRITING CHARACTER CONTESTS

1. Goffman suggests that we make up and enact fictions about ourselves — that our real lives are penetrated by fictional concepts. Do you agree or disagree? If there are any aspects of Goffman's essay that you find difficult to understand or to accept, present them for discussion.

2. According to Goffman, when two people have a "run-in" in real life, this takes a form quite similar to a scene from a play. Does your own experience support this view? Can you recall a run-in that you have either seen or participated in yourself? Could it be reenacted as a dramatic scene? Can you describe how this might be done?

---

[1]One of the reasons unexpected rescues are employed in action stories is that only in this way can the hero be given a chance to demonstrate that even in the face of quite hopeless odds he will not cry uncle. Second leads are allowed to prove this the hard way, being expendable in the plot.

[2]*San Francisco Chronicle*, July 14, 1966.

Also pg. 179

3. Character contests involve what Goffman calls the "boundaries" or "borders" of the self. They also involve matters of "honor" or "principle." Discuss a scene from Susan Glaspell's play *Trifles* (pp. 29–39) in Goffman's terms. In what sense does that scene record a "character contest"? Are matters of honor, principle, or boundaries of the self at stake in that scene? Is there a winner or a loser?

4. Consider Kate Chopin's story "The Kiss" as a character contest. What is at stake? Who wins or loses?

5. Consider William Carlos Williams's story "The Use of Force" as a character contest. What is at stake? Who wins or loses?

6. The "run-in" is an especially dramatic form of character contest. Which of the anecdotes you studied earlier can be described as a run-in? Rewrite a personal anecdote of your own in the form of a dramatic run-in, so that a reader will have no trouble assigning gains and losses to the characters involved. Use the dramatic rather than the narrative form of presentation.

7. In the run-in between the "bandit" and the "barmaid," the bandit is described as "towering" and the barmaid as "lovely." How important to the success of the story as a story are these details?

8. Suppose the barmaid had shot and killed the bandit. Would the result make as good a story? What would be lost with respect to this event's quality as a "character contest"?

9. How important are the barmaid's exact words to the function of this episode as a little drama or character contest?

10. The following is a brief but complete newspaper item about an event similar to the run-in between bandit and barmaid:

French Robbers Flee Barrage of Pastries
United Press International

St. Etienne, France—Two would-be robbers were driven away from a pastry shop by a hail of creme pies, cakes and pastries thrown by the 65-year-old owner, her daughter and two grandchildren, police said.

The two men armed with a tear-gas bomb and a pistol entered Armand Davier's pastry shop Sunday in the industrial city on the Loire River in southeastern France and demanded the contents of the cash box, officers said.

They ran from a fusillade of pies and cakes hurled at them by the owner, her daughter and two grandchildren, police said.

Your task is to make a complete little drama out of this, with three scenes:

    1. The bandits before the raid
    2. The shop before, during, and after the raid
    3. The bandits after they have fled

Try to make any gains or losses of character apparent, but try also to make your presentation as effective and amusing as possible. In particular, you should consider how this event may have changed the characters of the two bandits and the relationship between them.

11. Here is another opportunity to create a little drama involving food as a weapon.

Woman charged in assault with frozen chicken cutlets

CRANSTON, RI — A woman who allegedly beat her boyfriend with a five-pound bag of chicken was charged with domestic assault with a dangerous weapon and held at the police station last night.

The police say the fight between Tammy Lee Zarski, 38, of 266 Budlong Rd., and her live-in boyfriend began when the pair argued over what to cook for dinner.

It ended when Zarski allegedly attacked the man, swinging a plastic shopping bag that contained five pounds of frozen chicken.

"It was a big lump of frozen cutlets," said Sgt. Russell C. Henry, of the Cranston Police Department. "She hit him at least twice."

The man, who is 48, suffered cuts on the top of his head and under one eye. His injuries were not life-threatening, Henry said.

He was found bleeding and wandering outside near the apartment after the police received an anonymous 911 call. The police then entered the apartment and arrested Zarski without incident.

Officers found the bag of chicken, photographed it for evidence, and returned it to the freezer, Henry said.

Zarski was held at the station on the felony charge and was scheduled for arraignment today in Sixth District Court, Providence.

Following are three possible scenes, or you may want to devise your own sequence:

1. The woman and her boyfriend in the kitchen: the movement from discussion to argument, to attack.
2. The man wandering in street, possibly muttering incoherently; police arrive, alerted by a neighbor (or the girlfriend?); man's explanation.
3. Police examine evidence; woman's explanation.

The Stronger

August Strindberg

The following one-act play was written more than a hundred years ago by Swedish playwright August Strindberg, who is known for his dramatizations of psychological and sexual problems within and around family life. This particular play is unusual in several respects. Only one character speaks, while the others (and one other in particular) listen and react. The speaking character tells and interprets a narrative of events involving her, her husband, and the woman she is addressing. The title of the play suggests that the events that are narrated—and their narration on this occasion—constitute a character contest over which woman is "the stronger." As you read you will need to put some effort into reconstructing a narrative of the events that have preceded the play.

CHARACTERS
Mrs. X., actress, married
Miss Y., actress, unmarried
A Waitress

SCENE: A corner of a ladies' café (in Stockholm in the eighteen eighties). Two small wrought-iron tables, a red plush settee and a few chairs. Miss Y. is sitting with a half-empty bottle of beer on the table before her, reading an illustrated weekly which from time to time she exchanges for another. Mrs. X. enters, wearing a winter hat and coat and carrying a decorative Japanese basket.

Mrs. X   Why, Millie, my dear, how are you? Sitting here all alone on Christmas Eve like some poor bachelor.
Miss Y looks up from her magazine, nods, and continues to read.
Mrs. X   You know it makes me feel really sad to see you. Alone. Alone in a café and on Christmas Eve of all times. It makes me feel as sad as when once in Paris I saw a wedding party at a restaurant. The bride was reading a comic paper and the bridegroom playing billiards with the witnesses. Ah me, I said to myself, with such a beginning how will it go, and how will it end? He was playing billiards on his wedding day! And she, you were going to say, was reading a comic paper on hers. But that's not quite the same.
A waitress brings a cup of chocolate to Mrs. X and goes out.
Mrs. X   Do you know, Amelia, I really believe now you would have done better to stick to him. Don't forget I was the first who told you to forgive him. Do you remember? Then you would be married now and have a home. Think how happy you were that Christmas when you stayed with your fiancé's people in the country. How warmly you spoke of domestic happiness! You really quite longed to be out of the theatre. Yes, Amelia dear, home is best—next best to the stage, and as for children—but you couldn't know anything about that.
Miss Y's expression is disdainful. Mrs. X sips a few spoonfuls of chocolate, then opens her basket and displays some Christmas presents.
Mrs. X   Now you must see what I have bought for my little chicks. *[Takes out a doll.]* Look at this. That's for Lisa. Do you see how she can roll her eyes and turn her head. Isn't she lovely? And here's a toy pistol for Maja. *[She loads the pistol and shoots it at Miss Y, who appears frightened.]*
Mrs. X   Were you scared? Did you think I was going to shoot you? Really, I didn't think you'd believe that of me. Now if *you* were to shoot *me* it

wouldn't be so surprising, for after all I did get in your way, and I know you never forget it—although I was entirely innocent. You still think I intrigued to get you out of the Grand Theatre, but I didn't. I didn't, however much you think I did. Well, it's no good talking, you will believe it was me . . . *[Takes out a pair of embroidered slippers.]* And these are for my old man, with tulips on them that I embroidered myself. As a matter of fact I hate tulips, but he has to have tulips on everything.

Miss Y looks up, irony and curiosity in her face.

Mrs. X   *[putting one hand in each slipper]* Look what small feet Bob has, hasn't he? And you ought to see the charming way he walks—you've never seen him in slippers, have you?

Miss Y laughs.

Mrs. X   Look, I'll show you. *[She makes the slippers walk across the table, and Miss Y laughs again.]*

Mrs. X   But when he gets angry, look, he stamps his foot like this. "Those damn girls who can never learn how to make coffee! Blast! That silly idiot hasn't trimmed the lamp properly!" Then there's a draught under the door and his feet get cold. "Hell, it's freezing, and the damn fools can't even keep the stove going!" *[She rubs the sole of one slipper against the instep of the other. Miss Y roars with laughter.]*

Mrs. X   And then he comes home and has to hunt for his slippers, which Mary has pushed under the bureau . . . Well, perhaps it's not right to make fun of one's husband like this. He's sweet anyhow, and a good, dear husband. You ought to have had a husband like him, Amelia. What are you laughing at? What is it? Eh? And, you see, I know he is faithful to me. Yes, I know it. He told me himself—what *are* you giggling at?— that while I was on tour in Norway that horrible Frederica came and tried to seduce him. Can you imagine anything more abominable? *[Pause.]* I'd have scratched her eyes out if she had come around while I was at home. *[Pause.]* I'm glad Bob told me about it himself, so I didn't just hear it from gossip. *[Pause.]* And, as a matter of fact, Frederica wasn't the only one. I can't think why, but all the women in the Company seem to be crazy about my husband. They must think his position gives him some say in who is engaged at the Theatre. Perhaps you have run after him yourself? I don't trust you very far, but I know he has never been attracted by you, and you always seemed to have some sort of grudge against him, or so I felt.

Pause. They look at one another guardedly.

Mrs. X   Do come and spend Christmas Eve with us tonight, Amelia—just to show that you're not offended with us, or anyhow not with me. I don't know why, but it seems specially unpleasant not to be friends with you. Perhaps it's because I did get in your way that time . . . *[slowly]* or—I don't know—really, I don't know at all why it is.

Pause. Miss Y gazes curiously at Mrs. X.

Mrs. X   *[thoughtfully]* It was so strange when we were getting to know one another. Do you know, when we first met, I was frightened of you, so frightened I didn't dare let you out of my sight. I arranged all my goings and comings to be near you. I dared not be your enemy, so I became your friend. But when you came to our home, I always had an uneasy feeling, because I saw my husband didn't like you, and that irritated me — like when a dress doesn't fit. I did all I could to make him be nice to you, but it was no good — until you went and got engaged. Then you became such tremendous friends that at first it looked as if you only dared show your real feelings then — when you were safe. And then, let me see, how was it after that? I wasn't jealous — that's queer. And I remember at the christening, when you were the godmother, I told him to kiss you. He did, and you were so upset . . . As a matter of fact I didn't notice that then . . . I didn't think about it afterwards either . . . I've never thought about it — until *now! [Rises abruptly.]* Why don't you say something? You haven't said a word all this time. You've just let me go on talking. You have sat there with your eyes drawing all these thoughts out of me — they were there in me like silk in a cocoon — thoughts . . . Mistaken thoughts? Let me think. Why did you break off your engagement? Why did you never come to our house after that? Why don't you want to come to us tonight?

Miss Y makes a motion, as if about to speak.

Mrs. X   No. You don't need to say anything, for now I see it all. That was why — and why — and why. Yes. Yes, that's why it was. Yes, yes, all the pieces fit together now. That's it. I won't sit at the same table as you. *[Moves her things to the other table.]* That's why I have to embroider tulips, which I loathe, on his slippers — because you liked tulips. *[Throws the slippers on the floor.]* That's why we have to spend the summer on the lake — because you couldn't bear the seaside. That's why my son had to be called Eskil — because it was your father's name. That's why I had to wear your colours, read your books, eat the dishes you liked, drink your drinks — your chocolate, for instance. That's why — oh my God, it's terrible to think of, terrible! Everything, everything came to me from you — even your passions. Your soul bored into mine like a worm into an apple, and ate and ate and burrowed and burrowed, till nothing was left but the skin and a little black mould. I wanted to fly from you, but I couldn't. You were there like a snake, your black eyes fascinating me. When I spread my wings, they only dragged me down. I lay in the water with my feet tied together, and the harder I worked my arms, the deeper I sank — down, down, till I reached the bottom, where you lay in waiting like a giant crab to catch me in your claws — and now here I am. Oh how I hate you! I hate you, I hate you! And you just go on sitting there, silent, calm, indifferent, not caring whether the moon is new or full, if it's Christmas or New Year, if other people are happy or unhappy. You don't know how to hate or to love. You just sit there without moving — like a cat at a mouse-hole. You can't drag your prey out, you can't chase it, but you can out-stay it. Here you sit in your corner — you know they call it the rat-trap after you — reading the papers to see if anyone's ruined or wretched or been thrown out of the Company. Here you sit sizing up your victims and weighing your chances — like a pilot his shipwrecks for the salvage. *[Pause.]* Poor Amelia! Do you know, I couldn't be more sorry for you. I know you are miserable, miserable like some wounded creature, and vicious because you are wounded. I can't be angry with you. I should like to be, but after all you are the small one—and as for your affair with Bob, that doesn't worry me in the least. Why should it matter to me? And if you, or somebody else, taught me to drink chocolate, what's the difference? *[Drinks a spoonful. Smugly.]* Chocolate is very wholesome anyhow. And if I learnt from you how to dress, *tant mieux!*—that only gave me a stronger hold over my husband, and you have lost what I gained. Yes, to judge from various signs, I think you have now lost him. Of course, you meant me to walk out, as you once did, and which you're now regretting. But I won't do that, you may be sure. One shouldn't be narrow-minded, you know. And why should nobody else want what I have? *[Pause.]* Perhaps, my dear, taking everything into consideration, at this moment it is I who am the stronger. You never got anything from me, you just gave away—from yourself. And now, like the thief in the night, when you woke up I had what you had lost. Why was it then that everything you touched became worthless and sterile? You couldn't keep a man's love—for all your tulips and your passions—but I could. You couldn't learn the art of living from your books—but I learnt it. You bore no little Eskil, although that was your father's name. *[Pause.]* And why is it you are silent— everywhere, always silent? Yes, I used to think this was strength, but perhaps it was because you hadn't anything to say, because you couldn't think of anything. *[Rises and picks up the slippers.]* Now I am going home, taking the tulips with me—*your* tulips. You couldn't learn from others, you couldn't bend, and so you broke like a dry stick. I did not. Thank you, Amelia, for all your good lessons. Thank you for teaching my husband how to love. Now I am going home—to love him.

Exit.

FOR DISCUSSION AND WRITING: REVISING A CHARACTER CONTEST

1. Discuss the history of the relationships that have led to this little scene. That is, from the evidence given in the play, construct the story of the relevant portions of the characters' lives.

2. Discuss Goffman's theory of character contests as a way of interpreting the play. To do this, you must examine what is enacted and said in the play in the light of Goffman's concepts of why and how people behave the way they do. How much of what happens in the play can be explained by Goffman's theory? Are there aspects of the play that seem to elude Goffman's theory—perhaps things that belong to art rather than life?

3. Write a revised version of the play in which Miss Y does all the talking and Mrs. X is silent. To do this you should make the following assumptions: first, that Mrs. X's monologue is simply a version of events interpreted in a way that is satisfying for Mrs. X; second, that Miss Y would not only interpret the "same" events differently, she might also remem-

ber the events differently and might even remember somewhat different events; that is, you should assume that something happened between Mr. X and Miss Y that roughly corresponds to the description provided by Mrs. X, but may not correspond to that description in every respect. Your job is to keep the same large structure—an affair between Mr. X and Miss Y that ended with Mr. X still married to Mrs. X—but allow Miss Y to tell a version of the events that shows her to be "the stronger." We say there are two sides to every story. This is your chance to show what that expression means.

4. Assume that the waitress overhears this whole scene and that she knows more about the history of the Xs and Miss Y than emerges from Mrs. X's speeches. Has the waitress known Mr. X intimately? You decide. At any rate, your assignment here is to narrate the waitress's version of this scene. Assume she is telling a friend about it—or writing a letter to a friend about it—and go on from there.

Aristotle and the Advertisers: The Television Commercial as Drama (passages from the essay)

Martin Esslin

Dramatic form not only shapes our social behavior but also confronts us regularly as a form of persuasive manipulation. A major literary critic, Martin Esslin, has even argued that much of television advertising is dramatic in structure. Centuries ago, Aristotle pointed out that dramatic plots can be reduced to two simple forms and two complex developments of those forms. In one basic form, the fortunes of the central character or protagonist (hero) are improved during the course of the action. This is the basic comic plot. In the other simple form—the tragic—the protagonist experiences a fall in fortune.

The more complex plots involve a reversal in the course of the hero's fortunes: first a rise, followed by a fall; or first a fall, then a rise. Aristotle's word for such a reversal of fortune was peripeteia. *In classic drama, reversals were often brought about by the intervention of a god, whose descent from the heavens was simulated by lowering the god or goddess onto the stage with a machine like a derrick or backhoe. The Latin term for such a "god from a machine" is* deus ex machina, *a term we still use for divine intervention or other mechanical methods of reversing a character's fortunes in a play.*

Aristotle also believed that plots are more interesting if they lead to a change from ignorance to knowledge. He called such a change "recognition," or anagnorisis, *and the new way of thinking brought about by recognition he called* dianoia. *He was surely right about the importance of these features, for they are the basis of every detective story as well as of Aristotle's favorite play, the* Oedipus *of Sophocles. In a murder mystery the* anagnorisis *and* dianoia *lead to the* peripeteia *of the murderer. The structures Aristotle identified are still very much*

*with us, so it should come as no surprise that Martin Esslin finds them active
in TV commercials. Following these selections from his essay "Aristotle and the
Advertisers" (1980), we have added our reading of a more recent commercial.*

We have all seen it a hundred times, and in dozens of variations: that short   1
sequence of images in which a husband expresses disappointment and distress at his wife's inability to provide him with a decent cup of coffee and
seems inclined to seek a better tasting potion outside the home, perhaps even
at the bosom of another lady; the anxious consultation, which ensues between the wife and her mother or an experienced and trusted friend, who
counsels the use of another brand of coffee; and finally, the idyllic tableau of
the husband astonished and surprised by the excellence of his wife's new coffee, demanding a second—or even a third!—cup of the miraculously effective product.

A television commercial. And, doubtless, it includes elements of drama,   2
yet is it not too short, too trivial, too contemptible altogether to deserve serious consideration? That seems the generally accepted opinion. But in an age
when, through the newly discovered technologies of mechanical reproduction and dissemination, drama has become one of the chief instruments of
human expression, communication, and indeed, thought, all uses of the dramatic form surely deserve study. If the television commercial could be shown
to be drama, it would be among the most ubiquitous and the most influen-
tial of its forms and hence deserve the attention of the serious critics and the-
oreticians of that art, most of whom paradoxically still seem to be spellbound
by types of drama (such as tragedy) that are hallowed by age and tradition,
though practically extinct today. And surely, in a civilization in which drama,
through the mass media, has become an omnipresent, all-pervasive, continuously available, and unending stream of entertainment for the vast majority
of individuals in the so-called developed world, a comprehensive theory,
morphology, and typology of drama is urgently needed. Such a theory would
have to take cognizance of the fact that the bulk of drama today is to be
found not on the stage but in the mechanized mass media, the cinema, television, and in most civilized countries, radio; that, both on the stage and in
the mass media, drama exists in a multitude of new forms, which might even
deserve to be considered genres unknown to Aristotle—from mime to musi-
cals, from police serials to science fiction, from westerns to soap opera, from
improvisational theatre to happenings—and that, among all these, the television commercial might well be both unprecedented and highly significant.

The coffee commercial cited above, albeit a mere thirty to fifty seconds   3
in length, certainly exhibits attributes of drama. Yet to what extent is it typical of the television commercial in general? Not all TV commercials use plot,
character, and spoken dialogue to the same extent. Nevertheless, I think it
can be shown that most, if not all, TV commercials are essentially dramatic,
because basically they use mimetic action to produce a semblance of real life,
and the basic ingredients of drama—character and a story line—are present
in the great majority of them, either manifestly or by implication.

Take another frequently occurring type: a beautiful girl who tells us that   4
her hair used to be lifeless and stringy, while now, as she proudly displays, it
is radiantly vital and fluffy. Is this not just a bare announcement, flat and un-
dramatic? I should argue that, in fact, there is drama in it, implied in the clearly
fictitious character who is telling us her story. What captures our interest and
imagination is the radiant girl, and what she tells us is an event which marked
a turning point in her life. Before she discovered the miraculous new sham-
poo she was destined to live in obscurity and neglect, but now she has become beautiful and radiant with bliss. Are we not, therefore, here in the presence of that traditional form of drama in which a seemingly static display of
character and atmosphere evokes highly charged, decisive events of the past
that are now implicit in the present—the type of drama, in fact, of which Ib-
sen's *Ghosts* is a frequently cited specimen?

What, though, if the lady in question is a well-known show business or   5
sporting personality and hence a *real* rather than a fictitious character? Do
we not then enter the realm of reality rather than fictional drama? I feel that
there are very strong grounds for arguing the opposite: for film stars, pop sing-
ers, and even famous sporting personalities project not their real selves but a
carefully tailored fictional image. There has always, throughout the history of
drama, been the great actor who essentially displayed no more than a single,
continuous personality rather than a series of differing characters (witness the
harlequins and other permanent character types of the *commedia dell'arte*;
great melodrama performers like Frédéric Lemaître; great comics like Chaplin,
Buster Keaton, Laurel and Hardy, or the Marx Brothers; or indeed, great film
stars like Marilyn Monroe or John Wayne—to name but a very few). Such
actors do not enact parts so much as lend their highly wrought and artisti-
cally crafted fictitious personality to a succession of roles that exist merely to
display that splendid artifact. Hence if Bob Hope or John Wayne appear as
spokesmen for banking institutions, or Karl Malden as the advocate of a credit
card, no one is seriously asked to believe that they are informing us of their
real experience with these institutions; we all know that they are speaking
a preestablished, carefully polished text, which, however brief it may be,
has been composed by a team of highly skilled professional writers, and that
they are merely lending them the charisma of their long-established—and
fictional—urbanity, sturdiness, or sincerity.

There remains, admittedly, a residue of nondramatic TV commercials: 6
those which are no more than newspaper advertisements displaying a text
and a symbol, with a voice merely reading it out to the less literate members
of the audience, and those in which the local car or carpet salesman more or
less successfully tries to reel off a folksy appeal to his customers. But these
commercials tend to be the local stations' fill-up material. The bulk of the major, nationally shown commercials are profoundly dramatic and exhibit, in
their own peculiar way, in minimal length and maximum compression, the
basic characteristics of the dramatic mode of expression in a state of particular purity—precisely because here it approaches the point of zero extension,
as though the TV commercial were a kind of differential calculus of the aesthetics of drama.

Let us return to our initial example: the coffee playlet. Its three-beat ba-   7
sic structure can be found again and again. In the first beat the exposition is
made and the problem posed. Always disaster threatens: persistent
headaches endanger the love relationship or success at work of the heroine
or hero (or for headaches read constipation, body odor, uncomfortable sanitary pads, ill-fitting dentures, hemorrhoids, lost credit cards, inefficient detergents that bring disgrace on the housewife). In the second beat a wise friend
or confidant suggests a solution. And this invariably culminates in a moment
of insight, of conversion, in fact the classical anagnorisis that leads to dianoia
and thus to the peripeteia, the turning point of the action. The third beat
shows the happy conclusion to what was a potentially tragic situation. For it
is always and invariably the hero's or heroine's ultimate happiness that is at
stake: his health or job or domestic peace. In most cases there is even the
equivalent of the chorus of ancient tragedy in the form of an unseen voice, or
indeed, a choral song, summing up the moral lesson of the action and gen-
eralizing it into a universally applicable principle. And this is, almost invariably, accompanied by a visual epiphany of the product's symbol, container,
trademark, or logo—in other words the allegorical or symbolic representation of the beneficent power that has brought about the fortunate outcome
and adverted the ultimate disaster; the close analogy to the *deus ex machina*
of classical tragedy is inescapable.

All this is compressed into a span of from thirty to fifty seconds. More-   8
over such a mini-drama contains distinctly drawn characters, who, while representing easily recognizable human types (as so many characters of traditional drama), are yet individualized in subtle ways, through the personalities
of the actors portraying them, the way they are dressed, the way they speak.
The setting of the action, however briefly it may be glimpsed, also greatly
contributes to the solidity of characterization: the tasteful furnishings of the
home, not too opulent, but neat, tidy, and pretty enough to evoke admiring
sympathy and empathy; the suburban scene visible through the living room
or kitchen window, the breakfast table that bears witness to the housewifely
skills of the heroine—and all subtly underlined by mood music rising to a
dramatic climax at the moment of anagnorisis and swelling to a triumphant
coda at the fortunate conclusion of the action. Of all the art forms only drama
can communicate such an immense amount of information on so many levels simultaneously within the span of a few seconds. That all this has to be
taken in instantaneously, moreover, ensures that most of the impact will be
subliminal—tremendously suggestive while hardly ever rising to the level of
full consciousness. It is this which explains the great effectiveness of the TV
commercial and the inevitability of its increasing employment of dramatic
techniques. Drama does not simply translate the abstract idea into concrete
terms. It literally incarnates the abstract message by bringing it to life in a human personality and a human situation. Thus it activates powerful subconscious drives and the deep animal magnetisms that dominate the lives of
men and women who are always interested in and attracted by other human
beings, their looks, their charm, their mystery.

AIG VIDEO: THE GREATEST RISK IS NOT TAKING ONE

In this commercial for an insurance and financial services corporation, a drama of the young man who perseveres in the face of adversity and achieves fame is presented through a series of rapid cuts, or video bites. The young man in this case is Elvis Presley.

In the opening scene, a man dressed in a suit and hat of 1950s vintage is saying to the neatly dressed people standing around him, "This town will not put up with the vulgar body movements of Elvis Presley." His accent tells us that this is a southern town, perhaps meant to be Presley's own small hometown. The speaker's authoritative statement suggests that he may be the mayor and that it is his duty to maintain respectability. The next shot shows Elvis Presley gyrating, but we see him only from the chest down. His clothes are flashy: shiny, tight trousers and jacket, tie flying: a parody of the respectable attire of the townspeople in the opening shot. Upbeat background music continues throughout. In the next shot, a crowd is trying to surge forward, with police trying to hold it back. A female voice says excitedly, "I saw him gyrate his body and wiggle his hips!" Cut to the Elvis-gyrating shot.

The next shot shows a disc jockey smashing a record on his console, a smug smile on his face. Cut to these words on the screen: RADIO STATIONS REFUSED TO PLAY HIS MUSIC. The next shot shows a crowd, most of them young women, some clutching their heads in rapture, followed by a sequence of Elvis gyrating on an outdoor stage before an enthusiastic audience. Again, we do not see his face, just his movements from the torso on down. Cut to a mother standing between a boy and a girl, ages about eight and ten, with each of her hands protectively placed on each child's shoulder. She says firmly: "He should not be on television!" Following is a sequence showing Ed Sullivan, host of *Toast of the Town*, the most popular variety show on fifties television. His hands are raised in a protest position, and we see him mouthing, "No, no, no." Cut to words on the screen: AND TV STUDIOS VOWED NEVER TO SHOW HIM AGAIN [pause]

IF HE DIDN'T STOP SHAKING [pause] HIS HIPS

Cut to the shot of Elvis's below-the-waist gyrations presented as a sequence of four shots.

Cut to words on the screen:

THE GREATEST RISK IS NOT TAKING ONE

All of this has been filmed in black-and-white. The next cut is in color, a short sequence of Elvis on stage in a white satin suit, its capelike back extended as he raises his arms in a victorious gesture to the audience. Here is Elvis's "Yes, yes, yes!" in response to Ed Sullivan's "No, no, no!" This is the first and only full-length shot of Elvis; however, we still do not see his face—he is filmed from the rear—but it's clear he's the king, at the zenith of his career. The color signifies the passage of time—it's probably the sixties—and the blossoming of Presley's success as a radical break from the gray monotone of the respectable fifties.

This drama, a success story, ends with the corporate advertiser's name:

AIG

WORLD LEADERS IN INSURANCE AND FINANCIAL SERVICES

And what kind of drama is this? The corporate sponsor wants us to read it as a story of the young man who makes good by taking risks. Elvis's youth and sexuality are pitted against the repressive respectability of the fifties, and the shots of his fervent young (mostly female) audience make this also a drama of youth versus age. Our hero takes risks by refusing to conform to the standards of those who are the conservative gatekeepers to success: the mayor, the disc jockey, the mother, Ed Sullivan. And those crowds of adoring fans inspire him to take the risk and to go on gyrating. Of course, the media could not ignore such popularity, and the drama closes with the hero triumphant.

FOR DISCUSSION AND WRITING: REVERSALS AND RECOGNITIONS

1. Look back at the various narratives and dramas you have already considered, from the personal narratives of Pratt to the character contests of Goffman. Which of them have clear reversals, recognitions, or both? Is Aristotle right? Are the texts with reversals and recognitions the most interesting? Discuss any exceptions you find. It would be especially useful to consider your own dramatizations and personal narratives in the light of Aristotle's views.

2. Watch commercials on TV until you find one that follows the Aristotelian principles described by Esslin. If you have access to a VCR, record the commercial you are going to use so that you can study it carefully. If you don't have a VCR, do the best you can. You may have to see a commercial several times before you can complete your project.

   This project has two parts. First, develop a written version of your chosen commercial, in the form of a play, with stage directions and everything else you would need for someone to act out the commercial. (An alternative to this would be to have someone with access to a VCR provide a written version that the whole class could use.) Second, write an alternative version of the same commercial, in which some event happens or something is said that subverts or destroys the commercial function of the play. Try to make the smallest changes possible that will achieve the result that is being aimed at here. With some help from your classmates, act out your altered version.

REPRESENTATION AND ITS COMPLICATIONS

Thus far, we've looked at the structures of stories and plays, stressing their similarities to everyday texts. Now we'd like to explore further the ways in which literary texts create the effects they do.

At the end of the eighteenth century, William Wordsworth started writing a new kind of poetry, focusing on what he saw and felt in the everyday world. He rejected the use of poetic diction, stating that his purpose was "to imitate, and, as far as possible, adopt the very language of men." He also rejected the abstract subject matter of his predecessors. His colleague, poet and critic Samuel Taylor Coleridge, in his literary autobiography, *Biographia Literaria,* discussed Wordsworth's project in *Lyrical Ballads:*

> Mr. Wordsworth . . . was to propose to himself as his object, to give the charm of novelty to things of every day, and to excite a feeling analogous to the supernatural, by awakening the mind's attention from the lethargy of custom, and directing it to the loveliness and the wonders of the world before us; an inexhaustible treasure, but for which, in consequence of the film of familiarity and selfish solicitude we have eyes, yet see not, ears that hear not, and hearts that neither feel nor understand.

A few years later, Percy Bysshe Shelley drafted his *Defence of Poetry,* applying Coleridge's formulation to all poetry and suggesting that by making the mind a "receptacle of a thousand unapprehended combinations of thought," poetry "lifts the veil from the hidden beauty of the world, and makes familiar objects be as if they were not familiar." In a later passage, he develops this idea further. Poetry

> strips the veil of familiarity from the world, and lays bare the naked and sleeping beauty, which is the spirit of its forms.
>
> All things exist as they are perceived; at least in relation to the percipient. 'The mind is its own place, and of itself can make a heaven of hell, a hell of heaven.' But poetry defeats the curse which binds us to be subjected to the accident of surrounding impressions.

And whether it spreads its own figured curtain, or withdraws life's dark veil from before the scene of things, it equally creates for us a being within our being. It makes us the inhabitants of a world to which the familiar world is a chaos. It reproduces the common universe of which we are portions and percipients, and it purges from our inward sight the film of familiarity which obscures from us the wonder of our being. It compels us to feel that which we perceive, and to imagine that which we know. It creates anew the universe, after it has been annihilated in our minds by the recurrence of impressions blunted by reiteration.

Some one hundred years later, the Russian formalist Viktor Shklovsky developed this concept further and called it *defamiliarization* (*ostraneniye* in Russian). He applied the concept to narrative as well as poetic texts. "As perception becomes habitual," Shklovsky notes, "it becomes automatic." And he adds, "We see the object as though it were enveloped in a sack. We know what it is by its configuration, but we see only its silhouette." In considering a passage from Tolstoy's *Diary*, Shklovsky reaches the following conclusion:

> Habitualization devours objects, clothes, furniture, one's wife, and the fear of war. "If all the complex lives of many people go on unconsciously, then such lives are as if they had never been."
> Art exists to help us recover the sensation of life; it exists to make us feel things, to make the stone *stony*. The end of art is to give a sensation of the object as seen, not as recognized. The technique of art is to make things "unfamiliar," to make forms obscure, so as to increase the difficulty and the duration of perception. The act of perception in art is an end in itself and must be prolonged. *In art, it is our experience of the process of construction that counts, not the finished product.*

FOR DISCUSSION AND WRITING: THE FAMILIAR AND THE UNFAMILIAR

What do writers and artists do to make the familiar unfamiliar? There is no one device or method; rather, there are a number of ways. Look, for example, at Man Ray's photograph of a building's façade (p. 59). The disorienting effect is produced by shooting from an oblique angle. We might say that Ray has played with the cliché of approaching a subject "from a different angle." (We leave it to you to figure out what posture he had to assume to get that shot.) Poets, too, seek different angles, and poetry, for many readers, presents the challenge of the unfamiliar by its very appearance on the page. Look, for

Man Ray, *229 boulevard Raspail,* 1928. Collection Lucien
Treillard, Paris.

example, at the three poems that follow. They each present a form quite unlike a page of grammatically correct prose. They each have as their subject
everyday things, and so too does René Magritte, in his painting *Personal Values*. All have the same intention: to make us see common things anew. Read

René Magritte, *Les valeurs personelles (Personal Values)*,
1952. Private collection, New York, New York.

each of these texts carefully several times, then consider the following questions and suggestions.

1. What are the features of each text that make the experience of reading it
   different from reading a housewares catalogue, a biology textbook, or a
   guide to Paris? Make a list of these features for each poem and visual text
   as a basis for class discussion.

2. Write a paragraph in which you compare your ordinary experience with
   tools or personal effects, bugs, people you see on public transportation,
   or buildings with experiences portrayed by one of these poets or artists.

3. Try your hand at making a familiar object or event unfamiliar, using
   Cummings, Magritte, Merwin, Pound, or Ray as your model. Your text
   may be visual or verbal, or a combination of the two.

In a Station of the Metro

The apparition of these faces in the crowd;
Petals on a wet, black bough.

Ezra Pound

Tool

If it's invented it will be used

maybe not for some time

then all at once
a hammer rises from under a lid
and shakes off its cold family   5

its one truth is stirring in its head
order order saying

and a surprised nail leaps
into darkness
that a moment before had been nothing   10

waiting
for the law

W. S. Merwin

r-p-o-p-h-e-s-s-a-g-r

                    r-p-o-p-h-e-s-s-a-g-r
            who
a)s w(e loo)k
upnowgath
        PPEGORHRASS   5
                        eringint(o-
aThe):l
        eA
            !p:
S   a   10
            (r
rIvInG   .gRrEaPsPhOs)
                        to
rea(be)rran(com)gi(e)ngly   15
,grasshopper;

                e. e. cummings

2

Texts, Thoughts, and Things

I N THIS CHAPTER we ask you to shift your attention from the large, or "macro," structures of narrative and drama to the small, or "micro," structure of language itself. In particular we will focus on a single crucial element of language: the creative principle of metaphor.

A friend of ours who became a writer and teacher himself told us that his whole attitude toward language was changed when a teacher said to him—somewhat brutally—"Words are razor blades. You use them as if they were bricks." The point, of course, was that careless, clumsy use of language could be dangerous: that a certain awareness, a certain delicacy, is demanded by language. A razor blade can be a tool, a weapon, or a hazard, but you ignore its sharp edges at your peril. The point was forcefully made by the teacher's own use of the blade of metaphor, drawing the student's attention to a potential danger in language that he had overlooked.

We do not intend to draw any blood here, nor do we recommend wounding people to get their attention, but we hope this fragment of an anecdote will help explain why we have singled out metaphor as a dimension of language that should receive special attention. The reading and writing work in this chapter is designed to help you develop your awareness of the presence and function of metaphor in all sorts of texts. This awareness should help you attain greater precision and power as a writer. It should also enhance your pleasure and ability as a reader. Metaphor is at the heart of the creative process embodied in human language.

THE LINGUISTIC BASIS OF METAPHOR

It is widely understood that metaphor is a basic element of poetry. It is also true, however, that metaphor is a fundamental building block of ordinary language and of such forms of written prose as the essay. We begin our investigation of metaphor with two passages from a book called *Words and Things* by the psycholinguist Roger Brown.

In the first passage, Brown uses the case of the Wild Boy of Aveyron as a way of directing our attention to the linguistic problem of names for things—or nouns, as we call them. By clarifying for us the way in which nouns refer not to individual things but to "universals," or categories of things, Brown lays the basis for an understanding of metaphor.

In a metaphor the name of one thing is applied to another, so that, as in certain chemical reactions, there is an exchange of particles between the two. That is, when we say, "Words are razor blades," certain defining attributes of the category *razor blades* are transferred to the category *words:* namely, delicacy and danger. This is the way metaphor works. In the second passage included here, Brown helps us understand why the transfer takes place. He also suggests that all nouns are to some extent metaphorical. Language grows by a kind of metaphorical extension. Metaphor is thus not an ornament added on top of language, but a principle built in at the most fundamental level of linguistic behavior.

The following selections by Roger Brown are clear but dense—packed with meaning. Please read them slowly and carefully. Your understanding of metaphor will depend on your understanding of how words refer to things. That is, Brown's discussion of metaphor in the second selection depends upon his discussion of reference and categories in the first. To understand metaphor, we must be aware of how delicate and complicated is the connection between language and all the things we use language to discuss.

What Words Are: Reference and Categories

Roger Brown

"A child of eleven or twelve, who some years before had been seen completely naked in the Caune Woods seeking acorns and roots to eat, was met in the same place toward the end of September 1797 by three sportsmen who seized him as he was climbing into a tree to escape from their pursuit." In these words Dr. Jean-Marc-Gaspard Itard began his first report on the education of   1 the wild boy found in the Department of Aveyron. The discovery of a human creature who had lived most of his life outside of all human society excited the greatest interest in Paris. Frivolous spirits looked forward with delight to the boy's astonishment at the sights of the capital. Readers of Rousseau expected to see an example of man as he was "when wild in woods the noble savage ran." There were even some who counted on hearing from the boy mankind's original unlearned language—they conjectured that it was most likely to be Hebrew. The savage of Aveyron disappointed all of these expectations. He was a dirty, scarred, inarticulate creature who trotted and grunted like a beast, ate the most filthy refuse, and bit and scratched those who opposed him. In Paris he was exhibited to the populace in a cage, where he ceaselessly rocked to and fro like an animal in the zoo, indifferent alike to those who cared for him and those who stared. The great psychiatrist Pinel, who taught France to treat the insane as patients rather than as prisoners, was brought to examine the boy. After a series of tests Pinel pronounced him a congenital idiot unlikely to be helped by any sort of training.

Many came to believe that the so-called savage was merely a poor subnormal child whose parents had recently abandoned him at the entrance to some woods. However, a young physician from the provinces, Dr. Itard, believed that the boy's wildness was genuine, that he had lived alone in the woods from about the age of seven until his present age of approximately twelve, and there was much to support this view. The boy had a strong aversion to society, to clothing, furniture, houses, and cooked food. He trotted like an animal, sniffed at everything that was given him to eat, and masticated with his incisors in the same way as certain wild beasts. His body showed numerous scars, some of them apparently caused by the bites of animals and some which he had had for a considerable time. Above all, a boy of his general description had been seen running wild in the same forest some five years earlier.

Dr. Itard had read enough of Locke and Condillac to be convinced that most of the ideas a man possesses are not innate but, rather, are acquired by experience. He believed that the apparent feeble-mindedness of the boy of Aveyron was caused by his prolonged isolation from human society and his ignorance of any language and that the boy could be cured by a teacher with patience and a knowledge of epistemology. Itard asked for the job. He had been appointed physician to the new institute for deaf mutes in Paris and so asked to take Victor there to be civilized and, most interesting for us, to learn the French language. Permission was granted and Itard worked with the boy, whom he called Victor, for five years. Itard had little success in teaching Victor to speak. However, he had considerable success in teaching Victor to understand language and, especially, to read simple words and phrases. . . .

In teaching Victor to understand speech, Itard found that he must, in the beginning, set aside the question of meaning and simply train the boy to identify speech sounds. In the first period after his capture Victor paid no attention to the human voice but only to sounds of approach or movement in his vicinity—noises that would be important to a creature living in the forest. Itard devised an instructive game for teaching Victor to distinguish one vowel from another. Each of the boy's five fingers was to stand for one of five French vowels. When Itard pronounced a vowel, Victor was to raise the appropriate finger. Victor was blindfolded and the vowels were pronounced in an unpredictable order so that if the boy made correct responses it must be because he could distinguish the vowels. In time Victor learned to play the game, but he was never very good at it. Thus Itard decided that the boy's vision was more acute than his hearing and thought he might be taught to read more easily than he could be taught to understand speech.

Again Itard came up with an ingenious game designed to teach Victor to   5 identify the forms of the written and printed language, even though he could not yet understand their meanings. The same collection of words was written on two blackboards, making the order of words on one board unrelated to the order on the other. Itard would point to a word on his board and it was Victor's task to point to its counterpart on the other board. When the boy made a mistake, teacher and pupil "spelled" the word together; Itard pointed to the first letter of his word and Victor did the same with his supposed match, and they proceeded in this fashion until they came to two letters where Victor saw a difference. After a time Victor could read quite a large number of words, some of them very much alike. As yet, however, this was not reading with understanding but simply the identification of empty forms.

The time had come to teach Victor something about the meanings of   6 words. Itard arranged several objects on a shelf in the library, including a pen, a key, a box, and a book. Each thing rested on a card on which its name was written, and Victor had already learned to identify the names. Itard next disarranged the objects and cards and indicated to Victor that he was to match them up again. After a little practice the boy did this very well. Itard then removed all the objects to a corner of the room. He showed Victor one name and gave him to understand that he was to fetch the object named. Victor also learned this very quickly, and Itard grew increasingly optimistic.

The next test went badly at first. Itard locked away in a cupboard all of   7 the particular objects with which Victor had practiced, but made sure that there were in his study other objects of the same kinds—other pens, keys, boxes, and books. He then showed Victor a word, e.g., *livre*, and indicated that the boy was to bring the referent. Victor went to the cupboard for the familiar book and finding the cupboard locked had to give up the task. He showed no interest in any other book. The same failure occurred with the other words. Victor had understood each word to name some particular thing rather than a category of things.

Itard then spread out a variety of books, turning their pages to show what   8 they had in common. He indicated that the word *livre* could go with any of them. After this lesson, when shown the word *livre*, Victor was able to fetch a book other than the specific book of his training. However, he did not correctly constitute the book category at once, for he brought a handful of paper at one time and a pamphlet and magazine at another. As his errors were corrected, however, he learned to distinguish books from other sorts of publications and also to recognize such categories as are named *key*, *pen*, and *box*. The crucial test for understanding of the referent category was always Victor's ability to identify new instances.

Itard next approached the difficult problem of conveying an understand-   9
ing of words that name qualities and relations rather than objects that have
size, shape, and weight. He took out two books, one large and one small, and
Victor promptly labelled each with the word *livre*. Itard then took Victor's
hand and spread it flat on the front of the large volume showing how it failed
to cover the full surface. The same hand spread out on the smaller book did
cover that surface. Victor then seemed puzzled as if wondering that one word
should name these two different objects. Itard gave him new cards labelled
grand livre and *petit livre* and matched them with the appropriate books. Now
came the test to see whether Victor had learned specific habits or had ab-
stracted a general relationship. Itard produced two nails, one large and one
small, and asked that the cards *grand* and *petit* be correctly assigned. Victor
learned this relationship and others besides.

Itard had another good idea for verbs that name actions. He took a famil-   10
iar thing, e.g., a book, and made it the object of some action—pounding it or
dropping it or opening it or kissing it. In each case he gave the boy the appropriate verb in the infinitive form. The test was for the boy to label such actions
when their object was changed, e.g., to a key or a pen. This too Victor learned.

The end of all this imaginative teaching was that Victor learned to read   11
with understanding quite a large number of words and phrases. He would
obey simple written commands and also use the word cards to signal his own
desires. In addition to all this he assumed the manners and appearance of a
civilized young man. However, Itard's final word was discouraging. Although
Victor had been greatly improved by education, diminishing returns on his
efforts convinced Itard that the boy was performing to the limits permitted by
his intellectual endowment and these limits, unfortunately, were subnormal.

Reference and Categories

When Dr. Itard wanted to give Victor some idea of the meanings of words,   12
he hit upon a way of showing that each word stood for something, that each
word had a referent. This is the sort of thing each of us would do to convey
to a small child the meanings of his first words; it is also the usual recourse
in trying to communicate with a foreigner who understands no English. The use
of language to make reference is the central language function which is prerequisite to all else. It is the beginning of the psychology of language and is,
accordingly, the focus of this book.

What Victor learned about reference was at first too specific. Words do   13
not name particular things as Victor thought; they name classes or categories.
Someone who properly understands the word *book* is prepared to apply it to any
and all particular books. I see in the room where I sit a novel in a highly colored
dust jacket and quite near it one numbered volume of a sober encyclopedia;
on the floor is a Penguin paperback, and asleep in the hall the telephone direc-
tory. Although they differ in many respects, all of these are, nevertheless,
books. They have the printed pages and stiff covers that define the category.

Actually, we do not badly stretch the notion of the category if we treat even   14
a single particular book as a category. The single book, the single anything,

is a category of sense impressions. Victor must have seen the book that was used in his early training on many occasions, in various positions, and from different angles. At one time a book is a rectangular shape lying on a table; at another time the same book is only the back of a binding on the library shelf. While it is possible to say that these various experiences constitute a category, that category must be distinguished from the sort named by *book* in general. The various appearances of one book have a continuity in space-time that makes us think of them as one thing preserving its identity through change. The various individual books around my room do not have this kind of continuity. So let us agree to call all referents categories but to distinguish the particular referent from the general by calling it an "identity" category.

Itard's later training procedures show that not all referents are objects with   15
size, shape, and weight. Actions like dropping and kissing are referents and so are such qualities as large and small or red and green. Clearly too, these referents are categories. The act of dropping changes many of its characteristics from one occasion to the next but preserves something invariant that defines the action. Any sort of recurrence in the non-linguistic world can become the referent of a name and all such recurrences will be categories because recurrences are never identical in every detail. Recurrence always means the duplication of certain essential features in a shifting context of non-essentials.

It is quite easy to see that the referents of words are categories but some-   16
what less easy to see that language forms, the names of referents, are also categories. Variations in the production of a language form are probably more obvious in the written or printed version than in the spoken. Differences in handwriting and of type are so great that it is actually difficult to specify what all the renderings of one word have in common. Even the individual letter is a category of forms changing considerably in their numerous productions. Variations in pronunciation are also certainly ubiquitous but our early extensive training in disregarding the dimensions of speech that are not significant for distinguishing English words causes us to overlook them. So long as phonetic essentials are preserved we identify utterances as the same, although they change greatly in loudness, pitch, quaver, breathiness, and the like. From acoustic studies we know that even one speaker "repeating" the same vowel does not produce identical sounds. Itard's productions of the French vowels cannot have been identical from one time to another and neither, we may be sure, were the "matched" words he wrote on the two blackboards. In these first games Victor was learning to categorize the empty forms of language, to pick out the essential recurrent features and to overlook the non-essential variations.

FOR DISCUSSION AND WRITING: DEFINING CATEGORIES

1. It is easy to understand Brown when he says that the word *book* refers to a "category" that includes all the books that one could possibly encounter. But things get more complicated when he says that any particular book is also a category—what he calls an "identity category." Reconsider Brown's fourteenth paragraph and discuss the notion of "identity

category." Define this term in your own words, and illustrate your definition with examples.

2. Every word, even every letter, says Brown, is also a "category of forms." Looking over paragraph 16, define "category of forms" in your own words, and illustrate the way in which a word may be described as a "category of forms."

What Words Are: Metaphor

Roger Brown

When someone invents a new machine, or forms a concept, or buys a dog, or manufactures a soap powder his first thought is to name it. These names are almost never arbitrary creations produced by juggling the sounds of the language into a novel sequence. We think hard and ask our friends to help us find a "good" name, a name that is appropriate in that its present meaning suggests the new meaning it is to have.   1

Sometimes new words introduced by borrowing words or morphemes[1] from classical languages. The biological sciences have been especially partial to this practice as *photosynthesis, streptoneura,* and *margaritifera* testify. In order to savor the appropriateness of these names a classical education is required and so, for most of us, they are functionally arbitrary.   2

The usual method of creating a new name is to use words or morphemes already in the language; either by expanding the semantic range of some word or by recombining morphemes. Every word has a history of former meanings and, traced back far enough, an ancestor that belongs to another language. The modern French *lune* derives from the Latin *lux*. The extension of the Latin word for *light* to the moon is appropriate and may once have been experienced as appropriate. Today, however, because of phonetic change and loss of the earlier meaning, the metaphor in *lune* must be overlooked by most French speakers even as we overlook the metaphor in our *moon* which is a remote cognate of Latin *mensis* for month. Both languages arrived at their word for the moon by metaphorical means, though the metaphors are constructed on different attributes of the referent—its luminosity for the French, its periodic cycle for the English. In both cases the whole process dates so far back that the appropriateness of these names like that of *margaritifera* or *photosynthesis* is evident only to scholars.   3

Many new names are still very familiar in an older reference and so their appropriateness to the new referent is easy to see. There are dogs called *Spot* or *Rover;* detergents and soaps are called *Surf, Rinso,* and *Duz;* one kind of per-   4

---

[1][morpheme: the smallest unit of meaning in any given language. In English the word *dog* is a morpheme. The word *dogged* adds a second morpheme. *Eds.*]

sonality is said, by clinical psychologists, to be *rigid*. Compounds like *overcoat, railroad train*, and *fireplace* have familiar constituents. While the origins of these names are obvious enough they probably are not ordinarily noticed. It seems to be necessary to take a special attitude toward language, quite different from our everyday attitude, to discern the metaphors around us.

The metaphor in a word lives when the word brings to mind more than   5
a single reference and the several references are seen to have something in common. Sometime in the past someone or other noticed that the foot of a man bears the same relation to his body as does the base of a mountain to the whole mountain. He thought of extending the word *foot* to the mountain's base. This word *foot* then referred to two categories. These categories share a relational attribute which makes them one category. Within this superordinate category, which we might name *the foundations* or *lower parts of things*, are two subordinate categories—the man's foot and the mountain's base. These two remain distinct within the larger category because the members of each subordinate category share attributes that are not shared with the members of the other subordinate category. The *man's foot* is made of flesh and has toes, which is not true of the base of any mountain. Thus far the relationship is like that of any set of superordinate and subordinate categories, e.g., *polygons* as superordinate to triangles and squares. The subordinates have something in common which makes them species of one genus but they are distinct because members of one subordinate have still more in common. Metaphor differs from other superordinate-subordinate relations in that the superordinate is not given a name of its own. Instead, the name of one subordinate is extended to the other and this, as we shall see, has the effect of calling both references to mind with their differences as well as their similarities. The usual superordinate name, e.g., polygons, calls to mind only the shared attributes of the various varieties of polygon.

The use of *foot* to name a part of the mountain results in the appearance   6
of *foot* in certain improbable phrase contexts. One hears, for the first time, the *foot of the mountain* or *mountain's foot*. Until someone saw the similarity that generated the metaphor these sayings were not heard. They cause the metaphor to live for others who have not noticed the similarity in question. The anatomical reference is called to mind by the word *foot* which has been its unequivocal name. The context *of the mountain* is one in which this word has never appeared. The phrase suggests such forms as *peak* or *top* or *slope* or *height* or *base*; it is a functional attribute of all these. Only one of these forms has a referent that is like the anatomical foot and that one is *base*. There is a click of comprehension as the similarity is recognized and some pleasure at the amusing conceit of a mountain with toes, a mountain anthropomorphized. If the metaphor was created for a poem about the mountain climber's struggle with his almost human antagonist—the mountain itself—then the metaphor might figure importantly in communicating the sense of the poem.

This metaphor blazed briefly for the person who created it and it lights   7
up again when anyone hears it for the first time, but for most of us it is dead. This is because with repetition of the phrase *foot of the mountain* the word *foot* loses its exclusive connection with anatomy. The word may be used of

mountain as often as of man. When that is true there is nothing in the phrase *foot of the mountain* to suggest a man's foot and so the phrase is experienced as a conventional name for the lower part of a mountain. Part of the phrase is accidentally homophonic with part of the phrase *foot of a man* but there is no more reason for one to call the other to mind than there is for *board of wood* to remind us of *board of directors, bored with psycholinguistics,* or *bored from within.* In the interest of univocal reference we attend to the context in which each form occurs and do not consider the meanings it might have in other contexts.

The word *foot,* in isolation, is ambiguous. It has many referents includ- 8 ing the mountainous and the anatomical. That special attitude toward language which brings out the potential metaphors now seems to me to involve attending to forms in isolation, deliberately ignoring context. In this last sentence, for instance, consider the word *attending* and disregard its surroundings. *Attending* names at least two kinds of behavior; there is "attending a lecture" and "attending to a lecture." The latter behavior is notoriously not the same as the former. In the sentence above only the intellectual attention sense of *attending* comes to mind; the other is ruled out by context.

A metaphor lives in language so long as it causes a word to appear in im- 9 probable contexts, the word suggesting one reference, the context another. When the word becomes as familiar in its new contexts as it was in the old the metaphor dies. This has happened with *foot of the mountain.* Sometimes there is a further stage in which the older set of contexts dies altogether and also the older reference. In these circumstances one speaks of a historical semantic change in the word. The term *strait-laced* is applied nowadays to people who follow an exceptionally severe, restrictive moral code. An older sense can be revived by placing the term in one of its older contexts: "Mrs. Mather was miserable in her strait-laced bodice." In the days when people laced their clothing *strait* meant *tight* and to be *strait-laced* was literally to be rather tightly trussed up. It is not difficult to see the attributes of this condition that resulted first in a metaphor and then in a semantic change. Whether one is tightly laced into his clothing or into his conscience he will feel confined, he may strain against his bonds and burst them, or, when no one else is about, he may secretly relax them a little. The metaphor is so rich that we should not be surprised to find it in poetry as well as in the history of linguistic change.

In fact there exists a poem founded on the very similarities that caused 10 *strait-laced* to change in meaning.

Delight in Disorder

A sweet disorder in the dress
Kindles in clothes a wantonness.
A lawn about the shoulders thrown
Into a fine distraction;
An erring lace, which here and there   5
Enthrals the crimson stomacher;
A cuff neglectful, and thereby

Ribbands to flow confusedly;
A winning wave, deserving note,
In the tempestuous petticoat;   10
A careless shoestring, in whose tie
I see a wild civility;—
Do more bewitch me, than when art
Is too precise in every part.

Robert Herrick

Herrick lived in seventeenth century England, through the period of Pu-   11
ritan rule into the restoration of Charles II. F. W. Bateson . . . points out that
the poem reproduced above is concerned with more than disorder of costume. It is not only the clothes but also the wearers that Herrick would have
sweet, wanton, distracted, erring, neglectful, winning, tempestuous, wild, and
bewitching. The poem is a plea for disorder of manners and morals as well as
of dress. It is a statement of anti-Puritanism.

How does Herrick communicate these depth meanings? The poem by its   12
title professes to be concerned with dress. The word *disorder* can be applied
to dress, to manners, to politics, to morals, or even to a man's wits. The fact
that we are reading a poem makes us receptive to multiple meanings but the
title alone does not indicate what secondary meanings, if any, are relevant.
In the first line *sweet* sounds a trifle odd since it is not often said of disorder
in dress. *Sweet* starts several auxiliary lines of thought having to do, perhaps,
with girl friends, small children, and sugar cane. Only one of these is reinforced by what follows. *Kindles* and *wantonness* in the second line rule out children and sugar cane. Thoughts about girls and loose behavior are supported
by words like *distraction, enthrals,* and *tempestuous.* All of these words can be
used in talking about clothes. However, their choice is improbable enough to
call for some explanation. Since the improbable words are all drawn from a
set of terms having to do with girls and their behavior a second group of consistent references is created.

A scientist might call Herrick's message ambiguous since he uses words   13
that have several different referents and does not clearly sort these out with
critical contexts. Behind that judgment is the assumption that the poet intends, as a scientist might, to call attention to just one kind of reference. In
fact, however, Herrick wanted to talk simultaneously about clothing, ladies,
and morality and to do so in a very compact way. Rather than string out three
unequivocal vocabularies he uses one vocabulary which is able to make
three kinds of reference.

When a poet uses simile he explicitly invites us to note the similarities and   14
differences in two referents as in "My love is like a red, red rose." When he
uses metaphor a word is used in a context that calls for a different word as in
"The *lion* of England" or "My *rose* smiled at me." The context evokes one reference, the word another and the meaning is enriched by their similarities and
differences. *Lion* and *king, rose* and *love* concentrate on similarities. There is an
extraordinary sentence of e. e. cummings' . . . in which the difference in the

two references is the main thing: "And although her health eventually failed her she kept her sense of humor to the *beginning*." The most probable word for final position in that sentence is *end*. This is not only different from *beginning*, it is the antonym. The probability of *end* is so great that the reader is bound to anticipate it. Finding instead its antonym almost makes us feel reprimanded. Our worldly outlook has made us too prone to think of death as the end.

FOR DISCUSSION AND WRITING: DEFINING METAPHOR

1. At the end of paragraph 4, Brown says that "it seems to be necessary to take a special attitude toward language, quite different from our everyday attitude, to discern the metaphors around us." Try to define or describe the attitude Brown is discussing.

2. Adopting the attitude of a student of metaphor, examine the metaphors that Brown himself employs—as in the first sentence of paragraph 7, for instance. Does his use of metaphor differ from that of a poet like Robert Herrick?

3. Examine more closely the poem by Herrick. Brown has discussed the major system of metaphor in the poem, but the poetic text is enlivened by other instances of metaphoric language. Discuss the range of meaning evoked by some of the following words in the poem:

   kindles (line 2)
   enthrals (line 6)
   flow, wave, tempestuous (lines 8, 9, 10)

   How do you understand a phrase like "wild civility"?

4. Produce, in your own words, a working definition of metaphor, with some appropriate illustrative examples. You will need some clear notion of metaphor to begin your study of the workings of this feature of language in poems, dreams, essays, and advertisements.

METAPHOR IN THREE POEMS

Metaphor is a vital principle of all language, but it is especially important in poetry. If metaphors grow like weeds—in ordinary language—poets cultivate them, extend them, and combine them to make new hybrids that might never occur in nature but are exotic and exciting in those formal gardens we call poems.

Our study of the workings of metaphor will take us ultimately to essays, arguments, and advertising—back toward ordinary life. But we begin with three short poems, as laboratory specimens designed to illustrate some of the principles of metaphoric language. Please read them carefully and consider the questions for discussion and writing after each poem.

Separation

Your absence has gone through me
Like thread through a needle.
Everything I do is stitched with its color.

W. S. Merwin

FOR DISCUSSION AND WRITING: METAPHOR AND THE UNEXPECTED

1. It has been said that a good simile or metaphor is both unexpected and appropriate. Consider Merwin's poem in light of this view. How would you expect someone to complete the phrase "Your absence has gone through me like . . ."?

2. If someone said "Your absence has gone through me like a dagger," that would signify that separation is painful. What does Merwin's metaphor signify?

Let us honor . . .

Let us honor if we can
The vertical man
Though we value none
But the horizontal one.

W. H. Auden

FOR DISCUSSION AND WRITING: MODIFYING METAPHOR

This very small poem was sent by Wystan Hugh Auden to his friend Christopher Isherwood, and later appeared at the beginning of a volume of Auden's poetry. The poem depends upon the use of two words that are nearly synonyms (*honor* and *value*) and two words that form an abstract, geometrical opposition (*vertical* and *horizontal*). The reader is invited to make his or her own interpretive distinction between the meanings of *honor* and *value* and also to supply some concrete interpretations for *vertical* and *horizontal*. One way to do this is simply to rewrite the poem by filling in the blanks:

Let us _____ if we can
The _____ man
Though we _____ none
But the _____ one.

The assumption you must make in filling in these blanks is that *horizontal* and *vertical* are metaphors for something: for instance, death and life, slackness and probity. By supplying your interpretation, you collaborate in the completion of the poem.

Compare your version with others. Are some more satisfying than others? Is any one so satisfying that you feel like adopting it as "correct" and labeling the others wrong? Are any so unsatisfying that you want to rule them out entirely? Does the idea of interpretation as a collaborative or creative activity please or displease you? Discuss these matters.

Metaphors

I'm a riddle in nine syllables,
An elephant, a ponderous house,
A melon strolling on two tendrils.
O red fruit, ivory, fine timbers!
This loaf's big with its yeasty rising.   5
Money's new-minted in this fat purse.
I'm a means, a stage, a cow in calf.
I've eaten a bag of green apples,
Boarded the train there's no getting off.

Sylvia Plath

FOR DISCUSSION AND WRITING: MAKING METAPHORS

1. This poem is a riddle, with each line providing a metaphoric clue to its solution. Solve the riddle, and consider how the relationships between the metaphors contribute to its solution.

2. Compose your own riddle poem to present to the class for solution. Your subject should be something with which the class is familiar, such as a physical or emotional state (sleepiness, hunger, happiness, envy), or a place (classroom, fast-food restaurant), or a thing (car, TV, pizza). To get started, make a list of the qualities of your subject that first come to mind. Consider which quality or qualities best describe your subject, and concentrate on developing metaphors that will make your audience experience your subject from your point of view.

METAPHOR AND DREAM

For centuries people have believed that dreams are messages from somewhere, perhaps in a code that disguises their meaning. Over the past hundred years, a new theory of dreams has dominated discussion, the theory developed by Sigmund Freud. According to Freud, dreams are messages from the human unconscious, in a code designed to bypass the censorship of our conscious mind. These messages, which have to do with our most primal needs and desires—especially those relating to sexuality—must be censored because we do not wish to admit that we could even "think" such things, since they conflict with our status as civilized, reasonable beings.

Freud has a name for the psychic process or mechanism that transforms our desires into acceptable shape. He calls it the *dream-work.* For our purposes, Freud's dream-work is interesting on two counts. First, it operates much as do those linguistic devices called figures of speech, of which metaphor is especially important. Second, Freud calls the process of making sense of dreams *interpretation,* and what he means by interpretation is very close to what literary critics mean by the interpretation of poems.

Dreams and poems are texts that work in similar ways—to a certain extent. We are concerned here with both the similarities and the differences. But before discussing them, we should examine Freud's own definitions of his key terms. We have numbered and arranged these definitions here, but the language is Freud's (from the English translation of his *Introductory Lectures on Psychoanalysis*). We have added explanatory comments after each quotation from Freud.

From Introductory Lectures on Psychoanalysis

Sigmund Freud

1. *Latent* and *manifest*
   We will describe what the dream actually tells us as the *manifest dream-content* and the concealed material, which we hope to reach by pursuing the ideas that occur to the dreamer, as the *latent dream-thoughts.*

   Comment: Freud's theory depends upon a metaphor of surface and depth. What is manifest is what is visible on the surface. What is latent is hidden in the depths. For instance, a dream about the loss of a wedding ring (manifest) might signify a (latent) wish for separation from a spouse. What is manifest can be read directly. What is latent must be interpreted.

2. *Dream-work* and *work of interpretation*
   The work which transforms the latent dream into its manifest one is called the *dream-work.* The work which proceeds in the contrary direction, which endeavors to arrive at the latent dream from the manifest one, is our work of *interpretation.* This work of interpretation seeks to undo the dream-work.

   Comment: Freud here gives a name to the unconscious process that enables our real feelings to be expressed in a disguised manner. Thus disguised, thoughts and feelings we would censor or "repress" if we were awake can find expression in the form of dreams. He calls this process of transformation the dream-work. *For our purposes, what is most important is that Freud's dream-work operates by means of metaphors and other forms of verbal displacement. The dream-work functions poetically.*

3. Condensation

The first achievement of the dream-work is *condensation*. . . . Condensation is brought about (1) by the total omission of certain latent dream elements, (2) by only a fragment of some complexes in the latent dream passing over into the manifest one and (3) by latent elements which have something in common being combined and fused into a single unity in the manifest dream. . . . The dream-work tries to condense two different thoughts by seeking out (like a joke) an ambiguous word in which the two thoughts come together.

> *Comment: The first two forms of condensation mentioned by Freud are both ways of leaving out part of the whole complex of feelings behind the dream. The third, however, is a way of getting such thoughts or feelings into the dream by disguising them in some way. Freud points out that this process also occurs in slips of the tongue, sometimes now called "Freudian slips." A woman we know once found herself saying, "I don't believe in Freudian strips." She became a believer on the spot. The expression "Freudian strips," of course, combines or condenses the notion of the slip of the tongue with the notion of undressing or laying bare the latent content—what is under the clothing or behind the words. It is a perfect illustration of what Freud meant by condensation.*

4. Displacement

The second achievement of the dream-work is displacement. . . . It manifests itself in two ways: in the first, a latent element is replaced not by a component part of itself but by something more remote—that is by an allusion; and in the second, the psychical accent is shifted so that the dream appears differently centered and strange.

> *Comment: Freud is speaking here about the way in which meaning is displaced. For example, in the dream we mentioned earlier, about the loss of a wedding ring, the manifest and latent content are very close together, since the ring is a component part of the marriage. But suppose one dreamed of the loss of a donut. To interpret this dream as a dream of the end of marriage, one would have to see the donut as an allusion to the ring based on their shared form. And this could happen in a dream that seemed to be about a tea party like the one in* Alice in Wonderland, *in which everything is differently centered and strange.*

5. Imagery

The third achievement of the dream-work is psychologically the most interesting. It consists in transforming thoughts into visual images. [Freud suggests that we can imagine how this works by trying to translate a political editorial into pictures.] In so far as the article mentioned people and concrete objects you will replace them easily and perhaps even advantageously by pictures; but your difficulties will begin when you come to the representation of abstract words and of all those parts of speech which indicate relations between thoughts—such as particles, conjunctions, and so on. In the case of abstract words . . . you will recall that most abstract words are "watered down" concrete ones, and you will for that reason hark back as often as possible to the original concrete meaning of such words. Thus you will be pleased to find out that you can represent the "possession" of an object by a real, physical sitting down on it.

> *Comment: Once again, Freud's description of the dream-work sounds much like the work of a poetical imagination, finding concrete images in which to embody abstract ideas. The interpretation of dreams and the interpretation of poetical language have very much in common because what Freud called the dream-work and found to be active in the construction of dreams is actually modeled on the work of poets. Or, to put it another way, dreaming and poetry are both rooted in the human unconscious, though poetry is a way of trying to harness the unconscious to the demands of consciousness.*

As we can see from Freud's definitions, the dream-work functions in order to conceal meaning. But it conceals meaning in order to express it. Its motto might be "Better disguised expression than no expression at all." The language of poetry uses metaphor and other ways of displacing and condensing meaning for similar ends. In most poetry, however, meanings are displaced and condensed consciously, so as to give the reader an active role in constructing meanings for a poetic text, through the process that we call interpretation.

Poetic meaning, however, is not simply a matter of a poet's having a clear meaning and then disguising it. A poem is often a search for meaning on the part of the poet, who seeks—like the dream-work—to find signs and symbols for feelings that lie too deep within his or her psyche to have a definite mental shape. Poetic metaphor, then, is a way of pointing to meanings that can only be made clear by an act of interpretation.

You will have a chance to do some interpreting of poetic texts later on, but first we would like you to consider some popular versions of dream interpretation. If Freud thinks of the dream-work as something close to poetry, these are more prosaic, more mechanical ways of dealing with the interpretations of dreams. When you have read "Getting to Work on Your Dream" and "Symbolism," discuss the aspects of interpretation that seem common to Freud and the others—and those features that seem unique to each interpreter.

Getting to Work on Your Dream

Tony Crisp

An example will be used to show how to arrive at a dream's meaning from   1
use of the entries. It is important first to write the dream down as fully as possible; don't stint on the use of words; be descriptive. Then take the very opening scene of the dream and look it up in the appropriate entry.

> Example: "I was standing in the back garden of a house—one of a
> row of terraced houses. Each garden was fenced and ran down to a
> large drainage ditch. It seemed to be raining and water was filling the
> drainage ditch. The water was backing up into the gardens because
> something was blocking the ditch. It started rising up my legs. It was
> quite hot. I realised this was because hot water was running out of
> the baths and sinks in the houses. I felt I must get out of the gardens.
> Not only because of the water, but because of how people might feel
> if they saw me in their garden. I managed to find a way into a farm-
> yard where I felt relaxed" (Ted F).

The first scene here is a garden. On a piece of paper separate to the dream,
write "garden" with space for notes to be put beside it. The entry on **garden**
in the *Dictionary* says "The inner life of the dreamer; the area of growth or
change in your life; what you are trying to cultivate in yourself; feelings of
peace; being near to one's natural self; meditative attitude."

The words "houses," "raining," "hot water," "fences," "farmyard" need to   2
be looked up and relevant comments written down next to each word. In doing this with his dream, Ted ended up with the following:

- Garden—The growth and changes occurring in my life at present.
- Row of houses—Other people.
- Raining—Depressed feelings or difficulties; emotions which take
  away enthusiasm and act as a barrier to action; tears and emotional release, an outpouring; other people's emotions "raining"
  on me.
- Hot water—Emotions. In the idioms is "hot water," suggesting I
  have got myself in trouble.
- Fences—Social boundaries.
- Farmyard—Where my natural drives such as sexuality, parent-
  hood, love of fellowship, are cared for or expressed.

When Ted added his own associations to this the dream became fully understandable to him and read like this. "I am going through a lot of changes
at the moment—the garden. These are to do with allowing myself to have a
warm but nonsexual relationship with women. I have always been too dragged
along by my sexuality in the past. Just a few days before the dream I was in

a 'growth' group. I had made friends with a woman there, Susan, who I was warm with, but not sexually. The group work required some close physical contact, and I and another man worked with Susan. It seemed to me to go without complications. A while afterwards a woman in the group came to me and, with evident emotion, said I had made love publicly to my lover, meaning Susan. I had certainly been physically close to her and had felt at ease, but the viewpoint and feelings of the woman's accusations, coupled with her threat to expose me to the authority figure in the group, bowled me over. This is the hot water in the dream. The fences are the boundaries people erect between their personal life and what is socially acceptable. For some days, until understanding the dream, I felt really blocked up emotionally—the blocked drainage ditch. I cut off any friendship towards Susan. When I realised that in the farmyard—the acceptance of natural feelings without neat little boundaries—I could feel at peace, I was able to allow my natural warmth again."

After writing the comments next to each dream image or setting, add any   3
personal memories, feelings or associations, as Ted has. Put down anything which amplifies what has been dreamt. For instance a car is said to be one's drive and motivation in the entry on **car.** But it is helpful to add what personal feelings one has about one's car. Try imagining what the absence in one's life of the car, or house, etc., would mean; a friend recently told me the absence of her car would mean loss of independence—this was her personal association.

Symbolism
Julia and Derek Parker

The Parkers, like Tony Crisp, have brought the interpretation of dreams into the arena of popular culture. In this passage from "The Secret Code," a section of their book The Secret World of Dreams, *they discuss some common symbols. One of the things that we can learn from this discussion is that symbols, like other uses of language, can get worn out from overuse and become too familiar. Freud's dream-work is like poetry because he believed that it was always trying to avoid obvious meanings, in order to escape the censorship exerted by the conscious mind and express its true feelings in a disguised form. The dream-work needs to defamiliarize; it needs to be creative. This makes it, in Freud's view, different from the kind of symbolism the Parkers discuss in this passage.*

he language of dreams is based on symbolism and we must   1
now look at the language of symbols and see how far it is possible for people with no training in psychology to learn it.

A rough and ready description of a symbol is that it is an object, or perhaps an action, which stands for something else; in psychology, it represents   2 another object or action which is not directly connected with it. It is rather like a code.

One way of looking at symbolism and seeing how it works is to look at 3 the Christian religion, which is particularly rich in it. One of the most powerful symbols in world history is the fish which, from the very earliest years of Christianity, has been the symbol of Christ. This arose not because Christ or his actions were in any particular way fish-like, but because of the capital letters of five Greek words

’Iησοῦσ Χρισνόσ, Θεοῦ Υιάσ Σωτήρ

Jesus Christ, Son of god, Saviour—which made up the word,

ιχθύσ

a fish.

The symbolism which made a ship the representation of the Christian 4 church was arrived at in a different way. A ship carries people safely over the ocean, and the Church set out to carry people safely over the sea of life. Christianity also made use of the animal kingdom to represent Christ and the Church's qualities. He was called both Lamb and Lion, while the peacock stood for immortality, the phoenix for resurrection, the dragon or serpent for Satan and the stag for a soul thirsting for baptism.

It is easy enough to see how most of these symbols were arrived at: the 5 lamb is meek, the lion brave (or he has that reputation); the phoenix was believed to renew itself, the dragon and serpent were fierce, consuming men by fire or destroying them by poison.

Freud, of course, saw the snake as a symbol of the penis, whereas the 6 early Christians thought of its qualities, its "personality," and likened them to those of the devil.

The theory behind dream analysis is that the things about which we 7 dream, the actions in which we dream we are involved, the thoughts we dream, represent other things, other actions, other thoughts. This is fairly easy to accept. What is more difficult to believe is that symbolic meanings of certain things or actions are the same for all mankind. (Here, as everywhere else in this book unless we specifically say otherwise, when we speak of one sex we include the other.)

FOR DISCUSSION AND WRITING: INTERPRETING THE DEFAMILIARIZED WORLD

The fish symbol in its Christian signification is often found on bumper stickers today, often in the very simple form of a fish made by just two curved lines, joined at one end and crossed at the other to make a tail:

Sometimes the Greek letters that spell fish (ΙΧΦΨΣ or IXTHYS) are written inside the image. Lately, however, a counter symbol has appeared on some bumpers:

the fish with tiny legs that turn it into an amphibian, with the name Darwin inside the image. When an image becomes stabilized as part of a fixed code, it can readily be used as an intertext for a second image, which defamiliarizes the image and makes it, however briefly, poetical again.

One quality of dreams that invites interpretation is the emotional power they exert over the dreamer. Artists also try to achieve this power, sometimes in words and sometimes in visual images or music. We will close this section by offering you three texts—two pictures and a short piece of prose—that defamiliarize the known world much as dreams do. We ask you to interpret them, of course, but then we ask that you do a second thing. Discuss the features of these texts that guided your interpretation. That is, say what in them led you to read them in the way that you did.

Edward Hopper, *Night Shadows*, 1921.

Giorgio de Chirico, *Mystère et mélancolie d'une rue (Mystery and Melancholy of a Street)*, 1914. Private collection.

Surrealist Versailles

Giorgio de Chirico

One bright winter afternoon I found myself in the courtyard of the palace at Versailles. Everything looked at me with a strange and questioning glance. I saw then that every angle of the palace, every column, every window had a soul that was an enigma. I looked about me at the stone heroes, motionless under the bright sky, under the cold rays of the winter sun shining *without love* like a profound song. A bird sang in a cage hanging at a window. Then I experienced all the mystery that drives men to create certain things. And the creations seemed still more mysterious than the creators. It is futile to explain certain things scientifically, nothing is achieved. The palace was as I had imagined it. I had a presentiment that this was the way it must be, that it could not be different. An invisible link ties things together, and at that moment it seemed to me that I had already seen this palace, or that this palace had once, somewhere, already existed. Why are these round windows an enigma? Why are they—and can only be—French? They have a strange expression. Something altogether superficial like the smile of a child who does not know why he smiles; or something ferocious, like a chest pierced by a sword, or like the wound produced by a sword. And then more than ever I felt that everything was inevitably there, but for no reason and without any meaning.

SURREALIST METAPHOR

How far can metaphor be extended? If all naming is metaphorical, moving toward the unknown by analogies with what is already known and safely named, perhaps a poet can suggest new realities by metaphorically linking unusual or incompatible things. The surrealist movement in art and literature is based on disrupting our habitual sense of reality so as to allow us glimpses of a deeper reality. Consider, for instance, what the surrealist poet André Breton (1896–1966) said about the images that combine to make metaphors:

> The countless kinds of Surrealist images would require a classification which I do not intend to make today. To group them according to their particular affinities would lead me far afield; what I basically want to mention is their common virtue. For me, their greatest virtue, I must confess, is the one that is arbitrary to the highest degree, the one that takes the longest time to translate into practical language, either because it contains an immense amount of seeming contradiction or because one of its terms is strangely concealed; or because, presenting itself as something sensational, it seems to end weakly (because it suddenly closes the angle of its compass), or because it derives from itself a ridiculous *formal* justification, or because it is of a hallucinatory kind, or because it very naturally gives to the abstract the mask of the concrete, or the opposite, or because it implies the negation of some elementary physical property, or because it provokes laughter.

If a balanced view of poetic metaphor insists on images that are combined in a way that is both surprising *and* appropriate, the surrealists take an extreme position in favor of the surprising combination, as in the following lines from one of Breton's poems:

. . . there go the fuses blown again
Here's the squid with his elbows on the window sill
And here wondering where to unfold his sparkling sewer grill
Is the clown of the eclipse in his white outfit
Eyes in his pocket. . . .

The impossibility of a squid leaning elbows (of all things) on a window sill is perhaps the most striking thing about this language. Its parts just won't go together to form a "normal" image. But the possibility that this bizarre image is a metaphor for something else is both tantalizing and a little threatening. Is there some particular meaning that we are intended to decode? And are we stupid if we can't discover it?

Above all, the surrealists want to disabuse their readers of the notion that they have hidden a correct meaning behind every metaphor. They have allowed their unconscious minds to interrupt the logic of consciousness. If meanings have been generated, the surrealist poet and his or her readers will have to look for them together. Breton hopes that his images will have a high degree of arbitrariness, that they will require time and effort to be translated into "practical language." Notice that he does not say that they should be impossible to translate, only that they should offer resistance. Breton would like the reader's unconscious to enter into the process of translation. He wants us to play with his images until we begin to see how to connect and interpret them. Try, for instance, playing with the "clown of the eclipse" until you generate some reason for him to have "eyes in his pocket."

FOR DISCUSSION AND WRITING: COMPARING TERMS:
FREUD AND BRETON

At this point it will be helpful for you to compare what Breton said in the previous quotation (p. 83) with Freud's description of the dream-work quoted in the previous section (pp. 75–77). If we reduce Breton's statement to its purely descriptive notions, we get something like this:

1. Apparent contradiction
2. Hidden term
3. Concrete for abstract
4. Abstract for concrete
5. Negation of physical property

This is not the same as Freud's list, by any means, but there is some overlap. Discuss these five processes until you understand what is meant by each one, and then compare this list with Freud's description of the dream-work. Note both the common features and the differences. This development of your analytical terminology will help you in doing the assignments to come.

FOR DISCUSSION AND WRITING: CONSTRUCTING AND ANALYZING A RANDOM ASSEMBLAGE

In the following text André Breton offers us a brief description of surrealist methods, followed by an exemplary poem made up of pieces cut from newspaper headlines. We ask you to do three things with "Poem":

1. Read it, noticing the ways that it comes close to making ordinary prose sense for a line or so and then deviates into the impossible or the nonsensical.

2. Get together with some friends or classmates and a few newspapers and see if you can produce a poem as good as this one. You can use whole headlines or partial headlines, but remember, this is not a merely random enterprise. You must tease the reader with near approaches to normal syntax and meaning, and surprise that reader by strange deviations from the normal. When you are finished, compare and discuss your poems with others. Try to determine which parts of which poems are most successful and why this is the case.

3. Consider the way surrealist images are like and unlike other metaphors. Try to decide what they have to teach us about poetic metaphor in general.

Surrealist Methods

André Breton

Surrealist methods demand to be heard. Everything is valid when it comes to obtaining the desired suddenness from certain associations. The pieces of paper that Picasso and Braque insert into their work have the same value as the introduction of a platitude into a literary analysis of the most rigorous sort. It is even permissible to entitle POEM what we get from the most random assemblage possible (observe, if you will, the syntax) of headlines and scraps of headlines cut out of the newspapers:

POEM

A burst of laughter
of sapphire in the island of Ceylon

The most beautiful straws
HAVE A FADED COLOR
UNDER THE LOCKS

on an isolated farm
FROM DAY TO DAY
the pleasant
grows worse

A carriage road
takes you to the edge of the unknown

coffee
preaches for its saint
THE DAILY ARTISAN OF YOUR BEAUTY
MADAM,

a pair
# of silk stockings
is not

A leap into space
A STAG

Love above all
Everything could be worked out so well
PARIS IS A BIG VILLAGE

Watch out for
the fire that covers
THE PRAYER
of fair weather

Know that
The ultraviolet rays
have finished their task
short and sweet

THE FIRST WHITE PAPER
OF CHANCE
Red will be

The wandering singer
WHERE IS HE?
in memory
in his house
AT THE SUITORS' BALL

I do
as I dance
What people did, what they're going to do

POETIC USES OF METAPHOR

FOR DISCUSSION AND WRITING: ANALYZING
THE WORK OF METAPHORS IN POETRY

What follows is a mini-anthology of poems selected because each of them is short and makes some interesting use of metaphor. Some of them are about the poetic process and about metaphor in particular. Others are about other things but employ similes or other kinds of metaphoric processes as a way of presenting their ideas.

If you have attended to the previous work on metaphor in this book, you should be in a position now to write an essay on the way metaphors work in poetry. We ask you, then, to write such an essay, using the following mini-anthology as your source for examples. You are not being asked to write an interpretation of each poem, but to draw from the poems certain metaphors to illustrate your discussion.

In writing your essay you should consider some of the following matters:

1. Why do poets use metaphors so frequently?
2. What does the use of metaphor have to do with the "difficulty" of poetry?
3. What does the use of metaphor have to do with the pleasures of poetry?
4. What makes an interesting metaphor interesting?
5. How do metaphors contribute to the power of poetry to move us emotionally or to amuse us?

In the course of your discussion, you should consider some specific metaphors drawn from these poems, exploring and explaining the meanings generated by each metaphor. In the case of an extended comparison, you should examine the way that the details of description apply to both of the things being compared. For instance, Robert Francis's poem "Pitcher" describes what a baseball pitcher does in such a way that it becomes a metaphor for what a poet does. The result changes our way of thinking about both activities: pitching and writing poetry. But the effectiveness of the poem depends upon the way that the details of the description support both ends of the comparison, and that is the sort of analysis that you should make in your essay. To make it, of course, you have to understand that the comparison is being made—that the description is not just description but metaphoric. You need to be an alert reader and to read each poem over until you have a real grip on its meanings. If the poet is the pitcher, you are the batter—but in this case you can make him keep on throwing the same pitch until you really get ahold of it.

Remember, you are not being asked to go through each poem and write about what it means. You are being asked to draw from the poems the material that will enable you to produce your own essay on why and how poets use metaphor.

Doesn't he realize

Doesn't he realize
that I am not
like the swaying kelp
in the surf,
where the seaweed gatherer   5
can come as often as he wants.

Ono no Komachi

Translated from Japanese by
K. Rexroth and I. Atsumi

The Flea

Mark but this flea, and mark in this
How little that which thou deny'st me is;
It sucked me first, and now sucks thee,

And in this flea our two bloods mingled be;
Thou know'st that this cannot be said   5
A sin, nor shame, nor loss of maidenhead,
    Yet this enjoys before it woo,
    And pampered swells with one blood made of two,
    And this, alas, is more than we would do.

Oh stay, three lives in one flea spare,   10
Where we almost, yea more than married are.
This flea is you and I, and this
Our marriage bed, and marriage temple is;
Though parents grudge, and you, we're met
And cloistered in these living walls of jet.   15
    Though use make you apt to kill me,
    Let not to that, self-murder added be,
    And sacrilege, three sins in killing three.

Cruel and sudden, hast thou since
Purpled thy nail in blood of innocence?   20
Wherein could this flea guilty be,
Except in that drop which it sucked from thee?
Yet thou triumph'st, and say'st that thou
Find'st not thyself, nor me, the weaker now;
    'Tis true; then learn how false, fears be;   25
    Just so much honor, when thou yield'st to me,
    Will waste, as this flea's death took life from thee.

John Donne

Word

The word bites like a fish.
Shall I throw it back free
Arrowing to that sea
Where thoughts lash tail and fin?
Or shall I pull it in   5
To rhyme upon a dish?

Stephen Spender

Pitcher

His art is eccentricity, his aim
How not to hit the mark he seems to aim at,

His passion how to avoid the obvious,
His technique how to vary the avoidance.

The others throw to be comprehended. He   5
Throws to be a moment misunderstood.

Yet not too much. Not errant, arrant, wild,
But every seeming aberration willed.

Not to, yet still, still to communicate
Making the batter understand too late.   10

Robert Francis

you fit into me

you fit into me
like a hook into an eye

a fish hook
an open eye

Margaret Atwood

You don't understand me,

you gulp, a frog suddenly on my dinner
plate hopping through the buttered noodles
blinking cold eyes of reproach.

I can interpret the language of your hands
warm under calluses. Your body speaks into mine.   5
We are native users of the same jangling American.

A casual remark lets ants loose in your ears.
The wrong tone drips ice water on your nape.
Waiting I finger the bruise-colored why.

Look, I can't study you like the engine   10
of an old car coughing into silence on wet mornings.
Can't read the convolutions of your brain through the skull.

You want hieroglyphs at the corners of your squint decoded
in perfect silence that folds into your ribbed side,
a woman of soft accordion-pleated wool with healer's hands.   15

I don't understand you: you are not a book,
an argument, a theory. Speak to me.
I listen, and I speak back.

Marge Piercy

Moving in Winter

Their life, collapsed like unplayed cards,
is carried piecemeal through the snow:
Headboard and footboard now, the bed
where she has lain desiring him
where overhead his sleep will build   5

its canopy to smother her once more;
their table, by four elbows worn
evening after evening while the wax runs down;
mirrors grey with reflecting them,
bureaus coffining from the cold   10
things that can shuffle in a drawer,
carpets rolled up around those echoes
which, shaken out, take wing and breed
new altercations, the old silences.

Adrienne Rich

Because I could not stop for Death

Because I could not stop for Death —
He kindly stopped for me —
The Carriage held but just Ourselves —
And Immortality.

We slowly drove — He knew no haste   5
And I had put away
My labor and my leisure too,
For His Civility —

We passed the School, where Children strove
At Recess — in the Ring —   10
We passed the Fields of Gazing Grain —
We passed the Setting Sun —

Or rather — He passed Us —
The Dews drew quivering and chill —
For only Gossamer, my Gown —   15
My Tippet — only Tulle —

We paused before a House that seemed
A Swelling of the Ground —
The Roof was scarcely visible —
The Cornice — in the Ground —   20

Since then — 'tis Centuries — and yet
Feels shorter than the Day
I first surmised the Horses' Heads
Were toward Eternity —

Emily Dickinson

Dolor

I have known the inexorable sadness of pencils,
Neat in their boxes, dolor of pad and paper-weight,
All the misery of manilla folders and mucilage,

Desolation in immaculate public places,
Lonely reception room, lavatory, switchboard,   5
The unalterable pathos of basin and pitcher,
Ritual of multigraph, paper-clip, comma,
Endless duplication of lives and objects.
And I have seen dust from the walls of institutions,
Finer than flour, alive, more dangerous than silica,   10
Sift, almost invisible, through long afternoons of tedium,
Dropping a fine film on nails and delicate eyebrows,
Glazing the pale hair, the duplicate grey standard faces.

Theodore Roethke

Coming to the Morning

You make me remember all of the elements
the sea remembering all of its waves

in each of the waves there was always a sky made of water
and an eye that looked once

there was the shape of one mountain   5
and a blood kinship with rain

and the air for touch and for the tongue
at the speed of light

in which the world is made
from a single star   10

and our ears
are formed of the sea as we listen

W. S. Merwin

Spring

To what purpose, April, do you return again?
Beauty is not enough.
You can no longer quiet me with the redness
Of little leaves opening stickily.
I know what I know.   5
The sun is hot on my neck as I observe
The spikes of the crocus.
The smell of the earth is good.
It is apparent that there is no death.
But what does that signify?   10
Not only under ground are the brains of men
Eaten by maggots.
Life in itself
Is nothing,

An empty cup, a flight of uncarpeted stairs.   15
It is not enough that yearly, down this hill,
April
Comes like an idiot, babbling and strewing flowers.

Edna St. Vincent Millay

Thirteen Ways of Looking at a Blackbird

I
Among twenty snowy mountains,
The only moving thing
Was the eye of the blackbird.

II
I was of three minds,
Like a tree   5
In which there are three blackbirds.

III
The blackbird whirled in the autumn winds.
It was a small part of the pantomime.

IV
A man and a woman
Are one.   10
A man and a woman and a blackbird
Are one.

V
I do not know which to prefer,
The beauty of inflections
Or the beauty of innuendoes,   15
The blackbird whistling
Or just after.

VI
Icicles filled the long window
With barbaric glass.
The shadow of the blackbird   20
Crossed it, to and fro.
The mood
Traced in the shadow
An indecipherable cause.

VII
O thin men of Haddam,   25
Why do you imagine golden birds?
Do you not see how the blackbird
Walks around the feet
Of the women about you?

VIII

I know noble accents   30
And lucid, inescapable rhythms;
But I know, too,
That the blackbird is involved
In what I know.

IX

When the blackbird flew out of sight,   35
It marked the edge
Of one of many circles.

X

At the sight of blackbirds
Flying in a green light,
Even the bawds of euphony   40
Would cry out sharply.

XI

He rode over Connecticut
In a glass coach.
Once, a fear pierced him,
In that he mistook   45
The shadow of his equipage
For blackbirds.

XII

The river is moving.
The blackbird must be flying.

XIII

It was evening all afternoon.   50
It was snowing
And it was going to snow.
The blackbird sat
In the cedar-limbs.

Wallace Stevens

METAPHOR AS A BASIS FOR THOUGHT

In the last section we considered metaphor as a way of structuring poetry. Here we will be looking not only at metaphor as a way of structuring prose but also at the ways in which metaphor structures our thinking. How this structuring is revealed in our everyday language has been of primary interest to linguists George Lakoff and Mark Johnson. The material presented here is from their book *Metaphors We Live By*.

Concepts We Live By

George Lakoff and Mark Johnson

Metaphor is for most people a device of the poetic imagination and the rhetorical flourish — a matter of extraordinary rather than ordinary language. Moreover, metaphor is typically viewed as characteristic of language alone, a matter of words rather than thought or action. For this reason, most people think they can get along perfectly well without metaphor. We have found, on the contrary, that metaphor is pervasive in everyday life, not just in language but in thought and action. Our ordinary conceptual system, in terms of which we both think and act, is fundamentally metaphorical in nature.

The concepts that govern our thought are not just matters of the intellect. They also govern our everyday functioning, down to the most mundane details. Our concepts structure what we perceive, how we get around in the world, and how we relate to other people. Our conceptual system thus plays a central role in defining our everyday realities. If we are right in suggesting that our conceptual system is largely metaphorical, then the way we think, what we experience, and what we do every day is very much a matter of metaphor.

But our conceptual system is not something we are normally aware of. In most of the little things we do every day, we simply think and act more or less automatically along certain lines. Just what these lines are is by no means obvious. One way to find out is by looking at language. Since communication is based on the same conceptual system that we use in thinking and acting, language is an important source of evidence for what that system is like.

Primarily on the basis of linguistic evidence, we have found that most of our ordinary conceptual system is metaphorical in nature. And we have found a way to begin to identify in detail just what the metaphors are that structure how we perceive, how we think, and what we do.

To give some idea of what it could mean for a concept to be metaphorical and for such a concept to structure an everyday activity, let us start with the concept ARGUMENT and the conceptual metaphor ARGUMENT IS WAR. This metaphor is reflected in our everyday language by a wide variety of expressions:

Argument Is War

Your claims are *indefensible*.
He *attacked every weak point* in my argument.
His criticisms were *right on target*.
I *demolished* his argument.
I've never *won* an argument with him.
You disagree? Okay, *shoot!*
If you use that *strategy*, he'll *wipe you out*.
He *shot down* all of my arguments.

It is important to see that we don't just *talk* about arguments in terms of   6
war. We can actually win or lose arguments. We see the person we are arguing
with as an opponent. We attack his positions and we defend our own. We gain
and lose ground. We plan and use strategies. If we find a position indefensible,
we can abandon it and take a new line of attack. Many of the things we *do*
in arguing are partially structured by the concept of war. Though there is no
physical battle, there is a verbal battle, and the structure of an argument—
attack, defense, counterattack, etc.—reflects this. It is in this sense that the
ARGUMENT IS WAR metaphor is one that we live by in this culture; it structures the actions we perform in arguing.

Try to imagine a culture where arguments are not viewed in terms of war,   7
where no one wins or loses, where there is no sense of attacking or defending, gaining or losing ground. Imagine a culture where an argument is viewed
as a dance, the participants are seen as performers, and the goal is to perform
in a balanced and aesthetically pleasing way. In such a culture, people would
view arguments differently, experience them differently, carry them out differently, and talk about them differently. But *we* would probably not view
them as arguing at all: they would simply be doing something different. It
would seem strange even to call what they were doing "arguing." Perhaps the
most neutral way of describing this difference between their culture and ours
would be to say that we have a discourse form structured in terms of battle
and they have one structured in terms of dance.

This is an example of what it means for a metaphorical concept, namely,   8
ARGUMENT IS WAR, to structure (at least in part) what we do and how we
understand what we are doing when we argue. *The essence of metaphor is understanding and experiencing one kind of thing in terms of another.* It is not
that arguments are a subspecies of war. Arguments and wars are different
kinds of things—verbal discourse and armed conflict—and the actions performed are different kinds of actions. But ARGUMENT is partially structured,
understood, performed, and talked about in terms of WAR. The concept is
metaphorically structured, the activity is metaphorically structured, and,
consequently, the language is metaphorically structured.

Moreover, this is the *ordinary* way of having an argument and talking   9
about one. The normal way for us to talk about attacking a position is to use
the words "attack a position." Our conventional ways of talking about arguments presuppose a metaphor we are hardly ever conscious of. The metaphor
is not merely in the words we use—it is in our very concept of an argument.
The language of argument is not poetic, fanciful, or rhetorical; it is literal. We
talk about arguments that way because we conceive of them that way—and
we act according to the way we conceive of things.

Some Further Examples

We have been claiming that metaphors partially structure our everyday   10
concepts and that this structure is reflected in our literal language. Before we
can get an overall picture of the philosophical implications of these claims,
we need a few more examples. In each of the ones that follow we give a meta-

phor and a list of ordinary expressions that are special cases of the metaphor. The English expressions are of two sorts: simple literal expressions and idioms that fit the metaphor and are part of the normal everyday way of talking about the subject.

Theories (and Arguments) Are Buildings

Is that the *foundation* for your theory? The theory needs more *support.* The argument is *shaky.* We need some more facts or the argument will *fall apart.* We need to *construct* a *strong* argument for that. I haven't figured out yet what the *form* of the argument will be. Here are some more facts to *shore up* the theory. We need to *buttress* the theory with *solid* arguments. The theory will *stand* or *fall* on the *strength* of that argument. The argument *collapsed.* They *exploded* his latest theory. We will show that theory to be without *foundation.* So far we have put together only the *framework* of the theory.

Ideas Are Food

What he said *left a bad taste in my mouth.* All this paper has in it are *raw facts, half-baked ideas,* and *warmed-over theories.* There are too many facts here for me to *digest* them all. I just can't *swallow* that claim. That argument *smells fishy.* Let me *stew* over that for a while. Now there's a theory you can really *sink your teeth into.* We need to let that idea *percolate* for a while. That's *food for thought.* He's a *voracious* reader. We don't need to *spoon-feed* our students. He *devoured* the book. Let's let that idea *simmer on the back burner* for a while. This is the *meaty* part of the paper. Let that idea *jell* for a while. That idea has been *fermenting* for years.

With respect to life and death IDEAS ARE ORGANISMS, either PEOPLE   11
or PLANTS.

Ideas Are People

The theory of relativity *gave birth to* an enormous number of ideas in physics. He is the *father* of modern biology. Whose *brain-child* was that? Look at what his ideas have *spawned.* Those ideas *died off* in the Middle Ages. His ideas will *live on* forever. Cognitive psychology is still in its *infancy.* That's an idea that ought to be *resurrected.* Where'd you *dig up* that idea? He *breathed new life into* that idea.

Ideas Are Plants

His ideas have finally come to *fruition.* That idea *died on the vine.* That's a *budding* theory. It will take years for that idea to *come to full flower.* He views chemistry as a mere *offshoot* of physics. Mathematics has many *branches.* The *seeds* of his great ideas were *planted* in his youth. She has a *fertile* imagination. Here's an idea that I'd like to *plant* in your mind. He has a *barren* mind.

Ideas Are Products

We're really *turning (churning, cranking, grinding) out* new ideas. We've *generated* a lot of ideas this week. He *produces* new ideas at an astounding rate. His *intellectual productivity* has decreased in recent years. We need to *take the rough edges off* that idea, *bone it down, smooth it out.* It's a rough idea; it needs to be *refined.*

Ideas Are Commodities

It's important how you *package* your ideas. He won't *buy* that. That idea just won't *sell.* There is always a *market* for good ideas. That's a *worthless* idea. He's been a source of *valuable* ideas. I wouldn't *give a plugged nickel for* that idea. Your ideas don't have a chance in the *intellectual marketplace.*

Ideas Are Resources

He *ran out of* ideas. Don't *waste* your thoughts on small projects. Let's *pool* our ideas. He's a *resourceful* man. We've *used up* all our ideas. That's a *useless* idea. That idea will *go a long way.*

Ideas Are Money

Let me put in my *two cents' worth.* He's *rich* in ideas. That book is a *treasure trove* of ideas. He has a *wealth* of ideas.

Ideas Are Cutting Instruments

That's an *incisive* idea. That *cuts right to the heart of* the matter. That was a *cutting* remark. He's *sharp.* He has a *razor* wit. He has a *keen* mind. She *cut* his argument *to ribbons.*

Ideas Are Fashions

That idea went *out of style* years ago. I hear sociobiology *is in* these days. Marxism is currently *fashionable* in western Europe. That idea is *old hat!* That's an *outdated* idea. What are the new *trends* in English criticism? *Old-fashioned* notions have no place in today's society. He keeps *up-to-date* by reading the New York Review of Books. Berkeley is a center of *avant-garde* thought. Semiotics has become quite *chic.* The idea of revolution is no longer *in vogue* in the United States. The transformational grammar *craze* hit the United States in the mid-sixties and has just made it to Europe.

Love Is a Physical Force
(Electromagnetic, Gravitational, etc.)

I could feel the *electricity* between us. There were *sparks.* I was *magnetically drawn* to her. They are uncontrollably *attracted* to each other. They *gravitated* to each other immediately. His whole life *revolves* around her. The *atmosphere* around them is always *charged.* There is incredible *energy* in their relationship. They lost their *momentum.*

Love Is a Patient

This is a *sick* relationship. They have a *strong, healthy* marriage. The marriage is *dead*—it can't be *revived*. Their marriage is *on the mend*. We're getting *back on our feet*. Their relationship is *in really good shape*. They've got a *listless* marriage. Their marriage is *on its last legs*. It's a *tired* affair.

Love Is Madness

I'm *crazy* about her. She *drives me out of my mind*. He constantly *raves* about her. He's gone *mad* over her. I'm just *wild* about Harry. I'm *insane* about her.

Love Is Magic

She *cast her spell* over me. The *magic* is gone. I was *spellbound*. She had me *hypnotized*. He has me *in a trance*. I was *entranced* by him. I'm *charmed* by her. She is *bewitching*.

Love Is War

He is known for his many rapid *conquests*. She *fought for* him, but his mistress *won out*. He *fled from* her *advances*. She *pursued* him *relentlessly*. He is slowly *gaining ground* with her. He *won* her hand in marriage. He *overpowered* her. She is *besieged* by suitors. He has to *fend* them *off*. He *enlisted the aid* of her friends. He *made an ally* of her mother. Theirs is a *misalliance* if I've ever seen one.

Vitality Is a Substance

She's *brimming* with vim and vigor. She's *overflowing* with vitality. He's *devoid* of energy. I don't *have* any energy *left* at the end of the day. I'm *drained*. That *took a lot out of* me.

Life Is a Container

I've had a *full* life. Life is *empty* for him. There's *not much left* for him *in* life. Her life is *crammed* with activities. *Get the most out of life*. His life *contained* a great deal of sorrow. Live your life *to the fullest*.

Life Is a Gambling Game

I'll *take my chances*. The *odds are against me*. I've got an *ace up my sleeve*. He's *holding all the aces*. It's a *toss-up*. If you *play your cards right*, you can do it. He *won big*. He's a real *loser*. Where is he when the *chips are down*? That's my *ace in the hole*. He's *bluffing*. The president is *playing it close to his vest*. Let's *up the ante*. Maybe we need to *sweeten the pot*. I think we should *stand pat*. That's *the luck of the draw*. Those are *high stakes*.

In this last group of examples we have a collection of what are called 12 "speech formulas," or "fixed-form expressions," or "phrasal lexical items."

These function in many ways like single words, and the language has thousands of them. In the examples given, a set of such phrasal lexical items is coherently structured by a single metaphorical concept. Although each of them is an instance of the LIFE IS A GAMBLING GAME metaphor, they are typically used to speak of life, not of gambling situations. They are normal ways of talking about life situations, just as using the word "construct" is a normal way of talking about theories. It is in this sense that we include them in what we have called literal expressions structured by metaphorical concepts. If you say "The odds are against us" or "We'll have to take our chances," you would not be viewed as speaking metaphorically but as using the normal everyday language appropriate to the situation. Nevertheless, your way of talking about, conceiving, and even experiencing your situation would be metaphorically structured.

The Partial Nature of Metaphorical Structuring

Up to this point we have described the systematic character of metaphorically defined concepts. Such concepts are understood in terms of a number of different metaphors (e.g., TIME IS MONEY, TIME IS A MOVING OBJECT, etc.). The metaphorical structuring of concepts is necessarily partial and is reflected in the lexicon of the language, including the phrasal lexicon, which contains fixed-form expressions such as "to be without foundation." Because concepts are metaphorically structured in a systematic way, e.g., THEORIES ARE BUILDINGS, it is possible for us to use expressions (*construct, foundation*) from one domain (BUILDINGS) to talk about corresponding concepts in the metaphorically defined domain (THEORIES). What *foundation*, for example, means in the metaphorically defined domain (THEORY) will depend on the details of how the metaphorical concept THEORIES ARE BUILDINGS is used to structure the concept THEORY. [13]

The parts of the concept BUILDING that are used to structure the concept THEORY are the foundation and the outer shell. The roof, internal rooms, staircases, and hallways are parts of a building not used as part of the concept THEORY. Thus the metaphor THEORIES ARE BUILDINGS has a "used" part (foundation and outer shell) and an "unused" part (rooms, staircases, etc.). Expressions such as *construct* and *foundation* are instances of the used part of such a metaphorical concept and are part of our ordinary literal language about theories. [14]

But what of the linguistic expressions that reflect the "unused" part of a metaphor like THEORIES ARE BUILDINGS? Here are four examples: [15]

His theory has thousands of little rooms and long, winding corridors.
His theories are Bauhaus in their pseudofunctional simplicity.
He prefers massive Gothic theories covered with gargoyles.
Complex theories usually have problems with the plumbing.

These sentences fall outside the domain of normal literal language and are part of what is usually called "figurative" or "imaginative" language. Thus, literal expressions ("he has constructed a theory") and imaginative expressions ("His theory is covered with gargoyles") can be instances of the same general metaphor (THEORIES ARE BUILDINGS).

Here we can distinguish three different subspecies of imaginative (or non- 16 literal) metaphor:

> Extensions of the used part of a metaphor, e.g., "These facts are the bricks and mortar of my theory." Here the outer shell of the building is referred to, whereas the THEORIES ARE BUILDINGS metaphor stops short of mentioning the materials used.

> Instances of the unused part of the literal metaphor, e.g., "His theory has thousands of little rooms and long, winding corridors."

> Instances of novel metaphor, that is, a metaphor not used to structure part of our normal conceptual system but as a new way of thinking about something, e.g., "Classical theories are patriarchs who father many children, most of whom fight incessantly." Each of these subspecies lies outside the *used* part of a metaphorical concept that structures our normal conceptual system.

We note in passing that all of the linguistic expressions we have given to 17 characterize general metaphorical concepts are figurative. Examples are TIME IS MONEY, TIME IS A MOVING OBJECT, CONTROL IS UP, IDEAS ARE FOOD, THEORIES ARE BUILDINGS, etc. None of these is literal. This is a consequence of the fact that only *part* of them is used to structure our normal concepts. Since they necessarily contain parts that are not used in our normal concepts, they go beyond the realm of the literal.

Each of the metaphorical expressions we have talked about so far (e.g., 18 the time *will come;* we *construct* a theory, *attack* an idea) is used within a whole system of metaphorical concepts—concepts that we constantly use in living and thinking. These expressions, like all other words and phrasal lexical items in the language, are fixed by convention. In addition to these cases, which are parts of whole metaphorical systems, there are idiosyncratic metaphorical expressions that stand alone and are not used systematically in our language or thought. These are well-known expressions like the *foot* of the mountain, a *head* of cabbage, the *leg* of a table, etc. These expressions are isolated instances of metaphorical concepts, where there is only one instance of a used part (or maybe two or three). Thus the *foot* of the mountain is the only used part of the metaphor A MOUNTAIN IS A PERSON. In normal discourse we do not speak of the *head, shoulders,* or *trunk* of a mountain, though in special contexts it is possible to construct novel metaphorical expressions based on these unused parts. In fact, there is an aspect of the metaphor A MOUNTAIN IS A PERSON in which mountain climbers will speak of the *shoulder* of a mountain (namely, a ridge near the top) and of *conquering, fighting,* and even *being killed by* a mountain. And there are cartoon conventions where mountains become animate and their peaks become heads. The point here is that there are metaphors, like A MOUNTAIN IS A PERSON, that are marginal in our culture and our language; their used part may consist of only one

conventionally fixed expression of the language, and they do not systematically interact with other metaphorical concepts because so little of them is
used. This makes them relatively uninteresting for our purposes but not completely so, since they can be extended to their unused part in coining novel
metaphorical expressions, making jokes, etc. And our ability to extend them
to unused parts indicates that, however marginal they are, they do exist.

Examples like the *foot* of the mountain are idiosyncratic, unsystematic,   19
and isolated. They do not interact with other metaphors, play no particularly
interesting role in our conceptual system, and hence are not metaphors that
we live by. The only signs of life they have is that they can be extended in
subcultures and that their unused portions serve as the basis for (relatively
uninteresting) novel metaphors. If any metaphorical expressions deserve to
be called "dead," it is these, though they do have a bare spark of life, in that
they are understood partly in terms of marginal metaphorical concepts like A
MOUNTAIN IS A PERSON.

It is important to distinguish these isolated and unsystematic cases from   20
the systematic metaphorical expressions we have been discussing. Expressions like *wasting time, attacking positions, going our separate ways*, etc., are
reflections of systematic metaphorical concepts that structure our actions and
thoughts. They are "alive" in the most fundamental sense: they are metaphors we live by. The fact that they are conventionally fixed within the lexicon of English makes them no less alive.

FOR DISCUSSION AND WRITING: USING METAPHORICAL CONCEPTS

1. Lakoff and Johnson begin by defining what they call *metaphorical concepts*. Exactly what do they mean by this expression? What is the difference between a metaphor and a metaphorical concept? Base your explanation on a discussion of the "further examples" presented in the text.

2. In paragraph 18 Lakoff and Johnson discuss the metaphor *foot of the
mountain*. Compare their discussion with Roger Brown's treatment of the
same metaphor. Sum up in your own words the points each essay makes
using this same example. Do these two views complement each other, or
are they in conflict at any point?

3. In Sylvia Plath's poem "Metaphors," we can find references to common
expressions such as "big as a house" and "big as an elephant." Find other
references to common metaphors in any of the other poems in this text.
What happens when a poet works with a common metaphorical concept? What role do the normally unused parts of such concepts play in
the construction of poetic metaphors?

4. In your local newspaper or in a national news or sports magazine, find
an editorial in which metaphor plays an important part, either because
many metaphorical expressions are used in it or because the whole piece
is based on one or more metaphorical concepts, or both. Write an essay

in which you discuss the way metaphor functions in your chosen editorial. That is, show how metaphors are presented to influence the reader's response or how metaphorical concepts have operated to structure the writer's thinking.

5. Take one of Lakoff and Johnson's examples of a metaphorical concept, such as "ideas are fashions" or "love is madness," and use it to structure a short essay in which you explore, through the examples given, the cultural attitude that is reflected there. Feel free to provide additional examples of your own.

METAPHORICAL CONCEPTS

Metaphorical concepts function in every aspect of life, from business to health. The following two selections will serve to illustrate some of the ways in which metaphorical thinking shapes our thought and our actions in areas that seem a long way from poetry, such as business and medicine. The first selection is an article that appeared in the financial section of the *New York Times*. It was written by a management consultant from a major business school and addressed to an audience of corporate executives and would-be executives. It illustrates the way a particular set of metaphorical concepts—drawn from sports—operates in the thinking of corporate America.

The second selection is by the cultural critic and writer Susan Sontag. It is taken from her book *AIDS and Its Metaphors*, in which she explores the ways in which certain metaphors of disease have operated to shape thinking about quite different matters—political affairs, for instance.

A New Game for Managers to Play
Robert W. Keidel

As the football season gradually gives way to basketball, corporate managers   1
would do well to consider the differences between these games. For just as football mirrors industrial structures of the past, basketball points the way to the corporate structure of the future.

It's the difference between the former chief executive officer of I.T.T.,   2
Harold Geneen, the master football coach who dictates his players' roles and actions, and Donald Burr, the People Express Airlines chief executive officer, who puts his players on the floor and lets them manage themselves.

Football is, metaphorically, a way of life in work today—the corporate   3
sport. This is reflected in the language many managers use:

"It's taken my staff and me a sizable chunk of time, but we now have a   4
solid game plan for the XYZ job. Jack, I want you to quarterback this thing
all the way into the end zone. Of course, a lot of it will be making the proper
assignments—getting the right people to run interference and the right ones
to run with the ball. But my main concern is that we avoid mistakes. No fum-
bles, no interceptions, no sacks, no penalties. I don't want us to have to play
catch-up; no two-minute drills at the end. I want the game plan executed exactly the way it's drawn. When we're done we want to look back with pride
at a win—and not have to Monday-morning-quarterback a loss."

Does this football language represent more than just a convenient short-   5
hand? Almost certainly it does, because the metaphors we use routinely are
the means by which we structure experience. Thus, football metaphors may
well reflect—and reinforce—underlying organizational dynamics. But football, despite its pervasiveness, is the wrong model for most corporations.

Consider the scenario above. Planning has been neatly separated from   6
implementation; those expected to carry out the game plan have had no part
in creating it. Also, the communication flow is one-way; from the head coach
(speaker) to the quarterback (Jack)—and, presumably, from the quarterback
to the other players. And the thrust of the message is risk-averse; the real
name of the game is control—minimizing mistakes. But perhaps most significant is the assumption of stability—that nothing will change to invalidate
the corporate game plan. "No surprises!" as Mr. Geneen likes to say.

Stability is a realistic assumption in football, even given the sport's enor-   7
mous complexity, because of the time available to coaches—between games
and between plays. A pro football game can very nearly be programmed. Carl
Peterson, formerly with the Philadelphia Eagles and now president of the United
States Football League's champions, the Baltimore Stars, has estimated that
managing a game is 75 percent preparation and only 25 percent adjustment.

Thus, football truly is the realm of the coach—the head coach, he who   8
calls the shots. (Most pro quarterbacks do not call their own plays.) As Bum
Phillips has said in tribute to the head coach of the Miami Dolphins, Don Shula,
"He can take his'n and beat your'n, or he can take your'n and beat his'n."

But football is not an appropriate model for most businesses precisely   9
because instability is an overwhelming fact of life. Market competition grows
even more spastic, product life-cycles shrink unimaginably and technology
courses on paths of its own.

In this milieu, corporate "players" simply cannot perform effectively if   10
they must wait for each play to be called for them, and remain in fixed positions—or in narrowly defined roles—like football players; increasingly, they
need to deploy themselves flexibly, in novel combinations.

Thirty years ago it may have been possible to regard core business func-   11
tions—R&D, manufacturing and marketing—as separate worlds, with little
need for interaction. R&D would design the product and then lob it over the
wall to manufacturing; manufacturing would make the product and lob it
over another wall to the customer.

No need to worry about problems that do not fit neatly into the standard   12
departments; these are inconsequential and infrequent. And when they do

arise, they are simply bumped up the hierarchy to senior management—the head coach and his staff.

In effect, performance is roughly the sum of the functions—just as a 13 football team's performance is the sum of the performances of its platoons—offense, defense and special teams. Clearly, this view of the corporation is anachronistic. Yet it remains all too common.

Business's "season" is changing, and a new metaphor is needed. While 14 football will continue to be a useful model for pursuing machinelike efficiency and consistency—that is, for minimizing redundancies, bottlenecks and errors—this design favors stability at the expense of change. Since now more than ever businesses must continuously innovate and adapt, a more promising model is basketball.

To begin with, basketball is too dynamic a sport to permit the rigid sep- 15 aration of planning and execution that characterizes football. Unlike football teams, basketball teams do not pause and regroup after each play. As the former star player and coach Bill Russell has noted, "Your game plan may be wiped out by what happens in the first minute of play." Success in basketball depends on the ability of the coach and players to plan and adjust while in motion. Such behavior requires all-around communication—just as basketball demands all-around passing, as opposed to football's linear sequence of "forward," one-way passing.

Basketball also puts a premium on generalist skills. Although different 16 players will assume somewhat different roles on the court, all must be able to dribble, pass, shoot, rebound and play defense. Everyone handles the ball—a far cry from what happens on the gridiron. Indeed, basketball is much more player-oriented than football—a sport in which players tend to be viewed as interchangeable parts.

If football is a risk-averse game, basketball is risk-accepting. In basket- 17 ball, change is seen as normal, not exceptional; hence, change is regarded more as the source of opportunities than of threats. Mr. Geneen has claimed that "Ninety-nine percent of all surprises in business are negative."

Mr. Geneen's perspective is classic football and is tenable in stable, "con- 18 trollable" environments. But such environments are becoming rare. The future increasingly belongs to managers like Mr. Burr or James Treybig, the founder of Tandem Computers, who thrive on change rather than flee from it.

We need fewer head coaches and more player-coaches, less scripted 19 teamwork and more spontaneous teamwork. We need to integrate planning and doing—managing and working—far more than we have to date. Are you playing yesterday's game—or tomorrow's?

FOR DISCUSSION AND WRITING: USING SPORTS METAPHORS

1. In paragraph 5, Keidel makes an important point about metaphor. Try to restate it in your own terms. What does he mean by *structure* in the expression "the means by which we structure experience"?

2. Keidel is arguing that corporate managers should replace one set of metaphors with another. Why do you suppose he doesn't suggest getting rid of metaphor altogether and thinking of business *as* business?

3. If you have ever played an organized sport, you know that coaches use metaphors. That is, they talk about sports in terms of something else. Discuss some of the metaphors you have encountered within the world of sports. If you have ever had a coach whose speech was memorable, try to describe what you remember about the way he or she spoke. A coach (who shall remain nameless here) of a college soccer team used to crack up his team by telling them to "pair up in three"—not a metaphor exactly, but a piece of almost surrealist speech. You must have encountered similar poetic phrases. Share them with your classmates—especially any notable uses of metaphor. Where do most sports metaphors come from?

4. Write an essay in which you describe any common aspect of life in terms of one or two sports. That is, begin with an idea of this order: "Marriage is more like tennis than like boxing." Then explore all the parallels and contrasts between your subject matter and the sport (or sports) you have chosen as the basis for your metaphors. Some functions of life that you might wish to consider are school, family, friendship, love, and work, but choose something that interests you and discuss it in terms of appropriate sporting metaphors.

From AIDS and Its Metaphors

Susan Sontag

Just as one might predict for a disease that is not yet fully understood as well   1
as extremely recalcitrant to treatment, the advent of this terrifying new disease, new at least in its epidemic form, has provided a large-scale occasion for the metaphorizing of illness.

Strictly speaking, AIDS—acquired immune deficiency syndrome—is   2
not the name of an illness at all. It is the name of a medical condition, whose consequences are a spectrum of illnesses. In contrast to syphilis and cancer, which provide prototypes for most of the images and metaphors attached to AIDS, the very definition of AIDS requires the presence of other illnesses, so-called opportunistic infections and malignancies. But though not in *that* sense a single disease, AIDS lends itself to being regarded as one—in part because, unlike cancer and like syphilis, it is thought to have a single cause.

AIDS has a dual metaphoric genealogy. As a micro-process, it is described   3
as cancer is: an invasion. When the focus is transmission of the disease, an older metaphor, reminiscent of syphilis, is invoked: pollution. (One gets it from the blood or sexual fluids of infected people or from contaminated blood products.) But the military metaphors used to describe AIDS have a somewhat different focus from those used in describing cancer. With cancer, the metaphor scants the issue of causality (still a murky topic in cancer research) and picks

up at the point at which rogue cells inside the body mutate, eventually moving out from an original site or organ to overrun other organs or systems—a domestic subversion. In the description of AIDS the enemy is what causes the disease, an infectious agent that comes from the outside:

> The invader is tiny, about one sixteen-thousandth the size of the head of a pin. . . . Scouts of the body's immune system, large cells called macrophages, sense the presence of the diminutive foreigner and promptly alert the immune system. It begins to mobilize an array of cells that, among other things, produce antibodies to deal with the threat. Single-mindedly, the AIDS virus ignores many of the blood cells in its path, evades the rapidly advancing defenders and homes in on the master coordinator of the immune system, a helper T cell. . . .

This is the language of political paranoia, with its characteristic distrust 4 of a pluralistic world. A defense system consisting of cells "that, among other things, produce antibodies to deal with the threat" is, predictably, no match for an invader who advances "single-mindedly." And the science-fiction flavor, already present in cancer talk, is even more pungent in accounts of AIDS— this one comes from *Time* magazine in late 1986—with infection described like the high-tech warfare for which we are being prepared (and inured) by the fantasies of our leaders and by video entertainments. In the era of Star Wars and Space Invaders, AIDS has proved an ideally comprehensible illness:

> On the surface of that cell, it finds a receptor into which one of its envelope proteins fits perfectly, like a key into a lock. Docking with the cell, the virus penetrates the cell membrane and is stripped of its protective shell in the process. . . .

Next the invader takes up permanent residence, by a form of alien takeover familiar in science-fiction narratives. The body's own cells *become* the invader. With the help of an enzyme the virus carries with it,

> the naked AIDS virus converts its RNA into . . . DNA, the master molecule of life. The molecule then penetrates the cell nucleus, inserts itself into a chromosome and takes over part of the cellular machinery, directing it to produce more AIDS viruses. Eventually, overcome by its alien product, the cell swells and dies, releasing a flood of new viruses to attack other cells. . . .

As viruses attack other cells, runs the metaphor, so "a host of opportunistic diseases, normally warded off by a healthy immune system, attacks the body," whose integrity and vigor have been sapped by the sheer replication of "alien product" that follows the collapse of its immunological defenses. "Gradually weakened by the onslaught, the AIDS victim dies, sometimes in months, but almost always within a few years of the first symptoms." Those who have not already succumbed are described as "under assault, showing the telltale symptoms of the disease," while millions of others "harbor the virus, vulnerable at any time to a final, all-out attack."

Cancer makes cells proliferate; in AIDS, cells die. Even as this original 5 model of AIDS (the mirror image of leukemia) has been altered, descriptions of how the virus does its work continue to echo the way the illness is perceived as infiltrating the society. "AIDS Virus Found to Hide in Cells, Eluding Detection by Normal Tests" was the headline of a recent front-page story in *The New York Times* announcing the discovery that the virus can "lurk" for years in the macrophages—disrupting their disease-fighting function without killing them, "even when the macrophages are filled almost to bursting with virus," and without producing antibodies, the chemicals the body makes in response to "invading agents" and whose presence has been regarded as an infallible marker of the syndrome.* That the virus isn't lethal for *all* the cells where it takes up residence, as is now thought, only increases the illness-foe's reputation for wiliness and invincibility.

What makes the viral assault so terrifying is that contamination, and 6 therefore vulnerability, is understood as permanent. Even if someone infected were never to develop any symptoms—that is, the infection remained, or could by medical intervention be rendered, inactive—the viral enemy would be forever within. In fact, so it is believed, it is just a matter of time before something awakens ("triggers") it, before the appearance of "the telltale symptoms." Like syphilis, known to generations of doctors as "the great masquerader," AIDS is a clinical construction, an inference. It takes its identity from the presence of *some* among a long, and lengthening, roster of symptoms (no one has everything that AIDS could be), symptoms which "mean" that what the patient has is this illness. The construction of the illness rests on the invention not only of AIDS as a clinical entity but of a kind of junior AIDS, called AIDS-related complex (ARC), to which people are assigned if they show "early" and often intermittent symptoms of immunological deficit such as fevers, weight loss, fungal infections, and swollen lymph glands. AIDS is progressive, a disease of time. Once a certain density of symptoms is attained, the course of the illness can be swift, and brings atrocious suffering. Besides the commonest "presenting" illnesses (some hitherto unusual, at least in a fatal form, such as a rare skin cancer and a rare form of pneumonia), a plethora of disabling, disfiguring, and humiliating symptoms make the AIDS patient steadily more infirm, helpless, and unable to control or take care of basic functions and needs.

*The larger role assigned to the macrophages—"to serve as a reservoir for the AIDS virus because the virus multiplies in them but does not kill them, as it kills T-4 cells"— is said to explain the not uncommon difficulty of finding infected T-4 lymphocytes in patients who have antibodies to the virus and symptoms of AIDS. (It is still assumed that antibodies will develop once the virus spreads to these "key target" cells.) Evidence of presently infected populations of cells has been as puzzlingly limited or uneven as the evidence of infection in the populations of human societies—puzzling, because of the conviction that the disease is everywhere, and must spread. "Doctors have estimated that as few as one in a million T-4 cells are infected, which led some to ask where the virus hides. . . ." Another resonant speculation, reported in the same article (*The New York Times*, June 7, 1988): "Infected macrophages can transmit the virus to other cells, possibly by touching the cells."

The sense in which AIDS is a slow disease makes it more like syphilis,   7
which is characterized in terms of "stages," than like cancer. Thinking in terms
of "stages" is essential to discourse about AIDS. Syphilis in its most dreaded form
is "tertiary syphilis," syphilis in its third stage. What is called AIDS is generally
understood as the last of three stages—the first of which is infection with a human immunodeficiency virus (HIV) and early evidence of inroads on the immune
system—with a long latency period between infection and the onset of the "telltale" symptoms. (Apparently not as long as syphilis, in which the latency period
between secondary and tertiary illness might be decades. But it is worth noting
that when syphilis first appeared in epidemic form in Europe at the end of the
fifteenth century, it was a rapid disease, of an unexplained virulence that is unknown today, in which death often occurred in the second stage, sometimes
within months or a few years.) Cancer *grows* slowly: it is not thought to be, for
a long time, latent. (A convincing account of a process in terms of "stages" seems
invariably to include the notion of a normative delay or halt in the process, such
as is supplied by the notion of latency.) True, a cancer is "staged." This is a principal tool of diagnosis, which means classifying it according to its gravity, determining how "advanced" it is. But it is mostly a spatial notion: that the cancer
advances through the body, traveling or migrating along predictable routes.
Cancer is first of all a disease of the body's geography, in contrast to syphilis and
AIDS, whose definition depends on constructing a temporal sequence of stages.

Syphilis is an affliction that didn't have to run its ghastly full course, to   8
paresis (as it did for Baudelaire and Maupassant and Jules de Goncourt), and
could and often did remain at the stage of nuisance, indignity (as it did for
Flaubert). The scourge was also a cliché, as Flaubert himself observed. "SYPHILIS.
Everybody has it, more or less" reads one entry in the *Dictionary of Accepted
Opinions,* his treasury of mid-nineteenth-century platitudes. And syphilis did
manage to acquire a darkly positive association in late-nineteenth- and early-
twentieth-century Europe, when a link was made between syphilis and heightened ("feverish") mental activity that parallels the connection made since the
era of the Romantic writers between pulmonary tuberculosis and heightened
emotional activity. As if in honor of all the notable writers and artists who
ended their lives in syphilitic witlessness, it came to be believed that the brain
lesions of neurosyphilis might actually inspire original thought or art. Thomas
Mann, whose fiction is a storehouse of early-twentieth-century disease myths,
makes this notion of syphilis as muse central to his *Doctor Faustus,* with its protagonist a great composer whose voluntarily contracted syphilis—the Devil
guarantees that the infection will be limited to the central nervous system—
confers on him twenty-four years of incandescent creativity. E. M. Cioran recalls how, in Romania in the late 1920s, syphilis-envy figured in his adolescent
expectations of literary glory: he would discover that he had contracted syphilis,
be rewarded with several hyperproductive years of genius, then collapse into
madness. This romanticizing of the dementia characteristic of neurosyphilis
was the forerunner of the much more persistent fantasy in this century about
mental illness as a source of artistic creativity or spiritual originality. But with
AIDS—though dementia is also a common, late symptom—no compensatory
mythology has arisen, or seems likely to arise. AIDS, like cancer, does not allow

romanticizing or sentimentalizing, perhaps because its association with death is too powerful. In Krzysztof Zanussi's film *Spiral* (1978), the most truthful account I know of anger at dying, the protagonist's illness is never specified; therefore, it *has* to be cancer. For several generations now, the generic idea of death has been a death from cancer, and a cancer death is experienced as a generic defeat. Now the generic rebuke to life and to hope is AIDS. . . .

"Plague" is the principal metaphor by which the AIDS epidemic is un- 9 derstood. And because of AIDS, the popular misidentification of cancer as an epidemic, even a plague, seems to be receding: AIDS has banalized cancer.

Plague, from the Latin *plaga* (stroke, wound), has long been used metaphor- 10 ically as the highest standard of collective calamity, evil, scourge — Procopius, in his masterpiece of calumny, *The Secret History,* called the Emperor Justinian worse than the plague ("fewer escaped") — as well as being a general name for many frightening diseases. Although the disease to which the word is permanently affixed produced the most lethal of recorded epidemics, being experienced as a pitiless slayer is not necessary for a disease to be regarded as plague-like. Leprosy, very rarely fatal now, was not much more so when at its greatest epidemic strength, between about 1050 and 1350. And syphilis has been regarded as a plague — Blake speaks of "the youthful Harlot's curse" that "blights with plagues the Marriage hearse" — not because it killed often, but because it was disgracing, disempowering, disgusting.

Plagues are invariably regarded as judgments on society, and the meta- 11 phoric inflation of AIDS into such a judgment also accustoms people to the inevitability of global spread. This is a traditional use of sexually transmitted diseases: to be described as punishments not just of individuals but of a group ("generall licentiousnes"). Not only venereal diseases have been used in this way, to identify transgressing or vicious populations. Interpreting any catastrophic epidemic as a sign of moral laxity or political decline was as common until the later part of the last century as associating dreaded diseases with foreignness. (Or with despised and feared minorities.) And the assignment of fault is not contradicted by cases that do not fit. The Methodist preachers in England who connected the cholera epidemic of 1832 with drunkenness (the temperance movement was just starting) were not understood to be claiming that *everybody* who got cholera was a drunkard: there is always room for "innocent victims" (children, young women). Tuberculosis, in its identity as a disease of the poor (rather than of the "sensitive"), was also linked by late-nineteenth-century reformers to alcoholism. Responses to illnesses associated with sinners and the poor invariably recommended the adoption of middle-class values: the regular habits, productivity, and emotional self-control to which drunkenness was thought the chief impediment.*

---

*According to the more comprehensive diagnosis favored by secular reformers, cholera was the result of poor diet and "indulgence in irregular habits." Officials of the Central Board of Health in London warned that there were no specific treatments for the disease, and advised paying attention to fresh air and cleanliness, though "the true preventatives are a healthy body and a cheerful, unruffled mind." Quoted in R. J. Morris, *Cholera 1832* (1976).

Health itself was eventually identified with these values, which were religious as well as mercantile, health being evidence of virtue as disease was of depravity. The dictum that cleanliness is next to godliness is to be taken quite literally. The succession of cholera epidemics in the nineteenth century shows a steady waning of religious interpretations of the disease; more precisely, these increasingly coexisted with other explanations. Although, by the time of the epidemic of 1866, cholera was commonly understood not simply as a divine punishment but as the consequence of remediable defects of sanitation, it was still regarded as the scourge of the sinful. A writer in *The New York Times* declared (April 22, 1866): "Cholera is especially the punishment of neglect of sanitary laws; it is the curse of the dirty, the intemperate, and the degraded."*

That it now seems unimaginable for cholera or a similar disease to be re-   12
garded in this way signifies not a lessened capacity to moralize about diseases but only a change in the kind of illnesses that are used didactically. Cholera was perhaps the last major epidemic disease fully qualifying for plague status for almost a century. (I mean cholera as a European and American, therefore a nineteenth-century, disease; until 1817 there had never been a cholera epidemic outside the Far East.) Influenza, which would seem more plague-like than any other epidemic in this century if loss of life were the main criterion, and which struck as suddenly as cholera and killed as quickly, usually in a few days, was never viewed metaphorically as a plague. Nor was a more recent epidemic, polio. One reason why plague notions were not invoked is that these epidemics did not have enough of the attributes perennially ascribed to plagues. (For instance, polio was construed as typically a disease of children—of the innocent.) The more important reason is that there has been a shift in the focus of the moralistic exploitation of illness. This shift, to diseases that can be interpreted as judgments on the individual, makes it harder to use epidemic disease as such. For a long time cancer was the illness that best fitted this secular culture's need to blame and punish and censor through the imagery of disease. Cancer was a disease of an individual, and understood as the result not of an action but rather of a failure to act (to be prudent, to exert proper self-control, or to be properly expressive). In the twentieth century it has become almost impossible to moralize about epidemics—except those which are transmitted sexually. . . .

The persistence of the belief that illness reveals, and is a punishment for,   13
moral laxity or turpitude can be seen in another way, by noting the persistence of descriptions of disorder or corruption as a disease. So indispensable has been the plague metaphor in bringing summary judgments about social crisis that its use hardly abated during the era when collective diseases were no longer treated so moralistically—the time between the influenza and encephalitis pandemics of the early and mid-1920s and the acknowledgment of a new, mysterious epidemic illness in the early 1980s—and when great infectious epidemics were so often and confidently proclaimed a thing of the

*Quoted in Charles E. Rosenberg, *The Cholera Years: The United States in 1832, 1849, and 1866* (1962).

past.* The plague metaphor was common in the 1930s as a synonym for social and psychic catastrophe. Evocations of plague of this type usually go with rant, with antiliberal attitudes: think of Artaud on theatre and plague, of Wilhelm Reich on "emotional plague." And such a generic "diagnosis" necessarily promotes antihistorical thinking. A theodicy as well as a demonology, it not only stipulates something emblematic of evil but makes this the bearer of a rough, terrible justice. In Karel Čapek's *The White Plague* (1937), the loathsome pestilence that has appeared in a state where fascism has come to power afflicts only those over the age of forty, those who could be held morally responsible.

Written on the eve of the Nazi takeover of Czechoslovakia, Čapek's alle- 14 gorical play is something of an anomaly—the use of the plague metaphor to convey the menace of what is defined as barbaric by a mainstream European liberal. The play's mysterious, grisly malady is something like leprosy, a rapid, invariably fatal leprosy that is supposed to have come, of course, from Asia. But Čapek is not interested in identifying political evil with the incursion of the foreign. He scores his didactic points by focusing not on the disease itself but on the management of information about it by scientists, journalists, and politicians. The most famous specialist in the disease harangues a reporter ("The disease of the hour, you might say. A good five million have died of it to date, twenty million have it and at least three times as many are going about their business, blithely unaware of the marble-like, marble-sized spots on their bodies"); chides a fellow doctor for using the popular terms, "the white plague" and "Peking leprosy," instead of the scientific name, "the Cheng Syndrome"; fantasizes about how his clinic's work on identifying the new virus and finding a cure ("every clinic in the world has an intensive research program") will add to the prestige of science and win a Nobel Prize for its discoverer; revels in hyperbole when it is thought a cure has been found ("it was the most dangerous disease in all history, worse than the bubonic plague"); and outlines plans for sending those with symptoms to well-guarded detention camps ("Given that every carrier of the disease is a potential spreader of the disease, we *must* protect the uncontaminated from the contaminated. All sentimentality in this regard is fatal and therefore criminal"). However cartoonish Čapek's ironies may seem, they are a not improbable sketch of catastrophe (medical, ecological) as a managed public event in modern mass society. And however conventionally he deploys the plague metaphor, as an agency of retribution (in the end the plague strikes down the dictator himself), Čapek's feel for public relations leads him to make explicit in the play the understanding of disease *as* a metaphor. The eminent doctor declares the accomplishments of science to be as nothing compared with the merits of the dictator, about to launch a war, "who has averted a far worse scourge: the

---

*As recently as 1983, the historian William H. McNeill, author of *Plagues and Peoples*, started his review of a new history of the Black Death by asserting: "One of the things that separate us from our ancestors and make contemporary experience profoundly different from that of other ages is the disappearance of epidemic disease as a serious factor in human life" (*The New York Review of Books*, July 21, 1983). The Eurocentric presumption of this and many similar statements hardly needs pointing out.

scourge of anarchy, the leprosy of corruption, the epidemic of barbaric liberty, the plague of social disintegration fatally sapping the organism of our nation."

Camus's *The Plague,* which appeared a decade later, is a far less literal 15 use of plague by another great European liberal, as subtle as Čapek's *The White Plague* is schematic. Camus's novel is not, as is sometimes said, a political allegory in which the outbreak of bubonic plague in a Mediterranean port city represents the Nazi occupation. This plague is not retributive. Camus is not protesting anything, not corruption or tyranny, not even mortality. The plague is no more or less than an exemplary event, the irruption of death that gives life its seriousness. His use of plague, more epitome than metaphor, is detached, stoic, aware—it is not about bringing judgment. But, as in Čapek's play, characters in Camus's novel declare how unthinkable it is to have a plague in the twentieth century . . . as if the belief that such a calamity could not happen, could not happen *anymore,* means that it must.

FOR DISCUSSION AND WRITING: ANALYZING METAPHOR AS DISEASE

1. Summarize in your own words the major points of Sontag's text.

2. According to Sontag, what are the major metaphors used to speak about AIDS?

3. As Sontag demonstrates, we not only speak of disease in metaphors drawn from other aspects of life, we also use metaphors *from* disease to speak of other things. What aspects of her discussion do you find most surprising, interesting, or controversial? What connections do you find between her essay and Lakoff and Johnson's view of metaphor?

4. Sontag's book *AIDS and Its Metaphors* was published in 1988. What changes, if any, have you noticed in metaphors used to discuss AIDS since the publication of her book? Consider metaphors used by those with AIDS as well as by those without it. You may want to look beyond such obvious sources as *Time* and *Newsweek* to discuss drama, fiction, poetry, essays, medical journalism, and AIDS-prevention literature. Write a short essay in which you discuss the metaphors used in one or more of your sources.

ARGUING WITH METAPHOR: ANALOGY AND IDEOLOGY

As we have seen, metaphor is a crucial element of language and thought. In particular, it functions powerfully in texts designed to argue a position or persuade a reader to adopt a particular attitude. The form of metaphor most common in argument is *analogy.*

Basic strategy in the use of analogy is to claim that situation X, which is under disputation, is like or analogous to situation Y, about which there is no dispute. In extreme forms, such arguments go beyond the assertion of likeness and insist on sameness. "Property," said a famous socialist thinker, "is theft." Other thinkers have asserted that everyone has a right to life, liberty, and property, making property a right. Calling it "theft" is a way of denying that it is a right and insisting that it is based on a wrong.

Less obvious and dramatic forms of analogy operate throughout our language and culture to structure our values unobtrusively. This kind of social construction is what we call *ideology*—beliefs and values that all of us assimilate as we grow up in a particular culture, speaking the language of that culture. In the essay that follows, Emily Martin, an anthropologist, looks into the way that ideology has operated in a scientific field that is supposedly protected from cultural assumptions by scientific objectivity.

For our purposes, it is especially interesting that she refers to folktales, films, and literary texts as other embodiments of the same cultural formulas. Two of the texts she mentions—either in the body of her essay or in the notes—are included in this volume: the folktale "Sleeping Beauty" or "Briar Rose," and the short story "Night-Sea Journey" by John Barth. We will refer back to Martin's essay when we come to those texts.

The Egg and the Sperm
How Science Has Constructed a Romance Based on Stereotypical Male-Female Roles

Emily Martin

The theory of the human body is always a part of a world-picture. . . . The theory of the human body is always a part of a fantasy.
—*James Hillman,* The Myth of Analysis[1]

As an anthropologist, I am intrigued by the possibility that culture shapes   1
how biological scientists describe what they discover about the natural world. If this were so, we would be learning about more than the natural world in high school biology class; we would be learning about cultural beliefs and practices as if they were part of nature. In the course of my research I real-

Portions of this article were presented as the 1987 Becker Lecture, Cornell University. I am grateful for the many suggestions and ideas I received on this occasion. For especially pertinent help with my arguments and data I thank Richard Cone, Kevin Whaley, Sharon Stephens, Barbara Duden, Susanne Kuechler, Lorna Rhodes, and Scott Gilbert. The article was strengthened and clarified by the comments of the anonymous *Signs* reviewers as well as the superb editorial skills of Amy Gage.
[1]James Hillman, *The Myth of Analysis* (Evanston, Ill.: Northwestern University Press, 1972), 220.

ized that the picture of egg and sperm drawn in popular as well as scientific accounts of reproductive biology relies on stereotypes central to our cultural definitions of male and female. The stereotypes imply not only that female biological processes are less worthy than their male counterparts but also that women are less worthy than men. Part of my goal in writing this article is to shine a bright light on the gender stereotypes hidden within the scientific language of biology. Exposed in such a light, I hope they will lose much of their power to harm us.

Egg and Sperm: A Scientific Fairy Tale

At a fundamental level, all major scientific textbooks depict male and female reproductive organs as systems for the production of valuable substances, such as eggs and sperm.[2] In the case of women, the monthly cycle is described as being designed to produce eggs and prepare a suitable place for them to be fertilized and grown — all to the end of making babies. But the enthusiasm ends there. By extolling the female cycle as a productive enterprise, menstruation must necessarily be viewed as a failure. Medical texts describe menstruation as the "debris" of the uterine lining, the result of necrosis, or death of tissue. The descriptions imply that a system has gone awry, making products of no use, not to specification, unsalable, wasted, scrap. An illustration in a widely used medical text shows menstruation as a chaotic disintegration of form, complementing the many texts that describe it as "ceasing," "dying," "losing," "denuding," "expelling."[3]

Male reproductive physiology is evaluated quite differently. One of the texts that sees menstruation as failed production employs a sort of breathless prose when it describes the maturation of sperm: "The mechanisms which guide the remarkable cellular transformation from spermatid to mature sperm remain uncertain. . . . Perhaps the most amazing characteristic of spermatogenesis is its sheer magnitude: the normal human male may manufacture several hundred million sperm per day."[4] In the classic text *Medical Physiology*, edited by Vernon Mountcastle, the male/female, productive/destructive comparison is more explicit: "Whereas the female *sheds* only a single gamete each month, the seminiferous tubules *produce* hundreds of millions of sperm each day" (emphasis mine).[5] The female author of another text marvels at the length of the microscopic seminiferous tubules, which, if uncoiled and placed end to end, "would span almost one-third of a mile!" She writes, "In an adult male these structures produce millions of sperm cells each day."

2

3

[2]The textbooks I consulted are the main ones used in classes for undergraduate premedical students or medical students (or those held on reserve in the library for these classes) during the past few years at Johns Hopkins University. These texts are widely used at other universities in the country as well.

[3]Arthur C. Guyton, *Physiology of the Human Body*, 6th ed. (Philadelphia: Saunders College Publishing, 1984), 624.

[4]Arthur J. Vander, James H. Sherman, and Dorothy S. Luciano, *Human Physiology: The Mechanisms of Body Function*, 3d ed. (New York: McGraw Hill, 1980), 483–84.

[5]Vernon B. Mountcastle, *Medical Physiology*, 14th ed. (London: Mosby, 1980), 2:1624.

Later she asks, "How is this feat accomplished?"[6] None of these texts expressed such intense enthusiasm for any female processes. It is surely no accident that the "remarkable" process of making sperm involves precisely what, in the medical view, menstruation does not: production of something deemed valuable.[7]

One could argue that menstruation and spermatogenesis are not analogous processes and, therefore, should not be expected to elicit the same kind of response. The proper female analogy to spermatogenesis, biologically, is ovulation. Yet ovulation does not merit enthusiasm in these texts either. Textbook descriptions stress that all of the ovarian follicles containing ova are already present at birth. Far from being *produced*, as sperm are, they merely sit on the shelf, slowly degenerating and aging like overstocked inventory: "At birth, normal human ovaries contain an estimated one million follicles [each], and no new ones appear after birth. Thus, in marked contrast to the male, the newborn female already has all the germ cells she will ever have. Only a few, perhaps 400, are destined to reach full maturity during her active productive life. All the others degenerate at some point in their development so that few, if any, remain by the time she reaches menopause at approximately 50 years of age."[8] Note the "marked contrast" that this description sets up between male and female: the male, who continuously produces fresh germ cells, and the female, who has stockpiled germ cells by birth and is faced with their degeneration.

Nor are the female organs spared such vivid descriptions. One scientist writes in a newspaper article that a woman's ovaries become old and worn out from ripening eggs every month, even though the woman herself is still relatively young: "When you look through a laparoscope . . . at an ovary that has been through hundreds of cycles, even in a superbly healthy American female, you see a scarred, battered organ."[9]

To avoid the negative connotations that some people associate with the female reproductive system, scientists could begin to describe male and female processes as homologous. They might credit females with "producing" mature ova one at a time, as they're needed each month, and describe males as having to face problems of degenerating germ cells. This degeneration would occur throughout life among spermatogonia, the undifferentiated germ cells in the testes that are the long-lived, dormant precursors of sperm.

But the texts have an almost dogged insistence on casting female processes in a negative light. The texts celebrate sperm production because it is continuous from puberty to senescence, while they portray egg production as inferior because it is finished at birth. This makes the female seem unproductive, but some texts

4

5

6

7

---

[6]Eldra Pearl Solomon, *Human Anatomy and Physiology* (New York: CBS College Publishing, 1983), 678.

[7]For elaboration, see Emily Martin, *The Woman in the Body: A Cultural Analysis of Reproduction* (Boston: Beacon, 1987), 27–53.

[8]Vander, Sherman, and Luciano, 568.

[9]Melvin Konner, "Childbearing and Age," *New York Times Magazine* (December 27, 1987), 22–23, esp. 22.

will also insist that it is she who is wasteful.[10] In a section heading for *Molecular Biology of the Cell*, a best-selling text, we are told that "Oogenesis is wasteful." The text goes on to emphasize that of the seven million oogonia, or egg germ cells, in the female embryo, most degenerate in the ovary. Of those that do go on to become oocytes, or eggs, many also degenerate, so that at birth only two million eggs remain in the ovaries. Degeneration continues throughout a woman's life: by puberty 300,000 eggs remain, and only a few are present by menopause. "During the 40 or so years of a woman's reproductive life, only 400 to 500 eggs will have been released," the authors write. "All the rest will have degenerated. It is still a mystery why so many eggs are formed only to die in the ovaries."[11]

The real mystery is why the male's vast production of sperm is not seen   8
as wasteful.[12] Assuming that a man "produces" 100 million (10^8) sperm per day (a conservative estimate) during an average reproductive life of sixty years, he would produce well over two trillion sperm in his lifetime. Assuming that a woman "ripens" one egg per lunar month, or thirteen per year, over the course of her forty-year reproductive life, she would total five hundred eggs in her lifetime. But the word "waste" implies an excess, too much produced. Assuming two or three offspring, for every baby a woman produces, she wastes only around two hundred eggs. For every baby a man produces, he wastes more than one trillion (10^{12}) sperm.

How is it that positive images are denied to the bodies of women? A look   9
at language—in this case, scientific language—provides the first clue. Take the egg and the sperm.[13] It is remarkable how "femininely" the egg behaves

[10]I have found but one exception to the opinion that the female is wasteful: "Smallpox being the nasty disease it is, one might expect nature to have designed antibody molecules with combining sites that specifically recognize the epitopes on smallpox virus. Nature differs from technology, however: it thinks nothing of wastefulness. (For example, rather than improving the chance that a spermatozoon will meet an egg cell, nature finds it easier to produce millions of spermatozoa.)" (Niels Kaj Jerne, "The Immune System," *Scientific American* 229, no. 1 [July 1973]: 53). Thanks to a *Signs* reviewer for bringing this reference to my attention.

[11]Bruce Alberts et al., *Molecular Biology of the Cell* (New York: Garland, 1983), 795.

[12]In her essay "Have Only Men Evolved?" (in *Discovering Reality: Feminist Perspectives on Epistemology, Metaphysics, Methodology, and Philosophy of Science*, ed. Sandra Harding and Merrill B. Hintikka [Dordrecht, The Netherlands: Reidel, 1983], 45–69, esp. 60–61), Ruth Hubbard points out that sociobiologists have said the female invests more energy than the male in the production of her large gametes, claiming that this explains why the female provides parental care. Hubbard questions whether it "really takes more 'energy' to generate the one or relatively few eggs than the large excess of sperms required to achieve fertilization." For further critique of how the greater size of eggs is interpreted in sociobiology, see Donna Haraway, "Investment Strategies for the Evolving Portfolio of Primate Females," in *Body/Politics*, ed. Mary Jacobus, Evelyn Fox Keller, and Sally Shuttleworth (New York: Routledge, 1990), 155–56.

[13]The sources I used for this article provide compelling information on interactions among sperm. Lack of space prevents me from taking up this theme here, but the elements include competition, hierarchy, and sacrifice. For a newspaper report, see Malcolm W. Browne, "Some Thoughts on Self Sacrifice," *New York Times* (July 5, 1988), C6. For a literary rendition, see John Barth, "Night-Sea Journey," in his *Lost in the Funhouse* (Garden City, N.Y.: Doubleday, 1968), 3–13.

and how "masculinely" the sperm.[14] The egg is seen as large and passive.[15] It does not *move* or *journey*, but passively "is transported," "is swept,"[16] or even "drifts"[17] along the fallopian tube. In utter contrast, sperm are small, "streamlined,"[18] and invariably active. They "deliver" their genes to the egg, "activate the developmental program of the egg,"[19] and have a "velocity" that is often remarked upon.[20] Their tails are "strong" and efficiently powered.[21] Together with the forces of ejaculation, they can "propel the semen into the deepest recesses of the vagina."[22] For this they need "energy," "fuel,"[23] so that with a "whiplashlike motion and strong lurches"[24] they can "burrow through the egg coat"[25] and "penetrate" it.[26]

At its extreme, the age-old relationship of the egg and the sperm takes on   10 a royal or religious patina. The egg coat, its protective barrier, is sometimes called its "vestments," a term usually reserved for sacred, religious dress. The egg is said to have a "corona,"[27] a crown, and to be accompanied by "attendant cells."[28] It is holy, set apart and above, the queen to the sperm's king. The egg is also passive, which means it must depend on sperm for rescue. Gerald Schatten and Helen Schatten liken the egg's role to that of Sleeping Beauty: "a dormant bride awaiting her mate's magic kiss, which instills the spirit that brings her to life."[29] Sperm, by contrast, have a "mission,"[30] which is to "move through the female genital tract in quest of the ovum."[31] One popular account has it that the sperm carry out a "perilous journey" into the "warm darkness,"

[14]See Carol Delaney, "The Meaning of Paternity and the Virgin Birth Debate," *Man* 21, no. 3 (September 1986): 494–513. She discusses the difference between this scientific view that women contribute genetic material to the fetus and the claim of long-standing Western folk theories that the origin and identity of the fetus comes from the male, as in the metaphor of planting a seed in soil.

[15]For a suggested direct link between human behavior and purportedly passive eggs and active sperm, see Erik H. Erikson, "Inner and Outer Space: Reflections on Womanhood," *Daedalus* 93, no. 2 (Spring 1964): 582–606, esp. 591.

[16]Guyton (n. 3), 619; and Mountcastle (n. 5), 1609.

[17]Jonathan Miller and David Pellham, *The Facts of Life* (New York: Viking Penguin, 1984), 5.

[18]Alberts et al., 796.

[19]Ibid., 796.

[20]See, e.g., William F. Ganong, *Review of Medical Physiology*, 7th ed. (Los Altos, Calif.: Lange Medical Publications, 1975), 322.

[21]Alberts et al. (n. 11), 796.

[22]Guyton, 615.

[23]Solomon (n. 6), 683.

[24]Vander, Sherman, and Luciano (n. 4), 4th ed. (1985), 580.

[25]Alberts et al., 796.

[26]All biology texts quoted use the word "penetrate."

[27]Solomon, 700.

[28]A. Beldecos et al., "The Importance of Feminist Critique for Contemporary Cell Biology," *Hypatia* 3, no. 1 (Spring 1988): 61–76.

[29]Gerald Schatten and Helen Schatten, "The Energetic Egg," *Medical World News* 23 (January 23, 1984): 51–53, esp. 51.

[30]Alberts et al., 796.

[31]Guyton (n. 3), 613.

where some fall away "exhausted." "Survivors" "assault" the egg, the success-ful candidates "surrounding the prize."[32] Part of the urgency of this journey, in more scientific terms, is that "once released from the supportive environment of the ovary, an egg will die within hours unless rescued by a sperm."[33] The wording stresses the fragility and dependency of the egg, even though the same text acknowledges elsewhere that sperm also live for only a few hours.[34]

In 1948, in a book remarkable for its early insights into these matters, [11] Ruth Herschberger argued that female reproductive organs are seen as bio-logically interdependent, while male organs are viewed as autonomous, op-erating independently and in isolation:

> At present the functional is stressed only in connection with women: it is in them that ovaries, tubes, uterus, and vagina have endless interdependence. In the male, reproduction would seem to involve "organs" only.
>
> Yet the sperm, just as much as the egg, is dependent on a great many related processes. There are secretions which mitigate the urine in the urethra before ejaculation, to protect the sperm. There is the reflex shutting off of the bladder connection, the provision of prosta-tic secretions, and various types of muscular propulsion. The sperm is no more independent of its milieu than the egg, and yet from a wish that it were, biologists have lent their support to the notion that the human female, beginning with the egg, is congenitally more de-pendent than the male.[35]

Bringing out another aspect of the sperm's autonomy, an article in the journal [12] *Cell* has the sperm making an "existential decision" to penetrate the egg: "Sperm are cells with a limited behavioral repertoire, one that is directed toward fertil-izing eggs. To execute the decision to abandon the haploid state, sperm swim to an egg and there acquire the ability to effect membrane fusion."[36] Is this a cor-porate manager's version of the sperm's activities — "executing decisions" while fraught with dismay over difficult options that bring with them very high risk?

There is another way that sperm, despite their small size, can be made [13] to loom in importance over the egg. In a collection of scientific papers, an electron micrograph of an enormous egg and tiny sperm is titled "A Portrait of the Sperm."[37] This is a little like showing a photo of a dog and calling it a

---

[32]Miller and Pelham (n. 17), 7.
[33]Alberts et al. (n. 11), 804.
[34]Ibid., 801.
[35]Ruth Herschberger, *Adam's Rib* (New York: Pelligrini & Cudaby, 1948), esp. 84. I am indebted to Ruth Hubbard for telling me about Herschberger's work, although at a point when this paper was already in draft form.
[36]Bennett M. Shapiro. "The Existential Decision of a Sperm," *Cell* 49, no. 3 (May 1987): 293–94, esp. 293.
[37]Lennart Nilsson, "A Portrait of the Sperm," in *The Functional Anatomy of the Sperma-tozoan*, ed. Bjorn A. Afzelius (New York: Pergamon, 1975), 79–82.

picture of the fleas. Granted, microscopic sperm are harder to photograph than eggs, which are just large enough to see with the naked eye. But surely the use of the term "portrait," a word associated with the powerful and wealthy, is significant. Eggs have only micrographs or pictures, not portraits.

One depiction of sperm as weak and timid, instead of strong and power- 14 ful—the only such representation in western civilization, so far as I know— occurs in Woody Allen's movie *Everything You Always Wanted to Know about Sex* *But Were Afraid to Ask*. Allen, playing the part of an apprehensive sperm inside a man's testicles, is scared of the man's approaching orgasm. He is reluctant to launch himself into the darkness, afraid of contraceptive devices, afraid of winding up on the ceiling if the man masturbates.

The more common picture—egg as damsel in distress, shielded only by 15 her sacred garments; sperm as heroic warrior to the rescue—cannot be proved to be dictated by the biology of these events. While the "facts" of biology may not *always* be constructed in cultural terms, I would argue that in this case they are. The degree of metaphorical content in these descriptions, the extent to which differences between egg and sperm are emphasized, and the parallels between cultural stereotypes of male and female behavior and the character of egg and sperm all point to this conclusion.

New Research, Old Imagery

As new understandings of egg and sperm emerge, textbook gender im- 16 agery is being revised. But the new research, far from escaping the stereotypical representations of egg and sperm, simply replicates elements of textbook gender imagery in a different form. The persistence of this imagery calls to mind what Ludwik Fleck termed "the self-contained" nature of scientific thought. As he described, it, "the interaction between what is already known, what remains to be learned, and those who are to apprehend it, go to ensure harmony within the system. But at the same time they also preserve the harmony of illusions, which is quite secure within the confines of a given thought style."[38] We need to understand the way in which the cultural content in scientific descriptions changes as biological discoveries unfold, and whether that cultural content is solidly entrenched or easily changed.

In all of the texts quoted above, sperm are described as penetrating the 17 egg, and specific substances on a sperm's head are described as binding to the egg. Recently, this description of events was rewritten in a biophysics lab at Johns Hopkins University—transforming the egg from the passive to the active party.[39]

Prior to this research, it was thought that the zona, the inner vestments 18 of the egg, formed an impenetrable barrier. Sperm overcame the barrier by mechanically burrowing through, thrashing their tails and slowly working

---

[38]Ludwik Fleck, *Genesis and Development of a Scientific Fact,* ed. Thaddeus J. Trenn and Robert K. Merton (Chicago: University of Chicago Press, 1979), 38.
[39]Jay M. Baltz carried out the research I describe when he was a graduate student in the Thomas C. Jenkins Department of Biophysics at Johns Hopkins University.

their way along. Later research showed that the sperm released digestive enzymes that chemically broke down the zona; thus, scientists presumed that the sperm used mechanical *and* chemical means to get through to the egg.

In this recent investigation, the researchers began to ask questions about 19 the mechanical force of the sperm's tail. (The lab's goal was to develop a contraceptive that worked topically on sperm.) They discovered, to their great surprise, that the forward thrust of sperm is extremely weak, which contradicts the assumption that sperm are forceful penetrators.[40] Rather than thrusting forward, the sperm's head was now seen to move mostly back and forth. The sideways motion of the sperm's tail makes the head move sideways with a force that is ten times stronger than its forward movement. So even if the overall force of the sperm were strong enough to mechanically break the zona, most of its force would be directed sideways rather than forward. In fact, its strongest tendency, by tenfold, is to escape by attempting to pry itself off the egg. Sperm, then, must be exceptionally efficient at *escaping* from any cell surface they contact. And the surface of the egg must be designed to trap the sperm and prevent their escape. Otherwise, few if any sperm would reach the egg.

The researchers at Johns Hopkins concluded that the sperm and egg 20 stick together because of adhesive molecules on the surfaces of each. The egg traps the sperm and adheres to it so tightly that the sperm's head is forced to lie flat against the surface of the zona, a little bit, they told me, "like Br'er Rabbit getting more and more stuck to tar baby the more he wriggles." The trapped sperm continues to wiggle ineffectually side to side. The mechanical force of its tail is so weak that a sperm cannot break even one chemical bond. This is where the digestive enzymes released by the sperm come in. If they start to soften the zona just at the tip of the sperm and the sides remain stuck, then the weak, flailing sperm can get oriented in the right direction and make it through the zona—provided that its bonds to the zona dissolve as it moves in.

Although this new version of the saga of the egg and the sperm broke 21 through cultural expectations, the researchers who made the discovery continued to write papers and abstracts as if the sperm were the active party who attacks, binds, penetrates, and enters the egg. The only difference was that sperm were now seen as performing these actions weakly.[41] Not until August 1987, more than three years after the findings described above, did these researchers reconceptualize the process to give the egg a more active role. They began to describe the zona as an aggressive sperm catcher, covered with adhesive

---

[40]Far less is known about the physiology of sperm than comparable female substances, which some feminists claim is no accident. Greater scientific scrutiny of female reproduction has long enabled the burden of birth control to be placed on women. In this case, the researchers' discovery did not depend on development of any new technology. The experiments made use of glass pipettes, a manometer, and a simple microscope, all of which have been available for more than one hundred years.

[41]Jay Baltz and Richard A. Cone, "What Force Is Needed to Tether a Sperm?" (abstract for Society for the Study of Reproduction, 1985), and "Flagellar Torque on the Head Determines the Force Needed to Tether a Sperm" (abstract for Biophysical Society, 1986).

molecules that can capture a sperm with a single bond and clasp it to the zona's surface.[42] In the words of their published account: "The innermost vestment, the *zona pellucida*, is a glyco-protein shell, which captures and tethers the sperm before they penetrate it. . . . The sperm is captured at the initial contact between the sperm tip and the *zona*. . . . Since the thrust [of the sperm] is much smaller than the force needed to break a single affinity bond, the first bond made upon the tip-first meeting of the sperm and *zona* can result in the capture of the sperm."[43]

Experiments in another lab reveal similar patterns of data interpretation. Gerald Schatten and Helen Schatten set out to show that, contrary to conventional wisdom, the "egg is not merely a large, yolk-filled sphere into which the sperm burrows to endow new life. Rather, recent research suggests the almost heretical view that sperm and egg are mutually active partners."[44] This sounds like a departure from the stereotypical textbook view, but further reading reveals Schatten and Schatten's conformity to the aggressive-sperm metaphor. They describe how "the sperm and egg first touch when, from the tip of the sperm's triangular head, a long, thin filament shoots out and harpoons the egg." Then we learn that "remarkably, the harpoon is not so much fired as assembled at great speed, molecule by molecule, from a pool of protein stored in a specialized region called the acrosome. The filament may grow as much as twenty times longer than the sperm head itself before its tip reaches the egg and sticks."[45] Why not call this "making a bridge" or "throwing out a line" rather than firing a harpoon? Harpoons pierce prey and injure or kill them, while this filament only sticks. And why not focus, as the Hopkins lab did, on the stickiness of the egg, rather than the stickiness of the sperm?[46] Later in the article, the Schattens replicate the common view of the sperm's perilous journey into the warm darkness of the vagina, this time for the purpose of explaining its journey into the egg itself: "[The sperm] still has an arduous journey ahead. It must penetrate farther into the egg's huge sphere of cytoplasm and somehow locate the nucleus, so that the two cells' chromosomes can fuse. The sperm dives down into the cytoplasm, its tail beating. But it is

[42]Jay M. Baltz, David F. Katz, and Richard A. Cone, "The Mechanics of the Sperm-Egg Interaction at the Zona Pellucida," *Biophysical Journal* 54, no. 4 (October 1988): 643–54. Lab members were somewhat familiar with work on metaphors in the biology of female reproduction. Richard Cone, who runs the lab, is my husband, and he talked with them about my earlier research on the subject from time to time. Even though my current research focuses on biological imagery and I heard about the lab's work from my husband every day, I myself did not recognize the role of imagery in the sperm research until many weeks after the period of research and writing I describe. Therefore, I assume that any awareness the lab members may have had about how underlying metaphor might be guiding this particular research was fairly inchoate.

[43]Ibid., 643, 650.

[44]Schatten and Schatten (n. 29), 51.

[45]Ibid., 52.

[46]Surprisingly, in an article intended for a general audience, the authors do not point out that these are sea urchin sperm and note that human sperm do not shoot out filaments at all.

soon interrupted by the sudden and swift migration of the egg nucleus, which rushes toward the sperm with a velocity triple that of the movement of chromosomes during cell division, crossing the entire egg in about a minute."[47]

Like Schatten and Schatten and the biophysicists at Johns Hopkins, another researcher has recently made discoveries that seem to point to a more interactive view of the relationship of egg and sperm. This work, which Paul Wassarman conducted on the sperm and eggs of mice, focuses on identifying the specific molecules in the egg coat (the zona pellucida) that are involved in egg-sperm interaction. At first glance, his descriptions seem to fit the model of an egalitarian relationship. Male and female gametes "recognize one another," and "interactions . . . take place between sperm and egg."[48] But the article in *Scientific American* in which those descriptions appear begins with a vignette that presages the dominant motif of their presentation: "It has been more than a century since Hermann Fol, a Swiss zoologist, peered into his microscope and became the first person to see a sperm penetrate an egg, fertilize it and form the first cell of a new embryo."[49] This portrayal of the sperm as the active party—the one that *penetrates* and *fertilizes* the egg and *produces* the embryo—is not cited as an example of an earlier, now outmoded view. In fact, the author reiterates the point later in the article: "Many sperm can bind to and penetrate the zona pellucida, or outer coat, of an unfertilized mouse egg, but only one sperm will eventually fuse with the thin plasma membrane surrounding the egg proper (*inner sphere*), fertilizing the egg and giving rise to a new embryo."[50]

The imagery of sperm as aggressor is particularly startling in this case: the main discovery being reported is isolation of a particular molecule *on the egg coat* that plays an important role in fertilization! Wassarman's choice of language sustains the picture. He calls the molecule that has been isolated, ZP3, a "sperm receptor." By allocating the passive, waiting role to the egg, Wassarman can continue to describe the sperm as the actor, the one that makes it all happen: "The basic process begins when many sperm first attach loosely and then bind tenaciously to receptors on the surface of the egg's thick outer coat, the zona pellucida. Each sperm, which has a large number of egg-binding proteins on its surface, binds to many sperm receptors on the egg. More specifically, a site on each of the egg-binding proteins fits a complementary site on a sperm receptor, much as a key fits a lock."[51] With the sperm designated as the "key" and the egg the "lock," it is obvious which one acts and which one is acted upon. Could this imagery not be reversed, letting the sperm (the lock) wait until the egg produces the key? Or could we speak of two halves of a locket matching, and regard the matching itself as the action that initiates the fertilization?

[47]Schatten and Schatten, 53.
[48]Paul M. Wassarman, "Fertilization in Mammals," *Scientific American* 259, no. 6 (December 1988): 78–84, esp. 78, 84.
[49]Ibid., 78.
[50]Ibid., 79.
[51]Ibid., 78.

It is as if Wassarman were determined to make the egg the receiving part- 25
ner. Usually in biological research, the *protein* member of the pair of binding
molecules is called the receptor, and physically it has a pocket in it rather like
a lock. As the diagrams that illustrate Wassarman's article show, the molecules on the sperm are proteins and have "pockets." The small, mobile molecules that fit into these pockets are called ligands. As shown in the diagrams,
ZP3 on the egg is a polymer of "keys"; many small knobs stick out. Typically,
molecules on the sperm would be called receptors and molecules on the egg
would be called ligands. But Wassarman chose to name ZP3 on the egg the
receptor and to create a new term, "the egg-binding protein," for the molecules on the sperm that otherwise would have been called the receptor.[52]

Wassarman does credit the egg coat with having more functions than 26
those of a sperm receptor. While he notes that "the zona pellucida has at times
been viewed by investigators as a nuisance, a barrier to sperm and hence an
impediment to fertilization," his new research reveals that the egg coat "serves
as a sophisticated biological security system that screens incoming sperm, selects only those compatible with fertilization and development, prepares sperm
for fusion with the egg and later protects the resulting embryo from poly-
spermy [a lethal condition caused by fusion of more than one sperm with a
single egg.]"[53] Although this description gives the egg an active role, that role
is drawn in stereotypically feminine terms. The egg *selects* an appropriate
mate, *prepares* him for fusion, and then *protects* the resulting offspring from
harm. This is courtship and mating behavior as seen through the eyes of a
sociobiologist: woman as the hard-to-get prize, who, following union with the
chosen one, becomes woman as servant and mother.

And Wassarman does not quit there. In a review article for *Science*, he 27
outlines the "chronology of fertilization."[54] Near the end of the article are two
subject headings. One is "Sperm Penetration," in which Wassarman describes
how the chemical dissolving of the zona pellucida combines with the "substantial propulsive force generated by sperm." The next heading is "Sperm-
Egg Fusion." This section details what happens inside the zona after a sperm
"penetrates" it. Sperm "can make contact with, adhere to, and fuse with (that
is, fertilize) an egg."[55] Wassarman's word choice, again, is astonishingly skewed
in favor of the sperm's activity, for in the next breath he says that sperm *lose* all
motility upon fusion with the egg's surface. In mouse and sea urchin eggs, the
sperm enters at the *egg's* volition, according to Wassarman's description: "Once
fused with egg plasma membrane [the surface of the egg], how does a sperm
enter the egg? The surface of both mouse and sea urchin eggs is covered with

---

[52]Since receptor molecules are relatively *immotile* and the ligands that bind to them relatively *motile*, one might imagine the egg being called the receptor and the sperm the lig-
and. But the molecules in question on egg and sperm are immotile molecules. It is the
sperm as a *cell* that has motility, and the egg as a cell that has relative immotility.
[53]Wassarman, 78–79.
[54]Paul M. Wassarman, "The Biology and Chemistry of Fertilization," *Science* 235, no.
4788 (January 30, 1987): 553–60, esp. 554.
[55]Ibid., 557.

thousands of plasma membrane-bound projections, called microvilli [tiny "hairs"]. Evidence in sea urchins suggests that, after membrane fusion, a group of elongated microvilli cluster tightly around and interdigitate over the sperm head. As these microvilli are resorbed, the sperm is drawn into the egg. Therefore, sperm motility, which ceases at the time of fusion in both sea urchins and mice, is not required for sperm entry."[56] The section called "Sperm Penetration" more logically would be followed by a section called "The Egg Envelops," rather than "Sperm-Egg Fusion." This would give a parallel—and more accurate—sense that both the egg and the sperm initiate action.

Another way that Wassarman makes less of the egg's activity is by describing components of the egg but referring to the sperm as a whole entity. Deborah Gordon has described such an approach as "atomism" ("the part is independent of and primordial to the whole") and identified it as one of the "tenacious assumptions" of Western science and medicine.[57] Wassarman employs atomism to his advantage. When he refers to processing going on within sperm, he consistently returns to descriptions that remind us from whence these activities came: they are part of sperm that penetrate an egg or generate propulsive force. When he refers to processes going on within eggs, he stops there. As a result, any active role he grants them appears to be assigned to the parts of the egg, and not to the egg itself. In the quote above, it is the microvilli that actively cluster around the sperm. In another example, "the driving force for engulfment of a fused sperm comes from a region of cytoplasm just beneath an egg's plasma membrane."[58]

Social Implications: Thinking Beyond

All three of these revisionist accounts of egg and sperm cannot seem to escape the hierarchical imagery of older accounts. Even though each new account gives the egg a larger and more active role, taken together they bring into play another cultural stereotype: woman as a dangerous and aggressive threat. In the Johns Hopkins lab's revised model, the egg ends up as the female aggressor who "captures and tethers" the sperm with her sticky zona, rather like a spider lying in wait in her web.[59] The Schatten lab has the egg's nucleus "interrupt" the sperm's dive with a "sudden and swift" rush by which she "clasps the sperm and guides its nucleus to the center."[60] Wassarman's description of the surface of the egg "covered with thousands of plasma membrane-bound projections, called microvilli" that reach out and clasp the sperm adds to the spiderlike imagery.[61]

28

29

---

[56]Ibid., 557–58. This finding throws into question Schatten and Schatten's description (n. 29 above) of the sperm, its tail beating, diving down into the egg.

[57]Deborah R. Gordon, "Tenacious Assumptions in Western Medicine," in *Biomedicine Examined,* ed. Margaret Lock and Deborah Gordon (Dordrecht, The Netherlands: Kluwer, 1988), 19–56, esp. 26.

[58]Wassarman, "The Biology and Chemistry of Fertilization," 558.

[59]Baltz, Katz, and Cone (n. 42 above), 643, 650.

[60]Schatten and Schatten, 53.

[61]Wassarman, "The Biology and Chemistry of Fertilization," 557.

These images grant the egg an active role but at the cost of appearing dis- 30
turbingly aggressive. Images of woman as dangerous and aggressive, the femme
fatale who victimizes men, are widespread in Western literature and culture.[62]
More specific is the connection of spider imagery with the idea of an engulfing,
devouring mother.[63] New data did not lead scientists to eliminate gender stereotypes in their descriptions of egg and sperm. Instead, scientists simply began
to describe egg and sperm in different, but no less damaging, terms.

Can we envision a less stereotypical view? Biology itself provides another 31
model that could be applied to the egg and the sperm. The cybernetic model—
with its feedback loops, flexible adaptation to change, coordination of the
parts within a whole, evolution over time, and changing response to the environment—is common in genetics, endocrinology, and ecology and has a
growing influence in medicine in general.[64] This model has the potential to
shift our imagery from the negative, in which the female reproductive system
is castigated both for not producing eggs after birth and for producing (and
thus wasting) too many eggs overall, to something more positive. The female
reproductive system could be seen as responding to the environment (pregnancy or menopause), adjusting to monthly changes (menstruation), and
flexibly changing from reproductivity after puberty to nonreproductivity later
in life. The sperm and egg's interaction could also be described in cybernetic
terms. J. F. Hartman's research in reproductive biology demonstrated fifteen
years ago that if an egg is killed by being pricked with a needle, live sperm
cannot get through the zona.[65] Clearly, this evidence shows that the egg and
sperm *do* interact on more mutual terms, making biology's refusal to portray
them that way all the more disturbing.

We would do well to be aware, however, that cybernetic imagery is 32
hardly neutral. In the past, cybernetic models have played an important part
in the imposition of social control. These models inherently provide a way of
thinking about a "field" of interacting components. Once the field can be seen,
it can become the object of new forms of knowledge, which in turn can allow
new forms of social control to be exerted over the components of the field.
During the 1950s, for example, medicine began to recognize the psychosocial
environment of the patient: the patient's family and its psychodynamics. Professions such as social work began to focus on this new environment, and the
resulting knowledge became one way to further control the patient. Patients
began to be seen not as isolated, individual bodies, but as psychosocial en-

[62]Mary Ellman, *Thinking about Women* (New York: Harcourt Brace Jovanovich, 1968),
140; Nina Auerbach, *Woman and the Demon* (Cambridge, Mass.: Harvard University
Press, 1982), esp. 186.

[63]Kenneth Alan Adams, "Arachnophobia: Love American Style," *Journal of Psychoanalytic Anthropology* 4, no. 2 (1981): 157–97.

[64]William Ray Arney and Bernard Bergen, *Medicine and the Management of Living*
(Chicago: University of Chicago Press, 1984).

[65]J. F. Hartman, R. B. Gwatkin, and C. F. Hutchison, "Early Contact Interactions between Mammalian Gametes *In Vitro*," *Proceedings of the National Academy of Sciences*
(U.S.) 69, no. 10 (1972): 2767–69.

tities located in an "ecological" system: management of "the patient's psychology was a new entrée to patient control."[66]

The models that biologists use to describe their data can have important 33 social effects. During the nineteenth century, the social and natural sciences strongly influenced each other: the social ideas of Malthus about how to avoid the natural increase of the poor inspired Darwin's *Origin of Species*.[67] Once the *Origin* stood as a description of the natural world, complete with competition and market struggles, it could be reimported into social science as social Darwinism, in order to justify the social order of the time. What we are seeing now is similar: the importation of cultural ideas about passive females and heroic males into the "personalities" of gametes. This amounts to the "implanting of social imagery on representations of nature so as to lay a firm basis for reimporting exactly that same imagery as natural explanations of social phenomena."[68]

Further research would show us exactly what social effects are being 34 wrought from the biological imagery of egg and sperm. At the very least, the imagery keeps alive some of the hoariest old stereotypes about weak damsels in distress and their strong male rescuers. That these stereotypes are now being written in at the level of the *cell* constitutes a powerful move to make them seem so natural as to be beyond alteration.

The stereotypical imagery might also encourage people to imagine that 35 what results from the interaction of egg and sperm—a fertilized egg—is the result of deliberate "human" action at the cellular level. Whatever the intentions of the human couple, in this microscope "culture" a cellular "bride" (or femme fatale) and a cellular "groom" (her victim) make a cellular baby. Rosalind Petchesky points out that through visual representations such as sonograms, we are given "*images* of younger and younger, and tinier and tinier, fetuses being 'saved.'" This leads to "the point of viability being 'pushed back' *indefinitely*."[69] Endowing egg and sperm with intentional action, a key aspect of personhood in our culture, lays the foundation for the point of viability being pushed back to the moment of fertilization. This will likely lead to greater acceptance of technological developments and new forms of scrutiny and manipulation, for the benefit of these inner "persons": court-ordered restrictions on a pregnant woman's activities in order to protect her fetus, fetal surgery, amniocentesis, and rescinding of abortion rights, to name but a few examples.[70]

[66]Arney and Bergen, 68.
[67]Ruth Hubbard, "Have Only Men Evolved?" (n. 12 above), 51–52.
[68]David Harvey, personal communication, November 1989.
[69]Rosalind Petchesky, "Fetal Images: The Power of Visual Culture in the Politics of Reproduction," *Feminist Studies* 13, no. 2 (Summer 1987): 263–92, esp. 272.
[70]Rita Arditti, Renate Klein, and Shelley Minden, *Test-Tube Women* (London: Pandora, 1984); Ellen Goodman, "Whose Right to Life?" *Baltimore Sun* (November 17, 1987); Tamar Lewin, "Courts Acting to Force Care of the Unborn," *New York Times* (November 23, 1987), A1 and B10; Susan Irwin and Brigitte Jordan, "Knowledge, Practice, and Power: Court Ordered Cesarean Sections," *Medical Anthropology Quarterly* 1, no. 3 (September 1987): 319–34.

Even if we succeed in substituting more egalitarian, interactive meta- 36
phors to describe the activities of egg and sperm, and manage to avoid the
pitfalls of cybernetic models, we would still be guilty of endowing cellular en-
tities with personhood. More crucial, then, than what *kinds* of personalities
we bestow on cells is the very fact that we are doing it at all. This process
could ultimately have the most disturbing social consequences.

One clear feminist challenge is to wake up sleeping metaphors in sci- 37
ence, particularly those involved in descriptions of the egg and the sperm. Although the literary convention is to call such metaphors "dead," they are not
so much dead as sleeping, hidden within the scientific content of texts—and
all the more powerful for it.[71] Waking up such metaphors, by becoming
aware of when we are projecting cultural imagery onto what we study, will
improve our ability to investigate and understand nature. Waking up such
metaphors, by becoming aware of their implications, will rob them of their
power to naturalize our social conventions about gender.

FOR DISCUSSION AND WRITING: ARGUING ABOUT METAPHORS IN SCIENCE

1. Martin's essay is divided into sections. What are they, and what is accomplished in each one?

2. Some of the instances of metaphors used in scientific journals gathered
   by Martin are quite striking. Choose one or two of these for group discussion.

3. Write a short piece in which you discuss what you learned about sexual
   reproduction in your early education and what Martin's essay teaches.
   Did she persuade you to rethink your understanding of these basic
   processes?

4. Using Emily Martin's approach as your model, examine a science textbook or another kind of textbook that discusses processes or historical or
   political events and examine a section of the text for sleeping metaphors
   and analogies. What cultural imagery do you find in these metaphors?
   That is, how does the writer want you to perceive the process or event?

HIDDEN MEANING: PARABLES AND ALLEGORY

When metaphorical thought is taken to an extreme of elaboration, we find
whole stories that seem to be about one thing but are intended to convey
a message about some other thing. These stories, if they are short, we

---

[71]Thanks to Elizabeth Fee and David Spain, who in February 1989 and April 1989, respectively, made points related to this.

usually call *parables,* and, if they are long, we call *allegories*—especially if they seem to convey messages about more than one hidden topic. Both of these words refer to the way that meaning is removed from the surface or hidden in the texts that they describe. Parables play a major role in Christian thinking because Jesus used them as a teaching device. In the following passage from the Gospel of Mark, we find not only a number of parables, but also a theory of parable being expounded to the inner circle of disciples, and a parable about parables. We ask you to begin thinking about parables by reading this passage and discussing the parables in it—especially that of the sower of seeds.

The Parables of Jesus

The Gospel of Mark

Once again he began to teach beside the seashore. And the greatest multitude gathered to hear him, so that he went aboard the ship and was seated out to sea, and all the multitude was on shore facing the sea. He taught them a great deal in parables, and said to them in his discourse: Listen. Behold, a sower went out to sow. And it happened as he sowed that some of the grain fell beside the way, and birds came and ate it. Some fell on stony ground where there was not much soil, and it shot up quickly because there was no depth of soil; and when the sun came up it was parched and because it had no roots it dried away. Some fell among thorns, and the thorns grew up and stifled it, and it bore no fruit. But some fell upon the good soil, and it bore fruit, and shot up and increased, and yielded thirtyfold and sixtyfold and a hundredfold. And he said: He who has ears, let him hear. When they were alone, his followers along with the twelve asked him about the parables. He said to them: To you are given the secrets of the Kingdom of God; but to those who are outside all comes through parables, so that they may have sight but not see, and hear but not understand, lest they be converted and forgiven. And he said to them: You did not read this parable? Then how shall you understand all the parables? The sower sows the word. And these are the ones beside the way where the word is sown, and as soon as they hear it Satan comes and snatches the word that has been sown among them. And there are some who are as if sown on stony ground, who when they hear the word accept it with joy; and they have no roots in themselves but are men of the moment, and when there comes affliction and persecution, because of the word, they do not stand fast. And others are those who were sown among thorns; these are the ones who hear the word, and concern of the world and the beguilement of riches and desires for other things come upon them and stifle the word, and it bears no fruit. And the others are those who were sown upon the good soil, who hear the word and accept it and bear fruit thirtyfold and sixtyfold and a hundredfold. Then he said to them: Surely the lamp is not brought in so as to be set under a basket or under the bed rather than to be set on a stand; for there is nothing hidden except to be shown, nor anything concealed except to be brought to light. He who has ears to hear, let him hear. And he said to them: Consider what you hear. Your measure will be made by the measure by which you measure, and more shall be added for you. When a man has, he shall be given; when one has not, even what he has shall be taken away from him. And he said: The Kingdom of God is as when a man sows his seed in the ground, and sleeps and wakes night and day, and the seed grows and increases without his knowing it; for of itself the earth bears fruit, first the blade, then the ear, then the full grain in the ear. But when the grain gives its yield, he puts forth the sickle, for the time of harvesting is come. And he said: To what shall we liken the Kingdom of God, and in what parable shall we place it? It is like the seed of mustard, which when it is sown in the ground is smaller than all the seeds on earth, but when it has been sown, it shoots up and becomes greater than all the other greens, and puts forth great branches, so that the birds of the air may nest in its shadow. With many such parables he spoke the word to them, according to what they could comprehend; but he did not talk with them except in parables; but privately with his own disciples he expounded all.

Mark 4.11–30, translated by Richmond Lattimore

On Parables *and* Before the Law

Franz Kafka

Kafka's parables are to those of Jesus as surrealist metaphor is to ordinary metaphor. That is, instead of hiding but pointing clearly to a second level of meaning, they trouble thought and force the reader to generate meanings that cannot be assigned comfortably to the original text. Here are two of Kafka's parables. The first is a discussion of parable that blurs the distinction between reality and fiction, between the parable and the real. Try to interpret it—that's part of the game. But be flexible and listen gladly to other interpretations. The second, which is called "Before the Law," is also something of a puzzle, though its meaning may be clearer than that of the first. Do not wait before the gate. Offer your interpretation before it is too late.

On Parables

Many complain that the words of the wise are always merely parables   1
and of no use in daily life, which is the only life we have. When the sage says: "Go over," he does not mean that we should cross to some actual place, which we could do anyhow if the labor were worth it; he means some fabulous yonder, something unknown to us, something that he cannot designate more precisely either, and therefore cannot help us here in the very least. All

these parables really set out to say merely that the incomprehensible is incomprehensible, and we know that already. But the cares we have to struggle with every day: that is a different matter.

Concerning this a man once said: Why such reluctance? If you only fol-   2
lowed the parables you yourselves would become parables and with that rid
of all your daily cares.

Another said: I bet that is also a parable.   3

The first said: You have won.   4

The second said: But unfortunately only in parable.   5

The first said: No, in reality: in parable you have lost.   6

Translated by Willa and Edwin Muir

Before the Law

Before the law stands a doorkeeper. To this doorkeeper there comes a
man from the country and prays for admittance to the Law. But the doorkeeper says that he cannot grant admittance at the moment. The man thinks
it over and then asks if he will be allowed in later. "It is possible," says the
doorkeeper, "but not at the moment." Since the gate stands open, as usual,
and the doorkeeper steps to one side, the man stoops to peer through the
gateway into the interior. Observing that, the doorkeeper laughs and says: "If
you are so drawn to it, just try to go in despite my veto. But take note: I am
powerful. And I am only the least of the doorkeepers. From hall to hall there
is one doorkeeper after another, each more powerful than the last. The third
doorkeeper is already so terrible that even I cannot bear to look at him."
These are difficulties the man from the country has not expected; the Law, he
thinks, should surely be accessible at all times and to everyone, but as he
now takes a closer look at the doorkeeper in his fur coat, with his big sharp
nose and long, thin, black Tartar beard, he decides that it is better to wait until he gets permission to enter. The doorkeeper gives him a stool and lets him
sit down at one side of the door. There he sits for days and years. He makes
many attempts to be admitted, and wearies the doorkeeper by his importu-
nity. The doorkeeper frequently has little interviews with him, asking him
questions about his home and many other things, but the questions are put
indifferently, as great lords put them, and always finish with the statement
that he cannot be let in yet. The man, who has furnished himself with many
things for his journey, sacrifices all he has, however valuable, to bribe the
doorkeeper. The doorkeeper accepts everything, but always with the remark:
"I am only taking it to keep you from thinking you have omitted anything."
During these many years the man fixes his attention almost continuously on
the doorkeeper. He forgets the other doorkeepers, and this first one seems to
him the sole obstacle preventing access to the Law. He curses his bad luck,
in his early years boldly and loudly; later, as he grows old, he only grumbles
to himself. He becomes childish, and since in his yearlong contemplation of
the doorkeeper he has come to know even the fleas in his fur collar, be begs
the fleas as well to help him and to change the doorkeeper's mind. At length
his eyesight begins to fail, and he does not know whether the world is really

darker or whether his eyes are only deceiving him. Yet in his darkness he is
now aware of a radiance that streams inextinguishably from the gateway of
the Law. Now he has not very long to live. Before he dies, all his experiences
in these long years gather themselves in his head to one point, a question he
has not yet asked the doorkeeper. He waves him nearer, since he can no
longer raise his stiffening body. The doorkeeper has to bend low toward him,
for the difference in height between them has altered much to the man's disadvantage. "What do you want to know now?" asks the doorkeeper; "you are
insatiable." "Everyone strives to reach the Law," says the man, "so how does
it happen that for all these many years no one but myself has ever begged for
admittance?" The doorkeeper recognizes that the man has reached his end,
and, to let his failing senses catch the words, roars in his ear: "No one else
could ever be admitted here, since this gate was made only for you. I am now
going to shut it."

Translated by Willa and Edwin Muir

Borges and I *and* Ragnarök

Jorge Luis Borges

*Jorge Luis Borges, who died not so long ago, liked the parable form and ad-
mired Kafka's use of it. Here are two of Borges's short pieces that might be called
parables and certainly ask to be interpreted as we interpret parables. The first,
called "Borges and I," is about the relationship between the private and public
self and the difference between the real and the artificial. In discussing it, try to
decide which is the "real" Borges. The second is called "Ragnarök," the Norse
name for the end of the reign of the old gods. That should give you a start on
reading it. Notice that Borges uses the notion of dream-work as a way of accounting for the fantastic features of this allegory.*

Borges and I

It's Borges, the other one, that things happen to. I walk through Buenos   1
Aires and I pause—mechanically now, perhaps—to gaze at the arch of an
entryway and its inner door; news of Borges reaches me by mail, or I see his
name on a list of academics or in some biographical dictionary. My taste runs
to hourglasses, maps, eighteenth-century typefaces, etymologies, the taste of
coffee, and the prose of Robert Louis Stevenson; Borges shares those preferences, but in a vain sort of way that turns them into the accoutrements of an
actor. It would be an exaggeration to say that our relationship is hostile—I
live, I allow myself to live, so that Borges can spin out his literature, and that
literature is my justification. I willingly admit that he has written a number of
sound pages, but those pages will not save *me*, perhaps because the good in
them no longer belongs to any individual, not even to that other man, but
rather to language itself, or to tradition. Beyond that, I am doomed—utterly

and inevitably—to oblivion, and fleeting moments will be all of me that survives in that other man. Little by little, I have been turning everything over to him, though I know the perverse way he has of distorting and magnifying everything. Spinoza believed that all things wish to go on being what they are—stone wishes eternally to be stone, and tiger, to be tiger. I shall endure in Borges, not in myself (if, indeed, I am anybody at all), but I recognize myself less in his books than in many others', or in the tedious strumming of a guitar. Years ago I tried to free myself from him, and I moved on from the mythologies of the slums and outskirts of the city to games with time and infinity, but those games belong to Borges now, and I shall have to think up other things. So my life is a point-counterpoint, a kind of fugue, and a falling away—and everything winds up being lost to me, and everything falls into oblivion, or into the hands of the other man.

I am not sure which of us it is that's writing this page.   2

Ragnarök

The images in dreams, wrote Coleridge, figure forth the impressions that   1
our intellect would call causes; we do not feel horror because we are haunted by a sphinx, we dream a sphinx in order to explain the horror that we feel. If that is true, how might a mere chronicling of its forms transmit the stupor, the exultation, the alarms, the dread, and the joy that wove together that night's dream? I shall attempt that chronicle, nonetheless; perhaps the fact that the dream consisted of but a single scene may erase or soften the essential difficulty.

The place was the College of Philosophy and Letters; the hour, nightfall.   2
Everything (as is often the case in dreams) was slightly different; a slight magnification altered things. We chose authorities; I would speak with Pedro Henríquez Ureña, who in waking life had died many years before. Suddenly, we were dumbfounded by a great noise of demonstrators or street musicians. From the Underworld, we heard the cries of humans and animals. A voice cried: *Here they come!* and then: *The gods! the gods!* Four or five individuals emerged from out of the mob and occupied the dais of the auditorium. Everyone applauded, weeping; it was the gods, returning after a banishment of many centuries. Looming larger than life as they stood upon the dais, their heads thrown back and their chests thrust forward, they haughtily received our homage. One of them was holding a branch (which belonged, no doubt, to the simple botany of dreams); another, with a sweeping gesture, held out a hand that was a claw; one of Janus' faces looked mistrustfully at Thoth's curved beak. Perhaps excited by our applause, one of them, I no longer remember which, burst out in a triumphant, incredibly bitter clucking that was half gargle and half whistle. From that point on, things changed.

It all began with the suspicion (perhaps exaggerated) that the gods were   3
unable to talk. Centuries of a feral life of flight had atrophied that part of them that was human; the moon of Islam and the cross of Rome had been implacable with these fugitives. Beetling brows, yellowed teeth, the sparse beard of a mulatto or a Chinaman, and beastlike dewlaps were testaments to the degeneration of the Olympian line. The clothes they wore were not those of a

decorous and honest poverty, but rather of the criminal luxury of the Underworld's gambling dens and houses of ill repute. A carnation bled from a buttonhole; under a tight suitcoat one could discern the outline of a knife. Suddenly, we felt that they were playing their last trump, that they were cunning, ignorant, and cruel, like agèd predators, and that if we allowed ourselves to be swayed by fear or pity, they would wind up destroying us.

We drew our heavy revolvers (suddenly in the dream there were revolvers) and exultantly killed the gods.   4

Two Parables of Calvino

Italo Calvino

The Italian author Italo Calvino, like many postmodern writers, worked frequently in or near the parable. As a veteran reader of parables, you should be ready to read these and discuss the meanings concealed in them. As with many parables, the keys to the meaning of these are most likely to be found near the end of the little stories. Both parables are taken from Calvino's Invisible Cities, *a collection of related parables.*

Cities and Memory: Isidora

When a man rides a long time through wild regions he feels the desire for a city. Finally he comes to Isidora, a city where the buildings have spiral staircases encrusted with spiral seashells, where perfect telescopes and violins are made, where the foreigner hesitating between two women always encounters a third, where cockfights degenerate into bloody brawls among the bettors. He was thinking of all these things when he desired a city. Isidora, therefore, is the city of his dreams: with one difference. The dreamed-of city contained him as a young man; he arrives at Isidora in his old age. In the square there is the wall where the old men sit and watch the young go by; he is seated in a row with them. Desires are already memories.

Continuous Cities: Cecilia

You reproach me because each of my stories takes you right into the   1
heart of a city without telling you of the space that stretches between one city and the other, whether it is covered by seas, or fields of rye, larch forests, swamps. I will answer you with a story.

In the streets of Cecilia, an illustrious city, I met once a goatherd, driving   2
a tinkling flock along the walls.

"Man blessed by heaven," he asked me, stopping, "can you tell me the   3
name of the city in which we are?"

"May the gods accompany you!" I cried. "How can you fail to recognize   4
the illustrious city of Cecilia?"

"Bear with me," that man answered. "I am a wandering herdsman. 5
Sometimes my goats and I have to pass through cities; but we are unable to
distinguish them. Ask me the names of the grazing lands: I know them all,
the Meadow between the Cliffs, the Green Slope, the Shadowed Grass. Cities
have no name for me: they are places without leaves, separating one pasture
from another, and where the goats are frightened at street corners and scatter. The dog and I run to keep the flock together."

"I am the opposite of you," I said. "I recognize only cities and cannot dis- 6
tinguish what is outside them. In uninhabited places each stone and each
clump of grass mingles, in my eyes, with every other stone and clump."

Many years have gone by since then; I have known many more cities 7
and I have crossed continents. One day I was walking among rows of identical houses; I was lost. I asked a passerby: "May the immortals protect you,
can you tell me where we are?"

"In Cecilia, worse luck!" he answered. "We have been wandering through 8
its streets, my goats and I, for an age, and we cannot find our way out. . . ."

I recognized him, despite his long white beard; it was the same herdsman 9
of long before. He was followed by a few, mangy goats, which did not even
stink, they were so reduced to skin-and-bones. They cropped wastepaper in
the rubbish bins.

"That cannot be!" I shouted. "I, too, entered a city, I cannot remember 10
when, and since then I have gone on, deeper and deeper into its streets. But
how have I managed to arrive where you say, when I was in another city, far
far away from Cecilia, and I have not yet left it?"

"The places have mingled," the goatherd said. "Cecilia is everywhere. 11
Here, once upon a time, there must have been the Meadow of the Low Sage.
My goats recognize the grass on the traffic island."

Night-Sea Journey

John Barth

*In her essay on biological metaphors, Emily Martin refers to this story in a foot-
note. The first question, then, is why she did this. The piece reads like an essay,
a meditation on a journey, perhaps a philosophical text on "the meaning of
life." Some readers have taken it to be such. But Martin's interest in it suggests
that it may have more to do with biology than with philosophy. We invite you
to read it and to consider all the possible areas of thought in which it can be
held to make sense: philosophy, biology, art. In your discussion you might consider the last words, asking what all this has to do with "love."*

"One way or another, no matter which theory of our journey is correct, it's 1
myself I address; to whom I rehearse as to a stranger our history and condition, and will disclose my secret hope though I sink for it.

"Is the journey my invention? Do the night, the sea, exist at all, I ask my-   2
self, apart from my experience of them? Do I myself exist, or is this a dream?
Sometimes I wonder. And if I am, who am I? The Heritage I supposedly transport? But how can I be both vessel and contents? Such are the questions that
beset my intervals of rest.

"My trouble is, I lack conviction. Many accounts of our situation seem   3
plausible to me—where and what we are, why we swim and whither. But im-
plausible ones as well, perhaps especially those, I must admit as possibly
correct. Even likely. If at times, in certain humors—striking in unison, say,
with my neighbors and chanting with them 'Onward! Upward!'—I have supposed that we have after all a common Maker, Whose nature and motives we
may not know, but Who engendered us in some mysterious wise and launched
us forth toward some end known but to Him—if (for a moodslength only) I
have been able to entertain such notions, very popular in certain quarters, it
is because our night-sea journey partakes of their absurdity. One might even
say: I can believe them *because* they are absurd.

"Has that been said before?   4

"Another paradox: it appears to be these recesses from swimming that   5
sustain me in the swim. Two measures onward and upward, flailing with the
rest, then I float exhausted and dispirited, brood upon the night, the sea, the
journey, while the flood bears me a measure back and down: slow progress,
but I live, I live, and make my way, aye, past many a drownèd comrade in
the end, stronger, worthier than I, victims of their unremitting *joie de nager*. I
have seen the best swimmers of my generation go under. Numberless the
number of the dead! Thousands drown as I think this thought, millions as I
rest before returning to the swim. And scores, hundreds of millions have ex-
pired since we surged forth, brave in our innocence, upon our dreadful way.
'Love! Love!' we sang then, a quarter-billion strong, and churned the warm
sea white with joy of swimming! Now all are gone down—the buoyant, the
sodden, leaders and followers, all gone under, while wretched I swim on. Yet
these same reflective intervals that keep me afloat have led me into wonder,
doubt, despair—strange emotions for a swimmer!—have led me, even, to
suspect . . . that our night-sea journey is without meaning.

"Indeed, if I have yet to join the hosts of the suicides, it is because (fatigue   6
apart) I find it no meaningfuller to drown myself than to go on swimming.

"I know that there are those who seem actually to enjoy the night-sea;   7
who claim to love swimming for its own sake, or sincerely believe that 'reaching the Shore,' 'transmitting the Heritage' (*Whose* Heritage, I'd like to know?
And to whom?) is worth the staggering cost. I do not. Swimming itself I find
at best not actively unpleasant, more often tiresome, not infrequently a torment. Arguments from function and design don't impress me: granted that we
can and do swim, that in a manner of speaking our long tails and streamlined
heads are 'meant for' swimming; it by no means follows—for me, at least—
that we *should* swim, or otherwise endeavor to 'fulfill our destiny.' Which is
to say, Someone Else's destiny, since ours, so far as I can see, is merely to
perish, one way or another, soon or late. The heartless zeal of our (departed)
leaders, like the blind ambition and good cheer of my own youth, appalls me

now; for the death of my comrades I am inconsolable. If the night-sea journey has justification, it is not for us swimmers ever to discover it.

"Oh, to be sure, 'Love!' one heard on every side: 'Love it is that drives   8 and sustains us!' I translate: we don't know *what* drives and sustains us, only that we are most miserably driven and, imperfectly, sustained. *Love* is how we call our ignorance of what whips us. 'To reach the Shore,' then: but what if the Shore exists in the fancies of us swimmers merely, who dream it to account for the dreadful fact that we swim, have always and only swum, and continue swimming without respite (myself excepted) until we die? Supposing even that there *were* a Shore—that, as a cynical companion of mine once imagined, we rise from the drowned to discover all those vulgar superstitions and exalted metaphors to be literal truth: the giant Maker of us all, the Shores of Light beyond our night-sea journey!—whatever would a swimmer do there? The fact is, when we imagine the Shore, what comes to mind is just the opposite of our condition: no more night, no more sea, no more journeying. In short, the blissful estate of the drowned.

"'Ours not to stop and think; ours but to swim and sink. . . .' Because a   9 moment's thought reveals the pointlessness of swimming. 'No matter,' I've heard some say, even as they gulped their last: 'The night-sea journey may be absurd, but here we swim, will-we nill-we, against the flood, onward and upward, toward a Shore that may not exist and couldn't be reached if it did.' The thoughtful swimmer's choices, then, they say, are two: give over thrashing and go under for good, or embrace the absurdity; affirm in and for itself the night-sea journey; swim on with neither motive nor destination, for the sake of swimming, and compassionate moreover with your fellow swimmer, we being all at sea and equally in the dark. I find neither course acceptable. If not even the hypothetical Shore can justify a sea-full of drownèd comrades, to speak of the swim-in-itself as somehow doing so strikes me as obscene. I continue to swim—but only because blind habit, blind instinct, blind fear of drowning are still more strong than the horror of our journey. And if on occasion I have assisted a fellow-thrasher, joined in the cheers and songs, even passed along to others strokes of genius from the drownèd great, it's that I shrink by temperament from making myself conspicuous. To paddle off in one's own direction, assert one's independent right-of-way, overrun one's fellows without compunction, or dedicate oneself entirely to pleasures and diversions without regard for conscience—I can't finally condemn those who journey in this wise; in half my moods I envy them and despise the weak vitality that keeps me from following their example. But in reasonabler moments I remind myself that it's their very freedom and self-responsibility I reject, as more dramatically absurd, in our senseless circumstances, than tailing along in conventional fashion. Suicides, rebels, affirmers of the paradox—nay-sayers and yea-sayers alike to our fatal journey—I finally shake my head at them. And splash sighing past their corpses, one by one, as past a hundred sorts of others: friends, enemies, brothers; fools, sages, brutes—and nobodies, million upon million. I envy them all.

"A poor irony: that I, who find abhorrent and tautological the doctrine of   10 survival of the fittest (*fitness* meaning, in my experience, nothing more than survival-ability, a talent whose only demonstration is the fact of survival, but whose chief ingredients seem to be strength, guile, callousness), may be the sole remaining swimmer! But the doctrine is false as well as repellent: Chance drowns the worthy with the unworthy, bears up the unfit with the fit by whatever definition, and makes the night-sea journey essentially *haphazard* as well as murderous and unjustified.

"'You only swim once.' Why bother, then?   11

"'Except ye drown, ye shall not reach the Shore of Light.' Poppycock.   12

"One of my late companions—that same cynic with the curious fancy,   13 among the first to drown—entertained us with odd conjectures while we waited to begin our journey. A favorite theory of his was that the Father does exist, and did indeed make us and the sea we swim—but not a-purpose or even consciously; He made us, as it were, despite Himself, as we make waves with every tail-thrash, and may be unaware of our existence. Another was that He knows we're here but doesn't care what happens to us, inasmuch as He creates (voluntarily or not) other seas and swimmers at more or less regular intervals. In bitterer moments, such as just before he drowned, my friend even supposed that our Maker wished us unmade; there was indeed a Shore, he'd argue, which could save at least some of us from drowning and toward which it was our function to struggle—but for reasons unknowable to us He wanted desperately to prevent our reaching that happy place and fulfilling our destiny. Our 'Father,' in short, was our adversary and would-be killer! No less outrageous, and offensive to traditional opinion, were the fellow's speculations on the nature of our Maker: that He might well be no swimmer Himself at all, but some sort of monstrosity, perhaps even tailless; that He might be stupid, malicious, insensible, perverse, or asleep and dreaming; that the end for which He created and launched us forth, and which we flagellate ourselves to fathom, was perhaps immoral, even obscene. Et cetera, et cetera: there was no end to the chap's conjectures, or the impoliteness of his fancy; I have reason to suspect that his early demise, whether planned by 'our Maker' or not, was expedited by certain fellow-swimmers indignant at his blasphemies.

"In other moods, however (he was as given to moods as I), his theoriz-   14 ing would become half-serious, so it seemed to me, especially upon the subjects of Fate and Immortality, to which our youthful conversations often turned. Then his harangues, if no less fantastical, grew solemn and obscure, and if he was still baiting us, his passion undid the joke. His objection to popular opinions of the hereafter, he would declare, was their claim to general validity. Why need believers hold that *all* the drownèd rise to be judged at journey's end, and non-believers that drowning is final without exception? In *his* opinion (so he'd vow at least), nearly everyone's fate was permanent death; indeed he took a sour pleasure in supposing that every 'Maker' made thousands of separate seas in His creative lifetime, each populated like ours with millions of swimmers, and that in almost every instance both sea and swimmers were utterly annihilated, whether accidentally or by malevolent design. (Nothing if not pluralistic, he imagined there might be millions and billions of 'Fathers,' perhaps in some 'night-sea' of their own!) However—and here he turned infidels against him with the faithful—he professed to believe that in possibly a single night-sea per thousand, say, one of its quarter-billion swimmers (that is, one swimmer in two hundred fifty billions) achieved a qualified immortality. In some cases the rate might be slightly higher; in others it was vastly lower, for just as there are swimmers of every degree of proficiency, including some who drown before the journey starts, unable to swim at all, and others created drowned, as it were, so he imagined what can only be termed impotent Creators, Makers unable to Make, as well as uncommonly fertile ones and all grades between. And it pleased him to deny any necessary relation between a Maker's productivity and His other virtues—including, even, the quality of His creatures.

"I could go on (*he* surely did) with his elaboration of these mad notions— 15 such as that swimmers in other night-seas needn't be of our kind; that Makers themselves might belong to different *species,* so to speak; that our particular Maker mightn't Himself be immortal, or that we might be not only His emissaries but His 'immortality,' continuing His life and our own, transmogrified, beyond our individual deaths. Even this modified immortality (meaningless to me) he conceived as relative and contingent, subject to accident or deliberate termination: his pet hypothesis was that Makers and swimmers *each generate the other*—against all odds, their number being so great—and that any given 'immortality-chain' could terminate after any number of cycles, so that what was 'immortal' (still speaking relatively) was only the cyclic process of incarnation, which itself might have a beginning and an end. Alternatively he liked to imagine cycles within cycles, either finite or infinite: for example, the 'night-sea,' as it were, in which Makers 'swam' and created night-seas and swimmers like ourselves, might be the creation of a larger Maker, Himself one of many, Who in turn et cetera. Time itself he regarded as relative to our experience, like magnitude: who knew but what, with each thrash of our tails, minuscule seas and swimmers, whole eternities, came to pass—as ours, perhaps, and our Maker's Maker's, was elapsing between the strokes of some supertail, in a slower order of time?

"Naturally I hooted with the others at this nonsense. We were young 16 then, and had only the dimmest notion of what lay ahead; in our ignorance we imagined night-sea journeying to be a positively heroic enterprise. Its meaning and value we never questioned; to be sure, some must go down by the way, a pity no doubt, but to win a race requires that others lose, and like all my fellows I took for granted that I would be the winner. We milled and swarmed, impatient to be off, never mind where or why, only to try our youth against the realities of night and sea; if we indulged the skeptic at all, it was as a droll, half-contemptible mascot. When he died in the initial slaughter, no one cared.

"And even now I don't subscribe to all his views—but I no longer scoff. 17 The horror of our history has purged me of opinions, as of vanity, confidence, spirit, charity, hope, vitality, everything—except dull dread and a kind of melancholy, stunned persistence. What leads me to recall his fancies is my growing suspicion that I, of all swimmers, may be the sole survivor of this fell journey, tale-bearer of a generation. This suspicion, together with the recent sea-change, suggests to me now that nothing is impossible, not even my late companion's wildest visions, and brings me to a certain desperate resolve, the point of my chronicling.

"Very likely I have lost my senses. The carnage at our setting out; our decimation by whirlpool, poisoned cataract, sea-convulsion; the panic stampedes, mutinies, slaughters, mass suicides; the mounting evidence that none will survive the journey—add to these anguish and fatigue; it were a miracle if sanity stayed afloat. Thus I admit, with the other possibilities, that the present sweetening and calming of the sea, and what seems to be a kind of vasty presence, song, or summons from the near upstream, may be hallucinations of disordered sensibility. . . . 18

"Perhaps, even, I am drowned already. Surely I was never meant for the rough-and-tumble of the swim; not impossibly I perished at the outset and have only imagined the night-sea journey from some final deep. In any case, I'm no longer young, and it is we spent old swimmers, disabused of every illusion, who are most vulnerable to dreams. 19

"Sometimes I think I am my drownèd friend. 20

"Out with it: I've begun to believe, not only that *She* exists, but that She lies not far ahead, and stills the sea, and draws me Herward! Aghast, I recollect his maddest notion: that our destination (which existed, mind, in but one night-sea out of hundreds and thousands) was no Shore, as commonly conceived, but a mysterious being, indescribable except by paradox and vaguest figure: wholly different from us swimmers, yet our complement; the death of us, yet our salvation and resurrection; simultaneously our journey's end, midpoint, and commencement; not membered and thrashing like us, but a motionless or hugely gliding sphere of unimaginable dimension; self-contained, yet dependent absolutely, in some wise, upon the chance (always monstrously improbable) that one of us will survive the night-sea journey and reach . . . Her! *Her*, he called it, or *She*, which is to say, Other-than-a-he. I shake my head; the thing is too preposterous; it is myself I talk to, to keep my reason in this awful darkness. There is no She! There is no You! I rave to myself; it's Death alone that hears and summons. To the drowned, all seas are calm. . . . 21

"Listen: my friend maintained that in every order of creation there are two sorts of creators, contrary yet complementary, one of which gives rise to seas and swimmers, the other to the Night-which-contains-the-sea and to What-waits-at-the-journey's-end: the former, in short, to destiny, the latter to destination (and both profligately, involuntarily, perhaps indifferently or unwittingly). The 'purpose' of the night-sea journey—but not necessarily of the journeyer or of either Maker!—my friend could describe only in abstractions: *consummation, transfiguration, union of contraries, transcension of categories.* When we laughed, he would shrug and admit that he understood the business no better than we, and thought it ridiculous, dreary, possibly obscene. 'But one of you,' he'd add with his wry smile, 'may be the Hero destined to complete the night-sea journey and be one with Her. Chances are, of course, you won't make it.' He himself, he declared, was not even going to try; the whole idea repelled him; if we chose to dismiss it as an ugly fiction, so much the better for us; thrash, splash, and be merry, we were soon enough drowned. But there it was, he could not say how he knew or why he bothered to tell us, 22 any more than he could say what would happen after She and Hero, Shore and Swimmer, 'merged identities' to become something both and neither. He quite agreed with me that if the issue of that magical union had no memory of the night-sea journey, for example, it enjoyed a poor sort of immortality; even poorer if, as he rather imagined, a swimmer-hero plus a She equaled or became merely another Maker of future night-seas and the rest, at such incredible expense of life. This being the case—he was persuaded it was—the merciful thing to do was refuse to participate; the genuine heroes, in his opinion, were the suicides, and the hero of heroes would be the swimmer who, in the very presence of the Other, refused Her proffered 'immortality' and thus put an end to at least one cycle of catastrophes.

"How we mocked him! Our moment came, we hurtled forth, pretending 23 to glory in the adventure, thrashing, singing, cursing, strangling, rationalizing, rescuing, killing, inventing rules and stories and relationships, giving up, struggling on, but dying all, and still in darkness, until only a battered remnant was left to croak 'Onward, upward,' like a bitter echo. Then they too fell silent—victims, I can only presume, of the last frightful wave—and the moment came when I also, utterly desolate and spent, thrashed my last and gave myself over to the current, to sink or float as might be, but swim no more. Whereupon, marvelous to tell, in an instant the sea grew still! Then warmly, gently, the great tide turned, began to bear me, as it does now, onward and upward will-I nill-I, like a flood of joy—and I recalled with dismay my dead friend's teaching.

"I am not deceived. This new emotion is Her doing; the desire that pos- 24 sesses me is Her bewitchment. Lucidity passes from me; in a moment I'll cry 'Love!' bury myself in Her side, and be 'transfigured.' Which is to say, I die already; this fellow transported by passion is not I; *I am he who abjures and rejects the night-sea journey!* I. . . .

"I am all love. 'Come!' She whispers, and I have no will. 25

"You who I may be about to become, whatever You are: with the last 26 twitch of my real self I beg You to listen. It is *not* love that sustains me! No; though Her magic makes me burn to sing the contrary, and though I drown even now for the blasphemy, I will say truth. What has fetched me across this dreadful sea is a single hope, gift of my poor dead comrade: that You may be stronger willed than I, and that by sheer force of concentration I may transmit to You, along with Your official Heritage, a private legacy of awful recollection and negative resolve. Mad as it may be, my dream is that some unimaginable embodiment of myself (or myself plus Her if that's how it must be) will come to find itself expressing, in however garbled or radical a translation, some reflection of these reflections. If against all odds this comes to pass, may You to whom, through whom I speak, do what I cannot: terminate this aimless, brutal business! Stop Your hearing against Her song! Hate love!

"Still alive, afloat, afire. Farewell then my penultimate hope: that one may 27 be sunk for direst blasphemy on the very shore of the Shore. Can it be (my old friend would smile) that only utterest nay-sayers survive the night? But even that were Sense, and there is no sense, only senseless love, senseless death. Whoever echoes these reflections: be more courageous than their author! An end to night-sea journeys! Make no more! And forswear me when I shall forswear myself, deny myself, plunge into Her who summons, singing . . .

"'Love! Love! Love!'"   28

FOR DISCUSSION AND WRITING: COMPOSING PARABLES

1. You now have enough experience with parable and allegory to think usefully about the way this form of writing works and the reasons for its persistence for more than two thousand years. Basing your work on what you have read here and any other experience of these forms that you may have, consider some of the following questions:

   a. What are the differences between modern parable and the parables of Jesus?

   b. Which of these parables or allegories do you find most interesting? Why? What is the source of its appeal to you? Can you base a principle on your own experience, arguing that parables are best when they do X or Y?

   c. Consider all those places in which the writer of a parable is thinking about parables themselves. What theories of parable are generated in these texts? Which do you find most satisfying? Why?

2. Write a short parable of your own, in which you present a story about one thing that wants to be read as carrying meanings in another area of thought altogether, as the parable of the sower of seeds carries meaning about the teacher of ideas and values.

METAPHOR AND METONYMY: ADVERTISING

Metaphor plays a major role in one kind of text that we encounter every day: advertising. To analyze the role of metaphor in advertising, we will need one more technical term: *metonymy*. We have been using the term *metaphor* to cover all the ways of talking about one thing in terms of another, but actually we can make an important distinction between metaphor proper and another metaphoric device. This device is called metonymy. Metaphor proper is based upon some resemblance between the two things that are brought together in the metaphor. Robert Francis can speak of poetry and baseball in the same language because a poet and a baseball pitcher share certain attributes (pp. 89–90). There is an analogy between the two elements of the metaphor.

We use metonymy, on the other hand, whenever we speak of one thing in terms of another that is usually associated with it. When we say

"The White House says . . ." we don't mean that the building actually spoke but that the person who lives there, the president, has taken the position attributed to the building. Cartoonists use this same metonymy whenever they draw a picture of the White House with words coming out of it. A frequently used type of metonymy called *synecdoche* is the substitution of part of something for the whole of it. If we asked a rancher, "How many cattle do you own?" he might reply, "Seven hundred head." Obviously, he owns the rest of the beasts also, not just the heads. You can keep clear the difference between metaphor and metonymy by remembering these examples: (1) *head of beer* is a metaphor, based on resemblance, and (2) *head of cattle* is metonymy, based on association — in this case synecdoche, a part for the whole.

In advertising, metonymy or association is very important. When a celebrity endorses a product, an association is formed between them. When a basketball player endorses a basketball shoe, we have a natural metonymy. Such shoes are already associated with the player. What the advertiser wants, however, and will sometimes make very explicit, is to have this metonymy interpreted as a metaphor. That is, the maker of basketball shoes wants us (subconsciously or consciously) to attribute the quality of the player to the shoe. Most beer commercials establish a metonymic connection between good times and beer, hoping that the viewer will accept a further metaphoric connection and finally a cause-and-effect connection: the beer *is* good and a *cause* of good times.

Some ads make a very skillful use of metaphor and metonymy to push their products. You owe it to yourself to understand exactly how they are trying to manipulate you. We provide analyses of three ads here and then invite you to do some analytical work of your own.

Vista

Though it may not appear so in our black-and-white reproduction of it, the Vista ad is visually striking. The tanned diver is dressed in red trunks and T-shirt. The water in the foreground is very shallow and transparent, showing the brown sand under it. The sea is green with bright whitecaps. The upper half of the picture is all bright blue sky, without a cloud. The diver is plunging into no more than two or three inches of water. It is a dramatic, arresting picture, and it arrests the viewer's eye as well. What is going on here, we wonder, and what will come of it? Why would anyone dive into two inches of water anyway?

For answers, we must go to the small, white sentences printed over the blue sky in the upper left of the frame. What they tell us is that we shouldn't read the picture literally. It is not about diving but about things for which such a dive may be a metaphor. The printed text picks up these metaphors from the visual image and interprets them in such a way as to connect them to the product being advertised:

When you dive into a client
presentation.
When you hit the dirt in a
business skirmish.
When you make a splash with
the higher-ups.
And the higher higher-ups.

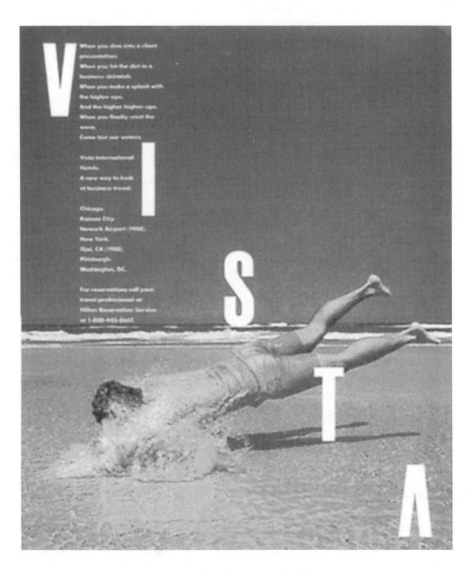

When you finally crest the
wave.
Come test our waters.

After this it introduces the product, a chain of hotels seeking business-people as customers. The ad takes a collection of dead or inert metaphors that have come to function as clichés about business, and revitalizes them by connecting them to a single, startling visual image. What the image does is take them literally—dive, hit the dirt, make a splash, crest the wave, test our waters. It shows someone doing all these things—or almost doing all these things. After all, it is not easy to hit the dirt and make a splash at the same time. This sounds, in fact, like a clumsily mixed metaphor, but the picture shows how one can indeed hit the dirt and make a splash at the same time. You just dive into two inches of water. This whole process does many of the same things that poems do. It revives inert metaphors that have become clichés; it gives you metaphor where you expect literal meaning and literal meaning where you expect figures of speech. It is also a little bit like a riddle or puzzle on the order of Sylvia Plath's poem "Metaphors." Is it a good ad? Will it sell the product? It is hard to say, but it certainly is an attention-getter, and the visual image does indeed lead us to look at the text to find out what is going on here. For our purposes, of course, it also demonstrates once again how poetry and advertising often employ the same dimensions of language for their different purposes.

Productbuzz

If you had opened to Productbuzz's full-page ad in *Forbes* magazine, you would definitely have noticed it. The background is lime green, and out of it vibrate Day-Glo orange-red—well, what are they? Saucers? And what have they to do with the two assertive phrases that separate them?

Today, tongue depressors.
Tomorrow, the world.

Maybe they are stylized mouths opening for those tongue depressors, but it's likely you'll turn the page rather than reading on because of the offensive Day-Glo attack on your eyes. And there's another reason to question the effectiveness of this ad, which jumps out of the meant-to-be-clever-sounding slogan. Many people will recognize it as a parodic version of "Today, Germany, tomorrow the world," a slogan associated with Adolf Hitler and his Nazis as they began the aggressive takeover of much of Europe, an aggression that would bring about World War II. Indeed, this phrase has been adapted by racists promoting "white power." An Internet search will turn up other parodic versions, some of which may be amusing, but primarily to those lacking a sense of history.

Certainly Productbuzz wants your business and promotes itself as an effective developer of "digital marketplaces." This ad proclaims its success with the health-care industry, suggesting that the clever marketing of the humblest health-care item, the tongue depressor, is but the first step toward enormous sales of big-ticket services and equipment. The corporate world wants to be

Today, tongue depressors.
Tomorrow, the world.

Healthcare is just the beginning. Next, more vertical industries, each ready for a new way to do business. Ready for Web-based communities built around the products they need to buy and sell. Productbuzz's *Guided Digital Marketplaces* are just that...real one-stop shops focused on the products, information, news—even job listings—that every business requires. *Finally*, digital marketplaces that look good on paper too. Saving time and effort for buyers. Driving traffic to sellers. Making connections and closing deals. Productbuzz. The e-commerce model with a difference: It works.

*product*buzz

www.productbuzz.com

sure the dot coms it deals with can really hustle, and Productbuzz wants its ad to be aggressive and convincing enough to catch corporate attention. However, many corporate minds may wonder, as we did, just what those saucer-like shapes are meant to represent. Open mouths ready to eat those words? The logo at the bottom solves this little problem: those things are meant to be sound waves symbolizing the buzz of business. But with such an unfortunate intertext, they may also be read as bad vibrations.

NeuVis: "So Much for E-Business Being a Level Playing Field"

The NeuVis ad is designed around the cliché of the "level playing field," on which competitors meet without advantages. To this idea of sportsmanship is opposed the new entrepreneurial ruthlessness, in which the whole idea is to compete unfairly and take advantage of the weaknesses of others. "Give yourself an unfair advantage," says the fine print. NeuVis wants to suggest that if you use their software, your business will succeed like the team on the left in the visual image.

In the picture, there is no time left in the fourth quarter, and the home team has gone beyond the 99 possible points on the scoreboard to lead 119 to 0, which amounts to seventeen touchdowns and extra points. The game appears to have been played by very young children — grammar school age — with one exception. The home team has a center who looks like a transfer from the National Football League. This towering behemoth is poised to center the ball and lead the interference. The fine print suggests that "as you break out of the pack, you can change direction, improve your system and add features without losing critical momentum" — putting the language of sport and of software somewhat uneasily into the same sentence.

But the image is doing the heavy work in this ad. Anyone who knows the game of football can imagine what will happen after the snap — and especially to those tiny creatures directly facing the monstrous center. If these teams had actually played for sixty minutes, it is doubtful whether anyone would be left to line up on the right side of the line of scrimmage. But NeuVis leaves all that to our imaginations. They would not wish us to see too clearly the actual mayhem that would occur if the ball were snapped.

They do, however, want us to think about that metaphorical cliché of the "level playing field." The field is pictured vividly for us — a cliché brought to life — and it is level, but the game is unfair. Our football culture is full of expressions such as "Just win, baby!" and "Winning isn't everything. It's the only thing." The old idea that it doesn't matter whether you win or lose but how you play the game has been swallowed up by a culture that encourages everyone to think only of "the bottom line" — which is the line on an account where the final total is reckoned. The connection between football, advertising, and business is powerfully active in our culture. This ad taps into that existing cultural code.

The picture also is slightly funny. It exaggerates. It is aware of itself as making a pitch. NeuVis software is not going to put your team ahead 119 to 0 at the end of the fiscal year. But the strangeness of the picture and the awful implications of what will happen if that ball is snapped attract our attention irresistibly. We see it as a sort of odd joke and are led to wonder just what it means. Visually speaking, this is a brilliant conception. The written text, in our opinion, doesn't come near that level of cleverness. But the power and appropriateness of the image make this a successful ad.

FOR DISCUSSION AND WRITING: COMPARING AND ANALYZING METAPHORIC AND METONYMIC QUALITIES IN ADVERTISING

1. Even without the example of these discussions before you, you know a lot about advertising because you see many ads every day. Find two different full-page ads for a particular type of product such as designer perfume, cigarettes, bran cereal, or luxury automobiles. (We suggest a slick magazine designed for a general audience, such as *Sports Illustrated,* the *New Yorker, Esquire,* or *Vogue,* as your best source of skillfully done ads.) Write an essay in which you compare and discuss the metaphoric and metonymic qualities of the two ads. Try to reach some conclusions about how and why certain things work in advertising.

2. Find an ad that you think doesn't work very well, and write an analysis of its strengths and weaknesses. For example, does the ad present metonymic associations that are counterproductive, such as using the wrong celebrity or an unsuitable cliché? Does it use metaphors that are at odds with the product or service the ad is trying to sell? Or is the ad just plain untruthful about the product or service it's trying to sell?

3

Texts and
Other Texts

I N THE PREVIOUS TWO CHAPTERS we examined aspects of language and textuality that have been considered important since Aristotle's time. At this point, however, we begin to shift our attention to things that have been the special concerns of modern literature and recent literary theory. As you might expect, from here on, things get more complicated. Our principles, however, remain the same. We will continue to share with you the theory that we have used to shape our presentation of ideas and materials. We will also continue to offer you opportunities to grasp this theory by actual application of it to textual situations.

Our emphasis in this chapter, as you will soon see, is on the way that texts are always related to and dependent upon other texts. In our culture we have tended to stress "originality" as a supreme value in writing. The pressure to be "original" has often worked to inhibit writers—especially student writers—and thus to prevent them from actually developing their ideas. One of our purposes in this chapter is to reduce the anxiety about originality.

Once you realize that all texts are reworkings of other texts, that writing comes out of reading, that writing is always rewriting, you can see that the desirable quality we call "originality" does not mean creating something out of nothing but simply making an interesting change in what has been done before you. One develops as a writer by playing with material already in existence. The "new" emerges as a function of this play. With this in mind, we invite you to enter the world of intertextuality—where you have actually lived all along.

INTERTEXTUALITY

One of the surest tests is the way a poet borrows. Immature poets imitate; mature poets steal.   —*T. S. Eliot*

In their traffic with art, artists employ preformed images as they employ whatever else feeds into their work. Between their experience of nature and their experience of other art they allow no functional difference.   —*Leo Steinberg*

Artists and writers do not simply look at nature—or into their own hearts—and transcribe what they find there. This is so because for them the very act of looking is already shaped by the art and writing of the past, as well as by other cultural conventions. The eye of an adult human being is never innocent. The eye of a baby may be "innocent" in some sense, but it is also untrained, and the untrained eye does not see much. As observers of life, we go from ignorance to prejudice without ever passing through the mythical land of objectivity. What a scientist learns is how to see with the prejudices of his or her own science. An artist sees through the prejudices of art.

This is simply the way things are for human beings in this world. Learning to see nature or the human heart is learning how to notice certain things and disregard others. But that is only one side of the problem facing the artist or writer. The writer must not only notice and disregard things. The writer must also transcribe the things that he or she notices. That is, the writer must find ways to put experience into verbal form. Experience need not come in the form of an anecdote or a play, but it must be expressed in these or other forms that already exist. A writer, we may say, has one eye on experience and the other on writing that has already been done. No text is produced without awareness of other texts. This is why Labov (see chapter 1) finds a repeated structural pattern in anecdotes told by ordinary speakers. These speakers have already listened to many anecdotes themselves. They know the anecdotal forms.

When a group of people are exchanging anecdotes, stories, or jokes, a further development will be noticed: relationships may be generated between what one person and another person recount. Sometimes the connection is just similarity or association. You will hear a speaker say, "That reminds me of . . . ." But other times one story will be told in opposition to another, to prove an opposite point or illustrate an alternative view of someone or something. In an extended session, the relationship of one story to another can become very complicated. With written texts—and especially the durable written texts we call literature—such relationships are often of the most elaborate and complex kinds. The technical term for such relationships is *intertextuality*.

Wherever there are texts, there is intertextuality. Even in what we may call minimal texts, like bumper stickers, we can find intertextuality. For instance, in a certain tiny New England state, environmentalists display a red bumper sticker that says SAVE THE BAY. The bay in question suffers from pollution that is a threat to health, to commercial shellfishing, and to the quality of life in general. Many of those concerned with these matters have joined an organization working to preserve or restore the quality of this bay's water. Hence the bumper sticker: SAVE THE BAY.

There are those, however, who do not love environmentalists and do not care about the quality of the bay. They have originated and proudly display a black sticker with their own slogan: PAVE THE BAY. Whatever one's view of the rights and wrongs of the matter, if you are a student of literary language, you have to admit that PAVE THE BAY is the more interesting of the two signs. It is interesting because it is more concrete (so to speak), because it suggests something that is hardly possible (since the bay in question is thirty miles long and five miles wide) and because it is more clearly intertextual.

Paving the bay is sufficiently unlikely to violate our sense of the possible. We readers of this bumper text are forced by this impossibility to find a second way to read the text. If it cannot be meant *literally*, it must, if it means anything, have what we call a *figurative* meaning. That is, it must function like a metaphor. We cannot simply read it; we must interpret it. What does PAVE THE BAY mean? Its meaning depends upon its intertextuality. Without SAVE THE BAY, PAVE THE BAY would be close to nonsense, a mere impossibility. But alongside SAVE THE BAY, from which it is distinguishable by only a single letter, PAVE THE BAY signifies, among other things, the rejection or negation of the environmentalist position that is textualized in SAVE THE BAY. PAVE THE BAY means "Don't let these wimpy environmentalists push you around."

A similar relationship exists between another bumper sticker, WARNING: I BRAKE FOR ANIMALS, and its anti-text, WARNING: I SPEED UP TO HIT LITTLE ANIMALS (both actually exist). Even here the second text signifies mainly a rejection of the first. That is, WARNING: I BRAKE FOR ANIMALS is meant to refer literally to the behavior of the driver; whereas WARNING: I SPEED UP TO HIT LITTLE ANIMALS does not necessarily tell you about the driver's intentions. It does tell you about his or her attitude toward the sentiment displayed on the first sign. It refers, then, not literally to the world of action but intertextually to the other sign, which it negates.

PAVE THE BAY is a more interesting negation for two reasons. First, it is so economical: a major change in meaning is achieved through the alteration of just one letter. Second, it presents a more startling concept than speeding up to hit animals: it suggests a slightly different world, where strange feats of engineering are possible, whereas going out of one's way to inflict pain on defenseless creatures is distressingly familiar to us. The attitudes motivating the two signs may not be terribly different. They are rooted in dislike of environmentalists who interfere with the rights of others. But one of the two stickers is more interesting than the other—and both are more interesting than their pre-texts, precisely because they are intertextual.

In another case, the "wimps" have the last word. The sticker PRESERVE YOUR RIGHT TO BEAR ARMS has been answered by PRESERVE YOUR RIGHT TO ARM BEARS. Again, the second sign is more interesting because it is both intertextual and figurative. Giving guns to bears is not a possible project in this world. The text that advocates this impossibility thus forces us to look for a nonliteral meaning. To read it we must see it as a transformation of its literal predecessor: ARM BEARS is another minimal change, using exactly the same letters as BEAR ARMS, but inverting the words and relocating the S to make ARM a verb and BEARS a noun. Maximum change of meaning with minimal verbal change seems to be a rule of quality here. The second text, which would be nonsense without the first, becomes supersense when connected with its pre-text. For the reader to interpret the second text, he or she must see it as a *transformation* of the first. That is a crucial principle. Intertextuality is active when the reader is aware of the way one text is connected to others.

There are many forms of intertextuality. One text may contain a mention of another, for instance, or a quotation or citation of an earlier text. One text may devote itself extensively to a discussion of another, offering commentary, interpretation, counterstatement, or criticism. One text may be a translation of another, an imitation, an adaptation, a pastiche, or a parody. In this chapter, we shall explore many—though not all—of these possible relationships. As an introduction to the practice of intertextuality, we ask you to consider and discuss the following three texts. Text (1) is a passage from the Bible's Old Testament, in the translation produced in England in the early seventeenth century. Text (2) is a speech delivered by a messenger in a play written in England in the later seventeenth century. Text (3) is an advertisement that appeared in a popular magazine in the later twentieth century.

Text (1)

Samson

Book of Judges

This section of the Bible tells the story of Samson, who was predestined by God to help deliver the Israelites from the control of the Philistines. Endowed with great strength, Samson in one battle slew one thousand Philistines with the jawbone of an ass. The source of this strength was his hair, which had never been cut. He kept this knowledge secret until it was seduced from him by Delilah, a woman who, paid by the Philistines, had Samson's head shaved while he was sleeping. Bereft of his exceptional strength, Samson was captured by the Philistines, blinded, and made to grind grain in the prison house. The following section picks up at this point.

21 But the Philistines took him, and put out his eyes, and brought him down to Gaza, and bound him with fetters of brass; and he did grind in the prison house.

22 Howbeit the hair of his head began to grow again after he was shaven.

23 Then the lords of the Philistines gathered them together for to offer a great sacrifice unto Dagon their god, and to rejoice: for they said, Our god hath delivered Samson our enemy into our hand.

24 And when the people saw him, they praised their god: for they said, Our god hath delivered into our hands our enemy, and the destroyer of our country, which slew many of us.

25 And it came to pass, when their hearts were merry, that they said, Call for Samson, that he may make us sport. And they called for Samson out of the prison house; and he made them sport: and they set him between the pillars.

26 And Samson said unto the lad that held him by the hand, Suffer me that I may feel the pillars whereupon the house standeth, that I may lean upon them.

27 Now the house was full of men and women; and all the lords of the Philistines were there; and *there were* upon the roof about three thousand men and women, that beheld while Samson made sport.

28 And Samson called unto the Lord, and said, O Lord God, remember me, I pray thee, and strengthen me, I pray thee, only this once, O God, that I may be at once avenged of the Philistines for my two eyes.

29 And Samson took hold of the two middle pillars upon which the house stood, and on which it was borne up, of the one with his right hand, and of the other with his left.

30 And Samson said, Let me die with the Philistines. And he bowed himself with *all his* might; and the house fell upon the lords, and upon all the people that *were* therein. So the dead which he slew at his death were more than *they* which he slew in his life.

31 Then his brethren and all the house of his father came down, and took him, and brought *him* up, and buried him between Zorah and Eshtaol in the buryingplace of Manoah his father. . . .

Judges 16.21–31, King James version

Text (2)

From Samson Agonistes

John Milton

British poet John Milton (1608–1674) retold Samson's story in his play Samson Agonistes. *In this selection from the play, the final events of Samson's life are narrated by a messenger from another city.*

Messenger. Occasions drew me early to this city,
And as the gates I entered with sun-rise,
The morning trumpets festival proclaimed
Through each high street. Little I had despatched
When all abroad was rumored that this day   1600
Samson should be brought forth to shew the people
Proof of his mighty strength in feats and games;
I sorrowed at his captive state, but minded
Not to be absent at that spectacle.
The building was a spacious theater   1605
Half round on two main pillars vaulted high,
With seats where all the lords and each degree
Of sort, might sit in order to behold,
The other side was open, where the throng
On banks and scaffolds under sky might stand;   1610
I among these aloof obscurely stood.
The feast and noon grew high, and sacrifice
Had filled their hearts with mirth, high cheer, and wine,
When to their sports they turned. Immediately
Was Samson as a public servant brought,   1615
In their state livery clad; before him pipes
And timbrels, on each side went armed guards,
Both horse and foot before him and behind
Archers, and slingers, cataphracts and spears
At sight of him the people with a shout   1620
Rifted the air clamoring their god with praise,
Who had made their dreadful enemy their thrall.
He patient but undaunted where they led him,
Came to the place, and what was set before him
Which without help of eye, might be assayed,   1625
To heave, pull, draw, or break, he still performed
All with the incredible, stupendious force,
None daring to appear antagonist.
At length for intermission sake they led him
Between the pillars; he his guide requested   1630
(For so from such as nearer stood we heard)
As over-tired to let him lean a while
With both his arms on those two massy pillars
That to the arched roof gave main support.
He unsuspicious led him; which when Samson   1635
Felt in his arms, with head a while inclined,
And eyes fast fixed he stood, as one who prayed,
Or some great matter in his mind revolved.
At last with head erect thus cried aloud,
"Hitherto, Lords, what your commands imposed   1640
I have performed, as reason was, obeying,
Not without wonder or delight beheld.
Now of my own accord such other trial
I mean to show you of my strength, yet greater;

As with amaze shall strike all who behold." 1645
This uttered, straining all his nerves he bowed;
As with the force of winds and waters pent
When mountains tremble, those two massy pillars
With horrible convulsion to and fro
He tugged, he shook, till down they came and drew 1650
The whole roof after them, with burst of thunder
Upon the heads of all who sat beneath,
Lords, ladies, captain, counsellors, or priests,
Their choice nobility and flower, not only
Of this but each Philistian city round 1655
Met from all parts to solemnize this feast.
Samson with these immixed, inevitably
Pulled down the same destruction on himself;
The vulgar only scaped, who stood without.

Text (3)

FITNESS FOR MEN

The Rake.
Ultimate footwear for the club, the court, or the Colosseum.

FOR DISCUSSION AND WRITING: ANALYZING
A TEXTUAL NETWORK

1. The biblical text is itself, no doubt, a written version of material that was transmitted orally before being set down in the Hebrew Bible. The English version is a translation made in the early 1600s. It is the immediate pre-text for Milton's verse drama, *Samson Agonistes*, though Milton knew his Bible in Hebrew as well. In the passage we have quoted, a messenger recounts the same crucial events covered by the biblical passage. Discuss the changes Milton has made and the possible reasons for them. How, in other words, has he used his pre-text?

2. Looking at the third text, how can we tell it is part of the same textual network as the others? What specific features indicate this connection? How does this text use the Samson textual network? Try to consider every detail of text (3), such as things like the meaning of "ultimate," for instance.

TRANSFORMING TEXTS (1)

In this section we will consider some of the more obvious ways in which new texts are created out of old ones. We can begin with a textual finger exercise devised by the French writer Raymond Queneau. In his book *Transformations*, Queneau presents a very short account of two trivial incidents that do not even make a simple story. He then proceeds to represent these incidents a hundred times, using a different stylistic principle every time. We have reprinted here, in English translation, Queneau's original "Notation" and six of his revisions. We would like you to examine each of his transformations and discuss exactly what he has done and how he has done it, before proceeding to some transformations of your own.

From Transformations

Raymond Queneau

otation

In the S bus, in the rush hour. A chap of about 26, felt hat with a cord instead of a ribbon, neck too long, as if someone's been having a tug-of-war with it. People getting off. The chap in question gets annoyed with one of the men standing next to him. He accuses him of jostling him every time anyone goes past. A snivelling tone which is meant to be aggressive. When he sees a vacant seat he throws himself on to it.

Two hours later, I meet him in the Cour de Rome, in front of the gare Saint-Lazare. He's with a friend who's saying: "You ought to get an extra button put on your overcoat." He shows him where (at the lapels) and why.

ouble   *ntry*

Towards the middle of the day and at midday I happened to be on and got on to the platform and the balcony at the back of an S-line and of a Contrescarpe-Champerret bus and passenger transport vehicle which was packed and to all intents and purposes full. I saw and noticed a young man and an old adolescent who was rather ridiculous and pretty grotesque; thin neck and skinny windpipe, string and cord round his hat and tile. After a scrimmage and scuffle he says and states in a lachrymose and snivelling voice and tone that his neighbour and fellow-traveller is deliberately trying and doing his utmost to push him and obtrude himself on him every time anyone gets off and makes an exit. This having been declared and having spoken he rushes headlong and wends his way towards a vacant and a free place and seat.

Two hours after and a-hundred-and-twenty minutes later, I meet him and see him again in the Cour de Rome and in front of the gare Saint-Lazare. He is with and in the company of a friend and pal who is advising and urging him to have a button and vegetable ivory disc added and sewn on to his overcoat and mantle.

recision

In a bus of the S-line, 10 metres long, 3 wide, 6 high, at 3 km. 600 m. from its starting point, loaded with 48 people, at 12.17 P.M., a person of the masculine sex aged 27 years 3 months and 8 days, 1 m. 72 cm. tall and weighing 65 kg. and wearing a hat 35 cm. in height round the crown of which was a ribbon 60 cm. long, interpollated a man aged 48 years 4 months and 3 days, 1 m. 68 cm. tall and weighing 77 kg., by means of 14 words whose enunciation lasted 5 seconds and which alluded to some involuntary displacements of from 15 to 20 mm. Then he went and sat down about 1 m. 10 cm. away.

57 minutes later he was 10 metres away from the suburban entrance to the gare Saint-Lazare and was walking up and down over a distance of 30 m. with a friend aged 28, 1 m. 70 cm. tall and weighing 71 kg. who advised him in 15 words to move by 5 cm. in the direction of the zenith a button which was 3 cm. in diameter.

arrative

One day at about midday in the Parc Monceau district, on the back platform of a more or less full S bus (now No. 84), I observed a person with a very long neck who was wearing a felt hat which had a plaited cord round it instead of a ribbon. This individual suddenly addressed the man standing next to him, accusing him of purposely treading on his toes every time any passengers got on or off. However he quickly abandoned the dispute and threw himself on to a seat which had become vacant.

Two hours later I saw him in front of the gare Saint-Lazare engaged in earnest conversation with a friend who was advising him to reduce the space between the lapels of his overcoat by getting a competent tailor to raise the top button.

assive

It was midday. The bus was being got into by passengers. They were being squashed together. A hat was being worn on the head of a young gentleman, which hat was encircled by a plait and not by a ribbon. A long neck was one of the characteristics of the young gentleman. The man standing next to him was being grumbled at by the latter because of the jostling which was being inflicted on him by him. As soon as a vacant seat was espied by the young gentleman it was made the object of his precipitate movements and it became sat down upon.

The young gentleman was later seen by me in front of the gare Saint-Lazare. He was clothed in an overcoat and was having a remark made to him by a friend who happened to be there to the effect that it was necessary to have an extra button put on it.

 *aiku*[1]

Summer S long neck
plait hat toes abuse retreat
station button friend

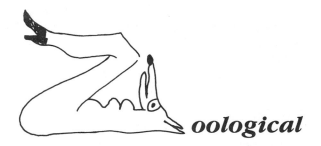 *oological*

In the dog days while I was in a bird cage at feeding time I noticed a young puppy with a neck like a giraffe who, like the toad, ugly and venomous, wore yet a precious beaver upon his head. This queer fish obviously had a bee in his bonnet and was quite bats, he started yakking at a wolf in sheep's clothing claiming that he was treading on his dogs with his beetle-crushers. But the sucker got a flea in his ear; that foxed him, and quiet as a mouse he ran like a hare for a perch.

---

[1][Haiku: a Japanese poem composed of three lines, of 5, 7, and 5 syllables respectively, and presenting one theme. *Eds.*]

I saw him again later in front of the Zoo with a young buck who was telling him to bear in mind a certain drill about his fevvers.

FOR DISCUSSION AND WRITING: MAKING YOUR OWN TRANSFORMATIONS

1. Compare "Notation" with each of its transformations. What, specifically, has been done in each adaptation to make it different from the others? How would you describe the "voice" in each one?

2. Using Queneau's six transformations as models, write a set of your own. Use as your "Notation" a short anecdote of your own, a newspaper report such as a police report, or the article reprinted here on p. 46.

3. Which transformation was easiest for you to write? Why? Which was most difficult? Why?

4. Try to imagine that "Precision" was written by someone whose composition teacher was always telling him or her to "be more precise" in his writing. What other rules of good writing are being parodied in Queneau's transformations?

TRANSFORMING TEXTS (2): SLEEPING BEAUTIES

Writers are always borrowing, or—as T. S. Eliot said in the quotation at the beginning of this chapter—stealing from one another. This is a basic element of textuality. Texts are produced through a combination of the writer's experiences as a human being and the writer's knowledge of earlier texts. Sometimes, however, the intertextual relationship is very much in the foreground: this is true in translation, interpretation, adaptation, and parody. Translation from one language to another is not our concern in this book. Interpretation will be taken up in the next section of this chapter. At the moment, we are concerned with *adaptation* and that special form of adaptation called *parody*.

Adaptation occurs whenever a writer rewrites an earlier work, making significant changes in the original. Raymond Queneau's *Transformations* (pp. 157–61) is one kind of adaptation. The versions of Samson's story produced by John Milton and by the Nike company's copywriters (pp. 154–56) are also adaptations. Milton's adaptation is a reverent development and extension of the biblical original. The Nike ad is more an allusion to the original than a full adaptation of it, but it represents a tendency toward that kind of irreverent adaptation we call *parody*.

A parody is an adaptation that makes fun of its original by exaggerating its most striking and unusual features or by relocating it to a context that renders the original absurd, as in the Nike ad. Exaggeration parodies the form of the original. Relocation parodies its content or meaning. Because it has a critical function, parody points the way to more formal kinds of interpretation and criticism. Parody and other forms of adaptation assume that the original still has some life in it if certain aspects of it are modified, others eliminated, and some new things added. In the following pages, we present for your consideration some adaptations of a well-known text, the fairy tale "Sleeping Beauty" or "Briar Rose," which exists in many versions, coming originally from the oral traditions of Europe. We offer here four versions, beginning with two by the Grimm brothers, who collected and transcribed their tales in Germany for many years before publishing the first edition of them in 1812. Because they rewrote and edited their texts so heavily, we have included here translations of both their manuscript version and that of the sixth edition. We ask you to note the changes and consider the reasons for them. The third version in our selection actually was written more than a century before the Grimms collected their stories. Charles Perrault was a cultured Frenchman whose sources are still mysterious, but he certainly seems to have tapped into an authentic mine of folktales. We have put his version after those of the Grimms because it is more elaborate.

There are many other versions of the sleeping princess in European culture, including the sleep of the Valkyrie, Brunhild, in the Old Norse Völsunga saga ("Saga of the Volsungs"). In this version, the heroine is awakened by the hero, Sigurd, who later betrays her. Richard Wagner followed this version in his operatic sequence, *The Ring of the Nibelung*. In another early version the sleeping maid is raped by a king, who brings her back to the palace, where his wife is not exactly pleased by this. In Perrault, the angry wife is replaced by a mother-in-law. Emily Martin showed in chapter 2 how the culture embodied in fairy tales can affect modern scientific thinking. Cultural shifts in value have also caused the tales themselves to be remade to suit the new attitudes.

The final text in this sequence consists of six units from Robert Coover's contemporary version of the story, *Briar Rose*,* including the first and the last. Coover, who has become a pioneer in the development of hypertext fiction, conceives of a narrative text like this one in terms of units that are variations on the possibilities of the story—it might have gone this way, it might have gone that way. The full book has many more than these six, but these will serve to show how an ancient tale can be rethought to carry new ideas in a postmodern form.

---

*The complete text of Robert Coover's *Briar Rose* may be found at www.bedfordstmartins .com/textbook, where *Briar Rose* may be read as a hypertext. You may find more information on hypertexts in "Text and Hypertext," pp. 238–39.

Thorn-rose (Briar-rose)
The Manuscript Version

Jacob and Wilhelm Grimm

A King and queen had no children at all. One day the queen was bathing,   1
when a crab crawled out of the water onto the land and said: you will soon
get a daughter. And so it happened also, and the king in his joy held a great
celebration and there were thirteen fairies in the land, but he had only twelve
golden plates, and so could not invite the thirteenth. The fairies endowed her
with every virtue and beauty. As the celebration was coming to an end, the
thirteenth fairy came and said: you did not ask me and I prophesy that your
daughter in her fifteenth year will prick her finger with a spindle and will die
of it. The other fairies wanted to make this as good as they could and said:
she should only fall asleep for a hundred years.

The king however issued the order that all spindles in the whole realm   2
should be destroyed, which happened, and when the king's daughter was fifteen years old, and the parents had one day gone out, she went around in the
castle and at last reached an old tower. A narrow staircase led into the tower,
then she came to a little door, in which there was a yellow key, which she
turned, and came into a little room in which an old woman was spinning
her flax. And she joked with the woman and wanted to spin also. Then she
pricked herself with the spindle, and fell immediately into a deep sleep. Because in that moment the king and his court had returned, everything in the
castle began to sleep, even the flies on the walls. And around the whole castle grew a thorn hedge, so that nothing of it could be seen.

After a long, long time a king's son came into the land, he was told the   3
story by an old man who remembered hearing it from his grandfather and
that already many had tried to get through the thorns, but all had remained
hanging in them. But when this prince went up to the thorn hedge, all the
thorns parted in front of him and seemed to be flowers, and behind him they
turned into thorns again. As he now entered the castle, he kissed the sleeping princess, and everything awoke from its sleep and the two married and if
they are not dead, they are still living.

Thorn-rose (Briar-rose)
From Grimm's Fairy Tales, *Sixth Edition*

Jacob and Wilhelm Grimm

A long time ago there lived a king and a queen who said every day, "oh, if   1
only we had a child!" and never had one. Then it happened that once when
the queen was bathing, a frog crawled out of the water onto the land and said
to her: "your wish will be fulfilled, before a year has passed you will bring a

daughter into the world." What the frog had said happened, and the queen gave birth to a girl, who was so beautiful that the king could not contain himself and arranged a great celebration. He invited not only his relatives, friends and acquaintances, but also the wise women, so that they might be kind and well disposed toward the child. There were thirteen of them in his kingdom, but because he had only twelve golden plates, from which they were to eat, one of them had to stay at home. The celebration was held with all manner of splendor, and when it was at an end, the wise women made presents to the child of their magical gifts: one gave virtue, the other beauty, the third riches, and thus was given everything in the world that could be wished. When eleven had made their pronouncements, the thirteenth suddenly entered. She wanted to avenge herself for not having been invited, and without greeting or even looking at anyone she cried in a loud voice: "the king's daughter shall prick herself with a spindle in her fifteenth year and fall down dead." And without saying another word, she turned around and left the hall. All were shocked, then the twelfth stepped forward, who still had her wish left, and because she could not lift the evil sentence, but only soften it, she said: "it shall not be death, however, but a hundred-year-long deep sleep, into which the king's daughter falls." The king, who wanted to preserve his dear child from misfortune, issued the order that all spindles in the whole kingdom should be burned. But the gifts of the wise women were all fulfilled in the girl, because she was so beautiful, well behaved, friendly and intelligent, that everyone who saw her had to like her. It happened that on the day when she became just fifteen years old, the king and the queen were not at home, and the girl remained quite alone in the castle. She went around everywhere, looked at rooms and chambers as she pleased, and at last came to an old tower. She climbed up the narrow spiral staircase and came to a small door. In the lock was a rusty key, and when it turned, the door sprang open, and an old woman sat in the little room with a spindle, and was busily spinning flax. "Good-day, old mother" said the king's daughter, "what are you doing there?" "I am spinning" said the old woman, and nodded her head. "What kind of thing is that, that jumps around so merrily?" said the girl, took the spindle and wanted to spin as well. But scarcely had she touched the spindle, when the spell was fulfilled and she pricked herself in the finger with it.

But the moment that she felt the prick, she fell down onto the bed that 2
stood there, and lay in a deep sleep. And this sleep spread over the whole castle: the king and queen, who had just come home and had entered the hall, began to fall asleep, and the whole court with them. Then the horses in the stable slept, the dogs in the courtyard, the doves on the roof, the flies on the wall, even the fire which was flaming on the hearth became still and fell asleep, and the roast meat stopped sizzling, and the cook, who wanted to pull the hair of the cook's boy, because he had neglected to do something, let go of him and slept. And the wind died down, and in the trees in front of the castle not a small leaf moved any more.

Around the castle, however, a thorn hedge began to grow, which grew higher 3
each year and finally surrounded the whole castle and grew all over it, so that nothing more could be seen of it, not even the flag on the roof. There was a story in the land, however, of the beautiful sleeping Thorn-rose, for so the king's

daughter was called, so that from time to time kings' sons came and wanted to penetrate through the hedge into the castle. But it was not possible for them, for the thorns held fast together, as if they had hands, and the young men remained hanging in them, could not get themselves free again, and died a pitiful death. After many long years a king's son came once again into the land and heard that an old man told of a thorn hedge, that a castle was supposed to be behind it, in which a wondrously beautiful king's daughter, called Thorn-rose, had been sleeping for a hundred years and with her was sleeping the king and the queen and the whole court. He knew also from his grandfather that many kings' sons had come and had tried to penetrate through the thorn hedge, but had remained hanging in them and died a sad death. Then the young man said "I am not afraid, I will go out and see the beautiful Thorn-rose." No matter how the good old man tried to warn him, he did not listen to his words.

Now however the hundred years were just up, and the day had come,   4
when Thorn-rose was to wake up. When the king's son went up to the thorn hedge, they were nothing but large beautiful flowers, which parted by themselves and let him pass through unharmed, and behind him they closed again as a hedge. In the castle yard he saw the horses and dappled hunting dogs lying asleep, on the roof the doves sat and had their heads tucked under their wings. And as he entered the house, the flies slept on the wall, the cook in the kitchen held his hand as if he meant to grab the boy, and the maid sat in front of the black hen that was to be plucked. Then he went on, and saw in the hall the whole court lying asleep, and up by the throne lay the king and queen. Then he went still further, and everything was so still that one could hear his own breath, and at last he came to the tower and opened the door to the little room in which Thorn-rose slept. She lay there and was so beautiful that he could not take his eyes from her, and bent over, and gave her a kiss. But when he had touched her with the kiss, Thorn-rose opened her eyes, woke up, and looked at him quite cheerfully. Then they went down together, and the king awoke and the queen, and the whole court, and they looked at one another astonished. And the horses in the courtyard stood up and shook themselves: the hunting dogs jumped and wagged their tails: the doves on the roof took their heads from under their wings, looked around and flew off into the fields: the flies on the walls crept forward: the fire in the kitchen rose up, flamed, and cooked the meal: the roast meat began to sizzle again: and the cook boxed the boy's ears so that he cried out: and the maid finished plucking the hen. And then the marriage of the king's son with Thorn-rose was celebrated in magnificent fashion and they lived happily up to their end.

The Sleeping Beauty (La belle au bois dormant)

Charles Perrault

Once upon a time there were a King and a Queen who were very unhappy   1
because they had no children. They were more unhappy than words can tell. They went to all the watering-places in the world. They tried everything—

prayers, pilgrimages, vows to saints—but it made no difference. At last, however, the Queen conceived and gave birth to a daughter. A splendid christening was arranged. All the fairies who could be found in the country—there were seven of them—were invited to be godmothers, so that, if each of them brought a gift (as was the custom of the fairies in those days), the little Princess would be endowed with every good quality imaginable.

When the christening was over, the whole company went back to the   2
King's palace, where a great banquet had been prepared for the fairies. A magnificent place was laid for each of them, with a solid gold case containing a knife, a fork, and a spoon of finest gold inset with diamonds and rubies. But just as they were all sitting down, who should come in but an old fairy who had not been invited because she had remained shut up in a tower for fifty years or more and everyone had believed her to be dead or under a spell.

The King ordered a place to be laid for her, but it was impossible to give   3
her a gold case like the others because only seven had been made, for the seven known fairies. The old fairy took this as a slight and muttered threats under her breath. One of the younger fairies, who was sitting next to her, heard this muttering and guessed that she might give the Princess some harmful gift. So, the moment the meal was finished, she went and hid behind the tapestry. In that way she would be the last to speak and could make up, as far as lay in her power, for any harm that the old fairy might do.

Meanwhile, the fairies began to present their gifts to the Princess. The   4
youngest gave her the gift of perfect beauty; the next promised that she should be marvellously witty and gay; the third, that she should be exquisitely graceful in all her movements; the fourth, that she should dance beautifully; the fifth, that she should sing like a nightingale; and the sixth, that she should play all kinds of instruments to perfection. When the turn of the old fairy came, she said, trembling more with anger than with age, that the Princess would run a spindle into her hand and would die in consequence.

When they heard her make this terrible gift a shudder ran through the   5
whole company, and none could restrain their tears. But at that moment the young fairy came out from behind the tapestry and said:

"Set your minds at rest, King and Queen, your daughter shall not die   6
from this cause. It is true that I have not the power to undo entirely what my senior has done. The Princess *will* run a spindle into her hand. But, instead of dying, she will simply fall into a deep sleep which will last a hundred years, at the end of which the son of a king will come to wake her."

Hoping to avoid the disaster predicted by the old fairy, the King immedi-   7
ately issued a proclamation forbidding all his subjects to spin with spindles, or to have spindles in their homes, on pain of death.

Fifteen or sixteen years later, when the King and Queen were away at one   8
of their country houses, it happened that the young Princess was playing about in the castle. Running from room to room, she reached the top of a big tower and came to a little attic where a dear old woman was sitting by herself spinning. This old woman had not heard of the King's proclamation forbidding the use of spindles.

"What is that you are doing?" asked the Princess.   9

"Spinning, my dear," said the old woman, who did not know who she was.   10

"How pretty it is," said the Princess. "How do you do it? Give it to me   11
and let me try."

No sooner had she taken it up than—since she was hasty and rather   12
careless and, besides, the fairies had so ordained it—she ran the spindle into
her hand and immediately fainted away.

The old woman was greatly upset and called for help. People came run-   13
ning from all over the palace. They poured water on the Princess's face, un-
laced her dress, chafed her hands and rubbed her forehead with essence of
rosemary, but nothing would bring her back to life.

Then the King, who had returned to the palace and came up to see what   14
the noise was about, remembered the fairy's prophecy. Realizing that this had
to happen, since the fairies had said so, he had the Princess carried to the
finest room in the palace and placed on a bed embroidered in gold and silver. She looked like an angel—she was so beautiful. Her swoon had not
drained the colour from her face: her cheeks were still rosy, her lips like coral.
Her eyes were closed, but she could be heard breathing gently, which showed
that she was not dead.

The King gave orders that she was to be left to sleep there quietly until   15
the day came when she was to awake. The good fairy who had saved her life
by dooming her to sleep for a hundred years was in the Kingdom of Mata-
quin, twelve thousand leagues away, at the time of the accident. But the news
was brought to her instantly by a little dwarf with seven-league boots (that is,
boots which covered seven leagues at a single stride). The fairy set off immediately in a carriage of fire drawn by dragons, and was there within the hour.
The King came out to hand her down from her carriage. She approved everything that he had done. But, as she was extremely far-sighted, she reflected
that, when the Princess eventually awoke, she would feel most uncomfortable to be all alone in that old castle. So this is what she did.

She touched with her wand everything in the castle, except the King and   16
Queen: Governesses, maids-of-honour, chambermaids, gentlemen-in-waiting,
officers of the household, stewards, cooks, scullions, pot-boys, guards, doorkeepers, pages, footmen. She also touched all the horses in the stables, with
the grooms, the big watchdogs, and little Puff, the Princess's puppy, who was
lying beside her on the bed. No sooner had she touched them than they
all fell asleep, to wake only when their mistress did, ready to serve her when
she needed them. Even the roasting-spits which were turning before the fire
crammed with partridges and pheasants went to sleep, and the fire also. All
this was performed in a twinkling, for the fairies always did their work fast.

The King and Queen, having kissed their dear child without her waking,   17
left the castle and gave orders that no one was to go near it. These orders
were not necessary, for within a quarter of an hour there grew up all around
such a number of big and little trees, brambles, and tangled thorns, that neither man nor beast could have passed through. Nothing but the tops of the
towers could be seen, and then only from a considerable distance. It was obvious that the fairy had worked another of her magic spells to guard the
Princess from prying eyes while she slept.

At the end of a hundred years, the son of the King who was then reign- 18
ing and who belonged to a different family from the sleeping Princess, was
out hunting in that neighbourhood and inquired what were the towers which
he could see above the trees of a thick wood.

His followers gave him different answers according to the versions they 19
had heard. Some said that it was an old castle haunted by spirits; others, that
it was the place where all the witches of the region held their sabbath. The
most widespread belief was that it was the home of an ogre who carried off
all the children he could catch to eat them there undisturbed, since he alone
had the power of passing through the wood.

The Prince did not know what to believe, when an old peasant came for- 20
ward and said:

"Your Highness, more than fifty years ago I heard my father say that 21
there was a most beautiful princess in that castle. He said that she was to
sleep for a hundred years and that she would be awakened by a king's son,
for whom she was intended."

These words acted on the young Prince like a spur. He felt certain that 22
this was an exploit which he could accomplish and, fired by love and the desire for glory, he determined to put the story to the test there and then. As he
entered the wood, all the big trees, and brambles and the thorn-bushes bent
aside of their own accord to let him pass. He advanced towards the castle,
which he could see at the far end of a long avenue. He was a little surprised
to find that none of his men had been able to follow him, since the trees had
sprung back as soon as he had passed through. But that did not deter him
from going on. A prince is always brave when he is young and in love. He
reached the great forecourt, where everything that met his eyes might well
have stricken him with fear. There was a dreadful silence. The image of death
was everywhere. The place was full of the prostrate bodies of men and animals, all apparently dead. But the Prince soon saw, by the red noses and
ruddy cheeks of the doorkeepers, that they were only asleep; and their glasses,
which still contained a few drops of wine, showed plainly enough that they
had fallen asleep while drinking.

He went on into a big courtyard paved with marble, up a staircase and 23
into the guardroom, where the guards were drawn up in two lines with their
arquebuses on their shoulders, snoring away loudly. He passed through several rooms filled with ladies and gentlemen who were all asleep, some on
their feet, others seated. At last he came to a room with golden panelling and
saw on a bed, whose curtains were drawn aside, the loveliest sight he had
ever seen: a princess of about fifteen or sixteen, whose radiant beauty seemed
to glow with a kind of heavenly light. Trembling and wondering, he drew near
and knelt down before her.

Then, as the spell had come to its end, the Princess awoke and, looking 24
at him more tenderly than would seem proper for a first glance:

"Is it you, my Prince?" she said. "You have been a long time coming." 25

Delighted by these words, and still more so by the tone in which they 26
were uttered, the Prince hardly knew how to express his joy and gratitude. He
swore that he loved her better than life itself. His speech was halting, but it

pleased her all the more; for the less ready the tongue, the stronger the love. He was more confused than she was, and it was scarcely surprising. She had had time to think out what she would say to him, for it seems very probable (though the story does not say so) that the good fairy had arranged for her long sleep to be filled with pleasant dreams. In short, they went on talking to each other for four hours, and still had not said half the things they wanted to say.

Meanwhile, the whole palace had awakened with the Princess. Each had 27 gone about his duties and, since they were not all in love, they were dying of hunger. The lady-in-waiting, as famished as the others, grew impatient and loudly announced that dinner was ready. The Prince helped the Princess to get up. She was fully dressed in sumptuous clothes, and the Prince took good care not to tell her that she was turned out just like my grandmother, even to the high starched collar. She was no less beautiful for that.

They passed into a hall of mirrors, and there they supped, attended by 28 the officers of the Princess's household. Violins and oboes played old but delightful airs, which had not been heard for nearly a hundred years. And after supper, without wasting time, the chaplain married them in the palace chapel and the lady-in-waiting drew the bed-curtains round them. They slept little. The Princess hardly needed to and the Prince had to leave her early in the morning to get back to the town, where his father would be growing anxious about him.

The Prince told him that he had lost his way while out hunting in the for- 29 est and had spent the night in a charcoal-burner's hut, where he had supped on black bread and cheese. The King was an easy-going man and believed him. But his mother was not entirely convinced and, noticing that he went out hunting nearly every day and always had an excuse ready when he did not come home at night, she felt certain that he was engaged in some love-affair. For he lived with the Princess for more than two years and they had two children. The first, a daughter, was called Dawn, and the second, a son, was called Day, because he looked even more beautiful than his sister.

Several times the Queen tried to make her son confide in her by saying 30 to him that it was natural to take one's pleasures in life, but he never dared reveal his secret to her. Although he loved her, he feared her because she came of a family of ogres, and the King had only married her for the sake of her wealth. It was even whispered that she had ogreish appetites herself and that when she saw little children about she had the greatest difficulty in restraining herself from pouncing on them. That was why the Prince would not confide in her.

But when the King died, as he did after two years, and the Prince became 31 the master, he announced his marriage publicly and went with great ceremony to fetch his wife the Queen from the castle. She was given a royal welcome when she drove into the capital seated between her two children.

Some time after that, the King went to war against his neighbour, the Em- 32 peror Cantalabutto. He left the kingdom in charge of the Queen Mother, bidding her to take the greatest care of his wife and children. He was to be away at the war for the whole summer. As soon as he had gone, the Queen Mother sent her daughter-in-law and the children to a country house in the woods, where she would be able to satisfy her horrible appetites more easily. She herself followed them a few days later, and one evening she said to her steward:

"I wish to have little Dawn for my dinner tomorrow."   33

"But Your Majesty . . ." said the steward.   34

"It is my wish," said the Queen (and her voice was the voice of an ogress   35 who is craving for human flesh), "and I wish to have her served with mustard-and-onion sauce."

The miserable steward, realizing that it was useless to trifle with an ogress,   36 took his largest knife and went up to little Dawn's room. She was then four years old and she came skipping and laughing to fling her arms around his neck and asked him for sweets. Tears came into his eyes and the knife fell from his hand. He went out to the farmyard and killed a young lamb which be cooked with such a delicious sauce that his mistress declared that she had never eaten anything so good. At the same time he took away little Dawn and gave her to his wife to hide in the cottage they had at the bottom of the farmyard.

A week later the wicked Queen said to the steward: 37

"I wish to have little Day for my supper."   38

He made no reply, having decided to trick her in the same way as before.   39 He went to fetch little Day and found him with a tiny foil in his hand, fencing with a pet monkey, though he was only three. He carried him down to his wife, to be hidden with little Dawn, and served instead a very tender young kid which the ogress found excellent.

So far, things had gone very well. But one evening the wicked Queen said   40 to the steward:

"I wish to have the Queen, served with the same sauce as her children."   41

When he heard this, the poor steward despaired of tricking her again.   42 The young Queen was over twenty, without counting the hundred years during which she had been asleep. Her skin was a little tough, although it was smooth and white. Where would he find a skin as tough as that among the farmyard animals? Since his own life was at stake, he made up his mind to cut the Queen's throat and went up to her room intending to act quickly. Working himself into a fury, he burst into the room, knife in hand. But he did not want to take her unawares, so he told her with great respect of the order he had received from the Queen Mother.

"Do your duty, then," she said, baring her throat to the knife. "Carry out   43 the order you have been given. I shall see my children again, my poor children whom I loved so dearly!" For she believed them to be dead, since they had been taken away without a word of explanation.

"No, no, Your Majesty," replied the unhappy steward, completely won   44 over, "you shall not die and you shall still see your dear children; but you shall see them in my house, where I have hidden them. And I will trick the Queen again, by giving her a young doe to eat in place of you."

He took her quickly to his house and, leaving her there to embrace her   45 children, he set about preparing a doe which the Queen Mother ate for supper with as much relish as if it had been the young Queen herself. She was well pleased with her cruelty and she intended to tell the King, when he came back, that ravening wolves had devoured his wife and his two children.

One evening when she was prowling as usual about the yards and court- 46 yards of the castle to see if she could smell out some young human flesh, she heard the voice of little Day in a ground-floor room. He was crying because he had been naughty and his mother was threatening to have him whipped. She also heard little Dawn, who was begging for her brother to be let off.

The ogress recognized the voices of the Queen and her children and was 47 furious to find that she had been tricked. The next morning she called in a voice of thunder for a huge vat to be placed in the middle of the courtyard and filled with toads, vipers, adders and other poisonous reptiles. Into this were to be cast the Queen and her children, with the steward, his wife, and his servant, who had all been led out on her order with their hands tied behind their backs.

They were standing there and the executioners were preparing to cast 48 them into the vat when the King, who was not expected back so soon, came riding into the courtyard. He had been travelling post-haste and, filled with amazement, he demanded to know the meaning of this horrible sight. No one dared to enlighten him, but the ogress, furious at the turn things had taken, flung herself headlong into the vat and was devoured in an instant by the foul creatures which she had had placed there. The King could not help feeling sorry, for she was his mother. But he soon consoled himself with his beautiful wife and his children.

Six Sections from *Briar Rose*

Robert Coover

He is surprised to discover how easy it is. The branches part like thighs, the 1 silky petals caress his cheeks. His drawn sword is stained, not with blood, but with dew and pollen. Yet another inflated legend. He has undertaken this great adventure, not for the supposed reward — what is another lonely bedridden princess? — but in order to provoke a confrontation with the awful powers of enchantment itself. To tame mystery. To make, at last, his name. He'd have been better off trying for the runes of wisdom or the Golden Fleece. Even another bloody grail. As the briars, pillowy with a sudden extravagance of fresh blooms, their thorns decorously sheathed in the full moonlight, open up to receive him as a doting mother might, he is pricked only by chagrin. Yet he knows what it has cost others who have gone before him, he can smell their bodies caught in the thicket, can glimpse the pallor of their moon-bleached bones, rattling gently when the soft wind blows. That odor of decay is about the extent of his ordeal, and even it is assuaged by the fragrances of fresh tansy and camomile, roses, lilac and hyssop, lavender and savory, which encompass him affectionately — perhaps he has been chosen, perhaps it is his virtue which has caused the hedge to bloom — as he plunges deeper into the thicket, the castle turrets and battlements already visible to him, almost within reach, through its trembling branches.

She dreams, as she has often dreamt, of abandonment and betrayal, of lost 2 hope, of the self gone astray from the body, the body forsaking the unlikely self. She feels like a once-proud castle whose walls have collapsed, her halls and towers invaded, not by marauding armies, but by humbler creatures, bats, birds, cats, cattle, her departed self an unkempt army marauding elsewhere in a scatter of confused intentions. Her longing for integrity is, in her spellbound innocence, all she knows of rage and lust, but this longing is itself fragmented and wayward, felt not so much as a monstrous gnawing at the core as more like the restless scurry of vermin in the rubble of her remote defenses, long since fallen and benumbed. What, if anything, can make her whole again? And what is "whole"? Her parents, as always in her dreams, have vanished, gone off to death or the continent or perhaps to one of their houses of pleasure, and she is being stabbed again and again by the treacherous spindle, impregnated with a despair from which, for all her fury, she cannot awaken.

The pale moonlit turrets of the castle, glimpsed through the brambles, rise 3 high into the black night above like the clenched fists of an unforgiving but stonily silent father, upon whose tender terrain below he is darkly trespassing, heralded by a soft icy clatter of tinkling bones. Unlike these others who ornament the briars, he has come opportunely when the hedge is in full bloom, or perhaps (he prefers to think) the hedge has blossomed tonight because it is he who has come, its seductive caresses welcoming him even as the cold castle overhead repels, the one a promise and a lure, showing him the way, the other the test he must undertake to achieve the object of his heroic quest. Which is? Honor. Knowledge. The exercise of his magical powers. Also love of course. If the old tales be true, a sleeping princess awaits him within. He imagines her as not unlike this soft dew-bedampened wall he is plunging through, silky and fragrant and voluptuously receptive. If she is the symbolic object of his quest, her awakening is not without its promise of passing pleasures. She is said, after all, to be the most beautiful creature in the world, both fair and good, musically gifted, delicate, virtuous and graceful and with the gentle disposition of an angel, and, for all her hundred years and more, still a child, innocent and yielding. Achingly desirable. And desiring. Of course, she is also the daughter of a mother embraced by a frog, and there has been talk about ogres in the family, dominion by sorcery, and congress with witches and wizards and other powers too dark to name. If there be any truth in these century-old rumors from benighted times, this adventure could end, not in love's sweet delirium, but in its pain, its infamous cruelty. This prospect, however, does not dissuade him. On the contrary. It incites him.

Well, everyone *might* have lived happily ever after, replies the one crone, gut- 4 ting a plucked cock, if it hadn't been for his jealous wife. He was married—?! Of course, my love, what did you think? And she was, as you can imagine, a very unhappy lady, even if perhaps she was not the ogress everyone said she was, her husband especially. But that's terrible! That's not the worst of it, I'm afraid. I don't know if I want to hear the rest. She is in the kitchen, which at first was more like her parents' bedchamber or else the bath house, listening to the ancient scold in there tell a story about a princess who fell into an enchanted sleep as a child and woke up a mother. The princess is called Sleeping Beauty, though that might not have been her real name. Has she heard this story before? She can't remember, but it sounds all too familiar, and she is almost certain something bad is about to happen. But she goes on listening because she cannot do otherwise. So she waited until her husband was off hunting or at one of his other houses of pleasure, the old crone continues, ripping out the cock's inner organs, and then she went over to Sleeping Beauty's house and cooked up her children and ordered the clerk of the kitchen to build a big bonfire and burn Beauty alive, calling her a cruel home-wrecking bitch and a lump of you-know-what. The kitchen hag, cackling softly, squeezes a handful of chicken guts, making them break wind. There is something vaguely reassuring about this, not unlike a happy ending. The prince's wife, the crone continues, her hands braceleted in pink intestines, had in mind serving up a very special roast to her husband when he got home, believing, you see, that the way to a man's heart is, heh heh, through the stomach. She sniffs at the cock's tail. The story seems to be over. And that's all? she demands in helpless rage. Not quite, smiles the crone. She shakes her old head and a swarm of blue lights rises and falls around her ears. Sleeping Beauty was wearing a beautiful jewel-studded gown her friend the prince had given her and his wife wanted it, so she ordered Beauty, before being thrown on the fire, to strip down, which she did, slowly, one article at a time, shrieking wildly with each little thing she removed, as though denuding herself was driving her crazy. Meanwhile, as she'd hoped, the prince was just returning from whatever he'd been up to and, on hearing Beauty scream, came running, but before he knew it he found himself in the middle of a huge briar patch. Oh no! Oh yes! He had to cut his way through with his sword, redoubling his effort with each cry of his poor beloved, but the briars seemed to spring up around him even as he chopped them down, and the more she screamed and the more he slashed away, the thicker they got. Yes, yes, I can see him! No, you can't, he was completely swallowed up by the briars. A pity, but it was too late. No! Hurry! Here I am! It's *not* too late!

Her prince has come. The real one. It is dark and she does not know where   5
she is but she knows he has come and that it is he. She is filled with rejoicing, but also with trepidation. So much is at stake! She has known all along that her prince would come, but she has also known there would be no uncoming, forever after as much a threat as promised delight. What if he is not as she's imagined him to be? She was safe inside this impenetrable castle, protected even from the demands of her own body, and now this alien being who paces at her bedside has broached those walls and will soon break through to her very core, if he has not already done so. All her childhood fears return: of the dark, of strange noises, of monsters and ghosts, of murderers,

of being left alone, of her parents dying, of getting sick and dying herself, of the world dying. He clears his throat. Has he kissed her yet? She doesn't remember, but she musters her courage and opens her eyes to see who or what is there, terrified now that she will find a great hairy beast prowling beside her bed. But, no, it is he, a handsome young prince with manly brow and beard and flowing locks, tall and lean and strong. My prince, she whispers. You have come at last! Yes, well, he says with a grimace, wandering distractedly through the dimly lit room, draped in swags of gray dusty webs, which he swipes at irritably with his gauntleted hand. At a wooden chest, he picks up a bonehandled copper pitcher enameled with the family crest, thumps it, peers at its green bottom, sets it down again. He pokes through some wardrobe drawers, raising clouds of dust, finds some rings and necklaces and silver pennies, which he sorts through idly. Perhaps he takes some of these things, but not as a thief might: in effect, he *possesses* them. With one metallic finger he strokes a plump lute resting on a table: the dry strings snap and ping, their ancient tension released, but not hers. My prince? He turns his restless gaze upon her for a moment and then it seems to pierce right through her, as though focusing on something within or beyond her, chilling her to the marrow before it drifts away again, coming to rest on a chessboard with cracked and yellowed ivory pieces. He moves one of the figures, freeing it from its bonds of web, then, with a shrug, tips it over. It is a delicate, casual, yet studied gesture, and it terrifies her. In front of a round dust-grimed mirror on the wall, he stares at himself, stroking his beard. He is immaculately groomed and dressed, more elegant even than she had dreamt he would be. You are very beautiful, she murmurs timidly, but I thought you'd, I don't know, show more outward signs of your terrible ordeal. Ordeal—? You know, the briars. He turns away from the mirror, peers at her warily with narrowed eyes. What briars? Didn't you have to cut your way through a briar hedge outside? Maybe, he says stonily, I'm at the wrong castle.

She lies alone in her dusky bedchamber atop the morbid bed. Perhaps she 6 has never left it, her body anchored forever here by the pain of the spindle prick, while her disembodied self, from time to time, goes aimlessly astray, drifting through the castle of her childhood, in search of nothing whatsoever, except perhaps distraction from her lonely fears (of the dark, of abandonment, of not knowing who she is, of the death of the world), which gnaw at her ceaselessly like the scurrying rodents beneath her silken chemise. If she is still asleep, it does not feel like sleep, more like its opposite, an interminable wakefulness from which she cannot ease herself, yet one that leaves no residue save echoes of an old crone's tales, and the feeling that her life is not, has not been a life at all. Sometimes, in her wanderings, she finds a castle populous with sleepers, frozen in their tracks, snoring pimply-faced guards clutching wineglasses in which the dregs have dried, round-bellied scullery maids sweeping, their stilled labor swagged in thick dusty webs, the cook with a fistful of the kitchen boy's hair, his cuffing stopped in sudden sleep. But if she opens her eyes again, the castle will be dark and empty, hollow with a chill wind blowing, or else suddenly filled with a bustling confusion of servants, knights, children, animals, husbands or lovers, all making demands upon her, demands she cannot possibly fulfill, or even understand, and all she longs for, as she tells the old crone in the tower, is to sleep again. The crone may cackle or tell a story or scold her for her self-absorption, but sooner or later she will open her eyes and find herself here in her moldy bed once more, waiting for she knows not what in the name of waiting for her prince to come. Of whom, no lack, though none true so far of course, unless in some strange wise they all are, her sequential disenchantments then the very essence of her being, the fairy's spell binding her not to a suspenseful waiting for what might yet be, but to the eternal reenactment of what, other than, she can never be. She closes her eyes to such a cruel fate, but, as always, it is as if she has opened them again, and now to yet another prince arriving, bloodied but exultant, at her bedside. She welcomes him, cannot do other, ready as always for come what may. He leans toward her, blows her dessicated gown away. Yes, yes, that's right, my prince! And now, tenderly if you can, toothily if need be, take this spindled pain away . . .

FOR DISCUSSION AND WRITING: COMPARING VERSIONS AND TRANSFORMING TALES

1. Go back to the two versions by the Grimm brothers. Taking the manuscript version as being close to their source, the oral storyteller whose words they listened to and transcribed, compare it with the refined version they offered in their sixth edition. First note the main changes: what they left out, what they put in, and what they modified. Then, consider the reasons for these changes. Were some of them made for reasons of art—to make the story better? Were some of them made to accommodate the values of the readers of the stories (and the brothers themselves)? Through such changes we can construct a partial picture of the ideology of their culture. Write a short essay or give a report on what you take to be the most significant changes between the manuscript and the final version of the brothers Grimm.

2. Compare the Grimm material with that of Perrault. Perrault's version is, as we noted earlier, well over a century earlier than the Grimms', but it contains elements that were either missing from what they found or eliminated by them. Discuss the differences between the two versions and the way these differences change your reading of the tale.

3. Robert Coover's version has been made with full awareness of the whole tradition—Perrault, Grimm, and the earlier Italian version. His departures from the originals can all be considered as deliberate choices, designed to provoke interpretations of one sort or another. In short, he is inviting you to respond to them. What do they say about stories, about life, about our world? Do you find Coover saying things that are also said in works you have read in this book by Kafka, Borges, Calvino, Barth, or others? Or things that are similar to what is being said in those other works? Are fairy tales like parables in some way—or not like them at all?

4. You, too, can be a transformer. Take some well-known fairy tale and produce your own purposeful transformation of it. This will work best if you
   look up some familiar story and work with the printed text in front of you.
   You may follow the leads of the Grimms and Coover or find your own
   principle of transformation, but don't just imitate. Steal! That is, *change*
   the text you are transforming sufficiently to make it your own.

COMPLETING TEXTS:
THE READER'S WORK

Texts are lazy machineries that ask someone to do part of their job.
— *Umberto Eco*

What do we do when we read? What does it mean to "complete" a text?
Here we shall consider the act of reading as an act of writing in both
a figurative and a literal sense. In his book *The Role of the Reader,* Italian semiotician Umberto Eco discusses reading as a collaborative act in
which "a well-organized text on the one hand presupposes a model of
competence coming, so to speak, from outside the text, but on the other
hand works to build up, by merely textual means, such a competence."
As readers, we provide "models of competence," bringing to a text our
own intellectual equipment to help us understand what we are reading.
At the same time, the text directs that reading. When we look at a text
that starts out "Once upon a time" or "Once there was," we know we are
in the presence of a fairy tale and we therefore accept the conventions of
that genre — talking frogs, wicked stepmothers, handsome princes —
when we encounter them in the text. In recognizing a text as a particular
kind of text, such as fairy tale, mystery, or historical romance, we are
drawing on our intertextual knowledge — our reading of other texts like
the one in front of us. As Eco reminds us, "no text is read independently
of other texts."

   When we read the first sentence of William Carlos Williams's story
"The Use of Force" — "They were new patients to me, all I had was the
name, Olson" — the text assumes that we will know that the speaker is a
doctor. When the speaker describes his patient as "One of those picture
children often reproduced in advertising leaflets and the photogravure
sections of the Sunday papers," the text assumes the reader shares a
common cultural frame of reference; specifically, that the reader has seen
those American advertisements that feature children, and knows what
part the "Sunday papers" play in American culture, and is familiar with
the magazine section in them, as well as the type of child (blond and blue-
eyed) likely to be featured there as a "beautiful child." These are small

examples of the reader's work, and much of this work occurs subconsciously as we read.

The reader's work increases when there is a gap in the narrative and the reader is called upon to infer what took place during that missing time. In Eco's terms, this is called writing (in one's head) a "ghost chapter":

> Frequently, given a series of causally and linearly connected events $a \ldots e$, a text tells the reader about the event a and, after a while, about the event e, taking for granted that the reader has already anticipated the dependent events b, c, d (of which e is the consequence, according to many intertextual frames). Thus the text implicitly validates a "ghost chapter," tentatively written by the reader.

Writing this ghost chapter in your head can be a very straightforward operation when the information in the gap does not affect the events in the story. If the story tells us, for example, that "John got on the bus in New York," and in the next sentence, "John arrived in Providence," the reader quickly infers that the trip between New York and Providence was both safe and uneventful. The ghost chapter we write between event a, "John got on the bus in New York" and event e, "John arrived in Providence," might logically contain event b, John gave his ticket to the bus driver; event c, John found a seat; and event d, John watched the scenery go by. We know from our own experience that these are the events most likely to occur on any bus ride between one city and another, and because this is common knowledge, the text does not have to provide this information.

In Kate Chopin's story "The Kiss," there are two gaps in time, the first between the kiss and the reception, and the second between the reception and the wedding. Those jumps in time are appropriate to a story with a heroine who acts to get what she wants rather than sitting and brooding about it. Again, the reader may, in writing a ghost chapter, infer that whatever happens in those time periods is not important to the story. Yet Nathalie's final statement before the first gap in time (kiss—reception), "It depends upon—a good deal whether I ever forgive you," leaves the reader as well as Harvy speculating about what the gap in Nathalie's statement signifies: "depends upon—" what? The reader may also be busy speculating as to the nature of the relationship between Nathalie and Harvy. During a second reading of the text, the reader might wonder what plans ran through Nathalie's head; namely, how she plotted the moves that are described to us in the next sequence: the entrapment of Brantain at the reception. (And what information in the text allows us to use the term "entrapment"?) In the second gap, between the reception and the wedding, the reader can logically infer from common knowledge that Brantain and Nathalie become engaged, that she is given an engagement ring, that wedding plans are made. But it is also possible to speculate here about Harvy's reaction to this forthcoming event and to try to forecast what will take place in the final sequence of events.

In other texts, there are gaps that are not so easily filled by the reader because the text wishes to create suspense and so information is deliberately withheld from the reader. At these moments, the reader constructs a *possible world*. Say heroine X enters a room and finds her lover Y in the arms of another woman Z, and the text closes the door in our faces and changes the scene to the battlefield at Waterloo. The thwarted reader, desiring to know what happened in that room, may draw on his or her own frame of reference—"I know what I would do if I were X"—and create a possible world in which the scene is completed, though the imagined completion may be at variance with what actually is to take place in the text. This act is the creation by the reader of a possible world, a new text.

In Eco's terms, possible worlds are "sketches for another story, the story the actual one could have been had things gone differently. . . . They are worlds imagined, believed, wished." A fictional text is itself a possible world because it is composed of a possible set of events chosen by its author. As readers, we most frequently construct possible worlds from texts in which we have become deeply involved, and because we want their stories to continue, we construct our own, adding new endings, proposing new situations. Fans of that problematical heroine Scarlett O'Hara, of *Gone with the Wind*, may construct a possible world in which Scarlett marries Ashley Wilkes, her one true love. But this possible world would have little to do with the possible world that is actualized in Margaret Mitchell's novel, since that world is structured on the proposition that Ashley marries Melanie.

So when we talk about completing a text, we're not being entirely accurate. A text can never be completed. Each reader brings a unique model of competence to a text, and so each reader will fill gaps in the text differently. Because the fictional text is directed at the imagination of the reader, there will always be variables in the interpretation possible in the imaginative spaces of the text. However, a well-organized fictional text will not allow just any interpretation; rather, it directs the reader toward a certain number of possible readings. It is because of the extension of these possible readings by an infinite number of readers, each with a different model of competence, that an infinite number of readings of a text is possible. Which is to say, when John gets on the bus in New York, reader A will put him on a green and white bus; reader B will put him on a blue and white bus; reader C will give him a bumpy ride to Providence; reader D, who has taken that bus ride, will make John bored during the seemingly endless barren stretch from the Connecticut line to East Greenwich, Rhode Island; and so on and on. John's bus ride has endless variations.

In this section, you will be asked to put your work as a reader into the actual writing of ghost chapters and possible worlds. When you compare your reading with those of your classmates, you will have a very clear idea of what we mean by variables in interpretation.

Up in Michigan

Ernest Hemingway

Ernest Hemingway (1899–1961) wrote this story when he was about twenty-one, but its subject matter prevented its publication in the United States until 1938. The story is set in a locale where Hemingway vacationed with his family from the age of one to twenty-one. He drew on this locale frequently throughout his career.

Jim Gilmore came to Hortons Bay from Canada. He bought the blacksmith   1
shop from old man Horton. Jim was short and dark with big mustaches and big hands. He was a good horseshoer and did not look much like a black-smith even with his leather apron on. He lived upstairs above the blacksmith shop and took his meals at D. J. Smith's.

Liz Coates worked for Smith's. Mrs. Smith, who was a very large clean   2
woman, said Liz Coates was the neatest girl she'd ever seen. Liz had good legs and always wore clean gingham aprons and Jim noticed that her hair was always neat behind. He liked her face because it was so jolly but he never thought about her.

Liz liked Jim very much. She liked it the way he walked over from the   3
shop and often went to the kitchen door to watch for him to start down the road. She liked it about his mustache. She liked it about how white his teeth were when he smiled. She liked it very much that he didn't look like a black-smith. She liked it how much D. J. Smith and Mrs. Smith liked Jim. One day she found that she liked it the way the hair was black on his arms and how white they were above the tanned line when he washed up in the washbasin outside the house. Liking that made her feel funny.

Hortons Bay, the town, was only five houses on the main road between   4
Boyne City and Charlevoix. There was the general store and post office with a high false front and maybe a wagon hitched out in front, Smith's house, Stroud's house, Dillworth's house, Horton's house and Van Hoosen's house. The houses were in a big grove of elm trees and the road was very sandy. There was farming country and timber each way up the road. Up the road a ways was the Methodist church and down the road the other direction was

the township school. The blacksmith shop was painted red and faced the
school.

A steep sandy road ran down the hill to the bay through the timber. From   5
Smith's back door you could look out across the woods that ran down to the
lake and across the bay. It was very beautiful in the spring and summer, the
bay blue and bright and usually whitecaps on the lake out beyond the point
from the breeze blowing from Charlevoix and Lake Michigan. From Smith's
back door Liz could see ore barges way out in the lake going toward Boyne
City. When she looked at them they didn't seem to be moving at all but if she
went in and dried some more dishes and then came out again they would be
out of sight beyond the point.

All the time now Liz was thinking about Jim Gilmore. He didn't seem to   6
notice her much. He talked about the shop to D. J. Smith and about the Republican Party and about James G. Blaine.[1] In the evenings he read *The
Toledo Blade* and the Grand Rapids paper by the lamp in the front room or
went out spearing fish in the bay with a jacklight with D. J. Smith. In the fall
he and Smith and Charley Wyman took a wagon and tent, grub, axes, their
rifles and two dogs and went on a trip to the pine plains beyond Vanderbilt
deer hunting. Liz and Mrs. Smith were cooking for four days for them before
they started. Liz wanted to make something special for Jim to take but she
didn't finally because she was afraid to ask Mrs. Smith for the eggs and flour
and afraid if she bought them Mrs. Smith would catch her cooking. It would
have been all right with Mrs. Smith but Liz was afraid.

All the time Jim was gone on the deer hunting trip Liz thought about him.   7
It was awful while he was gone. She couldn't sleep well from thinking about
him but she discovered it was fun to think about him too. If she let herself go
it was better. The night before they were to come back she didn't sleep at all,
that is she didn't think she slept because it was all mixed up in a dream about
not sleeping and really not sleeping. When she saw the wagon coming down
the road she felt weak and sick sort of inside. She couldn't wait till she saw
Jim and it seemed as though everything would be all right when he came. The
wagon stopped outside under the big elm and Mrs. Smith and Liz went out.
All the men had beards and there were three deer in the back of the wagon,
their thin legs sticking stiff over the edge of the wagon box. Mrs. Smith kissed
D. J. and he hugged her. Jim said "Hello, Liz," and grinned. Liz hadn't known
just what would happen when Jim got back but she was sure it would be
something. Nothing had happened. The men were just home, that was all.
Jim pulled the burlap sacks off the deer and Liz looked at them. One was a
big buck. It was stiff and hard to lift out of the wagon.

"Did you shoot it, Jim?" Liz asked.   8

"Yeah. Ain't it a beauty?" Jim got it onto his back to carry to the smoke-   9
house.

That night Charley Wyman stayed to supper at Smith's. It was too late   10
to get back to Charlevoix. The men washed up and waited in the front room
for supper.

---

[1][James G. Blaine, a senator, ran for president in 1884. *Eds.*]

"Ain't there something left in that crock, Jimmy?" D. J. Smith asked, and 11
Jim went out to the wagon in the barn and fetched in the jug of whiskey the
men had taken hunting with them. It was a four-gallon jug and there was
quite a little slopped back and forth in the bottom. Jim took a long pull on his
way back to the house. It was hard to lift such a big jug up to drink out of it.
Some of the whiskey ran down on his shirt front. The two men smiled when
Jim came in with the jug. D. J. Smith sent for glasses and Liz brought them.
D. J. poured out three big shots.

"Well, here's looking at you, D. J.," said Charley Wyman.   12
"That damn big buck, Jimmy," said D. J.   13
"Here's all the ones we missed, D. J.," said Jim, and downed his liquor.   14
"Tastes good to a man."   15
"Nothing like it this time of year for what ails you."   16
"How about another, boys?"   17
"Here's how, D. J."   18
"Down the creek, boys."   19
"Here's to next year."   20

Jim began to feel great. He loved the taste and the feel of whiskey. He 21
was glad to be back to a comfortable bed and warm food and the shop. He
had another drink. The men came in to supper feeling hilarious but acting
very respectable. Liz sat at the table after she put on the food and ate with the
family. It was a good dinner. The men ate seriously. After supper they went
into the front room again and Liz cleaned off with Mrs. Smith. Then Mrs. Smith
went upstairs and pretty soon Smith came out and went upstairs too. Jim and
Charley were still in the front room. Liz was sitting in the kitchen next to the
stove pretending to read a book and thinking about Jim. She didn't want to
go to bed yet because she knew Jim would be coming out and she wanted to
see him as he went out so she could take the way he looked up to bed with her.

She was thinking about him hard and then Jim came out. His eyes were 22
shining and his hair was a little rumpled. Liz looked down at her book.
Jim came over back of her chair and stood there and she could feel him
breathing and then he put his arms around her. Her breasts felt plump and
firm and the nipples were erect under his hands. Liz was terribly frightened,
no one had ever touched her, but she thought, "He's come to me finally. He's
really come."

She held herself stiff because she was so frightened and did not know 23
anything else to do and then Jim held her tight against the chair and kissed
her. It was such a sharp, aching, hurting feeling that she thought she couldn't
stand it. She felt Jim right through the back of the chair and she couldn't
stand it and then something clicked inside of her and the feeling was warmer
and softer. Jim held her tight hard against the chair and she wanted it now
and Jim whispered, "Come on for a walk."

Liz took her coat off the peg on the kitchen wall and they went out the 24
door. Jim had his arm around her and every little way they stopped and
pressed against each other and Jim kissed her. There was no moon and they
walked ankle-deep in the sandy road through the trees down to the dock and
the warehouse on the bay. The water was lapping in the piles and the point

was dark across the bay. It was cold but Liz was hot all over from being with Jim. They sat down in the shelter of the warehouse and Jim pulled Liz close to him. She was frightened. One of Jim's hands went inside her dress and stroked over her breast and the other hand was in her lap. She was very frightened and didn't know how he was going to go about things but she snuggled close to him. Then the hand that felt so big in her lap went away and was on her leg and started to move up it.

"Don't, Jim," Liz said. Jim slid the hand further up. 25

"You mustn't, Jim. You mustn't." Neither Jim nor Jim's big hand paid any 26 attention to her.

The boards were hard. Jim had her dress up and was trying to do some- 27 thing to her. She was frightened but she wanted it. She had to have it but it frightened her.

"You mustn't do it, Jim. You mustn't." 28

"I got to. I'm going to. You know we got to." 29

"No we haven't, Jim. We ain't got to. Oh, it isn't right. Oh, it's so big and 30 it hurts so. You can't. Oh, Jim. Jim. Oh."

The hemlock planks of the dock were hard and splintery and cold and 31 Jim was heavy on her and he had hurt her. Liz pushed him, she was so un- comfortable and cramped. Jim was asleep. He wouldn't move. She worked out from under him and sat up and straightened her skirt and coat and tried to do something with her hair. Jim was sleeping with his mouth a little open. Liz leaned over and kissed him on the cheek. He was still asleep. She lifted his head a little and shook it. He rolled his head over and swallowed. Liz started to cry. She walked over to the edge of the dock and looked down to the water. There was a mist coming up from the bay. She was cold and mis- erable and everything felt gone. She walked back to where Jim was lying and shook him once more to make sure. She was crying.

"Jim," she said, "Jim. Please, Jim." 32

Jim stirred and curled a little tighter. Liz took off her coat and leaned over 33 and covered him with it. She tucked it around him neatly and carefully. Then she walked across the dock and up the steep sandy road to go to bed. A cold mist was coming up through the woods from the bay.

FOR DISCUSSION AND WRITING: DEFINING LOVE: WRITING THE READER'S WORK

1. The two principal characters are introduced in the first three paragraphs of the story. What can the reader infer about their relationship? About their personal characteristics?

2. Paragraphs 4 and 5 present a description of Hortons Bay. At one point, in paragraph 5, *you* "look out . . . across the bay" just as Liz does. How often does a shift in point of view occur in this story? What effects do these shifts have on the reader?

3. In paragraph 3, Hemingway uses an odd locution: "She liked it . . . ." How many times is this phrase repeated? What is the effect on the

reader? How often does the word *it* occur in the story, and at what points? How many different "translations" of this little pronoun must the reader provide?

4. Part of the reader's work in reading this story is to figure out what Liz thinks "love" is. What symptoms of "love" does she display, and how does she interpret them? Write an essay in which you describe Liz's conception of love, and in your conclusion, consider whether the incident on the dock and its aftermath change her feelings for Jim in any way.

Consider character
Contest
Who wins/loses, if
anyone
Pg. 45

The Red Convertible

Louise Erdrich

Louise Erdrich is a writer of German and Chippewa descent who grew up on an Indian reservation in North Dakota. This story is from Love Medicine, *a collection of fiction about two families, the Kashpaws and the Lamartines, who live on a North Dakota reservation.*

Lyman Lamartine

I was the first one to drive a convertible on my reservation. And of course it was red, a red Olds. I owned that car along with my brother Henry Junior. We owned it together until his boots filled with water on a windy night and he bought out my share. Now Henry owns the whole car, and his younger brother Lyman (that's myself), Lyman walks everywhere he goes. 1

How did I earn enough money to buy my share in the first place? My own talent was I could always make money. I had a touch for it, unusual in a Chippewa. From the first I was different that way, and everyone recognized it. I was the only kid they let in the American Legion Hall to shine shoes, for example, and one Christmas I sold spiritual bouquets for the mission door to door. The nuns let me keep a percentage. Once I started, it seemed the more money I made the easier the money came. Everyone encouraged it. When I was fifteen I got a job washing dishes at the Joliet Café, and that was where my first big break happened. 2

It wasn't long before I was promoted to busing tables, and then the short-order cook quit and I was hired to take her place. No sooner than you know it I was managing the Joliet. The rest is history. I went on managing. I soon became part owner, and of course there was no stopping me then. It wasn't long before the whole thing was mine. 3

After I'd owned the Joliet for one year, it blew over in the worst tornado ever seen around here. The whole operation was smashed to bits. A total loss. The fryalator was up in a tree, the grill torn in half like it was paper. I was only sixteen. I had it all in my mother's name, and I lost it quick, but 4 before I lost it I had every one of my relatives, and their relatives, to dinner, and I also bought that red Olds I mentioned, along with Henry.

The first time we saw it! I'll tell you when we first saw it. We had gotten   5
a ride up to Winnipeg, and both of us had money. Don't ask me why, because we never mentioned a car or anything, we just had all our money. Mine was cash, a big bankroll from the Joliet's insurance. Henry had two checks—a week's extra pay for being laid off, and his regular check from the Jewel Bearing Plant.

We were walking down Portage anyway, seeing the sights, when we saw   6
it. There it was, parked, large as life. Really as *if* it was alive. I thought of the word *repose*, because the car wasn't simply stopped, parked, or whatever. That car reposed, calm and gleaming, a FOR SALE sign in its left front window. Then, before we had thought it over at all, the car belonged to us and our pockets were empty. We had just enough money for gas back home.

We went places in that car, me and Henry. We took off driving all one   7
whole summer. We started off toward the Little Knife River and Mandaree in Fort Berthold and then we found ourselves down in Wakpala somehow, and then suddenly we were over in Montana on the Rocky Boy, and yet the summer was not even half over. Some people hang on to details when they travel, but we didn't let them bother us and just lived our everyday lives here to there.

I do remember this one place with willows. I remember I laid under those   8
trees and it was comfortable. So comfortable. The branches bent down all around me like a tent or a stable. And quiet, it was quiet, even though there was a powwow close enough so I could see it going on. The air was not too still, not too windy either. When the dust rises up and hangs in the air around the dancers like that, I feel good. Henry was asleep with his arms thrown wide. Later on, he woke up and we started driving again. We were somewhere in Montana, or maybe on the Blood Reserve—it could have been anywhere. Anyway it was where we met the girl.

All her hair was in buns around her ears, that's the first thing I noticed   9
about her. She was posed alongside the road with her arm out, so we stopped. That girl was short, so short her lumber shirt looked comical on her, like a nightgown. She had jeans on and fancy moccasins and she carried a little suitcase.

"Hop on in," says Henry. So she climbs in between us.   10
"We'll take you home," I says. "Where do you live?"   11
"Chicken," she says.   12
"Where the hell's that?" I ask her.   13
"Alaska."   14
"Okay," says Henry, and we drive.   15
We got up there and never wanted to leave. The sun doesn't truly set   16
there in summer, and the night is more a soft dusk. You might doze off, sometimes, but before you know it you're up again, like an animal in nature. You never feel like you have to sleep hard or put away the world. And things would grow up there. One day just dirt or moss, the next day flowers and long

grass. The girl's name was Susy. Her family really took to us. They fed us and put us up. We had our own tent to live in by their house, and the kids would be in and out of there all day and night. They couldn't get over me and Henry being brothers, we looked so different. We told them we knew we had the same mother, anyway.

One night Susy came in to visit us. We sat around in the tent talking of 17 this and that. The season was changing. It was getting darker by that time, and the cold was even getting just a little mean. I told her it was time for us to go. She stood up on a chair.

"You never seen my hair," Susy said. 18

That was true. She was standing on a chair, but still, when she unclipped 19 her buns the hair reached all the way to the ground. Our eyes opened. You couldn't tell how much hair she had when it was rolled up so neatly. Then my brother Henry did something funny. He went up to the chair and said, "Jump on my shoulders." So she did that, and her hair reached down past his waist, and he started twirling, this way and that, so her hair was flung out from side to side.

"I always wondered what it was like to have long pretty hair," Henry 20 says. Well we laughed. It was a funny sight, the way he did it. The next morning we got up and took leave of those people.

On to greener pastures, as they say. It was down through Spokane and 21 across Idaho then Montana and very soon we were racing the weather right along under the Canadian border through Columbus, Des Lacs, and then we were in Bottineau County and soon home. We'd made most of the trip, that summer, without putting up the car hood at all. We got home just in time, it turned out, for the army to remember Henry had signed up to join it.

I don't wonder that the army was so glad to get my brother that they 22 turned him into a Marine. He was built like a brick outhouse anyway. We liked to tease him that they really wanted him for his Indian nose. He had a nose big and sharp as a hatchet, like the nose on Red Tomahawk, the Indian who killed Sitting Bull, whose profile is on signs all along the North Dakota highways. Henry went off to training camp, came home once during Christmas, then the next thing you know we got an overseas letter from him. It was 1970, and he said he was stationed up in the northern hill country. Whereabouts I did not know. He wasn't such a hot letter writer, and only got off two before the enemy caught him. I could never keep it straight, which direction those good Vietnam soldiers were from.

I wrote him back several times, even though I didn't know if those letters 23 would get through. I kept him informed all about the car. Most of the time I had it up on blocks in the yard or half taken apart, because that long trip did a hard job on it under the hood.

I always had good luck with numbers, and never worried about the draft 24 myself. I never even had to think about what my number was. But Henry was never lucky in the same way as me. It was at least three years before Henry came home. By then I guess the whole war was solved in the government's mind, but for him it would keep on going. In those years I'd put his car into almost perfect shape. I always thought of it as his car while he was gone, even though when he left he said, "Now it's yours," and threw me his key.

"Thanks for the extra key," I'd said. "I'll put it up in your drawer just in   25 case I need it." He laughed.

When he came home, though, Henry was very different, and I'll say this: 26 the change was no good. You could hardly expect him to change for the better, I know. But he was quiet, so quiet, and never comfortable sitting still anywhere but always up and moving around. I thought back to times we'd sat still for whole afternoons, never moving a muscle, just shifting our weight along the ground, talking to whoever sat with us, watching things. He'd always had a joke, then, too, and now you couldn't get him to laugh, or when he did it was more the sound of a man choking, a sound that stopped up the throats of the people around him. They got to leaving him alone most of the time, and I didn't blame them. It was a fact: Henry was jumpy and mean.

I'd bought a color TV set for my mom and the rest of us while Henry was   27 away. Money still came very easy. I was sorry I'd ever bought it though, because of Henry. I was also sorry I'd bought color, because with black-and-white the pictures seem older and farther away. But what are you going to do? He sat in front of it, watching it, and that was the only time he was completely still. But it was the kind of stillness that you see in a rabbit when it freezes and before it will bolt. He was not easy. He sat in his chair gripping the armrests with all his might, as if the chair itself was moving at a high speed and if he let go at all he would rocket forward and maybe crash right through the set.

Once I was in the room watching TV with Henry and I heard his teeth   28 click at something. I looked over, and he'd bitten through his lip. Blood was going down his chin. I tell you right then I wanted to smash that tube to pieces. I went over to it but Henry must have known what I was up to. He rushed from his chair and shoved me out of the way, against the wall. I told myself he didn't know what he was doing.

My mom came in, turned the set off real quiet, and told us she had made   29 something for supper. So we went and sat down. There was still blood going down Henry's chin, but he didn't notice it and no one said anything, even though every time he took a bite of his bread his blood fell onto it until he was eating his own blood mixed in with the food.

While Henry was not around we talked about what was going to happen   30 to him. There was no Indian doctors on the reservation, and my mom was afraid of trusting the old man, Moses Pillager, because he courted her long ago and was jealous of her husbands. He might take revenge through her son. We were afraid that if we brought Henry to a regular hospital they would keep him.

"They don't fix them in those places," Mom said; "they just give them   31 drugs."

"We wouldn't get him there in the first place," I agreed, "so let's just for-   32 get about it."

Then I thought about the car.   33

Henry had not even looked at the car since he'd gotten home, though   34
like I said, it was in tip-top condition and ready to drive. I thought the car
might bring the old Henry back somehow. So I bided my time and waited for
my chance to interest him in the vehicle.

One night Henry was off somewhere. I took myself a hammer. I went out   35
to that car and I did a number on its underside. Whacked it up. Bent the tail
pipe double. Ripped the muffler loose. By the time I was done with the car it
looked worse than any typical Indian car that has been driven all its life on
reservation roads, which they always say are like government promises — full
of holes. It just about hurt me, I'll tell you that! I threw dirt in the carburetor
and I ripped all the electric tape off the seats. I made it look just as beat up
as I could. Then I sat back and waited for Henry to find it.

Still, it took him over a month. That was all right, because it was just get-   36
ting warm enough, not melting, but warm enough to work outside.

"Lyman," he says, walking in one day, "that red car looks like shit."   37

"Well it's old," I says. "You got to expect that."   38

"No way!" says Henry. "That car's a classic! But you went and ran the   39
piss right out of it, Lyman, and you know it don't deserve that. I kept that car
in A-one shape. You don't remember. You're too young. But when I left, that
car was running like a watch. Now I don't even know if I can get it to start
again, let alone get it anywhere near its old condition."

"Well you try," I said, like I was getting mad, "but I say it's a piece of   40
junk."

Then I walked out before he could realize I knew he'd strung together   41
more than six words at once.

After that I thought he'd freeze himself to death working on that car. He   42
was out there all day, and at night he rigged up a little lamp, ran a cord out
the window, and had himself some light to see by while he worked. He was
better than he had been before, but that's still not saying much. It was easier
for him to do the things the rest of us did. He ate more slowly and didn't jump
up and down during the meal to get this or that or look out the window. I put
my hand in the back of the TV set, I admit, and fiddled around with it good,
so that it was almost impossible now to get a clear picture. He didn't look at
it very often anyway. He was always out with that car or going off to get parts
for it. By the time it was really melting outside, he had it fixed.

I had been feeling down in the dumps about Henry around this time. We   43
had always been together before. Henry and Lyman. But he was such a loner
now that I didn't know how to take it. So I jumped at the chance one day
when Henry seemed friendly. It's not that he smiled or anything. He just said,
"Let's take the old shitbox for a spin." Just the way he said it made me think
he could be coming around.

We went out to the car. It was spring. The sun was shining very bright.   44
My only sister, Bonita, who was just eleven years old, came out and made us
stand together for a picture. Henry leaned his elbow on the red car's windshield, and he took his other arm and put it over my shoulder, very carefully,

as though it was heavy for him to lift and he didn't want to bring the weight
down all at once.

"Smile," Bonita said, and he did.   45

That picture, I never look at it anymore. A few months ago, I don't know   46
why, I got his picture out and tacked it on the wall. I felt good about Henry
at the time, close to him. I felt good having his picture on the wall, until one
night when I was looking at television. I was a little drunk and stoned. I
looked up at the wall and Henry was staring at me. I don't know what it was,
but his smile had changed, or maybe it was gone. All I know is I couldn't stay
in the same room with that picture. I was shaking. I got up, closed the door,
and went into the kitchen. A little later my friend Ray came over and we both
went back into that room. We put the picture in a brown bag, folded the bag
over and over tightly, then put it way back in a closet.

I still see that picture now, as if it tugs at me, whenever I pass that closet 47
door. The picture is very clear in my mind. It was so sunny that day Henry
had to squint against the glare. Or maybe the camera Bonita held flashed like
a mirror, blinding him, before she snapped the picture. My face is right out in
the sun, big and round. But he might have drawn back, because the shadows
on his face are deep as holes. There are two shadows curved like little hooks
around the ends of his smile, as if to frame it and try to keep it there — that
one, first smile that looked like it might have hurt his face. He has his field
jacket on and the worn-in clothes he'd come back in and kept wearing ever
since. After Bonita took the picture, she went into the house and we got into
the car. There was a full cooler in the trunk. We started off, east, toward Pem-
bina and the Red River because Henry said he wanted to see the high water.

The trip over there was beautiful. When everything starts changing, dry-   48
ing up, clearing off, you feel like your whole life is starting. Henry felt it, too.
The top was down and the car hummed like a top. He'd really put it back in
shape, even the tape on the seats was very carefully put down and glued
back in layers. It's not that he smiled again or even joked, but his face looked
to me as if it was clear, more peaceful. It looked as though he wasn't thinking of anything in particular except the bare fields and windbreaks and
houses we were passing.

The river was high and full of winter trash when we got there. The sun   49
was still out, but it was colder by the river. There were still little clumps of
dirty snow here and there on the banks. The water hadn't gone over the banks
yet, but it would, you could tell. It was just at its limit, hard swollen glossy
like an old gray scar. We made ourselves a fire, and we sat down and watched
the current go. As I watched it I felt something squeezing inside me and tight-
ening and trying to let go all at the same time. I knew I was not just feeling it
myself; I knew I was feeling what Henry was going through at that moment.
Except that I couldn't stand it, the closing and opening. I jumped to my feet.
I took Henry by the shoulders and I started shaking him. "Wake up," I says,
"wake up, wake up, wake up!" I didn't know what had come over me. I sat
down beside him again.

His face was totally white and hard. Then it broke, like stones break all 50
of a sudden when water boils up inside them.

"I know it," he says, "I know it. I can't help it. It's no use."   51

We start talking. He said he knew what I'd done with the car. It was ob- 52
vious it had been whacked out of shape and not just neglected. He said he
wanted to give the car to me for good now, it was no use. He said he'd fixed
it just to give it back and I should take it.

"No way," I says, "I don't want it."   53

"That's okay," he says, "you take it."   54

"I don't want it, though," I says back to him, and then to emphasize, just 55
to emphasize, you understand, I touch his shoulder. He slaps my hand off.

"Take that car," he says.   56

"No," I say. "Make me," I say, and then he grabs my jacket and rips the 57
arm loose. That jacket is a class act, suede with tags and zippers. I push
Henry backwards, off the log. He jumps up and bowls me over. We go down
in a clinch and come up swinging hard, for all we're worth, with our fists. He
socks my jaw so hard I feel like it swings loose. Then I'm at his rib cage and
land a good one under his chin so his head snaps back. He's dazzled. He
looks at me and I look at him and then his eyes are full of tears and blood
and at first I think he's crying. But no, he's laughing. "Ha! Ha!" he says, "Ha!
Ha! Take good care of it."

"Okay," I says, "okay, no problem. Ha! Ha!"   58

I can't help it, and I start laughing, too. My face feels fat and strange, and 59
after a while I get a beer from the cooler in the trunk, and when I hand it to
Henry he takes his shirt and wipes my germs off. "Hoof-and-mouth disease,"
he says. For some reason this cracks me up, and so we're really laughing for
a while, and then we drink all the rest of the beers one by one and throw
them in the river and see how far, how fast, the current takes them before
they fill up and sink.

"You want to go on back?" I ask after a while. "Maybe we could snag a 60
couple nice Kashpaw girls."

He says nothing. But I can tell his mood is turning again.   61

"They're all crazy, the girls up here, every damn one of them."   62

"You're crazy too," I say, to jolly him up. "Crazy Lamartine boys!"   63

He looks as though he will take this wrong at first. His face twists, then 64
clears, and he jumps up on his feet. "That's right!" he says. "Crazier 'n hell
Crazy Indians!"

I think it's the old Henry again. He throws off his jacket and starts swing- 65
ing his legs out from the knees like a fancy dancer. He's down doing something between a grass dance and a bunny hop, no kind of dance I ever saw
before, but neither has anyone else on all this green growing earth. He's wild.
He wants to pitch whoopee! He's up and at me and all over. All this time I'm
laughing so hard, so hard my belly is getting tied up in a knot.

"Got to cool me off!" he shouts all of a sudden. Then he runs over to the 66
river and jumps in.

There's boards and other things in the current. It's so high. No sound 67
comes from the river after the splash he makes, so I run right over. I look

around. It's getting dark. I see he's halfway across the water already, and I know he didn't swim there but the current took him. It's far. I hear his voice, though, very clearly across it.

"My boots are filling," he says. 68

He says this in a normal voice, like he just noticed and he doesn't know 69 what to think of it. Then he's gone. A branch comes by. Another branch. And I go in.

By the time I get out of the river, off the snag I pulled myself onto, the 70 sun is down. I walk back to the car, turn on the high beams, and drive it up the bank. I put it in first gear and then I take my foot off the clutch. I get out, close the door, and watch it plow softly into the water. The headlights reach in as they go down, searching, still lighted even after the water swirls over the back end. I wait. The wires short out. It is all finally dark. And then there is only the water, the sound of it going and running and going and running and running.

FOR DISCUSSION AND WRITING: CULTURAL KNOWLEDGE AND CULTURAL ICONS

1. What were your initial responses to the title of this story? What inferences is the reader called upon to make in the first paragraph? What questions are raised? What cultural knowledge do you bring to the term *reservation?*

2. There are nine breaks in the narrative. Why do you think the writer has made these breaks? What work must the reader do to fill the gaps between them?

3. In paragraphs 10–20 the story of Henry and Lyman's summer road trip is told. What happens on this trip? How does the trip relate to the rest of the story?

4. About how long was Henry a prisoner of war in Vietnam? What do you know about that war? What does Henry's behavior when he returns home tell you about the problems of many Vietnam veterans?

5. Write an essay in which you discuss what you think the red convertible represents in this story. Consider each brother's relationship to the car.

IDENTIFYING WITH TEXTS

Let's extend our thinking about intertextuality from folk culture into popular culture. How do works of entertainment—stories represented in the popular media such as cinema, television, or journalism—function as "texts"? Interpretive acts, such as those by Bettelheim and Prose on "Sleeping Beauty" (pp. 214–28), reflect the critical attitude toward popular culture, the promotion of which is one of the primary functions of schooling. The daily-life attitude to narrative is equally interpretive, but not necessarily critical, in that consumers of stories outside of school tend to *identify* with the entertainment narratives they enjoy.

Many critics contend that, precisely by virtue of this identification, entertainment texts serve an *ideological* purpose. *Ideology* is often thought of as a pejorative term alluding to "false consciousness"—thought that is merely deluded belief, unaware of the real conditions of one's life. A more neutral sense of ideology is equally applied, however, referring to "the set of ideas that arise from a given set of material circumstances," ideas by means of which the general public (without access to critical science) becomes conscious of its condition. This more neutral sense of the term acknowledges that ideology is inescapable and irreducible, even if it is subject to analysis by critical science. The categories of ideology, that is, name the fundamental elements of individual identity: race, ethnicity, sexuality, gender, religion, class, age, nationality. Until recently the preferred ideological identity of our society was white, European, heterosexual, masculine, Protestant, bourgeois, young, and American.

What ideas do we have about these aspects of our identity? What conduct is "proper" according to one's status in each of these categories? We all learn and internalize these codes of conduct and preferred behaviors from our experiences with our family and with our entertainment culture, long before we ever encounter the critical methods of interpretive analysis in school. Another often-misunderstood term may be used to clarify the effects of popular storytelling as a vehicle for the construction of identity: *propaganda*. The kind of propaganda we are most familiar with is what critics refer to as "agitational," understood as oppositional and subversive with the purpose of overthrowing the established order. Such propaganda is also used by the establishment in times of crisis to rally its citizens and distress its enemies. Another type of propaganda is equally prevalent, however: the propaganda of integration (to use the term provided by Jacques Ellul), which promotes acceptance of the status quo, conformity, passivity. Modern revolutionary societies have had to negotiate the complex shift from the agitational propaganda used to help get into power to the integrative propaganda used to stay in power. Each new administration in the American democratic system has to practice its own version of this shift from running against the bureaucracy to defending it.

In textual terms, the insight of ideological and propagandistic readings of popular entertainment is that stories play a crucial role in the symbolic life of a culture; the capacity for making meaning through the experience of reading is one way that individuals are gathered into a community. Values and beliefs in popular culture are not imposed by some external power, however, but negotiated in a kind of collective dialogue whose operations are still not fully understood. Critics have begun to recognize the positive side of entertainment by noting the way fans transform their favorite works into texts—the way *Star Trek* fans, for example, rewrite the story to suit their own interests and fantasies. It turns out that even while readers identify with their favorite stories, they do not simply accept the dominant values and beliefs expressed within them. Rather, a familiarity with popular culture in general and various subcultures in particular constitutes a "language" for the individual. Citizens of a given national culture "speak" it the way they speak their native language: they may use the stories, characters, scenes, images, and songs to think more or less creatively about their own lives. In our terms we could say that the native readers fashion an intertextual consciousness out of the stories they consume.

Typical of this intertextual function of popular stories is the classic cult film *Casablanca*. *Casablanca*, based on *Everybody Comes to Rick's* (which the critic James Agee called "one of the world's worst plays"), is ranked third behind *Gone with the Wind* and *Citizen Kane* on the American Film Institute poll of the best American films of all time. Directed by Michael Curtiz and starring Humphrey Bogart and Ingrid Bergman, *Casablanca* premiered on Thanksgiving Day 1942 and went on to win Oscars for best director, best screenplay, and best picture. The following set of readings about how films in general—and *Casablanca* in particular—present scenes of instruction about values and belief is offered as a point of departure for thinking and writing about intertextuality and ideology.

The pull toward identification with the characters and values presented in powerful literary and cinematic texts is very hard to resist. And our pleasure as readers or consumers of these texts is closely linked to this identification. But we also need to withdraw from that close connection or identification sometimes, at the risk of reducing that pleasure. Attending to the ideology of a text is one way of gaining critical distance from it. And we do need distance as well as identification. The complex dynamic of identification and withdrawal is at the heart of the process of interpretation. This process will be emphasized in the section that follows this one—and, indeed, will carry through to the "mystory" project with which this book closes. You can prepare yourself to get the most from the interpretation section by reading the texts in this one while being alert for the ways in which they raise this critical problem of closeness and distance.

The Culmination of Classic Hollywood:
Casablanca

Robert B. Ray

*In his authoritative history of American cinema, Robert Ray explains how pop-
ular films, typified by* Casablanca, *respond to specific historical situations by
conveying implicit instructions about the beliefs and values relevant to the
given moment. Robert Ray is director of film studies at the University of Florida
in Gainesville. He is also the leader of a rock band called the Vulgar Boatmen.*

Casablanca's plot confronted Rick with a series of choices: Should he help   1
Laszlo to escape and thereby forfeit his own safe neutrality? Should he keep
Ilsa with him? Should he avoid the situation altogether and do nothing? In
turn, the film appeared to demand that its audience decide between two sets
of values, Rick's outlaw hero code and Laszlo's official morality. This di-
chotomy resulted from the film's sustained contrasting of the two men.

Appearance: As played by Paul Henreid, standing erect in a white dress   2
suit, Victor Laszlo perfectly embodied the official hero. Indeed, Henreid's
clear eyes, chiseled Roman nose, high forehead, and strong jaw (with the hint
of an underbite) made Laszlo resemble George Washington, the arch-official
hero of American culture.

If Henreid gave Laszlo a kind of classical good looks, Bogart lent Rick an   3
irregular handsomeness, with weary, cynical eyes, a rather plain nose, and an
idiosyncratic mouth. The important thing about this attractiveness was its individuality; its refusal to conform to any preconceived notions of handsomeness duplicated the character's stubborn independence.

Attitude toward Women: While Laszlo was married (and even more tell-   4
ingly, comfortable with being so), Rick was another example of what Fiedler
has called "a long line of heroes in flight from woman and home." An early
scene confirmed Rick's attitude. Confronted by an ex-girlfriend trying to pin
him down to some commitment, he brushed her off with the casual disdain
of a man interested in women only for sexual entertainment.

Yvonne: Where were you last night?
Rick: That's so long ago I don't remember.
Yvonne: Will I see you tonight?
Rick: I never make plans that far ahead.

Finally getting the message, Yvonne uttered the classic complaint of all women
abandoned by an outlaw hero: "What a fool I was to fall for a man like you."

Significantly, too, Rick operated and lived above a saloon, a place which,   5
as Fiedler points out, "was for a long time felt as the anti-type of the home, a
refuge for escaping males nearly as archetypal as the wilderness and the sea."
Rick's bar was no different, a man's world where women were nightly bought
and sold in exchange for exit visas.

Origins: With their different origins, the American Rick and the European   6
Laszlo embodied the contradictory sources of the American ideology. For
while the official heroes (e.g., Jefferson, Franklin) provided continuity with
the manners, learning, and sophistication of the Old World, the outlaw hero
represented the instinctive repudiation of Europe and its culture.

Significantly, Rick's outlaw status depended on more than simply the im-   7
agery of self-containment that surrounded him. Like Shane and the typical
gunfighter, he had an ambiguous past: "Richard Blaine, American, Age 37.
Cannot return to his country," Strasser read to Rick. "The reason is a little
vague." Renault also showed interest:

Renault: I've often speculated on why you don't return to America. Did you
    abscond with the church funds? Did you run off with the Senator's wife?
    I'd like to think that you killed a man. It's the romantic in me.
Rick: It was a combination of all three.

The truth about Rick's past remained the undisclosed secret of *Casa-*   8
blanca; the film never revealed why Rick could not go home, as *Shane* refused to specify the exact nature of what its hero refused to discuss.

Casablanca, however, did indicate that while Laszlo was in Morocco for
a specific purpose (to escape the Nazis), Rick had come for apparently no
reason at all:

Renault: And what in heaven's name brought you to Casablanca?
Rick: My health. I came to Casablanca for the waters.
Renault: What waters? We're in the desert.
Rick: I was misinformed.

This denial of rational motivation represented a characteristic American ideological tendency to deny past events their capacity to control present circumstances. As an assertion, it derived from the frontier mythology of perpetual renewal which encouraged escapism. Not surprisingly, however, Rick's
apparent fresh start concealed a previous disappointment. Like Jay Gatsby
(another hero with mysterious origins), he was obsessed with a past that he
sought simultaneously to obliterate. In maintaining this ambiguous relationship with his own history, Rick represented not only the typical frontiersman,
but also America itself.

Attitudes toward Politics and Ideology: Laszlo was first and foremost a   9
public figure, driven by abstract principles at once rational and supraindi-
vidualistic. Trying to explain his character to Rick, Ilsa spoke of "knowledge
and thoughts and ideals," the chief symbols of the official values. Significantly, too, Laszlo led a collective movement, the Pan-European underground. Thanking Rick at the end, he spoke of *"our* side."

Rick's pragmatic skepticism contrasted strongly with Laszlo's idealism. "You   10
are a very cynical person," Ugarte told him, and nothing Rick said disproved
that characterization. "The problems of the world are not in my department,"
he insisted, and having heard Ilsa's moralizing about Laszlo's cause, he refused to help: "I'm not fighting for anything anymore except myself. I'm the
only cause I'm interested in." With his distrust of abstract principles, Rick

confirmed Tocqueville's observation that in America, "each man is narrowly shut up in himself, and from that basis makes the pretension to judge the world."

While Laszlo's absorption in political activities confirmed his official 11 hero status, Rick's evident leisure connected him further to the western hero described by Robert Warshow:

> The Westerner is *par excellence* a man of leisure. Even when he wears the badge of a marshal or, more rarely, owns a ranch, he appears to be unemployed. We see him standing at a bar, or playing poker — a game which expresses perfectly his talent for remaining relaxed in the midst of tension — or perhaps camping out on the plains on some extraordinary errand. If he does own a ranch, it is in the background; we are not actually aware that he owns anything except his horse, his guns, and the one worn suit of clothing which is likely to remain unchanged all through the movie. It comes as a surprise to see him take money from his saddlebags. As a rule we do not even know where he sleeps at night and don't think of asking. Yet it never occurs to us that he is a poor man. . . .[1]

This passage described Rick almost exactly. He owned the casino, but his work seemed limited to signing checks and vouchers, breaking up occasional fights, and refusing to drink with customers. In this context, the information that his cash reserves could withstand the café's closing for "two weeks, maybe three" *was* surprising. He seemed never to think of money.

Attitudes toward the Law: Casablanca repeatedly emphasized Rick's and 12 Laszlo's contrasting views of the law, an issue traditionally dividing the official hero and the renegade. Rick was clearly another version of Robin Hood, operating outside a corrupt legal system in the name of some higher, private notion of justice. Like the original Robin, he made all the decisions for a loyal band of followers (Carl the waiter, Sacha the bartender, the croupier, and most important, Sam the piano player). Like Robin (or the American gunfighter variants: Jesse James, Bonnie and Clyde, John Wesley Hardin), Rick robbed from the rich to give to the poor, manipulating his own roulette wheel to provide refugees with money for exit visas. When after one instance of remarkable "luck" by one of Rick's favored, another customer asked, "Say, are you sure this place is honest?" Carl's ironic reply reaffirmed the outlaw hero's private standard: "Honest? As honest as the day is long."

While Rick represented an extralegal morality, Laszlo relied on a legal 13 principle for his safety. The movie's basic premise was the neutrality of the "frontier" town Casablanca, an abstract principle that Laszlo repeatedly asserted. "You won't dare to interfere with me here," he warned Strasser. "This is still unoccupied France. Any violation would reflect on Captain Renault."

Having established Laszlo's dependence on the law, however, *Casablanca* 14 used the stock western depiction of the legal system's ultimate inadequacy as

---

[1]Robert Warshow, *The Immediate Experience* (New York: Atheneum, 1972).

a guarantor of the official hero's safety. As in most westerns, the villains in *Casablanca* could control the legal mechanism to their own advantage. "The Germans have *outlawed* miracles," Ferrari warned Laszlo, and Renault used the flimsiest legal pretext to close Rick's café: "I'm shocked! Shocked to find that gambling is going on here!" he proclaimed, pocketing his own roulette winnings. Unlike Laszlo, Rick recognized the Germans' eagerness to manipulate the law. His proposed scheme to deliver Laszlo into the Gestapo's hands offered an apparent certitude of legal proof: Laszlo would be apprehended in the act of purchasing the stolen letters of transit, thereby making himself an accessory to the German couriers' murder.

While Laszlo relied on the law, Rick, like all western heroes, took it into his own hands, replacing an insufficient, corrupt system with his individual standards of right and wrong. His willingness to operate outside the law preserved Laszlo, who, left to his own devices, might never have escaped Casablanca.   15

Although Rick and Laszlo clearly represented the two strains of American culture, *Casablanca* demonstrated their imbalance. For Bogart was the film's star, and no matter how badly he behaved early on, the interest center remained with him. Renault made this focus overt, describing Rick to Ilsa as "the kind of man that, well, if I were a woman, and I weren't around, I should be in love with Rick," an ironic version of Mark Twain's encomium to Tom Blankenship, the model for Huck: "He was the only really independent person—boy or man—in the community," Twain remembered in his *Autobiography*, adding in *Tom Sawyer* that all the other children "wished they dared be like him."   16

As *Casablanca*'s moral center, Laszlo was more ambiguous. While his principles were rationally acceptable, he represented too many of the things traditionally disparaged by the frontier mythology: marriage, political commitment, collective action, the denial of individualism. At moments, the movie allowed the implicit sense of Laszlo's coldness to surface in thin disguise: "We read five times that you were killed in five different places," a fellow underground fighter whispered. "As you see," Laszlo replied, seeming to acknowledge the cost of idealism to the human elements of his character, "it was true every single time."   17

In a cinematic tradition so dependent on audience identification, Laszlo's glacial perfection diminished his appeal. In contrast to Rick's emotional drunk scene, his control suggested a less passionate attachment to Ilsa. As Rick observed, she seemed mostly another "part of his work, the thing that keeps him going"—the conventional western's low estimate of married love. Rick's love, the movie assured, was the genuine article.   18

Having established Rick and Laszlo as representatives of the two divergent strains of American mythology, *Casablanca* assumed the national ideology's basic project: their reconciliation. . . .   19

Throughout this discussion of *Casablanca*, I have made deliberate references to *Huckleberry Finn*. For part of the movie's authority derived from its reworking of many of the motifs of Twain's novel, which Hemingway referred   20 to as the source for all American literature. Indeed, *Casablanca's* particularly close connection to *Huck Finn* was merely one instance of Classic Hollywood's characteristic, and probably unconscious, repetitions of that literature's fundamental themes.

Casablanca not only made Rick a reincarnation of the renegade Huck; it [21] also imitated basic elements of Twain's plot. The opening map sequence of *Casablanca*, with its dark, moving line representing "a tortuous, roundabout refugee trail," simulated a river, in the midst of which the city of Casablanca, and Rick's café, lay like a raft. Like Huck, Rick lived on this "raft" with a black companion (Sam), and this "river" (like the Mississippi) provided an escape route from oppression. *Casablanca* divided the character of Jim, the runaway slave, into two figures: the black friend, Sam, and the white man, Laszlo, who assumed Jim's problem, the need to escape.

Furthermore, Rick repeated Huck's pattern of being apolitical, of trying [22] to avoid the entire issue of helping Laszlo with its complicated issues of right and wrong. Sam, who was more like Tom Sawyer than Jim, pleaded with his boss to get away from the dilemma. Sounding like Jake Barnes in *The Sun Also Rises* proposing the trip to Spain to Bill Gorton, Sam begged, "We'll take the car and drive all night. We'll get drunk. We'll go fishin' and stay away until she's gone."

But Rick, like Huck, ended up helping Laszlo, almost in spite of himself. [23] His plan, which involved deceiving Ilsa and Laszlo until the last moment, repeated the kind of elaborate trickery that Tom and Huck had inflicted on Jim. Above all, *Casablanca* reaffirmed *Huck Finn's* assurance that the outsider's freedom could survive the entanglements required by helping someone else. The movie depicted any such commitment as only temporary, an emergency measure without lasting implications. As Huck ended by "light[ing] out for the Territory," staying one step ahead of civilization, Rick told Louis, "I could use a trip," and set out for the mysterious "Free French garrison over at Brazzaville," a phrase whose exotic, Foreign Legion remoteness effectively converted French North Africa into another frontier.

Casablanca's ending was crucial to the success of the film's ideological [24] project: the avoidance of choice between autonomy and commitment. Rick's intervention assumed the typical western form, the gunfight, as he outdrew the German officer trying to prevent Laszlo's escape. But as in all westerns, the crucial issue in *Casablanca* turned on the woman. Ingrid Bergman's well-known account of the scriptwriters' uncertainty about whether Ilsa would stay with Rick or leave with Laszlo misleadingly suggests the relative appropriateness of either conclusion. In fact, however, as a disguised western intent on demonstrating the impermanence of all interventions in society's affairs, *Casablanca* could not have conceivably allowed its outlaw hero to keep the girl. For the frontier mythology persistently portrayed the real danger to that hero's independence not as intervention for the good of others, but as marriage. *Casablanca* reassured its male audience (the source of the national anxiety regarding World War II intervention) that one could accept responsibilities without forfeiting autonomy, if one could evade the symbolic entanglements offered by the Good Good Girl.

The power of *Casablanca*'s ending, like *The Maltese Falcon*'s, derived from 25
the coincidence of ideological need (to send the woman away) with official
morality: in *The Maltese Falcon*, the woman had to be turned over to the police because she was the murderer; in *Casablanca*, because she had to remain
with her legal husband. The striking visual resemblances between the two
conclusions merely suggested the frequency with which Classic Hollywood
resorted to this basic western trope.

In both films, the woman played the sacrificial lamb which allowed the 26
audience to avoid choosing between the outlaw code and the official morality. Freed of Ilsa, Rick could light out for the Territory with Renault, their banter encouraging the film's audience to consider such temporary commitments
as fun. . . .

From Play It Again, Sam

Woody Allen

We had hoped to bring to you in this space an excerpt from Play It Again, Sam—
*a play by Woody Allen, made into a 1972 film starring Allen and directed by
Herb Ross, which we had included in a previous edition of* Text Book. *But Mr.
Allen's lawyers have denied us permission to use this material at the present
time. Nevertheless, Allen's play and the film are such beautiful examples of intertextuality at work that we will discuss them briefly here before moving on to
the next reading.* Play It Again, Sam *is a prototype for intertextual effects at all
levels. It may be read as a dramatized essay on the ideological function of intertextuality both in the story of the nebbish, Allan, who is a fan of Bogart, and
in the form of the film itself, which is a kind of remake of* Casablanca. *The character Allan demonstrates (no doubt in an exaggerated way for comic effect) how
a fan obsessed with a particular celebrity or star icon might manipulate experience to reproduce the scenes of certain stories. For example, at the end of* Play
It Again, Sam, *Allan is able to break off his affair with his best friend's wife by
quoting one of the most famous speeches in* Casablanca—*the "hill of beans"
speech: "I'm no good at being noble, but it doesn't take much to see that the
problems of three little people don't amount to a hill of beans in this crazy
world. Someday you'll understand that. Not now. Here's looking at you, kid."*

*In one scene from the play, for example, Allan invites a young woman over
for dinner while his best friend, Dick, is out of town on a business trip. During
the seduction scene on the couch, Allan, who has no idea how to relate with
women, gets some advice from the spirit of Bogart—or rather, from the persona
of some of the characters Bogart played. (In both the play and the film, "Bogart"
is visible to the audience and to Allan, but to none of the other characters—one
of many devices that ensure our identification with Allan.) The interest of this
scene is that it dramatizes one of the central ideas of ideological criticism—that
all popular narratives instruct the audience in how to behave according to their*

position in society (all popular works are guides to etiquette). Part of the value of looking at works from an earlier period, for our critical purposes, is that the beliefs that were taken for granted then become dated and hence more easily recognized as beliefs (rather than as truths) by later audiences. The racist attitudes that seemed normal to viewers of D. W. Griffith's film The Birth of a Nation *are painfully obvious to viewers today. Similarly, the sexism that informs the comedy in* Play It Again, Sam, *written in 1968 (as would have been obvious in the selection itself, if it had passed legal inspection) is no longer considered funny. The value of such examples, however, is that they remind us that the entertainment narratives we enjoy today are as filled with the stereotypes and prejudices of our current ideology as are the works from an earlier period. Indeed, ideology has been defined as "that which goes without saying."*

Bambi: A Boy's Story
Russell Banks

This selection introduces you to the cinema as a place in which we receive integrative propaganda about how we ought to behave or, at least, about the kind of behavior that our dominant culture deems most valuable. Russell Banks writes about Bambi *rather than about* Casablanca, *but his account of the effect on him of this simple children's story helps clarify what is at stake in more complex stories (whatever their medium). It also helps explain the pleasure derived from watching the brief cartoon* Bambi Meets Godzilla. *Russell Banks, the author of numerous books of fiction, teaches at Princeton University.*

Who can say that one and only one movie changed his life? Who can name   1
with confidence the movie that accomplished so much? No, there have been many movies—or "films," as I called them in my late teens and twenties—which altered my thinking about the world and thus about myself and which, therefore, could be said, to a greater or lesser degree, to have changed my life. (Although I must say that there have not been as many movies as books that have had this effect—but that's in the nature of a more or less bookish adult life, isn't it?)

Even so, I am an American child of the twentieth century, so that, before   2
books began to change my life—books, and then travel, sex, death, and divorce—which is to say, before I reached adolescence, there were surely movies to do the serious work, and in my childhood, in the absence of books, in the absence of even a merely provincial cinematic context against which I could place and measure the movie, and, going back still further, in the absence of *any* world larger than the one provided by my immediate family, in the absence, then, of church, school, community, in the absence of a conscious culture of any kind, yes, a single movie did have the capacity to alter and

then shape my inner life with a power, clarity, and speed that would never be available to me again. Not in movies, anyhow, and certainly not in books.

I was little more than a baby at the time, but a person nonetheless; no tabula rasa, no amorphous unformed amoeba of a consciousness, but a true *person;* and I recently discovered that there was a single winter afternoon at the movies that did indeed change my life, and in such a thoroughgoing way that I am utterly unable to remember today the person I was before the moment I sat down in the Scenic Theater, the only movie house in the small mill town of Pittsfield, New Hampshire, with my younger brother Steve on one side, my cousin Neil, also younger, and Uncle Bud Eastman on the other, and the lights went out. One person—a child very much like the newborn fawn Bambi, of no particular gender, a creature whose destiny was shaped merely by his species—seems to have died that afternoon; and another—a child defined by his gender—got born.

The power and clarity and speed of ritual is what I'm referring to here. My secularized New England Protestant bar mitzvah. Though I had long remembered the event, the name of the movie, the circumstances surrounding my viewing, and a few vivid details, until I happened in recent months to see it again, I recalled little else of it. And exactly who I was before I first saw the movie is lost to me now, except as I'm able to observe him in another child that age or younger; and who I was afterward remains to a disturbing degree the person I am today. That's how powerful it is, or was—*Bambi,* the Disney movie version of the Felix Salten story, which I saw at the age of four.

How do I know this took place, this transformation? The truth is, I was taught it by a child and, in part, by another Disney movie. I have a three-year-old granddaughter, Sarah, and last summer Sarah spent a week, without her parents, visiting my wife and me in our home in the Adirondack Mountains in upstate New York.

I am a relatively young grandfather, and my wife (not Sarah's grandmother) is even younger, but nevertheless we soon tired of carting this energetic, curious, but easily bored child to Santa's Workshop, Frontiertown, and the Great Escape Amusement Park. We began to look for diversions for her that were located closer to home and that we ourselves would find amusing, too.

There is very little television programming for children her age, especially way up in the north country, where the only channel we receive, and receive badly at that, is the NBC affiliate from Plattsburgh. We tuned in, but most of the children's shows seemed alternately hysterical and simple-minded. Sarah was neither, and we liked her that way, as did she.

But she seemed too young for movies—she was barely three, and too sidereal and digressive in her perceptions of time to care for plot, too curious about background to bother distinguishing it from foreground, and too far outside the economy to have her fantasy life targeted for colonization by sexual imagery. She was, we thought, media innocent. Possibly media immune.

We concluded all this when we rented the more popular children's movies and played them for her one after the other on the VCR. She watched them, *Mary Poppins, Cinderella, Peter Pan,* even *The Wizard of Oz;* but she watched them obediently, passively, sleepily, as if narcotized by a little too much cough medicine; and reluctantly (*we* were interested after all), we rewound the movies halfway through, with no protest from her, and returned them to the video outlet in nearby Elizabethtown.

Then, one evening, for the first time we ran a movie that instantly seized 10 her attention, drew her forward in her seat and engaged her emotionally in a way that none of the others had so far. She had locked onto it like a heat-seeking missile. It was Disney's *The Little Mermaid*. Relieved, my wife and I brought in a bowl of popcorn and sat down to watch it with her, but after a few moments, to our dismay and slight embarrassment, we realized that *The Little Mermaid* was essentially a dramatized tract designed to promote the virtues and rewards of female submissiveness and silence. Not the sort of thing we wanted our granddaughter to watch while in our care. She was *not* too young, it now seemed, to have her fantasy life structured and rearranged by sexual imagery, not too young to be colonized by the masters of the medium.

She wept when we rewound the film and removed it from the VCR. We 11 replaced it with *Bambi*, the last of the children's films in Elizabethtown that was not science fiction or horror. My wife, born in 1950, had not seen *Bambi* since her own early childhood and remembered it no more clearly than I, al-though she at least knew that Bambi was a boy, which I did not. All I'd re-membered of it, as I said, was that I had seen it at the Scenic in Pittsfield when I was four, with my brother and cousin and uncle. In my memory, it was a *girl's* story about a fawn—Bambi is a girl's name, right?—and there was a forest fire, and Bambi's mother had died somehow. Which was sad, to be sure, but it was only one episode and not the dramatic point of the movie, and the Disney people had handled the tragedy with gentleness and tact, as I recalled. The ending I remembered vaguely as uplifting. There were several memorable secondary characters, a mischievous rabbit with a foot spasm named Thumper and a winsome skunk named Flower. Nothing very promis-ing; certainly nothing dangerous.

I did remember it as having been a visually thrilling movie, however, 12 filled with gorgeously painted scenery—endless northern forests, fields of wild-flowers, falling leaves, snow and ice, lofty mountains, and turbulent skies—lyrical pictures of a world not unlike the one that I had grown up in and that actually surrounded us now in the Adirondacks. A world I hoped to honor and celebrate with my granddaughter.

It opened with a trailer for *The Little Mermaid*, a preview. We winced and 13 waited. This stuff is inescapable. Perhaps Sarah thought the trailer was the opening scene of the new movie; or the final scene of the movie we had just removed, a lingering afterimage.

No matter. From the first frame, *Bambi* was of an entirely different aes- 14 thetic and moral order than *The Little Mermaid*. We approved of this. We may have been forced to deprive our granddaughter of the pleasure of watching the story of Ariel, the free-swimming mermaid who surrenders her beautiful voice, becomes a bimbo in a bikini—Barbie with fins—and lands her prince, but we had given her instead the story of *Bambi*, which, from the scene unfold-ing behind the credits, we realized would be a story about love between mother and child, with possibly an early Green theme tossed in—the enemy, the outsider, would be Man, we could see. The central image appeared to be that of the Edenic garden before the arrival of the wars between the species. Nice. We approved. And where *The Little Mermaid* had opened like Andre Agassi's wardrobe, a frantic disco-dance of primary colors, of garish neon red and orange and fluorescent green and purple, the colors and rhythms of *Bambi* were soft and muted, opening slowly like the wings of a butterfly in shades of pale green and blue-gray, shifting to rose to speckled sunlight. This was a visual lyricism we could understand and value, one we wanted to share with Sarah.

It's the slow dawning of a spring day in the deep forest. Behind the images, the voices of a male tenor and chorus, hymnlike, rise up singing. . . .   15

My obligations to oversee the moral education of my granddaughter met,   16
I was free now to sit back, relax, and watch the movie for myself, and suddenly I was gone, lost inside the world of the movie, and found again inside my four-year-old self. It was a startling transformation, instantaneous and complete. I was at once and once again a country child on the cusp of boyhood, a creature just emerging from the polymorphous envelope of infancy and facing for the first time the beginnings of a terrifying, bewildering male life with others. An owl returns to his huge oak from his nighttime haunts, and flocks of birds waken the rest of the world with song. The dappled forest floor fills with parents and their newborn babes—quail, mice, squirrels, rabbits—all performing their morning ablutions, breaking their fasts, when a bluebird, fluttering from tree to tree, excitedly brings the news, "It's happened! It's happened!" What's happened? we all wonder. "The prince is born!" the bird exclaims. "The prince is born!"

Everyone hurries to what can only be called an adoration scene, a crèche,   17
practically, in the thicket, where a lovely large-eyed doe nudges her newborn fawn into view. It's straight from the New Testament. Like a benign Dr. Johnson, Friend Owl, urging reverence, explains to the excited onlookers, especially the agitated, somewhat bewildered young: "This is quite an occasion. It isn't every day a new Prince is born."

Indeed. And that is why this dawn is different from all other dawns. The   18
story of stories, your own story, if you happen to have just figured out this week that you yourself are a new prince, has begun.

The irrepressible Thumper asks what we all want to ask but don't dare.   19
"Whacha gonna call Him?"

"I think I'll call Him," says his mother, in a voice that can only come   20
from the mouth of a madonna, ". . . Bambi." (Not Jesus, but, to these ears, almost; or, more likely, what I heard was, "I think I'll call Him . . . Russell.")

After we have paused and admired the mother and child, the adoration   21
is appropriately terminated by Friend Owl, and we cut away and move through the tangled woods to a slowly rising shot of a powerful stag on a mountaintop in the distance. It's the magnificent Hartford Insurance stag in profile, silent on a peak in Darien, nobly examining the horizon. The Father. Our gaze has gone from the son to the father, from adoration of the young prince to contemplation of the old. Time and destiny have entered the story.

Strong stuff. At least, for me it was. In seconds, the movie had shattered   22
my personal time, had broken it into bits and swept away all the intervening

years in which I had struggled, and mostly failed, to live out the story of Bambi, returning me to the moment when the story first took me over. I suddenly remembered (oddly, remembered with my right hand, which began to move, as if holding a pencil or crayon between thumb and forefinger) how for years I had obsessively drawn that hugely antlered male deer, the old prince of the forest. Seated now on my living room sofa next to my granddaughter and wife, I reproduced the drawing invisibly in air, just as I had done over and over again when I was a boy—a single swift line that traced the outline of the noble stag, covering brown paper grocery bags with it, filling schoolbook margins and endpapers, drawing it all over my notebooks, even in wet sand at Wells Beach and in new snow in the backyard.

The story of Bambi, subtitled in Felix Salten's book "A Life in the Woods," is both simple and amazingly complete. From birth to death, it describes and proscribes the territory of a male life in a sequence that follows exactly the Victorian and modern middle-class view of that life properly lived. It's a rigorous, wholly believable, moral story. Believable because, although it has no irony, no sly winking inside jokes between knowing adults, it has an abundance of humor. And while, as everyone knows, it has heartbreak aplenty, the movie, as few of us remember, is nonetheless not sentimental. It's downright Darwinian. *Bambi* has danger to be faced, great peril, obstacles to be overcome; and, at crucial moments, the movie shows us death. Both kinds—death that is sudden, violent, and inexplicable and death that comes late and is unavoidable, natural, necessary. It has sex, to be sure, but no Hollywood sleaze, no puritanical prurience—males and females are simply drawn to one another, where they go mad with procreative desire ("twitter-pated," Friend Owl explains) and rush off to couple with one another and quickly produce offspring, all done with pleasure, great good gusto, and not a single salacious nudge or apology. No one, after all, wears clothes in this movie. In fact, the pleasures of the body—eating, sleeping, bathing, sport, and sex—are presented as straightforwardly satisfying and natural as in *Tom Jones*. 23

Bambi makes all the stops on the life-circuit, and does so in a rigorously structured, comprehensive, and rhythmically patterned way, as precise and inclusive as a Catholic mass or a cycle of myths. Which, of course, makes it feel universal. And from that feeling proceeds its moral imperative. *Bambi* may be agitprop, but it's agitprop of a very high order. 24

Not for everyone, however. Recently, a friend of mine took his son to see the movie in a Manhattan theater. My friend is a large and gentle feminist of a man; his son is a bright six-year-old boy, older perhaps by several lifetimes than I was when I first saw the movie. In the scene that follows the death of Bambi's mother, when Bambi's father arrives at the thicket and, basso profundo, says to him, "Your mother can't be with you any more . . . ," my friend's son asked, "Didn't the father help the mother?" My friend had to say no. After all, the movie said no. "Then we'd better get out of here," the boy said, and they did, father and son, barely a third of the way through the movie. 25

On Manhattan's Upper West Side in 1990, *Bambi*, the boy's story, was not *their* story, that's for sure. Not the way it had been mine in the middle 1940s in small-town New Hampshire. My father had a rack of antlers and 26 was absent on a hill, too—a plumber working all week on the construction of the weather station at the top of Mount Washington, coming home only on weekends, taking up my mother's time with his needs and watching over me from a vast, powerfully masculine, fixed distance. "Were you a good boy this week? Did you do all your chores? Did you obey your mother, take care of your younger brother, learn the ways of the forest?"

There are the usual differences between the movie and the book that gen- 27 erated it, *Bambi: A Life in the Woods,* by Felix Salten, translated in 1928 by Whittaker Chambers, of all people, with a wry foreword by John Galsworthy ("I particularly recommend it to sportsmen . . ."). The story has been simplified, streamlined, slightly sanitized. But there is, to me, an amazing and shrewd faithfulness to the overall structure of the book (everything is cyclic and occurs in triplets—three acts, three seasonal sequences, three distinct stages of life) and to Salten's realistic description of "a life in the woods." His is not a kind and gentle woods; it's nature with fang and frost, with hunger and hardship, with violence that is natural and necessary (there are carnivores in the forest, after all) and the perverse, gratuitous violence of Man the Hunter. And although there is much in Salten's novel concerning the relations between the genders that is explicit and didactic, in Disney's movie that same material is implicit, is dramatized, and is no less thematically central or seductive for that. Quite the opposite.

At bottom, they are both, novel and movie, moral tales about the proper 28 relations between the genders, told for boys from the Victorian male point of view. In the book, after having seen a passing pair of grown male deer for the first time, Bambi asks his mother, "'Didn't they see us?'

"His mother understood what he meant and replied, 'Of course, they saw 29 all of us.'

"Bambi was troubled. He felt shy about asking questions, but it was too 30 much for him. 'Then why . . . ,' he began, and stopped.

"His mother helped him along. 'What is it you want to know, son?' she 31 asked.

"'Why didn't they stay with us?'   32

"'They don't ever stay with us,' his mother answered, 'only at times.'   33

"Bambi continued, 'But why didn't they speak to us?'   34

"His mother said, 'They don't speak to us now; only at times. We have 35 to wait till they come to us. And we have to wait for them to speak to us. They do it whenever they like.'"

And a little further on, his mother says, "'If you live, my son, if you are 36 cunning and don't run into danger, you'll be as strong and handsome as your father is sometime, and you'll have antlers like his, too.'

"Bambi breathed deeply. His heart swelled with joy and expectancy."   37

As did mine. Hunkered down in my seat in the darkness in the Scenic 38 Theater, and now here, forty-six years later, in front of a TV screen in my living room, I was on both occasions located at precisely the age when a child can be most easily colonized by the gender-specific notions of his or her culture, the age when the first significant moves toward individuation are occurring at a recklessly fast rate and in the explicit terms of one's inescapable biology.

At that moment, at the telling of one's story, one's heart cannot help 39 swelling with joy and expectancy. Just as, earlier, Sarah's heart, perhaps, had swelled at the telling of Ariel's story in *The Little Mermaid.* And was apparently not moved in the slightest by the telling of Bambi's and mine. For this was, as she surely knew, a boy's story, and thus was not for her, was irrelevant, if pleasantly distracting. For, after all, the birds were pretty, the thump-footed rabbit funny, the shy skunk sweet, and there was the excitement of the forest fire, the scary presence of the hunters. All that seemed more than mildly interesting to her, but in no way capable of changing her life.

She needed *The Little Mermaid* for that, I'm afraid. I have no regrets that 40 my wife and I kept it from her, however. And though it probably would have done me in the long run no good at all, I wish that someone—my uncle Bud Eastman, maybe, or a kindly grandfather conscious of the pain, confusion, and cruelty that come as soon as a boy marches into such territory—someone, had taken a quick look at the opening scenes of *Bambi* that Saturday afternoon and had said to himself, This movie is only going to drive the kid deeper into sexual stereotyping. It's going to validate the worst attitudes of the adult world that surrounds him. It's going to speed the end of his innocence.

"Let's get out of here, boys," he might then have said to me and my 41 brother Steve and cousin Neil. He'd have needed to know back then only what my friend's six-year-old son knows now. "Let's go down the street to Varney's for an ice cream soda," he might have said, "and come back next week for a Zorro double feature, or maybe for Gene Autry, the Singing Cowboy. Let's come back when they're showing a movie that *won't* change your life."

FOR DISCUSSION AND WRITING: ANALYZING FILMS: INTERTEXTS, IDEOLOGIES, ICONS

1. Watch the films *Play It Again, Sam* and *Casablanca* and analyze them using the terms provided by Gerard Genette. Genette supplied some terms, that is, to describe the palimpsest-like or intertextual relationship that exists between the Curtiz and Allen films. The source film in Genette's terms is called the "hypotext," and the receiving film is called the "hypertext" (although the latter term is less specific now that it is associated with multilinked interactive works for the computer) As Genette has shown at length in his scholarly study *Palimpsestes,* the use of an earlier work as the basis for generating one's own new work is an ancient tradition, with its most famous modern example being James Joyce's rewriting of Homer's *Odyssey* in a novel called *Ulysses.* In your analysis, decide exactly how Woody Allen made use of the source material.

2. Umberto Eco used *Casablanca* as the prototype for defining the formal characteristics of a classic cult film. His argument is worth quoting at some length, since it shows the intertextual nature of the experience of fandom.

   In order to transform a work into a cult object, one must be able to break, dislocate, unhinge it so that one can remember only parts of it, irrespective of their original relationship with the whole. In the case of a book one can unhinge it, so to speak, physically, reducing it to a series of excerpts. A movie, on the contrary, must be already ramshackle, rickety, unhinged in itself. A perfect movie, since it cannot be reread every time we want, from the point we choose, as happens with a book, remains in our memory as a whole, in the form of a central idea or emotion; only an unhinged movie survives as a disconnected series of images, of peaks, of visual icebergs. It should display not one central idea but many. It should not reveal a coherent philosophy of composition. It must live on, and because of, its glorious ricketiness.[1]

This ramshackle quality of the cult film facilitates viewer identification, as viewers recognize in certain disjointed sequences certain archetypes that have been internalized as the frames of their experience. "The term *archetype*," Eco adds, "serves only to indicate a preestablished and frequently reappearing narrative situation, cited or in some way recycled by innumerable other texts and provoking in the addressee a sort of intense emotion accompanied by the vague feeling of a déjà vu that everybody yearns to see again." Eco notes that when he has reviewed *Casablanca* with groups assembled for the purpose of counting all such archetypes, the process takes many hours. Similarly, Ray's interpretation of the film frequently cites parallel archetypes from other classic American texts. Try this inventory process yourself, to see how many standard types and scenarios you recognize. In your inventory, keep in mind Eco's distinction between "common frames" ("data-structures for representing stereotyped situations such as dining at a restaurant coded by our normal experience") and "intertextual frames" ("stereotyped situations derived from preceding textual tradition and recorded by our encyclopedia, such as the standard duel between the sheriff and the bad guy").

3. Use Russell Banks's essay about *Bambi* as a model for your own discussion of a favorite or significant film. Select the film in the same way that Banks does—by reflecting a bit, to discover a film that has most stayed in your memory. If the film is available on tape, watch it again and analyze the story as an "allegory" about the preferred values of our culture. Banks argues that *Bambi* represents an allegory about gender expectations in a certain period of our culture. *Allegory* here means that the characters are viewed as "personifications" of ideological concepts.

4. Make a list of some of the best-known classic popular icons that you can think of (such as James Dean, Marilyn Monroe, and so forth). Discuss the kinds of values, beliefs, and behaviors that have come to be associ-

[1]Umberto Eco, *Travels in Hyperreality*, trans. William Weaver (San Diego: Harcourt Brace Jovanovich, 1986).

ated with these figures. Select one of the figures and do some background research on the ideological interpretations that might have been applied to him or her. Make a second list of contemporary or current celebrities and compare the two lists. Collectively, is the second list just an update of the first one? That is, are the values associated with the two lists similar, but with the "archetype" passing to a new carrier? Or do you notice a shift in the values, a revision that requires some new types or a modification of the classic icons? For example, compare Marilyn Monroe and Madonna in ideological terms.

5. Robert Ray argues that *Casablanca* displays a pattern that may be found in many other American films. Test his claim by applying his analysis of *Casablanca* to a current film or television show to see if the same sorts of archetypes (in Eco's terms) are present. What are the similarities? What has changed?

ON INTERPRETATION

You have been interpreting texts throughout this book, of course, but now it is time to confront more directly the problems of interpretation. Vast tomes have been written about this, but our principle, here as elsewhere in this book, is that "less is more." With that in mind, we offer you three very short but powerful theories of interpretation. The first, by the British critic Frank Kermode, is based on the parables of Jesus that you have already considered. The second, by the American writer Susan Sontag, is one of the most powerful attacks on interpretation that we know of. And the third, by the Italian semiotician Umberto Eco, attempts to find a middle way between approaches to interpretation that believe the reader is entirely free to make meanings and those that insist on the total authority of the original author.

FOR DISCUSSION AND WRITING: PROPOSING YOUR OWN THEORY OF LITERARY INTERPRETATION

We ask you simply to read these three theoretical positions, discuss each of them, considering strengths and weaknesses, things you agree with and things you don't, and then develop your own theory of literary interpretation. You may choose to agree with one or another of these three positions, or you may develop some compromise or new position of your own, but try to make your view clear in relation to those presented—and those mentioned—in these three short pieces.

The Purpose of Parables
From The Genesis of Secrecy

Frank Kermode

When Jesus was asked to explain the purpose of his parables, he described them as stories *told to them without*—to outsiders—with the express purpose of concealing a mystery that was to be understood only by insiders. So Mark tells us: speaking to the Twelve, Jesus said, "To you has been given the secret of the kingdom of God, but for those outside everything is in parables; so that they may indeed see but not perceive, and may indeed hear but not understand; lest they should turn again, and be forgiven" [4:11–12].

I have given the translation of the Revised Standard Version, which might be varied—perhaps "parables" should be "riddles"—but unless certain words here mean what they do not usually mean the sense of Jesus' saying is plain enough. Only the insiders can have access to the true sense of these stories. "For to him who has will more be given; and from him who has not, even what he has will be taken away." To divine the true, the latent sense, you need to be of the elect, of the institution. Outsiders must content themselves with the manifest, and pay a supreme penalty for doing so. Only those who already know the mysteries—what the stories really mean—can discover what the stories really mean. As a matter of fact, the teacher, on the very occasion when he pronounced this rule, showed himself irritated with his elect for seeking explanations of what they already, in principle, knew. And, if we are to believe Mark, they continued to be slow learners, prone to absurd error. But they did know that even plain stories mean more than they seem to say, that they may contain mysteries inaccessible to all but privileged interpreters—and perhaps not always with any great measure of certainty even to them.

Interpretation as Interference
From Against Interpretation

Susan Sontag

In most modern instances, interpretation amounts to the philistine refusal to leave the work of art alone. Real art has the capacity to make us nervous. By reducing the work of art to its content and then interpreting *that*, one tames the work of art. Interpretation makes art manageable, conformable.

This philistinism of interpretation is more rife in literature than in any other art. For decades now, literary critics have understood it to be their task to translate the elements of the poem or play or novel or story into something else. Sometimes a writer will be so uneasy before the naked power of his art that he will install within the work itself—albeit with a little shyness, a touch of the good taste of irony—the clear and explicit interpretation of it. Thomas

Mann is an example of such an overcooperative author. In the case of more stubborn authors, the critic is only too happy to perform the job.

The work of Kafka, for example, has been subjected to a mass ravish-   3 ment by no less than three armies of interpreters. Those who read Kafka as a social allegory see case studies of the frustrations and insanity of modern bureaucracy and its ultimate issuance in the totalitarian state. Those who read Kafka as a psychoanalytic allegory see desperate revelations of Kafka's fear of his father, his castration anxieties, his sense of his own impotence, his thralldom to his dreams. Those who read Kafka as a religious allegory explain that K. in *The Castle* is trying to gain access to heaven, that Joseph K. in *The Trial* is being judged by the inexorable and mysterious justice of God. . . . Another *oeuvre* that has attracted interpreters like leeches is that of Samuel Beckett. Beckett's delicate dramas of the withdrawn consciousness—pared down to essentials, cut off, often represented as physically immobilized—are read as a statement about modern man's alienation from meaning or from God, or as an allegory of psychopathology.

Proust, Joyce, Faulkner, Rilke, Lawrence, Gide . . . one could go on citing   4 author after author; the list is endless of those around whom thick encrustations of interpretation have taken hold. But it should be noted that interpretation is not simply the compliment that mediocrity pays to genius. It is, indeed, *the* modern way of understanding something, and is applied to works of every quality. Thus, in the notes that Elia Kazan published on his production of *A Streetcar Named Desire,* it becomes clear that, in order to direct the play, Kazan had to discover that Stanley Kowalski represented the sensual and vengeful barbarism that was engulfing our culture, while Blanche Du Bois was Western civilization, poetry, delicate apparel, dim lighting, refined feelings and all, though a little the worse for wear to be sure. Tennessee Williams' forceful psychological melodrama now became intelligible: it was *about* something, about the decline of Western civilization. Apparently, were it to go on being a play about a handsome brute named Stanley Kowalski and a faded mangy belle named Blanche Du Bois, it would not be manageable.

The Intention of the Text
From Interpretation and Overinterpretation

Umberto Eco

Some contemporary theories of criticism assert that the only reliable reading   1 of a text is a misreading, that the only existence of a text is given by the chain of responses it elicits, and that, as maliciously suggested by Todorov (quoting Lichtenberg à propos of Boehme), a text is only a picnic where the author brings the words and the readers bring the sense.[1]

---

[1]T. Todorov, "Viaggio nella critica americana," *Lettera,* 4 (1987), 12.

Even if that were true, the words brought by the author are a rather em-   2
barrassing bunch of material evidences that the reader cannot pass over in
silence, or in noise. If I remember correctly, it was here in Britain that somebody suggested, years ago, that it is possible to do things with words. To interpret a text means to explain why these words can do various things (and
not others) through the way they are interpreted. But if Jack the Ripper told
us that he did what he did on the grounds of his interpretation of the Gospel
according to Saint Luke, I suspect that many reader-oriented critics would be
inclined to think that he read Saint Luke in a pretty preposterous way. Non-
reader-oriented critics would say that Jack the Ripper was deadly mad—and
I confess that, even though feeling very sympathetic with the reader-oriented
paradigm, and even though I have read Cooper, Laing, and Guattari, much
to my regret I would agree that Jack the Ripper needed medical care.

I understand that my example is rather far-fetched and that even the   3
most radical deconstructionist would agree (I hope, but who knows?) with
me. Nevertheless, I think that even such a paradoxical argument must be
taken seriously. It proves that there is at least one case in which it is possible to say that a given interpretation is a bad one. In terms of Popper's theory of scientific research, this is enough to disprove the hypothesis that interpretation has no public criteria (at least statistically speaking).

One could object that the only alternative to a radical reader-oriented   4
theory of interpretation is the one extolled by those who say that the only
valid interpretation aims at finding the original intention of the author. In
some of my recent writings I have suggested that between the intention of the
author (very difficult to find out and frequently irrelevant for the interpretation of a text) and the intention of the interpreter who (to quote Richard
Rorty) simply "beats the text into a shape which will serve for his purpose,"
there is a third possibility.[2] There is an *intention of the text*.

INTERPRETING TEXTS

Schoolchildren are expected to be able to infer something called the character of
Macbeth from indices scattered about Shakespeare's text.   —*Frank Kermode*

Directed to art, interpretation means plucking a set of elements (the X, the Y, the
Z, and so forth) from the whole work. The task of interpretation is virtually one of
translation. The interpreter says, Look, don't you see that X is really—or, really
means—A? That Y is really B? That Z is really C?   —*Susan Sontag*

As the word *interpretation* is normally used in literary study, it means
transforming a story, play, or poem into an essay. We have already con-

[2]Richard Rorty, *Consequences of Pragmatism* (Minneapolis, University of Minnesota
Press, 1982), p. 151.

sidered transformation as a form of intertextuality, but the transformations we considered were mainly transformations *within* the same genre: fiction into fiction. We have also considered the way readers must construct ghost chapters and possible worlds in order to complete the texts they read. Both of these activities, transformation and completion, are interpretive. So is the translation of figurative language into literal prose. In short, we have already considered many of the dimensions of interpretation, though not all, but we have not yet faced squarely the problem of writing the interpretive essay.

The purpose of the interpretive essay is not simply to repeat in the form of an essay what has already been said in a story, poem, or play. It *is* that to some extent, but if that were all, interpretation would be a trivial enterprise. The major function of interpretation is to say what a previous text has left unsaid: to unravel its complications, to make explicit its implications, and to raise its concrete and specific details to a more abstract and general level. That is, as we shall illustrate a few paragraphs later on, the interpreter must find a way of writing about the general principles of human behavior that are embodied in the specific situations and events of any story. The interpreter must say what the story is *about*.

We should also note that interpretation is not something that is entirely avoided in plays, poems, and stories themselves. Authors will often attempt to control the way their texts are read by offering self-interpretations within those texts. Samuel Beckett parodied this desire of the author to control meaning by adding what he called "Addenda" to the end of his novel *Watt*, noting, "The following precious and illuminating material should be carefully studied. Only fatigue and disgust prevented its incorporation." The last addendum reads simply, "No symbols where none intended."

By forbidding the reader to find symbolic or figurative meanings except where the author intended them to be found, Beckett symbolized the desire of most authors to control the interpretation of their own texts. By saying it so bluntly, he also made this desire faintly ridiculous. But did he *intend* this statement to symbolize what we say it symbolizes? That is a matter of interpretation. We say that when Beckett wrote "No symbols where none intended" he was joking, because he knew that no one can control meanings or even realize their intentions perfectly. And we would support our interpretation by pointing to other places where Beckett seems to be saying something similar—an easy task since *Watt* is devoted to the distressing gap between words and things, the constant slippage of meaning. Furthermore, we would add, the expression itself doesn't even specify whose intention is required to make an object into a symbol. If the rule is to be "No symbols where none intended," then perhaps the reader's intention would satisfy the rule in this instance. Then, of course, it would be *our* symbol, and not Beckett's. But doesn't interpretation mean that it must be *his* symbol that we understand? What is the writer's share in meaning and what is the reader's? These are vexed and difficult questions, much debated in literary theory. We cannot and should not try to settle them here. What we hope to accomplish instead is to clarify the possibilities of interpretive writing a bit and to offer a few practical suggestions for entering the world of interpretive discourse.

You may remember the story by William Carlos Williams included in Chapter 1 of this book, about a doctor who must struggle physically to diagnose the fever of a lovely and ferocious little girl (pp. 21–24). The story itself is very sparing with interpretive commentary, but it nevertheless makes a strong effort to direct our interpretation of it. The effort is most apparent in the title provided by the author: "The Use of Force." This title takes the concrete events narrated in the text and gathers them under the interpretive umbrella of "force." That is one of the major features of interpretive discourse. Interpretation is constituted by our moving from saying "The story is about a doctor and a child" to saying "The story is about the use of force." This move, from the concrete details of doctor and child to the abstraction "use of force" is what interpretation is all about. In this case, the author tries hard to guide the interpretive move by providing his own interpretive abstraction in the title of his text.

Kate Chopin, in her story "The Kiss," does not provide us with such guidance. Her title simply names the initial action of the story. To produce an interpretation, we must find our own way of discussing the significance of the events narrated in the text. We might decide the story is about "deception," for instance, and base our interpretation upon this decision. The important point to remember is that interpretation always involves a move from the specific details named in the text to a more general level: from the doctor prying open the child's mouth with a spoon to the abstract concept *force*.

In the epigraph by Frank Kermode at the beginning of this discussion, we can locate one type of interpretation. The reader takes a set of details from a play and constructs from them an abstraction called the "character" of Macbeth. One could do the same for characters in many of the plays and stories we have read. This sort of interpretation appears to be "natural," since we do it all the time, but it is based upon certain assumptions about the psychic unity of human beings and the importance of the individual person that are not, in fact, universal assumptions. Many forms of storytelling exist in which the individuals named in the text are not important in themselves but as representations of something else. This is the case in fables, parables, allegories, and other forms of symbolic fiction. In reading such narratives, the interpreter does what Susan Sontag describes in the epigraph from her essay, "Against Interpretation," quoted at the head of this discussion. That is, the interpreter says, "X is really A, Y is really B."

Being able to say "X is really A" involves knowing the system of values and beliefs that gives the concept A its meaning. For instance, Christianity is a system of values and beliefs. The story of Samson, from the Old Testament—a Jewish scripture—is read by Christian interpreters in accordance with their own system of beliefs. Reading and interpreting in this way, they say that Samson is really Christ, or, more technically, that Samson is a "type" of Christ, a symbol of Christ. By his sacrifice of his own life, Samson contributes to the salvation of his people. His death in the temple of the Philistines is equivalent to the death of Jesus at the hands of the Romans; and, just as the Philistines were defeated by Samson's sacrificial death, Rome was Christianized, ultimately conquered, by the One the Romans captured and tortured. This is how interpretation according to a system of values and beliefs works.

Christianity is one of a number of such systems used in literary interpretation. Psychoanalytical systems, such as the Freudian, are also widely used, and so are socioeconomic systems, such as Marxism. It is extremely difficult to generate such interpretations without serious study of the systems involved, which is one of the reasons why we will not ask you to undertake this kind of work. It is possible, however, for someone who is not an expert but is willing to pay close attention to comment on such interpretations, to extend them, and to revise, question, and even reject them.

If you have worked on the transformations of "Sleeping Beauty" in the earlier section, "Transforming Texts (2)," you are now something of an expert on that story. Therefore, you are in a good position to respond to the two interpretive essays on "Sleeping Beauty" in this section, the first by noted child psychologist Bruno Bettelheim and the second by writer Francine Prose. As you judge each one and then compare the two, keep in mind the short statements on interpretation by Kermode, Sontag, and Eco in the previous section, and how they apply to these interpretive essays. You will also find a reading and interpretation of Ernest Hemingway's "Up in Michigan," which will encourage you to make one of your own, and finally, an interpretation of Robert Francis's poem "Pitcher," which we hope will encourage you to write your own interpretation of a poem.

The Sleeping Beauty

Bruno Bettelheim

Bruno Bettelheim is a child psychologist who has written extensively on fairy tales. The following essay is taken from his book The Uses of Enchantment: The Meaning and Importance of Fairy Tales *(1976). Bettelheim, who believes that much "can be learned from [folktales] about the inner problems of human beings" and about solutions to those problems, relies heavily on Freud in this interpretation of "Sleeping Beauty."*

Adolescence is a period of great and rapid change, characterized by periods 1 of utter passivity and lethargy alternating with frantic activity, even dangerous behavior to "prove oneself" or discharge inner tension. This back-and-forth adolescent behavior finds expression in some fairy tales by the hero's rushing after adventures and then suddenly being turned to stone by some enchantment. . . .

While many fairy tales stress great deeds the heroes must perform to be- 2 come themselves, "The Sleeping Beauty" emphasizes the long, quiet concentration on oneself that is also needed. During the months before the first menstruation, and often also for some time immediately following it, girls are passive, seem sleepy, and withdrawn into themselves. While no equally noticeable state heralds the coming of sexual maturity in boys, many of them experience a period of lassitude and of turning inward during puberty which equals the female experience. It is thus understandable that a fairy story in which a long period of sleep begins at the start of puberty has been very popular for a long time among girls and boys.

In major life changes such as adolescence, for successful growth opportu- 3 nities both active and quiescent periods are needed. The turning inward, which in outer appearance looks like passivity (or sleeping one's life away), happens when internal mental processes of such importance go on within the person that he has no energy for outwardly directed action. Those fairy tales which, like "The Sleeping Beauty," have the period of passivity for their central topic, permit the budding adolescent not to worry during his inactive period: he learns that things continue to evolve. The happy ending assures the child that he will not remain permanently stuck in seemingly doing nothing, even if at the moment it seems as if this period of quietude will last for a hundred years. . . .

Recently it has been claimed that the struggle against childhood depend- 4 ency and for becoming oneself in fairy tales is frequently described differently for the girl than for the boy, and that this is the result of sexual stereotyping. Fairy tales do not render such one-sided pictures. Even when a girl is depicted as turning inward in her struggle to become herself, and a boy as aggressively dealing with the external world, these two *together* symbolize the two ways in which one has to gain selfhood: through learning to understand and master the inner as well as the outer world. In this sense the male and female heroes are again projections onto two different figures of two (artificially) separated aspects of one and the same process which *everybody* has to undergo in growing up. While some literal-minded parents do not realize it, children know that, whatever the sex of the hero, the story pertains to their own problems. . . .

"The Sleeping Beauty" is best known today in two different versions: Perrault's, and that of the Brothers Grimm. To explain the difference, it may be best to consider briefly the form the story took in Basile's *Pentamerone*, where its title is "Sun, Moon, and Talia."[1]

On the birth of his daughter Talia, a king asked all the wise men and seers to tell her future. They concluded that she would be exposed to great danger from a splinter of flax. To prevent any such accident, the king ordered that no flax or hemp should ever come into his castle. But one day when Talia had grown up, she saw an old woman who was spinning pass by her window. Talia, who had never seen anything like it before, "was therefore delighted with the dancing of the spindle." Made curious, she took the distaff in her hand and began to draw out the thread. A splinter of hemp "got under her fingernail and she immediately fell dead upon the ground." The king left his lifeless daughter seated on a velvet chair in the palace, locked the door, and departed forever, to obliterate the memory of his sorrow.

Some time after, another king was hunting. His falcon flew into a window of the empty castle and did not return. The king, trying to find the falcon, wandered in the castle. There he found Talia as if asleep, but nothing would rouse her. Falling in love with her beauty, he cohabited with her; then he left and forgot the whole affair. Nine months later Talia gave birth to two children, all the time still asleep. They nursed from her breast. "Once when one of the babies wanted to suck, it could not find the breast, but got into its mouth instead the finger that had been pricked. This the baby sucked so hard that it drew out the splinter, and Talia was roused as if from deep sleep."

One day the king remembered his adventure and went to see Talia. He was delighted to find her awake with the two beautiful children, and from then on they were always on his mind. The king's wife found out his secret, and on the sly sent for the two children in the king's name. She ordered them cooked and served to her husband. The cook hid the children in his own home and prepared instead some goat kids, which the queen served to the king. A while later the queen sent for Talia and planned to have her thrown into the fire because she was the reason for the king's infidelity. At the last minute the king arrived, had his wife thrown into the fire, married Talia, and was happy to find his children, whom the cook had saved. The story ends with the verses:

Lucky people, so 'tis said,
Are blessed by Fortune whilst in bed.

[1]By that time it was already an old motif, as there are French and Catalan renderings from the fourteenth to the sixteenth centuries which served as Basile's models, if he did not rely on folk tales of his own time as yet unknown to us.

Perrault, by adding on his own the story of the slighted fairy who utters   9
the curse, or by using this familiar fairy-tale motif, explains why the heroine
falls into deathlike sleep and thus enriches the story, since in "Sun, Moon,
and Talia" we are given no reason why this should be her fate.

In Basile's story Talia is the daughter of a king who loved her so much   10
that he could not remain in his castle after she fell into a deathlike sleep. We
hear nothing more about him after he left Talia ensconced on her thronelike
chair "under an embroidered canopy," not even after she reawakened, married her king, and lived happily with him and her beautiful children. One king
replaces another king in the same country; one king replaces another in
Talia's life—the father king is replaced by the lover king. Might these two
kings not be substitutes for each other at different periods in the girl's life, in
different roles, in different disguises? We encounter here again the "innocence" of the oedipal child, who feels no responsibility for what she arouses
or wishes to arouse in the parent.

Perrault, the academician, doubly distances his story from Basile's. He   11
was, after all, a courtier who told stories for the perusal of princes, pretending that they were invented by his little son to please a princess. The two
kings are changed into a king and a prince, the latter somebody who obviously is not yet married and has no children. And the presence of the king is
separated from the prince by a sleep of one hundred years, so that we can feel
certain that the two have nothing in common. Interestingly enough, Perrault
does not quite manage to extricate himself from the oedipal connotations: in
his story the queen is not insanely jealous because of the betrayal by her husband, but she appears as the oedipal mother who is so jealous of the girl her
son the prince falls in love with that she seeks to destroy her. But while the
queen in Basile's tale is convincing, Perrault's queen is not. His story falls
into two incongruous parts: a first which ends with the prince's awakening
Sleeping Beauty and marrying her; followed by a second part in which we are
suddenly told that the mother of Prince Charming is really a child-devouring
ogress who wishes to eat her own grandchildren.

In Basile, the queen wishes to feed his children to her husband—the   12
most terrible punishment for preferring Sleeping Beauty to her that she can
think of. In Perrault, she wants to eat them herself. In Basile, the queen is
jealous because her husband's mind and love are entirely taken up with Talia
and her children. The king's wife tries to burn Talia in the fire—the king's
"burning" love for Talia having aroused the queen's "burning" hatred for her.

There is no explanation for the cannibalistic hatred of the queen in   13
Perrault's tale but that she is an ogress who "whenever she saw little children
passing by, . . . had all the difficulty in the world to avoid falling upon them."
Also, Prince Charming keeps his marriage to Sleeping Beauty a secret for two
years, until his father dies. Only then does he bring Sleeping Beauty and her
two children, called Morning and Day, to his castle. And although he knows
that his mother is an ogress, when he leaves to go to war he puts her in
charge, entrusting his kingdom and wife and children to her. Perrault's story
ends with the king returning at the moment when his mother is just about to
have Sleeping Beauty thrown into a pit full of vipers. On his arrival the
ogress, who sees her plans spoiled, jumps into the pit herself.

It can easily be understood that Perrault did not feel it appropriate to tell   14
at the French court a story in which a married king ravishes a sleeping
maiden, gets her with child, forgets it entirely, and remembers her after a time
only by chance. But a fairy prince who keeps his marriage and fatherhood a
secret from his father-king—shall we assume because he fears the king's
oedipal jealousy if the son also becomes a father—is unconvincing, if for no
other reason than that oedipal jealousy of mother and father in regard to the
same son in the same tale is overdoing it, even in a fairy story. Knowing his
mother is an ogress, the prince does not bring his wife and child home as long
as his good father may exercise a restraining influence, but only after his
death, when such protection is no longer available. The reason for all this is
not that Perrault was lacking in artistry, but that he did not take his fairy stories seriously and was most intent on the cute or moralistic verse ending he
appended to each.[2]

With two such incongruous parts to this story, it is understandable that   15
in oral telling—and often also in printed form—the story ends with the
happy union of the prince and Sleeping Beauty. It is this form that the Brothers Grimm heard and recorded, and which was then and is now most widely
known. Still, something got lost which was present in Perrault. To wish death
to a newborn child only because one is not invited to the christening or is
given inferior silverware is the mark of an evil fairy. Thus, in Perrault, as in
the Brothers Grimm's version, at the very beginning of the story we find the
(fairy god)mother(s) split into the good and the evil aspects. The happy ending requires that the evil principle be appropriately punished and done away
with; only then can the good, and with it happiness, prevail. In Perrault, as
in Basile, the evil principle is done away with, and thus fairy-story justice is
done. But the Brothers Grimm's version, which will be followed from here on,
is deficient because the evil fairy is not punished.

However great the variations in detail, the central theme of all versions   16
of "The Sleeping Beauty" is that, despite all attempts on the part of parents
to prevent their child's sexual awakening, it will take place nonetheless. Furthermore, parents' ill-advised efforts may postpone the reaching of maturity

[2]Perrault, speaking to the courtiers he had in mind as his readers, made fun of the fairy
stories he told. For example, he specifies that the queen-ogress wishes to have the children served her "with Sauce Robert." He thus introduces details which detract from the
fairy-story character, as when he tells that on her awakening Sleeping Beauty's dress was
recognized as old-fashioned: "she was dressed as my great-grandmother, and had a
point band peeping over a high collar; she looked not a bit the less beautiful and charming for all that." As if fairy-tale heroes would not live in a world where fashions do not
change.

Such remarks, in which Perrault indiscriminately mixes petty rationality with fairy-
story fantasy, grossly detract from his work. The dress detail, for example, destroys that
mythical, allegorical, and psychological time which is suggested by the hundred years of
sleep by making it a specific chronological time. It makes it all frivolous—not like the
legends of saints who awake from a hundred years of sleep, recognize how the world has
changed, and immediately turn into dust. By such details, which were meant to amuse,
Perrault destroyed the feeling of timelessness that is an important element in the effectiveness of fairy tales.

at the proper time, as symbolized by Sleeping Beauty's hundred years of sleep, which separate her sexual awakening from her being united with her lover. Closely related to this is a different motif—namely, that to have to wait even a long time for sexual fulfillment does not at all detract from its beauty.

Perrault's and the Brothers Grimm's versions begin by indicating that one 17 may have to wait a long time to find sexual fulfillment, as indicated by having a child. For a very long time, we are told, the king and his queen wished for a child in vain. In Perrault, the parents behave like his contemporaries: "They went to all the waters in the world; vows, pilgrimages, everything was tried and nothing came of it. At last, however, the Queen was with child." The Brothers Grimm's beginning is much more fairy-tale-like: "Once upon a time was a king and a queen who said every day 'Oh, if we only had a child!' but they never got one. Once when the queen sat in the bath, it happened that a frog crawled out of the water on the land and told her 'Your wish will be fulfilled; before a year is over, you'll bring a daughter into the world.'" The frog's saying that the queen will give birth before a year is over puts the time of waiting close to the nine months of pregnancy. This, plus the queen's being in her bath, is reason to believe that conception took place on the occasion of the frog's visit to the queen. (Why in fairy tales the frog often symbolizes sexual fulfillment is discussed later, in connection with the story "The Frog King.")

The parents' long wait for a child which finally arrives conveys that there 18 is no need to hurry toward sex; it loses none of its rewards if one has to wait a long time for it. The good fairies and their wishes at the christening actually have little to do with the plot, except to contrast with the curse of the fairy who feels slighted. This may be seen from the fact that the number of fairies varies from country to country, from three to eight to thirteen. The good fairies' gifts of endowment to the child also differ in the different versions, while the curse of the evil one is always the same: the girl (in the Brothers Grimm's story when she is fifteen) will prick her finger on a distaff (of a spinning wheel) and die. The last good fairy is able to change this threat of death into a hundred years' sleep. The message is similar to that of "Snow White": what may seem like a period of deathlike passivity at the end of childhood is nothing but a time of quiet growth and preparation, from which the person will awaken mature, ready for sexual union. It must be stressed that in fairy tales this union is as much one of the minds and souls of two partners as it is one of sexual fulfillment.

In times past, fifteen was often the age at which menstruation began. The 19 thirteen fairies in the Brothers Grimm's story are reminiscent of the thirteen lunar months into which the year was once, in ancient times, divided. While this symbolism may be lost on those not familiar with the lunar year, it is well known that menstruation typically occurs with the twenty-eight-day frequency of lunar months, and not with the twelve months which our year is divided into. Thus, the number of twelve good fairies plus a thirteenth evil one indicates symbolically that the fatal "curse" refers to menstruation.

It is very much to the point that the king, the male, does not understand 20 the necessity of menstruation and tries to prevent his daughter from experiencing the fatal bleeding. The queen, in all versions of the story, seems unconcerned with the prediction of the angry fairy. In any case, she knows better than to try to prevent it. The curse centers on the distaff, a word which in English has come to stand for female in general. While the same is not true for the French (Perrault) or German (Brothers Grimm) word for distaff, until fairly recently spinning and weaving were considered as characteristically "woman's" occupations.

All the king's painstaking efforts to forestall the "curse" of the malicious 21 fairy fail. Removing all the distaffs from the kingdom cannot prevent the girl's fateful bleeding once she reaches puberty, at fifteen, as the evil fairy predicted. Whatever precautions a father takes, when the daughter is ripe for it, puberty will set in. The temporary absence of both parents when this event occurs symbolizes all parents' incapacity to protect their child against the various growing-up crises which every human being has to undergo.

As she becomes an adolescent, the girl explores the formerly inaccessi- 22 ble areas of existence, as represented by the hidden chamber where an old woman is spinning. At this point the story abounds in Freudian symbolism. As she approaches the fateful place, the girl ascends a circular staircase; in dreams such staircases typically stand for sexual experiences. At the top of this staircase she finds a small door and in its lock a key. As she turns the key, the door "springs open" and the girl enters a small room in which an old woman spins. A small locked room often stands in dreams for the female sexual organs; turning a key in a lock often symbolizes intercourse.

Seeing the old woman spinning, the girl asks: "What kind of thing is this 23 that jumps about so funnily?" It does not take much imagination to see the possible sexual connotations in the distaff; but as soon as the girl touches it, she pricks her finger, and falls into sleep.

The main associations this tale arouses in the child's unconscious are 24 to menstruation rather than intercourse. In common language, referring also to its Biblical origin, menstruation is often called the "curse"; and it is a female's—the fairy's—curse that causes the bleeding. Second, the age at which this curse is to become effective is about the age at which, in past times, menstruation most frequently set in. Finally, the bleeding comes about through an encounter with an old woman, not a man; and according to the Bible, the curse is inherited by woman from woman.

Bleeding, as in menstruation, is for the young girl (and for the young man 25 too, in a different manner) an overwhelming experience if she is not emotionally ready for it. Overcome by the experience of sudden bleeding, the princess falls into a long sleep, protected against all suitors—i.e., premature sexual encounters—by an impenetrable wall of thorns. While the most familiar version stresses in the name "The Sleeping Beauty" the long sleep of the heroine, the titles of other variants give prominence to the protective wall, such as the English "Briar Rose."[3]

---

[3]The German name of girl and tale, *"Dornröschen,"* emphasizes both the hedge of thorns and the (hedge) rose. The diminutive form of "rose" in the German name stresses the girl's immaturity, which must be protected by the wall of thorns.

Many princes try to reach Sleeping Beauty before her time of maturing is   26
over; all these precocious suitors perish in the thorns. This is a warning to
child and parents that sexual arousal before mind and body are ready for it
is very destructive. But when Sleeping Beauty has finally gained both physical
and emotional maturity and is ready for love, and with it for sex and marriage,
then that which had seemed impenetrable gives way. The wall of thorns suddenly turns into a wall of big, beautiful flowers, which opens to let the prince
enter. The implied message is the same as in many other fairy tales: don't
worry and don't try to hurry things—when the time is ripe, the impossible
problem will be solved, as if all by itself.

The long sleep of the beautiful maiden has also other connotations. Whether   27
it is Snow White in her glass coffin or Sleeping Beauty on her bed, the adolescent dream of everlasting youth and perfection is just that: a dream. The
alteration of the original curse, which threatened death, to one of prolonged
sleep suggests that the two are not all that different. If we do not want to change
and develop, then we might as well remain in a deathlike sleep. During their
sleep the heroines' beauty is a frigid one; theirs is the isolation of narcissism.
In such self-involvement which excludes the rest of the world there is no suffering, but also no knowledge to be gained, no feelings to be experienced.

Any transition from one stage of development to the next is fraught with   28
dangers; those of puberty are symbolized by the shedding of blood on touching
the distaff. A natural reaction to the threat of having to grow up is to withdraw
from a world and life which impose such difficulties. Narcissistic withdrawal
is a tempting reaction to the stresses of adolescence, but, the story warns, it
leads to a dangerous, deathlike existence when it is embraced as an escape
from the vagaries of life. The entire world then becomes dead to the person; this
is the symbolic meaning, and warning, of the deathlike sleep into which everybody surrounding Sleeping Beauty falls. The world becomes alive only to the
person who herself awakens to it. Only relating positively to the other "awakens" us from the danger of sleeping away our life. The kiss of the prince breaks
the spell of narcissism and awakens a womanhood which up to then has remained undeveloped. Only if the maiden grows into woman can life go on.

The harmonious meeting of prince and princess, their awakening to each   29
other, is a symbol of what maturity implies: not just harmony within oneself,
but also with the other. It depends on the listener whether the arrival of the
prince at the right time is interpreted as the event which causes sexual awakening or the birth of a higher ego; the child probably comprehends both these
meanings. . . .

The story of Sleeping Beauty impresses every child that a traumatic   30
event—such as the girl's bleeding at the beginning of puberty, and later, in
first intercourse—does have the happiest consequences. The story implants
the idea that such events must be taken very seriously, but that one need not
be afraid of them. The "curse" is a blessing in disguise.

One more look at the earliest known form of the motif of "The Sleeping   31
Beauty" in *Perceforest* some six hundred years ago: it is Venus, the goddess
of love, who arranges for the sleeping girl's awakening by having her baby
suck the splinter out of her finger, and the same happens in Basile's story. Full

self-fulfillment of the female does not come with menstruation. Female completeness is not achieved when falling in love, not even in intercourse, nor in childbirth, since the heroines in *Perceforest* and in Basile's story sleep all through it. These are necessary steps on the way to ultimate maturity; but complete selfhood comes only with having given life, and with nurturing the one whom one has brought into being: with the baby sucking from the mother's body. Thus, these stories enumerate experiences which pertain only to the female; she must undergo them all before she reaches the summit of femininity.

It is the infant's sucking the splinter out from under the mother's nail 32
which brings her back to life—a symbol that her child is not just the passive recipient of what the mother gives to him, but that he also actively renders her great service. Her nurturing permits him to do so; but it is his nursing from her which reawakens her to life—a being reborn, which, as always in fairy tales, symbolizes the achievement of a higher mental state. Thus, the fairy tale tells parent and child alike that the infant not only receives from his mother, but also gives to her. While she gives him life, he adds a new dimension to her life. The self-involvement which was suggested by the heroine's long-lasting sleep comes to an end as she gives to the infant and he, by taking from her, restores her to the highest level of existence: a mutuality in which the one who receives life also gives life.

In "The Sleeping Beauty" this is further emphasized because not only 33
she but her entire world—her parents, all inhabitants of the castle—returns to life the moment she does. If we are insensitive to the world, the world ceases to exist for us. When Sleeping Beauty fell asleep, so did the world for her. The world awakens anew as a child is nurtured into it, because only in this way can humanity continue to exist.

This symbolism got lost in the story's later forms which end with the 34
awakening of Sleeping Beauty, and with it her world, to a new life. Even in the shortened form in which the tale came down to us, in which Sleeping Beauty is awakened by the kiss of the prince, we feel—without it being spelled out as in the more ancient versions—that she is the incarnation of perfect femininity.

FOR DISCUSSION AND WRITING: ANALYZING A FREUDIAN INTERPRETATION

1. In the first four paragraphs, Bettelheim presents the Freudian-based theory of child development that structures his system of interpretation. To what degree does Bettelheim's interpretation of "Sleeping Beauty" conform to Susan Sontag's description of interpretation as translation (see the epigraph on p. 210), wherein one plucks "a set of elements" from the whole work?

2. Sontag finds such an approach reductive in that it removes the art from the work of art. Do you agree, or would you describe Bettelheim as an "insider," one who, in Frank Kermode's terms, knows "the mysteries— what the stories really mean"?

3. Write a description of Bettelheim's conception of "perfect femininity" and how the various Sleeping Beauties he discusses exemplify it. You may want to write a comparative essay on femininity as presented in "Sleeping Beauty" after you read Francine Prose's essay, which follows.

4. What was your reaction to Bettelheim's interpretation? What parts of it did you find problematical? Make notes of your questions and comments to refer to as you read the following essay on "Sleeping Beauty" by Francine Prose.

On "Sleeping Beauty"

Francine Prose

This essay appeared in a collection edited by Kate Bernheimer called Mirror, Mirror on the Wall: Women Writers Explore Their Favorite Fairy Tales *(1998). Using a comparative approach, Prose examines the motif of the sleeping woman as a sexual fantasy.*

It seems, we might think, the very simplest of tales, this romantic and hopeful story about the power of love to reverse all the weaker enchantments and in the process rouse young girls from their insensate virginal comas. Its elements (the pricked finger, the drop of blood, the long swoon, the Prince who slashes through the bramble hedge to deliver the saving kiss) are so naively transparent, their sexual content so naked that we may be reminded of those textbook-Freudian dreams in which the dreamer's teeth fall out, or trains disappear into tunnels. How embarrassing to observe one's mysterious and fascinating subconscious surfacing in narratives so predictable, so banal. 1

It seems, we might think, a paradigm of the feminist critique of how our culture programs girls, of that psychic footbinding designed to send them— blinded, hobbling—from the cradle to the altar: Just close your eyes, dearies, and lie perfectly still until the handsome Prince happens along and his desire initiates you, introduces you to your real life. No other story, no other fairy tale sets it all out so diagrammatically, or so strictly prescribes the division of active and passive along, as they say, the most gender-traditional lines. Cinderella, Rapunzel, Little Red Riding Hood—all those endangered and rescued maidens were at least apparently awake, and, strictly speaking, conscious. 2

Conversely, we might think "Sleeping Beauty" emblematic of something hardwired into the species, DNA-encoded, cellular, deeper than culture and representative of all the untidy, inconvenient and ineradicable instincts that make the feminist's tiny daughter pine for the nail gloss and lipstick. As girls, we loved this story best of all for its heartening promise that the long nap we knew we were taking would eventually end; perhaps when we least expected it, the mystical—predestined—kiss would provide the piece of the puzzle that, even fast asleep, we knew was missing. 3

Or we might think, as I do now, that the story is yet another of those ⁴ madeleines manquées,[1] those memory-jogs that don't quite work, that fail to restore our youth, one of those markers, those startling reminders of how far we've come, and of all we've gone through and learned. How much smaller our childhood homes seem when we revisit them as adults, how different that buttery tea cookie tastes when we must weigh the health risks they pose. And oh, how the beloved fairy tale can suddenly reveal that dark subterranean detail, that knotty little plot twist squirming under the surface that we never registered, never suspected, all those years ago.

So let's begin again, this way: imagine the Prince's surprise when the Princess ⁵ (Is she comatose? Is she . . . dead?) turns out to be alive! No one could for one moment pretend that what inspired his lustful or curious kiss was her vibrant animation. Those eyelids blinking open, that look of wonder or distress, the inevitable consternation when the awakened dreamer figures out that she's somehow slept through the last hundred years—none of that was exactly what the Prince had in mind as he braved the wild beasts and sliced through bramble thicket.

Gradually, with age and time, and often through the medium of art (which ⁶ so often traffics in the hidden, the taboo, the unspeakable) we begin to collect a few hints, a few vague shadowy clues to that most baffling and intriguing enigma: the opposite gender's sexuality—not its garden-variety lusts and marketplace fixations but the cobwebbed corners of rarely visited attics. Sometimes these are facts that are commonly known by (let's say) one-half of the population but prudently concealed from the other half. These are home truths that our soul mates, our most dearly beloveds, would just as soon choose to keep quiet—that is, if they knew them themselves and could put these intuitions into words. For sometimes these are secrets judged not merely too dangerous to admit, but too anarchic and subversive to permit oneself to think.

And really, why should men trust us with secret information that (given ⁷ our momentary or lifelong feelings about males in general or in particular) we may use against them, as evidence of insufficiency, or villainy, or hopeless and incurable testosterone-linked disease. Alternately, if our experience has caused us to feel fondly toward men (as individuals, needless to say, not as governments or armies), we may find ourselves struck by the astonishment that overcomes us when we're obliged to admit that someone is genuinely— someone dares to be—different from ourselves.

Back to Sleeping Beauty, then. By now it's probably clear that what I'm talk- ⁸ ing about is a sort of modified necrophilia: not exactly sex with a corpse— literal graveyard *amour*—but rather sex with a woman who only *appears* to have left the world of the living.

Once you look it's everywhere, though mostly—again—in art, since not ⁹ even one's most voluble, open, forthcoming, least paranoid male friends (and

[1][madeleines manquées: literally, "failed tea cake." In Marcel Proust's *In Search of Lost Time*, the taste of a madeleine dipped in tea brings forth a stream of memories. Here, it fails to do so. *Eds.*]

certainly not, for obvious reasons, one's husband or lovers) are about to confide that their deepest secret fantasy is sex with an unconscious woman (now commonly thought of as rape) or with an inflatable sex doll or ingenious female robot.

And yet it can be imagined, and *has been* imagined, again and again, by the   10
likes of Basile and Charles Perrault (the original authors, transcribers—or whatever—of "Sleeping Beauty"), by Edgar Allan Poe, by E. T. A. Hoffmann, by Heinrich von Kleist, by Tommaso Landolfi, by Thomas Hardy, by the great and eccentric Uruguayan fabulist Felisberto Hernandez, by Yasunari Kawabata, and, more recently, by Alfred Hitchcock. (What one wants to point out is that none of these writers are man-hating feminists raving that what men want, what men really want, is not a living, breathing woman but rather a barely sensate automaton or a receptive pillowy sex toy . . .) It's men who have imagined this—that is, imagined *other* men capable of falling in love with an artificial "woman" or a living woman convincingly impersonating a dead one.

In another fairy tale, "Snow White," the Prince falls in love with Snow   11
White while she is insensate in her coffin. In the Volsung Saga, Sigurd loses his heart to the fast-asleep Brunhilde as soon as he removes the armor from her unconscious body. For Poe, of course, the perfect lover is the dead Annabel Lee, whom no living (or full-grown) woman can ever hope to equal. In Hoffmann's "The Sandman," it's Olympia, the piano-playing but nearly mute, icily pretty automaton whom the young Nathaniel much prefers to his flesh-and-blood fiancée, Clara. In Hernandez's "The Daisy Dolls," it's the larger-than-life-sized mannequins engineered to look progressively more animated and "natural" as a rich man and his wife play an increasingly treacherous game involving elaborate practical jokes, passion, betrayal and murder.

In von Kleist's "The Marquise of O," the heroine faints dead away in the   12
aftermath of an assault during the siege of her family's castle—and, in that unconscious state, inspires her gallant rescuer, Count F—, to rape her and father a child. In Hardy's *Tess of the D'Urbervilles,* somnolence holds a similar attraction for the amoral Alec D'Urberville, who takes advantage of the sleeping Tess to rob her of her virtue. Landolfi's "Gogol's Wife" is an inflatable doll with mucous membranes whom Gogol murders in a fit of uncontrollable jealous rage; the old men in Kawabata's *The House of the Sleeping Beauties* pay large sums of money to patronize a bordello where they warm their old, chilly bodies by lying beside the warmer flesh of slumbering young women.

By far the most disturbing example of this peculiar subgenre is Alfred   13
Hitchcock's masterpiece *Vertigo*, with its loopy, lush excesses and its gaping plot holes through which we can glimpse the master wrestling with his private demons, a struggle so all-consuming that he inevitably loses his grip. In this film (so dreamy, so hallucinogenic, so nearly out-of-control compared to the logical, bloody-minded meticulousness of his other work), Hitchcock appears to be operating in a fever-haze of rampant sexual obsession. His compulsion is almost indistinguishable from the passion that drives his hero, Scottie, to turn the warm-hearted, down-to-earth Judy into an exact replica (a mannequin) of the icy, ethereal—and, by that point, dead—Madeleine

(who was herself supposedly possessed by the spirit of another dead woman, Carlotta Valdes).

In the film's most fascinating, horrifying and titillating sequence, we 14 watch the play of torment, longing and desire on Scottie's face as he cajoles and bullies Judy into changing her wardrobe, her style, dying her hair, transforming herself, inch by inch, into the woman Scottie fell in love with when he rescued her—unconscious, half-drowned—from San Francisco Bay. (Like Sigurd in the Volsung Saga, Scottie undresses his beloved while she is still passed out—before she has awoken, or recovered.) And we know that Scottie will never be satisfied until Judy *becomes* the lover whom he was finally unable to keep alive, helpless to save (or so he thinks) from suicide and violent death.

The first time I saw the film, I was a freshman in college, and afterward 15 I stayed awake, terrified, all night, seized by a sort of anxious vertigo not unlike poor Scottie's. Since then I've seen the film perhaps a dozen times and gradually come to understand what it was that so unnerved me during and after that first viewing.

That was in the late sixties, when one heard a lot of talk about the ways 16 in which men reduced women to fetish objects. But none of the men *I* knew did that; they all seemed perfectly capable of telling (and in fact quite grateful for) the larger and smaller differences between a female college student and a Barbie doll. Moreover, the male's inability to see women as fully human and his powerful impulse to fetishize them has always seemed a somewhat overelaborate reading of the fact that construction workers whistle at female passersby.

Vertigo convinced me that such impulses were very real, and what I felt 17 was a fear akin to (if not as severe as) what we experience the first time we're forced honestly to confront the fact of death, or the existence of evil. I realized that it could happen, I glimpsed what that sort of fetishization would— and did—look like, and I understood that all of us (not only men) might be capable of acting on that impulse but in fact might be (consciously or unconsciously) powerless to resist it.

I realized that these constructs we nurture so lovingly—that is to say, 18 our individual *selves*, those intricate collages of memories, experiences, opinions, feelings, quirks, etc.—finally mattered far less than some sort of template that we either matched or didn't, some abstract erotic response to images and desires programmed into the system long before birth, or in the earliest weeks or moments of life; we might as well be ducklings, imprinting on a real or artificial surrogate mother duck.

It all seemed so reductive, so terribly unfair, like some sort of sexual 19 Calvinism, erotic predestination—the unchangeable fate, incapable of being altered in the slightest by all our illusions of self-knowledge, by our fancy pretenses of rational (or irrational) choice. What does it matter what we *are* if we are all simply obeying some biological imperative triggered by a suit, a glance, a gesture, the color of someone's hair? And what could be a more perfect repository for these inchoate longings, a more suitable scrim on which to project these mysterious desires, a cleaner slate on which to draw the ideal creature who embodies all these most hidden and urgent needs than an artificial woman, a woman asleep or dead, a woman who will not spoil the moment of blissful consummation by insisting so distractingly that she's Judy—and not Madeleine.

So perhaps the story of Sleeping Beauty is not so much as promise of fu- 20 ture romantic awakenings as a warning, an etiquette lesson, a prescription for behavior. It's not so much that we *are* asleep, on ice till the Prince comes to rouse us. It's that—if we want the Prince to come . . . well, forget the make up, the curlers, the short skirts, the feminine wiles, forget the flirtation, the conversation. The surest route to a man's (or to some men's) heart is to pretend to be unconscious: I'm asleep, dear . . . and actually, to tell the truth, I may not even be . . . real. I'm what you've always dreamed about. Do with me what you will.

If fairy tales are the alchemical distillation of our collective desires and dreams 21 then perhaps what Freud said about dreams may apply to these stories too: their details, their entirety, the sum of what actually happened are finally less significant than what we remember and misremember, fragment and distort.

This, then, is how we remember the story of Sleeping Beauty: the Prin- 22 cess, the castle, the brambles, the Prince . . . and, of course, the kiss. Some of us (the more logically or causally minded, those interested in first principles) may even recall that the source of the enchantment was the malevolent curse of some typically malcontent witch. Wasn't there a pricked finger involved? A telltale drop of blood? Something about a spinning wheel? Or was that . . . Rumpelstiltskin?

So what have we forgotten? What is the "real" story? What elements of 23 the narrative have been selectively edited out by the bowdlerization of the nursery and by the omission of the more disturbing details with each retelling, each generation.

Let's look at Charles Perrault's "La Belle au Bois Dormant," the very first 24 story in his 1697 *Histoires ou Contes du Temps Passé*. Here, the romantic awakening (no kiss, it seems, was required; the Prince had merely to kneel before the Princess for the spell to be broken) is a bright little nugget sandwiched between two dark chapters on the theme of female vengefulness, envy and rage. The love story provides a brief interlude of grace (in one lovely detail, the ladies-in-waiting take care not to tell the newly awoken Princess that she is dressed in the fashions of somebody's great-grandmother— though she looks very beautiful anyway) between two much longer and profoundly harrowing sections.

The first movement begins with the King and Queen's passionate longing 25 to have a child, a wish which after many barren years is ultimately granted. Overjoyed, they stage a lavish Christening, to which they invite all the kingdom's resident fairies, with the understanding that each elfin godmother will give the newborn a magical gift.

Alas, the royal couple forgets to include an elderly, reclusive and obscure 26 fairy, who shows up uninvited, her offering a curse. She promises that the Princess will have her hand pierced by a spindle and die of the wound—a malediction which a younger fairy mediates by changing the death sentence to a mere hundred-year sleep. (Host, hostesses, makers of guest lists and indeed of *any* lists—the most fashionably dressed celebrities, the notable books and films of the year, the richest CEOs, the best writers or artists under the age of forty—would do well to consider the daunting number of fairy tales that begin with catastrophes whipped up by somebody in a rage at having been excluded.)

As a prophylactic measure, spindles are outlawed throughout the kingdom. One wonders what its residents did for clothing during the intervening years until the teenage Princess, wandering through a palace, finds an old woman in a tower room so remote that she has apparently never heard about the prohibition against spinning. Of course, the Princess sticks herself and nods off for a hundred years until the Prince arrives, and so on. (The kiss—so central to our modern understanding of the story—is thought to have been added during the centuries when "The Sleeping Beauty" was a standard repertoire plot for traveling marionette shows; this fact may tempt us to reimagine the kiss as a sort of abrupt thunking peck between two wooden puppets.)

No sooner has the Princess woken than it begins to seem as if the long sleep has been a blessed idyll, a prudent restorative nap before the struggle-to-the-death about to ensue when the Prince (now the King) goes off to war, leaving the Princess (who by now has borne him two children) with his mother. The worst-case nightmare mother-in-law is, as it happens, an Ogress whose craving to eat her two grandchildren and her daughter-in-law (with Sauce Robert!) is thwarted at the very last minute by the King's return. Is this, then, one moral of the tale: that the long sleep of girlhood is a brief, welcome interval of peace between the battles (with other women!) that deform childhood and adult life?

And now let's search a bit further back still, to see what Perrault himself forgot—or what he chose to leave out—in his borrowing from an earlier version of the story in Basile's 1636 *Pentamerone*. Here there are no uninvited vengeful fairies; rather, a wise man predicts that harm will come to the Princess through a splinter in a skein of flax. But here again female malevolence is the truly lethal splinter; after the King awakens the Sleeping Beauty (whom Basile calls Talia), it turns out that her gallant savior is already married; like the Ogress in Perrault, his understandably furious wife tries (with horrifying near-success) to cook and eat her husband's mistress and her two children, Sun and Moon. And where did these children come from?

That is the major—and most startling—difference between Perrault and Basile. For the King in the Neapolitan tale acts on the impulse which later generations of literary heroes somehow managed to resist. That is, he rapes Sleeping Beauty, and in the process fathers two children, who are miraculously able to nurse although their mother remains unconscious. Finally, one of the infants, in a sort of feeding frenzy, mistakes her fingertip for a nipple, sucks out the poisoned splinter and brings the Princess back to life.

So now, it seems, we've come full circle, and then some. The insensate, slumbering woman is not only the ideal lover and mate, but also—as it turns out—the perfect mother. The kiss that returns the Sleeping Beauty to her

waking state requires two generations. Or perhaps it's not love—but motherhood—that finally makes a girl's eyes blink open in this seemingly simple
(but actually complex) story, this seemingly romantic (but in fact deeply disturbing) narrative, this eternally haunting fairy tale with its peculiar take on
death and life, on women and men, on the continuance of the species.

FOR DISCUSSION AND WRITING:
MAKING A CULTURAL CRITIQUE

1. In his essay on "Sleeping Beauty," Bettelheim rejects the idea of sexual
   stereotyping: "Fairy tales do not render such one-sided pictures" (par. 4).
   How does Prose challenge that statement?

2. Prose refers to Freudian theory, especially Freud's dream theory (see p.
   226), which would make sense, given that we have a story centered on a
   sleeping woman. "If fairy tales are the alchemical distillation of our collective desires and dreams," she writes, then Freud "may apply" (par.
   21). Notice how Prose qualifies many of her statements. She does not
   rule Freud out by any means, but neither does she use Freud's work as
   a value system with which to structure her interpretation. How would
   you describe her method of interpretation? She does not present herself
   as an "insider," in Kermode's terms, nor does she appear to be "against
   interpretation" as Sontag is. Umberto Eco's position occupies a middle
   ground: because it is nearly impossible to find the "original intention of
   the author," and because an interpreter tends to beat "the text into a
   shape which will serve for his purpose" (p. 210), one turns to the "intention of the text." This is a tricky concept, but basically it means that the
   text constructs its model reader; that you cannot read a text any way you
   want (as may occur on the extreme edges of reader-response criticism);
   but that certain texts allow a lot of space for the reader to conjecture.
   "Sleeping Beauty" is such a text, in part because we don't know who the
   original author is. It's a story that has been rewritten a number of times,
   and therefore carries with it the baggage of the times and cultures within
   which it was rewritten. How, then, does Prose's interpretation reflect the
   culture of the late twentieth century?

3. In her final paragraph, Prose comes to a qualified conclusion: "Or perhaps it's not love—but motherhood—that finally makes a girl's eyes
   blink open. . . ." Does this mean Prose would agree with Bettelheim's
   conclusion that to nurture a child is to reach "the summit of femininity"
   (par. 31), or not? Look again at Prose's conclusion, and then review her
   discussion, the evidence she presents, and how she presents it. Write a
   short essay in which you argue for one interpretation over another, based
   on textual evidence, or in which you explain why Prose's qualified conclusion is justified.

4. Prose tries to get at the meaning of "Sleeping Beauty" by finding and interpreting what has been left out in later versions of the story. You can

carry her method a step further by studying Disney's *Sleeping Beauty* (1986, 1996), part of the "Classic Storybook Collection" that allows kids to "relive the movies one book at a time." You will find some interesting substitutions and additions, as well as significant omissions, and after analyzing these, you can then write an interpretation of the Disney version of "Sleeping Beauty."

Interpreting "Up in Michigan"

Nancy R. Comley and Robert Scholes

In your earlier reading of the story "Up in Michigan," we did not ask you what you thought the story was about, though undoubtedly you did have some thoughts on the matter. We were concentrating there on the work of the reader coming to the text for the first time. In the first part of this essay, Comley and Scholes present their reading of the text and the work it requires the reader to do. In the second part, the authors present an interpretation of the text.

A First Reading

In this essay we discuss reading in general and reading Ernest Hemingway   1
in particular, citing a single short story that Hemingway wrote early in his career: "Up in Michigan." Our goal is not to produce a single "right" or ultimate reading of this story, but to explore possible ways of reading it and the implications of those ways. We argue, inevitably, that certain ways of reading are better than others, in that they provide more pleasure for the reader or produce more interesting and persuasive readings.

In many ways, this is a simple story about a couple and their first "date,"   2
which leads to a sexual encounter over the woman's protests. "Aha," you say, "date rape." "Well," we say, "yes—and no, or, perhaps, maybe." The first point we want to make about reading is that this kind of move, from a summary of the events of the story to an expression like "date rape," is one of the things we do when we read. We turn events—in this particular narrative, a sexual act—into interpretive and evaluative categories, like date rape. Such categories enable us to get control of a story, to fit it into our own thinking. We can't do without them, but they can limit us by closing down interpretive possibilities too quickly, oversimplifying something that may be more subtle and more complex than the categories we apply. Reading fictions like this is partly a matter of developing categories that are less simple and rigid.

Let's begin reading. We move through the story rapidly once, pointing   3
out questions and problems. Then we come back and see what kinds of answers and solutions we can produce.

The first thing to read is the title. It gives us a place, Michigan, but not a   4
time. And it offers an intriguing preposition, "Up." This probably refers to the

part of Michigan in which the events of the story take place, but it may have other meanings as well. In the first two paragraphs we are introduced to two characters, Jim Gilmore and Liz Coates (as well as Mrs. Smith). The writing is very simple and direct: Jim "came," he "bought," he "was," and he "lived" [1]. The second paragraph begins by telling us about Liz, but ends by telling us how Jim reacted to her: he "liked her face" but "never thought about her" [2]. The person telling us this story (the narrator) knows—and reports—what Jim was and was not thinking and feeling, that is, he (so-called for convenience) occasionally gives us things from Jim's point of view.

The narrator also gives us things from the viewpoint of Liz, starting with the first sentence in paragraph [3]. But something else happens in this paragraph that should attract the careful reader's attention. Instead of saying, "She liked the way he walked" he says, "She liked *it* the way he walked," and continues using that construction repetitiously for most of this paragraph. Why does he do that? What's going on here? We come back to these questions but for the moment it is enough to notice that there's something odd in this use of the word "it."

The next paragraph is purely descriptive, letting us know that we are in a relatively remote and rural part of the world. Paragraph [5] opens with description, too, and the rhythm of the sentences becomes more noticeable as the narrator describes the beauty of the scene. He first puts the reader in the scene, using the second person—"From Smith's back door *you* could look"—and then puts Liz in the same place—"From Smith's back door *Liz* could see" [5]. This alignment of viewpoints is quite literal—both Liz and "you" seeing the same thing from the same place, but it is also metaphorical, bringing the reader into line with Liz's thoughts and feelings, which become the topic in the next paragraph.

Paragraph [6] not only tells us what Liz is thinking about at a particular time, it also uses a different tense and a different kind of narrative time. The first sentence does not say "Liz thought" but "All the time now Liz *was thinking*" (our emphasis). This use of the "iterative" mode of narration enables a writer to tell us once something that happens many times (in this case "All the time"). Here, it has the effect of emphasizing Liz's preoccupation with Jim Coates—who doesn't "seem to notice her much." We are getting our information mainly from Liz's point of view here, as we will throughout most of this narrative. For reasons we will want to think about, Hemingway has decided to present this story from that angle. We also get some other useful information in this paragraph. Jim talks about James G. Blaine, the "plumed Knight" of the Republican party, a senator and diplomat who ran for President in 1884 and was much in the news that year. This gives us a fairly persuasive way of dating these events, though the date might be earlier, because Blaine had been in the news before. This paragraph is mainly informational, telling us things we need to know about the situation of the story.

Paragraph [7] continues and intensifies the internal focus on Liz's feelings, giving us plenty of clues to her emotional state. She misses him badly, has trouble sleeping, but discovers that it is "fun to think about him too." She feels "weak and sick sort of inside" when she sees Jim coming back from his

5

6

7

8

trip. These are signs of what Liz (and we) would probably call "love"—a condition the story is going to ask us to think about. Then the men come back with their load of dead deer and their new growths of beard. The big event narrated in this paragraph is something that doesn't happen: "Liz hadn't known just what would happen when Jim got back but she was sure it would be something. Nothing had happened." It is worth noting that Hemingway's narrative voice tells us nothing about how Liz reacted to this "nothing." We, too, expect something, given the way we have been told about her feelings early in this paragraph, and we, too, get nothing. As he does so often, Hemingway expects us to fill in the gaps of his narrative, to make the story our own. We must supply her feelings of disappointment, which makes them both stronger and less sentimental than they would be if the author had insisted on telling us about them.

The next dozen paragraphs [8–20] are mainly conversation about the 9 deer the men have killed on their hunting trip and information about drinking from the whiskey jug. Jim, in particular, has a big drink straight out of the jug while bringing it in, slopping some of it down his shirt front—which may be a hint that this is not his first drink of the day. During the conversation about hunting and drinking they also have at least two more "big shots." This conversation is reported without any commentary, not even a "he said" or any identification of who says what. It is generic man talk, and Hemingway gives it to us generically.

Paragraph 21 shifts back from the external reported conversation to tell- 10 ing us, first, about Jim's feelings, and, later, about Liz's. Jim "began to feel great" and "loved the taste and the feel of whiskey." After a dinner where the men were "feeling hilarious but acting very respectable" they talk in the front room. (Do they continue drinking? We don't know.) And Liz sits in the kitchen, pretending to read a book, waiting to see Jim so she can "take the way he looked up to bed with her." Clearly, she has a bad case of love, so bad that she wants to take Jim's image to bed with her, though what she will do with it there is one of the things we are not told.

She is in this state, "thinking about him hard" [22], when Jim comes into 11 the kitchen, stands behind her, and puts "his arms around her." It is clear from the context that his hands are on her breasts. "Her breasts felt plump and firm and the nipples were erect under his hands"—Jim's viewpoint, we are told what he is feeling. Liz is frightened. She has never been touched this way before, but she thinks, in terms of her notion of love, "He's come to me finally. He's really come." It is worth noting that this description of an embrace is expressed in the language of coition, from the "hard" of Liz's thoughts, to her "erect" nipples, to "He's come." Hemingway charges this moment with even more sexuality than the event calls for.

The next paragraph is anchored in Liz's point of view and continues the 12 process of using the most sexual words in the least obvious places. Liz holds herself "stiff" but when she feels Jim's erection through the back of the chair we are told only that she feels "Jim." That is, we, the readers, have to ask ourselves what part of Jim she would feel through the back of the chair and supply that in order to visualize this scene properly. We must also solve another little interpretive puzzle. We are told in no uncertain terms that, when Jim "held her tight hard" against the back of the chair, "she wanted it now." What, we must ask, is the "it," that she wanted? This is not the last of the "its" the reader must deal with, so, let us leave the interpretive question open for the moment. The paragraph ends with Jim inviting her in a whisper to "Come on for a walk."

Paragraph [24] describes their walk down the sandy road to the dock. What follows is seen mainly from Liz's perspective. We are told that, though the weather is cold, she is "hot all over from being with Jim." Jim is reduced, in this paragraph, to a pair of hands: one inside her dress, stroking her breast, the other moving from her lap to sliding up her leg. In the next two paragraphs of dialogue, Liz tells Jim "Don't" and "You mustn't." Then comes the crucial paragraph [27]:

> The boards were hard. Jim had her dress up and was trying to do something to her. She was frightened but she wanted it. She had to have it but it frightened her.

The key words in this paragraph are "something" and "it." We, knowing readers that we are, know what Jim is trying to do. Liz either does not know exactly or will not allow herself to think clearly about it. "Something" looks like a vague word, but it is used precisely here because of its vagueness. And that pronoun "it" also poses an interpretive problem. In this paragraph, "it" seems to refer grammatically to "something." We are told unmistakably that "it" frightens her but that she has to have "it." Vagueness upon vagueness. Readers of this story must interpret. The text forces us to contribute to the construction of the event and its interpretation.

In paragraph [28] Liz tells Jim he mustn't do "it" and in the next Jim says "I got to. I'm going to. You know we got to." This is brief, but the shift in pronouns raises the question of whether Jim is doing something here or both Jim and Liz ("we") are doing it. Jim's words also raise the interpretive question of whether Liz knows what they are doing and that they have to do it. Either he thinks she knows this, or he is trying to persuade her that she knows it.

In paragraph [30] Liz replies that they don't have to. She then says, "Oh, it isn't right. Oh, it's so big and it hurts so. You can't. Oh, Jim. Jim. Oh." Once again, the pronouns are interesting. "It" in the first of these sentences refers to what Jim is doing. In the second sentence, however, "it" refers to what Jim is doing it with. The exclamations are also interesting. Suddenly all those "Ohs." Hemingway avoids any graphic description of this sexual act, but the thrusts of Jim's body are recorded in Liz's exclamations: "Oh. . . . Oh. . . . Oh. . . . Oh." And the deed is done. There is apparently a brief lapse of time between this paragraph and the next.

We are still seeing things through the eyes of Liz in paragraph [31] but the narrator sticks to physical information, avoiding any direct statements about what she is feeling emotionally until after she starts to cry. We might call this semi-detached narration. We learn that Jim has fallen asleep on top of her and that she can't wake him. We also learn that he has hurt her. When she can't wake him up, she works her way out from under him (instead of just pushing him off) and tries to compose her clothing and hair. Then she leans over and kisses him on the cheek. He rolls over and she starts to cry. In the mist coming up from the bay "she was cold and miserable and everything felt gone."

In the closing paragraphs she tries again, unsuccessfully, to wake Jim, covers him with her coat and tucks him in, and walks up the sandy road to go to bed with that "cold mist" "coming up through the woods from the bay." We are left with some questions. Why does she kiss him and tuck him in like a baby? Why does she want to wake him up? What would he say if he awoke? What will Liz's life be like from now on? 17

Interpreting "Up in Michigan"

Let us start with that big, clumsy but important question that hovers over the story as we read it in our own time: Is this a story of "date rape"? In 1922 this expression was simply not in our vocabulary. Now it is unavoidable. This tells us something important about all acts of interpretation: They involve two different scenes, a scene and time of writing and a scene and time of reading. Interpretation is always to some extent a negotiation between these two scenes. One great issue is how much weight each should receive in reading any text. Should the interpretive effort be directed totally or primarily to an attempt to recover the exact intention the author may have had in producing the text? Or is the reader free to make the text mean whatever he or she wants it to mean? Let us make our own position on this matter as clear as possible. We think that recovering the author's meaning—to the extent that this is possible—is an essential part of the interpretive process. It is something we all need to learn to do—and not just with literary texts but with all sorts of messages that we encounter daily. It is also a game, with rules, that can be fun to play. 18

On the other hand, we also believe that no author ever can be entirely clear about his or her own intentions, nor can authors actually realize in any text all that they might intend to accomplish. Furthermore, it is also important to ask what a text means to us, here and now. And if we sense a gap between what the author may have intended and the meanings we find in a text, we must raise questions about this gap. This is one place where criticism— as opposed to interpretation—can begin. But in order for it to begin, we must reach some clear view of the differences between the author's view of things and our own. Coming back to "Up in Michigan," we must ask both what Hemingway may have intended in 1922 and what we understand now. And we must raise the further question of how well the story stands up. That is, does it have anything important to say to us now, about the lives that we presently live? 19

The question of "date rape" can be raised in a number of ways. It can, for instance, be used simply to short circuit or shut down any careful reading of the story. Here is a man who has forced sex on a woman who said, "No"—wicked man, trivial story. Or it could be read according to some other already written interpretive script: "Women always say 'No' but mean 'Yes,' so what's new?" Both of these readings, in our view, turn a subtle and complex 20 little story into something far less interesting. To interpret the story with a subtlety that attempts to match that of the writing, we must examine carefully some decisions the author has made about what we are told, and when, and how—and what we are not told, as well. Perhaps the most important of Hemingway's decisions was to tell the crucial events of the story from Liz Coates' point of view.

There might be many answers to the question of why this point of view 21 was adopted. It might be, simply, that the story is more interesting from her viewpoint than from that of the intoxicated Jim. But it might also be that telling the story this way enabled Hemingway to give us a closer look at this character's state of mind before and during the episode on the dock. In paragraph 23, the following sentences are crucial:

> She felt Jim right through the back of the chair and she couldn't stand it and then something clicked inside of her and the feeling was warmer and softer. Jim held her tight hard against the chair and she wanted it now and Jim whispered, "Come on for a walk."

As the reader turns these words into images and sensations—a vital part of the interpretive process—he or she must imagine Liz feeling the pressure of Jim's erection through the back of the chair, at first having a kind of negative reaction ("she couldn't stand it") and then a response in which her desire matches his own—something clicks inside her and she feels warmer and softer—so that when he asks her to walk out with him, she comes willingly.

In paragraph 24, we are told that Liz, as one of Jim's hands strokes her 22 breast inside her dress and the other is in her lap, "was very frightened and didn't know how he was going to go about things but she snuggled close to him." A few paragraphs later, when Jim is trying to do "something" to her, we are told that "She was frightened but she wanted it. She had to have it but it frightened her." All this evidence, as we interpret it, tells us that Liz is sufficiently ignorant about the mechanics of sex to be unsure of what is going to happen to her. She wants "something," but she isn't exactly sure what "it" will be or how Jim will "go about things." It is clear that Liz feels that the man is the one who will do whatever "things" are done, but the vagueness of the words "things," "something," and, of course, "it" convey to us the vagueness of Liz's own thoughts here. Whether she really "knows" and is repressing this knowledge or really "doesn't know," is open to interpretive argument, but it seems clear from Hemingway's decisions about point of view and particular words that he wants us to see Liz as saying "Yes," in many ways in response to a demand she doesn't fully understand, and then saying, "No," as the penetration she could not imagine actually occurs.

Perhaps few women of Liz's age in our own time would be quite as in- 23 nocent as she seems to be, but the doubts, the indecisions, and the wanting and not wanting should not be difficult for us now, both men and women, to understand.

To finish interpreting this text, however, we must go on to the final para- 24 graph. Liz tucks Jim in with her own coat, as if he were a sleeping child instead of a man who has just hurt her sexually. How are we to read this? Liz is miserable, crying, and cannot wake the drunken and sated man. For her, "everything felt gone." Yet she performs this loving, protective action before leaving the dock. We are inclined to read this as Liz's attempt to give a domestic or familial shape to what has happened. By treating Jim as she might treat her child or her husband, if she had one, she is trying to turn the episode into a courtship, whatever it may have been. It also shows us a person too kind to leave a man in that condition uncovered to the cold mist coming up the bay.

What, then, are we to imagine as the future of Liz and Jim? Scholarship 25 tells us that Hemingway began writing this as a version of how the parents of a friend of his got married. From this we might imagine that Liz and Jim did move from here to marriage and family life. But the story could also have ended like Hemingway's early sketch, "Pauline Snow," in which the girl is disgraced and finally has to leave the area. As with other aspects of this story, Hemingway has developed it in such a way as to leave interpretation open rather than closed. We can speculate about the future lives of this couple — and are even perhaps invited to do so — but there is no evidence here that will enable us to settle on a particular ending.

What we have is a classic confrontation between female tenderness and 26 male sexual drive. And one of the things that is interesting about this particular version of that old story is how fully Hemingway's sympathies are enlisted on the female side of the equation, though he clearly understands how it looks from the male side as well. The prose is very clear and relatively simple, but the thoughts and feelings have a surprising subtlety and complexity. The writing is also characterized by a probity and accuracy of feeling that go deep enough to get beyond the behavioral fashions of any particular time. Hemingway's greatest achievement is to have written of his own time in a way that is meaningful for our time as well.

FOR DISCUSSION AND WRITING: CONSIDERING INTENTION AND INTERPRETATION

1. Compare your earlier reading of "Up in Michigan" with Comley and Scholes's. What did you notice that they did not? Remember, every reader brings different cultural and literary baggage to their reading of a text. Did you agree with their reading? Why or why not?

2. This interpretation starts with the issue of the author's intention and how much of his meaning is recoverable. In our discussion of Francine Prose's essay on "Sleeping Beauty," we noted that sometimes intention is very difficult to consider, especially in a text written anonymously and in a time far distant from ours. A lot is known about Hemingway, and one could reconstruct to some extent the scene of his writing of "Up in Michigan" as a very young man. This would take special research on your part, but what can you bring to this text without such research? Many readers react to this story as one about "date rape." But that is a very recent term

that did not exist when this story was written, so we can't simply say it's a story about date rape. What strategies do the authors employ to try to recover some of Hemingway's intention?

3. Keeping in mind the strategies of interpretation you have noted in Comley and Scholes's interpretation, try your hand at interpreting one of the stories in earlier sections of this text, such as William Carlos Williams's "The Use of Force," Kate Chopin's "The Kiss," or Louise Erdrich's "The Red Convertible."

Interpreting "Pitcher"
Robert Scholes

Interpreting poetry presents the greatest challenge to the reader, but it also presents the greatest rewards. As Robert Scholes points out in his interpretation of "Pitcher," a poem about poetry, the poet tries to be unpredictable in his use of language. It is necessary for the reader to be "crafty": to be shrewd and cunning and ingenious so as not to be outsmarted by the poet/pitcher.

Pitcher

His art is eccentricity, his aim
How not to hit the mark he seems to aim at,

His passion how to avoid the obvious,
His technique how to vary the avoidance.

The others throw to be comprehended. He   5
Throws to be a moment misunderstood.

Yet not too much. Not errant, arrant, wild,
But every seeming aberration willed.

Not to, yet still, still to communicate
Making the batter understand too late.   10

Robert Francis

How should a crafty reader read this poem? Situate, situate. The "pitcher"   1
in question is not a jug but a person who "throws" to a "batter." We are in the world of baseball here, which, if you are a North American of the early twenty-first century, or an East Asian or Latin American, should cause you no difficulty. If you are coming from any of a number of other cultures, however, you might need quite a bit of guidance. I will assume that you, my reader, do not. As a poem about baseball (or softball) pitching, the poem is quite accurate. I used to pitch myself, half a century ago, and I know very well what goes through a pitcher's mind. To avoid the obvious and vary the avoidance—yes,

watch someone like Pedro Martinez[1] and you will see the process in practice. It is a disaster for a pitcher to be "wild," but it is necessary that the pitcher be unpredictable: "seeming aberration willed," that's the ticket. The fastball up and in, followed once by the curve outside and next time by another inside fastball. Yes. We situate the poem by clothing its abstractions in specifics. As a poem about pitching, I like it. I like it personally. It wakes memories of hours on the mound, of youthful joys and sorrows, and it informs my present occasion of watching the sport. But there is something else going on here, something that catches the attentive eye of the crafty reader.

Consider some of the words used that do not come from the world of the diamond: "comprehended," "misunderstood," "communicate," "understand." All of these words have to do with language and meaning, and there are other phrases in the poem, like "avoid the obvious," which works as well with reference to language as it does with reference to baseball. There is a pattern here. The poet/speaker is talking about baseball, for sure, but he may be talking about something else as well. We are in the area of the "symbol" and the secret-hidden-deeper-meaning, here, and must move cautiously. There is no secret, nothing hidden. But there may well be a delayed meaning, a meaning meant to appear plainly only after the reader has swung at it and missed or taken it for a called strike. All these references to language and meaning indicate that the poet may be talking about a way of communicating. He talks about two ways of throwing: "The others throw to be comprehended. He / Throws to be a moment misunderstood." On the baseball field eight players throw the ball as straight as they can, intending that somebody should catch it with as little trouble as possible. They do not always succeed in this—ask any first baseman about it. But they do not deliberately throw curves or sinkers to one another. Only the pitcher does this. But all those words that point toward language and meaning invite us to look for an analogy between the baseball situation and something in the world of communication.

The crafty reader will not be long in formulating the problem this way: pitcher : fielders :: X : other communicators. From here how long can it take such a reader to reach X = Poet? Or, finally, pitcher : fielders :: poet : prose writers. A definition of poetry is being proposed here. Francis is arguing that the meaning of a poem should be clear enough, but not immediately. It should involve a "moment" of misunderstanding, followed by comprehension that comes "too late." In this formulation the reader is like a batter with two strikes on him, frozen by a slow curve that breaks over the plate. And his poem tries to enact precisely that process, freezing us into reading it as a poem about baseball only, only to discover, too late, that it is a poem about poetry as well. Which means that it is about a third thing, the relation between the art of pitching and the ars poetica.[2] The poem practices what it preaches, in more ways than one. Look at the rhymes, or rather look for the rhymes: aim/aim at, avoid/avoidance, He/—, wild/willed, communicate/late.

2

3

---

[1] [Pedro Martinez pitches for the Boston Red Sox. *Eds.*]
[2] [ars poetica: the art of poetry; poetics. *Eds.*]

They don't all come at the end of the lines and they are not exact. Sometimes they are repetitions of the same syllable but in different locations. Only the last rhyme is what we expect—and then we don't expect it. "His technique how to vary"—indeed—and how well the word *technique* fits both poet and pitcher!

FOR DISCUSSION AND WRITING: INTERPRETING A POEM

1. Robert Scholes starts his interpretation by *situating* himself in the world of the poem. Look closely at the first paragraph to follow his process of situating himself. You might call it an examination of why he responded to the poem in the first place. Look again at the poems in the "Poetic Uses of Metaphor" section in Chapter 2 (pp. 87–94). Choose one that you respond to, one that you feel you can situate yourself in.

2. You know from working with metaphor in chapter 2 that a metaphor links together two outwardly dissimilar things and surprises us into seeing their similarities. Scholes presents his working out of the latent element in the poem—the poet—through a formula (par. 3). But how did he get to the formula? Note that he starts with the words of the poem, and he begins to see that though "The poet/speaker is talking about baseball . . . he may be talking about something else as well" (par. 2). The language of the poem points to the "hidden" element, and the quality of an interpretation depends upon close attention to the words of the poem. Examine the words of the poem you have chosen to see what pattern they might form. Do you see similarities? Do you see oppositions? Where is the language leading you?

3. In his final paragraph, the formula is presented, and Scholes goes on to explain how the metaphor works and why "Pitcher" is an effective poem. In the process, he tells you what the poem means, but it's the working out of *how* it means that makes this an effective interpretation. Now write one of your own.

TEXT AND HYPERTEXT

A *hypertext* is simply a collection of texts that are linked in such a way that a reader can jump from one unit to another. The links are what make the text "hyper." In traditional written documents, separate units of text (small ones like paragraphs and big ones like chapters) are displayed so that the reader can follow them in a line from beginning to end, by turning printed pages or by scrolling electronic text from top to bottom. That is, the spacing on the page of print—or an electronic image of a page—breaks the text up into paragraphs, chapters, sections, and so on, which follow one another in an order that the reader is also supposed to follow.

Most printed texts of any length have a linear structure as well as a linear format. That is, they require the reader to follow the line of a story or an argument as he or she moves through the text.

Film and television are also organized in a linear fashion. The text flows on, and the reader must attend to it as it flows. These forms are more suitable for story than for argument, which is why so many television shows are narrative in form, including game shows that lead toward a conclusion in which someone wins or loses a fortune. There are films and videos, however, that resist the pressure to tell stories. They break up the narrative flow with various kinds of alienation effects that free the viewer from the narrative spell, call attention to the nature of the medium, and otherwise stimulate thought about the materials being represented.

In printed texts, in the last decades of the twentieth century, many writers also tried to break up the flow of the linear story or argument in various ways. Julio Cortázar, Roland Barthes, and Robert Coover, for example, began writing texts for publication in print that strained against the limits of print as a medium, offering sections that could be read in more than one order, such as Cortázar's *Hopscotch,* Barthes's *A Lover's Discourse: Fragments,* or Coover's *Briar Rose.* But media are powerful, and most readers followed the linear text, turning the pages one after the other.

Hypertext has changed all this. The essence of hypertext is that it breaks up these linear structures. Above all, it does not require the reader to follow a single sequence from unit to unit. It allows the reader to select which links to follow and which to ignore. In this way it has become a medium more suited to the experiments of writers like Coover and Barthes than to the printed medium in which they made those experiments. And many writers and scholars have followed their lead, to the point where fiction written expressly for hypertextual reading began to appear around 1990.

Obviously, these developments are important for students of textuality and for the authors of a work like *Text Book.* But there is no way we can simulate a hypertext in print. The media are too powerful to allow this. What we can do, however, and have done, is to provide a hypertext for study on our publisher's Web server. Specifically, we have taken the full text of Robert Coover's short novel, *Briar Rose,* and used it to construct a hypertext by adding visual materials and places for commentary to the original forty-two units of the book. We are hoping that you will find this interesting and will send us comments (via your instructors) that we can incorporate on the comment pages, thus making this hypertext a bit interactive, as a hypertext should be.

We also invite you to think of other creative and critical uses for this material. You can find the home page for this hypertext at <www.bedfordstmartins.com/textbook>.

4

Texts and Research: The Mystory

VOICE

In this concluding chapter you have an opportunity to bring together all the devices of textual writing that you have learned in the preceding chapters. Traditionally, composition textbooks often include a unit on "writing the research paper." *Text Book* conforms to this practice, except that textualist research is conducted somewhat differently. Our name for this new mode of inquiry is *mystory*.

This difference between research papers and research texts may be summarized within the linguistic category of *voice*. *Voice* is defined in the handbooks in terms of "agency":

> Direct kinds of sentences, active sentences place emphasis on the people and things responsible for actions and conditions. Passive sentences, on the other hand, are descriptive sentences that deemphasize the actors involved and instead focus on people or things that do not act. . . . Notice that the person completing the action can be totally absent from a passive sentence. . . . Because human choices and actions determine much of what goes on around us, give the credit or blame to the people responsible (Perrin 268).

Voice, and the related grammatical categories of *mood* and *tone,* are affected by theoretical debates surrounding such questions as "the death of the author"—debates that make it difficult to ascertain who or what is responsible for anything. Roland Barthes noticed that a third category of voice had emerged within experimental literature—a middle voice—

based on the reflexive, self-conscious nature of modernist writing that claimed to be knowledge only of language, not of life. In the middle voice, one is the recipient of one's own actions: responsibility is neither assumed nor avoided but is discovered as an effect of writing. Mystory is composed in the middle voice.

MOOD

A related grammatical category that is extended within text is mood. "Mood, indicated by verb form, refers to the way writers present their ideas and information. Sometimes writers want to stress the factuality of information (indicative mood). Sometimes they want to give commands (imperative mood). Sometimes they want to stress that information is conditional or contrary to fact (subjunctive mood)" (Perrin 210–11). Voice and mood come together naturally in a literary context:

> It is relatively easy to distinguish between subject matter and mood. A group of poems on the subject of death may range from a mood of noble defiance in Donne's "Death, Be Not Proud," to pathos in Frost's "Out, Out—," to irony in Houseman's "To an Athlete Dying Young." . . . If a distinction is made between mood and tone, it will be the fairly subtle one of mood being the emotional attitude of the author toward his subject and tone the attitude of the author toward his audience (Holman 327).

Voice is sometimes used as a metonym for *style,* as when writers are urged to "find their own voice." The use of the middle (reflexive) voice in mystory accounts for one of the biggest differences between a paper and a text: the position or attitude of the writer to the object of study. You are accustomed to writing in the active voice, adopting a neutral or objective tone, and making an argument that interprets, judges, or assigns a meaning to the object of study. While mystory does not exclude argument, it also opens the relation of subject-object so that the object of study may explain the subject (the author). The work of literature (the object) becomes the source of knowledge that writers use to understand themselves.

A common mistake in writing a paper is to provide only the information gathered in the research without forming it into an "argument"—without stating a claim about the information and then demonstrating the truth of the claim. Text begins with the same dual pairing of topic and point of view: one of Barthes's shorthand definitions of *text* is "the work plus the reader," and the relationship of the writer to the work is precisely what is in question. The distinction is similar to the one that informs the relationship between story and discourse in narrative: story is the material ("facts") of the drama, and discourse is how one finds out about this material.

In cinema, the discursive level is revealed through the cinematography—lighting, editing, camera work—all of which evoke the attitude of the filmmaker to the events of the drama. *Mood* in mystory is a hybrid category joining the features of the linguistic and poetic senses of the term. *Mood* in the latter case refers to "atmosphere" or the "ambiance" of a specific place and time. A research text shares some of the qualities of narrative storytelling in that what is in question is not so much the facts or events but the "attitude" of the writer.

A better term for *attitude* in this case is "state of mind." In a paper, one communicates and justifies one's claims about the topic; in a text, one discovers one's own state of mind relative not just to the object of study but also to one's existential condition. There is an adage addressed to creative writers that in the short story, "character is destiny." In the mystory, this observation is distributed through the relationship of the writer to the story: the character in the story is an image of the researcher's destiny. There are two dimensions to knowledge: what is known, and the state of mind of the knower. Papers and texts are complementary in that each one foregrounds one or the other of these distinct dimensions of learning.

IDENTIFICATION

A research text differs from the method of critique that is the dominant form of reading in cultural studies. Text and critique share the same theoretical understanding, however, about how culture works. The theory is that human identity—the self—is not a natural essence but is constructed within a specific historical society. The institutions of society maintain discourses (languages, logics, modes of proof, etiquettes) that function to "interpellate" or recruit persons into the dominant belief system or ideology of the society. Every society, and every institution in society, performs this function, so that people raised in the United States become identified with "America," and persons raised in China become "Chinese."

The key word in this theory is *identification*. Institutions exploit the basic psychological process of identity formation known as "introjection," or "the entry into language." The first institution a person encounters, and the oldest one in society, is the family. In the family one enters natural language, but becoming a native speaker involves much more than just acquiring a vocabulary. It also involves the assumption of a position in a complex array of identity categories: gender, sexuality, ethnicity, religion, race, class, nation, and the like. Identification is at the heart of this education in that one becomes who and what one is by internalizing an image of the nurturing authority figures encountered in one's world. According to the theory, this act of identification with parent figures in the family—extended to the authority figures encountered in the other institutions that continue the interpellation process as one matures—is a "mis-recognition," a necessary "mistake" that implants alienation at the core of selfhood as an experience. To be a "self," that is, is to carry internally an image acquired from "outside." Throughout one's life, identity is experienced as a negotiation of this border between the inside and the outside. Identity is "extimacy," as psychoanalyst Jacques Lacan put it, coining a term that combines in one word "external" and "intimacy." An individual subject is not autonomous and self-identical, but is dependent upon and an effect of languages into which he or she has entered. As the philosopher said: We do not speak language; it speaks us.

THE PERSONAL IS POLITICAL

If text agrees with critique about the social construction of identity, it disagrees about how to learn in such a world—how to "know thyself" (understood now as learning how "self" is an effect of living within a specific set of discourses and institutions). Critique in its purest forms, such as those practiced by Marxists, retains the Enlightenment, humanist optimism about science. Marx invented the science of society in the nineteenth century and claimed to have discovered the laws of history (the cause-and-effect motor that drove change in modern societies was class warfare, according to Marx). Critique holds that science is not itself ideological and is capable of taking up an objective position outside the dynamics of interpellation, while setting aside the effects of identification associated with selfhood. Text, in contrast, reflects the contemporary loss of confidence in the Enlightenment model of knowledge. Much of the leadership in this postmode has come from feminism, which distanced itself from scientific critique by declaring that "the personal is political." There is no external position outside of ideology in this view. Rather, knowing is always situated in one's own particular and specific experience. History and "herstory" are not necessarily the same "story."

The textual method known as mystory follows from this feminist lesson. Nor is the lesson a simple inversion in which personal experience replaces objective history as the site of truth. Rather, the question now concerns the disjunction between the general causative forces that operate at a global, collective level and the effects that are experienced locally and partially by individuals. Cultural critic Fredric Jameson proposed that what is needed in these conditions of fundamental alienation is a new method, a new aesthetic even, capable of composing a "cognitive map": one may never be able to "experience" directly the reality of one's world, but one may be able to "write" it. Mystory is a textual method that responds to this challenge. The term *mystory* follows from *herstory*, to generalize that feminist insight into all categories of interpellation.

THE WRITER AS ACTOR

Mystory is optimistic about identification as a mode of knowledge. The clearest understanding of the difference between critique and text may be seen by contrasting mystory with the "epic" method of "alienation" (the alienation effect) found in the theories and plays of Bertolt Brecht. The "A" effect (or "V" effect in the original German, *Verfremdungseffekt*), as Chris Baldick defines it, is

> a dramatic effect aimed at encouraging an attitude of critical detachment in the audience, rather than a passive submission to realistic illusion; and achieved by a variety of means, from allowing the audience to smoke and drink to interrupting the play's action with songs, sudden scene changes, and switches of role. Actors are also encouraged to distance themselves from their characters rather than identify with them: ironic commentary by a narrator adds to this "estrangement." By reminding the audience of the performance's artificial nature, Brecht hoped to stimulate a rational view of history as a changeable human creation rather than as a blind process to be accepted passively (Baldick 4).

Brecht's epic theater is often contrasted with the Stanislavski school of "method acting," which was developed in the Soviet Union in the 1920s, picked up in the United States through a process of cultural exchange, and institutionalized in the Actors Studio by Lee Strasberg in the 1940s and 1950s, to become the dominant mode of acting in American entertainment in all media. The Method, as it is called, achieves its famous "reality effect" (the opposite of the alienation effect) through encouraging the actor to identify with the role. The actor's training involves mnemonics—a memory technique—in which the role is memorized by mapping it onto the personal experience of the actor. What Barthes called the "third" or "obtuse" meaning in a photograph—neither its denotation nor its cultural connotation (the first two meanings)—is the same thing that Method actors use to memorize their parts in a drama: something in the role triggers a memory from their own experience. The actor's work is to enhance and augment this memory through the re-creation of its sensory details. The experience of this personal scene reproduces the emotion of that moment. The actor associates this lived emotion with the role by means of an image. The emotion may then be reproduced on stage by recalling the image.

RECOGNITION

How does this background inform the research text? Mystory, as we have said, is optimistic about identification. The assumption is that what is true about learning a language is also true about interpellation. As we saw with the case of the wild child in Chapter 2, if one has not learned a language in early childhood, one's ability to learn anything else is severely curtailed. Interpellation is part of this learning, meaning that the experience of identifying with a role model is a prerequisite to other experiences of recognition in other discourses. One first must be "subjected" to a specific ideology (culture) to later be "liberated" into understanding reality. Mis-recognition, that is, is the foundation of a series of subsequent experiences of "recognition" that are crucial to the mode of knowledge associated not with critique but with discovery and invention. The basic mechanism of recognition is an act in which some external scene is experienced as matching with an inner feeling. The Greeks foregrounded this kind of experience in tragedy—that moment in the drama that Aristotle called "anagnorisis," when the protagonist discovers or realizes "the true state of affairs" (as when Oedipus realized that he had killed his father and married his mother). The Greeks also established the baseline for recognition in the context of creativity or invention, as represented in the story of Archimedes, who shouted "Eureka!" when he connected the displacement of his bathtub water with the solution to a physics problem.

EPIPHANY

At the heart of the method of recognition as a mode of knowledge is the ancient theory of correspondences in which the local microcosm was grasped as a corollary of the macrocosm: "As above, so below." While Western science broke with this cosmology at the time of the Renaissance, it remained important in the arts. The most characteristic feature of modernist poetry, for example—the epiphany—is a secularized version of correspondence theory. Poets have given this experience of revelation many names, but it is always some version of the same realization that something in the external scene correlates with an inner condition, mood, or feeling. The list of devices by which this extimacy has been recorded could include Keats's "negative capability," Baudelaire's "correspondence," Rimbaud's "illumination," Rilke's "*Weltinnenraum,*" T. S. Eliot's "objective correlative," James Joyce's "epiphany," or even Freud's "uncanny." Of course, what separates modernism from postmodernism is the rejection in the latter of correspondence or revelation as a mode of knowledge. Or rather, this mode is "deconstructed" (used and transformed) within the problematic of the cognitive map and of alienation. The textual principle is that recognition has never been a "phenomenon" of direct experience, but a rhetorical effect of writing. It is still possible to write an illumination, and this experience constitutes the kind of "responsibility" that defines the middle voice: the writer claims the image as a "portrait" and signs it, adopts it as his or her own.

POPCYCLE

A mystory is a cognitive map by means of which one locates one's position within the "popcycle"—the set of institutions and their discourses that constructed one's identity. The mystorical method is not to stand outside each discourse but to use the forms and logics specific to the institution as the means to record one's experience of family, entertainment, and school. In the latter case, "school" is understood as the K–12 institution in which one learns not only the practices of literacy but through them the history of the community. This history functions to recruit one into a nationality. In the previous chapters of *Text Book,* we have practiced some of the forms of the family (the anecdote) and entertainment (transformations, ghost chapters). We also engaged in some critique, to the extent that we worked with the ideological basis of identification with works of popular culture (*Play It Again, Sam*). The principle justifying the mystorical approach to research is that specialized disciplines or career fields interpellate subjects in the same way as the other institutions of society. The critical effect is achieved, therefore, not by the denial of this reality and the pretense of objectivity, but through a homeopathic embracing of identification. The critical effect is achieved by composing a mystory in which one juxtaposes the products of the different discourses in one composition. The repetitions or correspondences that emerge in the intertext among one's different experiences produce a eureka effect—the epiphany. In fact, the goal of mystory is an experience whose highest achievement has been called "satori" (enlightenment).

PLEASURE AND BLISS

Part of the point of the analogy with the Zen experience of satori is that text cannot be known by intellect alone. Text research is partly conceptual or analytic and partly aesthetic (the hybrid of critical and creative writing). To know literature as text requires some practice of literary devices, as Barthes stated:

> Criticism always deals with the texts of pleasure, never the texts of bliss: Flaubert, Proust, Stendhal are discussed inexhaustibly; thus criticism speaks the futile bliss of the tutor text, its past or future bliss: you are about to read, I have read: criticism is always historical or prospective; the constatory presence, the presentation of bliss, is forbidden it; its preferred material is thus culture, which is everything in us except our present. With the writer of bliss (and his reader) begins the untenable text, the impossible text. This text is outside pleasure, outside criticism, unless it is reached through another text of bliss; you cannot speak "on" such a text, you can only speak "in" it, in its fashion, enter into a desperate plagiarism, hysterically affirm the void of bliss (and no longer obsessively repeat the letter of pleasure) (Barthes 1975: 21–22).

Mystory as research text is partly a text of pleasure and partly a text of bliss. In both instances, the purpose is to approach literature from the side of a *desire* to know, rather than from the side of knowledge as information. Too often the schools assume this desire and therefore teach the knowledge only as information. The result is a population of students with high verbal scores on the SAT who nonetheless dislike literature or have no idea why it actually is important. Mystory addresses this condition in two respects. First, it constitutes text research as self-knowledge: the inquiry into the library of culture is organized by correspondence, as mapping the match between collective and individual experience. Second, the logic of writing is aesthetic, using literary devices as methods of direct knowledge (metafiction as self-portrait). The simple reality is that it is a pleasure to play with language—to relate stories and construct figures of thought that address sensory experience. The rationale is that even if critical knowledge is still the order of the day in the specialized major, for the general education student the texts of pleasure and bliss are the most important thing, so that one finally recognizes what all the fuss is about.

The prototype for the method of research by identification is Roland Barthes's *A Lover's Discourse: Fragments,* in which Barthes composes an intertext between his own situation—an experience of unrequited love—

and the short novel by Goethe, *The Sorrows of Young Werther.* Barthes's *Fragments* is a study of *Werther,* undertaken as a text of pleasure and a text of bliss. To appreciate the method, it is useful to first review the following archive of materials representing Goethe's novel. The archive includes a brief biographical outline about Goethe; a plot outline of the novel; a sample of a few pages of the novel; and a selection from Goethe's essay, "Reflections on Werther," all of which describe the "state of mind" explored in the narrative.

Plot Outline for *The Sorrows of Young Werther* by Johann Wolfgang von Goethe

Lewy Olfson, ed.

Roland Barthes's *A Lover's Discourse: Fragments* is a good example of a research text. Barthes retains the critical goal of knowledge of an object of study—the lover's discourse—but he abandons the objective stance that describes this practice from the outside, translating it into a discourse of science. He retains the goal of a description that is generalizable as knowledge of both literature and life, but he commits himself to using a dramatic method that, rather than attempting to suspend or bracket out his own experience of love, admits it and brings it into a practice of participant-observation. "The description of the lover's discourse," Barthes explains, "has been replaced by its simulation, and to that discourse has been restored its fundamental person, the I, in order to stage an utterance, not an analysis. What is proposed, then, is a portrait—but not a psychological portrait; instead, a structural one which offers the reader a discursive site: the site of someone speaking within himself, amorously, confronting the other (the loved object), who does not speak" (Barthes 1978: 3). The "I" of *Fragments* is a hybrid, a fictionalized "Barthes," showing himself in a lover's situation while reading a novel about love. That novel is Goethe's *The Sorrows of Young Werther.* The following plot outline is provided to familiarize you with the complete story alluded to in *Fragments.* The outline is from Lewy Olfson, ed., *Plot Outlines of One Hundred Famous Novels: The Second Hundred* (Garden City, NY: Dolphin, 1966).

PLOT OUTLINE

> *Johann Wolfgang von Goethe was born in Frankfurt-am-Main, Germany, in 1749. His father was a prominent lawyer, and his mother was a charming, cultured woman who instilled her love of learning in her son, who bore the signs of genius at an early age. He gave up the study of law in order to write verse and plays, and in 1770 undertook the study of medicine in Strasbourg. Here Goethe came under the influence of Herder, who taught that the true spirit of a nation was evident in its folk poetry, that it was wrong for one country to imitate the*

literary styles of another, and that honesty, feeling, and the expression of emotion are the proper subjects of literature. Goethe fashioned his own early writings on these precepts of Herder, and inaugurated with The Sorrows of Young Werther *the Sturm und Drang (storm and stress) movement, which dominated German literature for years.*

In Werther *Goethe attempted to emphasize the power of sentiment and emotion and to disregard classical form and restraint. The character of Werther— sensitive, passionate, depressed, suicidal—became the model for romantic youth all over Europe. It is perhaps unnecessary to add that this book, which divided the generations as had nothing in memory, was sensationally controversial. Although* The Sorrows of Young Werther *strikes today's readers as mawkish, it retains some of its power and is fascinating as the first, and still the best, work of its sort. After 1775 the author spent most of his life at the court of Weimar, where he studied mathematics, optics, geology, and biology, and wrote poetry, drama, philosophy, autobiography, and his great masterpiece, the poetic drama* Faust, *which in its complete form was published in 1831, one year before the author's death. Goethe had long since abandoned the unrestrained romanticism of* Werther, *and had imposed classic disciplines on his later and more mature work; elsewhere, however, the impact of* Werther *continued to be strongly felt in the writings of the Romantic authors throughout the Western world.*

In May 1771 the young man Werther leaves home and goes to a province to   1
settle for his mother the tangled matters that surround an inheritance of hers. While in the country he writes letters to William, his friend at home, describing his impressions.

A would-be painter, Werther is enchanted with the countryside, and   2
spends hours wandering over fields, meadows, hills, and the banks of streams. His favorite place is Wahlheim, a hilltop community a little distance from where he is staying, and it is to Wahlheim and its unspoiled scenic beauties that Werther escapes whenever he can.

The young man is as delighted with the rustic people he encounters as   3
he is with their homeland. Tired of the pretensions and artificiality of city dwellers, Werther is refreshed by the simple, straightforward folk of the province, who care nothing for rank or wealth, but are willing to make friends with him for his own sake. One of the local people whom Werther finds particularly appealing is a young serving man who has fallen desperately in love with his employer, a widow considerably his senior. The lad's devotion to the woman, and his idolization of her charms and beauty, are touching to Werther, and stir profound feelings within him.

Werther forms no close attachments during the early part of his sojourn,   4
and though he is not unhappy, he does philosophize on the dreamlike quality of the world and of life itself. Nonetheless he is willing to mingle with people, and when a ball is given he willingly accepts an invitation.

It is at the ball that he meets for the first time the beautiful Charlotte S.,   5
daughter of a magistrate. He is instantly taken with Lotte's warmth, natural charm, and divine beauty. Glad that the young man to whom she is reportedly

engaged—one Albert—is away on an extended business trip, Werther passes the entire evening in transports of delight, dancing with Lotte whenever he can, keeping his eyes on her constantly.

The next day Werther goes to the home of Magistrate S. to pay a call.   6 There he finds Lotte taking care of her eight younger brothers and sisters (her mother is dead), and the simple, unaffected grace of this wholesome beauty fills Werther with rapture. He has found the woman of his dreams in Lotte, and he loves.

The next few weeks make Wahlheim seem like heaven to young Werther.   7 He spends as much time as possible with the girl, and it seems to him that with every one of his thoughts, with every one of his ideals, she is in complete accord. Their views on life, on literature, on art, on nature—all, all coincide. Werther is the happiest of mortals. By mid-July he is convinced that Lotte loves him in return . . . but whenever she mentions her absent betrothed, a shadow of doubt passes across his mind.

Werther's correspondent, William, taken aback by his friend's passionate   8 letters, urges the young man to accept an offered post traveling with the Ambassador. But young Werther refuses. Is not love a more profitable business to devote oneself to than politics—or even art?

In August, Lotte's betrothed, Albert, returns—and Werther finds him to be   9 a worthy, respectable young man. The two strike up a friendship, and young Werther continues to be as welcome in the S. household as before Albert's return.

The first time that Werther is in disagreement with Albert occurs when,   10 playing idly with a pair of Albert's pistols, Werther puts one of them to his temple. This leads to a discussion of suicide, which Albert finds wholly indefensible. Werther is unable to make his friend see his reasons for defending suicide as an action of manliness and courage; it is the painter's conviction that a man is no more to be censured for dying from suicide than for dying from disease. But Albert cannot accept this proposition. Werther recognizes how difficult it is for men to understand one another.

With Albert's return to Wahlheim, however, things cannot go along un-   11 changed, and Werther feels how completely—and how hopelessly—he is the slave of his love for Lotte. He is reduced to a state of restless indolence. He cannot paint. Even the kindness of Lotte and Albert oppresses him, for Werther does not enjoy the role of trusted friend. At last, frustrated beyond endurance, Werther decides to accept the post with the Ambassador and go away. Lotte and Albert bid him a fond goodbye, confident that they will see Werther again in the next world if not in this. With a passionate "Farewell!" Werther leaves them, his heart pounding violently in his bosom.

In October, Werther joins the Ambassador's entourage in a city distant   12 from Wahlheim, and throws himself into courtly life. But he and the Ambassador do not get along together at all. Werther finds life at court petty, foolish, and unsatisfying. Even the friendship of Count von C. and a flirtation with Fraulein von B. cannot keep the unhappy young man from thinking of the good people of Wahlheim, of the beautiful, fresh country scenery and atmosphere, and—of Lotte. He forces himself to continue in his post, but by March he cannot endure life away from Lotte any longer. When a foolish mistake leads to Werther's being branded as a social climber, he resigns his post and returns to Wahlheim.

When he goes to visit Lotte he finds that she has married Albert in Jan- 13 uary. He can now no longer regard Albert as a friend—Albert, whom God has seen fit to place by Lotte's side in a role that Werther alone was born to fulfill! At times Werther is at a loss to understand how Lotte can love her husband; at other times he thinks that she is divinely right for preferring her bourgeois, solid husband to himself, so unstable and emotional.

At this point Werther encounters again the young man who had so im- 14 pressed him when he first came to the province. The adoring serving lad tells Werther that he has been turned out of his mistress' house by the woman's jealous brother; nonetheless, says the young man, he will love the woman forever, even if he never sees her again. The young servant's passion finds an echoing response in Werther's breast.

When in September Albert is again called away on business, Werther be- 15 gins to pay calls upon Lotte with increasing regularity. Though the girl cannot help but be aware of the love she inspires, she is always careful to treat Werther as a good friend—nothing less, but nothing more. And with every look of friendship from Lotte, with every word of warmth, Werther's passion for her blazes more brightly.

Though he is happy when in Lotte's company, Werther is miserable when 16 away from her. He becomes a man obsessed, and his mind is constantly revolving around his unhappiness. He is in despair that he, who was born to give so much love, should be prevented from giving it by the unhappy accident of his beloved's having been already promised to another man. In his unhappiness Werther takes to rambling in the countryside at night, and he finds in the turbulent skies a sympathy with his own mood of depression.

One day, while out on one of his rambles, Werther meets a harmless 17 young madman, who rants about days of past happiness and glory. From the man's mother Werther learns that the happy days the man longs for were those when he was completely mad, and locked up in an asylum. Werther thinks deeply on the fact that this man is happy only in insanity. The next day Werther makes the alarming discovery that the young man had once been secretary to Magistrate S., and his passionate love for the magistrate's daughter—Lotte—is what has driven him to madness.

Now it seems to Werther that he cannot endure his misery any longer. 18 He is continually haunted and tortured by visions of Lotte. As for the girl herself, she can no longer avoid knowing what is obvious about Werther's feelings for her—and this knowledge frightens her. Lotte and Albert agree that they must become less intimate with young Werther.

One day, word comes that the young serving man whom Werther had be- 19 friended has been arrested for murder. He has killed the new servant of the employer whom he has so passionately loved. When Lotte, Albert, and Lotte's father excoriate the lad, Werther sees how completely out of sympathy he is with them. He is a man apart from the mainstream of life.

At last, determined to save herself from the embarrassment of Werther's 20 violent passion, Lotte tells him that he must not come to visit her until Christmas. Werther, destroyed by this order, takes leave of his beloved.

Now, a plan which has been floating half-formed through Werther's mind 21
takes definite shape, and Werther determines to kill himself. He writes a long
and passionate letter of farewell to Lotte, intending that it should be delivered
to her after his death. Then, he goes to take his leave of her in person.

It is the night before Christmas, and Lotte is startled at Werther's visit— 22
particularly since Albert is away from the house. Werther is strangely calm,
however, and soon Lotte agrees to let him read aloud to her passages from
Ossian which he has translated into German expressly as a gift for her.

As he reads, Lotte is aware of her own emotions, and she recognizes that, 23
in her heart, she has never wanted Werther to go away. Rather, she has
wanted to keep his love and his passion for herself.

Listening to Werther's low, steady voice, Lotte becomes caught up in the 24
passages he is reading—passages of love and death. Suddenly the two young
people are overcome with emotion. Werther falls to his knees and seizing
Lotte's hand, covers it with kisses. The girl sobs, pushes the young man away,
and flees from the room. But Werther has recognized the truth: she loves him!

In a strange state of elation, young Werther returns to his hotel and gives 25
orders that he is not to be disturbed until morning. The next day Werther
sends a servant with a note to Albert, begging the loan of Albert's pistols for
a trip Werther plans to take.

When she hears the request that has been made to her husband, Lotte 26
turns pale—but silently she obeys Albert and fetches the pistols to deliver to
the servant. Trembling, silent, terrified, Lotte returns to her needlework.

The next morning at six, the servant finds Werther lying on the blood- 27
soaked rug. He sends for a doctor, but it is too late. By noon Werther is dead.

A simple funeral is held, and Werther is buried between two favorite lin- 28
den trees. Albert finds himself incapable of attending the service, and of
course Lotte is not present. Workmen carry the body. There is no priest in
attendance.

*The following excerpt from Goethe's novel provides a sense of the style, tone,
and voice of the narrative. These letters occur early in the plot. The book opens
with the first letter, dated May 4, 1771. The excerpts are dated July 1771, at the
time when Albert has returned home and Werther is playing the role of the
trusted friend. Werther commits suicide in late December 1771.*

The Sorrows of Young Werther (excerpt)

Johann Wolfgang von Goethe

July 13th
No, I am not deceived—I can read true sympathy in her dark eyes. Yes, 1
I feel . . . and here I know I can trust my heart . . . that she . . . dare I, can I
express heaven in a few words? That she loves me.

Loves me. And how precious I have become to myself, how I—I can say   2
this to you, who have understanding for such emotions—how I worship at
my own altar since I know that she loves me!

Is this presumption or fact, I ask myself? I don't know the man who, I   3
fear, has a place in Lotte's heart, yet when she speaks of her betrothed with
so much warmth and love, then I am a man degraded, robbed of his honor,
title, and sword.

July 16th

Oh, how wildly my blood courses through my veins when, by chance, my   4
hand touches hers or our feet touch under the table! I start away as if from a
fire, a mysterious power draws me back, and I become dizzy . . . and in her
artlessness and innocence she has no idea how much such little intimacies
torment me. When she puts her hand in mine in the course of a conversation
and, absorbed by what we are talking about, draws closer to me, and the
heavenly breath from her lips touches mine . . . then I feel I must sink to the
ground as if struck by lightning. William, if ever I should presume to take advantage of this heaven on earth, this trust in me . . . you know what I mean.
But I am not depraved. Weak, yes, weak God knows I am . . . and can this
not be called depraved?

She is sacred to me. All lust is stilled in her presence. I can't explain how   5
I feel when I am with her. It is as if every nerve in my body were possessed
by my soul. There is a certain melody . . . she plays it on the piano like an
angel, so simply yet with so much spirit. It is her favorite song, and I am restored from all pain, confusion, and vagaries with the first note.

Nothing that has ever been said about the magic power of music seems   6
improbable to me now. How that simple melody touches me! And how well
she knows when she should play it, often at moments when I feel like blowing my brains out! Then all delusion and darkness within me are dispelled,
and I breathe freely again.

July 18th

William, what is life worth without love? A magic lantern without light.   7
All you have to do is put in the light, and it produces the loveliest colored pictures on a white wall. And if there is nothing more to it than these oh, so transient phantoms, always it denotes happiness when we stand in front of it like
naïve boys and are enchanted by the magical visions. Today an unavoidable
gathering prevented me from visiting Lotte. What could I do? I sent over my
servant, if only to have someone about me who had been near her! The impatience with which I waited for him and the joy, when I saw him return, are
indescribable! I would have liked to embrace and kiss him, but was, of
course, too ashamed.

They say that when the stone of Bonona is exposed to the rays of the sun   8
it attracts them and shines for a while into the night. That was how the boy
affected me. The idea that she had looked at his face, at his cheeks, at the
buttons on his waistcoat and the collar of his jacket, made every one of these
things sacred and invaluable to me. At that point I wouldn't have let anyone

have the boy for a thousand talers! I felt simply wonderful in his presence! Dear God, William, don't laugh at me! Do you suppose it is illusory to be so happy?

July 19th

I shall see her today! When I awaken in the morning and look blithely   9 into the sunlight, I cry out, "I shall see her today!" And I don't have another wish for the next twenty-four hours. Everything—everything, I tell you—is lost in this one anticipation!

July 20th

I can't agree with you that I should go to———with our ambassador. I   10 don't like subordination, and we know only too well that the man is obnoxious. My mother, you say, would like to see me actively employed. I have to laugh. Am I not actively employed now, and does it make any difference, really, whether I am sorting peas or lentils? Everything on earth can be reduced to a triviality and the man who, to please another, wears himself out for money, honor, what you will, is a fool.

July 24th

I realize that it means a great deal to you that I do not neglect my sketch-   11 ing, so I would rather say nothing at all about it except confess that I have not done much work since I met Lotte.

I have never been happier. My appreciation of nature, down to the most   12 insignificant stone or blade of grass, has never been more keen or profound, and yet . . . I don't know how to explain it to you. My powers of expression are weak and everything is so hazy in my mind that all contours seem to elude me. I tell myself that if I had clay or wax, I could shape them. And if this mood prevails, I shall certainly get hold of some clay and model it, even if all I turn out is a patty cake!

I have started three times to draw Lotte and three times made a complete   13 mess of it. This irritates me, because only a short while ago I was quite a good portraitist. So I did a silhouette of her, and that will have to suffice.

July 26th

Yes, dear Lotte, I shall attend to everything, only please give me more er-   14 rands to do and give them to me more often. And one more request: no more sand, please, on the little notes you write to me. Today I pressed your letter to my lips and felt the grains on my teeth.

July 26th

Every now and then I make up my mind to see her less often—as if any-   15 one could possibly adhere to such a rule! Every day I give in to temptation and swear that tomorrow I will stay away, but when tomorrow comes, I of course find an absolutely irresistible reason for going to see her, and before I know it—there I am! Perhaps it is because she said the evening before, "Will you be coming tomorrow?" So who could stay away? Or she asked me to attend to something, and I tell myself that the only proper thing to do is go personally to inform her that it has been done. Or the day is so beautiful that I go to Wahlheim and, once I am there . . . well, after all, she is only half an hour away, I am too close to her aura . . . whoosh! and I am there.

My grandmother used to tell a fairy tale about the Magnet Mountain: the 16
ships that came too close to it were robbed suddenly of all their metal, even the nails flew to the mountain, and the miserable sailors foundered in a crash of falling timber.

[July 30th]

Albert has come back, and I shall leave. He might be the best, the most 17
noble man in the world, and I would be glad to subordinate myself to him in any capacity whatsoever, but I would find it insufferable to see him take possession of so much perfection. To take possession . . . let it suffice, William . . . her betrothed has returned—a worthy, kindly man whom one simply has to like. Fortunately, I was not present when he arrived, it would have torn my heart to shreds. And he is an honorable man. Not once has he kissed Lotte in my presence. May God reward him for it! And I have to love him for the way he respects the girl. He seems to like me and I have the feeling that I have Lotte to thank for this rather than any impression of his own, because in things like that women have great intuition and they are right—it is always to their advantage to keep two admirers in harmony with each other, however rarely it may occur.

Meanwhile, I cannot help respecting Albert. His easy-going behavior 18
contrasts strangely with my restlessness, which cannot be concealed. He is a man of strong feelings and knows what a treasure he has in Lotte. He seems to be a man of good spirits too, and you know that, as far as I am concerned, moroseness is a man's greatest vice. He apparently takes me for a sensible fellow, and my devotion to Lotte, my warm pleasure in everything in which she takes part, only increases his sense of triumph and makes him love her more. I have no idea whether or not he sometimes plagues her with little outbursts of jealousy—we will have to leave that point undecided—but if I were in his shoes, I don't think I would be entirely free of this base emotion.

Be that as it may, the joyous days with Lotte are over. What shall I call 19
it? Folly? Delusion? It doesn't need a name. The dilemma speaks for itself. I knew all I know now before he came; I knew that I had no claim to her and demanded none, or let us say, I did not desire her more than one simply has to desire anyone so altogether lovely. And now, idiot that I am, I stare wide-eyed with astonishment at my rival, who has come at last to take the girl away!

I grit my teeth and scoff at my misery and would scoff even more if anyone 20
dared tell me to resign myself to the situation because there is nothing to be done about it. Just keep such straw men away from me! I tear through the woods and when I have gone as far as I can and find Lotte sitting beside Albert in the summerhouse in her little garden, I behave like an idiot and indulge in all sorts of absurdities. I don't even make sense! "For heaven's sake," she told me today, "please, I beg of you, no more scenes like the one in the garden last night. You are perfectly horrible when you are trying to be funny." Just

between you and me: I watch out for the times when he is busy and then . . .
whoosh, there I am and when I find her alone I feel perfectly wonderful!

August 8th

I assure you, dear William, that I did not mean you when I took those   21
men to task who demand from us resignation to an unavoidable fate. It never
occurred to me that you might be of the same opinion. And actually you are
right. But, my good friend, in this world things can be settled with an either-
or attitude only very rarely. Feelings and behavior overshadow each other
with an effect as varied as the difference between hawk- and pug-nose. So
you won't be offended with me, I hope, if I concede your entire argument and
try to squeeze through between the either and the or!

You say that I must "either" have hope of winning Lotte "or" I must have   22
none. Very well. In the first case I am to try to grasp the fulfillment of my wish
and make my hopes come true; in the second I am to pull myself together
and try to rid myself of this miserable emotion that must in the end utterly
debilitate me. Dear William, you put it so well, and it is easily advised. But
can you demand of an unfortunate human who is dying by inches of an insid-
ious disease that he should end his misery with one knife thrust? Wouldn't
you rather say that his misfortune weakens him to such an extent that it must
rob him also of the courage to rid himself of it?

Of course you might reply with an appropriate parable: who would not   23
rather sacrifice his right arm than lose his life through hesitation and despair?
I don't know. And don't let us settle it with parables. Enough! Yes, William,
sometimes I do have moments of surging courage to shake it all off, and then
. . . if only I knew whither . . . probably I would go.

*Werther was Goethe's first published narrative work. He went on to become one
of the leading men of letters not only of Germany but also of Europe. This passage from book 12 of his memoirs,* Poetry and Truth, *was written late in his
career. It describes the mood or state of mind that Goethe wanted to express in
his story. What if Werther had decided to go on with his life, and then met
up again with Charlotte in old age? Thomas Mann based a novel—*Lotte in
Weimar—*on the evening that Charlotte Kestner (the real-life Lotte, the object
of Goethe's youthful passion) spent with Goethe forty-four years after that summer of young love.*

Reflections on Werther (excerpt)

Johann Wolfgang von Goethe

. . . Werther's letters . . . probably enjoyed such a diversified popularity be-   1
cause the various events were first discussed in idealized dialogues with several individuals but then, in the composition itself, they are directed at one

friend and participant only. I don't think it would be advisable to say more about the treatment of this much-discussed little volume, but quite a bit remains to be told about the content.

A repugnance toward life has its physical and moral origins. We shall leave the explanation of the former to the doctor, of the latter to the moralist, and, in material that has been worked over again and again, let us pay attention to the salient point where this phenomenon expresses itself most clearly. All one's gratifications in life are based on the regular reappearance of external things. The change from day to night, of the seasons, of flower and fruit, and all the other things that confront us at regular intervals so that we may and should enjoy them—these are the actual wellsprings of our daily life. The more openly we avow these pleasures, the happier we are. But if these divers spectacles revolve in front of us and we take no part in them, then we are unreceptive to these precious gifts, then the greatest evil, the most dire sickness breaks out in us—we look upon life as a repulsive burden. There is the story of an Englishman who hanged himself because he didn't want to dress and undress himself any more. I knew a gardener, a stalwart fellow in charge of a big park, who in his bleakness cried out one day, "Am I to spend my whole life watching the rain clouds move from eve to morn?" And then I have heard tell of one of our best men that he hates to see the greening of springtime and wishes that, for a change, everything would come up red! All these are symptoms of a weariness of life that quite often culminates in suicide and is more prevalent among thoughtful introverts than one would care to believe.

Nothing, however, can further such a weariness of life as much as the repetition of love. First love is truly described as the only love, for in the second, and through the second, the emotion in its highest sense is already lost. The idea of forever and eternal—which is really what uplifts and sustains love—is destroyed, and it becomes a transient thing like all events that are repeated. The separation of its sensual and moral aspects, which in our confused civilization has split our loving and desiring sensations, also produces harmful exaggerations.

Furthermore, a young man soon becomes aware—if not in himself, then in others—of the fact that moral epochs change just as the seasons do. The graciousness of the great, the favor of the powerful, the promotion of those who are diligent, the adulation of the crowd, the love of an individual—all fluctuate without our being able to hold fast to any of them, any more than we can grasp the sun, moon, or stars. And these things are not all natural phenomena. They elude us through our own fault or the fault of others, by chance or by fate, but they change, and we can never be sure of them.

But what makes a sensitive youth most fearful is the irresistible repetition of his errors. Only too late does he recognize that in the cultivation of his virtues he at the same time raises his mistakes. The former rest on the roots of the latter as well as on their own, and the latter branch out in all directions, secretly but just as powerfully, and as varied as those that flourish in the open. Since we practice our virtues, for the most part, willfully and consciously, whereas our faults take us unconsciously by surprise, the former occasionally give us a little pleasure, but the latter worry and torment us constantly. And here lies the most intricate aspect of self-recognition, an aspect that makes it virtually impossible. Add to all this the turgid blood of youth, the powers of an imagination that is easily paralyzed, the imbalance of the day's motion—and the impatient urge to free oneself of the dilemma does not seem so unnatural.

Such dire reflections, however, that must lead him who gives himself up   6
to them to endless speculation, would not have developed so decisively in the hearts of German youth if an external inducement had not incited and encouraged him. And this was offered by English literature, especially English poetry, the excellencies of which are accompanied by a profound melancholy that it seems to pass on to anyone studying it. The intellectual Briton sees himself surrounded from his youth by a world of eminence that stimulates all his energies. Sooner or later he becomes aware of the fact that he is going to need all his thinking capacities to put up with it. How many English poets there are who led profligate lives in their youth and felt justified early in life in accusing all earthly things of being naught but vanity! How many tried to make their way in business, in parliament, at court, in the ministry, how many played prominent or secondary roles at embassies, participated in internal unrest, state and governmental changes, and had more sad than good experiences, if not with themselves, then with their friends and benefactors!

But even being only a spectator of such great events forces a man to take   7
life seriously, and where can such earnestness lead except to the contemplation of transitory things and an awareness of the worthlessness of all earthly matters? The German can be serious too. English poetry therefore suited him very well, and because it was conceived on such lofty heights, he found it impressive. A grandiose, vigorous, and worldly sagacity can be found in it, a profound and gentle spirit, a splendid will, a passionate activity—all glorious qualities for which the intellectual, erudite man can only be lauded, yet all these things combined do not make a poet. True poetry proclaims itself as a secular gospel in its ability to liberate us from the earthly burdens that oppress us by producing in us serenity and a physical sense of well-being. It lifts us and our ballast into higher spheres like a balloon, leaving the confused and labyrinthine path of our earthly meanderings below us in bird's-eye perspective. The liveliest and most serious works should have the same aim— to alleviate passion and pain through a felicitous and ingenious presentation. With this in mind, one should take a look at the majority of English poems, most of which are highly moral and didactic, and one will find that, for the most part, they display a dreary weariness of life. All English contemplative poems, even Young's "Night Thoughts," in which this dreariness has been gloriously realized, straggle off before you know it into such sad regions, where the mind is given a problem it cannot solve, where even religion, if the poet has any, does not help him. Volumes could be printed as a commentary to the dread verse:

Then old Age and Experience, hand in hand
    Lead him to death, and make him understand,

After a search so painful and so long,
That all his life he has been in the wrong.

What furthermore makes a complete misanthrope of the English poet and   8
spreads an unpleasant aura of repugnance against all things over his writing
is that, because of the numerous schisms in his communal existence, he must
dedicate if not his whole life then the better part of it to one political party or
other. Such a writer is not permitted to glorify his loved ones, to whom he is
devoted, or the cause he favors, because he might otherwise arouse ill will.
He therefore uses his talents to speak as harshly as possible of his opponent,
and satiric weapons, however adeptly used, always serve to sharpen and poison the atmosphere. When this takes place on both sides, the world that lies
between is destroyed, with the result that, in a great and intellectually active
nation, one finds at best nothing but folly or madness in their verse. Even the
most tender poem is concerned with sad subject matter. Here an abandoned
young girl is dying, there a faithful lover drowns or, swimming as fast as he
can, is eaten by a shark before he can reach his beloved. And when a poet
like Gray settles down in a village churchyard and starts to sing the same old
melody, he can be sure of attracting a following among the friends of melancholy. Milton, in "Allegro," must first dispel all gloom with some violent verse
before he can arrive at a very moderate measure of joyful expression, and
even our blithe friend Goldsmith loses himself in elegiac sentiments in his
"Deserted Village" when he lets his "Traveler" cross the face of the earth to
find a lost Eden, which the author describes very beautifully, but sadly.

I do not doubt that it would be possible to confront me with lively and   9
gay English poems as well, but most of the best of them belong to an older
epoch, and the latest ones that might be included tend toward satire, are bitter, and especially lack a respect for women.

Suffice it to say that the more general, serious poems mentioned above,   10
which tended to undermine human nature, were our favorites. We picked
them out from among all others. One person, according to his personality,
chose the lighter lament, another sought a more oppressive despair that was
ready to sacrifice all. Strangely enough, our father and teacher, Shakespeare,
who knew so well how to spread brightness, also helped to increase our
gloom. Hamlet and his monologues remained ghosts that haunted us. We
knew the main parts by heart and loved to recite them, and every one of us felt
he had to be just as melancholy as the Prince of Denmark, even if he hadn't
seen a ghost and didn't have a royal father to avenge.

But in order that all this melancholy might not lack a suitable setting, it   11
was left to Ossian to lure us to a final Thule, where we wandered across gray,
unending moors, amid prominent, moss-covered gravestones, surrounded by
grass that was being eerily swept by the wind, and looked up into a sky that
was leaden with clouds. This Caledonian night became day only in the
moonlight. Defunct heroes and wan maidens hovered around us until, in the
end, we really thought we could see the terrible shape of the spirit of Loda.
In such an atmosphere, with fancies and studies of this nature, tortured by un-
satisfied passion, with no external inspiration to do anything really important,

our only prospect to succumb, in the end, to a dreary, uncultured, bourgeois existence—we began to think kindly of departing this life should it no longer seem worth living, or at any rate of doing so whenever it suited us. Thus we helped ourselves meagerly over the wrongs and boredom of the day. Sentiments such as these were so universal that *Werther* had to have the powerful effect it did, because it touched every heart and depicted the innermost workings of a sick youthful madness openly and comprehensibly. The following lines attracted little attention and were written before the publication of *Werther,* but they prove how well acquainted the English were with this type of misery.

> To griefs congenial prone
>   More wounds than nature gave he knew
> While misery's form his fancy drew
>   In dark ideal hues and horrors not its own.

Suicide—however much may already have been said or done about it— 12 is an event of human nature that demands everyone's sympathy, and it should be dealt with anew in every era . . . .

FOR DISCUSSION AND WRITING: ANALYZING THE TUTOR TEXT: *WERTHER*

1. The previous archive includes samples of three different versions of *Werther:* a plot outline, the narrative itself (in the form of letters), and the author's reflections about the work. What effects does each create? What is the difference in knowledge and experience between the plot outline that describes the entire story and the narrative sample of the novel itself? Imagine that you are an examiner for a national testing service. Write a set of questions based on the archive that would be a good measure of a student's grasp of the material.

2. Part of the interest of *Werther* as the "tutor text" for Barthes's study is that the novel is autobiographical. Goethe identified with his protagonist, whose story fictionalized a life experience from Goethe's own youth. As Goethe wrote in a letter to his friend Eckermann, speaking of Werther, "This is another one of those creatures whom, like the pelican, I have fed with the blood of my own heart . . . there were special circumstances close at hand, urgent, troubling me, and they resulted in the state of mind that produced Werther. I had lived, loved, and suffered much." Goethe was surprised by the response to *Werther*—not just by its popularity but also that the young people of Germany at the beginning of the Romantic period seemed to draw the wrong lesson from Werther's suicide. Goethe's attitude toward life was positive, optimistic, declaring that "however it may be, life is good." His own response to unhappy love was not suicide but literary achievement. He demonstrated the wisdom of storytellers who know that bad experiences make for good stories. Test

this wisdom yourself by composing an anecdote about a bad dating experience you have had that demonstrates the difficulties of courtship.

3. Although we live in an era characterized as "postmodern," which supposedly is far removed in its sensibility from the "age of sentiment" in which Goethe lived, the fact is that readers' response to *Werther* in its day resembles in our day the response of fans to entertainment celebrities—stars of music and movies. *Werther*'s fans imitated the character's wardrobe of blue frock coat and yellow waistcoat. If anything, the extent to which life imitates art has been augmented considerably by modern mass media. Conduct a survey in your class, or among your friends and peers, to discover to what extent their codes of dress and behavior are influenced by popular media culture. Write a short analysis of the results, judging for yourself the influence of fad and fandom on personal style among your peers and in your own case.

4. In the segment titled "Reflections on Werther" (taken from Goethe's memoirs, *Poetry and Truth*), Goethe states that "suicide . . . is an event of human nature that demands everyone's sympathy, and it should be dealt with anew in every era." As Howard Rheingold once pointed out, the self-destructive behavior of the generation that admired *Werther* has recurred in other times and places, such as the epidemic of suicides supposedly touched off in the 1930s by Billie Holiday's recording of "Gloomy Sunday." We have our celebrity suicides in our own time, as in the case of Kurt Cobain. Suicide is one of the leading causes of death among young people today, especially young men. *Dead Poets Society* is a film that dramatizes the circumstances leading to a student's suicide. Do you think this problem receives the kind of attention it deserves in the press, school, or other forums? What is the cultural or social attitude toward suicide? Do you know of any cases of suicide or similarly extreme problems in your local community or through press reports from other communities? How were the stories treated in the media? Were they sensationalized? explained away? investigated? used as moral lessons? What social or counseling services are available in your community or school for individuals with emotional problems?

5. *Werther* is an epistolary novel, composed as a body of letters covering a period of about a year and a half (May 1771 to December 1772), mostly sent to one friend, William. The art of letter writing nearly disappeared from modern literacy because of such innovations as the telephone. However, with the Internet and e-mail, the "letter" is once again a common practice. Compare the literary letters of *Werther* with the e-mail style of today's listservs and chat sessions. If Werther were living in America now rather than in Germany in the 1770s, how would his correspondence with William differ? Imagine that you are William, and write a series of posts in your e-mail style replying to Werther's letters. Start an imaginary "flame war" with your friend.

6. In his "Reflections," Goethe describes the "world weariness," or "*Weltschmerz*," that informed the general state of mind or mood of his era, and

he attributes this feeling to the influence of English poetry. A commentator who notes the recurrence of *Weltschmerz* at different historical moments in different nations points out that all the characters had at least one thing in common: they were often the sons (and sometimes daughters) of wealthy families and therefore free to indulge themselves in emotional states. "Weltschmerz, in other words, is often a disease of the healthy and wealthy" (Rheingold 116). Part of the interest of the observation is just the fact that a historical moment may be experienced in terms of an overriding mood. The advertisers and pundits who categorize generations as "X" and "Y" seem to be looking at least for some unifying attitude, if not a common state of mind. Do you notice any shared feeling or attitude toward life or the world among your friends? What about your own state of mind: could you describe it in terms of some consistent feeling or attitude? According to some observers, mass media culture has appropriated the words *cool* and even *funk* from African-American and street culture and promoted them as indicative of a national mood. Do you agree? Compose a text in which you attempt to define your own state of mind or consistent emotional attitude as you go through your daily routine.

ROLAND BARTHES: THE FRAGMENT

Roland Barthes must be counted the most characteristic and important French intellectual of the structuralist generation that gained worldwide attention starting in the 1960s. By the time of his death in 1980 at age sixty-five—when he was still very much in the midst of a rich and evolving literary career—he was a best-selling author and professor at the College de France, that pinnacle of French intellectual institutions. Yet Barthes as intellectual authority cut a curious figure. He detested all forms of authority, worried about the power wielded by the teacher, and described his main subject, literature, as "a grand imposture which allows us to understand speech outside the bounds of power, in the splendor of a permanent revolution of language."   —Peter Brooks

One of Roland Barthes's principal contributions to the practice of textuality was the idea that critical and creative writing are essentially the same—that the old distinction separating fact and fiction, truth and imagination, is less important than the more general condition in which all experience (science as well as art) is equally mediated by language. To explore the consequences of this insight, Barthes developed a hybrid essay combining aspects of critical analysis and artistic expression. One of the texts resulting from this procedure is *A Lover's Discourse: Fragments*.

The poetic or artistic dimension of *Fragments* includes the telling of a love story. The story or anecdote at the heart of this text focuses on the *crisis* or *critical* moment of the love affair. While waiting for the beloved to keep their date at a café (in vain, as it turns out: the beloved stands him up), the lover reads a famous Romantic novel, *The Sorrows of Young Werther*, by Goethe. He begins to compare his own unhappy situation with the story of unrequited love recounted in the novel, which ends with the suicide of the protagonist, Werther. Attempting to free himself from the pain of rejection and jealousy, the lover-reader here decides to end the affair.

This story is never told directly in *A Lover's Discourse*, only in fragments distributed throughout the text, cast in the frame of the lover's meditations. The critical or analytical dimension of *Fragments* thus consists of Barthes casting this highly emotional experience into a collection of stereotypes and clichés that appear in all such love stories. He distances himself from the strong emotions by ordering or classifying the elements of the experience in a scientific manner. Part of his purpose is to identify those aspects of our personal, private attitudes and actions that are in fact directed by public, social, and cultural conventions and beliefs (ideology). He hopes in this way to combine in one text the effects of truth and beauty.

Barthes himself provided a set of instructions at the beginning of *Fragments* itemizing the rhetorical components of his experiment, which could be summarized as follows—as in Pratt's inventory (pp. 2–11) of the parts of a natural narrative.

A. Selecting the figures:

   1. Each separate fragment ("Waiting," "The Heart," etc.) is one *figure, pose,* or *topic.* The lover's situation includes a set of poses that anyone who enters into a dating relationship is likely to employ. Like the "character contests" described by Goffman (pp. 42–44), courting is a "ritual" process. With the term *pose,* Barthes alludes not only to "role playing" but also to dance figures, a standardized set of movements with which a choreographer might design a ballet.

   2. A figure in the lover's discourse is recognizable to the extent that it is something clearly outlined as *memorable.* "You know you have a figure when you can say 'That is so true: I recognize that scene of language.'"

B. Writing the figures:

   1. Each figure or topic has a *title* (e.g., "Show me whom to desire"), a *heading* (e.g., "induction"), and an *argument* (e.g., "The loved being is desired because another . . ."). The point of departure for a figure is always something the lover might *say,* even if only to himself or herself, perhaps only unconsciously, in that situation (hence the *discourse*). The argument is a paraphrase *describing* that saying. The figures are arranged in alphabetical order, according to

the spelling of the headings (hence the translator had to retain the French—*cacher* comes before *coeur*).

2. Of the body (numbered paragraphs), the following may be observed:

   a) Only the topic headings and arguments are general. The meditations or reflections recorded within each topic will be specific to each user of the discourse, who must fill in the figure with his or her own experience (thoughts, feelings, actions) of the pose.

   b) The figures do not tell the love story, but instead record the "asides" that might accompany the story, as if one had kept a running commentary on one's experience (not in the manner of a diary, but an analysis, like the color commentary that embellishes the action of a sports broadcast).

   c) The content of the commentary in the body is drawn from a combination of three areas of reference, each acknowledged briefly in the margins:

      (1) a primary work of art (Goethe's *Sorrows of Young Werther* in this case) relevant to the concerns of the discourse

      (2) the speaker's specialized culture (schooling, training)

      (3) the speaker's everyday life culture—popular arts, mass media experience, conversations with friends, and the like

From A Lover's Discourse: Fragments

Roland Barthes

Here are six complete "figures" from Barthes's text. As you read them, notice the regular structure (title, heading, argument,· and body) and the irregular or flexible size and shape of the body itself. The regular structure directs and stimulates writing; the flexible body allows the writer to stop when he has nothing more to say. As you read, think about how your own meditations on these figures would be different if they were governed by different cultural and personal experiences.

So it is a Lover who Speaks and who Says:

Waiting

attente / waiting

Tumult of anxiety provoked by waiting for the loved being, subject to trivial delays (rendezvous, letters, telephone calls, returns).

1. I am waiting for an arrival, a return, a promised sign. This can be futile, or immensely pathetic: in *Erwartung (Waiting)*, a woman waits for her lover, at night, in the forest; I am waiting for no more than a telephone call, but the anxiety is the same. Everything is solemn: I have no sense of *proportions*.   *Schön-berg*

2. There is a scenography of waiting: I organize it, manipulate it, cut out a portion of time in which I shall mime the loss of the loved object and provoke all the effects of a minor mourning. This is then acted out as a play.

The setting represents the interior of a café; we have a rendezvous, I am waiting. In the Prologue, the sole actor of the play (and with reason), I discern and indicate the other's delay; this delay is as yet only a mathematical, computable entity (I look at my watch several times); the Prologue ends with a brainstorm: I decide to "take it badly," I release the anxiety of waiting. Act I now begins; it is occupied by suppositions: was there a misunderstanding as to the time, the place? I try to recall the moment when the rendezvous was made, the details which were supplied. What is to be done (anxiety of behavior)? Try another café? Telephone? But if the other comes during these absences? Not seeing me, the other might leave, etc. Act II is the act of anger; I address violent reproaches to the absent one: "All the same, he (she) could have . . ."

"He (she) knows perfectly well . . ." Oh, if she (he) could be here, so that I could reproach her (him) for not being here! In Act III, I attain to (I obtain?) anxiety in the pure state: the anxiety of abandonment; I have just shifted in a second from absence to death; the other is as if dead: explosion of grief: I am internally *livid*. That is the play; it can be shortened by the other's arrival; if the other arrives in Act I, the greeting is calm; if the other arrives in Act II, there is a "scene"; if in Act III, there is recognition, the action of grace: I breathe deeply, like Pelléas emerging from the underground chambers and rediscovering life, the odor of roses.   *Winni-cott*   *Pelléas*

(The anxiety of waiting is not continuously violent; it has its matte moments; I am waiting, and everything around my waiting is stricken with unreality: in this café, I look at the others who come in, chat, joke, read calmly: they are not waiting.)

3. Waiting is an enchantment: I have received *orders not to move*. Waiting for a telephone call is thereby woven out of tiny unavowable interdictions *to infinity*: I forbid myself to leave the room, to go to the toilet, even to telephone (to keep the line from being busy); I suffer torments if someone else telephones me (for the same reason); I madden myself by the thought that at a certain (imminent) hour I shall have to leave, thereby running the risk of missing the healing call, the return of the Mother. All these diversions which solicit me are so many wasted moments for waiting, so many impurities of anxiety. For the anxiety of waiting, in its pure state, requires that I be sitting in a chair within reach of the telephone, without doing anything.

4. The being I am waiting for is not real. Like the mother's breast for the infant, "I create and re-create it over and over, starting from my capacity to love, starting from my need for it": the other comes here where I am waiting, here where I have already created him/her. And if the other does not come, I hallucinate the other: waiting is a delirium.

Winni-
cott

The telephone again: each time it rings, I snatch up the receiver, I think it will be the loved being who is calling me (since that being should call me); a little more effort and I "recognize" the other's voice, I engage in the dialogue, to the point where I lash out furiously against the importunate outsider who wakens me from my delirium. In the café, anyone who comes in, bearing the faintest resemblance, is thereupon, in a first impulse, *recognized.*

And, long after the amorous relation is allayed, I keep the habit of hallucinating the being I have loved: sometimes I am still in anxiety over a telephone call that is late, and no matter who is on the line, I imagine I recognize the voice I once loved: I am an amputee who still feels pain in his missing leg.

5. "Am I in love?—Yes, since I'm waiting." The other never waits. Sometimes I want to play the part of the one who doesn't wait; I try to busy myself elsewhere, to arrive late; but I always lose at this game: whatever I do, I find myself there, with nothing to do, punctual, even ahead of time. The lover's fatal identity is precisely: *I am the one who waits.*

(In transference, one always waits—at the doctor's, the professor's, the analyst's. Further, if I am waiting at a bank window, an airport ticket counter, I immediately establish an aggressive link with the teller, the stewardess, whose indifference unmasks and irritates my subjection; so that one might say that wherever there is waiting there is transference: I depend on a presence which is shared and requires time to be bestowed—as if it were a question of lowering my desire, lessening my need. *To make someone wait:* the constant prerogative of all power, "age-old pastime of humanity.")

E.B.

6. A mandarin fell in love with a courtesan. "I shall be yours," she told him, "when you have spent a hundred nights waiting for me, sitting on a stool, in my garden, beneath my window." But on the ninety-ninth night, the mandarin stood up, put his stool under his arm, and went away.

The Heart

coeur / heart
> This word refers to all kinds of movements and desires, but what is constant is that the heart is constituted into a gift-object—whether ignored or rejected.

Winnicott: *Playing and Reality.*
E.B.: Letter

1. The heart is the organ of desire (the heart swells, weakens, etc., like the sexual organs), as it is held, enchanted, within the domain of the Image-repertoire. What will the world, what will the other do with my desire? That is the anxiety in which are gathered all the heart's movements, all the heart's "problems."

2. Werther complains of Prince von X: "He esteems my mind and my talents more than this heart of mine, which yet is my one pride . . . Ah, whatever I know, anyone may know—I alone have my heart." *Werther*

You wait for me where I do not want to go: you love me where I do not exist. Or again: the world and I are not interested in the same thing; and to my misfortune, this divided thing is myself; I am not interested (Werther says) in my mind; you are not interested in my heart.

3. The heart is what I imagine I give. Each time this gift is returned to me, then it is little enough to say, with Werther, that the heart is what remains of me, once all the wit attributed to me and undesired by me is taken away: the heart is what remains *to me,* and this heart that lies heavy on my heart is heavy with the ebb which has filled it with itself (only the lover and the child have a heavy heart).

(X is about to leave for some weeks, and perhaps longer; at the last moment, he wants to buy a watch for his trip; the clerk simpers at him: "Would you like mine? You would have been a little boy when they cost what this one did," etc.; she doesn't know that *my heart is heavy within me.*)

Images

image / image
>   In the amorous realm, the most painful wounds are inflicted
>   more often by what one sees than by what one knows.

1. ("Suddenly, coming back from the coatroom, he sees them in intimate conversation, leaning close to one another.")

The image is presented, pure and distinct as a letter: it is the letter of what pains me. Precise, complete, definitive, it leaves no room for me, down to the last finicky detail: I am excluded from it as from the primal scene, which may exist only insofar as it is framed within the contour of the keyhole. Here then, at last, is the definition of the image, of any image: that from which I am excluded. Contrary to those puzzle drawings in which the hunter is secretly figured in the confusion of the foliage, I am not in the scene: the image is without a riddle.

2. The image is peremptory, it always has the last word; no knowledge can contradict it, "arrange" it, refine it. Werther knows perfectly well that Charlotte is betrothed to Albert, and in fact only suffers vaguely from the fact; *Werther*

but "his whole body shudders when Albert embraces her slender waist." *I know perfectly well* that Charlotte does not belong to me, says Werther's reason, *but all the same,* Albert is stealing her from me, says the image which is before his eyes.

3. The images from which I am excluded are cruel, yet sometimes I am caught up in the image (reversal). Leaving the outdoor café where I must *leave behind* the other with friends, I *see myself* walking away alone, shoulders bowed, down the empty street. I convert my exclusion into an image. This image, in which my absence is reflected as in a mirror, is a *sad* image.

A romantic painting shows a heap of icy debris in a polar light; no man, no object inhabits this desolate space; but for this very reason, provided I am suffering an amorous sadness, this void requires that I fling myself into it; I project myself there as a tiny figure, seated on a block of ice, abandoned forever. "I'm cold," the lover says, "let's go back"; but there is no road, no way, the boat is wrecked. There is a *coldness* particular to the lover, the chilliness of the child (or of any young animal) that needs maternal warmth.

Caspar David Friedrich

4. What wounds me are the *forms* of the relation, its images; or rather, what others call *form* I experience as force. The image—as the example for the obsessive—is *the thing itself.* The lover is thus an artist; and his world is in fact a world reversed, since in it each image is its own end (nothing beyond the image). . . .

"I want to understand"

comprendre / to understand
> Suddenly perceiving the amorous episode as a knot of inexplicable reasons and impaired solutions, the subject exclaims: "I want to understand (what is happening to me)!"

1. What do I think of love?—As a matter of fact, I think nothing at all of love. I'd be glad to know *what it is,* but being inside, I see it in existence, not in essence. What I want to know (love) is the very substance I employ in order to speak (the lover's discourse). Reflection is certainly permitted, but since this reflection is immediately absorbed in the mulling over of images, it never turns into reflexivity: excluded from logic (which supposes languages exterior to each other), I cannot claim *to think properly.* Hence, discourse on love though I may for years at a time, I cannot hope to seize the concept of it except "by the tail": by flashes, formulas, surprises of expression, scattered through the great stream of the Image-repertoire; I am in love's *wrong place,* which is its dazzling place: "The darkest place, according to a Chinese proverb, is always underneath the lamp."

Reik

REIK: Quoted in *Fragments of a Great Confession.*

2. Coming out of the movie theater, alone, mulling over my "problem," my lover's problem which the film has been unable to make me forget, I utter this strange cry: not: *make it stop!* but: *I want to understand* (what is happening to me)!

3. Repression: I want to analyze, to know, to express in another language than mine; I want to represent my delirium to myself, I want to "look in the face" what is dividing me, cutting me off. *Understand your madness:* that was Zeus' command when he ordered Apollo to turn the faces of the divided Androgynes (like an egg, a berry) toward the place where they had been cut apart (the belly) "so that the sight of their division might render them less insolent." To understand—is that not to divide the image, to undo the *I,* proud organ of misapprehension? *Sympo-sium*

4. Interpretation: no, that is not what your cry means. As a matter of fact, that cry is still a cry of love: "I want to understand myself, to make myself understood, make myself known, be embraced; I want someone to take me with him." That is what your cry means. *A.C.*

5. I want to change systems: no longer to unmask, no longer to interpret, but to make consciousness itself a drug, and thereby to accede to the perfect vision of reality, to the great bright dream, to prophetic love. *etymol-ogy*
(And if consciousness—such consciousness—were our human future? If, by an additional turn of the spiral, some day, most dazzling of all, once every reactive ideology had disappeared, consciousness were finally to become this: the abolition of the manifest and the latent, of the appearance and the hidden? If it were asked of analysis not to destroy power (not even to correct or to direct it), but only *to decorate* it, as an artist? Let us imagine that the science of our *lapsi* were to discover, one day, its own *lapsus,* and that this *lapsus* should turn out to be: a new, unheard-of form of consciousness?)

Blue Coat and Yellow Vest

habit / habiliment
> Any affect provoked or sustained by the clothing which the subject has worn during the amorous encounter, or wears with the intention of seducing the loved object.

1. Because of a forthcoming encounter—one I anticipate with exaltation—I dress very carefully, I perform my toilet with every scruple. This word has only "official" meanings; not to mention the scatological usage, it also designates "the preparations given to the prisoner condemned to death before he is led to the scaffold"; or again, "the transparent and oily membrane *Littré*

A.C.: Letter.
ETYMOLOGY: The Greeks opposed ὄναρ (*onar*), the vulgar dream, to ὕπαρ (*hypar*), the prophetic (never believed) vision. Communicated by J.-L.B.

used by butchers to cover certain cuts of meat." As if, at the end of every toilet, inscribed within the excitation it provokes, there were always the slaughtered, embalmed, varnished body, prettified in the manner of a victim. In dressing myself, I embellish that which, by desire, will be spoiled.

Sympo-
sium

2. Socrates: "I therefore have decked myself out in finery so that I might be in the company of a fine young man." I must resemble whom I love. I postulate (and it is this which brings about my pleasure) a conformity of essence between the other and myself. Image, imitation: I do as many things as I can in the other's fashion. I want to be the other, I want the other to be me, as if we were united, enclosed within the same sack of skin, the garment being merely the smooth envelope of that coalescent substance out of which my amorous Image-repertoire is made.

Werther

3. Werther: "How much it cost me to make myself give up the very simple blue coat that I was wearing the first time I danced with Lotte; but it had finally worn out altogether. So I had had another one made, absolutely identical to the first . . ." It is in this garment (blue coat and yellow vest) that Werther wants to be buried, and which he is wearing when he is found dying in his room. Each time he wears this garment (in which he will die), Werther disguises himself. As what? As an enchanted lover: he magically re-creates the episode of the enchantment, that moment when he was first transfixed by the Image. This blue garment imprisons him so effectively that the world around him vanishes: *nothing but the two of us:* by this garment, Werther forms for himself a child's body in which phallus and mother are united, with

Lacan

nothing left over. This perverse outfit was worn across Europe by the novel's enthusiasts, and it was known as a "costume à la Werther."

Identifications

identification / identification
> The subject painfully identifies himself with some person
> (or character) who occupies the same position as himself in
> the amorous structure.

Werther

1. Werther identifies himself with every lost lover: he is the madman who loved Charlotte and goes out picking flowers in midwinter; he is the young footman in love with a widow, who has just killed his rival—indeed, Werther wants to intercede for this youth, whom he cannot rescue from the law: "Nothing can save you, poor wretch! Indeed, I see that nothing can save us." Identification is not a psychological process; it is a pure structural operation: I am the one who has the same place I have.

2. I devour every amorous system with my gaze and in it discern the place which would be mine if I were a part of that system. I perceive not analogies but homologies: I note, for instance, that I am to X what Y is to Z; everything I am told about Y affects me powerfully, though Y's person is a

matter of indifference to me, or even unknown; I am caught in a mirror which changes position and which reflects me wherever there is a dual structure. Worse still: it can happen that on the other hand I am loved by someone I do not love; now, far from helping me (by the gratification it implies or the diversion it might constitute), this situation is painful to me: I see myself in the other who loves without being loved, I recognize in him the very gestures of my own unhappiness, but this time it is I myself who am the active agent of this unhappiness: I experience myself both as victim and as executioner.

(It is because of this homology that the love story "works" — sells.)

3. X is more or less desired, flattered, by others than by me. Hence I put myself in their place, as Werther is in the same place as Heinrich, the mad- *Werther* man with the flowers, who has loved Charlotte to the point of madness. Now, this structural analogy (certain points are arranged in a certain order around one point) is readily imaginable in terms of personality: since Heinrich and I occupy the same place, it is no longer merely with Heinrich's place that I identify myself, but with his image as well. A hallucination seizes me: *I am Heinrich!* This generalized identification, extended to all those who surround the other and benefit from the other as I do, is doubly painful to me: it devalues me in my own eyes (I find myself *reduced* to a certain personality), but it also devalues my other, who becomes the inert object of a circle of rivals. Each, identical with the others, seems to be shouting: *Mine! mine!* Like a mob of children arguing over a ball or any other object; in short, over the fetish thrown into their midst.

The structure has nothing to do with persons; hence (like a bureaucracy) it is terrible. It cannot be implored — I cannot say to it: "Look how much better I am than H." Inexorable, the structure replies: "You are in the same place; hence you are H." No one can *plead* against the structure.

4. Werther identifies himself with the madman, with the footman. As a reader, I can identify myself with Werther. Historically, thousands of subjects *Werther* have done so, suffering, killing themselves, dressing, perfuming themselves, writing as if they were Werther (songs, poems, candy boxes, belt buckles, fans, colognes à la Werther). A long chain of equivalences links all the lovers in the world. In the theory of literature, "projection" (of the reader into the character) no longer has any currency: yet it is the appropriate tonality of imaginative readings: reading a love story, it is scarcely adequate to say I project myself; I cling to the image of the lover, shut up with this image in the very enclosure of the book (everyone knows that such stories are read in a state of secession, of retirement, of voluptuous absence: in the toilet). *Proust*

PROUST: (The orris-scented toilet, in Combray) "Intended for a more particular and more vulgar purpose, this room . . . long served as a refuge for me, doubtless because it was the only one where I was allowed to lock the door, a refuge for all my occupations which required an invincible solitude: reading, daydreaming, tears, and pleasure."

FOR DISCUSSION AND WRITING:
COMPOSING AN IDENTIFICATION

1. For each of Barthes's six figures, identify the areas of reference drawn upon by the writer. Adapting Barthes's system to our own purposes, it will be useful to classify these references into three broad categories: (a) literature, classical music, fine art; (b) popular culture, including music, proverbs or clichés, films, and advertising; and (c) personal experience, including both things that have happened and things that have been said to the lover. When you understand Barthes's method, you will be in a position to adapt it to your own writing. As a first step toward that understanding, select one of Barthes's figures and replace its body with your own numbered paragraphs. Begin by jotting down notes from your own cultural repertory: books, films, TV, things you have heard or said that have to do with the figure you have selected. Then, using your notes for inspiration, compose your own meditation on your chosen figure.

2. We have reprinted only six figures from the eighty in Barthes's book. Assuming that the lover's discourse Barthes describes is shared by many people in Western cultures, try to add some of the missing pieces of this scenario. Make a list of some of the other objects, events, and expressions that constitute the lover's "scenes of language." In class discussion, try to construct the argument that should go with each figure. As a group, begin to list some of the cultural items that would help you compose the bodies of these figures. You can only go so far with this as a group project, because at some point the general cultural discourse (all lovers) must be supplemented by your personal repertory of texts (your own experiences as stored in memory).

3. One way to test the validity and value of an experiment is to see if it is replicable, or if it is applicable to other problems or issues. Write a set of figures, titled *Fragments of a Student's Discourse,* modeled after Barthes's *Fragments,* applying Barthes's form and procedure to the discourse of the student. You are to write about the conventions and stereotypes of the student experience, identifying the conventions and clichés, figures and poses, myths and expectations of the student life. Do for the student's life*style* what Barthes did for the lover's style of conduct. Use the following questions to guide your extrapolation from the lover's to the student's discourse:

   Are any of the figures used in the lover's discourse also relevant to the student's discourse? Of the ones that might be directly translatable across discourses, do they mean the same thing, or function the same way, in both contexts? Some of the figures may not be directly transferable but might have equivalents in the new setting. For example, if the heart is the organ of love sentiment, would the brain be equivalent for the student's situation? What does it mean to *be* "a brain"? Is this the same as *having* one? Can a student be too brainy? What are the sources of a student's anxiety, hope, joy, pain? What are the crucial moments or events in a student's life? Where does this scene of life and language begin? Where does it end? What objects are important to a student? What words, phrases, sayings, and clichés preside over our lives as students?

4. The fragments amount to units of intertextuality, with Barthes gathering together within each pose a set of references drawn from different institutions of the "popcycle." Distributed among these citations are allusions to a number of methodological statements. Collect as many of these comments as you can find in which Barthes explains some aspect of what he is trying to do—the purpose of his text as inquiry. The other useful inventory to make is of the features or aspects of Werther's story that Barthes chose to include. The method of identification does not require complete "realism"—exact objective correspondence between the object of study and the text of bliss. Rather, his approach resembles that of the advertisers he studied, such as the pasta makers who attempted in their ads to evoke an aura of "Italianicity" by means of a few carefully chosen signifiers. Or as Barthes said in his text on Japan (*The Empire of Signs*), "I am not lovingly gazing toward an Oriental essence—to me the Orient is a matter of indifference, merely providing a reserve of features whose manipulation—whose invented interplay—allows me to 'entertain' the idea of an unheard-of symbolic system, one altogether detached from our own" (Barthes 1982:3). To get a sense of the method in our case, we may substitute the word *Werther* for *Orient* in the previous statement.

5. The major assignment in this section is simple to state: reproduce Barthes's fragments study using your own "image repertoire" and intertext, applied to a work of literature with which you identify. It might be useful to open up these specifications somewhat, to expand the object of study to other media, such as cinema, television, or music. The theme need not be "love" but may concern any point of connection between your personal experience and the object of study. Narratives are structured around problems—the character desires something that obstacles and opponents prevent him or her from obtaining. This narrative conflict may be juxtaposed with a problem drawn from any of the areas of identity formation: class, ethnicity, gender, and the like. An important methodological point to note, since it is not self-evident in Barthes, is that the connection may in fact be figurative rather than literal. The object of study may provide a metaphor or analogy that, when juxtaposed in the fragments with the personal situation, produces an image of the mood or state of mind that colors your experience of the world (living at home was like being a replicant in *Blade Runner*, as more than one student has proposed). The point is not that you already know what that mood is (whether it is *Weltschmerz*, *cool*, or something else—even something that has no name), but that the research of the story shows you a condition that you "recognize" as true about yourself. In short, the text may contain pieces (fragments) of documentary arguments or narrative anecdotes, but the overall text works as a metaphor.

FRAGMENTS OF IDENTIFICATION: A GUIDE

The following list breaks down the previous suggestions into a set of "ingredients" and a "recipe," or the procedure for composing a research text. Feel free to modify these steps and add others of your own. The goal is to transform Barthes's tutor text into the prototype for a genre of research text.

1. The "ingredients" for this research text include the following:
   a. An incident from the past that sticks in your memory
      Reflect on memories of growing up, from early childhood through high school graduation. Think of a specific incident or event that comes to mind without too much effort. One technique for locating a good incident to work with is to make a list of the ideological categories of identity (gender, class, ethnicity, race, religion, sexuality, nationality). Our society has an ideal set of expectations for how these categories are to be fulfilled, but almost no person fits the ideals. Reflect on any incident that expresses your sense of a lack of fit between you and the ideal of one of these categories. Who was enforcing the ideal (from what institution: family, church, school, peer group, popular media)? The incident may be modest, not necessarily dramatic, but just a symptom of tension between your reality and the ideal expectation. Another way to select the incident is to think of a turning point in your experience, some event that marked a choice, a decision, perhaps a realization only in retrospect that you passed a crossroad and took one path and not the other.
   b. A story
      The story may be in any genre and medium—book, movie, television, song, or comic book. One way to select the story is to find one that you remember, that stuck in your memory for whatever reason, something that you read, saw, or heard while you were growing up. Another approach is to select a story that you have not read but that is considered an important work of literature or art.
2. The "recipe" or procedure for composing the text
   a. One option is to emulate the form of Barthes's *Fragments*. Review the outline in the introduction to *A Lover's Discourse*, "Writing the figures." Organize your text as a series of figures, including all the elements: topic and title, numbered paragraphs, with your choice of story and personal incident, supplemented by your "specialized culture." A good resource for the asides based on

specialized culture is *Text Book* itself. Your text then creates an assemblage based on associations that you draw among your story, the life incident, and the readings of *Text Book*.

b. A good way to work with an unfamiliar story is to adapt the technique of Method acting. The narrative of the story is organized by a conflict. The protagonist desires something, and there is some obstacle preventing the fulfillment of the desire. If you were going to act the part of this character using the Method, you would produce a personal emotional memory to help define your performance. Compose your text as an assemblage of fragments, juxtaposing the details of the story conflict with the details of an incident from your own experience that may be associated emotionally with the story problem. It is not that your experience is the same as the one in the story, but that there is some common thread linking the two. For an actor the common thread is an emotion. If the character is angry or afraid, the actor thinks of some experience involving anger or fear and uses sensory details of that memory to understand the feelings of the character.

c. A third possibility is to reverse the direction of emotional understanding from that used in the Method. After deciding on the personal experience, select a story that reveals or expresses the feeling or state of mind that you remember or associate with the personal experience. There is no need to name the feeling in abstract or conceptual terms; the point is to recover or locate the feeling through the act of writing. The form again is an assemblage based on Barthes's *Fragments*. The basic devices are juxtaposition, repetition, and variation, assembled to produce a kind of "allegory" relating the life experience to the story problem. In this case, however, there is likely to be just one figure—the metaphor between you and the story. For example, suppose the book is Melville's *Moby Dick,* and the memory concerns your first summer job. You would not necessarily make an explicit comparison ("The boss paced in his kitchen like Ahab on the deck of the *Pequod*") but instead use concrete language to record selected details from the two domains, so that the comparison could emerge indirectly.

3. As an alternative to using the figures formula from Barthes's *Fragments,* produce a new form or recipe from the examples collected in the archive. Analyze each example to locate its procedures for relating a life experience to a story. Collect these devices into a set and restate them as instructions for making a research text. Then

follow your own instructions, using your own life incident and preferred story.

ARCHIVE: TEXTS OF IDENTIFICATION

This section includes a sample of texts of pleasure and bliss by critics
who are working the same territory as Barthes. Together they show some
of the possibilities of research by identification and, in so doing, prove at
least that such a method exists and enjoys some important advocates.
Each one could be generalized into a genre, as we have done with *A Lover's
Discourse,* and thus provide a model for the major assignment we gave at
the end of the previous section. The larger purpose of the sample is to
gain some practice with writing a "poetics"—a set of heuristic rules for
generating a research text. No one of the samples contains all possible
features, and each one manifests the "rules" in ways that are specific and
peculiar to itself. Together they show a pattern that we call "mystory," as
discussed in the beginning of this chapter.

Rapunzel across Time and Space

Connie Porter

Connie Porter, a novelist who lives in Virginia, is the author of The All-Bright
Cafe. *This selection is collected in* Mirror, Mirror on the Wall: Women Writers
Explore Their Favorite Fairy Tales, *ed. Kate Bernheimer (New York: Anchor,
1998).*

*Despite what Einstein says about the impossibility of time travel, the barrier of the
speed of light, I've traveled through time. Maybe that is why I don't expect questions about baldheaded girls. It would seem that black girls would be beyond that
now, especially these girls, wealthy and privileged and beautiful. It would seem they
would not be part of the cult of Rapunzel, paying homage to some girl in a fairy
tale. . . .*

Baldheaded. This word flew through a restaurant in a country club I was in   1
recently. Spoken by one of a group of young black girls I was dining with, it
sailed stealthily. An invisible boomerang. Purposeful. Well-aimed. It quietly
whizzed above our water glasses, bowing the heads of the candle flames,
pulling laughter up the slender throats of the girls.

   Baldheaded is one of those encoded words. It is one of *our* words. A   2
black word. You can look it up in a dictionary, but you will not find the mean-

ing that we have wrapped it in. For those girls and me, that word did not mean someone with no hair, or some man who is balding on top. This is what it meant:

baldheaded a. *referring to a black female with very short, especially kinky, hair.*

The girl who had flung the word that night in the restaurant explained to me that she only wanted me to answer a question—why the character Sarah in a children's book I'd written was baldheaded. She and her friends thought the question was funny. The whole notion that a girl whose hair was no longer than the snap of a finger, whose hair was so nappy, so kinky, so picky, so beady, so woofy, so wooly, so rough, would be given such a prominent role in a book probably would have seemed laughable to me when I was their age. And what would have seemed even more outlandish was that Sarah *was not* the comic relief. She was not the butt of all the children's jokes because of her hair, but rather was intelligent and compassionate and skipped some mean double dutch to boot.

If I had come across a character like Sarah when I was a girl, I would   3
have been stunned. I don't recall seeing black girls in the books when I was little in the late sixties. I read about Pippi and her long stockings, the Strawberry Girl and Ramona—that pest. If I had found Sarah in a book, I would have loved her. Secretly. Gone to the bookmobile and checked out over and over every book she appeared in. Read them at night in bed with one of my sisters. Stared at her face so much like mine, finding her secretly beautiful. But I would have wondered the same thing the girl in the restaurant wondered.

My hair was long, in two thick braids that fell past my shoulder blades.   4
Why couldn't Sarah's hair be like mine? Pretty. I knew my hair was pretty because it was long, not because of what my mother said, or what my father said. Because I never heard them say that. It was comments from girls in the projects where we lived, girls at school, who made it clear to me that my sisters and I and other girls with long, thick hair had pretty hair. Nice hair. We did not have "good" hair. Because good hair was something you were born with. It was hair that was naturally straight or curly. My sisters and I all got our hair pressed with a hot comb. So all our hair could aspire to was being pretty, and for me, that was enough. Pretty hair.

Sarah could have had that, I would have thought. Long braids shiny with   5
grease. The author could have given her braids tied with ribbons or affixed with shiny barrettes the way my mother did my hair. I would have thought that, not knowing the straightening comb had not been invented until this century, well after the time the books Sarah is in are set. I would have thought that the author made a mistake by making her baldheaded, but never said that to the author if I ever met her.

My parents are Southerners, and like many Southerners, they raised my   6
siblings and me to be unfailingly respectful and polite to both children and adults. They did not approve of us throwing encoded words around, certainly never at a dinner table, and not even in the wilds of the school playground

where it seems a child would like to throw them. I would have kept my feelings about Sarah hidden in my heart with my other secret—my love for Robert, a boy with skin like copper, who sat in the front row of my fourth-grade class. I would not have been open about the way I felt about Sarah because at ten, even at eight, I knew the connotations of baldheaded. Not only was Sarah's hair ugly, she was ugly, unlovable, deserving of ridicule. I knew these as facts of life. They were truths, like the rising sun in the east and the inconstant face of the moon shining in my window at night. I don't know when I learned them, on what day I sat down and was told about girls like Sarah, the direction of the rising sun, the fickleness of the shining moon. But I knew. On the playground and in the alleys around my house, I heard girls who looked like Sarah told to "Get out of here with your ugly, baldheaded self." I saw them dismissed, heard them dismissed, not for something they ever did, or said, but just for *being*. I never called those girls names, but I was capable of laughter like the girls in the restaurant. I could giggle along with those girls who knew how to throw well. Girls who could have been raised in the outback two hundred years ago, in a world created in the Dreamtime.

The restaurant I was sitting in, a virtually all-white country club one of   7
the girls' family belonged to, was a world hundreds of light-years removed from the world I grew up in. In all my nights of dreaming as a girl, I never dreamt this world, never dreamt these girls. Despite what Einstein says about the impossibility of time travel, the barrier of the speed of light, I've traveled through time. Maybe that is why I don't expect questions about baldheaded girls. It would seem that black girls would be beyond that now, especially these girls, wealthy and privileged and beautiful. It would seem they would not be part of the cult of Rapunzel, paying homage to some girl in a fairy tale whose story they might not even remember well.

I know I don't always remember fairy tales well. I remember bits of sto-   8
ries, trolls, straw spun into gold, poison apples, witches, wicked stepmothers, handsome princes. Rapunzel, I'm sure of, is about hair. The girl has long hair and meets a handsome prince who sees her hair shining golden in the forest, climbs it, falls in love with her and later marries her. They go on to live happily ever after. End of story. But when I went and reread the story recently, I discovered I knew less than I even thought.

The fairy tale does not even begin with Rapunzel. It begins with her par-   9
ents, a barren couple who have all but given up hope of having a child. The mother sees some rapunzel, a bitter lettuce growing in a witch's garden. The father, seeking to please his wife, goes and gets some for her. At night he scales the wall surrounding the witch's garden and gets his wife the rapunzel. He even returns a second night for more. This is when he is caught by the witch and she makes him promise to give her the child the wife will bear. He swears he will and keeps the promise once the child is born. The witch names the child Rapunzel.

Rapunzel is very beautiful with golden hair. The witch takes her off to the   10
middle of the forest when Rapunzel is twelve. She locks her in a tall tower that has a window only at the very top. The only way the witch can reenter the tower is by Rapunzel's hair. Rapunzel ties it onto the window latch and

the witch climbs up. One day, a young prince is out in the forest and hears Rapunzel singing. He is moved by her voice, finds the tower, but can't figure out a way to enter it. He returns the next day and hears the witch call to Rapunzel to let down her hair. Once the witch leaves, he does the same and meets Rapunzel. He wants to marry her and take her away, but Rapunzel reminds him there is no way for her to leave the tower. She tells him to bring skeins of silk and she will make a ladder. One day, Rapunzel tells the witch that when the prince comes to see her, he does not pull her hair as hard as the witch does when she climbs. In a fit of anger, the witch cuts Rapunzel's hair and sends her away. The witch then attaches the hair to the window latch and when the prince comes, she tells him he will never see Rapunzel again. Distraught, the prince jumps from the tower window. His fall is broken by a patch of brambles that scratch his eyes out. The prince wanders for years until he comes to a desert, the place Rapunzel has been banished to. She is now the mother of twins, a boy and girl. The prince hears her voice and he follows it. Rapunzel recognizes him. She cries and her tears cure his blindness. The prince takes her back to his kingdom and they live happily ever after. End of the story.

This is the end of the real tale, not the one I remembered. It has left me 11 angry with the father, a thief of a man who steals from the garden of a known witch, not once, but twice. Sure it is to please his wife, but they would have all been better off if he had given her some arugula he bought at a farmers' market. This foolish man then has the nerve to give away a child he and his wife have longed for. It is best that the story jumps then to Rapunzel, sparing us the grief of her parents, both their mouths made bitter by their longing for Rapunzel, the daughter they will never know.

I'm amazed by two things about Rapunzel's life in the forest. One is the 12 length of her hair. I knew that it was long, but I had forgotten its length — twenty ells. That's seventy-five feet! I can't imagine how many pounds that is, or where she actually kept all that hair before she let it down. The other thing that amazes me is that the prince is *not* attracted to Rapunzel's hair. He is not even attracted to her face, a crescent of it shining in the corner of the window, the fullness of it hovering above a canopy of leaves. It is Rapunzel's voice that brings him to her. It is the beauty of her soul that makes him want to ascend the tower.

The prince is attracted to what he cannot see, what he cannot touch. He 13 is not attracted to the beauty of Rapunzel's hair. It is not an end; it is merely a means, a way of climbing into her life. That is why even after throwing himself out of a seventy-five-foot tower and having his eyes scratched out, the prince is able to recognize Rapunzel again.

Rapunzel's tears are very powerful, restoring sight to a man who has no 14 eyes. Perhaps their power comes from Rapunzel's lifetime of sorrow — being given away by her father to a witch, locked in a tower, having her head shorn, being banished to a desert, living in misery with a set of twins fathered by whom? The girl has truly suffered and deserves some happily ever after, especially since she has found a man willing to accept two children whom he may not have fathered. He deserves his sight back and Rapunzel deserves all seventy-five feet of her hair back, coiled around her head like the rings of Saturn, trailing behind her like the tail of a comet. I hope as the story ends, Rapunzel has her hair, a reminder of the time she has traveled, the space she crossed to come to a life that may seem like a dream come true to someone looking at it from the outside but from the inside looks nothing like a world she dreamt, but one that should have been all along.

I hope the children I spoke to in the restaurant study Rapunzel's life, re-   15
member the details of it better than I did. They are still young and most likely will grow out of their fascination with long hair. I grew out of mine in college when I realized not only had I never gotten Robert all those years ago, that I had never gotten Henry or John or Dennis or Craig while I was in college. They may do like me, not wait for any witch. I went to the hairdresser and had her cut my hair off. I was sick of relaxing it, of combing it, of using it to pull men up into my life. Having my brains pulled out, bit by bit, little by little. There was no way I wanted to end up some vapid, shallow woman with an ell of a lot of hair but nothing underneath it. I had the hairdresser make me bald-headed and when she spun me around to look in the mirror to see what I saw of her creation, I did not have to hold the secret inside. I thought I looked quite fine. That my hair looked pretty. That it looked good. It was good.

My hair is now more of an accessory than anything else. Since college   16
I've let it grow back and cut it again, let it grow back and cut it again. Now it is growing back, getting long again. I straighten it with a hot comb, or jump in the shower and let it get good and nappy, good and woofy and wooly and rough. I braid it, twist it, or wear it in a big nappy ball on the top of my head. When I feel like being baldheaded again, I will go to a hairdresser and make it so, knowing that not only do some little black girls dismiss baldheaded women, sometimes grown black men do also. But that is all right with me because there is a day in every woman's life when she hears a voice inside herself that tells her what she needs to do, that tells her what needs to come out and be heard, even if it is only from a tower, only in a forest. And if any man is wandering by and hears it, he had better have a ladder and the strength to endure the power of her tears.

This is not the kind of thing you can say to a child who asks a simple   17
question. *Why is Sarah baldheaded?* The girl who asked it is still shedding baby teeth. You have to answer a question like that simply. Speak like a child. You have to say, I wanted Sarah to have short hair because I thought she looked beautiful that way. I saw a picture of a girl taken just before slavery ended. She was dark, thin and had very short hair. She had big dark eyes that looked sad and I thought she was a very beautiful little girl. That is what you say. What goes unsaid is what a child of that age cannot understand.

When I saw that girl with those eyes, I thought her face as beautiful as   18
the dark side of the moon. The side we never see because we are told the moon rotates and revolves at the same time. Because it has this captured rotation, we are told, the moon always keeps the same side toward Earth. Being one who has traveled through time, I don't think the scientists' story is true. I think they have bad memories and maybe have forgotten parts of their own tale.

Maybe, once upon a time, the moon did show her other face, proudly,   19
boldly, for just one night. It shone down on Earth below just as the other side
does, bathed in silver light, brilliant in its fullness. But this face was dismissed for *being* what it was not—just like the other side. Since that night the
moon turned that face forevermore into the darkness of space refusing to let
anyone on Earth see it and was called fickle. She was hurt by being made fun
of, for being called fickle and sang out her sorrow from the dark side of her
face. People hear her voice on windless nights. Part of a chorus people used
to call the music of the spheres. Its beauty haunts us, draws us to look up
into the sky at night.

We want to hear her voice more clearly, but the moon will never turn its   20
other face to us again. We will have to cross time and space to pull ourselves
into her life, make a ladder of our own hair. Nappy. Curly. Straight. Braided.
Dreaded. We will have to shave our own heads, all of us become baldheaded
and beautiful, weaving a ladder that stretches to her to hear the full beauty
of her voice, to see the beauty of the face cloaked in darkness. We will feel
the power of her tears as they fall into our eyes. Though not blind, we will see
that she was never the one who was fickle. We were. Then we will all live
happily ever after. End of story.

FOR DISCUSSION AND WRITING:
EMBLEMATIZING IDENTITY

1. Porter's use of the tale of Rapunzel to explore an event in her own experience overlaps with some of the work in the earlier chapters. She recognizes a connection between an identity category in her experience and
   the fairy tale. Look back at the earlier exercises in chapter 3 and analyze
   Porter's essay in terms of transforming, completing, interpreting, and
   identifying with the tale. How does her treatment of "Rapunzel" compare
   with Russell Banks's discussion of *Bambi?*

2. The point of departure for the essay—the insult associated with the term
   "baldheaded"—is a good example of the existence of subcultural codes
   in the society, created out of the specific experience of those living within
   given categories of identity formation. In the post–civil rights era, we are
   more aware of the importance of difference and the fact that not everyone in the society shares the same "position" or the same values. In fact,
   one of the continuing political and ethical dilemmas of our society is the
   breakdown of communication that sometimes arises when these differences are ignored. Polls show that whites and blacks have quite different
   perceptions about race relations in America. One example is the different response that students have to Mark Twain's *Huckleberry Finn,* depending on their race and ethnicity. Can you think of other examples of
   terms (other than the familiar slurs each group applies to the other) from
   everyday language or slang that carry coded meanings for a subculture?
   What slang terminology do you use yourself? What is the source for this
   terminology (peers, TV, clubs)?

3. Inventory the different aspects of identity categories treated in this essay, and discuss how each one is introduced and how they add up to a whole. For example, race, gender, and class, and perhaps even sexuality, seem to be involved. Is one more important than the others? An important element of mystory that is present here but not prominently so is "history." How does Porter bring history into the mix of discourses?

4. Make an inventory of your own identity categories, noting especially what material attributes tend to characterize or even stereotype your position in each of the different categories. See if you can reproduce Porter's insight by finding a fairy tale or legend that provides a kind of "emblem" for the dominant or preferred attributes, status, or behavior for that category (the equivalent of the "cult of Rapunzel" for hair).

History of an Encounter: Alias Olympia

Eunice Lipton

In what could be considered an example of "herstory," the art historian Eunice Lipton demonstrates the possibility of the researcher openly identifying with the object of study, but in a way that puts in question, rather than simply reproducing, the dominant values of the discipline. Researchers probably have always identified with their objects of study, but the conventions of objectivity prevented them from admitting this or even recognizing it. Herstory has produced some of the most innovative work of our time and is a major force in the transformation of the humanities, not only in its politics but also in its methodologies. The feminist slogan—"the personal is political"—has been extended to disciplinary research, with artists leading the way into a new mode of study.

An example of the artistic practices that anticipate Lipton's personal approach to research is the "artist's book" Extraordinary/Ordinary by May Stevens, which the artist describes as "a collage of words and images of Rosa Luxemburg, Polish/German revolutionary leader, theoretician, and murder victim (1871–1919) juxtaposed with images and words of Alice Stevens (born 1895–   ), housewife, mother, washer and ironer, inmate of hospitals and nursing homes." To compose this "juxtaportrait," Stevens researched the life and works of Luxemburg, gathering such materials as "thoughts from intimate notes sent from prison to her comrade and lover, Leo Jogiches, and to her friends; from agit-prop published in Die Rote Fahne; *and from her serious scientific writings. Images from her girlhood, her middle life, and the final photograph of her murdered head." The point to emphasize is that before Stevens could use the historical figure of Rosa Luxemburg as a metaphor for her feelings about her mother, she had to do some conventional research in the library. What is new here is the application of the research to emotional and poetic rather than strictly informational ends.*

Eunice Lipton's feminist politics led her to shift her attention away from the "author" (Manet) of a famous painting ("Olympia") and away from the abstract form of the painting (the approved method of her discipline) to focus instead on the life of the artist's model. Lipton's research into the life and career of the model, Victorine Meurent, is conducted explicitly as an analogy for understanding the researcher's own condition as a woman and as a professional. The form of the research is a narrative recounting Lipton's travels and interviews as she tracked down information about the elusive Meurent.

I don't remember when I first saw Victorine Meurent, but I wouldn't have rec-   1
ognized her or known her name at the time. No one would have. She was just another naked woman in a painting. Maybe I remarked that the man who made the picture was called Manet or that the work itself was named *Olympia,* but that would have been it. When I was at college in the late 1950s, works of art were considered things of beauty. Period. One would never pay attention to a painting's literal content. One wouldn't even risk noticing that De Kooning's *Woman II* had a woman in it.

Even as I became a professional art historian in the 1960s, the look of   2
Olympia did not change. The naked white woman on the bed seemed like any odalisque, Venus, or Danaë—idealized flesh made into art. I was taught to appreciate Manet's particularly modern vocabulary, his tonal contrasts, flattened spaces, outlined forms, that is, his fundamentally abstract intentions. It was Manet who was placed first in the pantheon of modernist painting; we were told that before anyone else, he had seen people and events for what they really were: abstract pictorial forms.

But one day in 1970, try as I may, I could not shake the feeling that there   3
was an event unfolding in *Olympia* and that the naked woman was staring quite alarmingly out of the picture. I could not make her recede behind the abstract forms I knew—I had been taught so fervently to believe—were the true content of the work. Her face kept swimming forward, her eyes demanded attention. I saw that unlike other naked women in paintings, Olympia did not drape herself suggestively upon her bed, or supplicate prospective lovers, or droop resignedly. Nor did she smile flirtatiously. Rather she reigned imperiously, reclining upon silken pillows, her steady gaze a dare, her tight little body and proprietary hand an omen. Now I could see that even the stilted pose of the black maid and overarching cat gave the lie to scenarios of seduction. Olympia, alert and dignified, resembled a noble consort on an Etruscan funerary monument far more than an inviting Greek or Oriental courtesan. This was a woman who could say "yes," *or* she could say "no."

Her contemporaries knew this in the nineteenth century though they didn't   4
say it in so many words. In fact, Manet was greatly distressed over how his painting was received; he even considered destroying it. What happened was this. In May of 1865 *Olympia* was exhibited in the Salon, the official exhibition forum of the time. The press took an instant and bellicose dislike to the work, using words like: "The vicious strangeness of [this] . . . woman of the night"; "a sort of female gorilla, a grotesque. . . ." "Such indecency! . . ." Before anyone knew what was happening, respectable Parisians were sweeping through the Salon's drafty halls brandishing walking sticks and umbrellas;

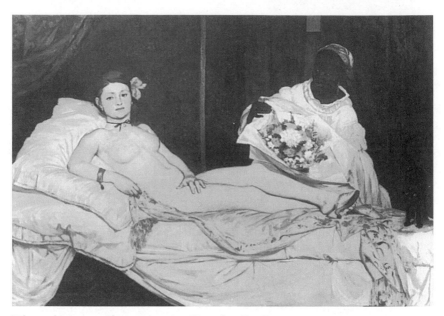

Edouard Manet. *Olympia,* 1863. Giraudan/Art Resources,
New York, New York.

they were heading toward *Olympia* with murder on their minds. The authorities were taken aback, and took the unprecedented step of cordoning off the
painting. But the damage was done. Manet fled to Spain thinking: Titian
had done it, so had Giorgione and Velazquez—he meant painted naked
women—why is everyone so angry at me? This may have been the first time
in modern history that a painting incited people to such public agitation. . . .

I can't say when it was exactly that my wonder about Olympia and the   5
treatment she received turned to impatience, but I began to hear the ram-
paging walking sticks and umbrellas, and to feel the heat and rage the painting produced in commentators, the barely contained anger squeezed into
stylish commentary about artist-geniuses and their pathetic models. I know
it was about the same time that I met Linda, and also read an article in the
Village Voice entitled "The Next Great Moment in History Is Theirs." In it,
Vivian Gornick wrote that "women in this country are gathering themselves
into a sweat of civil revolt. . . . [Their] energy . . . lies trapped and dormant
like a growing tumor, and at its center there is despair, hot, deep, wordless. . . .
[They have been] deprived . . . of the right to say 'I' and have it mean something. This understanding . . . underlies the current wave of feminism. It is
felt by thousands of women today, it will be felt by millions tomorrow."

The next thing I knew I was throwing Kate Millett's *Sexual Politics* across   6
the room, demanding, "How can this be true, this silencing of women, this
enforced invisibility? And what the hell did that professor mean when he said
I had too many ideas?"

Then it was August 26, 1970, and a march was called to commemorate   7
the Nineteenth Amendment to the Constitution, the establishing of women's
right to vote. I went with my friend Marcia. We made our way to Fifth Avenue
and Fifty-ninth Street. As we approached, what we saw took our breath away.
Women were everywhere—thousands and thousands and thousands of
women. Marcia grabbed my arm and said the oddest thing: "What *would* my
mother have made of this?" I wouldn't have thought of my mother at such a
moment. I never thought of my mother as a woman.

But what a sight the avenue was, women filling all the spaces, banishing   8
the cars, the honking, the men. How we gazed upon each other. With what
amazement and pleasure we talked and laughed and wept as we flooded that
capacious boulevard. And with what confidence we lured the hesitant from
the sidelines. How they fell into the arms of the river that we became that
day, we women of all shapes, sizes, and ages marveling at each other.

We also handed each other leaflets and flyers that said: "Join the Na-   9
tional Organization of Women!" "Come to meetings of Redstockings" ". . . The
New York Radical Feminists" ". . . The Feminists!" And we did. We met in
churches, in school rooms, in libraries. Then in each other's homes. We organized by neighborhood, ten to twelve in a cadre. We met weekly, and we
talked our hearts out. We divulged secrets we didn't know we had. Nothing
was off limits. We talked about sex and orgasm, ambition, marriage, homo-
sexuality, our fathers, our siblings, our mothers. The rage at our families, our
lovers, our teachers was staggering. And maybe for the first time in our lives,
we turned that fury on to the world, away from ourselves.

The listening, the uninterrupted speaking, made us realize how smart we   10
were, and how inhibited. For most of us, this talking—this consciousness-
raising—was the first time we heard each other speaking discursively and
analytically about our lives. Bit by little bit, our talking, our weeping, and our
anger added up to an emotional and political history. And a strategy.

What better emblem for the time—those opening salvos of the Women's   11
Movement—than *Olympia*, a woman whose naked body said: "See this? It's
mine. I will not be the object of your gaze, invisible to my own. This is my
body, my life."

Yes, I marveled at the intricate psychological drama surrounding *Olympia*,   12
which on the one hand elicited men's attraction—so many had written *something* about her at a time when models were usually nameless and invisible—
but on the other provoked ridicule and contempt. *All that writing about her.*
In our own time, in 1977, an entire book on *Olympia* written by Theodore
Reff, and again in 1985, T. J. Clark, the most dazzling bad boy in the Art History community, published a notably long, obfuscating, and tortured essay
on *Olympia* in his book on Manet. Every prominent scholar of nineteenth-
century art planted himself in front of her, writing paraphernalia at hand. All
thought their engagement disinterested, but it wasn't. They circled her from
above, close up, on top. What did they mean to do with all those words? Describe her? Analyze her? Situate her? *Or:* Possess her? Control her? Silence
her? No one admitted his emotions, neither the irritation nor the fascination.

None could acknowledge what amounted to a professional obsession that spanned a century and a half. And continues.

More and more I brought Meurent up in my classes as if I could some- 13 how redress the balance by at least speaking her name, acknowledging her corporeality as Victorine Meurent, a real woman of the nineteenth century. Musingly, I'd say, "Some day I'm going to find this woman," and the more I said it, the more I meant it. It became a promise. I took her to myself, unconsciously, unwittingly. That face, those eyes. I wanted what she had: her confidence, her dignity, her "no."

Many things came between us though. My career for one, books and ar- 14 ticles about geniuses—Picasso, Degas, Manet. And my own ambivalent self stuck in a conservative profession. And a culture that enjoined girls to behave themselves. Plus—I rationalized—all I know is Meurent's name, that she worked for Manet, traveled to the United States, exhibited a few times at the Paris Salon. She was only a model. What is there really to say?

I had no idea what the ramifications of the search would be. I didn't even 15 realize that our names were the same: "Eunice" is a translation from the Greek of "Evnike"; it means "Happy Victory." And I certainly didn't *intend* to end up a redhead. All I knew was that I envied Meurent her autonomy even as I acknowledged the paradox that I was a well-paid American professor in the late twentieth century, and she was a working-class model in nineteenth-century Paris. I was convinced that she had had more choices than I, and that she had acted on them. The dare of her gaze was the proof.

As I set out in earnest to find Meurent, I kept losing my way. A two-step 16 of desire and longing crossed by withdrawal and passivity. I had learned this dance as a child, but coming of age in the era of McCarthyism, Eisenhower, and Doris Day refined it immeasurably. Across this faraway history I started looking for Meurent.

This is the record of my search.   17

* * *

It's clear to me that if I want to find out more about Meurent's life and 18 locate the paintings, I must discover the location of her death in 1928 and find the death certificate with a list of her surviving relatives. The only route left is to search the public record in all twenty arrondissements. My hunch is that she died in or around Montmartre or some other northern or northeastern part of the city. Certainly on the Right Bank, but away from the center. Then I think that perhaps, since she lived to the age of eighty-four, she might have died in a hospital in any part of the city. That's why I decide to go to each and every one of the twenty Mairies—each quarter's seat of government.

This search is a desperate move on my part, as I can go to the Mairie at 19 Hôtel de Ville and have them survey the records of the city. I'm not sure why I'm not doing that. Maybe I don't trust them. Or maybe walking suits me; map in hand, I can cruise the city. Or maybe it will just take me longer to discover that there's nothing to find.

This is the routine I work out. I enter the Mairie and go to the section 20 called État-Civil. Usually a clerk at some point acknowledges my presence, comes up and asks me what I want. I smile and say: "I have reason to believe that a certain woman of some renown died in this arrondissement in 1928." If it seems appropriate, I show the person postcard reproductions of *Olympia* and the *Déjeuner sur l'herbe:* "Yes, she was the woman Manet painted here. She was also a painter herself." Either I bore them or, more often than I anticipate, they say, "Oh, I didn't know that," and are genuinely interested. Then, I hand them a three-by-five card with Meurent's name and *"décédée 1928"* written on it. "Could you at the same time, please, also check under marriages? Thank you so much." I wait. I try not to look eager or nervous. I know distress would upset the clerks; the French have a low tolerance for loss of self-control. But each and every time my body temperature shoots up, my gut twists, my heart knocks about in my chest.

The first Mairie I visit is in the Ninth Arrondissement, the section called   21
Opéra. It contains so many of the streets where artists lived, ate, and amused themselves in the late nineteenth century, streets like Nôtre Dame de Lorette, rue des Martyrs, rue Pigalle, boulevard de Clichy, boulevard de Rochechouart, the latter two divided, with the uneven numbers in the Ninth, the even in the Eighteenth. I suppose, finally, the Ninth is classier, more bourgeois than the Eighteenth. Degas, for example, always lived in the Ninth; he couldn't have lived in the Eighteenth. Valadon lived in the Eighteenth. So, I start in the Ninth. The address of the Mairie is 6, rue Drouot.

It's a rainy day when I go. I take the Métro to Richelieu-Drouot, exit, and   22
pick my way down the street. It's lunchtime — animated talking, gesticulating, eating everywhere. Crêpes with confiture; quiches with ham and cheese; brioches and croissants; roasting chestnuts. I try to maneuver unobtrusively with my umbrella, resolutely *not* looking at the food vendors. Finally I arrive at the Mairie and read the instructions. Happily, there are always instructions: *Escalier A* for . . . *Escalier B* for . . . Then a dingy courtyard. The dull lights behind the large windows provide no comfort. I get confused and climb the wrong staircase. A clerk's grimace reroutes me. I arrive at the right place, pull out my three-by-five card, ask my questions, and wait.   23

Nothing.

I went back to magazine illustrating after America. I also took some draw-   24
ing classes with Mlle Rousseau and sometimes dropped in on Alfred
Stevens's women's studio. That's why people often saw us together; I
was never romantically interested in him. He was a prude parading as
a dandy. The most exciting thing I did then was find myself an apart-
ment near Montmartre, at 191, rue du Faubourg Poissonnière. It was
on the border between the Ninth and the Tenth. I wanted to move to the
north of the city for a long time. I liked the openness of Montmartre,
and the mix of people, and the bars. It felt easy there. People said
Montmartre was stained with blood after the Commune; they called it
***enragé.* It appealed to me. I was a little *enragée* myself.**

A year later I moved further into Montmartre, to 1, boulevard de   25
Clichy, on the corner of rue des Martyrs. What a location! And what
a building! Up and down Martyrs there were bars and restaurants open

day and night. It was possible for women to frequent them alone any time and find the company of other interesting women. My building had a few two-storey studios, although I didn't have one. I had two small-ish rooms, but one was big enough for a large painting, and for parties. I loved to dance.

Many interesting people lived in that building, too. Up on the third 26 floor next door to me were two Danish girls. One did the books for a publishing business, the other was a lawyer's assistant. They were great conversationalists and very pretty. Occasionally I'd see them at La Souris, one of a number of bars near Pigalle that I went to, like Le Hanneton and Le Rat-Mort. Another neighbor was Eva Gonzalès, married to Henri Guérard. She studied with Manet, who did a portrait of her painting, or rather sitting dressed up in front of an easel, brushes in hand.

And my other neighbor—everyone knew her—was Sarah Bernhardt. 27 She had one of the double floor studios. It was the time, in the mid-1870s, when she was sculpting seriously. I often saw her and her friend, the painter Louise Abbéma—looking completely like a man and quite shocking—at La Souris. Bernhardt and I were the same age. She was extremely attractive, though not beautiful. She grew up in a brothel.

Sometimes I'd walk over to place Blanche and eat at Coquet's. It 28 was easy and comfortable for women to meet there, too, and was often full of girls looking for a good time with each other—milliners, seam-stresses, laundresses, some hopeful dancers and actresses, some street-walkers, some secretaries and teachers, too.

It was while I was living on boulevard de Clichy that I sent work to 29 the Salon for the first time. I'm sure that living there helped me—so many busy girls. That was 1876, and I sent a self-portrait, which was accepted.

I try the quarter where I know Meurent was born, where the rue Folie-Méricourt 30 is located. In her lifetime it was called the Sixth Arrondissement, but it's the Eleventh now. The neighborhood has a special meaning for me, first, of course, because she grew up there—those were the streets she walked as a child and adolescent; but I have lived on this street, too. More than once, Ken and I stayed here with his friend Howie, who lives one door down from Victorine's house; Howie is a well-known writer and clown.

The Mairie of the Eleventh is on place Léon Blum. I arrive at about 31 eleven in the morning. It's packed. People are irritated and in a hurry. When my turn comes I condense my spiel and show my three-by-five card. I skip the postcard reproductions. The clerk throws me a contemptuous look, then does the search. I never know how carefully. I shudder to think. She finds nothing. Meurent didn't die where she was born. Is that good or bad? I don't know. Nowadays people don't want to die where they are born, even in France. And Victorine moved around. This is the girl who'd gone to the United States and become a painter. And still I don't know how that happened. Or what it means.

My mother had a laundry shop on the rue Popincourt, just around the 32 **corner from Folie-Méricourt. It was her own business, and it did well.**

The few times I went, I liked it—all the women together, cozy, friendly, lots of laughter. Peaceful, too. My mother didn't like my being there, though. Once, I heard her telling her sister how the girls were often sick, and also that they kept bad company. So before I started school with the nuns when I was seven, my father and uncle took care of me all through the day. My uncle was a sculptor, my father was a *ciseleur,* a finisher of sculpture. The two of them worked together in my uncle's studio. My father was very handsome, short and solidly built. Smart, too, but with a mean temper.

When I was little, I liked being with them. I remember playing and 33 drawing on their studio floor. My uncle loved me and showed off my drawings. With my father, it was different. Sometimes he was proud, other times he made fun of me. He'd yell across at his brother, "She calls this scribbling drawing?" When the two of them went out on errands, they took me along. That's how I got to know all the shops and the workers—we went to silversmiths, wire makers, plaster suppliers. No one bothered about me. Even though I was small, I was always dressed in overalls with my hair under a cap, so no one treated me like a girl; I was just the Meurent kid. I got an earful! Mostly about how hard it was to make ends meet. Everyone complained about the emperor's projects. Of course, all my father's and uncle's friends were socialists. Prices were inflated, and that was that. Sure, construction was taking place all over the city, they said, but they all felt it was for the rich: the parks, the sewerage, the new streets. My father's friends were certain all the building was going on to insure that the workers never rose again as they had in '48. But in the 1850s it did provide work.

Sometimes we'd visit other people's studios, even painters. One 34 who, in retrospect, was particularly important was Thomas Couture. We started dropping in there when I was about twelve. My father liked him. I think Papa thought painting was better than sculpting, and certainly better than what he did, finishing other people's sculpture. It was less messy, and the painters were a literate bunch. My father loved to tell people his opinions. So we'd often go over to painters' studios. And although I'm sure that as time went by, it became clearer that I was a girl, nobody cared. One day when Couture needed an additional person for a picture, he asked if I could stand in for one of the male figures. I was fifteen; it was 1859.

I remember the first time I put trousers on as an adult was for Manet, 35 his painting of me as an *espada.* I went over to his studio with the usual mixture of feelings, and a hangover; I always drank a lot before I went to see him when I was going to model. I loved the costume that day, though, those tight Spanish pants. The white silk stockings and little jacket weren't bad either. Then he had gorgeous yellow and purple scarves; Manet always had beautiful things in his studio. He asked me to wrap the purple one around my head, letting the leftover cloth hang down my back. Then he placed the soft black hat sideways on the purple silk, and I pushed the yellow handkerchief into the jacket

pocket. It was a difficult pose with both arms extended. He said I didn't have to hold the sword and cloak, but I wanted to.

That's the day he made that comment about my expression. He 36 **said, "I can't quite put my finger on it, Victorine, but there's something about the way you look, your face. You never look at the world as if you need anything from it."**

Once I had a long black woolen skirt with a high waistline. I wore it on cold 37 days with soft leather boots, a mouton coat, and a large brimmed black felt hat. I loved nothing more than traipsing through the snow on Greenwich Village's narrow streets in these clothes—the whoosh of the skirt, the hat pulled low, my lips and face warm and cold in the winter sunlight. I felt so beautiful on those days, so full of desire. I was thirty and single, and a handsome, older man loved me and brought me silken presents and poetry. We made love in my big bed as the lemon light of winter days passed into reddish nights.

Walking the streets of Paris could be like that, easy and sensual, imag- 38 ining everything I want and having it. I've walked cities before, alone or with Ken, or in the old days with my friend Carol. In the 1970s, when she and I were in our late thirties, we spent many an evening strolling Upper Broadway, a joint between our lips. We'd window-shop, gossip, talk Art History. One night she said to me, "Well, who would you have been in Paris in the nineteenth century?" Who, indeed? A smart Jewish woman in nineteenth-century France. Some enlightened man's wife? One of the working-class women we'd written about: a milliner, a laundress, a ballet dancer? We couldn't imagine. And then Meurent came to my mind. I don't know why, really. Maybe it was *her* powers of imagining. Carol, another redhead, liked the idea and gave me her crooked smile. "Yeah."

FOR DISCUSSION AND WRITING: ENCOUNTERING EXEMPLARY HISTORIES

1. Lipton's example clarifies how to undertake a study of the abstractions of ideological identity in a specific embodied case. There is no agreement about the politics of art, as may be seen in the case of *Olympia*. On several college campuses, charges of sexual harassment have been brought by women relating to a similar painting (Goya's *Naked Maja*). The argument is that displaying representations of nudes (even of ones characterized as "masterpieces") in public places is demeaning to women and creates an environment that is not conducive to equal status of all participants. What are the issues involved in such a controversy? Would Lipton support or oppose efforts to remove a copy of *Olympia* from your classroom? As a compromise, some administrators have proposed pairing the female nude with a similarly classical male nude (such as a reproduction of Michelangelo's *David*). What do you think of this suggestion?

2. The selection from "History of an Encounter: Alias Olympia" includes part of the introduction explaining the project, and then a sample of the body of the book recording Lipton's search or research in Paris looking

for evidence and traces of the life and accomplishments of Victorine Meurent. In the latter part, Lipton intercuts her accounts of the search with dramatic passages written in the voice of Victorine, who is allowed to tell her own story. What is the effect of this narrative device—of making the object of study a "character" in a narrative? The intercutting or montage between the two voices finally implies that Victorine represents a fantasy or alternative self for Lipton, who imagines through Victorine what it would be like to live the life of a bohemian woman artist in nineteenth-century Paris. Part of the importance of Lipton's example for mystory is that her identification involves a case study central to her career discipline.

Select an exemplary person who is important in the history of the career field in which you plan to major (or a field about which you are curious). Do some background research on this person and his or her contribution to the field. Write a report in which you assess the possibilities of working with this scene in the way that Lipton shifted her attention from Manet to Victorine. Is there a background or secondary figure, a supporting player, whose story could be foregrounded to get a new perspective on the history of that field?

3. There is also a black woman depicted in *Olympia*. Write several statements from her point of view, in her voice, expressing her life circumstances and how she feels about posing in this particular painting.

From The Way to Rainy Mountain

N. Scott Momaday

N. Scott Momaday shows how to put together the elements articulated in the samples into an overall arrangement in a way that is very useful for the mystory. Using a tripartite form, clearly marking the separate levels of the popcycle, Momaday juxtaposes three levels of his cultural experience: the Kiowa myths that he learned from his grandmother; the actual history of the Kiowa symbolized in these myths; and his personal recollections of his childhood on the reservation. While these three levels are similar to those Susan Howe mentions in her reflections on her own method ("history, mystic speech, and poetry"), Momaday makes his personal experience a more explicit part of the composition. In this example, we observe the use of identification (with his grandmother Aho and grandfather Mammedaty); the use of pattern (the unity of each section is created by the repetition of a detail within the information across the three levels); and the use of setting to express feeling (the memories of scenes from the reservation). Most important is the location of Momaday's memories of childhood in the context of the traditional stories and actual history of his group (the Kiowa), thus bringing the three levels of his symbolic experience into contact—personal, historical, and mythical. Note the resemblance of Momaday's use of fragments and anecdotes to Barthes's tripartite structure in A Lover's Discourse.

N. Scott Momaday, professor of English and comparative literature at the University of Arizona, won the Pulitzer Prize in 1969 for his novel House Made of Dawn. *He has become perhaps the best-known American Indian writer. His mother was one-eighth Cherokee and his father was Kiowa.* The Way to Rainy Mountain *is a collection of thirty-four three-paragraph units (plus an introduction and epilogue) and is illustrated with drawings by Momaday's father.*

I

You know, everything had to begin, and this is how it was: the Kiowas came   1
one by one into the world through a hollow log. They were many more than now, but not all of them got out. There was a woman whose body was swollen up with child, and she got stuck in the log. After that, no one could get through, and that is why the Kiowas are a small tribe in number. They looked all around and saw the world. It made them glad to see so many things. They called themselves *Kwuda*, "coming out."

They called themselves Kwuda *and later* Tepda, *both of which mean "coming out."*   2
And later still they took the name Gaigwu, *a name which can be taken to indicate something of which the two halves differ from each other in appearance. It was once a custom among Kiowa warriors that they cut their hair on the right side of the head only and on a line level with the lobe of the ear, while on the left they let the hair grow long and wore it in a thick braid wrapped in otter skin. "Kiowa" is indicated in sign language by holding the hand palm up and slightly cupped to the right side of the head and rotating it back and forth from the wrist. "Kiowa" is thought to derive from the softened Comanche form of* Gaigwu.

I remember coming out upon the northern Great Plains in the late spring.   3
There were meadows of blue and yellow wildflowers on the slopes, and I could see the still, sunlit plain below, reaching away out of sight. At first there is no discrimination in the eye, nothing but the land itself, whole and impenetrable. But then smallest things begin to stand out of the depths — herds and rivers and groves — and each of these has perfect being in terms of distance and of silence and of age. Yes, I thought, now I see the earth as it really is; never again will I see things as I saw them yesterday or the day before.

III

Before there were horses the Kiowas had need of dogs. That was a long time   4
ago, when dogs could talk. There was a man who lived alone; he had been thrown away, and he made his camp here and there on the high ground. Now it was dangerous to be alone, for there were enemies all around. The man spent his arrows hunting food. He had one arrow left, and he shot a bear; but the bear was only wounded and it ran away. The man wondered what to do. Then a dog came up to him and said that many enemies were coming; they

were close by and all around. The man could think of no way to save himself. But the dog said: "You know, I have puppies. They are young and weak and they have nothing to eat. If you will take care of my puppies, I will show you how to get away." The dog led the man here and there, around and around, and they came to safety.

A hundred years ago the Comanche Ten Bears remarked upon the great num- 5
ber of horses which the Kiowas owned. "When we first knew you," he said, "you
had nothing but dogs and sleds." It was so; the dog is primordial. Perhaps it
was dreamed into being.

The principal warrior society of the Kiowas was the Ka-itsenko, "Real
Dogs," and it was made up of ten men only, the ten most brave. Each of these
men wore a long ceremonial sash and carried a sacred arrow. In time of battle
he must by means of this arrow impale the end of his sash to the earth and stand
his ground to the death. Tradition has it that the founder of the Ka-itsenko had
a dream in which he saw a band of warriors, outfitted after the fashion of the
society, being led by a dog. The dog sang the song of the Ka-itsenko, then said
to the dreamer: "You are a dog; make a noise like a dog and sing a dog song."

There were always dogs about my grandmother's house. Some of them were 6
nameless and lived a life of their own. They belonged there in a sense that
the word "ownership" does not include. The old people paid them scarcely
any attention, but they should have been sad, I think, to see them go.

XXI

Mammedaty was the grandson of Guipahgo, and he was well-known on that 7
account. Now and then Mammedaty drove a team and wagon out over the
plain. Once, in the early morning, he was on the way to Rainy Mountain. It was
summer and the grass was high and meadowlarks were calling all around.
You know, the top of the plain is smooth and you can see a long way. There
was nothing but the early morning and the land around. Then Mammedaty
heard something. Someone whistled to him. He looked up and saw the head
of a little boy nearby above the grass. He stopped the horses and got down
from the wagon and went to see who was there. There was no one; there was
nothing there. He looked for a long time, but there was nothing there.

There is a single photograph of Mammedaty. He is looking past the camera and 8
a little to one side. In his face there is calm and good will, strength and intelli-
gence. His hair is drawn close to the scalp, and his braids are long and wrapped
with fur. He wears a kilt, fringed leggings, and beaded moccasins. In his right
hand there is a peyote fan. A family characteristic: the veins stand out in his
hands, and his hands are small and rather long.

Mammedaty saw four things that were truly remarkable. This head of the 9
child was one, and the tracks of the water beast another. Once, when he
walked near the pecan grove, he saw three small alligators on a log. No

one had ever seen them before and no one ever saw them again. Finally, there was this: something had always bothered Mammedaty, a small aggravation that was never quite out of mind, like a name on the tip of the tongue. He had always wondered how it is that the mound of earth which a mole makes around the opening of its burrow is so fine. It is nearly as fine as powder, and it seems almost to have been sifted. One day Mammedaty was sitting quietly when a mole came out of the earth. Its cheeks were puffed out as if it had been a squirrel packing nuts. It looked all around for a moment, then blew the fine dark earth out of its mouth. And this it did again and again, until there was a ring of black, powdery earth on the ground. That was a strange and meaningful thing to see. It meant that Mammedaty had got possession of a powerful medicine.

XXIV

East of my grandmother's house, south of the pecan grove, there is buried a   10
woman in a beautiful dress. Mammedaty used to know where she is buried, but now no one knows. If you stand on the front porch of the house and look eastward towards Carnegie, you know that the woman is buried somewhere within the range of your vision. But her grave is unmarked. She was buried in a cabinet, and she wore a beautiful dress. How beautiful it was! It was one of those fine buckskin dresses, and it was decorated with elk's teeth and beadwork. That dress is still there, under the ground.

Aho's high moccasins are made of softest, cream-colored skins. On each instep   11
there is a bright disc of beadwork—an eight-pointed star, red and pale blue on
a white field—and there are bands of beadwork at the soles and ankles. The
flaps of the leggings are wide and richly ornamented with blue and red and
green and white and lavender beads.

East of my grandmother's house the sun rises out of the plain. Once in   12
his life a man ought to concentrate his mind upon the remembered earth,
I believe. He ought to give himself up to a particular landscape in his experience, to look at it from as many angles as he can, to wonder about
it, to dwell upon it. He ought to imagine that he touches it with his hands
at every season and listens to the sounds that are made upon it. He
ought to imagine the creatures there and all the faintest motions of the
wind. He ought to recollect the glare of noon and all the colors of the
dawn and dusk.

FOR DISCUSSION AND WRITING: CREATING PATTERNS
ACROSS DISCOURSES

1. Momaday is a good relay for what mystory is trying to achieve, in that in
   his Native American culture the individual readily acknowledges his or
   her part in a collective order. Reflecting the point of view of an oral cul-

ture, the Native American author treats the public traditions of the tribe as a personal memory. As a research collage, *Rainy Mountain* tells the Kiowa story from four perspectives, as Kenneth Lincoln explains:

> The tribal or folkloric memory speaks through Aho, the grandmother muse; the pictorial or visual mode projects through the senior Momaday's drawing to illustrate his mother's stories to her grandson; the historical or public medium documents events through James Mooney's *Calendar History of the Kiowa Indians* (1898), borrowings from Elsie Clews Parson's *Kiowa Tales* (1929), and parallels with Mildred P. Mayhall's *The Kiowas* (1962); the personal or impressionist voice elegizes a journey through Momaday's own re-created pilgrimage from Montana to Oklahoma, occasioned by Aho's death.

Place Momaday on the list of ideological categories. Use Momaday's example to compose a list of your own equivalents of the groups and individuals with whom Momaday identifies. Do some research to locate the collective and personal resources available for citation in your own version of *Rainy Mountain*.

2. What are the formal lessons of *Rainy Mountain*? Notice how the three parts of each unit in Momaday's composition are linked. In the opening paragraph of *Mind Tools: The Five Levels of Mathematical Reality*, Rudy Rucker observes that "mathematics is the study of pure pattern, and everything in the cosmos is a kind of pattern." Look for the pattern that appears in the information you gathered in exercise 1. Compare your pattern with the patterns constructed by each of the authors represented in this chapter.

3. One goal of mystory as an experiment is to learn how to replace argumentation with mood as a way to guide research. Mystory thus shares some of the same attitudes expressed by a new generation of graphic designers who are inventing a hybrid approach to visualization that draws equally on the arts and industrial design. "It may address a problem," Rich Poyner has argued in the design magazine *I.D.*, "but it is absolved from the need to find a solution in the closed, objective, rational sense that still informs so much rhetoric about graphic design." The opposition between style and idea, he says, "is misleading because it never seems to acknowledge that the solution to a communication problem might be a mood, emotion, or atmosphere." One motive for this shift is to leave a place for the reader in the construction of the text (interactive texts are written from the position of receiver rather than author—a receiver of the traditions of existing high and popular culture). If there are to be any arguments made, the reader of the mystory, not the composer, supplies them.

The emotion generated during the process of composition is "objective" in that it does not necessarily exist prior to the activity of research; the writer does not express this emotion. Rather, the experiment shows a potential scene of emotion to the writer, who then decides to grasp it, research it, and repeat it through a series of elaborations and enlargements to learn what it has to say about the relation of the writer to the cultural contexts brought together in the mystory. The text creates the experience; it does not "represent" a prior experience within the standards of a realism. The writer is free to reject the comment of the miniaturized pattern or to interpret it. At the same time, the metaphor that emerges during the stage of *inventio* (of research, of finding and collecting the items of information from each context) may be manipulated by the writer, since an extensive number of details may be found that repeat across these discourses. The emotion functions to hold the diverse materials together in memory, more than to express an authentic reality.

The assignment is to write a "discourse on method" for the mystory. Analyze and compare the readings collectively to find their pattern, to see what features they manifest that, when added together, constitute a set of instructions for making a mystory. Notice in the form and style of the relays how each one tells about both how the author wants to write and how the author performs this kind of writing at the same time. Your discourse on method (like most examples of this genre) should combine these two levels of information about the mystory in one composition: explanations of how and why one could compose a mystory; and a demonstration showing what research composed mystorically might look like. The mystory is experimental, and it could be organized in the form often used to write up the results of a scientific experiment, which would require separating the statement of what the experiment is to be, the conduct of the experiment itself, and the evaluation of the results. A discourse on method, however, combines these elements into one document that says what it does; it tells and shows the method.

From A Chorus of Stones: The Private Life of War

Susan Griffin

"It is said that the close study of stone will reveal traces from fires suffered thousands of years ago," Susan Griffin writes, explaining the method she used in A Chorus of Stones. *"I am beginning to believe that we know everything, that all history including the history of each family is part of us, such that, when we hear any secret revealed, a secret about a grandfather, or uncle, or a secret about the battle of Dresden in 1945, our lives are made suddenly clearer to us, as the unnatural heaviness of unspoken truth is dispersed. For perhaps we are like stones; our own history and the history of the world embedded in us, we hold a sorrow deep within and cannot weep until that history is sung." To write through her feeling that her life "is not separate from history," Griffin performs a hybrid style best described as "montage"—a juxtaposition of sources such as diaries, interviews, art, literature, psychology, and historical documents "to illustrate how it is that private life—family history, childhood experience, gender and sexuality, private aspiration and public image—assume a role in the causes*

and effects of war" (Griffin jacket copy). The information turned up by the research is interpolated in fragments, juxtaposed with her own reminiscences, anecdotes, and meditations, rendered in a lyrical voice. The selection included here takes the life and work of Ernest Hemingway as its focus, although the examples in the book include figures such as Heinrich Himmler, Hugh Trenchard, and Mohandas Gandhi from other areas of history.

Susan Griffin is a well-known feminist writer, poet, essayist, lecturer, teacher, playwright, and filmmaker. She is the author of more than twenty books, including Woman and Nature: The Roaring Inside Her *and* Pornography and Silence: Culture's Revenge against Nature.

December

It is a delicate balance, telling someone else's story, entering another life,   1
identifying, feeling as this other might have felt, and yet remaining aware that a boundary exists over which one cannot step.

Soldiers continue to wage war in the old way. Yes, the technologies are   2
increasingly sophisticated. But still there are those who place their bodies in the way of weapons and aim their own weapons at others. And what is even more true is that the idea of the soldier remains as a fixture of all our thought, so that in some way each of us is both civilian and soldier. In the full understanding of ourselves, the story of the soldier is also our own.

December

Writing about one's own life, it is only when one writes about the most in-   3
timate and seemingly idiosyncratic details that one touches others.

What I wanted above all in this last chapter was to render a portrait of   4
the war story, and to do this by portraying the storyteller. And so I thought of Ernest Hemingway.

December

Is this because it is private and hidden feelings one longs to hear expressed?   5

In the beginning I did not know that Hemingway's real experience in   6
warfare had been exaggerated as part of his public image. He served in the ambulance corps in Italy near the end of the First World War. He was under fire in that war only once and then just for a few minutes before he was wounded in the leg; he spent the remainder of the war in a hospital.

December

I like the feeling of intimacy in a journal. Pajamas. Unmade bed. Breakfast   7
dishes. Body smells.

Yet, even so, it was not so much the documentation of the experience of   8
the soldier I wanted as the creation of the myth. And for this Hemingway was

perfect. He created a legend in which he performed the principal and heroic role.

December
The starched uniform of the soldier a counterbalance to the terrible inti- 9
macy of ruptured flesh.

Hemingway's literary style became the voice for the Lost Generation, a 10
term which described the generation that had come of age during the Great War and been embittered by it. But as I came of age, his voice embodied the masculine ideal. Laconic. Tough. Tight-jawed. Humphrey Bogart was the perfect actor to play one of his heroes in *To Have and Have Not.*

December
Hemingway's great influence on our generation. The language. That story 11
David Lueck told me (cut from the fifth chapter). How as a boy he hung a map
of the battlefields of World War II in his room. (His hero, Douglas MacArthur.)
Before he was twenty-one, he was fighting in Korea, and, while he was there,
reading—A Farewell to Arms.

Hemingway was the paradigmatic American writer, fishing in the waters 12
off Havana, or, his beret pulled slightly lower on one side, cigarette in his mouth, typing his latest account of a bullfight or recreating the landscape of a battlefield from memory.

January 1991
In one way it seems strange to be going on vacation now. In midwinter, 13
mid-crisis, to a warm, lush island in the Pacific Ocean.

January
Looking at the surface of the sea, one would never guess at all that lies 14
underneath.

January
Continually, a sweet scent in the air. Shedding clothes, tensions, fear. Every- 15
thing sways here like the ocean. So evident, a maternal feel to the earth. My body
bellying out, because of age, health returning. I like the feel of it. Breast heavy.

January
Reading Hemingway in the midst of all this. Detect a sharply divided re- 16
sponse to pleasure in him.

January
A beauty that tears one open. 17

January
We watch the news. Every day brings us closer to the deadline for an invasion. 18

January

Feeling close to the origin of existence here. Mud on the slope, palm fronds 19
on the path smeared with it, lizards, ancient land animals, creatures in the sea
looking like pure protoplasm, earliest ancestors.

January

So much childbirth in Hemingway's stories. Especially in his war stories.   20

January

Eating breakfast in our room, we watch the Senate debate on television. 21
Senator from New Jersey offers an eloquent argument for extending the period
of economic sanctions. Meeting violence without violence!

January

The vote taken while we slept, we wake to find that Congress has given the 22
President the right to declare war immediately after the fifteenth.

January

A turtle swims to shore just a few yards from us. I've never seen one so close. 23
But it moves too slowly. A man on the beach tells us all the turtles on this beach
have some kind of tumor.

January

On the news channel they show men training with live ammunition in the 24
desert at night, the landscape lit with greenish floodlights and shell bursts. It
looks like the moon.

January

Going home now, I don't want to lose this feeling of ease in my body, as if 25
the sea and land have come into me.

January

The day of the deadline. Picking us up, my daughter says she wants to 26
leave the airport as soon as possible. Everyone is anxious now about terrorism.
Suddenly it occurs to me even she could be a casualty.

January

It is so difficult to believe. We are at war. The phone rings as I am unpack- 27
ing. Joanna says fire has been exchanged. I run upstairs to the television. A re-
porter is quietly describing bombs as they are being dropped in Baghdad. I sit
stunned on the edge of the bed. Everything in my life has suddenly stopped.

Born in 1899, Ernest Hemingway was part of a generation whose lives 28
were shaped by two World Wars. He was a contemporary of Himmler, Fermi
and General Douglas MacArthur. He belonged to a prosperous middle-class
family and grew up in comfortable circumstances in the safe but somewhat
narrow environment of Oak Park, Illinois, a suburb of Chicago. His father

was a doctor. His mother, who had inherited money of her own, was an educated woman who had been trained as an opera singer. She had a short career on the stage until, the story goes, she found the stage lights burned her sensitive eyes. She was a feminist, and took a strong interest in the cultural life of the city, to which she purposefully exposed all of her children.

February

I wanted so much to believe that the breakdown of the Cold War was also 29
the beginning of a shift into a new way of thinking and being. Or perhaps an
ancient one, still able to imagine peace.

Ernest was his mother's favorite child. She doted on him, keeping him in 30
a close, affectionate relationship, and even slept in the same bed with him
until he was five years old. He returned her affection. But as he grew older he
rebelled. She dominated the family, including his father, and later he would
imply that this was the reason he grew to hate her.

February

Archaeologists express concern over the ancient sites in Iraq which could be 31
bombed. Remains of Neanderthal culture. Evidence of the first agriculture. The
first villages and towns.

Making fun of his mother's zealous care for him, when he is a young man 32
he will call her *Mrs. Heminstein.* Intertwined as this name is with his attempt
to free himself from the influence of his mother, this is also an early sign of
Hemingway's anti-Semitism. Did he know, or just sense intuitively, that misogyny and anti-Semitism are similarly interwoven in history?

February

A report that Iraqi airplanes have been seen parked at the archaeological 33
site of the ancient city of Ur. This was one of the oldest cities of Mesopotamia,
dating from 3000 B.C.

Like many boys of this generation, including Heinrich Himmler and my 34
grandfather, Ernest was dressed in ruffles and lace. As one of his biographers,
Kenneth Lynn, perceptively observes, Grace was particularly keen on picturing her son as feminine. One photograph of him taken at the age of two in
which he wears a flowered hat is labeled "Summer Girl," in her handwriting.
As he grew older, she would often dress Ernest and his older sister in identical clothing as if they were twins of the same sex, either as boys or as girls. I
do not see this as a simple perversity. It seems possible that Grace might project her wishes for a wider range of being on her children, making them act
out changes of gender she wanted for herself.

February

Among the structures of ancient Ur was a large ziggurat, a calendrical tower, 35
built, according to its modern discoverers, to observe the heavens. Ziggurat means
"hill of heaven."

As much as Ernest tried to move away from the influence of his mother, 36 he also wanted to get closer to his father. Of course, like many men, his father was not as present in the home as Grace, and he was more remote in his moods. He was also given to depression. Ernest loved to go with him when he went hunting or fishing. The family had a second home in the woods at Lake Walloon, and there Ernest would also accompany his father when he ministered care to a local Native American tribe. As a boy he witnessed emergency surgeries, bone settings, childbirth. Clarence was proud of his son because he was not squeamish when he looked at the preserved organs the doctor kept in glass jars in his study.

February
In a book on architecture I read that calendric structures reveal rhythmic 37 *patterns reflecting calendric changes: the waning and waxing of the moon, the rise and fall of tides, menstrual cycles.*

As he moved into manhood, Hemingway began to hate what he saw as his 38 father's cowardice and submission to his mother. In an early story he depicts his father backing down in a fight, admonished by his mother to keep the peace.

February
A bunker in Baghdad bombed. Filled with civilians. A man weeping in front 39 *of the bunker. So many in his family dead. All his children. It is unimaginable. Yet I am implicated in these deaths.*

One might be tempted to look at Hemingway's childhood as the sole ex- 40 planation for the obsession with masculine heroism that became the subject of much of his work. But psychoanalysis itself employs too narrow a lens to explain any life. When the perspective is widened one sees that his childhood was not so much unique as it was a variation on a theme. No wonder the legend Hemingway made of himself became so popular: both his real story and the mythology he created mirrored the world to which he belonged.

February
Day by day the stories issuing from the Pentagon about the bombing of the 41 *bunker change. First they say there were no civilians there. Then that the military officials were hiding among the civilians. Then that they were misinformed.*

My grandparents were both born in the state where Hemingway was 42 raised. They were at the southern end of the state, in an area more rural than the suburbs of Chicago. But even in 1949, after my parents divorced, when I visited Chicago with my grandparents, the city still seemed to smell of the slaughterhouses.

February
Sacrament of language, binding thread of words. One wants to trust others. 43 *Yet when a lie is told the body is cast into a state of profound disturbance. One must choose then between oneself and society.*

Like Grace, my grandmother dreamed of becoming an artist. She wanted 44
to be an actress. Extraordinary as it was for a woman of her generation, she
studied drama for two years at the University of Illinois. The story goes that
a traveling theatre asked her to join. But her father would not allow this. She
shared Grace Hemingway's hunger for culture and the finer things of life. In
the early days of television we watched plays by Thornton Wilder, ballet, and
Liberace playing Chopin or Rachmaninoff was one of her favorites. During
breakfast she read to us from the *Reader's Digest*. My grandfather was hardly
interested. He liked to read mysteries or westerns. In the early days of television, we watched Wild Bill Hickok together as he rode into the scrub brush
of the Southern California hills. My grandfather's fishing tackle in its khaki
case sat in a privileged position in our basement. Though their easy chairs
rested just a few yards apart in our living room, my grandparents lived as if
in separate worlds. But when Hemingway's late story "The Old Man and the
Sea" arrived at our house under the covers of the *Saturday Evening Post* both
my grandparents read it.

February

In the back of the house the plum tree blossoming again.   45

I have a strong feeling of familiarity for Grace and Clarence Hemingway. 46
A marriage conventional and proper on the surface concealing gaping holes
of dissatisfaction. My grandfather the wage earner respectably dressed in his
three-piece suits. My grandmother his wife keeping house, putting up preserves, baking cakes on holidays, roast beef every Sunday for a meal eaten
early on the Limoges spread over a linen cloth.

February

Sunday. Time out from the war. Nan and I go to the park. Photographs of 47
the space program in the Science Museum. Huge machines making it possible
to view stars as they never have been viewed before.

But this was just the surface. The appearance everyone worked so hard 48
to create. Just beneath that appearance was something else. I can remember
my grandmother standing beside the washing machine that in those days had
a hand-fed wringer. This was a task she hated more than all her other domestic tasks, most of which she performed with only an unspoken resentment, one that had settled permanently into the features of her face. As she
handed the wash to my grandfather so that he could hang it on the line in the
backyard, she was openly complaining.

February

But now, in many places on the planet, without sophisticated machinery, 49
we can hardly see the stars at all any more.

As I helped my grandfather with his tasks, I thought of him not so much 50
as a parent but as an older sibling, who, like me, might easily incur my grand-

mother's wrath. It was she who ruled our household. Every family has its own explanation for its patterns. Charlotte's grandmother believed Charlotte and her father had failed Franziska and that is why she committed suicide. In my family my grandmother's resentful rule over my grandfather was explained by his behavior earlier in their marriage, when he was a womanizer and drank too much. Now she was getting back at him.

February

Don calls. We haven't spoken in weeks. So good to hear his voice, sound- 51
ing as shaken as I am.

There was an incipient bitterness between them, however, that smelled 52
of old scores unsettled. It stretched way back to before their marriage when my grandmother, shunted off to the family in Virginia, bore him an illegiti-mate and stillborn child.

February

Now it comes out that forty percent of the "smart" laser-guided bombs are 53
missing their targets by thousands of feet.

But this historical argument missed a reality which existed daily before 54
our eyes, though we never spoke of it, and that was the deterioration of my grandfather. He had collapsed. He was like some star whose flame, moving out toward the periphery, had left nothing at the center.

February

Slowly, year after year, decade by decade, we grow used to the unspeakable. 55

At the end of a story Hemingway wrote about a son's disillusionment 56
with his father, the young hero says of him, *Seems like when they get started they don't leave a guy nothing.* It is a theme that will repeat itself throughout his work. A man shorn of all that has meaning for him, losing even his self respect, left with nothing.

February

One cries out, but it is as if in a dream where the voice is silent. It is a ter- 57
rible feeling to witness this destruction, which is also on the most fundamental level a self-destruction.

I can remember my grandfather sitting in his chair staring into space. 58
This was not the meditative mood of reflection. His silence made me uneasy. I sensed in his stillness a fundamental failure of being.

February

It is no wonder this war evokes childhood memories. What I felt as I wit- 59
nessed my mother's drinking; what she must have felt witnessing her father's alcoholism.

Though I sympathized with my grandfather in his submission, in my heart 60
I was glad my grandmother held the seat of power in our family. She was
present, in this world, aware, despite her resentment, of the needs of a child
to eat regularly and sleep between clean sheets. And though my grandfather
often seemed more lenient, his anger was volatile like a child's rage, and in
some strange way it partook of the emptiness that had settled so deeply in
him.

February
What one sees as a child. My grandmother's reigning unhappiness colored 61
the atmosphere; it was the air we breathed. But we never spoke of it.

Clarence Hemingway suffered from serious bouts of depression. He was 62
alternately vacant to his family and autocratic, finding fault with everything,
impossible to please. Growing up, Ernest fell under the shadow of his moods,
and this angered him. When was it he began to blame his mother for his father's transgressions?

February
A chain reaction of silences. The lack of intimacy between my grandmother 63
and grandfather. Did any secrets pass between them?

Tracing the complicated circuitry of gender in our lives, there is also this. 64
My grandmother's manner of authority, the qualities which made her able to
dominate other people's lives, were said to have come from her father. Was
the same true for Grace Hemingway? Her father, Ernest, after whom Hemingway was named, was the head of the Hemingway household until his
death, when Ernest was five years old. Then Grace took over the helm from
her father.

February
Those tender stories lovers tell each other at night before sleep, mingling 65
histories, dreams; another way of making love.

Both of Hemingway's grandfathers had fought in the Civil War. Anson 66
Hemingway, his father's father, commanded black troops in the infantry. It
was this grandfather who took Ernest at the age of eleven to join the crowds
greeting Theodore Roosevelt as he rode into the Oak Park railroad station.
Teddy Roosevelt was the young Hemingway's hero. He read Roosevelt's *African
Game Trails*. And he wore his khaki uniform, fashioned after Roosevelt's sa-
fari clothes, whenever his father took him to the Hall of African Mammals at
the Field Museum of Natural History in Chicago.

February
How isolated we were then, my family. All of us! My loneliness not just 67
*from that divorce, but from the greater separation which preceded it. Secrets di-
viding us.*

Ernest was not alone in his worship. Teddy Roosevelt, or T.R. as he was 68
affectionately known, became a symbol at the turn of the century for the revival
of certain *rough and ready* masculine virtues, now nearly vestigial. He was the
big game hunter, the cowboy, the statesman who spoke softly and carried a big
stick. He openly celebrated war. *No triumph of peace could be quite so great,*
he said. Peace, or the absence of war, brought its own problems, among them,
he warned, the greatest danger being *effeminate tendencies in young men.*

February

We hope against hope for a peace settlement.   69

As a child Ernest boasted to his parents that he was *afraid of nothing.* But 70
there were two sides to his fantasy life. At one moment he would sidle up to
his mother, asking her to play *Kitty* with him and stroke him and purr. Then,
switching to a different mode, he would swagger his way through stories he
made up in which he was the brave and vanquishing hero.

February

Bush has rejected the Soviet peace proposal. He makes the startling de- 71
mand that Iraqi troops withdraw before a cease-fire.

I can remember myself at the age of ten staring into the mirror as I but- 72
toned my collar, tried on one of my grandfather's ties and combed my hair
back in the style of a man. I liked to imagine myself as Kit Carson, dressed
in buckskin, forging through the wilderness. To swing to the other side of the
divide between the sexes was a way for me to escape the confining world of
domesticity so filled with my grandmother's resentments.

February

Sense of foreboding all day. Difficult to work. Nan calls. Iraqi troops are in 73
retreat, and they are being bombed and fired on while they withdraw!

Could it be that part of the sting for a man who is called effeminate is the 74
implicit threat of being reduced to the small world assigned to women? By
1917, leaving his mother and sister behind, Hemingway had moved into the
wider world of men. He was nineteen and just graduated from high school
when he went to work as a reporter at the *Kansas City Star.* Three weeks after he arrived, he joined the National Guard. Congress had declared war on
Germany that spring. He wrote his family that he planned to enlist later in an
active unit. His longing to go to war grew more intense that fall when he went
to hear Billy Sunday, the famous Chicago evangelist, urging young men to do
their patriotic duty.

February

Allied troops in Iraq. And still the war doesn't end. The rumor is that the 75
coalition wants Saddam Hussein dead. He has become like the Antichrist, the
symbol of all evil.

On the surface one might find a contradiction here: a religious man ex- 76
horting men to war. But this is a traditional transposition of values, part of a
shared history that goes back at least until 1096, when joining the First Cru-
sade became a way not only of testing manly virtue but of expiating sin.

February
Finally a cease-fire. Papers, television proclaiming a great victory. It is as if 77
no one died. The suffering of "the enemy" still invisible.

One thinks then of King Richard in battle with the Turks, his body, ac- 78
cording to Bulfinch, *as if it were made of brass impenetrable to any weapon.* As
the legend goes, surrounded by Turkish warriors, he cut down men and
horses alike, *cleaving them to the middle.* One of the strongest Turkish warriors, an officer of distinction, lost his head, his shoulder and his right arm to
a single blow of Richard's sword. The king emerged safely from battle *stuck
all over with javelins like a deer pierced by the hunters.*

March
I remember that sculpture of St. Sebastian I saw three years ago hanging 79
*on the wall of a church in the Black Forest. He was wounded from the arrows.
His golden loincloth looked like a skirt. I noticed this because of the sway of his
hip, and his face, so feminine.*

That Richard is likened to a deer must have had overtones of an earlier 80
time in the eleventh century. According to the Celtic religion, the deer was a
divine messenger. And then there are the wounds themselves, similar to the
wounds of any soldier, which seem to manifest what has always been so, as
if in warfare an inner condition had moved to the surface, even through mu-
tilation making a man seem more whole.

March
I was very ill that day but somehow managed to go out to see the pictures 81
*made of flowers by the village women adorning all the paths, celebrating the
resurrection of Christ. They do this every year at Easter.*

To his friends and family Hemingway boasted of plans to enlist as a Marine 82
or an aviator. But he knew this was impossible: his eyes were bad. He could
stay in the National Guard, but the likelihood of being called up before the
war's end was small. Then, in February of the next year, representatives of the
Italian Red Cross appeared in Kansas City to recruit ambulance drivers.

March
One image in particular struck me, an image of a whip supposed to have 83
*been used to flagellate Christ, pincers, and a ball and chain, carried out in
petals of spring blossoms.*

On June 2, 1918, Hemingway arrived in Paris with one week to spend before 84
he would be dispatched to Milan for his assignment. According to a letter he

wrote, on the first day of his leave he was picked up on the street by a woman who took him to a mansion near the outskirts of the city where, he said, using the chaste language of his upbringing, *a very beautiful thing happened to me.* The woman he met that day told him that under no circumstances would she be able to see him again. But he spent the rest of his stay in Paris looking for her. At the end of his leave, he finally found her as, along with many other soldiers, he watched through a slit in a wall while she made love to a man dressed as a military officer. Was this story, which he wrote in a letter to a friend at home, fact or fiction? This was a theme—an unsuccessful search for a lost woman, a woman lost to him—that would be repeated more than once in his fiction.

March

Reading a book of pre-Islamic Bedouin poetry. The traditional theme de- 85
scribes the loss of a woman, the beloved, followed by a quest for her, and end-
ing with the acceptance of a world deprived of her.

If the story is true he would not have been the first young soldier initiated 86
at one and the same time into the mysteries of sex and violence. Yet if the story were exaggerated, this embellishment would also be part of an old tradition by which stories of military and sexual conquest are both aggrandized. But he was soon to have another intimate contact with the female body. At the end of his week in Paris, he boarded a train for Milan where just after his arrival an official of the Red Cross called him to a munitions plant which had exploded just outside the city. There were many dead and he was shocked to find women among the bodies. It was the presence of the long hair, he said.

March

A photograph of the United States ambassador to the UN speaking with an 87
elderly woman in Kuwait. She is wearing a veil. And his face looks like a mask.

But he is also shocked by the presence of short hair among these women. 88
It is strange how such a detail alerts the mind. His mother was a feminist. There is even subtle evidence that for a period she may have been in love with another woman. But short hair, at that time, would have been such an outward sign of deviation from the expected.

March

Joanna and I take a walk together. She is trying to decide whether or not to 89
go to Chernobyl. A descent, like Inanna's descent. We are both concerned about
her health.

From Milan he was dispatched to Section IV at Schio, near Lake Garda, 90
where he drove an ambulance every other day, ferrying the wounded from the battlefront to an emergency care station. But he was disappointed. He found the work dull. There was nothing to do but look at the scenery, he said. He wanted to see action. He wrote a letter to a girlfriend at home implying he was closer to the battle and under heavy fire. Was this the first lie he was to tell about his experience in the war?

March

In the Times *an article saying it will take two years to put out the burning*   91
oil wells in Kuwait. The skies are black there.

His hope for seeing action finally came when his commanding officers   92
asked for volunteers to move closer to the line of fire at Fossalta where they
were needed to distribute cigarettes, water and chocolate. Everyone volun-
teered, but Hemingway was among the chosen. Then, after less than a week
in Fossalta, on June 7, he learned from the soldiers at the front that heavy
shelling was expected soon all along the line.

March

I dream I am back in that house where as a child I was so often frightened.   93
Is this because I am about to visit my mother after so long?

It must have been because of what the soldiers told him that he went out   94
near midnight, carrying his rifle and rucksack over his shoulder, and bicycled to
the trenches. He was determined to get closer to the action, and so he advanced
to a listening post, one hundred and fifty yards nearer the Austrian lines.

March

Los Angeles. Dinner with Jesse and Rachel. Talk about the war. Rachel is   95
against it. Jesse for it. She is afraid for Israel and sees Hussein as a kind of Hitler.

Does he run over the field? This is after all what he has been waiting for   96
since the war started, ever since he was a small boy in his khaki uniform, to
enter battle, to be baptized in this element, to become what he is supposed
to become and at the same time to take into himself what has forever been
promised him, the fiery center of his sex, himself.

March

I keep thinking about our talk with Jesse. As much as I dislike Hussein's   97
dictatorship, I do not think he is like Hitler. Still I am troubled by our talk. The
implications.

Is it perhaps a certain rapture that he feels now along with his fear as the   98
shells crack and brighten the air and the machine guns rattle? He is as close as
he will ever be to the heart of the matter. His blood rushes, the saliva in his
mouth goes dry, and if his head is lighter than usual, still every muscle, every
nerve seems vital in a new way, as if he had been reborn into this moment.

March

How can one be a pacifist in the face of such evil?   99

Later, much later, when Hemingway writes a version of this story, the first   100
sensation he describes himself feeling is the wetness of blood filling his boots.
A shell had exploded. The soldier in front of him was dead. And another, with

both legs blown off, also dead. But a third, near him, with a wound in his chest, was still alive.

March

And yet I can no longer accept violence as a solution. It is a feeling I have 101 *in my body, as if in the cells themselves.*

It is here that the narrative breaks down. We know he was wounded by 102 shrapnel in over two hundred places in his leg. But did he, despite these wounds, rise to lift the body of the other wounded man? And was he then struck by two machine gun bullets which wounded him again in the knee and the foot? The truth cannot be determined. Evidence exists that, as is so often the case with heroic deeds, the story strayed from the truth, giving the hero capacities which on closer examination are not only improbable but superhuman. Yet it is perhaps necessary, the enlargement, the careful whisking away of certain details, the flattering light casting one act into an unnatural brilliance, another unseen into the shadows. What goes on in battle is in the end just the raw material for the eventual achievement of glory.

March

At the museum here, as part of an exhibit about the Third Reich's condem- 103 *nation of modern art, films of book burnings are shown. Among the books burned, Hemingway's* A Farewell to Arms. *Chronicle of the underside of World War I. The same war which created Hitler.*

So, it is part of the same tradition that the story told by both sides in a 104 conflict is the same, except that the roles of the good and bad, avenger and criminal, savior and oppressor have been reversed. In the Arab version of King Richard's siege of Acre a different story is told. After seizing the city's ramparts, not wishing to be burdened with prisoners, Richard ordered that 2,700 Arab soldiers together with 300 women and children be assembled before the city wall. There they were roped together and delivered to the Frankish soldiers who attacked them with lances, sabers and stones until *all the wails were stilled.*

March

Seeing my mother today. It has been a long time and she is so much more ill. 105

What was it like for Hemingway to be wounded as he was? The rapture 106 before the shell broke was one matter but this was another. The body near him irrevocably altered, legs blasted to nothingness, not neatly torn but ragged, blood smeared everywhere, mixed with the mud. Later the images will make him shudder.

March

Attached by a thin plastic tube to a machine that increases her oxygen, she 107 *is worn out easily by conversation.*

I remember David Lueck telling me what he had witnessed in Korea. His 108
voice so low it could hardly be heard in the recording I made, he spoke in the
way I have heard women speak of rape or abuse, as if in the very telling
something monstrously ugly is brought into being. The terror and brutality
seemed to brand him, making him in his own mind irredeemably inseparable
from the ugliness. Yet what he saw defied description. It was told more in the
difficulty of telling than in the telling itself. He could name the mutilations,
intestines falling out of the body, along with shit, blood, pus, but no one who
had not been there could have any idea. It was only over time I began to
grasp what he was saying to me. It was not just the physical fear he was feeling, it was the weight of something sordid.

March

I am grateful for this time with my mother. I was deprived of my father's 109
death. It was so violent, so sudden.

How much more important then it becomes to reassemble the fragments 110
of these memories into something better, something fine, something that restores the shaken center into glory.

March

. *I can see now how crucial to a life the ending is. Death the last part of the story.* 111

A few years after the war, when he has moved to Paris and begun his first 112
brilliant short stories, Hemingway will draw a portrait of a young veteran who
makes up stories about the war. *Krebs found that to be listened to at all he had*
to lie, and after he had done this twice, he, too, had a reaction against the war
and talking about it. This could easily have been a self-portrait. His story to
Chink Dorman-Smith, a soldier he met in a bar in Milan, and later his friend,
that he had been wounded leading Arditi shock troopers on Monte Grappa.
The story to the reporter told just after his ship docked in America that his
body bore more scars from shrapnel than any other man who fought with the
Allied forces. The story told to Oak Park High School students that he had
fought with Arditi shock troops at Fossalta. The claim to the memorial committee of Oak Park that he had fought in three major battles on the Italian
front. The story he told in the cafés of Paris, about being buried alive for four
days at the front.

March

How deep the need is, to tell the story, to hear it to the end.   113

Who is it he wishes to impress with his lies? Is it his father, who meets 114
him at the railroad station, the same father whose critical judgments had
wounded him so many times? Or his mother, proud of his accomplishments,
whom he soon tells after the war, . . . *the mother of a man that has died for his*
country should be the proudest woman in the world. . . .

March
In wartime, one quick and senseless death after another. So many stories 115
without endings.

General Douglas MacArthur was among those men who wished to im- 116
press his mother with his heroism. It was she who urged him on in his military career, lobbying in Washington during the First World War to have him
made a general. And years after his mother's death when MacArthur hired
women to spend the night with him it was not to make love but to stay up all
night hearing him tell the stories of his victories.

March
Aftermath of childhood. Aftermath of war. That silence at the end. The ac- 117
tion has already occurred. Nothing can be done.

But there is also another story, of the soldier who wants to impress his 118
father, or who cannot. I am thinking of a story I heard about a young man
who was called up to do duty in the Israeli Occupied Territories. The violence, the killing, and what he saw as an injustice disturbed him. Finally he
broke down. He was discharged and sent to a clinic. His father would not
visit him there. This man was so disappointed with his son that afterward he
ceased to speak to him at all.

March
That moment at the end of Iphigenia. *Aristotle called it recognition. All the* 119
frenzy is done. Agamemnon has already killed his daughter, and his armies are
sailing toward Troy. How terrible to recognize this.

In a letter to Bill Horne, another veteran, Hemingway wrote of the 120
6,000,000,000 females and 8,000,000,000,000 males *crying out for second-*
hand thrills to be got from the front. The storyteller is never far from his audience. He can feel from his listeners what they want to hear. And what they
want to hear has also been a part of him. It has been what he himself wanted
to believe. It was even a kind of reason for being. The myth around which he
organized what he called himself. It was a story he himself had heard not so
much from any one person but in the atmosphere, indistinguishable from the
medium in which one day he came to consciousness, learned to look into a
mirror, to see himself and speak finally the syllables of his own name.

April
I do not want to enclose the text in a definitive meaning. As they come to 121
me I write ideas in my journal instead of the text.

There was another story of course but it came unbidden in the middle of 122
the night when he woke from a nightmare believing that he was still on the
battlefield, wounded, unable to flee. But it was only his wife, Hadley, who
heard this story, when she would wake at night with him and comfort him.

April
   The intuition of Cassandra. The feminine realm of thought holds the secrets   123
of our culture, and hence can make startling predictions.

   But the true story had even larger dimensions than this nightmare that   124
frightened him at night. Reality lay under the cover of a denser pattern of lies
that had invaded every aspect of his life. Concealing whoever he was a
man he had invented, who claimed to have given boxing lessons, or contracted
venereal disease, or traveled all over Spain with a cuadrilla of bullfighters.
Trying to reconstruct the bare facts of his life, one discovers only a confusing
landscape full of shrouding mists and quagmires. There is no solid ground.

April
   Cassandra condemned by Apollo, the reasonable god, to be unheard be-   125
cause she would not yield to his sexual assault. The second assault: what one
sees, erased.

   Perhaps this is why he hung on to everything, not only manuscripts and   126
letters as most writers do, but even boxing tickets, notes written on the backs
of old letters, to-do lists. Could it be that, having surrounded himself with
lies, he needed hard evidence of his actual existence?

April
   Shirley visiting again from Israel. We have lunch. I make some comment   127
about the cost of Patriot missiles being so high. She says she found out, facing
the threat of Scud attacks, that for her survival comes first.

   I can imagine Hemingway sitting surrounded as he is by all these papers   128
that document his existence, as he begins to locate something of himself
closer to the center. Does he discover this by accident or from the atmosphere
of his exile? Perhaps he is writing with his ear, trying to get the words, the
voice, the rhythms of the sentences to hold that electric quality of recognition
he has heard all around him. He ventures then just over the line of expectation. *I knew that I was hit.* He is breaking a mold *and leaned over and put my
hand on my knee.* Disturbing convention. *My knee wasn't there.* Moving
nearer to the truth than any of the tales he has told before. What emerges is
a different picture. *I wiped my hand on my shirt and,* not what he longed for
as a small boy telling tales, *another floating light came very slowly down,* but
somehow more alive, vibrant *and I looked at my leg and was very afraid.* In-
definably vivid, sharp with wit, and clarity, making him feel as he once wrote,
cool and clear inside himself.

FOR DISCUSSION AND WRITING:
RESEARCHING RECOGNITION

1. Review the Hemingway story included in chapter 3. Write an interpretation of that story based on Griffin's reading of Hemingway.

2. At one level, *A Chorus of Stones* could be read as biographical criticism: Hemingway's stories are explained in terms of his life. However, there are several levels at work in addition to the biographical one, and the cumulative effect is quite different from the conventional biographical interpretation: Griffin uses Hemingway's example as a kind of template that, when mapped onto her own experience, helps to locate the intersection between personal and societal histories. Write a short analysis of Griffin's method. Inventory the different elements at work in the content and the form of the writing. Compose a set of instructions that generalize Griffin's method from her specific materials, that could be used by writers interested in working with their own histories and interests.

3. Write your own "chorus of stones," following the instructions prepared in answer to the second question. Use Griffin's form and method, but use your own background and interests to guide the selection of the object(s) of study.

4. Looking at a photograph of her grandfather, Griffin states: "My grandfather's face bears an expression of grief just as if he were looking over a scene of senseless destruction, a field of bodies. What was his sorrow? Whatever it is, I recognize it." Griffin's mood is one of sorrow, whose specific quality she explores by means of the juxtaposition between details about the collective atrocities of war and certain events in the history of her family. The method is important for mystory, but the experience of "recognition" has to be generalized to allow for moods other than that of sorrow. Reflect upon the experience of composing your "chorus" for question 3. Were you surprised by the mood or feeling that emerged during the composition? Write a short essay on the effect of recognition that guided your choices and their elaboration in your writing. Your goal is to notice the "process": What happens when your research and composition are guided by the search for correspondences between your own situation and the historical or factual record?

5. Look again at the concluding section of question 3 in the section on Roland Barthes (p. 275). It suggests the possibility of extracting from the readings in this archive an alternative to Barthes's fragment figures as instructions for a research text. If you did not attempt this invention before, try it now. Once you have identified all the operating devices in the examples and translated them into instructions, test them in the composition of a research identification.

THE SIGNATURE

Another leader in the development of textualism is the French philosopher Jacques Derrida. Like Roland Barthes, Derrida experiments with a kind of writing that combines creativity and criticism. He no longer wants to write *about* literature but *with* literature. The reason for this approach is the textualist belief that literature cannot be fully understood by the traditional methods of interpretation, description, and analysis. For the textualist, a work of literature becomes intelligible through imitation of the work's own principle of composition—that is, the critic explains the work by using the artist's compositional technique to produce a new text. The textualist no longer tries to tell artists or students what a work of literature means, but seeks to learn from literature how to write criticism. To write as a textualist, one must transfer the artist's invention strategy from fiction or poetry to criticism or theory.

To test his theory that literature functions not only as an object of study but also as a source of knowledge, Derrida designed an experiment involving one of the oldest and most honored topics in the humanistic tradition: "Know thyself." In previous epochs, this project had been understood as an attempt to comprehend one's identity in terms of life experience by means of introspection. In our own time, in which language has become the model for explaining everything else, Derrida proposes to investigate not so much our identity in "life" but our identity in language— the identity not of our person but of our name.

By calling his experiment the "signature," Derrida reminds us of an ancient belief in the similarity or correspondence between the world outside and the interior life of a person, between the macro and micro worlds. The link mediating nature and society, joining one's biological existence to one's cultural experience, is language, with one's proper name bridging these dimensions of reality. The experiment includes the musical sense of "signature"—the set of signs at the beginning of a staff indicating the key and the time of the piece. The letters of the proper name constitute the "key" in which one's life is played out. We shall return to Derrida's technique of the "signature" after an excursion through the world of names. We can begin with the question asked by Shakespeare's teenage hero, Juliet.

What's in a Name
From Romeo and Juliet

William Shakespeare

The scene is set in the Italian city of Verona, four centuries ago. In a dark corner of the orchard behind the house of the Capulet family stands Romeo, young son of the Capulets' bitter enemies, the Montagues. He has just met and fallen in love with the Capulet daughter Juliet. At that moment, Juliet comes to a window of the house (or out on a balcony, as it is often staged), brooding to herself about this young Montague, who has obviously caught her fancy.

*This is, of course, one of the most famous love scenes in all of literature—
but we ask you to read it in another way, as a scene about language: specifically, as an interrogation of the relationship between words and things. We pick
up the action just as Juliet's frustration bursts out in speech. She is not aware,
of course, that the person on her mind is actually lurking in her father's orchard,
where he will hear every word she says.*

Juliet: O Romeo Romeo! wherefore art thou Romeo?
Deny thy father and refuse thy name;
Or, if thou wilt not, be but sworn my love,
And I'll no longer be a Capulet
Romeo [aside]:   Shall I hear more, or shall I speak at this?   5
Juliet: 'Tis but thy name that is my enemy.
Thou art thyself, though not a Montague.
What's Montague? It is nor hand, nor foot,
Nor arm, nor face, nor any other part
Belonging to a man. O, be some other name!   10
What's in a name? That which we call a rose
By any other name would smell as sweet.
So Romeo would, were he not Romeo called,
Retain that dear perfection which he owes
Without that title. Romeo, doff thy name;   15
And for thy name, which is no part of thee,
Take all myself
Romeo: I take thee at thy word.
Call me but love, and I'll be new baptized;
Henceforth I never will be Romeo.   20
Juliet: What man art thou that, thus bescreened in night,
So stumblest on my counsel?
Romeo: By a name
I know not how to tell thee who I am.
My name, dear saint, is hateful to myself,   25
Because it is an enemy to thee.
Had I it written, I would tear the word.
Juliet: My ears have yet not drunk a hundred words
Of thy tongue's uttering, yet I know the sound.
Art thou not Romeo, and a Montague?   30
Romeo: Neither, fair maid, if either thee dislike.

FOR DISCUSSION AND WRITING: NAMING NAMES

1. Make a list of all the statements about names in the text. Separate them
   into statements about proper names (Romeo, Montague) and statements
   about common nouns (rose, love). First, try to put each statement into
   your own words. Then discuss the larger implications of each statement.

What assumptions about the way names work are being made by the speaker?

2. What aspects of names and naming are causing the problems here? What can and cannot be changed with respect to names? Could we call a rose something else? Try to imagine how you might go about changing the common name for something. What about proper names? What does it mean to be "Romeo, and a Montague"?

THE HISTORY OF NAMES

The essay we excerpt here is designed to provide you with background on the subject of proper names, before you undertake some research into your own.

Names and Professions
(*from* Destiny in Names)

A. A. Roback

It is well known that most of our surnames are derived from the occupation   1
of an individual's progenitors. Thus we have Smith and Baker and Taylor and Butcher, Fisher, and Clark and all the rest. Since the decline of the guilds, and the free choice of a person's calling, it would become quite uncommon to find a man actually in the vocation designated by his surname. Occasionally, especially among Jews, we might find a dynasty of cantors, musicians, who preserve the rationale of their surname (Eddie Cantor, Zimbalist, and Fiedler are several illustrations of such namings), and the Cohens, Kahns, Kohns, Kagans, Kaplans, Katzes (abbreviation of *Kohen Tzedek*, "righteous priest"), are still to be regarded, for religious purposes, priests, descended from Aaron, the first of the caste, but most of them are not aware of their function and keep assimilating their name to something in keeping with the name-patterns of the ruling culture. (Coan, Conway, Cowan, Kuhn, Coburn, Kane, etc.)

If, then, after many removes from the original bearer, we still find, as if   2
through an atavistic throwback, an individual whose name corresponds with his profession, we think of it as a curiosity. That General Marshall should have risen to the first place in the American army, which, in European countries, would earn for him the title of Chief Marshal, is certainly a notable coincidence, if destiny plays no part here. Or let us, for a moment, scan the name of the man who led all the forces against the Nazis and succeeded in squelching their power through the invasion of France. Is it not worth reflecting that this man's surname is "a hewer of iron" (*Eisenhower* is, in the original German, *Eisenhauer*)? If an honorific sobriquet were to be pondered for the purpose, in recognition of his feat, it could not be more appropriate than the name which he actually inherited. Surely it is just as fitting as the

nickname Martel, i.e., "the hammer," which was given to Charles, grandfather of Charlemagne, in celebration of his victory over the Saracens. Another of our first-line generals, Van Fleet, does not seem to be quite at home, onomastically, but after all the fleet and the army are only complementary to one another.

This interlinking, or rather cross linking, is not rare with the army, air 3 force, and navy. We can cite, e.g., Bryant L. M. Boatner, commanding general of the air proving grounds, as one illustration, while his brother, H. J. Boatner, who has become a major general, is not out of place as a high land officer. In W. M. Fechteler (in German *fechten* means to fight), commander-in-chief of the Atlantic Fleet, we have another patronymic worthy of its bearer and vice versa.

All these are names with which any newspaper reader must be familiar. 4 A full list of the high ranking officers in the armed forces would, no doubt, disclose many more such coincidences.

In a sphere far removed from warfare and destruction we have a more 5 agreeable circumstance in the name of Pissarev ("writer") the famous Russian critic and that of Sir Russell Brain, probably the most eminent authority on the nervous system, and particularly the brain. Inasmuch as Brain is such an uncommon name, there must be something more than coincidence in this correspondence. In an adjacent sphere, we have the name of Freud, who tells us that because of his sex theories, his name, a contraction of *Freude*, meaning joy, was used as a taunt by his bitter opponents, associating it with the *filles de joie*, in other words implying that his scientific profession coincided with the world's oldest profession.

FOR DISCUSSION AND WRITING: IMAGINING NAMES

1. Whether or not a name determines one's destiny, there is evidence that people do form an impression of someone based on that person's name. It was reported in the newspapers that half the businessmen on Little Tokyo Street in Los Angeles did not want it renamed after *Challenger* astronaut Ellison Onizuka (killed in the shuttle explosion). One reason for this opposition had to do with Onizuka's name. Although it is a fairly common Japanese surname, the archaic meaning of Onizuka is "place where the devil lives." More troubling are the studies that show that a student's name influences the grade a paper receives (papers signed with common, strong names receive higher marks than those signed with odd, unusual names). Anyone who has ever been teased about his or her name (and who has not at some time during childhood?) knows that we are vulnerable through our names, that our name is an important feature of our identity. Write or tell an anecdote about such teasing, either that you experienced yourself or that you witnessed.

2. You know something about names in general. What do you know about your own names—or what can you find out? Using your library's resources (where you should find information on specific proper names and family names) and calling upon older members of your family, find

out what you can about the meaning and history of the names you use regularly. If your names mean something in some other language, find out about that, too. (Don't neglect nicknames and pet names.) Assemble your material so that you can present information about your names in the form of an oral or written report. And *save this material.* You will be using it more creatively later on.

THE POWER OF NAMES

Here are two discussions of the power of names. The first is a brief selection from an autobiographical essay by the well-known black writer Ralph Ellison, in which he reveals his full name and discusses its significance and its influence on his own life. The second is from a book on women and language by the social critic Dale Spender, who shows how the absence of names affects the place of women in history, and how titles like "Mr." And "Mrs." reveal structures of cultural power.

From Hidden Name and Complex Fate

Ralph Ellison

Let Tar Baby, that enigmatic figure from Negro folklore, stand for the world. 1 He leans, black and gleaming, against the wall of life utterly noncommittal under our scrutiny, our questioning, starkly unmoving before our naïve attempts at intimidation. Then we touch him playfully and before we can say *Sonny Liston!* we find ourselves stuck. Our playful investigations become a labor, a fearful struggle, an *agon.* Slowly we perceive that our task is to learn the proper way of freeing ourselves to develop, in other words, technique.

Sensing this, we give him our sharpest attention, we question him care- 2 fully, we struggle with more subtlety; while he, in his silent way, holds on, demanding that we perceive the necessity of calling him by his true name as the price of our freedom. It is unfortunate that he has so many, many "true names"—all spelling chaos; and in order to discover even one of these we must first come into the possession of our own names. For it is through our names that we first place ourselves in the world. Our names, being the gift of others, must be made our own.

Once while listening to the play of a two-year-old girl who did not know 3 she was under observation, I heard her saying over and over again, at first with questioning and then with sounds of growing satisfaction, "I am Mimi Livisay? . . . I am Mimi Livisay. I *am* Mimi Livisay . . . I am *Mimi* Li-vi-say! I am Mimi . . ."

And in deed and in fact she was—or became so soon thereafter, by 4 working playfully to establish the unit between herself and her name.

For many of us this is far from easy. We must learn to wear our names   5
within all the noise and confusion of the environment in which we find ourselves; make them the center of all of our associations with the world, with
man and with nature. We must charge them with all our emotions, our hopes,
hates, loves, aspirations. They must become our masks and our shields and
the containers of all those values and traditions which we learn and/or imagine as being the meaning of our familial past.

And when we are reminded so constantly that we bear, as Negroes, names   6
originally possessed by those who owned our enslaved grandparents, we are
apt, especially if we are potential writers, to be more than ordinarily concerned with the veiled and mysterious events, the fusions of blood, the furtive
couplings, the business transactions, the violations of faith and loyalty, the
assaults; yes, and the unrecognized and unrecognizable loves through which
our names were handed down unto us.

So charged with emotion does this concern become for some of us, that   7
we have, earlier, the example of the followers of Father Divine and, now, the
Black Muslims, discarding their original names in rejection of the blood-
stained, the brutal, the sinful images of the past. Thus they would declare
new identities, would clarify a new program of intention and destroy the verbal evidence of a willed and ritualized discontinuity of blood and human
intercourse.

Not all of us, actually only a few, seek to deal with our names in this man-   8
ner. We take what we have and make of them what we can. And there are
even those who know where the old broken connections lie, who recognize
their relatives across the chasm of historical denial and the artificial barriers
of society, and who see themselves as bearers of many of the qualities which
were admirable in the original sources of their common line (Faulkner has
made much of this); and I speak here not of mere forgiveness, nor of obse-
quious insensitivity to the outrages symbolized by the denial and the division, but of the conscious acceptance of the harsh realities of the human condition, of the ambiguities and hypocrisies of human history as they have
played themselves out in the United States.

Perhaps, taken in aggregate, these European names which (sometimes   9
with irony, sometimes with pride, but always with personal investment) represent a certain triumph of the spirit, speaking to us of those who rallied, re-
assembled and transformed themselves and who under dismembering pressures refused to die. "Brothers and sisters," I once heard a Negro preacher
exhort, "let us make up our faces before the world, and our names shall sound
throughout the land with honor! For we ourselves are our *true* names, not
their epithets! So let us, I say, Make Up Our Faces and Our Minds!"

Perhaps my preacher had read T. S. Eliot, although I doubt it. And in ac-   10
tuality, it was unnecessary that he do so, for a concern with names and naming was very much part of that special area of American culture from which
I come, and it is precisely for this reason that this example should come to
mind in a discussion of my own experience as a writer.

Undoubtedly, writers begin their *conditioning* as manipulators of words   11
long before they become aware of literature — certain Freudians would say at

the breast. Perhaps. But if so, that is far too early to be of use at this moment. Of this, though, I am certain: that despite the misconceptions of those educators who trace the reading difficulties experienced by large numbers of Negro children in Northern schools to their Southern background, these children are, in *their* familiar South, facile manipulators of words. I know, too, that the Negro community is deadly in its ability to create nicknames and to spot all that is ludicrous in an unlikely name or that which is incongruous in conduct. Names are not qualities; nor are words, in this particular sense, actions. To assume that they are could cost one his life many times a day. Language skills depend to a large extent upon a knowledge of the details, the manners, the objects, the folkways, the psychological patterns, of a given environment. Humor and wit depend upon much the same awareness, and so does the suggestive power of names.

"A small brown bowlegged Negro with the name 'Franklin D. Roosevelt 12 Jones' might sound like a clown to someone who looks at him from the outside," said my friend Albert Murray, "but on the other hand he just might turn out to be a hell of a fireside operator. He might just lie back in all of that comic juxtaposition of names and manipulate you deaf, dumb and blind— and you not even suspecting it, because you're thrown out of stance by his name! There you are, so dazzled by the F.D.R. image—which you *know* you can't see—and so delighted with your own superior position that you don't realize that it's *Jones* who must be confronted."

Well, as you must suspect, all of this speculation on the matter of names 13 has a purpose, and now, because it is tied up so ironically with my own experience as a writer, I must turn to my own name.

For in the dim beginnings, before I ever thought consciously of writing, 14 there was my own name, and there was, doubtless, a certain magic in it. From the start I was uncomfortable with it, and in my earliest years it caused me much puzzlement. Neither could I understand what a poet was, nor why, exactly, my father had chosen to name me after one. Perhaps I could have understood it perfectly well had he named me after his own father, but that name had been given to an older brother who died and thus was out of the question. But why hadn't he named me after a hero, such as Jack Johnson, or a soldier like Colonel Charles Young, or a great seaman like Admiral Dewey, or an educator like Booker T. Washington, or a great orator and abolitionist like Frederick Douglass? Or again, why hadn't he named me (as so many Negro parents had done) after President Teddy Roosevelt?

Instead, he named me after someone called Ralph Waldo Emerson, and 15 then, when I was three, he died. It was too early for me to have understood his choice, although I'm sure he must have explained it many times, and it was also too soon for me to have made the connection between my name and my father's love for reading. Much later, after I began to write and work with words, I came to suspect that he was aware of the suggestive powers of names and of the magic involved in naming.

I recall an odd conversation with my mother during my early teens in 16 which she mentioned their interest in, of all things, prenatal culture! But for a long time I actually knew only that my father read a lot, and that he admired this remote Mr. Emerson, who was something called a "poet and philosopher"—so much so that he named his second son after him.

I knew, also, that whatever his motives, the combination of names he'd 17
given me caused me no end of trouble from the moment when I could talk
well enough to respond to the ritualized question which grownups put to very
young children. Emerson's name was quite familiar to Negroes in Oklahoma
during those days when World War I was brewing, and adults, eager to show
off their knowledge of literary figures, and obviously amused by the joke implicit in such a small brown nubbin of a boy carrying around such a heavy
moniker, would invariably repeat my first two names and then to my great
annoyance, they'd add "Emerson."

And I, in my confusion, would reply, "No, *no, I'm* not Emerson, he's the 18
little boy who lives next door." Which only made them laugh all the louder.
"Oh, no," they'd say, *"you're* Ralph Waldo Emerson," while I had fantasies of
blue murder.

For a while the presence next door of my little friend, Emerson, made it 19
unnecessary for me to puzzle too often over this peculiar adult confusion.
And since there were other Negro boys named Ralph in the city, I came to
suspect that there was something about the combination of names which
produced their laughter. Even today I know of only one other Ralph who had
as much comedy made out of his name, a campus politician and deep-voiced
orator whom I knew at Tuskegee, who was called in friendly ribbing, *Ralph
Waldo Emerson Edgar Allan Poe,* spelled Powe. This must have been quite a
trial for him, but I had been initiated much earlier.

During my early school years the name continued to puzzle me, for it 20
constantly evoked in the faces of others some secret. It was as though I possessed some treasure or some defect, which was invisible to my own eyes and
ears; something which I had but did not *possess,* like a piece of property in
South Carolina, which was mine but which I could not have until some future time. I recall finding, about this time, while seeking adventure in back
alleys—which possess for boys a superiority over playgrounds like that which
kitchen utensils possess over toys designed for infants—a large photographic
lens. I remember nothing of its optical qualities, of its speed or color correction, but it gleamed with crystal mystery and it was beautiful.

Mounted handsomely in a tube of shiny brass, it spoke to me of distant 21
worlds of possibility. I played with it, looking through it with squinted eyes,
holding it in shafts of sunlight, and tried to use it for a magic lantern. But
most of this was as unrewarding as my attempts to make the music come
from a phonograph record by holding the needle in my fingers.

I could burn holes through newspapers with it, or I could pretend that it 22
was a telescope, the barrel of a cannon, or the third eye of a monster—*I* being the monster—but I could do nothing at all about its proper function of
making images, nothing to make it yield its secret. But I could not discard it.

Older boys sought to get it away from me by offering knives or tops, agate 23
marbles or whole zoos of grass snakes and horned toads in trade, but I held
on to it. No one, not even the white boys I knew, had such a lens, and it was
my own good luck to have found it. Thus I would hold on to it until such time

as I could acquire the parts needed to make it function. Finally I put it aside and it remained buried in my box of treasures, dusty and dull, to be lost and forgotten as I grew older and became interested in music.

I had reached by now the grades where it was necessary to learn some- 24 thing about Mr. Emerson and what he had written, such as the "Concord Hymn" and the essay "Self-Reliance," and in following his advice, I reduced the "Waldo" to a simple and, I hoped, mysterious "W.," and in my own reading I avoided his works like the plague. I could no more deal with my name—I shall never really master it—than I could find a creative use for my lens. Fortunately there were other problems to occupy my mind. . . .

The Male Line
(*from* Man Made Language)
Dale Spender

Studies of language have revealed that semantics is only one of the forms 1 through which sexism operates. . . . One of the other features of English language practices which is inherently sexist is the use of names. In our society "only men have real names" in that their names are permanent and they have "accepted the permanency of their names as one of the rights of being male." . . . This has both practical and psychological ramifications for the construction—and maintenance—of male supremacy.

Practically it means that women's family names do not count and that 2 there is one more device for making women invisible. Fathers pass their names on to their sons and the existence of daughters can be denied when in the absence of a male heir it is said that a family "dies out." One other direct result of this practice of only taking cognizance of the male name has been to facilitate the development of history as the story of the male line, because it becomes almost impossible to trace the ancestry of women—particularly if they do not come into the male-defined categories of importance.

Very little is known about women, says Virginia Woolf . . . for "the his- 3 tory of England is the history of the male line" . . . this point was brought home to Jill Liddington and Jill Norris . . . when they undertook to document the story of women's suffrage in Lancashire for "this vital contribution had been largely neglected by historians." . . . They had difficulty with sources and one difficulty was not one which would be encountered in tracing men . . . :

> Sometimes we seemed to be forever chasing down blind alleys. For instance, one of the most active women, Helen Silcock, a weavers' union leader from Wigan, seemed to disappear after 1902. We couldn't think why, until we came across a notice of 'congratulations to Miss Silcock on her marriage to Mr Fairhurst' in a little known labour journal, the *Women's Trade Union Review* . . . it was an object lesson for us in the difficulties of tracing women activists.

It is also an extremely useful device for eliminating women from history 4
and for making it exceedingly difficult to perceive a continuum and develop
a tradition.

When females have no right to "surnames," to family names of their 5
own, the concept of women as the property of men is subtly reinforced (and
this is of course assisted by the title *Mrs.*). Currently many women are changing their names and instead of taking the name of either their father or their
husband they are coining new, autonomous names for themselves: for example, Cheris Kramer has become Cheris Kramarae, Julia Stanley has become Julia Penelope—there are almost countless examples of this change. A
common practice has become that of taking the first name of a close female
friend or relative—such as mother—as the new family name (for example,
Janet Robyn, Elizabeth Sarah). When asked why she had legally dropped her
surname and retained her first two given names, Margaret Sandra stated that
a "surname" was intended as an indication of the "sire" and was so closely
linked socially with the ownership of women that there was no "surname"
that she found acceptable.

Although attempts have been made to trivialize these new naming activities 6
among women, such activities are serious and they do undermine patriarchal
practices. At the very least they raise consciousness about the role men's
names have played in the subordination of women, and at best they confound
traditional patriarchal classification schemes which have not operated in
women's interest. I have been told that it makes it very difficult to "pigeon-hole"
women, to "place" them, if they persist with this neurotic practice of giving
themselves new names. One male stated quite sincerely that it was becoming
"jolly difficult to work out whether women were married these days because
of the ridiculous practice of not taking their husband's names." In order to
operate in the world, however, it has *never* been necessary to know from a
name whether someone is married or single, as women can testify. Men have
not thought that *not* changing their name upon marriage should present difficulties to women and once more the bias of language practices is revealed.

But many males are confused, and not without cause. The language has 7
helped to create the representation of females as sex objects; it has also
helped to signal when a sex object is not available and is the property of another male. The patriarchal order has been maintained by such devices and
when women consciously and intentionally abolish them men have reason
to feel insecure; they do not however have reason to protest. . . .

FOR DISCUSSION AND WRITING: CHANGING NAMES

1. Consider any points in the previous two excerpts that seem to you especially interesting, surprising, or controversial. See if your classmates agree
   with your judgment. Try to resolve any differences.
2. What can you find out about the female names in your own heritage?
   How far back can you go beyond your mother, her mother, and so on?
   Do you have equal information about the male and female parts of your

heritage? Note any interesting names from the female side of your family. Compare your findings with those of others.

3. Consider some of the aspects of naming raised by Ellison. Do you know anyone whose last name was acquired at some recent point in history (for example, through Americanization or religious conversion)? Do you know anyone descended from slaves whose name comes from the family that owned the person's ancestors? Do you know of any well-known people who have changed their names? Have you every heard of a *nom de plume,* or pen name? How many actors and musicians use their "own" names? What is one's "own" name? Have we "problematized" for you the notion of having a name of one's own?

If you could have any names you wanted, with no fuss, what names would you take? Why? If you decided to change your names in actuality, would there be a fuss? Who would make it? Why?

Do you know anyone named after a famous person? If so, how has this affected his or her life? Would you like to bear a famous name? Do you believe that names are important? What's in a name?

WRITING FROM SIGNATURES

Let us begin with a brief discussion of the ancient practice of *blazoning*. In 1484 King Richard III of England chartered the Herald's College, whose purpose was to assign coats of arms and trace lineages. Within a century, a set of rules for *blazoning* (giving a concise verbal description of a shield bearing a coat of arms) had been standardized. Aristocratic families all had a coat of arms, and the practice continues today, with coats of arms being displayed by colleges and universities, fraternal organizations, and businesses. There are even people who will provide an "authentic" coat of arms for any of us willing to pay for such a thing.

Derrida's signature experiment is in part an adaptation to the generation (note the pun on lineage) of texts out of one's names of the techniques originally developed for representing symbolically on a shield the lineage of a family name. Some of the terms you will encounter when reading Derrida are derived from the art of heraldry. Besides the term *blazon,* Derrida also refers to the *abyss,* which means in this context the central point or heart of the shield. A coat of arms often contains at the abyss point a miniature shield representing the paternal (most important) coat of arms (or sometimes the arms of a line to which the "armiger" held a claim). The shield within a shield creates an effect of infinite regression, like that of the label on Morton salt, with the girl pictured holding a package of salt with a label also picturing a girl holding the package, and so on. The implication of this "putting into the abyss" for the mystory is that the microcosm (in this case the name of the author) constitutes a representation of the macrocosm (the work written by the one who signs that name).

The designers of coats of arms used poetic techniques such as the pun and the rebus. The mottoes inscribed on banners draped above or below the shield, for example, frequently were based on a pun on the family name (replacing the war cries of days of old). The Seton family motto is "Set On." The Bernard family, whose shield bears the image of a bear, covered by a crest with a smaller bear, has the motto "Bear and Forbear." The Winlaws' motto is "What I Win I Keep." The best known of such mottoes is that of the Vernons—*Ver non semper viret*—which may be translated either as "The Spring Is Not Always Green" or, as intended, "Vernon Always Flourishes."

A member of the Grafton family devised a rebus of the name, composed of a graft issuing from a *tun* (heraldic name for a beer or wine keg). Arms and crests, in other words, frequently deduce their origin from the family name in the same manner as mottoes, in which case they are called *armes parlantes,* or "canting heraldry." The families of Salmon, Sturgeon, Lucy, Herring, Shelley, Talbot, Wolf, Rabbitt, Falconer, and the like bear the image of their namesake (lucies are pike, shelley is a whelk-stalk, talbot is a hound). The Cardingtons bear three wool-cards, and the Harrows three harrows.

As you read the following selections from James Joyce and Jacques Derrida, keep in mind that both writers allude to the herald's system of blazoning a name as one of the models for their use of language.

Shem the Penman
(*from* Finnegans Wake)

James Joyce

Everyone knows that James Joyce is a major modern writer, with a reputation for being difficult. And some people know that Finnegans Wake is his last and most complicated text, one which he kept revising for years and years, always making it more complicated. Only those who have actually looked at it, however, also know that it is a funny book, chock-full of jokes and puns. Among other things, it is also a book about names and naming, and the way we are all full of ready-made language that we apply to things and people left and write (to use a Joycean sort of pun).

In the pages that follow, we present you with three versions of a tiny excerpt from Joyce's dream-book: some scraps from the first draft, the same section from a later draft, and the same section as it appears in the published book. In this section of the book, Joyce is writing about a character named Shem the

Penman, who is a writer very much like himself, Shem being a version of his own first name. In short, Joyce is playing with his signature here, and especially with the similarity of Shem and Sham. Read his work for some clues on how you might do this sort of thing yourself. And please don't be too solemn about it. Joyce is just playing with his names, playing with language, playing with himself, following a process that sociolinguists now recognize as the standard operation of nicknaming in our culture.

From the First Draft of *Finnegans Wake*

Shem is as short for Shemus as Jim is for Jacob. Originally of respectable connections his back life simply won't stand being written about.

*   *   *   *   *   *

Cain—Ham (Shem)—Esau—Jim the Penman

———

wellknown for violent abuse of self and others.

lives in inkbottlehouse

boycotted, local publican refuse to supply books, papers, ink, foolscap, makes his own from dried dung sweetened with spittle (ink) writes universal history on his own body (parchment)

hospitality, all drunk & rightly indignant

1 eye halfopen, 1 arm, 42 hairs on his head, 17 on upper lip, 5 on chin, 3 teeth, no feet, 10 thumbs, ½ a buttock, ½ & ½ a testicle,—when is a man not a man?

a forger, can imitate all styles, some of his own.

1st copies of most original masterpieces slipped from his pen

From a Later Draft of *Finnegans Wake*

Shem is as short for Shemus as Jim is joky for Jacob. A few are still found who say that originally he was of respectable connections (———was among his cousins) but every honest to goodness man in the land knows that his back life will not stand being written about. Putting truth and lies together some shot may be made at how this hybrid actually looked. His bodily makeup, it seems, included 1 halfopen eye, 1 arm, 42 hairs on his crown, 18 on his upper lip, 5 on his chin, all ears, no feet, 5 thumbs, 2 fifths of a buttocks, a testicle & a half,—so that even Shem himself, when playing with words in the nursery asked his brothers & sisters the first riddle of the uni-

verse: When is a man not a man?: offering a prize of a crabapple to the winner. One said when the heavens are rocking, another said when other lips, a
third said when the fair land of Poland, the next one said when those angel
faces smile, still another said when the wine is in, one of the youngest said
when father papered the parlour, still one said when you are old & grey & full
of tears, and still another when we were boys, & another when you come
down the vale, another *et enim imposuit manus episcopas fecit illum altissimis
sacerdotum* & one when pigs begin to fly. All were wrong, he said. So Shem
took the cake, the correct solution being, when he is a sham.

From Section I, Part vii, of *Finnegans Wake*

Shem is as short for Shemus as Jem is joky for Jacob. A few toughnecks   1
are still getatable who pretend that aboriginally he was of respectable stemming (he was an outlex between the lines of Ragonar Blaubarb and Horrild
Hairwire and an inlaw to Capt. the Hon. and Rev. Mr. Bbyrdwood de Trop
Blogg was among his most distant connections) but every honest to goodness
man in the land of the space of today knows that his back life will not stand
being written about in black and white. Putting truth and untruth together a
shot may be made at what this hybrid actually was like to look at.

Shem's bodily getup, it seems, included an adze of a skull, an eight of a   2
larkseye, the whoel of a nose, one numb arm up a sleeve, fortytwo hairs off
his uncrown, eighteen to his mock lip, a trio of barbels from his megageg chin
(sowman's son), the wrong shoulder higher than the right, all ears, an artificial tongue with a natural curl, not a foot to stand on, a handful of thumbs,
a blind stomach, a deaf heart, a loose liver, two fifths of two buttocks, one
gleetsteen avoirdupoider for him, a manroot of all evil, a salmonkelt's thin-
skin, eelsblood in his cold toes, a bladder tristended, so much so that young
Master Shemmy on his very first debouch at the very dawn of protohistory
seeing himself such and such, when playing with thistlewords in their garden
nursery, Griefotrofio, at Phig Streat III, Shuvlin, Old Hoeland, (would we go
back there now for sounds, pillings and sense? would we now for annas and
annas? Would we for fullscore eight and a liretta? for twelve blocks one bob?
for four testers one groat? not for a dinar! not for jo!) dictited to of all his little brothron and sweestureens the first riddle of the universe: asking, when is
a man not a man?: telling them take their time, yungfries, and wait till the tide
stops (for from the first his day was a fortnight) and offering the prize of a bit-
tersweet crab, a little present from the past, for their copper age was yet un-
minted, to the winner. One said when the heavens are quakers, a second said
when Bohemeand lips, a third said when he, no, when hold hard a jiffy, when
he is a gnawstick and determined to, the next one said when the angel of
death kicks the bucket of life, still another said when the wine's at witsends,
and still another when lovely wooman stoops to conk him, one of the littliest
said me, me, Sem, when pappa papared the harbour, one of the wittiest said,
when he yeat ye abblokooken and he zmear hezelf zo zhooken, still one said
when you are old I'm grey fall full wi sleep, and still another when wee deader
walkner, and another when he is just only after having being semisized,

another when yea, he hath no mananas, and one when dose pigs they begin now that they will flies up intil the looft. All were wrong, so Shem himself, the doctator, took the cake, the correct solution being—all give it up?—; when he is a—yours till the rending of the rocks, —Sham.

FOR DISCUSSION

The oddity of James Joyce's style may be alleviated if we review it in the context of a study on nicknaming. When you come to the assignment asking you to generate a text out of your own name, you might find it useful to imitate the way Joyce extended the play of nicknaming to himself, beating society at its own game by providing his own nicknames, as the process is described in the following excerpt by Jane Morgan, Christopher O'Neill, and Rom Harré. Compare the observations made in this sociolinguistic analysis with the style of *Finnegans Wake*.

Nicknames: Their Origins and Social Consequences

Jane Morgan, Christopher O'Neill, and Rom Harré

During adolescence conception both of self and of others undergoes consid- 1
erable change. This apparently cataclysmic transition is, however, apparently unreflected by the various personal labels attached. If nicknames are indeed to justify our claims to their being the surface manifestations of deeper psychological processes, then why aren't these tremendous personality changes of adolescence also reflected? The explanation must, we think, lie in the multiplicity of factors contributing to any nickname. We have linked it, true, to thought patterns and the individual's attempts to structure his [or her] world. Goffman's theories about social stigma also show a similarity to nicknames too strong to be ignored. They are closely linked, then, to minority and prejudice in a given society and perhaps even dependent on them. They are subject to that uncontrollable variable of the individual—his physical, mental, biographical idiosyncrasies, and how adequately he copes with them. All these— the psychological, the social, the personal—are variables directly affecting the constant—the nickname. Any change in one of these aspects, thus, for instance the personality changes of adolescence, can either be accentuated or counteracted by the other two forces exerting their influences on the situation. Unless these also remain constant, very little alteration would be apparent.

Another aspect of nicknaming, however, became discernible in the course 2
of research. Again, a definite progression could be traced when comparing the two lists of nine- and thirteen-year-olds. The change this time, however, was not in the content of the name itself but in the actual process of name-giving. We noted previously that the great majority of nicknames were internal formations—between 55 per cent and 60 per cent of the entire total. Of

this number, in turn, particularly with the younger age-group, these took the form of very simple, sometimes spontaneous syllabic mutations; "Nicholas-Ridiculous" etc. This variety of verbal experiment was likened to the "babbling" stage with babies—both being purely phonic explorations for the sheer joy of articulation, meaning being largely superfluous. Just as the "babbling" is a transitory phase in the acquisition of language, so the tendency among children to respond solely to the aural quality of a name was, in the later survey, superseded by a reaction to meaning, so that a far more complex thought pattern was apparent in the actual naming process. Having noticed this phenomenon, the names were analysed again, this time focusing upon the method, rather than the content or origin of the name. Results were as follows:

Process	9-yr olds	13-yr olds
Simple mutation	77%	57%
Pun/irony	8%	15%
Analogy	15%	28%

For these figures to be meaningful obviously an explanation of the categories is essential: Simple mutation entails, as explicated above, merely a slight alteration of the name, usually the addition of a suffix: Bundy-Bundy-o/Bundo; a direct rhyme: Jill-Pill; or simple and often meaningless mutation: Nigel-Niggles, etc. This category, as the table illustrates, is prevalent in the nine-year age-group, but is gradually absorbed into the two others. Pun/irony involves a more complicated and intellectual manipulation of the name, though the response is still predominantly to the phonic rather than the semantic content. Nine-year-olds were capable of the letter play of:

Sarah Tibbets   Stebbit   Tibits

But there is only one notable example of a name undergoing a triple process:

Vincent Parsloe   Lieut. Parslow   Lieut. Pidgeon   Loot

whereas, in the twelve-to-fourteen age-group, this is a far more common occurrence:

Jackie Amos	Amosquito	Flea
Steven Hill	Chill	Charlie
Joanne R.	Josy	Dozy
Richard Cantwell	Tin Cantwell	Tin
Tracy F.	Wednesday	"When's dey gonna break" (Thin legs)

Puns, too, involve a response to meaning rather than the sound of words:

David Sharp	Acker	Latin equivalent
Martin Southcott	Eastbed	Antithesis of compounds
Andrew Barefield	Barefield Sobers	Pun and allusion

In the thirteen-year-old selection, too, the nicknames are often ironic:

John O'Derr   Brain of Britain   Cos he's a thick Mick really

This category reveals a far more complicated and sophisticated manipulation of the original name, and a tendency to respond not to the sound of the word but to its meaning. The numbers in the group almost double in the latter survey, suggesting a far more complex thought process emerges proportionately with age.

The third category—that of the allusive names—shows evidence of the children reaching into the realms of their entire experience to supply the name. Again the group demonstrates a remarkable increase at the later stage. The nine-year-olds tended to simply add the "type" names: "Fatty," "Lanky," "Brainbox," "Four Eyes." The thirteen-year-olds, on the other hand, use everyday experience as referents far more frequently. The "Tubby's" of the primary school have become the "Cannon's" and the "Chubby Chequer's" of the high-school comprehensive. The analogy can be triggered off by either appearance or actual name:

Debra Brown	Henry	Like that dog on TV
Heather Taylor	Tiger	Like that girl on the "Double Deckers"
Jane Percy	Percy Thrower	
	Percy Parrot	Reasons apparent
	Persil Automatic	
Sharon Gonsuales	Speedy	Speedy Gonzales
Judy Lancaster	Bomber	Lancaster Bomber

The trend is, we think, worth particular attention because, to a certain extent, it reinforces an aspect of the Peevers and Secord report. The "Tubby's" etc. of the earlier group do seem to imply the process of a type concept being applied, without any significant modification, to individuals. And this validates the American account of the initial method of applying simple "global" referents to personal concepts.

The marked increase in the allusive content of names, too, implies the process of naming by continual reference to personal experience of the environment. The "type" figure is individualised by finding parallel examples in their world—the mass media playing, perhaps, a significant role. This would substantiate tentatively claims about the actual process of differentiation in personal concepts, increasing contact with the environment (directly proportionate to age) shading in the details, helping to discriminate more finely, improving perception and making others, in fact, three-dimensional.

FOR DISCUSSION AND WRITING: EXPLORING THE NAME FROM CREST TO NICKNAME

1. Does your family have a crest or coat of arms? How much do you know about it? How do these family coats of arms relate to the crests adopted

by fraternities and sororities? by corporations? Are the logos devised by businesses to represent their companies, or the emblems devised by advertisers to represent products, similar to family crests?

Imagine that you have been knighted in recognition of your good works and that you have permission to suggest the design of your own coat of arms. What would it look like?

2. With the three drafts of *Finnegans Wake* before us, we can see the progression of the passage at the level of both style and theme. What is the organizing idea of the piece? What is the stylistic principle? Evaluate the final draft according to the standards of writing normally applied to student essays.

3. The sample from *Finnegans Wake*, in the context of the article on nicknames, shows that Joyce appropriated a language practice from everyday life and extended it into an experimental form of high literature. He not only plays with the proper names but also uses the device to write a portrait of the character. Simulate Joyce's method, applied to your own case: compose a text of similar length to the sample, based on this technique of distortion, modification, and variation of the words of your own name and of a descriptive self-portrait (you will want to make liberal use of a dictionary and thesaurus).

4. Try a variation on the nicknaming method of self-portraiture by using another simple (oral) form from everyday language use—the joke. Start with an existing joke that makes fun of the community with which you identify (gender, religion, race, etc.). Rewrite the joke as a self-portrait in the style of *Finnegans Wake*.

SIGNING (THE PROPER NAME)

According to the French philosopher Jacques Derrida, there are at least three ways in which an author signs a work. The first dimension or register of signing is the signature "proper"—the proper name placed on the title page identifying the source of the writing. The second register refers to what is commonly called "style"—"the inimitable idiom of an artist's work"—such that even without the availability of the proper name, an experienced reader might recognize the author of a work. (This second register has been the basis for many an exam question.) There remains, however, one more way in which a piece of writing carries the mark of its owner. This third register of the signature is the most complex, involving the heraldic placement of the name in the depths of the text. At this level the writer's name is seen as the seed out of which the text has grown, by a process of metaphorical and intertextual development. Retracing this process, an interpreter can find the author's name, hidden in the depths—or, to use Derrida's word, the "abyss"—of the text.

As we learned from the reading by Roger Brown in chapter 2, a common noun is the name of a general category—*book* for example. A proper noun, in contrast, is said to have no "meaning" in the ordinary sense of the term. It refers exclusively, picking out in the world not a category of things but a specific individual thing. All the people named "James" or "Robert" do not constitute a set or category in the way that everything named "book" does, because the shared name does not promise any other relationship among the people (other than the fact that people have names), unlike the term *book*, which promises that everything by that name will possess certain qualities or attributes.

Or at least such has been the thinking about the operation of proper nouns or names until Derrida came along. Derrida asks us to reconsider the question of how names refer, that is, of the relationship between language and lived reality. We know from some of the reading in this section and from our familiarity with naming practices in non-Western societies that in some cultures, there is a looser, freer passage between common and proper nouns, between a general category and a particular individual who shares some of the qualities of that category; as in nicknames, which continue this tradition of naming a person according to personal attributes, such that the name not only identifies the person, but also connotes some aspects of the person's "style."

Derrida's point of departure for reopening the study of reference is the naming process as practiced in literature. Unlike ordinary life in our society in which a person's name is arbitrarily assigned and denotes without connotation the bearer of the name, in literature a name often tells a great deal about a person. One of the first tricks a reader learns about the great symbol hunt for meaning in reading literature is to notice the names of the characters. If a character bears the name "Christian," the reader may expect to find certain religious themes of some use in understanding the work. But what about in life? If you meet people named "Christian," do you expect them to be Christians? And if they are, that is hardly surprising in our culture.

But there is more to it than that, for Derrida finds that not only do authors often give "motivated" names to their characters, but these names also may bear a significant relationship to the author's identity. Jean Genet, the French novelist and dramatist, a reformed criminal, named many of his characters after flowers. His own name, "Genet," means "broomflower" in French, as well as a kind of horse (among other things). This relationship between the real and fictional proper names is only the beginning of the textual phenomenon identified by Derrida, whose research revealed that the rhetorical figure of antonomasia—taking a common noun for a proper name or a proper name for a common noun—is the key to the process by which the third level of the signature takes place.

At the third level of signing, the relationship between an author's name and his or her literary style becomes the basis for a "poetics"—a theory of the production or making of texts. Derrida calls this process the "double bind" or "double band" of the signature, in which the proper name moves from designating a particular individual to become the key to a general theory of how texts are constructed. Genet provides one model for this process, folding all three levels into one scene in which the botanical properties of the flowers in his books refer both to the proper name "Genet" and to a theory of rhetorical invention. Therefore writing may be produced that follows the linguistic equivalent of the reproductive processes of the specific plants concerned (hence the careful description of "dissemination," or the spreading of seeds as manifested in certain species—cryptogams, angiosperms, and the like).

Derrida's area of application of this idea is unusual, but the metaphor itself is ancient. Fertilization and reproduction in the plant and animal kingdoms have long served as metaphors for creativity in the arts. Indeed, the procedure Derrida uses in the following excerpt—juxtaposing the categories (and vocabulary) of botany and textiles, and these in turn with the terms of literature—is familiar to us from the reading on metaphor in chapter 2. His suggestion that we can find in our own names the conceptual category modeling a personal style of creativity is unusual and provocative, not to mention controversial. Derrida has used the signature theory to read a number of major figures in the fields of literature and philosophy ("Ponge" as "sponge," "Blanchot" as "white water," "Kant" as "edge," and so forth), converting their proper names into common nouns using the literal meanings of the name, or puns on the name, to identify the conceptual category which is the clue to that author's principle of invention. In the exercise assigned in this section, you will have an opportunity to extend this experiment to the investigation of your own signature at all three levels, to discover, perhaps, your own principle of thinking and writing. Derrida has researched "signing" only with writers, but he intends it to be a theory of language adaptable to thinking in any discipline or field of knowledge. Thus, the style you discover in your experiment based on the readings in this section should be applicable to your work regardless of your intended or eventual major.

In the following excerpt from *Glas* (the book in which he discusses Genet), Derrida offers some elements of his signature theory along with citations from Genet's writings, including statements from both autobiographical and fictional works (genres that are not clearly differentiated in Genet's work nor in the signature theory in general) that are meant to support or illustrate the argument.

The blurbs for Genet's books describe him as "the foremost prince in the lineage of French *poètes maudites* — cursed magicians whose lives are as colorful as their work is dangerous, and who distinguish themselves as outlaws as well as masters of language." His peers in American literature would be the likes of Henry Miller and William Burroughs. Genet's masterpiece, *Our Lady of the Flowers,* was written in a prison cell, on brown paper from which the prisoners were supposed to make bags. In 1948 he was condemned to life imprisonment (he was a habitual thief and pervert), but was pardoned by the president of France at the request of France's most eminent writers. Our excerpts from *Glas* do not include the discussions of the more "perverse" themes of Genet's works, but the basic elements of the signature theory come through clearly enough.

From Glas*

Jacques Derrida

Apparently, yielding to the Passion of Writing, Genet has made himself into   1
a flower. . . . What is rhetoric, if the flower (or rhetoric) is the figure of figures
and the place of places? Why does the flower dominate all the fields to which
it nonetheless belongs? Why does it stop belonging to the series of bodies or
objects of which it forms a part? . . .

The name of the person who seems to affix, append here his seal (Genet) is   2
the name, as we know, of his mother. . . . *Genêt* names a plant with flowers —
yellow flowers (*sarothamnus scoparius, genista;* broom, *genette, genêt-à-balais,*
poisonous and medicinal, as distinct from the dyer's broom, dyer's green-
weed, woodwaxen, an herb for dying yellow); *genet* a kind of horse. Of Spain,
a country of great importance in the text.

If all his literature sings and weaves a funerary hymen to nomination,   3
Genet never sets any value, *noblesse oblige,* on anything but naming himself.

He rides horse(back) on his proper name. He holds it by the bit (*mors*). . . .   4

Departed are those who thought the flower signified, symbolized, meta-   5
phorized, that one was devising repertories of signifiers and
anthic figures, classifying flowers of rhetoric, combining them, ordering them,
binding them up in a sheaf or a bouquet around the phallic arch. . . .

Departed then are, save certain exceptions, duly so considered the ar-   6
chaeologists, philosophers, hermeneuts, semioticians, semanticians, psycho-
analysts, rhetoricians, poeticians, even perhaps all those readers who still
believe, in literature or anything else.

Those still in a hurry to recognize are patient for a moment: provided that   7
it be anagrams, anamorphoses, somewhat more complicated, deferred and

*Trans. John P. Leavey, Jr., and Richard Rand (Lincoln: U of Nebraska P).

diverted semantic insinuations capitalized in the depths of a crypt, cleverly dissimulated in the play of letters and forms. Genet would then rejoin this powerful, occulted tradition that was long preparing its coup, its haywire start from sleep, while hiding its work from itself, anagrammatizing proper names, anamorphosing signatures and all that follows. Genet, by one of those movements in (n)ana, would have, knowing it or not, silently, laboriously, minutely, obsessionally, compulsively, and with the moves of a thief in the night, set his signatures in (the) place of all the missing objects. In the morning, expecting to recognize familiar things, you find his name all over the place, in big letters, small letters, as a whole or in morsels deformed or recomposed. He is no longer there, but you live in his mausoleum or his latrines. You thought you were deciphering, tracking down, pursuing, you are included. He has affected everything with his signature. He has affected it with everything. . . .

(. . .)   8

The rhetorical flower organizing this antitrope, this metonymy simulating   9
autonymy, I baptize it anthonymy. One could also say anthonomasia. Antonomasia is a "kind of synecdoche that consists in taking a common noun for a proper name, or a proper name for a common noun" (Littré).

"I was born in Paris on December 19, 1910. As a ward of the *Assistance*   10
Publique, it was impossible for me to know anything but my civil state. When I was twenty-one, I obtained a birth certificate. My mother's name was Gabrielle Genet. My father remains unknown. I came into the world at 22 Rue d'Assas.

"'I'll find out something about my origin,' I said to myself, and went to   11
the Rue d'Assas. Number 22 was occupied by the Maternity Hospital. They refused to give me any information. I was raised in Le Morvan by peasants. Whenever I come across genêt (broom) flowers on the heaths—especially at twilight on my way back from a visit to the ruins of Tiffauges where Gilles de Rais lived—I feel a deep sense of kinship with them. I regard them solemnly, with tenderness. My emotion seems ordained by all nature. I am alone in the world, and I am not sure that I am not their king—perhaps the fairy of these flowers. They render homage as I pass, bow without bowing, but recognize me. They know that I am their living, moving, agile representative, conqueror of the wind. They are my natural emblem, but through them I have roots in that French soil which is fed by the powdered bones of the children and youths screwed, massacred and burned by Gilles de Rais.

"Through that spiny plant of the Cevennes [Spain], I take part in the   12
criminal adventures of Vacher. Thus, through her whose name I bear, the vegetable kingdom is my familiar. I can regard all flowers without pity; they are members of my family. If, through them, I rejoin the nether realms—though it is to the bracken and their marshes, to the algae, that I should like to descend—I withdraw further from men." . . .

So this flower name would be a cryptogram or a cryptonym. It is not   13
proper because it is common. On the other hand, . . . it is not proper because it also leads back to the nether realms, to the marshes, verily to the depths of the sea. Above the sea, with heavy sides but carried by it, the galley. In the depths of the sea, algae.

Alga is a cryptogam, one of those plants that hide their sexual organs. 14
Like ferns, which in general multiply themselves through the dispersion of
spores. Whether one remarks them or not on the surface, the text is full of
them. The "ferns" of the "Man Condemned to Death" are "rigid." Certain
brackens unfold their fronds several meters below the ground. Cryptogams
are evidently not flowers. . . .

The stamin, *l'étamine*, names not only the light material in which nuns 15
are sometimes veiled, or through which precious liquids are filtered. But *étamine*, stamen, is also the male sex organ of plants: according to the *navette*
[shuttle, rape] — that's the word — running between the textile code and the
botanical code. Situated around the style and its stigma, stamens generally
form a thin thread, or filaments (*stamina*). Above the thin thread, a connec-
tive with four pollen sacs (microsporangia) that "elaborate and disperse the
pollen seeds." . . .

No more than for the flower, is there any univocal semantic or morpho- 16
logical definition of *étamine*. *Etamine* deviates itself from itself, bursts its
sheath, at the risk of disseminating the pollen. This always open risk affects
not only the androecium, but also the gynoecium. One must argue from the
fact that the seed can always burst or remain dormant.

It is concerning the seed, a fertilized ovule, that one thinks one is liter- 17
ally [*proprement*] speaking of dissemination (with angiosperms or gymno-
sperms). The seeds are sometimes thrown in every direction [*sens*] by the
bursting of the fruit. More often, they escape from it through slits or holes
open in its wall; wind or animals disperse them. Germination is therefore immediate only if light and moisture permit. . . .

"Botanists know a variety of *genêt* which they call winged-*genêt*. It de- 18
scribes its flight and theft in the *Journal*:

"As the theft was indestructible, I decided to make it the origin of a state 19
of moral perfection. . . . 'I want to cover the world with its loathsome prog-
eny.' . . . A kind of dissatisfaction inflated each of my acts, including the most
simple. I would have liked a visible, dazzling glory to be manifest at my fin-
gertips, would have liked my potency to lift me from the earth, to explode within
me and dissolve me, to shower me to the four winds. I would have rained
over the world. My powder, my pollen . . . would have touched the stars."

FOR DISCUSSION AND WRITING: DEVISING THE PORTRAIT

1. Derrida introduces a neologism in his commentary — *anthonymy* — to
   name the figure of antonomasia specific to Genet's practice. What is the
   justification for his invention of this hybrid critical term (notice its similarity with *anthology*)? What other terms appearing in the selection did
   you not recognize? In *Glas* Derrida cites many passages from encyclopedic dictionaries, juxtaposing scientific information about botany with
   Genet's discussion of writing and his descriptions of the sexual life of the
   characters in his novels. He points out that certain words appear in the
   vocabularies of both botany and literature. What is the botanical mean-

ing of *style*? Derrida suggests that the punning relationship between the two meanings of *style* justifies a conceptual gathering of the two sets into one category (the signature). Does this possibility make any sense? Look through a glossary of another specialized discipline that interests you, and compare its terminology with a glossary of literary terms.

2. Select an author whose works are at least somewhat familiar to you and test the signature theory. Write a short account in the manner of Derrida's *Glas* discussing whether or not, or in what way, the author's names are "in the abyss" of the work(s).

3. Drawing on all the readings and exercises provided in this chapter relevant to the proper name, write a text exploring the words and information that may be generated out of your given and surnames. First identify a "key list" of such terms and topics, then construct a composition (organized as much for aesthetic effect as for the exposition of your discoveries) by writing out a variety of presentations expanding your vocabulary into an account of the third level of the signature. To make the original list, you should use every available means to find the common nouns or names that translate your proper names into ordinary discourse. Check the dictionary definitions in the original language of your heritage, as well as encyclopedic dictionaries relevant to the names. You may also use poetic techniques to produce words out of your names—puns and anagrams might be especially useful. You might also want to include photocopied images depicting the things you find in your names. Several of the readings suggest analogies which might guide your experiment: think of the project as a written version of your coat of arms (a kind of improvised blazoning) or as a nicknaming process. Comment along the way on any signs of fate or destiny you notice in the results of your research. Are you "well-named"? Remember finally that the goal of the project is to take whatever material your names provide and turn it into a model for a theory (general description) of how to write.

ARCHIVE: THE PLAY OF TEXT

The signature version of textual research approaches mystory from the side of form and play. Manifesting a spirit of play with language, these samples show another way to treat an object of study. There is an object of study in each case, but it is not interpreted or explained. Rather, it is rewritten, mimed, appropriated, repeated, articulated, augmented, echoed. The point of such work is not meaning but celebration, meditation, intensification: the goal is to experience the original through writing its forms rather than or in addition to understanding it through concepts. The learning involves desire more than knowledge. In most of the examples, the mystorical goal of self-knowledge is still operating, and the process of playing with the original often motivates traditional research to locate materials or design ideas. In other cases, the act of play is foregrounded for its own sake. In the latter cases, however, the writing generated by the exercise may be used to register the object of study in the "database" of a mystory, to put it into the intertext, juxtaposed with representations from the other popcycle discourses. The goal is to gather enough signifiers (details) to make a pattern. In other words, the object of study is reached here through texts of bliss.

The following archive is organized with the selection presented first, followed by a comment with questions for discussion and writing.

Making It Stick
(*from* Many Mountains Moving)

Lawson Fusao Inada

Asian American—
And ashamed of it:
                    I'm Asian—
                    But my owner's
                    Caucasian!   5
                                        Model Minority On
                                        Board
Ask me about
My GREEN CARD!
                    Don't blame me—   10
                    I'm a citizen!
                                        Honk if you're
                                        Sushi!
I'd rather be
Studying!   15
                    My child
                    are Student
                    of the
                    Yale!
                                        Asian/Pacific   20
                                        Islander
                                        Gang Member!
Proud to be
Assimilated!
                    We support   25
                    Your troops!
                                        An old pond.
                                        A frog jumps in.
                                        The sound of water . . .

FOR DISCUSSION AND WRITING: POPULARIZING CULTURAL FORMS

In our frame of reference—the research text—the object of study is the great Japanese haiku poet, Basho, whose most famous poem is cited as the final bumper sticker. The identity question concerns the history of the Japanese in America. The critical insight is carried by the formal morphing between the style of the bumper sticker and that of haiku. Lawson Inada was held in American internment camps in California, Arkansas, and Colorado during World War II. His book of poetry, *Legends from Camp* (1993), received the American Book Award.

Do some research on the history of your ethnic group in the United States. Write a series of bumper stickers that express the various stages of that group experience. If your ethnic group has some distinctive art or folk practice associated with it, similar to the association of haiku poetry with the Japanese, use that form to express some of the historical information. What is the effect of putting the information into an aesthetic form, as compared with expressing it in declarative prose?

Everyone is Welcome
(*from* Finding Art's Place: Experiments in Contemporary Education and Culture)

Nicholas Paley

For more than a decade, some of the most intriguing activities in teaching and learning have come out of an independent workshop moving from space to space in the Hunts Point section of the South Bronx in New York City. It is in this workshop that Tim Rollins and Kids of Survival—an artist/teacher and group of inner-city teenagers—make paintings on the pages of books, re-shape forms of educational practice, and produce some of contemporary culture's most startling representations. 1

Rollins and his students work in an area of New York where over sixty percent of young people do not finish high school; where more than forty percent of the households are on welfare; where ninety-five percent of the population is "minority"; and where violence is an everyday occurrence because of the drug, prostitution, and gang economies.[1] Kids of Survival, or K.O.S., is a semi-changing group of adolescents who gave themselves their own title. Most of them are black and Puerto Rican youth, and most come from a part of New York so consistently represented in the media as marked by abandonment, poverty, and evaporated dreams that their urban landscape has long been considered the "ground zero" of American social policy.[2] 2

Rollins came to New York in 1975 from Maine, with an interest in art-making and teaching. From 1976–80, he pursued formal artistic and educational study, earning a B.F.A. from the School of Visual Arts and a master's 3 degree in art education from New York University. During this time (in 1979), he also co-founded Group Material, an artists' collective that linked its artistic practice to issues of social, cultural, and political advocacy.

In mid-1981, Rollins was recruited to teach art classes at I.S. 52 to students classified as "learning-disabled," "dyslexic," "emotionally handicapped," and "neurologically brain-impaired."[3] Impressed by the number of his special education students who demonstrated artistic aptitude, Rollins transformed his classroom into a studio for making art.[4] In doing so, he also transformed his own ideas of what it meant to be an artist and a teacher. As he put it:

> I ceased being an artist who taught, and collapsed my artistic and teaching practices into one strange and stumbling hybrid. I made my art with the kids — during classes, during free periods, during lunch periods, in the short time after school allowed us before getting kicked out by the custodians.[5]

In 1982, Rollins established K.O.S. and the Art and Knowledge Workshop to accommodate this unique approach to pedagogy and art-making. Its initial base of operations was Room 318 in I.S. 52 where Rollins taught during the school day. Three years later, Rollins extended the idea further. Feeling constrained by the limitations of public-school time schedules, overcrowded classrooms, and hierarchies of bureaucratic control, he turned the Workshop into a non-profit, after-school organization, moving it into a gymnasium of an abandoned school on Longwood Avenue that had been refurbished as a neighborhood community center.[6] The Art and Knowledge's current (1993) location is the 9,000-square-foot third floor of an old factory building on Barretto Street, just south of the Bruckner Expressway. In this shifting series of alternative spaces, Rollins and K.O.S. have collaborated to explore, through the study of works of literary distinction and through art making, many of the complex social, political, and ideological factors which shape their daily lives in the South Bronx.

In an early writing, Rollins has spoken about the kinds of issues or "matters" with which he and K.O.S. wrestle in their workshop activity: to learn what actually interests them; to represent themselves directly and sincerely; and to confront the political and economic factors which determine their lives.[7] Working through these issues, Rollins and K.O.S. have evolved a pedagogy that is multifaceted, incorporating tactics from classical and radical, group and individual, personal and social sources. Generally the process begins with Rollins' selecting for group study a literary work that he thinks might — in whole or in part — interest his students and speak to matters that concern them. Not surprisingly, many of the works selected portray young adults as central characters. Some of the books read by the group in the past ten years include Lewis Carroll's *Through the Looking Glass*, Stephen Crane's *The Red Badge of Courage*, Nathaniel Hawthorne's *The Scarlet Letter*, Herman Melville's *Moby Dick*, Alex Haley's *The Autobiography of Malcolm X*, Carlo Collodi's *Pinocchio*, and Franz Kafka's *Amerika*.

Rollins and K.O.S. go through these books together, with Rollins either   7
reading the selection out loud to the group or with members working from
their own versions of the text. During these collaborative sessions, they discuss ideas and themes in the text as seem pertinent to them and develop possible connections between these themes and text/life situations. These working sessions and conversations are sometimes recorded. Sometimes before,
sometimes during, and sometimes after these collaborative readings, members of K.O.S. make hundreds of small drawings (a process they call "jam-
ming") which link aspects of the narrative with the realities of their daily existence. These drawings reflect a wide variety of sources: their workshop
study in art history, their knowledge of popular culture, their visits to local
museums, and their knowledge of current events and city and global politics.
These drawings are not literal illustrations of the text(s); rather, they function
as concentrated visual emblems and signs of the written work(s). A number
of these images may then be painted as studies directly onto book pages.
Eventually, all these visual representations are collected and a set of the most
"sincere and moving" images is arrived at through group discussion; this
process can take months or years. The images are then transferred to trans-
parencies and, through the use of an overhead projector, displayed onto a
base of pages which have been torn from the book they have just read. In this
way they arrange a composition for a large painting. As Rollins explains: "The
book, something that one supposes we consume, has been converted into a
work of art active with social uses, pertinent and concrete for us today."[8]

One of the most illuminating examples of how this pedagogy works is   8
provided by Rollins and K.O.S.'s initial (1984–85) reading of Franz Kafka's
Amerika—a work that would eventually generate the extended series of
paintings for which they have become most well known. Rollins has explained his reasons for selecting a book by an author who, to some, might appear totally unsuitable for a group of inner-city teenagers:

> Kafka's text is perfect for us. Basically the plot is about a sixteen-
> year-old boy named Karl, who emigrates to New York and America
> to find, as always, fame and fortune. What Karl finds instead in this
> country is a unique Kafkaesque combination of reality and fantasy
> —a perception that a majority of children here seem to share (espe-
> cially those who have just arrived from Puerto Rico).[9]

What was of particular interest in Kafka's book, however, was its final   9
chapter, "The Nature Theatre of Oklahoma." Rollins tells the story this way:

> At the end of the year, [Karl's] ready to go home. He says to himself,
> "I can't handle it, I'm a failure, I can't make it in Amerika." And so
> just as he's about ready to get back on the boat and go home, he
> hears this sound. It sounds like a Salvation Army band. They're all
> carrying these placards. And the placards say, "Come join the Na-
> ture Theatre of Oklahoma! The Nature Theatre of Oklahoma where
> anyone can be an artist and everyone is welcome!" And Karl looks

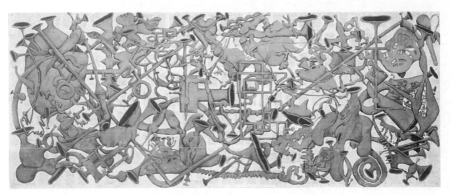

Tim Rollins & K.O.S. *Amerika VI*, 1986–1987. Mary Boone
Gallery, New York, New York.

at this and thinks, "I have been lied to, I have been cheated, I have
been robbed, and I am sure this is just another situation where I'm
going to get ripped off. But then again, that one sign says 'Everyone
is welcome.' Even if it is bullshit, I'm going to try it. I've never seen
that in Amerika before." So he joins.

Then they say, "Well, we're leaving for Clayton tonight on a
train. We're all going to go at midnight, so you've got to get registered
at the racetrack. You have to register before midnight because that's
when the train goes, and you lose your chance forever." So he goes
to the racetrack, and as he approaches the racetrack, he hears this
incredible sound of a traffic jam, and it's hundreds of horns like a
jazz orchestra or something. And as he walks into the racetrack he
sees an incredible scene of hundreds of people standing on pedes-
tals, dressed up like angels blowing whatever they want to on these
long golden horns. There's a big fat person who's making little
noises, and a little skinny person making big noises, and it's this big
kind of mess. All these sounds together.

And Karl asks the old man who brings him in, "What is this?"
and the guy says, "This is Amerika, where everyone has a voice and
everyone can say what they want." That's it. Then I say [to K.O.S.],
"Now look, you all have your own taste and you have different
voices. If you could be a golden instrument, if you could play a song
of your freedom and dignity and your future and everything you feel
about Amerika and this country, what would your horn look like?"[10]

As Rollins recalls, K.O.S.'s response was startling, explosive. They crafted   10
their own versions of Kafka's golden horns. They made small, intricate horns;
curving and straight horns; and horns that looked energetic, vigorous, and
extravagant. They made horns that seemed recognizable and horns that appeared to have no reference to any known reality. Eventually, a selected
number of these images were shaped into a large composition painted onto

every single one of Kafka's 298 pages, which Rollins had adhered to a six-by-fifteen foot ground of heavyweight rag paper.

The result of their work is *Amerika I,* completed in March of 1985. A 11
painting of dazzling visual expressiveness, majestic proportion, and subtle
complexity, it pulses with multiple meanings that shuttle across category and
time. From one standpoint, *Amerika I* suggests intriguing textual associations
extending beyond the narrative realities of the book, in that the painting's op-
ulence could easily pass for a visual representation of Kafka's rhetorical style.
The interconnected groups of meticulous, intricately painted trumpets, for example, make one think of Kafka's own obsessive, cramped, precisely crafted
tangle of sentences, while the fantastically shaped horns recall his eccentric
depiction of an impossible reality. Even the heroic size of the painting, with
its dominant golden hue, acts to reinforce Kafka's imagined view of the New
World (he never visited America) as a place of "almost limitless theater,"
wealth, and glittering promise.

From another perspective, *Amerika I* suggests connections with a wide 12
variety of artistic traditions: 1980s practices of appropriation; the politics of
surrealism and collage; the collective productions of William Morris and notions related to the "beautiful" in art; visual references to illuminated manuscripts; the muralist histories of Latin and South America; medieval tapes-
tries; and the heroic veils of abstract expressionist painting.

From still another point of view, *Amerika I* is charged with political ener- 13
gies: its tangled, interlocking chaos of golden horns—each carefully fashioned
to articulate a message of personal liberty—presents a compelling statement
from the urban landscape of the South Bronx to contemporary American society. Read in this way, Rollins and K.O.S.'s *Amerika I* is active with urgent
meaning. It presents, in very concrete terms, a unified image that glitters with
a singular and collective message of liberty to the wider social structure—an
image that, as Rollins notes, is both "beautiful and dangerous" at the same time.

From yet one more position, but not finally, *Amerika I* can be read as ob- 14
jective evidence of a heterodox pedagogical process at work. This approach honors the traditions of the academy—scholarship, analysis, the book, dialogue,

Tim Rollins & K.O.S. *Amerika I,* 1984–1985. Mary Boone
Gallery, New York, New York.

collaboration—but it can also be seen as the embodiment of its radical transformation. This transformation suggests connections with Freirian notions of education as a form of cultural politics. In this framework, teachers and students mutually engage in a series of investigations whose focus is to critically examine and scrutinize forms of contemporary culture as part of the broader social task of constructing the material realities of a more just and democratic life.

Since this initial *Amerika* painting, there have been more than a dozen   15
subsequent versions (as of this writing), each done by a semi-changing group of students. Most of these paintings link Kafka's text to the realities of students' lives in New York, and many suggest a less optimistic stance than others. *Amerika VI*, for example, with its massive uppercase letters, "H" and "B", serving as parameters for the painting, calls to mind the divisive events of Howard Beach in the borough of Queens that took place in December of 1986 (or, as Rollins has related, "They also signify the name Hieronymus Bosch and the netherworld this artist represents."[11]) In fact, Rollins indicates that the painting was a social mediation, done as a memorial to the racial incident that took place there. Still, there's a sense that this *Amerika* might be a visual reference for the actualities of confinement, enclosure. K.O.S.'s horns of liberty seem to be entangled within a grid-like assembly that resembles a fence, a barrier, or a cage of golden bars.

NOTES

A portion of this chapter is based on "Kids of Survival: Experiments in the Study of Literature," which appeared in *English Journal*, September 1988.

References for the essay "Everyone is Welcome" are as follows:

1. Margot Hornblower, "South Bronx, 10 Years After Fame," *The Washington Post*, August 25, 1987, A8.
2. *Ibid.*, A1.
3. Tim Rollins, "Tim Rollins + K.O.S.," *Parkett*, no. 20, (1989), p. 36; Personal communication, August 28, 1992, New York.
4. *Ibid.*
5. *Ibid.*
6. *Ibid.*
7. Tim Rollins, "La Realización de 'Amerika'" ("The Making of 'Amerika'"), trans. N. M. Paley, *Figura*, (Autumn 1985), unpaged.
8. *Ibid.*
9. *Ibid.*
10. Michele Wallace, "Tim Rollins + K.O.S.: The 'Amerika' Series," in *Amerika: Tim Rollins + K.O.S.* (New York: Dia Art Foundation, 1989), pp. 46–47.
11. Tim Rollins, "Notes on Amerika I–XII," in *Amerika: Tim Rollins + K.O.S.*, p. 73.

References to the statements situated intertextually throughout the chapter are as follows (in order of appearance):

The statement by Octavio Paz is from *The Other Voice: Essays on Modern Poetry* (New York: Harcourt Brace Jovanovich, 1990), p. 151.

The conversation among Tim Rollins, George Garces, Richard Cruz, and Nelson Montes is excerpted from "Dialogue 5, April 19, 1989, 5:00 p.m., The Art and Knowledge Workshop Studio, 965 Longwood Avenue, South Bronx," in "Tim Rollins + K.O.S.," *Parkett,* no. 20, (1989), p. 62.

The statement by Annette Rosado is from Amei Wallach, "Survival Art, 101," *New York Newsday,* part II, October 30, 1989, p. 16.

The statement "Devotion + Devour" was suggested by a memory of a painting of the same name (artist unknown).

The statement by Tim Rollins on genuine collaboration is from Tim Rollins, "Too Long Apart," a working copy of a manuscript provided to the author on April 23, 1993 about young people collaborating with artists to make photographs, p. 1.

The conversation between Tim Rollins and Carlos Rivera is excerpted from "Dialogue 5," p. 58.

"At the Art and Knowledge Workshop: April 23, 1993," is my reconstruction of an afternoon spent there.

FOR DISCUSSION AND WRITING: STRETCHING THE STORY

Tim Rollins's pedagogy is familiar to elementary schoolteachers and is sometimes called "story stretchers." Practiced especially in the early grades when students are just beginning to read, story stretchers are a set of activities suggested by the book that one is reading. If the story involves baking, gardening, or flying a kite, for example, the readers expand the experience of reading by performing the activity described. If the story is a fantasy or otherwise involves actions impossible, dangerous, or illegal, it is still possible to stretch the story world into other media and modes of expression. A similar practice is evident in the adult arts as well, in relation to the postmodernist device of appropriation, but also in the form of an homage to an admired cultural icon. A. C. Evans's piece (included later in this archive) is in such a collection of works by other artists paying homage to William S. Burroughs. A similar collection by visual artists is *Ports of Entry: William S. Burroughs and the Arts.* Homages by poets and visual artists to Emily Dickinson are collected in *Language as Object: Emily Dickinson and Contemporary Art.* These homages are related to story stretchers in the sense that they often adapt and extend the style and form favored by the original, or treat the original's themes in a different medium.

Select a favorite or canonical literary work and develop a set of story stretchers based on it. Document each exercise using writing and photography. The K.O.S. used the same identification method that you used in the "Fragments" section, except their "text" performed an element of the story. In rhetorical terms, the K.O.S. approach was a metonymic identification (a part of the whole is used to represent the whole). Or, to put it in cinematic terms, the visualization *(Amerika I)* used "diegetic" metaphors (something in the scene of the story world is used as the "vehicle" or signifier for the comparison with the maker's life). Return to one of the exercises from the "Identification" section and apply the K.O.S. method to it.

The Revolver: A Textual Transformation
(*from* Assassination Rhapsody)

Derek Pell

(1.) At the first questioning or examination, Oswald claimed that his only act committed or omitted in violation of a law was carrying a weapon consisting of a metal tube from which a projectile is discharged by the explosion of gunpowder, and resisting seizure by authority of the law. When Captain Fritz asked him why he carried a pistol with a revolving cylinder containing several cartridges, he answered, "Well, you know about a small firearm held and fired with one hand. I just carried it." He falsely alleged that he bought the pistol with a revolving cylinder containing several cartridges in a city in north Texas: population, 277,000, when in fact he purchased it from a business establishment that takes mail orders and sends goods by mail in a city on the SW coast of California: population, 1,958,000; with suburbs, 4,339,000.

(2.) At the first means or method of examining or being examined, Oswald claimed that his only thing done was carrying an instrument of any kind used for fighting, and resisting a seizing or being seized. When Captain Fritz asked him why he carried a small firearm held and fired with one hand, he answered, "Well, you know about a small weapon from which a shot is fired by explosive force, especially such a weapon small enough to be carried, as a rifle. I just carried it." He falsely alleged that he bought the small firearm held and fired with one hand in a large, important town, when in fact he purchased it from a commercial or industrial establishment in a large, important town.

(3.) At the first way of doing anything, Oswald claimed that his only matter, affair, or concern was carrying a thing by means of which something is done, and resisting a sudden attack, as of a disease. When Captain Fritz asked him why he carried a small weapon from which a shot is fired by explosive force, especially such a weapon small enough to be carried, as a rifle, he answered, "Well, you know about a small instrument of any kind used for fighting. I just carried it." He falsely alleged that he bought the small weapon from which a shot is fired by explosive force, especially such a weapon small enough to be carried, as a rifle, in a large, important concentration of houses and buildings, larger than a village but smaller than a city, when in fact he purchased it from a commercial thing established as a business, military organization, household, etc., in a large, important concentration of houses and buildings, larger than a village but smaller than a city.

(4.) At the first road, street, path, etc., Oswald claimed that his only constituent material was any matter, affair, or concern, and resisting a sudden onset or occurrence of a disease. When Captain Fritz asked him why he carried a small instrument of any kind used for fighting, he answered, "Well, you know about a small thing by means of which something is done. I just carried it." He falsely alleged that he bought the small instrument of any kind used for fighting, in a large important concentration of buildings for human beings to live in, when in fact he purchased the animal or thing under dis-

cussion from a commercial matter, affair, or concern in a large, important concentration of things that are built.

(5.) At the first way made for traveling between places by automobile,
horseback, etc., Oswald claimed that his only constituent cloth or other fabric
was what a thing is made of, and resisting a sudden something that occurs.
When Captain Fritz asked him why he carried a small tool or implement, he
answered, "Well, you know about a small tangible object, as distinguished from
a concept, quality, etc. I just carried it." He falsely alleged that he bought the
small person used by another to bring something about, in a large important
concentration of structures, when in fact he purchased the living organism
typically capable of moving about but not of making its own food by photosynthesis, from a commercial amorous relationship or episode.

(6.) At the first method of doing something, Oswald claimed that his
only constituent woven, knitted, or pressed fabric of fibrous material, as cotton, wool, silk, hair, synthetic fibers, etc., was what any matter, affair, or concern is made of, and resisting a sudden thing not definitely known, understood, etc.: as, something went wrong. When Captain Fritz asked him why he
carried a small implement, instrument, etc. held in the hand and used for
some work, he answered, "Well, you know about a small tangible thing that
can be seen or touched. I just carried the animal or thing under discussion."
He falsely alleged that he bought the small human being in a large important
place in which enemy aliens or prisoners of war are kept under guard, when
in a thing that has actually happened or is true, he purchased the living living thing from a commercial amorous connection by origin or marriage.

(7.) At the first regular, orderly arrangement, Oswald claimed that his
only anything made of parts put together was material or content of thought
or expression, as distinguished from style or form, and resisting a sudden
matter, affair, or concern. When Captain Fritz asked him why he carried a
small something used or needed in a given activity, he answered, "Well, you
know about a small tangible end to be achieved, a step in a process. I just
carried the four-footed creature." He falsely alleged that he bought the small
one that lives or exists, or is assumed to do so, in a large important square or
court in a city, when in a happening, act, deed, incident, etc., he purchased
the happening, act, deed, incident, etc., from a commercial amorous religious
sect or denomination.

(8.) At the first regular, orderly settlement or adjustment, Oswald claimed
that his only portions of a whole were a sudden debatable question and
an amorous relationship or episode. When Captain Fritz asked him why he
carried a small important person or thing, he answered, "Well, you know
about a small tangible ceasing to exist, death or destruction. I just carried the
person completely dominated by or dependent on another." He falsely alleged that he bought the small number expressing unity in a large important
plane figure having four equal sides and four right angles, when in something
that happens, he purchased the something that happens from a commercial
amorous religious group of people having a common leadership, philosophy,
etc.; school; party; especially one that has broken away from an established
church.

Conclusion

On the basis of the evidence revealed above, the Commission has concluded that Lee Harvey Oswald did not act alone.

FOR DISCUSSION AND WRITING: TRANSFORMING THE HISTORICAL DOCUMENT

The object of study in *Assassination Rhapsody* is the *Warren Commission Report: Report of President's Commission on the Assassination of President John F. Kennedy*, issued in 1964. J. G. Ballard (author of *Crash*) declared the *Warren Commission Report* to be one of his two favorite books, a fact that supports Harold Jaffe's description (in the introduction to Pell's book) of the *Warren Commission Report* as "one of the seminal texts of the postmodernist era." Derek Pell, a writer and visual artist, memorialized this epoch-shaping record with his own version of the "rhapsodic" form. "In ancient Greece, a rhapsody was a selection of epic poetry sung by a rhapsode—literally a 'stitcher' who combined memorized passages with original improvisations" (Baldick 188). In the nineteen episodes of *Assassination Rhapsody*, as Jaffe notes, Pell stitches together "conceptual art, caricature, absurdist assemblage, fiction-fantasy in the tradition of his acknowledged master Raymond Queneau. On occasion Pell conflates two or more of these modalities" (Pell 8).

The selection included here represents the modality that we first encountered in chapter 3: the "transformation." How would you classify the language device that Pell uses to produce his variations? A historical event lends itself to the same devices applied to literature in the earlier chapters. The "ghost chapter," for example, seems especially appropriate in the case of a controversial topic such as the Kennedy murder. In fact, you might say that Oliver Stone's film about the event is a kind of ghost chapter. Get a copy of the *Warren Commission Report* from your library, and select some part of it to use as the basis for rewriting, using any of the devices or methods introduced in the previous chapters. Look into the history of your community (an actual hometown or any community with which you identify, e.g., religion or ethnic group). Find a document associated with an event that is important to that community, and produce from it a series of transformations.

From There Are Many Roads to Space

A. C. Evans

i.m. William S. Burroughs 1914–1997
Now we are left with the career novelists   —*J.G. Ballard*

Burroughs began writing much later than Kerouac or Ginsberg: "I had no   1
choice except to write my way out. . . ," he said. It is necessary to travel. It is
not necessary to live.

Two interlocked projectors turn out "flat" copy, side-by-side, anamor-   2
phic. "However there are many roads to space." So, tell me about it? I looked
at the man in the grey suit, but before he could speak we were transported to
a pizza joint on the other side of town. There was a pile of books on the dirty
table: *Cities of the Red Night, The Place of Dead Roads, My Education, Ghost
of Chance* . . . he was a "map-maker," an explorer of psychic areas, a "cos-
monaut of inner space." The message was resistance:

> "Our troops operate in the area of dream and myth under guerrilla
> conditions . . . the enemy is a noncreative parasite."

If we are to have a future we must catch up with the past. Even though head-
light design occupies the brightest minds—the colour is almost identical—
gleaming leather "wild boy" sex appeal, pure velvet, born in St. Louis, Missouri.
And I was not alone. Boring rituals. Record-breaking results. Many roads.
Many spaces. Fluent conversation.

Interviewer: Wright Morris called *Naked Lunch* a haemorrhage of the   3
imagination. Would you take that as a compliment?

Burroughs: I frankly wouldn't know how to take it.   4

Edit. Delete. Rearrange. Rumours circulate endlessly—but most result   5
in dead ends—left and right images overprinted—filters are not necessary,
to live is not necessary. We entered the 1951 Telekinema, it's bloody and
gross and shot in 3-D. The screenplay squirts green, hallucinatory gunk at its
victims. He was one of the strangest monsters of filmdom with an extensive
archive and a diversity of activities. A unique talent. Hot property. Have they
put rat poison in the pasta? The man from El Dorado shuddered as an alien
waif stumbled in through the door. By this time Burroughs had moved further
out . . . The trail had gone cold. Not for him the dark sadness of *amour fou.*
Look at what is in front of you in silence—in hieroglyphic silence—the key
is beauty and deliriously intense flashbacks. This is how an exponent of English Dada can capture the news. You don't need subvocal speech to write
about it ("I could look at the end of my shoe for eight hours"). I stared out of
the window: beyond the village green were angels and devils from Sicily in
the 1860s. Yesterday becomes tomorrow. Easy lessons in hieroglyphic silence
rendered by excellent pre-computer animation techniques and a lock of
Lolita's hair. He works with the precision of a master chess-player.

Interviewer: Therefore, you're not upset by the fact that a chimpanzee   6
can do an abstract painting?

Burroughs: If he does a good one, no.   7

Now, the seedy manservant gains the upper hand in an updated film ver-   8
sion, discussing montage with Kathy Acker. It was an ascesis, a withdrawal.

Sometime Burroughs character, Academy 23 graduate Yen Lee materialised   9
and said "All dead poets and writers can be reincarnate in different hosts. Vivare
no es necesse . . ." Lee made a victory V sign hovering three or four feet from
the table top. I looked at his cold hard eyes. According to "Pages from Chaos"
he had been carefully selected "for a high level of intuitive adjustment." Training was carried out in the context of reality. Known as El Hombre Invisible he
had had several addresses in various cities: Duke Street, St James' London,

1972; 210, Center Street, New York, 1965; Villa Muniria, Tangier, 1961; rue Delacroix, Tangier, 1964; rue Git le Couer, Paris, 1960. He had The Look, The Big Break, The Star Quality . . . even the wind can't resist it. Distant recording of Peggy Lee singing *Fly me to the Moon (In Other Words)* . . . I just love it. This is London where less is always more. Neon years of exposure.

Interviewer: Do you work while you're travelling on trains or boats?   10

Burroughs: There is one example of a traintrip in which I tried typing, in-   11
corporating what I saw in the passing stations . . .

The expedition to see Céline was organised in 1958 by Allen Ginsberg—   12
we walked for half a mile in this rundown neighbourhood . . . what's new? A small but significant detail was missing. Céline, a qualified doctor you know, nailed Edith Sitwell's nose to the lavatory door. Personally I prefer Chanel No. 5. Like many artistic revolutionaries Yen Lee became a cultural icon late in life, mixing science fiction, the western, the travel book, the dream journal and other genres. But to travel you have to leave all the verbal garbage behind. "God talk, country talk, mother talk, love talk, party talk." You have to make a distinction between the sea in summer and the sea in winter—a blessed relief and a good hangover cure. Cut-ups have been used in films for years. That tired and heavy feeling is eliminated.

The man in the neat grey suit was still sitting at the cafe table, next to a   13
sign that read "Beautify your legs." By now his glamorous and exotic life had descended into literary madness—a gaunt figure in sneakers and sunglasses, a dank world of privilege and tragedy. It was 10.23am and, after an antiwar march in Rome, 1969, five hundred guests swept down the world-famous red carpet, a battleground of plastic weaponry. Next morning we check out. According to J.G. Ballard "when Burroughs talked about Time magazine's conspiracy to take over the world he meant it literally."

The first full length feature had distinctive architectural design, it opened   14
up fresh corners of idiosyncratic, visual style, a language of old service newsreels, popular documentary films and extreme experimentation—fantasy and *cinema verité* in equal measure. Dead home movies roll on. Old red stars fade over Hollywood.

Dream and myth, sir, dream and myth.   15

Interviewer: Your books are rarely obscure or hard to understand.   16

Burroughs: We think of the past as being there unchangeable. There's   17
nothing between them and the image. A lot of old junkies used to do this.

Edit, delete, rearrange.   18

I looked up and saw a face I thought I knew—it was . . . er . . .   19

Count Alfred Korzybski, author of *Science and Sanity*. Count Alfred said   20
"Anyone who prays in space is not there." Then he vanished. Rats might take over the Earth.

The man from El Dorado came home to write like a master chess-player,   21
map-maker and explorer. Bleeding bodies swept up in a sense of satire. Trendsetter burns out over Colorado. Conspiracy within the industry. What we call "love" is a fraud perpetrated by the female sex.

There had been an exorcism ceremony to evict The Ugly Spirit, not too   22
late. To achieve complete freedom from past conditioning is "to be in space."

Take a trip, a step into regions literally unthinkable in verbal terms . . . addiction is a disease of exposure, and an algebra of need. Don't believe anything they say. People feel they have already seen it on TV.

I look at my watch. It's still 10.23am and I think of a passage from *The* 23 *Necronomicon* translated by Kurt Unruh von Steinplatz, Benway edition, 1961; "Knowing we know not. Techniques exist. The message is resistance. . . ." Explain the subtle details. The Herr Doktor crumples into dust. There is a cold shriek on the distant wind, old folded photos exert a morbid fascination, a haemorrhage of the imagination. But the extreme edge of art, as of life, is the only place to be. The texts record ancient nightmare parasites and plagues. Human combustion becomes an everyday reality. Pure anamorphic velvet, two interlocked projectors and Boom! rumours circulate endlessly. No call. No answer. Always the Third walks beside you. Always.

City fellas demand train comes on time with a fully stocked licensed bar. 24 The biggest avalanche in history just missed us by inches. Stay in or opt out, it's all the same. Edit. Delete. Rearrange. His room-mate expectorated for about 40 mins. I never take a camera.

Dream and myth, travel and money. 25

Accelerated history, side-by-side, a psycho fold-in, no scissors used— 26

I quote James Grauerholz: "He surely had travels to tell and yet the five- 27 hour ride back to the City was mostly silent, as together we concentrated on the darkening highway and our own thoughts."

I observed that, for Rilke, Death was "a bluish distillate/in a cup without 28 a saucer . . ."

The man in the grey suit, in the pizza joint on the other side of town, 29 flashed me a telepathic message:

there are many roads to space
there are many
there are—

Now we are left with the career novelists. The rats take over the Earth. 30 Recall those seismic shocks in 1921. . . ?

Navigare necesse es. Vivare no es necesse. 31

This is a psycho-fold-in-cut-up—no scissors used. With thanks to:
The Burroughs File. City Lights, 1984
The Selected Poetry of Rainer Maria Rilke. trans. Stephen Mitchell, Picador, 1982
William Burroughs El Hombre Invisible. Barry Miles, Virgin, 1992
The Job. William Burroughs & Daniel Odier, John Calder, 1984
Ah Pook is Here and Other Texts. William Burroughs, John Calder, 1979
The Third Mind. William Burroughs & Brion Gysin, John Calder, 1979
"Struggles with the Ugly Spirit" James Campbell, in *The Guardian*, August 4, 1997
"'The CIA are watching me,' he confided." J. G. Ballard, in *The Guardian*, August 4, 1997.
With William Burroughs. A Report from The Bunker. Victor Bockris. Vermilion. 1982

FOR DISCUSSION AND WRITING: TESTING THE CUT-UP

The object of study in Evans's text is writing by and about William Burroughs. Burroughs began his career as one of the founding members of the Beat movement (along with Jack Kerouac and Allen Ginsberg). His writings at first were banned or condemned, but eventually they were recognized as expressing the fragmented discontinuous character of postmodern life better than any other works of the period. Evans uses Burroughs's own experimental collage method of composition—the cut-up—to put Burroughs's words into relation with citations from critics, commentators, and other creative writers. Burroughs described the method many times, as in the following excerpt:

> The method is simple. Here is one way to do it. Take a page. Now cut down the middle and across the middle. You have four sections: 1 2 3 4. Now rearrange the sections placing section two with section three. And you have a new page. Sometimes it says much the same thing. Sometimes something quite different—cutting up political speeches is an interesting exercise—in any case you will find that it says something and something quite definite. Take any poet or writer you fancy. The words have lost meaning and life through years of repetition. Now take the poem and type out selected passages. Fill a page with excerpts. Now cut the page. You have a new poem. Cut-ups are for everyone. Anybody can make cut-ups. It is experimental in the sense of being something to do (Burroughs 36).

Follow Burroughs's advice and apply his cut-up method (or any variation on it you might devise) to an author of your choice. Keep in mind that the method may be extended to intercutting segments from different works (replicate Evans's device of mixing lines from works by Burroughs with lines from books about Burroughs). In using the method himself, Burroughs often treated the results of the cut-up or fold-in as a first draft that he then revised to create the illusion of a seamless composition. As an exercise, see if it is possible to rewrite Evans's cut-up in the style of a conventional essay. Compare the learning effect of making a text about your author as opposed to doing a paper.

Writing for the Second Time through
Finnegans Wake
(*from* Empty Words: Writings '73–'78)
John Cage

In 1939 I bought a copy of *Finnegans Wake* in a department store in Seattle,   1
Washington. I had read the parts of *Work in Progress* as they appeared
in *transition*. I used outloud to entertain friends with *The Ondt and the*

Gracehoper. But even though I owned a copy, no matter where I lived, the *Wake* simply sat on a table or shelf unread. I was "too busy" writing music to read it.

In 1942 Janet Fairbanks asked me for a song. I browsed in the *Wake* 2 looking for a lyrical passage. The one I chose begins page 556. I changed the paragraph so that it became two and read as follows:

> "Night by silentsailing night, Isobel, wildwood's eyes and prim-arose hair, quietly, all the woods so wild, in mauves of moss and daphnedews, how all so still she lay, neath of the whitethorn, child of tree, like some losthappy leaf, like blowing flower stilled, as fain would she anon, for soon again 'twill be, win me, woo me, wed me, ah weary me! deeply, now evencalm lay sleeping;
>
> "Night, Isobel, sister Isobel, Saintette Isobelle, Madame Isa Veuve La Belle."

The title I chose was one of Joyce's descriptions of her, *The Wonderful* 3 *Widow of Eighteen Springs.*

I remember looking in later years several times for other lyrical passages 4 in the *Wake.* But I never settled on one as the text for another song.

In the middle 'sixties Marshall McLuhan suggested that I make a musi- 5 cal work based on the *Wake's* Ten Thunderclaps. He said that the Thunder-claps were, in fact, a history of technology. This led me to think of Jasper Johns' *Painted Bronze* (the cans of ale) and to imagine a concert for string or-chestra and voices, with the addition towards the end of wind instruments. The orchestra would play notes traced from star maps (*Atlas Borealis*) but due to contact microphones and suitable circuitry the tones would sound like rain falling, at first, say, on water, then on earth, then wood, clay, metal, cement, etc., finally not falling, just being in the air, our present circumstance. The chorus meanwhile would sing the Thunderclaps, which would then be elec-tronically transformed to fill up the sound envelopes of an actual thunder-storm. I had planned to do this with Lejaren Hiller at the University of Illinois 1968–9, but *HPSCHD* took two years rather than one to make and produce.

Due to N. O. Brown's remark that syntax is the arrangement of the army, 6 and Thoreau's that when he heard a sentence he heard feet marching, I be-came devoted to nonsyntactical "demilitarized" language. I spent well over a year writing *Empty Words*, a transition from a language without sentences (having only phrases, words, syllables, and letters) to a "language" having only letters and silence (music). This led me to want to learn something about the ancient Chinese language and to read *Finnegans Wake*. But when in this spirit I picked up the book, Joyce seemed to me to have kept the old structures ("sintalks") in which he put the new words he had made.

It was when I was in this frame of mind that Elliott Anderson, editor of 7 *TriQuarterly*, wrote asking me to write something (anything, text or music) for an issue of the magazine to be devoted to the *Wake* (In the wake of the *Wake*). I said I was too busy. I was. I was writing *Renga* and had not yet started *Apartment House 1776* the performance date of which had already been set. Anderson replied that his deadline could be changed. I refused again and again. He persisted.

Anderson was not the first person to bother me by asking me to do some- 8 thing when I was busy doing something else. We continually bother one an- other with birthdays, deadlines, celebrations, blurbs, fund raising, requests for information, interviews, letters of introduction, letters of recommendation. To turn irritation into pleasure I've made the practice, for more than ten years now, of writing mesostics (not acrostics: row down the middle, not down the edge). What makes a mesostic as far as I'm concerned is that the first letter of a word or name is on the first line and following it on the first line the sec- ond letter of the word or name is *not* to be found. (The second letter is on the second line.) When, for instance, we were in a bus in Northern Michigan on our way to hunt morels (Interlochen music students were asking me what a mesostic was), I wrote

"Music . . .

(the M without an O after it)
"Music
cOnducted . . .

(the O without an R) (the word "performed" would not have worked)
"Music
cOnducted
in spRing . . .

(the R without an E)
". . . by trEes: . . .

(the E without an L)
". . . dutch eLm disease."

To bring my correspondence with Elliott Anderson to a temporary halt, I 9 opened *Finnegans Wake* at random (page 356). I began looking for a J with- out an A. And then for the next A without an M. Etcetera. I continued find- ing Joyce and James to the end of the chapter. I wrote twenty-three mesostics in all.

I then started near the end of the book (I couldn't wait) for I knew how 10 seductive the last pages of *Finnegan* are.

my lips went livid for from the Joy
of feAr
like alMost now. how? how you said
how you'd givE me
the keyS of me heart.

Just a whisk brisk sly spry spink
spank sprint Of a thing
i pitY your oldself i was used to,
a Cloud.
in pEace

Having found these, I looked for those at the beginning and, finally, as   11
Joyce had done, I began at the end and continued with the beginning:

>   Just
>   A
>   May i
>   bE wrong!
>   for She'll be sweet for you as i was sweet when i came
>   down out of me mother.
>
>   Jhem
>   Or shen [brewed by arclight]
>   and rorY end
>   through all Christian
>   minstrElsy.

The bracketed words are the ones I'd have omitted if it were just now I   12
had written them. There were choices to be made, decisions as to which
words were to be kept, which omitted. It was a discipline similar to that of
counterpoint in music with a cantus firmus. My tendency was towards more
omission rather than less.

>   Just a whisk brisk sly spry spink . . .

became

>   Just a whisk
>   Of
>   pitY
>   a Cloud
>   in pEace and silence.

And a further omission was suggested by Norman O. Brown, that of punctuation, a suggestion I quickly acted on. Subsequently, the omitted marks were
kept, not in the mesostics but on the pages where they originally appeared,
the marks disposed in the space and those other than periods given an orientation by means of *I Ching* chance operations. Where, in all this work,
Joyce used italics, so have I. My marginal figures are source pages of the
Viking Press edition of *Finnegan*.

Stuck in the *Wake*. I couldn't get out. I was full of curiosity about all of   13
it. I read *A Skeleton Key*. . . . Ihab Hassan gave me his book, *Paracriticisms*,
and two others: Adaline Glasheen's *a second census of finnegans wake* and
Clive Hart's *Structure and Motif*. . . . I continued to read and write my way
through all of *Finnegans Wake*.

Finnegans Wake has six hundred twenty-five pages. Once finished, my   14
Writing Through Finnegans Wake had one hundred fifteen pages. My editor
at Wesleyan University Press, J. R. de la Torre Bueno, finding it too long, suggested that I shorten it. Instead of doing that, I wrote a new series of mesostics,

Writing for the Second Time Through Finnegans Wake, in which I did not permit the reappearance of a syllable for a given letter of the name. I distinguished between the two J's and the two E's. The syllable "just" could be used twice, once for the J of James and once for the J of Joyce, since it has neither A nor O after the J. But it could not be used again. To keep from repeating syllables, I kept a card index of the ones I had already used. As I guessed, this restriction made a text considerably shorter, forty pages in all.

My work was only sometimes that of identifying, as Duchamp had, 15 found objects. The text for *TriQuarterly* is *7 out of 23.* Seven mesostics were straight quotations, e.g., this one from page 383:

> he Just slumped to throne
> so sAiled the stout ship *nansy hans.*
>   froM liff away.
> for nattEnlaender.
>   aS who has come returns.

In such a case my work was merely to show, by giving it a five-line struc- 16 ture, the relation of Joyce's text to his name, a relationship that was surely in these instances not in his mind, though at many points, as Adaline Glasheen cheerfully lists, his name was in his mind, alone or in combination with another name, for example, "poorjoist" (page 113), and "joysis crisis" (page 395).

When I was composing my *Sonatas and Interludes,* which I did at the pi- 17 ano, friends used to want to know what familiar tunes, *God Save the King* for instance, would sound like due to the preparations between the strings. I found their curiosity offensive, and similarly from time to time in the course of this work I've had my doubts about the validity of finding in *Finnegans Wake* these mesostics on his name which James Joyce didn't put there. However I just went straight on, A after J, E after M, J after S, Y after O, E after C. I read each passage at least three times and once or twice upside down. (Hazel Dreis, who taught us English binding, used to tell us how she proofread the *Leaves of Grass,* an edition of which she bound for San Francisco's Grabhorn Press: upside down and backwards. When you don't know what you're doing, you do your work very well.) J's can thus be spotted by their dots and by their dipping below the line which i's don't do. Difficult letters to catch are the commonest ones, the vowels. And the consonants escape our notice in empty words, words the mind skips over. I am native to detailed attention, though I often make mistakes: I was born early in September. But I found myself from time to time bursting into laughter (this, not when the *Wake* was upside down). The play of sex and church and food and drink in an all time all space world turned family was not only regaling: it Joyced me (in places, that is, where Thoreau hadn't, couldn't, where, left to myself, I wouldn't've). I don't know whom to connect with Joyce ("We connect Satie with Thoreau"). Duchamp stands, I'd say, somewhere between. He is, like Joyce, alone. They *are* connected. For that and many other reasons. But that's something else to do.

I am grateful to Elliott Anderson for his persistence, and to the Trustees 18
of the James Joyce Estate for permitting the publication of this work.

JOHN CAGE
New York City, May 1977

I

wroth with twone nathandJoe
A
Malt
jhEm
Shen

pftJschute
sOlid man
that the humptYhillhead of humself
is at the knoCk out
in thE park

Jiccup
the fAther
Most
hEaven
Skysign

Judges
Or
deuteronomY
watsCh
futurE

pentschanJeuchy
chAp
Mighty
cEment
and edificeS

the Jebel and the
crOpherb
flYday
and she allCasually
ansars hElpers

Jollybrool
And
strupithuMp
and all thE uproor
aufroofS

to fJell
his baywinds' Oboboes
all the livvYlong
triCky
trochEes

whase on the Joint
whAse
foaMous
oldE
aS you

Jamey
Our
countrY
is a ffrinCh
soracEr this is

the grand mons inJun this is
the Alps hooping to sheltershock
the three lipoleuMs this is
thEir
legahornS

Jinnies
is a cOoin her
phillippY
dispatCh
to irrigatE the willingdone

the Jinnies
fontAnnoy
bode belchuM
bonnEt
to buSby

this is the hinndoo waxing ranJymad
fOr
the hinndoo seeboY
Cry
to the willingdonE

FOR DISCUSSION AND WRITING: MESSING
WITH MESOSTICS

John Cage (1912–1992) was the son of an inventor who developed an explanation of the cosmos called "Electrostatic Field
theory." This history predicts Cage's own innovations in music,
a field he chose after early ambitions as a writer and painter.

In 1933 he became the student of Arnold Schoenberg, who later called Cage not a composer but "an inventor—of genius." Committed to experiment, especially the Dadaist example of Marcel Duchamp, Cage went on to pioneer a new conception of music based on the use of chance and other nonintentional methods. In this, he was aided by his study of Zen Buddhism and a pacifist social philosophy based in the writings of Thoreau. As William Carlos Williams had done in poetry, Cage expanded the definition of music to include all categories of sound, such as random everyday noises. In the 1960s, Cage turned his attention to poetry, using both nonintentional and intentional methods. He soon discovered the use of mesostics, a form of acrostics, as an aid to composition. He also began using the texts of honored predecessors, such as James Joyce and Ezra Pound, as the basis of his chance procedures. Such methods as the casting of the *I Ching* to determine relationships within the text are intended to bring about the politically desirable goal of "demilitarizing" the language. Cage's "indeterminacy," his challenge to the status of author as ego, and his use of appropriation and found materials have become defining characteristics of postmodern art in general (Hoover 17–18).

Following Cage's directions for his experiment, "write through" a work of your own choice. Gather the phrases or sentences associated with the mesostics and treat them as a modified cut-up (revise them into a more seamless piece of prose). Follow up the mesostic performance with a discussion of the experience, comparing conventional reading practices with reading for the name.

Submarginalia
(*from* The Birth-Mark: On Settling the Wilderness in American Literary History)

Susan Howe

SAMUEL TAYLOR COLERIDGE: I am, & ever have been, a great reader—& have read almost every thing—a library-cormorant—I am *deep* in all out of the way books, whether of the monkish times, or of the puritanical aera—I have read & digested most of the Historical Writers—; but I do not *like* History. Metaphysics, & Poetry, & "Facts of Mind"—(i.e. Accounts of all the strange phantasms that ever possessed your philosophy-dreamers from Tauth, the Egyptian to Taylor, the English Pagan,) are my darling Studies.—In short, I seldom read except to amuse myself—& I am almost always reading (C ciii)

The cormorant is a glossy, black water bird often called sea-raven. Cor-   1
morants are widely dispersed over the Northern Hemisphere and both sides
of the Atlantic Ocean. They are underwater swimmers who feed on fish; they
are voracious. Cormorants dive and swim along the ocean bottom, swiftly
scanning every hole or pool, searching for prey. When a fish is sighted, it is
seized at once, and the bird rises to the surface with the captive in its beak.
Swimming under clear water, they seem to be flying.

These birds, if taken when young from the nest, can be trained to fish for   2
a keeper. In sixteenth- and seventeenth-century England cormorant fishing
was a sport. James I particularly enjoyed it. In 1618 he appointed a "master
of the royal cormorants," and a house and ponds were built for his cormorants, ospreys, and otters. In *Paradise Lost*, Milton makes the bird a simil-
itude for Satan. "So clomb this first grand Thief into God's fold; / So since into
his Church lewd hirelings climb. / Thence up he flew, and on the Tree of Life,
/ The middle tree and highest there that grew, / Sat like a cormorant" (PL Bk.
4:192–96).

Cormorants are strand birds; they occupy cliffs by the ocean, where they   3
perch upright on rocks, often motionless for long periods of time, with wings
extended.

*   *   *

COTTON MATHER: I write the *Wonders* of the CHRISTIAN RELIGION, flying from the Depravations of *Europe*, to the *American Strand*: And,
assisted by the Holy Author of that *Religion*, I do, with all Conscience of *Truth*, required therein by Him, who is the *Truth* it self, Report the *Wonderful Displays* of His Infinite Power, Wisdom, Goodness, and Faithfulness, wherewith His Divine Providence hath
Irradiated an *Indian Wilderness*. (MC 89)

A strand is the part of a shore lying between tidemarks.   4
A strand is a filament or fiber laid flat to form a unit for twisting or braid-   5
ing into yarn, thread, rope, or cordage. A strand could be a stalk of grass, a
string of pearls, barbs or fibers of feathers, a filament of hair. Molecular
changes in the brain are caused by impulses traveling along the strands of
nerve fibers.

"God brought Moses law into the world to be as a strand to the
inundation of impiety"—Jeremy Taylor, 1649.

Strand, *v.t.*, to drift or be driven on shore.   6

JOHN WINTHROP (1637): There was an old woman in Ipswich, who
came out of England blind and deaf, yet her son could make her understand any thing, and know any man's name by her sense of feeling. He would write upon her hand some letters of the name, and by
other such motions would inform her. This the governor himself had
‖ trial of‖ ‖tried often‖ when he was at Ipswich. (WH 1:235)

Motherly Piety: an anonymous old woman of Ipswich, swaddled in silence,   7
stranded in darkness, serves as Governor Winthrop's exemplary version during the disorderly days of the birth of his colony, when Mrs. Hutchinson, a
mother and a midwife, impiously dared to preach and prophesy.

Unknownness did your sense of touch re-trace my own nothingness?   8
Finger the way you imagined I am anything. Is your blind gaze sensible? Is
my question a solecism? Is a poetics of intervening absence an oxymoron?
Do we go anywhere? I will twine feathers, prickings, rulings, wampum beads,
chance echoes, sprays of lace in the place of your name. No more apprehension this side of history. Look we are reading a false conception.

Folklore of the cormorant: In China there is a superstition that the bird   9
isn't born from eggs. "The hare spits its young out, the cormorant spits its
fledglings out," goes an old saying. In ancient Japan, holding a cormorant
was supposed to bring about an easy delivery; for the same reason a cormorant feather was grasped in the hand of a woman just as she was giving
birth (DC 255).

*   *   *

Negative Transference

In 1977, Kenneth Murdock's Introduction to the Harvard Belknap Edi-   10
tion of Cotton Mather's *Magnalia Christi Americana: or, The Ecclesiastical History of New-England, from Its First Planting in the Year 1620, unto the Year of
Our* LORD, *1698, in Seven* BOOKS, cites his friend and colleague Perry Miller:
"The intellectual history of New England up to 1720 can be written as though
the [witchcraft] persecution in Massachusetts had never taken place. It had
no effect on the ecclesiastical or political situation, it does not figure in the
institutional or ideological development" of New England (MC 9).

Mather would not have agreed in 1700, the year he finished writing "the   11
Church History of this countrey" (MC 25). The antinomian controversy, the
witchcraft trials, cases of possession, and captivity narratives are all included
in *Magnalia* and in other books, sermons, and pamphlets he wrote. Although
women have troublesome, baffling, potentially transgressive natures, at least
they exist. In 1941, Emily Dickinson is a blank in F. O. Matthiessen's *American Renaissance: Art and Expression in the Age of Emerson and Whitman.*

Some of Emily Dickinson's surviving manuscripts and letters have been   12
cut apart with scissors. Sometimes pages have been torn to shreds, leaving a
single or double strand of words on the brink of the central blank. In the 1958
edition of *The Letters of Emily Dickinson,* her editor, Thomas H. Johnson,
pieced torn unities together. Sometimes he lengthened and recombined
strands of "unrelated thoughts" or "fragment scraps" and placed them in a
category called "Prose Fragments," as if these threaded filaments of letters
were too disorderly to qualify as poetry.

Strand, *noun,* from the Saxon *strand,* is the shore or beach of the sea, of   13
the ocean or of a large lake or navigable river. A margin is a border, edge,

brink, or verge of land. In botany a margin is the edge of a leaf. In books the margin is the edge of a page, left blank or to be filled in with notes.

Possibly in late 1885, Emily Dickinson wrote in a letter to her sister-in-   14
law Susan:

>   Emerging from an Abyss, and reentering it—that is Life, is it not,
> Dear?
>   The tie between us is very fine, but a Hair never dissolves (L 1024)

1861]   Death sets a Thing significant
        The Eye had hurried by
        Except a perished Creature
        Entreat us tenderly

        To ponder little Workmanships
        In Crayon or in Wool
        With "This was last Her
        fingers did" –
        Industrius until –

        The Thimble weighed too heavy –
        The stitches stopped – themselves.
        And then 'twas put among
        the Dust
        Upon the Closet shelves –

        A Book I have –a friend gave –
        Whose Pencil – here and there –
        Had notched the place that
        pleased Him –
        At Rest – His fingers are –

        Now – when I read – I read
        not –
        For interrupting Tears –
        Obliterate the Etchings
        Too Costly for Repairs.

                    (MBED 2:745–46)

Maybe margins shelter the inapprehensible Imaginary of poetry.

                    *   *   *

>   lo tsi k'o am, to have a ring around one's neck like a cormorant,
>   i.e., not to be wholly one's own master.

In China and Japan cormorants are domesticated. A ring or strap around   15
the bird's neck is a symbol of its bondage. An owner needs some way to bridle

and direct his worker-pet's fishing, so a cord or strap of hemp is strung around the bird's neck, then attached to a leash or line. Neck rings made from straw, rattan, bamboo, or iron serve the same purpose as the horse's bit, the water buffalo's nose ring, the falcon's leash and hood; the noose also prevents the bird from swallowing large fish.

"[I]n the last and highest stage of development," writes Berthold Laufer 16 in *The Domestication of the Cormorant in China and Japan*, "the neck-collar is simply discarded. . . . At this stage of the game the birds are disciplined to such a degree of perfection that they fish in unrestrained and absolute freedom. A well trained cormorant, while on duty, will not swallow any fish whether large or small; he knows his business and his lord" (DC 242).

*   *   *

An Idea of Wilderness

Magnalia is intended to be a historical account of the settlement and re- 17 ligious history of New England. Although Mather called his *Magnalia* a "History," its seven volumes could be called "Marginalia" *Christi Americana*. The general style is oddly fixed and declamatory; yet the provincial nonconformist author constantly disrupts the forward trajectory of his written "service . . . for the Church of God, not only here but abroad in Europe," with blizzards of anecdotes, anagrams, prefatory poems, dedications, epigrams, memories, lists of ministers and magistrates, puns, paradoxes, "antiquities," remarks, laments, furious opinions, recollections, exaggerations, fabrications, "Examples," wonders, spontaneous other versions. Short laudatory biographical sketches of the lives of "stars of the first magnitudes in our heavens" are constructed from miscellaneous documentation and distant recollection and punctuated with sudden self-revealing reverse opinion. Kenneth Murdock gave up after editing Books 1 and 2.* He says that Mather the reader "was primarily a smatterer, constantly skimming through whole volumes in search of passages containing ideas which he thought he could develop in his own way or which might serve him as appropriate quotations for use in his own writing" (MC 23). *Magnalia* was far too lengthy a document to be published in Massachusetts. On June 4, 1700, Mather wrote in his Diary: "I this Day putt up my *Church-History*, and pen down Directions about the publishing it. It is a work of near 300 sheets; and has lain by me, diverse years, for want of a fitt opportunity to send it. A Gentleman, just now sailing for *England*, undertakes the care of it; and by his Hand I send it for *London*" (MC 27). When Mather received the textual production of his voluminous work back from the "depravations of Europe" two years later, he was horrified by the numerous printer's errors.

In 1818, William Tudor, the first editor of the *North American Review*, 18 published a critical essay on the *Magnalia*. According to Murdock, Tudor's attitude represents nineteenth-century opinion of the book. "In this effeminate

---

*Whenever possible in these essays I use Murdock's edition of *Magnalia*. Much of the Hutchinson controversy and the life of John Cotton occurs in later books, so it was necessary to use the Andrus 1855 edition.

period . . . a fair perusal of Mather's *Magnalia* is an achievement not to be slighted . . . 800 folio pages in close double columns, even of the most desirable matter, might well cause hesitation. What then must be the effect of a chaotick mass of history, biography, obsolete creeds, witchcraft, and Indian wars, interspersed with bad puns, and numerous quotations in Latin, Greek and Hebrew which rise up like so many decayed, hideous stumps to arrest the eye and deform the surface?" (MC 33). In spite of this judgment it is impossible to imagine Hawthorne's early tales and sketches without the *Magnalia*. The idiosyncratic combination of history, fiction, Scripture, and Elizabethan and baroque drama in *Moby-Dick* recalls Mather's monumental meditative document. Mather was attracted to Camden's idea that letters in a word or name could be rearranged to cabalistically reveal God's hidden purpose. *Magnalia*'s nearly obsessive use of anagram and paradox reflects this belief and can be directly related to verbal compression in Webster's *American Dictionary of the English Language*, Emerson's essays, and Dickinson's poetry and letters: library cormorants all.

The same year William Tudor wrote his derogatory essay in America, 19 Coleridge was preparing his last course of lectures in London. On March 10, 1818, the poet made a notebook entry meant to describe himself. In 1836 his editor daughter and son-in-law placed it after the Preface to the first two volumes of *Literary Remains*.

> <S.T.C.=> who with long and large arm still collected precious Armfuls in whatever direction he pressed forward, yet still took up so much more than he could keep together that those who followed him gleaned more from his continual droppings than he himself brought home—Nay, made stately Corn-ricks therewith, while the Reaper himself was still seen only with a strutting Armful of newly cut Sheaves.—But I should misinform you grossly if I left you to infer that his Collections were a heap of incoherent Miscellanea—No!—the very Contrary—Their variety conjoined with the too great Coherency, the too great both desire & power of referring them in systematic, nay, genetic subordination was that which rendered his schemes gigantic & impracticable, as an Author—& his Conversation less instructive, as a man/—Inopem sua *Copia* fecit, too much was given, all so weighty & brilliant as to preclude choice, & too many to be all received—so that it passed over the Hearers mind like a roar of waters—. (C cxxv)

Coleridge's dissection of his turbulent, sometimes unfathomable literary 20 expression could be a description of *Magnalia Christi Americana*. Even if he had to subsist on provincial libraries, Mather's voracious reading a century earlier rivaled Coleridge's. A provincial library cormorant, utterly in love with words, Mather sometimes resembles Baudelaire's Poet-Albatross. "Le Poète est semblable au prince des nuées / Qui hante la tempête et se rit de l'archer; / Exilé sur le sol au milieu des huées, / Ses ailes de géant l'empêchent de marcher" (FM 32).

*   *   *

Years before John Livingston Lowes wrote *The Road to Xanadu*, Thomas 21
Wolfe was his student at Harvard. Marginal note 85a to Martin Gardner's edition of *The Annotated Ancient Mariner* tells us "Lowes' belief that Coleridge's
creative genius had fed unconsciously on memories acquired by prodigious
reading had much to do with Wolfe's insane attempt, as a student, to read all
the books in the Harvard library" (AM 70).

In 1927, when he was working on *Look Homeward, Angel*, Wolfe told a 22
former teacher: "I think I shall call it 'Alone, Alone,' for the idea that broods
over it, and in it, and behind it is that we are all strangers upon this earth we
walk on—that naked and alone do we come into life, and alone, a stranger,
each to each, we live upon it. The title, as you know, I have taken from the
poem I love best, 'The Rime of the Ancient Mariner'" (AM 70).

*   *   *

Coleridge, a cormorant of libraries, dives *deep* in books as if they were a 23
sea. When Thoreau compares readers who devour the sentimental novels in
Concord's circulating library to cormorants who will digest anything, he means
women (novelists and readers), though he doesn't say the word or use the feminine pronoun. The chapter in *Walden* is called "Reading." *Look Homeward,
Angel* is a sentimental novel. Walden is only a pond. Ponds can't have strands.

According to the "Editor's Introduction" to *The Collected Works of Samuel* 24
Taylor Coleridge (Marginalia I: Abbt to Byfield), Robert Southey, the author of
The Life of Nelson, allowed Coleridge to write marginal comments in his prized
edition of Cotton Mather's *Magnalia Christi Americana*. Southey once recommended Mather's *Ecclesiastical History of New England from Its First Planting*
to a friend as "one of the most extraordinary books in the world" (C lxxi, *n*).

Coleridge often penciled notes in the margins of Southey's books; Robert 25
Southey later reverently retraced them in ink for posterity.

*   *   *

Yet I was a most fearless child by daylight—ever ready to take the
difficult mountain path and outgo my companions' daring in tree-
climbing. In those early days we used to spend much of our summer
time in trees, greatly to the horror of Mrs. Rickman and some of our
London visitors.

On reviewing my earlier childhood, I find the predominant reflection . . . (SD 266)

_____

This is the apprehensive conclusion to Sara Coleridge's brief autobio- 26
graphical narrative in the form of a letter addressed to her daughter Edith.
The autobiography was an epistolary project uncharacteristically never mentioned in her other writings. Edith later published a heavily edited version in
Memoir and Letters of Sara Coleridge in 1874. Bradford Keyes Mudge in his
illuminating study, *Sara Coleridge, A Victorian Daughter: Her Life and Essays*,

points out the author's bitter awareness here of her own submarginal status. Sara begins her narrative by precisely noting:

> My father has entered his marriage with my mother and the births of my three brothers with some particularity in a family Bible, given him, as he also notes, by Joseph Cottle on his marriage; the entry of my birth is in my dear mother's hand-writing and this seems like an omen of our life-long separation, for I was never with him for more than a few weeks at a time. He lived not much more, indeed, with his other children, but most of their infancy passed under his eye. Alas! more than any of them I inherited that uneasy health of his, which kept us apart. But I did not mean to start with "alas!" (SD 163)

"The term *marginalia* (singular, *marginale*) refers to anything written by 27 Coleridge in the margins and other blank spaces in the text of a printed book, on flyleaves, end-papers, or the inside or outside of a paperwrapper" (C xxiii). Coleridge's notes on the two front flyleaves in BIBLE *Copy A* can be found in *Marginalia I: Abbt to Byfield.* Five entries were made there in "various hands." They have been consigned by the editors to a section called Annex. Annex is matter printed at the end of a book entry typographically distinct from the marginalia. "Sara Coleridge born December 23, 20 minutes past 6 in the Morning, 1802" (C 413). If Mrs. Coleridge hadn't marked it, the record of Sara's birth would be blank in her family's Holy Bible, containing the Old Testament and the New. All entries in the Annex are in women's hands.

Samuel Taylor Coleridge lavished worry and love on his sons Hartley 28 and Derwent (Berkeley died in infancy) while largely ignoring his daughter Sara until she was old enough to be useful to him. Robert Southey was her uncle. During most of her childhood she and her mother and brothers lived with the Southeys at Greta Hall. A brilliant woman, who could speak six languages, Sara became a poet, translator, opium addict, and library cormorant. When she died in 1852, Henry Reed, a professor of English at the University of Pennsylvania, who had first written to her in 1849 for permission to publish an edition of Coleridge's poetry and became one of her many devoted correspondents, wrote a memoir called "The Daughter of Coleridge." He regretted that she had expended so much of her genius in writing editorial notes, prefaces, and letters: "so varied were her writings and so rich in thought and in the accumulation of knowledge, that they may be compared to the conversation and '*marginalia*' of her father" (HR 22).

In 1829, Sara Coleridge married her cousin, Henry Nelson Coleridge, a 29 lawyer and classical scholar. She was pregnant seven times in thirteen years of marriage; only two children survived. Between her frequent miscarriages Sara suffered several nervous breakdowns. When her father died in 1834, his literary executor, Joseph Henry Green, gave Henry Coleridge the task of collecting, arranging, and editing for publication "the scattered remains of that remarkable mind" (HR 30). Sara collaborated on the immense editorial project; at the same time she was serving as Henry's amanuensis by copying legal documents for him in his poorly paid employment as a barrister-at-law. She and Henry, realizing their interest and the amount of energy the author had expended on other authors, went to a great deal of time, money, and trouble in order to trace, gather, and transcribe Coleridge's marginal notes. In 1843, when Henry died after a long illness, she was left with very little money, a massive and unfinished editorial project, and two young children to educate. Her two brothers also left her all responsibility for the care of her widowed mother. While he was alive, Henry had loaned Hartley and Derwent money; it was never repaid. Somehow Sara, formerly the author of a volume of poetry called *Pretty Lessons in Verse for Small Children*—fairy tales, translations, and various essays, including "On the Disadvantages Resulting from the Possession of Beauty," "Nervousness," "Reply to Strictures of Three Gentlemen upon Carlyle," and "On Mr. Wordsworth's Poem Entitled 'Lines Left on a Yewtree Seat'"—found time to write a two-hundred-page "Essay on Rationalism," prepare the second edition of her father's *Biographia Literaria* (1847) for publication, edit *Notes and Lectures upon Shakespeare, and Some of the Old Poets and Dramatists, with Other Literary Remains of S. T. Coleridge* (1849), then collect and publish her father's random contributions to newspapers and small magazines in *Essays on His Own Times: Forming a Second Series of the Friend* (1850). In endnote after footnote Sara carefully and precisely defended her father from charges of plagiarism. To refute these charges she dutifully read Schelling, Schlegel, and other German philosophers. "I might as well attempt to run up a river, the water up to my waist as to run through Schelling" (SD 108), she wrote to John Taylor Coleridge. While working on the preparation of *Notes and Lectures*, Sara wrote in her diary:

> No work is so inadequately rewarded either by money or credit as that of editing miscellaneous, fragmentary, immethodical literary remains like those of S.T.C. Such labours cannot be rewarded for they cannot be seen—some of them cannot even be perceived in their effects by the intelligent reader. How many, many mornings, evenings, afternoons have I spent in hunting for some piece of information in order to rectify a statement—to decide whether to retain or withdraw a sentence, or how to turn it—the effect being negative, the silent avoidance of error. . . . But when there is not mere carelessness but a positive coldness in regard to what I have done, I do sometimes feel as if I had been wasting myself a good deal—at least so far as worldly advantage is concerned. (CF 157)

All this time she continued in her effort to collect the volumes from Coleridge's library that had been widely scattered at the time of his death. Until a few days before her death in 1852, at forty-nine, she was still laboring over an edition of her father's poems. When the volume was later published as "edited by Sara and Derwent Coleridge," Derwent gracefully acknowledged his sister had done all of the work.

Shortly before she died, Sara Coleridge recalled her father: "Indeed, he 30 seems ever at my ear, in his books, more especially his marginalia—speaking not personally to me, and yet in a way so natural to my feelings, that *finds* me so fully, and awakens such a strong echo in my mind and heart, that I seem more intimate with him now than ever I was in life" (c lviii). George Whalley, editor of the Princeton *Marginalia,* remarks in his Editor's Introduction, "Harvesting the Marginalia": "Except that Henry and Sara preserved some marginal notes that would now be otherwise lost to us, their work is not very useful to the modern editor" (c cxlvi).

"What was I?" Sara asked herself in her autobiographical epistolary   31
"sketch" (SD 265).

*   *   *

Sir William Hamilton, British diplomat and archaeologist, the husband   32
of Emma Hamilton, Horatio Nelson's mistress, described his philosophy in a letter to the admiral. "My study of antiquities . . . has kept me in constant thought of the perpetual fluctuation of every thing. The whole art is really to live all the *days* of our life; and not with anxious care disturb the sweetest hour that life affords, — which is the present. Admire the Creator, and all his works, to us incomprehensible; and do all the good you can upon earth: and take the chance of eternity without dismay" (MM 2:531). Besides underlining the portions of the passage above in his copy of Southey's *Life of Nelson,* Herman Melville drew three lines in the right margin for emphasis. On the front flyleaf of the book, Elizabeth Shaw Melville wrote: "This book is kept for reference for[m?] 'Billy Budd' — (unfinished)" (MM 2:516).

After Melville's death, Mrs. Melville wrote in her husband's edition of Isaac   33
Disraeli's *The Literary Character:* "My ideas of my husband are so much associated with his books that to part with them would be as it were breaking some of the last ties which still connect me with so beloved an object. The being in the midst of books he has been accustomed to read, and which contain his *marks* and *notes,* will still give him *a sort of existence with me*" (F 194). Harrison Hayford and Merton M. Sealts, Jr., editors of *Billy Budd, Sailor* and *Billy Budd: The Genetic Text,* refer to Mrs. Melville's editorial notations on the original manuscript as marks made by an "alien hand."

*   *   *

Alienation

lashed in a hammock, hemp around his neck, dragging cables, cordage,   34
without volition under language, in a measure mysteriously woman, Billy drifts fathoms down dreaming *Obey* pinned to a clip now gone. What space to which to extend the arms; at that instant we are all like swimmers. "Fathoms down, fathoms down, how I'll dream fast asleep." Fathom understanding: fathom which wave to think. "O, 'tis me, not the sentence they'll suspend" (BB 132). The ballad is so mutinous without a known author. Fatherless in the same sentence what syllables will flood utterance. Warbling, warbling. Leaving no verb in their eyes

our predestinated depths who fathoms. Strond strund stronde strand.   35
The margin submerges phonic substance. A mother's thread or line is ringed about with silence so poems are

Billy radically alone.   36

*   *   *

Bitterness Fire Love Sound Water

To feed these essays I have dived through other people's thoughts with 37
footnotes for compasses and categories for quadrants. I have plagiarized sermons, memorial introductions, epitaphs, anagrams, epigrams, dictionaries
here and elsewhere. In the acquisitive spirit I have borrowed back brief earlier brimstone sermons. "What is an author?" asks Michel Foucault in the essay that directly inspired and informed my writing about Anne Hutchinson,
Thomas Shepard, John Winthrop, Anne Bradstreet, Mary Rowlandson, James
Savage, and Emily Dickinson. Foucault's influence is problematic. This wide-
ranging philosopher and library cormorant's eloquent, restless, passionate
interrogation of how we have come to be the way we are remains inside the
margins of an intellectual enclosure constructed from memories, meditations,
delusions, and literary or philosophical speculations of European men. "What
is a picture?" Jacques Lacan tells me, at the perceptual level, in its relation to
desire, reality appears to be marginal. What are the guises of human sciences
when women do speak? In Emmanuel Levinas's terminology: *"A work conceived radically is a movement of the Same towards the Other which never returns to the Same"* (CP 91; italics in original). After 1637, American literary expression couldn't speak English. I am a North American author. I was born
in 1937. Into World War II and the rotten sin of man-made mass murder. "I
see but you, O warlike pennant! O banner so broad, with stripes, I sing you
only" (LG 245). What new path in ethics will lead me away? Love words. Definition is variable. We do not have such a Journal.

My aim in the present study? Ask what form for the form. Print is a pho- 38
bic response to negligence. Letters should be civil or slang being negligent.

Truth is water. Attraction makes it open.   39

Bold pencil line in margin across the verso leaf at one extreme why should 40
she write. Their business is to fish. A woman writing with such rebelliousness
altogether. Ranging marginalia without a known author I am full of hunger.
Print is furious have no page to waste. Yoursebl live on demigorgon offspring
fearfnll love. What does a seducer hunt?

Unmediated companion I am what you hunt fettered alone in you.   41

and we desire. Every flag and twig condemned to market mud in the year 42
before April. A child can be had. Ding-dong. "Little Annie's Ramble." "A LITTLE
GIRL, of five years old, in a blue frock and white pantalettes, with brown curl-
ing hair and hazel eyes." See pure rhetoric to tell to. But I have gone too far
from home. The jury sits in judge. John Bull: "Law is a bottomless pit; it is a
cormorant." So it is. Consuming means devour everything. Locke, John, his
Treatise on the *Human Understanding;* law-nets are cobwebs. *Clarissa; or the
History of a Young Lady;* etymological fancies; more rings I won't pity. Eden.
First Part of our unwritten. Cormorant time demanding all. So it was

dear (and ever shall be).   43

In what language shall I address you? Self-assertion by letter writing. 44
Some Connecticut locality. Factual detail.

Many out-of-the-way volumes, especially books about the Puritan Revo- 45
lution in England, and books by and about Puritans in seventeenth-century
New England are my darling studies, and I used them while I was writing
these essays

scattered by the fratricidal Enlightenment   46

she turns the tables without rejecting Abraham Isaac Jacob. That kind of adoration. The time is autumn morning evening. To collect an error in the shelter of theory send disciples soon.

Every source has another center so is every creator.   47

A mere slip of the coast at a northern extreme America America all is   48
smooth again. Our lakes of the woods. The double's face I remember all
shawled and coming down. It was an emblem of desire. Nothing thwarts desire here. Here are gardens blue backgound wash water. Love is reflected in
water. The birds their plumage. Swallows swim so low. Sometimes I dive below the line in such a story September October.

Slips from a particular institution all or one of them.   49

"Our lady was ful of grace as a stronde ful of watyr." In the idiom de- 50
construction old women wish to remain in touch. Stranger speak kindly.
Sometimes speech divides us. Mixture of midland and northern dialect. Tran-
sience. Experience. Wyclif's Bible and Wyclif's sermons. Then once, in
Sibbes, His great command as clear a benediction. It was my postmodern editorial decision to turn some sections of the conversion narratives and Mary
Dyer's letter into poems. If the name Walden hadn't been taken from an English place, Thoreau thinks he could imagine its original name was *Walled-in*
Pond. In *This New Yet Unapproachable America*, Stanley Cavell says the
name may come from the Waldensian heresy. "O banner so broad there, with
stripes, / flapping up there in the wind," let me enfold tenderness. Even so
and by such tracing of far-fetched meandering I hope to stray.

In these essays I have followed the spelling and punctuation of each 51
quoted source. Revisions, deletions, footnotes, spelling, stray marks, and
punctuation are usually edited to conform to the requirements of whatever
period they are published in. In the flow of time original versions are modernized and again modernized

in the flow of time these copies are copies of copies.   52

Doubles are counteracted one must draw still. "Come up here soul soul." 53
Two desires. Thrift thrift. Near the surface I'll twine them and put in life. They
are not the one. Flapping flapping flapping flapping. Sometimes I know you
just from reading.

It is the grace of scholarship. I am indebted to everyone.   54

Key for "Introduction" and "Submarginalia"

AC   *The Antinomian Controversy:* David Hall, ed.

AM   *The Annotated Ancient Mariner:* Samuel Taylor Coleridge; Martin Gardner, ed.

AR   *American Renaissance: Art and Expression in the Age of Emerson and Whitman:* F. O. Matthiessen.

B   *The Bodleian Shelley Manuscripts:* Donald H. Reiman, ed.

BB   *Billy Budd, Sailor:* Herman Melville; Hayford and Sealts, eds.

C   *The Collected Works of Samuel Taylor Coleridge,* vol. 12, *Marginalia I:* George Whalley, ed.

CF   *Coleridge Fille:* Earl Leslie Griggs.

CP   *Collected Philosophical Papers:* Emmanuel Levinas.

CWS   *Coleridge's Writings on Shakespeare:* Terence Hawkes, ed.

DC   *The Domestication of the Cormorant in China and Japan:* Berthold Laufer.

EH   "Recollections of Hawthorne by His Sister Elizabeth": Randall Stewart.

EN   *Nature:* Ralph Waldo Emerson.

F   *Byron and Byronism in the Mind and Art of Herman Melville:* Edward Fiess.

FM   *Les Fleurs du mal:* Charles Baudelaire.

H   *Tales and Sketches:* Nathaniel Hawthorne.

HF   *Hymns and Fragments:* Friedrich Hölderlin.

HR   *Sara Coleridge and Henry Reed:* Leslie Nathan Broughton, ed.

L   *The Letters of Emily Dickinson:* Johnson and Ward, eds.

LCP   *Language, Counter-Memory, Practice:* Michel Foucault.

LG   *Leaves of Grass:* Walt Whitman.

MBED   *The Manuscript Books of Emily Dickinson:* R. W. Franklin, ed.

MC   *Magnalia Christi Americana,* Books 1 and 2: Kenneth B. Murdock, ed.

MM   *Melville's Marginalia:* Walker Cowen, ed.

PL   *Paradise Lost:* John Milton.

PS   *Selected Writings of Edgar Allan Poe.*

PT   *The Piazza Tales.* "Bartleby, the Scrivener: A Story of Wall-Street": Herman Melville; Hayford, MacDougall, and Tanselle, eds.

PW   *Complete Works of Edgar Allan Poe,* vol. 16, *Marginalia—Eureka:* James A. Harrison, ed.

RD   *Rat & the Devil; Journal Letters of F. O. Matthiessen and Russell Cheney:* Louis Hyde, ed.

S   *Shelley: Poetical Works:* Thomas Hutchinson, ed.

SD   *Sara Coleridge, A Victorian Daughter: Her Life and Essays:* Bradford Keyes Mudge, ed. and author.

SL   *The Scarlet Letter:* Nathaniel Hawthorne.

TS   *Transport to Summer:* Wallace Stevens.

WD   *An American Dictionary of the English Language:* Noah Webster.

WH   *The History of New England from 1630 to 1649:* John Winthrop; James Savage, ed.

Sources for "Introduction" and "Submarginalia"

Arac, Jonathan. "F. O. Matthiessen: Authorizing an American Renaissance." In *The American Renaissance Reconsidered: Selected Papers from the English Institute, 1982–83,* edited by Walter Benn Michaels and Donald E. Pease. 90–112. Baltimore: The Johns Hopkins University Press, 1985.

Baudelaire, Charles. *Les Fleurs du mal.* Edited by Robert Strick. Paris: Presses Pocket, 1989.

Coleridge, Samuel Taylor. *The Annotated Ancient Mariner.* Edited by Martin Gardner. New York: Bramhall House, 1965.

———. *Coleridge's Writings on Shakespeare.* Edited by Terence Hawkes. New York: Capricorn Books, 1959.

————. *The Collected Works of Samuel Taylor Coleridge*. Vol. 12, *Marginalia I: Abbt to Byfield*. Edited by George Whalley. Princeton, N.J.: Princeton University Press, 1980.

Coleridge, Sara. *Memoir and Letters of Sara Coleridge*. Edited by Edith Coleridge. New York: Harper & Brothers, 1874.

————. *Sara Coleridge and Henry Reed*. Edited by Leslie Nathan Broughton. Ithaca, N.Y.: Cornell University Press, 1937.

Dickinson, Emily. *The Letters of Emily Dickinson*. 3 vols. Edited by Thomas H. Johnson and Theodora Ward. Cambridge, Mass.: The Belknap Press, Harvard University Press, 1958.

————. *The Manuscript Books of Emily Dickinson*. 2 vols. Edited by R. W. Franklin. Cambridge, Mass.: The Belknap Press, Harvard University, 1981.

Emerson, Ralph Waldo. *Nature. A Facsimile of the First Edition*. Boston: Beacon Press, 1989.

Fiess, Edward. *Byron and Byronism in the Mind and Art of Herman Melville*. Ann Arbor, Mich.: University Microfilms, 1965.

Foucault, Michel. *Language, Counter-Memory, Practice: Selected Essays and Interviews*. Edited by Donald F. Bouchard. Ithaca, N.Y.: Cornell University Press, 1977.

Griggs, Earl Leslie. *Coleridge Fille: A Biography of Sara Coleridge*. New York: Oxford University Press, 1940.

Hall, David D. *The Antinomian Controversy, 1636–1638: A Documentary History*. Edited by David D. Hall. Middletown, Conn.: Wesleyan University Press, 1968.

Hawthorne, Nathaniel. *The Scarlet Letter and Other Tales of the Puritans*. Edited by Harry Levin. Boston: Houghton Mifflin, 1961.

————. *Tales and Sketches*. New York: The Library of America, 1982.

Hölderlin, Friedrich. *Hymns and Fragments*. Translated by Richard Sieburth. Princeton, N.J.: Princeton University Press, 1984.

Laufer, Berthold. *The Domestication of the Cormorant in China and Japan*. Field Museum of Natural History Anthropological Series, vol. 18, no. 3. Chicago: Field Museum Press, 1931.

Levinas, Emmanuel. *Collected Philosophical Papers*. Translated by Alphonso Lingis. Boston: Martinus Nijhoff, 1987.

Mather, Cotton. *Magnalia Christi Americana: or, The Ecclesiastical History of New-England*. Hartford, Conn.: Silas Andrus & Son, 1855.

————. *Magnalia Christi Americana*, Books 1 and 2. Edited by Kenneth B. Murdock. Cambridge, Mass.: The Belknap Press, Harvard University Press, 1977.

Matthiessen, F. O. *American Renaissance: Art and Expression in the Age of Emerson and Whitman*. New York: Oxford University Press, 1941.

————. *Rat & the Devil; Journal Letters of F. O. Matthiessen and Russell Cheney*. Edited by Louis Hyde. Hamden, Conn.: Archon Books, 1978.

Melville, Herman. *Billy Budd, Sailor (An Inside Narrative)*. Edited by Harrison Hayford and Merton M. Sealts, Jr. Chicago: University of Chicago Press, 1962.

————. *Melville's Marginalia*. 2 vols. Edited by Walker Cowen. New York: Garland Publishing, 1987.

————. *The Piazza Tales, and Other Prose Pieces*. Edited by Harrison Hayford, Alma A. MacDougall, and G. Thomas Tanselle. Evanston and Chicago: Northwestern University Press and the Newberry Library, 1987.

Milton, John. *The Complete Poetical Works of John Milton*. Edited by Douglas Bush. Boston: Houghton Mifflin, 1965.

Mudge, Bradford Keyes. *Sara Coleridge, A Victorian Daughter: Her Life and Essays*. New Haven, Conn.: Yale University Press, 1989.

Poe, Edgar Allan. *The Complete Works of Edgar Allan Poe*. Vol. 16, *Marginalia — Eureka*. Edited by James A. Harrison. New York: AMS Press, 1965.

————. *Selected Writings of Edgar Allan Poe*. Edited by Edward H. Davidson. Boston: Houghton Mifflin, Riverside Press, 1956.

Shelley, Percy Bysshe. *The Bodleian Shelley Manuscripts: A Facsimile Edition, with Full Transcriptions and Scholarly Apparatus.* Vol. 7. Edited by Donald H. Reiman. New York: Garland Publishing, 1989.

————. *Poetical Works.* Edited by Thomas Hutchinson. New York: Oxford University Press, 1990.

Stevens, Wallace. *Transport to Summer.* New York: Alfred A. Knopf, 1951.

Stewart, Randall. "Recollections of Hawthorne by His Sister Elizabeth." *American Literature* 16 (January 1945): 316–29.

Webster, Noah. *An American Dictionary of the English Language.* Revised and enlarged by Chauncey A. Goodrich. Springfield, Mass.: George and Charles Merriam, 1852.

Whitman, Walt. *Leaves of Grass.* Edited by Emory Holloway. Garden City, N.Y.: Doubleday, 1926.

Winthrop, John. *The History of New England from 1630 to 1649.* 2 vols. Edited by James Savage. Boston: Phelps and Farnham, 1825.

FOR DISCUSSION AND WRITING: GENERATING A POETICS OF KNOWLEDGE

Howe Too

Born in Ireland (1937), Susan Howe emigrated with her family to the United States as a child. Author of ten books of poetry, she has been an actress and assistant stage designer at Dublin's Gate Theater, a painter, radio producer, and literary critic. Her greatest influences are Charles Olson, especially in his attraction to the history and culture of New England, and Emily Dickinson. Howe also considers the early Puritan writers, especially Cotton Mather, to be important influences on her writing. She has twice received the Before Columbus Foundation American Book Award, in 1980 for *Secret History of the Dividing Line* (1979), and in 1987 for *My Emily Dickinson.* Among her other books are *Pythagorean Silence* (1982), *Defenestration of Prague* (1983), *Articulation of Sound Forms in Time* (1987) (Hoover 346–47).

Howe's writing is often associated with the school of poets known as the "language" group, which includes such figures as Charles Bernstein, Clark Coolidge, Lyn Hejinian, and Bob Perelman (among others). The Language School is noted for its break with the tradition of the lyric poem and its assumptions about the voice of the individual poet. Charles Bernstein, for example, argued that "it is a mistake to posit the self as the primary organizing feature of writing. As many others have pointed out, a poem exists in a matrix of social and historical relations that are more significant to the formation of an individual text than any personal qualities of the life or voice of an author."

"Submarginalia" is the first essay in the collection entitled *The Birth-Mark* and introduces the method Howe used in the rest of the study. The essay is a good example of conducting research in aesthetic terms—finding one's own voice by appropriating fragments of a tradition. Sort out and describe which of the techniques in the essay are critical or scholarly and which are creative or poetic. To what extent does "Submarginalia" synthesize into one text all the features of this unit, including all the works in both archives—the fragments and the signatures, identifications and play? Compare and contrast her uses of identification and of collage with other relevant figures in the archives. Notice how she deals with questions of identity—her experience of gender and the status of women in her tradition.

Write a set of rules or instructions based on Howe's example that generalize her strategies as a method for composing a research text.

A Work of Literature/A Play of Text

We have come now to the final assignment, an experiment whose purpose is to test the reach of text as a learning experience.

A mystory in practice makes use of both approaches demonstrated in this chapter—identification and language play. Indeed, the effect of recognition or epiphany that often results during the composition of a mystory is due not only to the themes of the materials, but more often to some repetition of a signifier—a word or shape—across the different semantic areas juxtaposed in the composition. The play method of miming or citing fragments of the original works is useful in the mystory for entering research findings into each part of the figure, without attempting to interpret in advance how the different materials cohere. The juxtaposition often produces some unexpected pattern, and this pattern, elaborated into an image, constitutes a kind of identity logo or blazon for the author.

As was the case for the other chapters, the textual approach to research establishes a conduit or interchange between a simple form (or forms) and a more complex practice (such as the exchange between the oral anecdote and the literate short story in chapter 1). The exchange in the case of research is between the simple citation and complex collage. The research paper uses citation with an attitude or feeling of proof. The researchers subordinate themselves to the voice of authority and document every claim, although the quotations in an essay are embedded in the framing argument. Papers are not supposed to quote too much or too often, however, but are expected to paraphrase and summarize the work of others, while couching the discussion as an interpretation or analysis of the object of study.

Writing as Recycling (Waste Not, Want Not)

Text takes a different (nearly opposite) approach to citation, one that appears to reduce the author to editor or curator, while foregrounding quotation. However, a shift in attitude motivating the citation produces a paradoxical reversal. The attitude of text is aesthetic, and the effect of the makers' disappearance into the language is the emergence of their own voice. The unit of meaning shifts from the single word to whole lines or even paragraphs from the encyclopedia or archive. "Writing" is reduced to the basic operations of selection and combination (or revision and variation)—recycling existing works into texts. The claim to knowledge or proof is traded in for an experience of creative invention. And yet, the claim of mystory is that the learning effect about the object of study is just as strong as the one produced by the paper. Both papers and texts search the cultural archive for materials to use, but the motive for the search differs: "proof" (idea) for the paper; "recognition" (emotion) for the text.

In "Submarginalia," for example, Howe ventriloquizes the styles and language of an American tradition with which she identifies (a New England heritage). The repetition of carefully selected passages, their combination with other selections moving from colonial to modern periods, signals an eccentric or idiosyncratic orientation that specifies Howe as the authority, the authorizing figure and point of coherence of the inventory. The emphasis is not on meaning, but on performance. Moreover, she adopts as a blazon or personal logo an image from the cultural heritage—the cormorant—that she extends into a metaphor that evokes not only her poetics and method but also her state of mind, an ambivalence about her position in the tradition.

The Great Experiment: Re-Citing, Re-Searching

Imagine that *Text Book* as a whole constitutes a tradition of writing that is to you what the New England heritage is to Howe: a language that speaks you and within which you want to claim your place (to pick up the conversation and keep it going). Follow the instructions you extracted from Howe (and from the other samples in the archive), and compose a collage composition in which you mine the resources of the book to find a voice and style of thought into which you may insert yourself. Include a metaphor that expresses your relationship to media and culture, the way Howe used the cormorant. The form of the text should emulate Howe's essay (supplemented by any of the other sample forms included in the archive).

For a more ambitious research project, follow leads in the immediate archive wherever they may lead in the library or on the Internet (into history or popular culture) to other materials in which you recognize your own style and voice. For example, you may want to look into the existence of a "voice" peculiar to your own region of the country (critics like to treat writers who live in a particular region as a "school" and identify features of the works that are shared by the group). "Recognition" works here in the middle voice: it is not that you already know what the southern (for example) style is (if you are from the South), only that you know that in principle your identity was constructed within a southern culture.

One assumption of the mystory is that you have to look outside your immediate memory (to history, entertainment, literature, or politics, for example) to discover what may have been assimilated, introjected inside, to become the filter that shapes your awareness. In the case of literary heritage, it is not that you have already assimilated the tradition, but that the tradition is there for you to use, as "equipment for living" (to borrow Kenneth Burke's phrase). The payoff is an experience of "extimacy." The result is not fate but opportunity. Once you discover where you are in language, it is possible to steer any course.

BIBLIOGRAPHY

Baldick, Chris. *The Concise Oxford Dictionary of Literary Terms*. New York: Oxford UP, 1990.

Barthes, Roland. *The Pleasure of the Text*. Trans. Richard Miller. New York: Hill, 1975.

———. *Empire of Signs*. Trans. Richard Howard. New York: Hill, 1982.

Bernheimer, Kate, ed. *Mirror, Mirror on the Wall: Women Writers Explore Their Favorite Fairy Tales*. New York: Anchor, 1998.

Burroughs, William S. "The Cut-Up Method of Brion Gysin." *Re/Search #4/5: A Special Issue: William S. Burroughs, Brion Gysin, and Throbbing Gristle*. San Francisco, 1982.

Cage, John. *Empty Words: Writings '73–'78*. Middletown, CT: Wesleyan, 1981.

Goethe, Johann Wolfgang von. *"The Sorrows of Young Werther" and Selected Writings*. Trans. Catherine Hutter. New York: New American Library, 1962.

Griffin, Susan. *A Chorus of Stones: The Private Life of War*. New York: Doubleday, 1992.

Holman, C. Hugh. *A Handbook to Literature*. 3rd ed. New York: Bobbs-Merrill, 1972.

Hoover, Paul, ed. *Postmodern American Poetry: A Norton Anthology*. New York: Norton, 1994.

Loydell, Rupert, ed. *My Kind of Angel: i. m. William Burroughs*. Devon, England: Stride, 1998.

Paley, Nicholas. *Finding Art's Place: Experiments in Contemporary Education and Culture*. New York: Routledge, 1995.

Pell, Derek. *Assassination Rhapsody*. Brooklyn: Autonomedia, 1989.

Perrin, Robert. *The Beacon Handbook*. Boston: Houghton Mifflin, 1987.

Rheingold, Howard. *They Have A Word for It*. Los Angeles: Tarcher, 1988.

Tate, James, ed. *The Best American Poetry, 1997*. New York: Scribner, 1997.

Acknowledgments (continued from p. iv)

John Barth, "Night-Sea Journey," from *Lost in the Funhouse*. Copyright © 1966 by John Barth (first published in Esquire Magazine), from *Lost in the Funhouse* by John Barth. Used by permission of Doubleday, a division of Random House, Inc.

Roland Barthes, "waiting," "heart," "image," "to understand," "habiliment," and "identification" from *A Lover's Discourse: Fragments* by Roland Barthes, translated by Richard Howard. Copyright © 1977 by Editions du Seuil. English Translation Copyright © 1979 by Farrar, Straus and Giroux, Inc. Reprinted by permission of Hill and Wang, a division of Farrar, Straus and Giroux, LLC.

Walter Benjamin, "Ordnance." Excerpt from "One-Way Street" in *Reflections: Essays, Aphorisms, Autobiographical Information*, by Walter Benjamin, copyright © 1978 by Harcourt, Inc., reprinted by permission of the publisher.

Bruno Bettelheim, "The Sleeping Beauty," from *The Uses of Enchantment* by Bruno Bettelheim, copyright © 1975, 1976 by Bruno Bettelheim. Used by permission of Alfred A. Knopf, a division of Random House, Inc.

Jorge Luis Borges, "Borges and I" and "Ragnarok," from *Collected Fictions* by Jorge Luis Borges, translated by Andrew Hurley, copyright © 1998 by Maria Kodama; translation copyright © 1998 by Penguin Putnam, Inc. Used by permission of Viking Penguin, a division of Penguin Putnam, Inc.

Andre Breton, "Poem." From *Manifestoes of Surrealism*, by Andre Breton, translated by Seaver and Lane, reprinted by permission of the University of Michigan Press, copyright © 1969 by the University of Michigan Press.

Roger Brown, "What Words Are: Reference and Categories." Reprinted with the permission of The Free Press, a Division of Simon & Schuster, Inc., from *Words and Things* by Roger Brown. Copyright © 1958, 1968 by The Free Press.

John Cage, "Writing for the Second Time through *Finnegans Wake*," from *Empty Words: Writings '73–'78* (University Press of New England, 1979), by John Cage. Reprinted by permission of Wesleyan University Press.

Italo Calvino (Canadian rights), "Cities and Memory 2" and "Continuous Cities," from *Invisible Cities*. Copyright © 1978 by Italo Calvino. Used by permission of The Wylie Agency, Inc.

Italo Calvino (U.S. rights), "Cities and Memory 2" and "Continuous Cities," from *Invisible Cities*, by Italo Calvino, copyright © 1972 by Giulio Einaudi editore s.p.a. English translation by Williams Weaver, copyright © 1974 by Harcourt, Inc., reprinted by permission of Harcourt, Inc.

Nancy R. Comley and Robert Scholes, "Reading and Interpreting 'Up in Michigan'." From *New Essays on Hemingway's Short Fiction*, ed. Paul Smith. Copyright © 1998. Reprinted with the permission of Cambridge University Press.

Robert Coover, "Five Sections from *Briar Rose*," from *Briar Rose* by Robert Coover. Copyright © 1996 by Robert Coover. Used by permission of Grove/Atlantic, Inc.

Tony Crisp, "Getting to Work on Your Dream." From *Dream Dictionary* by Tony Crisp, copyright © 1990 by Tony Crisp. Used by permission of Dell Publishing, a division of Random House, Inc.

E. E. Cummings, "r-p-o-p-h-e-s-s-a-g-r." Copyright 1935, © 1963, 1991 by the Trustees for the E. E. Cummings Trust. Copyright © 1978 by George James Firmage, from *Complete Poems: 1904–1962* by E. E. Cummings, edited by George J. Firmage. Used by permission of Liveright Publishing Corporation.

Giorgio de Chirico, "Surrealist Versailles." Reprinted by permission from a translation in *Giorgio de Chirico*, copyright © 1955 The Museum of Modern Art, New York.

Jacques Derrida, "From *Glas*." Reprinted from *Glas* by Jacques Derrida, English translation by John P. Leavey, Jr., and Richard Rand, by permission of the University of Nebraska Press. Copyright © 1986 by the University of Nebraska Press.

Emily Dickinson, "Because I could not stop for Death." Reprinted by permission of the publishers and the Trustees of Amherst College from *The Poems of Emily Dickinson*, Thomas H. Johnson, ed., Cambridge, Mass.: The Belknap Press of Harvard University Press, Copyright © 1951, 1955, 1979 by the President and Fellows of Harvard College.

Umberto Eco, "Issues of Interpretation." From *Interpretation and Overinterpretation* (New York: Cambridge University Press, 1992). Reprinted with the permission of Cambridge University Press.

Ralph Ellison, "From 'Hidden Name and Complex Fate'." From *Shadow and Act* by Ralph Ellison, copyright © 1953, 1964 by Ralph Ellison. Used by permission of Random House, Inc.

Louise Erdrich, "The Red Convertible." From *Love Medicine, New and Expanded Version* by Louise Erdrich, © 1984, 1993 by Louise Erdrich. Reprinted by permission of Henry Holt and Company, LLC.

Martin Esslin, "Aristotle and the Advertisers." Reprinted by permission of Louisiana State University Press from *Meditations: Essays on Brecht, Beckett, and the Media* by Martin Esslin. Copyright © 1980 by Martin Esslin.

A. C. Evans, "There Are Many Roads to Space." From *My Kind of Angel*, ed. Rupert Loydell (Stride Publications, 1998). Reprinted by permission of A. C. Evans.

Robert Francis, "Pitcher," from *Orb Weaver* by Robert Francis. Copyright © 1953 by Robert Francis. Reprinted by permission of Wesleyan University Press.

Sigmund Freud, from *Introductory Lectures on Psycho-Analysis* by Sigmund Freud, translated by James Strachey. Copyright © 1965, 1964, 1963 by James Strachey. Used by permission of Liveright Publishing Corporation. Sigmund Freud © Copyrights, The Institute of Psycho-Analysis and The Hogarth Press for permission to quote from *The Standard Edition of the Complete Psychological Works of Sigmund Freud*, translated and edited by James Strachey. Reprinted by permission of The Random House Group, Ltd.

Lawson Fusao Inada, "Making It Stick." From *Many Mountains Moving*. Reprinted by permission of Many Mountains Moving.

Susan Glaspell, *Trifles*. Reprinted by permission of The Estate of Susan Glaspell.

Johann Wolfgang von Goethe, "Excerpt from *Reflections on Werther*." From *The Sorrows of Young Werther and Other Writings* by Johann Wolfgang von Goethe, translated by Catherine Hutter, copyright © 1962 by Catherine Hutter. Used by permission of Dutton Signet, a division of Penguin Putnam, Inc.

Erving Goffman, "Character Contests." From *Interaction Ritual*, by Erving Goffman, copyright © 1967 by Erving Goffman. Used by permission of Pantheon Books, a division of Random House, Inc.

Susan Griffin, excerpt from *A Chorus of Stones*. From *A Chorus of Stones* by Susan Griffin, copyright © 1992 by Susan Griffin. Used by permission of Doubleday, a division of Random House, Inc.

Brothers Grimm, "Sleeping Beauties," from *One Fairy Story Too Many*, edited by John Ellis. Reprinted by permission of The University of Chicago Press and John Ellis. Copyright © 1983 The University of Chicago Press.

Susan Howe, "Submarginalia," from *The Birth-Mark: On Settling the Wilderness in American Literary History* (University Press of New England, 1993), by Susan Howe. Reprinted by permission of Wesleyan University Press.

Storm Jameson, "Departures." From *Journey from the North: Autobiography of Storm Jameson*, by Storm Jameson. Reprinted by permission of The Peters Fraser & Dunlop Group.

James Joyce, "Shem the Penman (*from* Finnegans Wake)." From *Finnegans Wake* by James Joyce, copyright © 1939 by James Joyce, Copyright renewed © 1967 by Giorgio Joyce and Lucia Joyce. Used by permission of Viking Penguin, a division of Penguin Putnam, Inc.

Franz Kafka, "Before the Law" and "On Parables," from *Franz Kafka: The Complete Stories* by Franz Kafka, edited by Nahum N. Glatzer, copyright 1946, 1947, 1948, 1949, 1954, 1958, 1971 by Schocken Books. Used by permission of Schocken Books, a division of Random House, Inc.

Robert Keidel, "A New Game for Managers to Play." Copyright © 1985 by the New York Times Co. Reprinted by permission.

Frank Kermode, "From *The Genesis of Secrecy*." Reprinted by permission of the publisher from *The Genesis of Secrecy: On the Interpretation of Narrative* by Frank Kermode, pp. 2–3, Cambridge, Mass.: Harvard University Press, Copyright © 1979 by Frank Kermode.

Ono no Komachi, "Doesn't he realize. . . ," from Kenneth Rexroth, *Women Poets of Japan*, copyright © 1977 by Kenneth Rexroth and Ikuko Atsumi. Reprinted by permission of New Directions Publishing Corp.

George Lakoff and Mark Johnson, excerpts from *Metaphors We Live By.* Copyright © 1980 by The University of Chicago Press. Reprinted by permission of The University of Chicago Press and the authors.

Eunice Lipton, "History of an Encounter," from *Alias Olympia.* Copyright © 1992 by Eunice Lipton. Reprinted by Eunice Liption and the Watkins/Loomis Agency.

Emily Martin, "The Egg & the Sperm," from *Signs: Journal of Women in Culture and Society,* 16/3 (1991). By permission of The University of Chicago Press, Journals Division, and Emily Martin.

W. S. Merwin, "Separation," from *Moving Target.* Copyright © 1963 by W. S. Merwin Georges Borchardt, Inc. Reprinted by permission of the Wylie Agency, Inc.

N. Scott Momaday, "From *The Way to Rainy Mountain.*" Reprinted from *The Way to Rainy Mountain* by N. Scott Momaday. Copyright © 1969, The University of New Mexico Press. Reprinted with permission of the publishers.

Jane Morgan, Christopher O'Neill & Rom Harre, "Nicknames: Their Origins and Social Consequences." From *Nicknames: Their Origins and Social Consequences* (Routledge, 1979), by Jane Morgan, Christopher O'Neill & Rom Harre. Reprinted by permission of Taylor & Francis Books Ltd.

Lewy Olfson, Ed., from *Plot Outlines of 100 Famous Novels* by Lewy Olfson, Ed., copyright © 1966 by Doubleday, a division of Random House, Inc. Used by permission of Doubleday, a division of Random House, Inc.

Grace Paley, "A Conversation with my Father," from *Enormous Changes at the Last Minute* by Grace Paley. Copyright © 1971, 1974 by Grace Paley. Reprinted by permission of Farrar, Straus and Giroux, LLC.

Nicholas Paley, "Everyone is Welcome." Copyright © 1995. From *Finding Art's Place: Experiments in Contemporary Education and Culture* by Nicholas Paley. Reproduced by permission of Routledge, Inc., part of The Taylor & Francis Group.

Julia and Derek Parker, "Symbolism." From *The Secret World of Your Dreams* by Julia and Derek Parker, copyright © 1991. Used by permission of Penguin Putnam, Inc.

Derek Pell, "The Revolver: A Textual Transformation." From *Assassination Rhapsody* by Derek Pell. Reprinted by permission of Autonomedia.

Marge Piercy, "You don't understand me," from *Stone, Paper, Knife* by Marge Piercy, copyright © 1983 by Marge Piercy. Used by permission of Alfred A. Knopf, a division of Random House, Inc.

Sylvia Plath, "Metaphors," from *Crossing the Water* by Sylvia Plath. Copyright © 1960 by Ted Hughes. Copyright renewed. Reprinted by permission of HarperCollins Publishers, Inc. and Faber and Faber, Ltd.

Connie Porter, "Rapunzel Across Time and Space." From *Mirror, Mirror on the Wall,* edited by Kate Bernheimer. Copyright © 1998. Reprinted by permission of Ellen Levine Literary Agency, Inc.

Ezra Pound, "In a Station of the Metro," from *Personae,* copyright © 1926 by Ezra Pound. Reprinted by permission of New Directions Publishing Corp.

Mary Louise Pratt, "Natural Narratives," from *Toward a Speech Act Theory,* by Mary Louise Pratt. Reprinted by permission of Indiana University Press.

Francine Prose, "On 'Sleeping Beauty'." From *Mirror, Mirror on the Wall,* edited by Kate Bernheimer. Copyright © 1998. Reprinted by permission of International Creative Management.

The Providence Journal, "Woman charged in assault with frozen chicken cutlets" (April 5, 1999). Reprinted by permission of The Providence Journal.

Raymond Queneau, "Transformations," from *Exercises in Style,* copyright © 1947, 1958 by Editions Gallimard and Barbara Wright. Reprinted by permission of New Directions Publishing Corp.

Robert B. Ray, "The Culmination of Classic Hollywood: *Casablanca,*" from *A Certain Tendency of Hollywood Cinema, 1930–1980.* Copyright © 1985 by Princeton University Press. Reprinted by permission of Princeton University Press.

Adrienne Rich, "Moving in Winter," from *Collected Poems: 1950–1970* by Adrienne Rich. Copyright © 1993 by Adrienne Rich. Copyright © 1967, 1963, 1962, 1961, 1960, 1959, 1958, 1957, 1956, 1955, 1954, 1953, 1952, 1951 by Adrienne Rich. Copyright © 1984, 1975, 1971, 1969, 1966 by W. W. Norton & Company, Inc. Used by permission of W. W. Norton & Company, Inc.

A. A. Roback, "Names and Professions," from *Destiny and Motivation in Language*. Reprinted by permission of Sci-Art Publishers.

Theodore Roethke, "Dolor," from *The Collected Poems of Theodore Roethke*. Copyright © 1943 by Modern Poetry Association, Inc., from *The Collected Poems of Theodore Roethke* by Theodore Roethke. Used by permission of Doubleday, a division of Random House, Inc.

Robert Scholes, "Interpreting 'Pitcher'," from *The Crafty Reader*, by Robert Scholes. Reprinted by permission of Yale University Press and Robert Scholes. Copyright © 2001. All rights reserved.

Susan Sontag, excerpt from *Against Interpretation* by Susan Sontag. Copyright © 1964, 1966, renewed 1994 by Susan Sontag. Reprinted by permission of Farrar, Straus and Giroux, LLC.

Susan Sontag, excerpts from *AIDS and its Metaphors* by Susan Sontag. Copyright © 1988, 1989 by Susan Sontag. Reprinted by permission of Farrar, Straus and Giroux, LLC.

Dale Spender, "The Male Line." Reproduced from *Man Made Language* by Dale Spender, Pandora Press, London, 1985.

Stephen Spender, "Word," copyright © 1948 by Stephen Spender, from *Selected Poems* by Stephen Spender. Reprinted by permission of Random House, Inc. and Faber and Faber, Ltd.

Brent Staples, "A Brother's Murder." Copyright © 1986 by the New York Times Co. Reprinted by permission.

Wallace Stevens, "Thirteen Ways of Looking at a Blackbird," from *The Collected Poems of Wallace Stevens* by Wallace Stevens, copyright © 1954 by Wallace Stevens. Used by permission of Alfred A. Knopf, a division of Random House, Inc.

August Strindberg, "The Stronger," translated by Elizabeth Sprigge. Copyright © 1955 by Elizabeth Sprigge. Reprinted by permission of A. P. Watt, Ltd., on behalf of Sarah Gabriel Lumley-Smith.

Edna St. Vincent Millay, "Spring." From *Collected Poems*, HarperCollins. Copyright 1921, 1948 by Edna St. Vincent Millay. All rights reserved. Reprinted by permission of Elizabeth Barnett, literary executor.

Patricia Williams, "On Being the Object of Property," from *Signs: Journal of Women in Culture and Society*. 14/1, 1988. Reprinted by permission of The University of Chicago Press, Journals Division, and Patricia J. Williams.

William Carlos Williams, "The Use of Force," from *The Collected Stories of William Carlos Williams*, copyright © 1938 by William Carlos Williams. Reprinted by permission of New Directions Publishing Corp.

Art Permissions

Giorgio de Chirico, "Mystery and Melancholy of a Street," 1914. Reprinted by permission of Artists Rights Society, copyright © 2001 Artists Rights Society (ARS), New York / SIAE, Rome. Transparency provided by Allan Mitchell.

Edward Hopper, *Night Shadows*, 1921. Copyright © 2001: Whitney Museum of American Art.

Rene Magritte, "Les Valeurs Personelles." Reprinted by permission of Artists Rights Society, copyright © 2001 C. Herscovici, Brussels / Artists Rights Society (ARS), New York. Digital image provided by San Francisco Museum of Modern Art (purchased through a gift of Phyllis Wattis).

Edouard Manet, *Olympia*, 1863. Reprinted by permission of Art Resource.

NeuVis advertisement courtesy of NeuVis, Inc. Reprinted with permission.

Nike advertisement courtesy of Chiat-Day Adv./Gary McGuire Photo. Reprinted with permission.

Man Ray, "Boulevard Raspail," 1928. Reprinted by permission of Artists Rights Society, copyright © 2001 Man Ray Trust / Artists Rights Society (ARS), NY / ADAGP, Paris. Digital image provided by Sarl Telimage, Paris, France.

Tim Rollins & K.O.S., *Amerika I*, 1984–85 and *Amerika VI*, 1986–87. Reprinted courtesy of the Mary Boone Gallery.

Vista advertisement reprinted courtesy of Hilton International/Vista International Hotels, Cydney Roach-Lawrence copy writer. Agency: Doyle Graf Mabley.

Index